On the Road to Autonomy

Promoting Self-Competence in Children and Youth with Disabilities

Edited by

Laurie E. Powers, Ph.D.
Oregon Health Sciences University
Portland, Oregon

George H.S. Singer, Ph.D.
University of California
Santa Barbara, California

Jo-Ann Sowers, Ph.D.
University of New Hampshire
Concord, New Hampshire

·P A U L·H·
BROOKES
PUBLISHING Co.

Baltimore • London • Toronto • Sydney

Paul H. Brookes Publishing Co.
Post Office Box 10624
Baltimore, Maryland 21285-0624

Typeset by Signature Typesetting & Design, Baltimore, Maryland.
Manufactured in the United States of America by
Vail-Ballou Press, Binghamton, New York.

The poem "A Conversation with Cerebral Palsy" by Jill Allen
is used by permission of the author.

Names used in case examples are pseudonyms.

Library of Congress Cataloging-in-Publication Data

On the road to autonomy : promoting self-competence in children and youth with disabilities /
    edited by Laurie E. Powers, Gearge H.S. Singer, Jo-Ann Sowers.
        p. cm.
    Includes bibliographical references and index.
    ISBN 1-55766-235-5
    1. Handicapped children.   2. Handicapped youth.   3.   Self-esteem in children.
    4. Autonomy (Psychology).   I. Powers, Laurie.   II. Singer, George H.S.   III. Sowers, Jo-Ann.
    HV888.055   1996
    362.4'083—dc20
                                      96-10802
                                         CIP

British Library Cataloguing-in-Publication data are available from the British Library.

Contents

Contributors

Jill Allen
3 Oakwood Lane
Essex Junction, VT 05452

Carol Andrew, Ed.D., OTR
Pediatrics and Adolescent Medicine
One Medical Center Drive
Dartmouth-Hitchcock Medical Center
Lebanon, NH 03756-0001

Sara N. Burchard, Ph.D.
Psychology Department
Dewey Hall
University of Vermont
Burlington, VT 05405

Elizabeth Cooley, Ph.D.
West Ed
730 Harrison Street
San Francisco, CA 94107

W. Carl Cooley, M.D.
Dartmouth Center for Genetics and
   Child Development
Dartmouth-Hitchcock Medical Center
One Medical Center Drive
Lebanon, NH 03756-0001

Patty Cotton
Institute on Disability
Concord Center
10 Ferry Street, Unit 14
Concord, NH 03301

Robin Ellison
Hood Center for Family Support
Dartmouth-Hitchcock Medical Center
One Medical Center Drive
Lebanon, NH 03756-0001

Sharon Field, Ed.D.
441 Education Building
College of Education
Wayne State University
Detroit, MI 48202

Ann E. Glang, Ph.D.
Teaching Research–Eugene
Western Oregon State College
99 West 10th Avenue, Suite 337-C
Eugene, OR 97401

Tiffany Goupil
12 Badger Street
Nashua, NH 03060

Laura Hershey
P.O. Box 9004
Denver, CO 80209

Alan Hoffman, Ed.D.
341 College of Education
Wayne State University
Detroit, MI 48202

Larry Irvin, Ph.D.
Teaching Research–Eugene
99 West 10th Avenue, Suite 370
Eugene, OR 97401

Wendy Kliewer, Ph.D.
Psychology Department
Box 842018
Virginia Commonwealth University
Richmond, VA 23284-2018

Eric Knowles
Granite State Independent Living
  Foundation
P.O. Box 7268
Concord, NH 03301

Paula D. Kohler, Ph.D.
Transition Research Institute
51 Gerty Drive, Room 113
University of Illinois at
  Urbana-Champaign
Champaign, IL 61820

Jeanne Matuszewski
2366 Elm Street
Manchester, NH 03104

Rick McAllister
Institute on Disability
University of New Hampshire
Concord Center
10 Ferry Street, Unit 14
Concord, NH 03301

Maggie Nesbitt
Portland Public Schools
531 S.E. 14th
Portland, OR 97214

Jan Nisbet, Ph.D.
Director, Institute on Disability
312 Morrill Hall
University of New Hampshire
Durham, NH 03824

Ardis L. Olson, M.D.
Department of Pediatrics and
  Adolescent Medicine
Dartmouth-Hitchcock Medical Center
One Medical Center Drive
Dartmouth Medical School
Lebanon, NH 03756-0001

Laurie E. Powers, Ph.D.
Child Development and Rehabilitation
  Center
Oregon Health Sciences University
P.O. Box 574
707 Southwest Gaines
Portland, OR 97207

George H.S. Singer, Ph.D.
Graduate School of Education
University of California
Santa Barbara, CA 93106-9490

Joanne Singer, Ph.D.
Graduate School of Education
University of California
Santa Barbara, CA 93106-9490

Jessie Skinner
115 Farm Lane
Portsmouth, NH 03801

Bridget Smith-Horn, Ph.D.
85575 Pine Grove Road
Eugene, OR 97405

Jo-Ann Sowers, Ph.D.
Institute on Disability
University of New Hampshire
Concord Center
10 Ferry Street, Unit 14
Concord, NH 03301

Kathleen Mongan Thies, Ph.D., R.N.
28 Windsong Avenue
Bedford, NH 03310

Bonnie Todis, Ph.D.
Teaching Research–Eugene
99 West 10th, Suite 370
Eugene, OR 97401

Nancee Tracy, Ed.M.
Department of Pediatrics and
  Adolescent Medicine
Dartmouth-Hitchcock Medical Center
One Medical Center Drive
Lebanon, NH 03756-0001

Ann P. Turnbull, Ed.D.
Beach Center on Families and Disability
3111 Haworth Hall
University of Kansas
Lawrence, KS 66045

H. Rutherford Turnbull, III, LL.B., LL.M.
Beach Center on Families and Disability
3111 Haworth Hall
University of Kansas
Lawrence, KS 66045

Alison Turner
Hood Center for Family Support
Dartmouth-Hitchcock Medical Center
One Medical Center Drive
Lebanon, NH 03756

Judith Voss, M.A.
Teaching Research—Eugene
Western Oregon State College
99 West 10th Avenue, Suite 337-C
Eugene, OR 97401

Michael J. Ward, Ph.D.
Office of Special Education and
    Rehabilitative Services
400 Maryland Avenue, S.W.
Switzer Building, Room 4624
Washington, DC 20202

Michael Wehmeyer, Ph.D.
Department of Research and
    Program Services
The Arc National Headquarters
500 East Boarder Street, Suite 300
Arlington, TX 76010

Foreword

Adrienne Asch

It takes a village to raise a child, says the African proverb and the 1996 book by First Lady Hillary Rodham Clinton. All too many children in North America and the world over inhabit "villages" that offer less nurturance, guidance, and love than they deserve or need. For children who have characteristics termed "disabilities," the lack of nurturance, guidance, and welcome has all too often been even more severe and detrimental to any hope that they could take their place as fulfilled, contributing, and valued members of the community.

Since the 1960s, parents, professionals, and disability rights activists have struggled to improve the opportunities for young people and adults who have disabilities, and *On the Road to Autonomy: Promoting Self-Competence in Children and Youth with Disabilities* contains messages crucial to all the members of the village in which today's and tomorrow's youth will find themselves. The book testifies to the spirit and principles of the parent and disability rights movements in its underlying belief that merely having a disability need not be the precursor to an unhappy, passive existence. "Self-esteem" and "self-competence" have currency in discussions about many groups of disadvantaged young people, and undoubtedly there is some truth to the suspicion that girls' low math scores or minority youth drop-out rates stem in part from low self-esteem. The contributors to this volume recognize that self-competence flows from the experiences of children with disabilities with parents, siblings, peers, teachers, counselors, the parents of schoolmates, and myriad others who can appreciate, enjoy, and include or can thwart, demean, and exclude. Everyone who cares about enhancing opportunities for young people with disabilities should heed the suggestions about school and classroom arrangements, the value of friendship, and the significance of teaching that all people have various challenges and that meeting those challenges can itself be a source of pride. The hard-won insights of adults who have grown up with disabilities infuse the text and demonstrate the value of helping young people hear stories of those who are "like them."

Fortunately, the book's message is more than simply that youth with disabilities need role models who have disabilities or that they must make friends without disabilities. These two ideas, while explicit and valuable, have their own pitfalls, and the text avoids them. In fact, all people probably need peers and adults whom they can admire and from whom they can learn. Ideally, those people may be anyone anywhere regardless of sex, race, age, or disability status. Whom one admires and whom one is "like" should be based as much on interests, tastes, hopes, and goals as on those characteristics the world often sees as defining—such as race, sex, or disability. One of this book's strengths is its appreciation of the idea that young people can learn from all kinds of people and experiences, even cruel and negative ones, if they can get help from people who consistently affirm their worth and their contribution to family, school, and community.

Today I write as what many would call a successful adult with disabilities, a role model, although I have never sought such a label. I love my work as a college teacher, prize the companionship of many friends, and take joy in knowing that I can contribute to people's lives. Is that self-competence, self-esteem? Perhaps. Even as I write these words, I know how much strangers' foolish and patronizing questions or friends' well-intentioned but misplaced exclusion can sting and jar me and test my sense of place. Self-competence is not taught and learned once for all time. It is tested constantly in a discriminatory, patronizing, and sometimes cruel world that does not recognize people with disabilities as fully deserving or capable of a multifaceted life. All who read this book should know that the young people they care about are likely to meet institutional and personal obstacles that will test their sense of worth and value. Young people with disabilities will profit from knowing that they have talents, skills, and love to give to those who will notice who they are; they must be supported in continually striving to find people, work, and activities that help them thrive. The readers of this book are in the best position to promote such self-competence in youth. I hope that the messages in these pages will somehow reach the many teachers, counselors, doctors, and youth workers who do not recognize that youth can have disabilities and be proud. They need this book so that they do not undermine all the work that the disability rights movement, dedicated parents, and caring professionals struggle to do to foster self-efficacy and self-determination in youth with disabilities. Read this book and spread its message widely. Everyone will benefit.

Adrienne Asch, Ph.D.
Wellesley College
Wellesley, Massachusetts

REFERENCE

Clinton, H.R. (1996). *It takes a village and other lessons children teach us.* New York: Simon & Schuster.

Preface

The impetus for this book comes from the experiences of children, adolescents, adults, and families affected by disability and ongoing challenges with whom we have had the privilege to work and learn from. Professional perspectives of disability and challenge have expanded to encompass both better understanding of the problems faced by young people with ongoing challenges and respect for the capabilities and resilience demonstrated by children and teenagers as they develop personal meanings for their experiences, manage their challenges, and go about the business of typical living. This book seeks to integrate these perspectives of disability through a comprehensive examination of the multidimensional construct of self-competence.

The preparation of this volume provided us with valuable opportunities for thought, study, and discussion related to the development and expression of self-competence among children with disabilities and ongoing challenges. The project challenged us to question our basic assumptions about the nature of disability; differences in meaning that underlie the language professionals, families, and children use to describe ongoing physical, cognitive, learning, health, emotional, and behavioral challenges; and the responsibility of professionals in acknowledging and supporting the self-competence of children and youth.

We have become sensitized to the importance of understanding these issues from the perspectives of children, youth, and adults with disabilities, as well as their families. Back in the 1970s, professionals typically decided what was best for people with disabilities. Since the 1980s, however, we have realized that it is critical to listen to people with disabilities and to design supports that address their expressed needs and wants. Many of the contributions in this book challenge us to take an additional step to recognize the competence of children with disabilities and to develop partnerships that provide children and youth with a voice in both defining their experience and identifying and implementing strategies to promote their well-being.

To successfully accomplish this shift requires us to regard children and youth with disabilities as informed experts from whom we must learn if we are to be helpful. It requires that we replace our reliance on subjective interpretations of children's experiences with more direct dialogue with children and youth about what is important, what they need to do for themselves, and the supports they want from us. It requires that we involve children and youth in evaluating the efficacy of the supports professionals provide. It requires professionals to carefully evaluate their personal assumptions regarding ways to support children and youth with disabilities to develop enhanced self-competence.

The quality of this volume is reflective of the thoughtful and enthusiastic work of its contributors, to whom we are indebted. We also appreciate the help provided by Connie Loesch and Cindi LaPointe in preparing the manuscripts and correspondence and in the numerous other activities required to complete the volume. Finally, we want to acknowledge the encouragement and support that we received from our colleagues, friends, and families, from whom we derive inspiration and self-competence.

On the Road to Autonomy

I

FOUNDATIONS

1

Self-Competence and Disability

Laurie E. Powers, George H.S. Singer, and Jo-Ann Sowers

Recent expansion in our understanding of the nature and expression of self-competence and the identification of effective practices to promote self-competence offers great promise for facilitating the development and well-being of children and youth with and without disabilities. These advances are grounded both in knowledge regarding the promotion of self-competence emergent in typical child development and in recognition of personal and contextual challenges that may have an impact on self-competence among children with disabilities. Effective approaches to support and bolster self-competence focus on a multidimensional array of issues including self-acceptance, social inclusion, achievement, and autonomy. Emphasis on these topics reflects a major shift in societal and professional perspectives on self-competence and disability. The purpose of this chapter is to describe this shift, to provide a conceptual framework for the promotion of self-competence, and to offer an overview of the specific influence of family factors on the emergence of self-competence during childhood and adolescence.

The preparation of this chapter was supported in part by Grant Nos. H158K20006, H023T80013, and H086U20006 from the U.S. Department of Education. The opinions expressed herein are exclusively those of the authors and no official endorsement should be inferred.

SHIFTS IN PERSPECTIVES ON SELF-COMPETENCE AND DISABILITY

Adjustment to disability emerged as a major area of investigation and discourse in association with societal and professional emphasis on rehabilitation in the 20th century. During this period, deficit model interpretations of disability either as a catalyst for psychological maladjustment or, in the most severe instance, as a reflection of underlying psychological disturbance reinforced notions that disability was inherently associated with impaired adjustment. The goal of treatment was to reduce dysfunction and facilitate optimal, but likely less than typical, levels of adjustment. Rehabilitation efforts generally failed to apply traditional interpretations of child competence to children with disabilities and instead focused on documenting impairment among children with disabilities and proposing treatments to ameliorate their problems and their family's assumed maladjustment (Eiser, 1990).

In many ways, disability and self-competence have traditionally been regarded as antithetical: The goal of most intervention has been to help children and families manage, given their unfortunate circumstances, rather than to validate and promote their capacities for competence. Little attention has been focused on acknowledging either that children with disabilities are foremost typical, developing human beings or that children with disabilities can and do demonstrate self-competence.

Recent decades have witnessed a gradually emerging revolution in the social construction of disability and perspectives regarding its impact on psychological adjustment. Much of the impetus for this revolution has been stimulated by consumer and parent activism in the disability civil rights movement (Powers, 1995). This movement has redefined disability in sociopolitical terms and shifted the locus of maladjustment from personal tragedy to societal stigma (Shapiro, 1993). Findings on resilience and positive adaptation have provided additional impetus for attention to the important role of self-competence in facilitating childhood adjustment to adverse circumstances (Garmezy, 1991; Werner & Smith, 1992). Finally, unprecedented levels of successful participation of people with disabilities in our society has directly challenged deficit interpretations of disability.

Key characteristics of this shift in understanding of the relationship between disability and competence are shown in Table 1. Epidemiologic evidence confirms that the presence of disability is a risk factor for adjustment difficulties (Cadman, Boyle, Szatmari, & Offord, 1987; Gortmaker, Walker, Weitzman, & Sobol, 1990), and it is clear that some children with disabilities, under certain conditions, experience impaired self-competence (Garrison & McQuiston, 1989; Prout, Marcal, & Marcal, 1992). Howev-

Table 1. Perspectives on self-competence and disability

Traditional	Contemporary
Universally negative impact	Potential for positive contributions
Sole determinant of dysfunction	One risk factor
Intrapersonally defined	Socioculturally defined
Disability-specific differences	Cross-disability similarities
Global dysfunction	Individual strengths
Locus of pathology	Adaptation, resilience
Treatment for dysfunction	Promotion and prevention
External resources	Internal resources for self-help
Professional help	Peer support
Individual intervention	Contextual intervention

er, there is increasing evidence suggesting that most children with disabilities do not manifest psychological disturbance or maladjustment (Garrison & McQuiston, 1989). Growing attention is also being directed to the potential positive life contributions that can be associated with self-awareness and discovery of capabilities gained through experience with managing disability. In fact, personal accounts by people with disabilities suggest that acknowledgment of the positive contributions of disability is key to positive adjustment (Brown, 1995). Similarly, parent conceptions of positive contributions to family life associated with rearing their children with disabilities appears to facilitate parent well-being (Turnbull et al., 1993). Such perspectives do not deny the existence of disability-related obstacles. Rather, they broaden our meanings of disability by asserting its capacity to create opportunities for different life experiences that can stimulate personal and societal development.

In contrast to traditional notions of disability as having an inherently negative impact on well-being, research findings suggest that the presence of disability is one risk factor for adjustment difficulty, the impact of which is a function of its interaction with numerous other within-disability factors, generic child factors, and contextual risk factors. Within-disability factors, such as level of functional challenge (Breslau, 1985), duration of disability (Orr, Weller, Satterwhite, & Pless, 1984; Pless & Roghmann, 1971), and personal perceptions of disability (Drotar & Bush, 1985) appear to be important predictors of adjustment. Generic factors such as attributional style have an impact on adjustment for all children, including those with disabilities (Schoenherr, Brown, Baldwin, & Kaslow, 1992). Contextual factors such as poverty, family discord, and social isolation also interact with disability to substantially increase risk for impaired adjustment (Cadman et al., 1987). The focus of investigation has shifted to defining models that explain the impact of and relationship between these multiple factors that may cause disability to increase risk for impaired adjustment (Bennett, 1994). This approach also acknowledges that disability is but one aspect of life experience for children and that other factors essential for the optimal development of all children also apply to children with disabilities (Sinnema, 1991).

In contrast to focusing on the impact of specific disability characteristics, contemporary perspectives highlight the importance of understanding the impact of cross-disability factors (Stein & Jessop, 1989). This approach has catalyzed recognition of generic disability characteristics such as predictability, perceived impact, visibility, and family burden as they complement or interact with condition-specific challenges. Such a cross-disability focus increases the feasibility of designing generic supports while also fostering a sense of common identity among children and families with various disabilities and the formation of cross-disability coalitions essential for promoting destigmatization (Becker & Arnold, 1986).

These shifts toward a deeper understanding of the relationship between disability and adjustment have highlighted the fallacy of traditional stereotypes of disability as synonymous with dependence, incompetence, and biological inferiority. Contemporary perspectives increasingly define disability in sociopolitical terms, shaped by both individual and societal response to the differences imposed by disability (Zola, 1991). This redefinition has prompted growing acknowledgment of the importance of public accommodation and the redress of discrimination that prevents people with disabilities from functioning as full members of society (Hahn, 1985). Rather than construing disability as reflective of personal weakness, sociopolitical perspectives embrace tenets of self-acceptance, diversity, personal choice, inclusion, and access to and control of supports and advance efforts to reduce the adverse impact of disability through contextual interventions, such as family support, educational inclusion, and legislative advocacy.

Increasing attention has also been directed toward understanding the nature of coping and resilience among children with disabilities. This work has taken two primary forms. The first includes research that explores the capacities of children with disabilities to successfully adapt to disability. Findings suggest that children with disabilities often demonstrate resilience to adverse circumstances such as hospitalization (Shannon, Fergusson, & Dimond, 1984), physical challenge (Wells & Schwebel, 1987), and teasing (see Chapter 11). Research also suggests that children with disabilities may, in some instances, manifest particular adaptive strengths in association with managing their challenges. For example, Olson, Johansen, Powers, Pope, and Klein (1993) found that children with severe juvenile arthritis developed problem-solving capabilities that exceeded those of youth with more mild disabilities or of their peers without disabilities.

The second line of resilience research has begun to identify the adaptive role that coping mechanisms normally considered dysfunctional may have for children with disabilities. For instance, research has highlighted the adaptive benefits of focusing on strengths and denying limitations (Timberlake, 1985) and the adaptive expression of anxiety and sorrow during episodes of acute illness (Mattsson, 1972). Much traditional evaluation of self-competence among children with disabilities has focused on comparison of their psychosocial functioning to groups of children who do not experience disabilities or to standardized norms for outcome measures without attention to the role of situation-specific differences in explaining the adaptive value of responses among children managing disabilities. This approach is gradually being deemphasized in favor of research that explores within-group variability among children with disabilities (Harper, 1991). It is likely that this shift will facilitate the identification of additional adaptive strategies utilized by children and families.

Enhanced focus on competence and resilience among children with disabilities has fueled prevention and promotion efforts. Interventions such as coping skills training, health education, self-determination and leadership development, family support, mentoring, and peer support provide a few examples of emerging approaches aimed at assisting children and families to identify and maximize their personal strengths and adaptive skills. Evidence suggests that such approaches enhance child psychosocial adjustment and disability management and minimize the adverse impacts of disability (Pantell, Lewis, & Sharp, 1989; Powers, Sowers, & Stevens, 1995; Singer & Powers, 1993; Sinnema, 1991; also see Chapter 14). Additional prevention and promotion interventions to enhance social problem solving, self-esteem, and stress management have been largely validated with children who do not experience identified disabilities, and these interventions hold promise for bolstering the self-competence of children with disability (e.g., Dubrow, Schmidt, McBride, Edwards, & Merk, 1993; Henderson, Kelbey, & Engebretson, 1992; Pope, McHale, & Craighead, 1988).

One important outcome of emerging findings and approaches to promoting self-competence is a shift from an emphasis on professionally driven models to increasing acknowledgment of the value of consumer control and peer support among people with disabilities and their families (Jones & Ulicny, 1986; Santelli, Turnbull, Lerner, & Marquis, 1993; Williams & Shoultz, 1984). Through interaction with peers who experience similar challenges, people with disabilities and parents of children with disabilities have opportunities for mutual support and for sharing information about resources and strategies for managing barriers. The proliferation of peer counseling programs in schools signals our growing acknowledgment of the benefits of mutual support between children. Peer support is also regarded as an essential element of effective coping interventions for children with disabilities (Garrison & McQuiston, 1989). The popularity of these approaches highlights the important benefits of self-help for promoting adjustment and bolstering self-perceptions of competence.

CONCEPTUAL FRAMEWORK FOR UNDERSTANDING SELF-COMPETENCE

Although there is widespread agreement regarding the importance of self-competence for understanding behavior and adjustment, self-competence is a multidimensional construct for which the literature does not provide a consistent definition. Rather than undertaking a detailed analysis and comparison of the various interpretations of self-competence, this discussion offers an overview of what seem to be its most predominant properties: perceptions of efficacy and worthiness. We also explore the manifestation of self-competence through expression of self-esteem, self-determination, and effective coping.

Efficacy and Worthiness: Foundations for Self-Competence

Self-competence is foremost a self-reflective, evaluative, phenomenological process. As shown in Figure 1, the primary elements that contribute to perceptions of self-competence are efficacy and worthiness. Perceptions of efficacy tend to be behaviorally based, whereas perceptions of worthiness are more affectively derived. Perceptions of efficacy and worthiness are cognitively mediated by beliefs and attitudes about per-

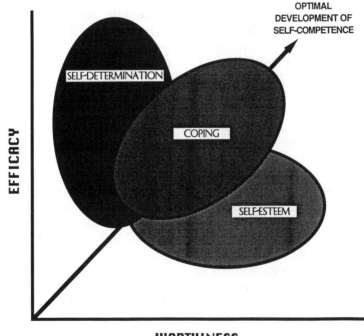

Figure 1.   Foundations for self-competence.

sonal ideals and though social comparison (Harter, 1993; James, 1980). Efficacy generally refers to beliefs about personal agency or one's capabilities to attain desired outcomes or manage undesirable circumstances (Bandura, 1986). Efficacy is derived most intensively from success in domains that are personally valued. Worthiness refers to self-evaluations of personal regard and value as a human being (Rosenberg, 1965). Although self-competence is intuitively most often associated with high efficacy, perceptions of efficacy cannot be isolated from perceptions of worthiness; efficacy promotes self-worth, and self-worth facilitates striving toward efficacy (Branden, 1969).

Efficacy and worthiness are related to one another, in part, by values regarding the meaning or quality of what we do and our purpose in life. Those who exhibit high levels of efficacy and low levels of worthiness may perceive that they are competent in areas that are not central to their judgment of personal worth. These people may be perceived by others as successful; however, they are sensitive to their personal inadequacies or they do not derive pride from their capabilities. People who exhibit low levels of efficacy and low levels of worthiness typically perceive themselves as ineffectual and of little use to themselves or others. They are most at risk for marginal lifestyles and psychopathology. Those who exhibit low levels of efficacy and high levels of worthiness typically avoid or do not value achievement and instead focus on their inherent value as human beings. They may be viewed by others as underachievers; however, they may experience positive regard for their place in life. Finally, those who exhibit high levels of efficacy and high levels of worthiness generally perceive themselves to be effective in conducting their lives while also inherently valuable as human beings, regardless of temporary accelerations or setbacks in their achievement. They are perceived by others to be successful and self-confident.

Inherent within this elucidation of the relationship between worthiness and efficacy is an assumption of correspondence between their subjective and objective expression; that is, we assume that the perceiver is "accurate" in his or her judgments of personal capabilities and value based on life experience. Some theorists make the point that extremely high levels of illusory worthiness may lead one to miss or neglect opportunities to develop one's capabilities, thus ultimately decreasing self-competence (Baumeister, 1993; Mruk, 1995). Likewise, inaccurate self-perceptions of efficacy may place one at risk for ignoring information or feedback that might prevent underachievement or failure experiences. As most of our perceptions are illusory to some degree, it is likely that the maintenance of mildly positive illusions about our worthiness and efficacy is promotive of well-being.

Self-competence is grounded in perceptions of personal worthiness and self-efficacy derived from actual experience. Variables that influence self-perceptions of worthiness include family climate, gender, birth order, and perceived value or lack thereof by others (Bednar, Wells, & Peterson, 1989; Harter, 1990; Mruk, 1995). Conditions that promote perceptions of efficacy include mastery experiences, successful management of challenges, vicarious learning, social influence, and positive physiologic feedback (Bandura, 1986; Harter, 1985).

Perceptions of worthiness and efficacy are acquired through developmental experiences such as positive attachments with caregivers, opportunities for expression of increasing levels of independence and autonomy, and friendship. These perceptions emerge over time, in conjunction with progression in social–cognitive development (see Chapter 2). Most researchers agree that the development of perceptions of efficacy is situation specific; that is, children differentiate among their capabilities in various social and task-related domains (Bandura, 1986; Harter, 1990). There is less agreement regarding whether perceptions of worthiness are global or situation specific. Theorists such as Rosenberg (1965) and Harter (1990) emphasize the importance of global self-worth, whereas Bandura (1990) suggests that worthiness is likely multidimensional. Most likely, self-perceptions of worthiness have global and situation-specific aspects.

These definitions and characteristics of worthiness and efficacy have potentially positive applications for children with disabilities. First and most important, conditions facilitative to the development of worthiness and efficacy for all children are also accessible to children with disabilities. Second, the situation-specific nature of the development of efficacy perceptions supports the capacity of children with disabilities to learn to emphasize their unique skills and abilities. Third, development of global and specific perceptions of worthiness support children with disabilities learning to appreciate themselves in totality, while concurrently responding to their particular strengths and challenges. Finally, the influence of social factors on the development of self-perceptions of efficacy and worthiness provides acknowledgment of the importance of sociocultural meanings, specifically stigma. Additional research in this area is essential if we are to both better understand the influence of sociocultural factors on self-competence and identify strategies to promote self-competence through social and political change.

Perceptions of efficacy and worthiness provide a foundation for the development of self-competence. The expression of self-competence is manifested, in part, through self-esteem, self-determination, and effective coping. The following discussion provides a brief, necessarily oversimplified, overview of some of the unique and overlapping elements of self-esteem, self-determination, and coping. Our purpose is to provide the reader with an introduction to these constructs and their relationships with one another, laying a foundation for the more detailed discussion found in the succeeding chapters of this volume. We preface this discussion by acknowledging that the definitions of these constructs and their relationships are highly ambiguous and much additional research is needed to clarify their convergent and discriminant properties.

Self-Esteem

Self-esteem is an elusive construct with many different definitions and perhaps the broadest overlap with the underlying aspects of self-competence previously described. Some theorists, such as Rosenberg (1965), have emphasized perceptions of self-regard in their definitions of self-esteem. Others have emphasized judgments of self-worth as demonstrated through behavior (Coopersmith, 1967) and accurate self-perceptions (Bednar et al., 1989). Still other theorists have defined self-esteem comparatively, emphasizing social comparison (Harter, 1985) or judgments of the congruence between one's current self-perceptions and aspired-for self perceptions (Pope et al., 1988). Mruk (1995) derives a definition of self-esteem that is based on perceptions of worthiness and competence, highlighting its developmental nature as "the lived status of one's individual competence and personal worthiness at dealing with the challenges of life over time" (p. 21). Although self-esteem is generally viewed as having affective, cognitive, and behavioral elements, most theorists identify the essence of self-esteem in perceptions of personal worthiness. Thus, as depicted in Figure 1, when related to self-determination and coping on dimensions of worthiness and efficacy, self-esteem is most strongly grounded in worthiness.

High self-esteem appears to be associated with self-confidence, effective coping, and psychosocial well-being (Bednar et al., 1989; Harter, 1993; Wells & Marwell, 1976). In contrast, low self-esteem is associated with depression, substance abuse, and delinquency (Harter, 1993; Jung, 1994; Kaplan, Martin, & Johnson, 1986). The evidence is mixed regarding the impact of disability on self-esteem. For example, Zeltzer, Kellerman, Ellenberg, Dash, and Rigler (1980) found that adolescents with disabilities did not exhibit different levels of self-esteem than did their typical peers. However, adolescents' perceptions of the impact of disability on their lives was inversely related to their self-esteem. In a review of controlled studies with large cohorts of children with ongoing medical conditions, McArarney (1985) found no overall differences in levels of self-esteem between children with and without identified conditions. Magill and Hurlbut (1986) found that disability was significantly associated with impaired self-esteem among adolescents; however, this relationship became nonsignificant when gender (being female) was considered. Other studies have associated disability with lowered self-esteem, particularly for children with cognitive, emotional, or learning challenges (Heyman, 1990; Prout et al., 1992). Factors cited earlier, such as predictability of disability, demographics, family stress, functional impact, and social isolation, appear to put children with disabilities at increased risk for low self-esteem.

Self-Determination

The construct of self-determination has been the focus of much recent attention, and an understanding of the definition and impact of self-determination is just beginning to take shape. Ward (1988) conceptualized self-determination as "the attitudes which lead people to define goals for themselves and the ability to take the initiative to achieve those goals" (p. 2). Field and Hoffman (1994) referred to self-determination as "the ability to identify and achieve goals based on a foundation of knowing and valuing oneself" (p. 164). Wehmeyer (1992) defined self-determination as "acting as the primary causal agent in one's life and making choices and decisions regarding one's quality of life, free from external influence or interference" (p. 305). Finally, Powers et al. (Chapter 15) describe self-determination as

> personal attitudes and abilities that facilitate an individual's identification and pursuit of goals...reflected in personal attitudes of empowerment, active participation in decision-making, and self-directed action to achieve personally valued goals. (p. 292)

Much of the research on self-determination has been conducted by those in the field of disability. As such, the construct integrates an empowerment and personal rights focus that is less evident in conceptualizations of self-esteem and coping.

Like self-esteem, self-determination is typically conceptualized as a multidimensional, developmental phenomenon associated with a variety of other psychosocial constructs, such as locus of control, self-efficacy, self-regulation, autonomy, learned helplessness, mastery motivation, empowerment, and quality of life. Although this construct embraces definitional elements of worthiness and efficacy, most would agree that the essence of self-determination is founded in self-perceptions of efficacy and behavioral manifestations of efficacy. To express self-determination is most basically to decide and act on one's own behalf. Thus, as shown in Figure 1, when related to self-esteem and coping on dimensions of worthiness and efficacy, self-determination is most strongly grounded in efficacy.

Less is directly known about the characteristics of children with high and low self-determination because specific measures of the global construct are currently being developed and validated. However, studies examining the impact of particular elements of self-determination suggest that people with high levels of self-determination behave more autonomously, are more effective social problem solvers, are more assertive, and exhibit higher levels of self-efficacy and self-esteem than do individuals with low levels of self-determination (Wehmeyer, Kelchner, & Richards, in press). Likewise, adolescents who learn self-determination core skills, such as decision making, problem solving, and interpersonal negotiation, exhibit significantly higher levels of empowerment, psychosocial adjustment, and goal setting than do their peers who do not learn self-determination skills (Powers, Turner, et al., 1995).

Successful Coping

Coping generally refers to individual responses to manage stressful situations (Compas, 1987; Lazarus & Folkman, 1984). Coping can encompass many different types of responses, such as direct efforts to manage the stressor, managing feelings stimulated by the stressor, or thinking differently to reduce the threat of the stressor. Thus, coping responses are generally classified as problem-focused, emotion-focused, or perception-focused. Coping success is a function of the utility of those responses selected to reduce perceived stress. Coping success appears to be a function of self-perceptions of both efficacy and worthiness (Mruk, 1995). Thus, as depicted in Figure 1, coping is positioned between self-esteem and self-determination on dimensions of worthiness and efficacy.

Coping is a highly complex, situation-specific process: The same coping response may reduce perceived stress in one situation and make it worse in another situation. Likewise, a response such as denial may be used effectively to initially manage panic when a person is confronted by a serious threat, but this response may ultimately become counterproductive if the person fails to acknowledge the threat and identify problem-focused responses to reduce it. Generally, problem-focused responses are most useful in situations in which the threat can be managed, whereas emotion-focused or perception-focused responses are most useful in stressful situations that cannot be controlled (Folkman & Lazarus, 1980). With regard to perception-focused coping, generally responses that emphasize situational, depersonalized, and temporary interpretations of stressful events promote resilience (Seligman, 1990). Coping becomes increasingly differentiated as children develop. Youth who possess the broadest repertoires of different coping strategies are most prepared to respond effectively to stress (Compas, 1987).

Cognitive appraisal of the threat and coping alternatives is key for successful coping (Lazarus & Folkman, 1984). Appraisal of the potential impact of a stressor or "what's at stake" appears particularly salient for children with disabilities. For example, Ireys, Werthamer-Larsson, Kolodner, and Gross (1994) found that adolescents' perceptions of the impact of their health conditions mediated the association between the characteristics of their conditions and mental health problems. Interestingly, in a comparative study of adolescents with and without disabilities, Zeltzer et al. (1980) found no differences among youth in their ratings of the impact of illnesses they experienced. Apparently youth without disabilities who experience intermittent, typical health problems felt that their problems were as disruptive as those experienced by youth with disabilities. The authors suggested that these findings may highlight the resilience of children with ongoing health problems to disruptions caused by disability. In a similar study, Adams and Weaver (1986) found that adolescents with chronic physical conditions exhibited lower levels of perceived stress and higher levels of self-esteem than a comparison group of youth without chronic conditions who had recently visited an outpatient clinic. Much additional research is needed to clarify the coping patterns of children with disabilities, in particular of youth with learning and emotional challenges.

Summary

The preceding discussion highlights the importance and complexity of self-competence in promoting the psychosocial well-being of children and youth with disabilities. The convergence of self-esteem, self-determination, and effective coping is associated with optimal well-being. These perceptions interrelate to potentiate the impact of one another while also reducing the likelihood of highly illusory self-perceptions by stimulating cross-checking of one perception against the other.

It is clear that many factors interrelate to facilitate self-esteem, self-determination, and successful coping. Much of our discussion to this point has centered on the role of child factors. We now turn our attention to an exploration of the role of family, the most crucial source of social influence upon child well-being and development of self-competence.

FAMILY LIFE, PARENTING, AND SELF-COMPETENCE

The study of self-determination, coping, and (to a lesser extent) self-esteem in young people with disabilities is very new. In fact, many of the chapters in this volume represent the first generation of work in this important area. It should come as no surprise, then, that there is little information available about the family conditions and parenting practices that help to promote these adaptive characteristics. Instead, it is necessary to cull the literature on child rearing for children who do not experience disabilities as well as research on the contributors to related characteristics of children with disabilities. Ultimately, we hope researchers will be able to generate helpful recommendations to parents and siblings about what kinds of family experiences and practices help to produce self-competent adults. For now, we must be content with roughing in a suggestive picture of how family life and parenting can promote coping skills, high self-esteem, and self-determination.

Family Environment

Parenting takes place in the context of a family. The values, interactions, and structure of relationships within the larger family unit have a strong influence on parent–child relationships. Recent efforts to categorize types of families and the impacts of these types on children with disability highlight the importance of family resources and the general tenor of family relationships. One form of measurement used in the study of families aims to characterize the general tenor of the family as a single unit. This overall characterization of the family has been conceptualized in different ways by different researchers. One of the most influential approaches was developed by Moos and colleagues (Moos & Moos, 1991), who describe an overall view of the family as the *family climate.* In order to measure the family climate they used Moos's Family Environment Scale, a widely used measure that aims to characterize key elements of the environment and the individual's interpretation of them . Three scales are designed to measure the general tenor of relationships in the home: *family cohesion, family expressiveness,* and *family conflict.* A personal growth domain is made up of four scales that aim to measure the family's *independence, achievement orientation, active–recreational orientation,* and *moral–religious emphasis.* A System Maintenance domain measures the extent to which rules and organization are applied to give form to family life. The items in these scales are all worded so that they refer to the family as a whole unit.

The most authoritative study of the impact of family climate on the development of children with disabilities was conducted by Mink, Nihira, and Meyers (1983). Their studies are particularly relevant for readers of this volume because they examined the impact of family climate and parenting practices on children's school and community adaptation. They studied families of children with moderate mental retardation and families of children with mild cognitive disabilities. Of particular interest are their findings on the predictors of children's self-esteem, community self-sufficiency, and personal-social responsibility as these dimensions of adaptation logically appear to overlap with the areas of self-determination, coping, and self-esteem that are the focus of this volume. They were interested in developing a taxonomy of family types and then relating these different profiles to children's adaptation.

Two family types emerged from the analysis of Mink et al. as providing the conditions that help children with moderate mental retardation to have high self-esteem community independence skills, and positive personal-social adjustment. Both of these generative family types were characterized by family climates that were high in cohesion and relatively low in conflict. Both had households that provided a variety of active stimulation for the children and, as is discussed in more detail here, used parenting practices that were characterized by high levels of involvement with and pride in the children.

Other findings also suggest that cohesive family climates with relatively low levels of conflict are good environments for children with disabilities as well as their siblings. Dyson, Edgar, and Crnic (1989) found that families marked by high cohesion, low conflict, and relatively high expressiveness were most likely to foster positive self-concepts among their children with disabilities and their siblings. Children in these families also had fewer behavior problems than did children from less cohesive and more conflicted families. An additional variable that was a contributor to the children's adaptation was parent stress. The more parents reported that they experienced stress associated with parenting a child with disabilities, the more the siblings and child with disability were likely to have negative self-concepts. In keeping with these findings, Mink et al. (1983) reported that the family type that had the worst child outcomes was characterized by relatively low cohesion, high conflict, and a general climate of low morale.

The Marital Dyad   Moving from the whole family as a unit to its subunits, the marital dyad has received a lot of attention in the general literature on child development and has begun to receive attention from researchers in the disability field. It is very likely that in two-parent families, one of the main contributors to overall family cohesion is a positive marital relationship. Less is known about family climate in single-parent families.

Cummings and Davies (1994) reviewed the extensive literature on the impact of marital discord on children. While there is some conflict in almost all marriages, research suggests that the intensity, frequency, and resolution of parental conflict all have an impact on children. Conflict that takes place in the context of a family that is generally marked by a positive emotional climate has less of a negative effect on children than conflict in a home that is generally marked by anger or emotional distance. When fights are of moderate intensity and end in problem-solving resolutions, children generally are not negatively effected. Some studies suggest that older children benefit from seeing their parents argue so long as they also see them resolve the disagreement in a constructive fashion.

However, conflicts must stay within certain bounds. Conflicts that erupt into physical violence are particularly harmful to children. For example, emotional and behavioral problems are roughly four times more common in children of battered women than in children whose mothers have not been victims of a partner's violence. An atmosphere of frequent spousal anger that goes unresolved is detrimental. Parental conflict is translated into troubled parent–child interactions in different ways. One of the strongest links between problems in the parental dyad and the parent–child subsystem appears to be the emotional tone of interactions. When parents are in conflict, they are more likely to be depressed, irritable, or angry. These emotions spill over into interactions with children. As discussed later, the general emotional tone of parent–child relationships matters a lot to children's well-being and self-concept. Parents who are angry or depressed from a distressed marital relationship are at risk of having a negatively toned relationship with their child, which can erode the child's development of a positive self-concept.

Research on single-parent families and the impact of divorce on children with disabilities is almost nonexistent. There is considerable evidence from the general literature on families to suggest that children in single-parent families are at risk of doing less well in school and having more emotional and behavioral problems than do children in two-parent families (Hernandez, 1995). A major cause of these problems is economic distress. In 1992, approximately 45% of families with children headed by single mothers were living below the poverty line, compared with 8.4% of families with two parents (McLanahan & Sandefur, 1994). Because economic disadvantage is a predictor of poorer outcomes for children with disabilities (Mink et al., 1983), it is likely that single parenthood is correlated with poorer outcomes. However, this does not mean that children invariably do worse in single-parent homes. In the Mink et al. (1983) study, one of the family types that was found to be most supportive for children was made up predominantly of single mothers. Extrapolating from related studies, we would expect that single parents who have sufficient economic resources and who are not under severe stress are more likely to do well with their children, particularly if they are able to establish promotive parenting practices.

Parenting Practices

A discussion of parenting practices brings us to the level of interactions between parents and children where most of the direct home influence of childhood development takes place. Zetlin, Turner, and Winick (1986) studied parenting practices during the adolescence of adults with mental retardation. They categorized the families that they studied into three groups: *supportive, dependency-producing,* and *conflict-ridden.* Supportive families had a warm relationship with their teenager that generally included a high degree of interest in the teenager and interactions with a positive affective tone. The parents in these families were a stable source of support to the young people. In addition, they encouraged them to develop independence and to acquire skills that would help them with self-care and community living. Dependency-producing families also had warm relationships with their teenagers with mild mental retardation, but, instead of encouraging development of skills and judgment, their styles of providing support and regulating conduct did not allow for independence. Conflict-ridden relationships, as the name implies, were marked by emotional coldness or anger and by arguments and fights. These parents exercised control over their adolescents that continued into adulthood, but with decreased support.

The supportive parenting configuration was associated with the best outcomes in early adulthood. In keeping with our belief that research on families should lead to ways to help family members in practical ways, it is necessary to develop a much fuller picture of what attitudes, beliefs, and behaviors constitute productive family environments and which are conflicted or contribute to helplessness.

A research tradition that began with classic studies by Baumrind (1967, 1971, 1973) provides a promising framework for examining the complex nature of parenting practices. By studying many families in open exploratory fashion, Baumrind developed a schema for classifying parenting practices. As shown in Figure 2, this schema orders parenting practices in a grid generated across two dimensions. One dimension represents disciplinary practices and extends between two poles: firm and lax. The second axis represents the emotional tone of the parent toward the child and ranges from indifferent to loving; one pole is marked by emotional coldness, the other by warmth.

When combined, these two dimensions represent four parenting styles: authoritarian, authoritative, neglectful, and indulgent. Authoritarian parents were high on control and low on emotional warmth. Authoritarian parents were likely to control their children according to an absolute set of standards. They valued obedience, respect for authority, work, tradition, and the preservation of order. They tended to exercise extensive control over their children and used punishment, including physical punishment. Children of authoritarian parents were found to show little independence in middle childhood and to exhibit moderate levels of social responsibility. At the opposite extreme, permissive parents were low on control and high on emotional warmth. They were found to avoid exercising control, to allow the child to regulate his or her behavior and activities as much as possible, to use little punishment, and to behave in accepting and positive ways toward the child's impulses. Children from these homes were observed to be relatively dependent and to lack social responsibility.

Authoritative parents were high on the control dimension and also high on the dimension of emotional warmth. They were likely to direct the child and not hesitate to exercise parental control. In doing so, they would give reasons for setting limits or making rules, and they allowed children to make choices and sometimes to negotiate changes in the rules. They used verbal encouragement as a main way of influencing children. Authoritative parents showed high levels of interest and spoke positively about their children. These children were found to be high on measures of indepen-

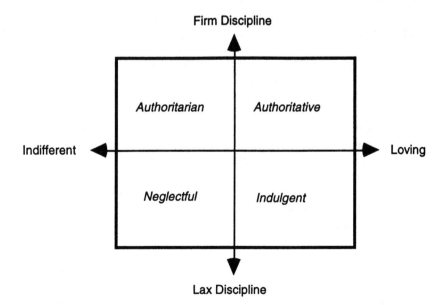

Figure 2.   Four styles of parenting created by dichotomizing and crossing the dimensions of intimacy and power. Adapted from Maccoby and Martin (1983).

dence and on measures of social responsibility (Baumrind, 1971, 1973). Baumrind did not describe the fourth quadrant of the schema, neglectful parents. Practices in these families would be marked by emotional coldness and disengagement and by little structure or control of children's behavior.

Other researchers have built upon Baumrind's work. Of particular interest is a study by Grolnick and Ryan (1989) of the relationship between Baumrind's parenting styles and teenagers' school adaptation. They interviewed 96 couples who were parents of high school–age students in order to characterize their parenting practices. To measure the teenagers' school adaptation, they obtained teacher ratings and achievement scores. They also asked the teenagers to respond to self-report instruments designed to measure their abilitites to regulate their own behavior in regard to doing school work and participating in class and to respond to an instrument designed to measure the teenagers' sense of control over their own lives. Consistent with Baumrind's findings about younger children, they found that the children of parents who were warmly involved and who encouraged their teenagers' autonomy were rated highest by teachers on academic competence and scored the highest on self-reported cognitive competence. Children from homes that were highly structured and where parents used controlling and punitive disciplinary practices had more problems in school and were less confident in their own capabilities. Children of parents who were warm but did not provide structure also did relatively poorly in school and lacked a clear sense of being able to control their own lives and understand the causes of events in their lives.

One of the valuable contributions made by Grolnick and Ryan is the clarification of Baumrind's schema of parenting practices and into clear dimensions. Figure 3 illustrates the dimensions of parenting that Grolnick and Ryan refined from their research. This representation is useful because it begins to identify specific attitudes and behavioral practices that could be used as the basis for parent training. Grolnick and Ryan identified three dimensions of parenting: *support for autonomy, structure,* and *involvement.* As shown in Figure 3, support for autonomy involves parental attitudes or values about the child's independence, parents' use of techniques that promote or impede the child's autonomy, and parental behavior related to directiveness. Authoritarian parents valued obedience and conformity over autonomy, used power-based control techniques including physical punishment and controlled use of rewards rather than reasoning or encouragement and empathetic limit setting, and imposed their agenda on the teenagers rather than offering choices and involving the teenagers in problem solving.

The parenting dimension of *structure* had two elements, information and consistency. Parents who provided little structure gave unclear information to teenagers about what was expected of them. Parents who were low on the structure variable also tended to be inconsistent in stating and applying rules. Parents low on the structure dimension were like the permissive parents in Baumrind's study of younger children— low on control and high on emotional warmth.

The dimension of parent *involvement* consisted of parental knowledge about the psychological and behavioral aspects of their children's lives. Knowledgeable parents were able to describe their children's thoughts and feelings and their behavior, whereas less knowledgeable parents were more unaware of these aspects. A second dimension of involvement concerned time spent with the teenager, and the final dimension of involvement focused on the level of enjoyment or the emotional tone of the relationship. Parents who were low in enjoyment of their children tended to be negative, angry, or cold as opposed to emotionally positive and warm.

Support for Autonomy

Values Obedience	Autonomy	Values Autonomy
Conformity	▲	Independence

Power-Based Physical Punishment	Autonomy Oriented Techniques	Reasoning, Empathic Limit Setting
Controlling Use of Rewards	▲	Encouragement

Imposes Agenda	Directiveness	Involves Children in Problem Solving
Few Choices	▲	Many Choices

Structure

Kind of Clarity	Information	Provides
Value Rules Unclear Consequences	▲	Clear Rules Expectations Guidelines Stipulates Consequences

Inconsistent	Consistency	Consistent
Rules Stated Irregularly Applied Irregularity	▲	Rule Promoted Applied Consistency

Involvement

Unaware	Knowledge	Aware
Poor Monitoring	▲	Monitors Child Closely

Low	Time Spent	High
	▲	

Negative	Enjoyment	Positive
Cold or Angry	▲	Warm

Figure 3.   Dimensions of parenting.

To summarize, parents who had the best-adjusted teenagers at school were those who valued their child's autonomy and used reasoning and empathic limit setting rather than controlling or punitive discipline. They involved the teenagers in problem solving and provided choices rather than imposing an agenda. They provided a consistent structure for teenagers through their statement of clear rules and expectations and by stipulating guidelines for, as well as consequences of, behavior. They were involved with their children, spent time with them regularly, were observant and aware of their feelings and behavior, and enjoyed their children in a relationship that was generally marked by positive, warm affect.

This line of research was carried out with parents of children without identified challenges. The next question that arises is this: Do these same configurations of parenting practices describe parents of children with disabilities, and do the same practices also have the same impact on children? A second, more sophisticated question also arises: How do parents have to modify their practices associated with autonomy, involvement, and structure to adapt to a child's disability?

Disability and Promotive Family Factors

A little information is available regarding whether these parenting practices and outcomes apply to parents of children with disabilities. As mentioned earlier, Zetlin et al. (1986) found that young adults with mental retardation adapted best in families labeled as supportive. As defined by Zetlin et al., supportive families appear to have some of the same characteristics of Baumrind's authoritative parents and appear to value autonomy as described by Grolnick and Ryan (1989).

In their taxonomic studies of families, Mink et al. (1983) employed a questionnaire designed to measure Baumrind's parenting dimensions. They designed a scale to measure these dimensions and examined the dimensions as one set of several variables that predicted the child's adaptation to school and community. Unfortunately, their findings collapse the parenting variables into a few subscale scores so that it is difficult to interpret in a way that links specific parenting practices with child outcomes. The two family types that provided the best environments for encouraging a child's adaptation to school and community were both characterized by high scores on a subscale designed to measure parenting quality as defined by Baumrind. Mink et al. described these families as warm, caring, and supportive, suggesting that they would be high on involvement and positive emotional commitment. They described the families as flexible in response to their child's behavior, suggesting that parents did not use power-oriented control techniques or rigid rules. An ethnographic description in a later report (Mink, 1986) notes that these families also encouraged their children with mental retardation to take part in family chores, such as walking the family dog, suggesting that the parents provided a structure that promoted autonomy. A parent in the second positive family type encouraged her son to ride a bicycle around the neighborhood and is described as good with the child and as genuinely liking him, suggesting a warm emotional tone and the use of encouragement to provide structure.

The family type associated with the poorest outcomes for children with mental retardation had poorer quality in parenting practices. In her 1986 report, Mink described one family in this group as somewhat passive, restrictive of their child's activities, unaware of how to raise their child, and emotionally overwhelmed. It is more difficult to fit this description into the framework of Baumrind and of Grolnick and Ryan. However, the description suggests that these parents provided less consistency, were less knowledgeable about their child, and did not support autonomy. Children from families like this had the lowest adaptive behavior, the most maladaptive behavior, and the lowest self-esteem. In summary, the answer to the question of whether families of children with disabilities can be usefully categorized as authoritarian, permissive, or authoritative must be very tentative at this point, somewhere between a "probably" and a "maybe."

The second question, regarding how parents might modify practices associated with autonomy, involvement, and structure to adapt to a child's disability, has also been addressed only minimally by researchers. However, at least two important studies suggest that this is the question research ought to focus on to offer practical help to parents in learning how best to raise a child with a disability. These two studies both used qualitative methodology to examine how adults with disabilities described their childhood and their relationships with their families.

Ferguson and Asch (1989) summarized published accounts by adults with disabilities who wrote about their families of origin. They found four patterns of parenting in these accounts: 1) parents who were overprotective, 2) parents who ignored or denied their child's disability, 3) parents who tried to fix the disability or minimize its impact, and 4) parents who tried to minimize the disability and ensure that the child had a full life. Figure 4 illustrates a new set of dimensions that enter into the puzzle of parenting when a child has a disability: standards or expectations and attitude toward the disability.

The first of these dimensions concerns the goals and standards that parents should apply in day-to-day interactions with their child. Formulation of these standards requires consideration of issues such as how much to require of the child in regard to chores, homework, polite behavior, participation in family activities, and involvement in the neighborhood, and the nature of hopes for the child's future. The other added dimension in parenting a child with a disability concerns attitude toward the disability—the parents' beliefs regarding how much effort should be made to remediate the disability, how much time should be devoted to remedial activities and therapies, and, perhaps most important, parental beliefs regarding the extent to which disability defines the child as a person. Ferguson and Asch found that when parents tended to be excessively focused on the child's disability and held low expectations of the child, their children really struggled as adults to become more independent and autonomous. Parents who denied their child's disability and did not make efforts to explain it, provided adaptive equipment and special training, or provided other accommodations also appeared to cause distress to their children when they became adults.

Another set of accounts (Ferguson & Asch, 1989) described parents who placed too much emphasis on the disability at the expense of appreciating the child as a person whose disability was but one of many characteristics. These parents tended to push the children too much to try to overcome their disability. The adults who recalled their early relationships with their parents in the most positive light described them as providing training and equipment to help them maximize their abilities while at the same time helping them to have as full a life as possible in a way that emphasized their personhood as multidimensional, with disability being but one element of it.

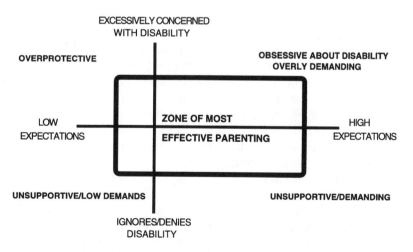

Figure 4.   Parental attitude toward disability.

The account of Powers, Singer, and Todis (see Chapter 4) will, we hope, be a further contribution to our limited knowledge about effective parenting practices for children with disabilities. Interviews with successful adults with disabilities revealed major themes pertaining to the way that parents raised them. These themes overlap in some ways with the Baumrind schema and also add some new dimensions that have not been emphasized in previous parenting research. For example, successful adults recalled how their parents modeled assertiveness for them and taught them how to be persistent and strong in dealing with other people. Other themes such as the importance of including children in typical family leisure activities appear to echo Baumrind's findings regarding a warm emotional tone in the family as well as the finding that family cohesion is associated with positive child-rearing outcomes.

In summary, some parenting practices are more effective than others in encouraging positive self-esteem, a strong sense of self-determination, and coping skills in children. It is likely that parents do better at raising children if they use disciplinary practices that are not rigid and punitive but set clear and consistent limits and explain the reasons for these limits. It is also likely that parents who are engaged with their children, are knowledgeable about their feelings and behavior, and who enjoy their children are also likely to do better than parents who are disengaged or angry and rejecting. Families that provide structure and that promote opportunities to learn skills that contribute to independence and social inclusion are also likely to do better than families that are chaotic or have expectations that are too low. Some evidence has begun to suggest that parents' attitudes toward the child's disability, the accommodations they provide, the extent to which they provide the child with typical experiences and opportunities, and whether or not they model proactive strategies such as assertiveness to manage disability barriers are also dimensions that contribute to positive outcomes.

Future research should aim to further illuminate this new territory. It is hoped that the focus of future parent skill development and parent support interventions will expand to help parents with the many day-to-day and minute-to-minute judgments they must make in raising a child with a disability.

CONCLUSION

Changing perspectives of disability, in conjunction with enhanced understanding of child psychosocial adjustment, are stimulating new levels of awareness regarding the emergence and expression of self-competence among children and youth with disabilities. This new awareness acknowledges both the potential risk to psychosocial adjustment associated with disability and the capacities of children with disabilities to develop self-esteem, self-determination, and coping repertoires effective for negotiating typical and disability-related stress. Factors essential to the optimal promotion of self-competence among children with disabilities include child capacities, within-disability characteristics and cross-disability features, family resources, and societal acceptance of accommodation to diversity.

This chapter is intended to provide an overview of shifting perspectives on self-competence and disability; to provide a conceptual framework for the expression of self-competence though self-esteem, self-determination, and effective coping; and to discuss the essential role of family in promoting and supporting child self-competence. The following chapters in this volume detail comprehensive quantitative, qualitative, and personal accounts of information and interventions essential to the emergence, expression, and promotion of self-competence among children and youth with various disabilities that encompass learning, physical, health, and emotional challenges.

The first section of this volume includes chapters that provide a foundation for the understanding of self-competence. Consistent with our perspective that children with disabilities are first and foremost children whose development and expression of self-competence follows typical patterns, this volume begins with chapters that describe development and coping among children without identified disabilities. The second section includes chapters that address contextual factors essential to the facilitation of self-competence for children with disabilities: educational practices, support for families, social relationships, and medical care. The final section of this volume includes chapters that describe innovative approaches to promote self-competence across childhood and adolescence in areas including skill-development for children, families, and educators; friendship and leisure; employment; early childhood care and education; and mentoring. These chapters comprise much of our current knowledge and thinking related to self-competence and disability. It is hoped that this work will stimulate a second generation of research and demonstration that further elevates our understanding and capacities to promote the development and expression of self-competence among children and youth with disabilities.

REFERENCES

Adams, J.A., & Weaver, S.J. (1986). Self-esteem and perceived stress in young adolescents with chronic disease. *Journal of Adolescent Health Care, 7,* 173–177.

Bandura, A. (1986). *Social foundation of thought and action: A social cognitive theory.* Englewood Cliffs, NJ: Prentice Hall.

Bandura, A. (1990). Conclusion: Reflections on nonability determinants of competence. In R.J. Sternberg & J. Kolligan, Jr. (Eds.), *Competence considered* (pp. 315–362). New Haven: Yale University Press.

Baumeister, R. (Ed.). (1993). *Self-esteem: The puzzle of low self-regard.* New York: Plenum.

Baumrind, D. (1967). Child care practices anteceding three patterns of preschool behavior. *Genetic Psychology Monographs, 75,* 43–88.

Baumrind, D. (1971). Current patterns of parental authority. *Developmental Psychology Monographs, 4,* 1–103.

Baumrind, D. (1973). The development of instrumental competence through socialization. In A. Pick (Ed.), *Minnesota symposium on child psychology* (Vol. 7, pp. 3–46). Minneapolis: University of Minnesota Press.

Becker, G., & Arnold, R. (1986). Stigma as a social and cultural construct. In S.C. Ainlay, G. Becker, & L.M. Coleman (Eds.), *The dilemma of difference: A multidisciplinary view of stigma* (pp. 37–57). New York: Plenum.

Bednar, R.L., Wells, M.G., & Peterson, S.R. (1989). *Self esteem: Paradoxes and innovations in clinical theory and practice.* Washington, DC: American Psychological Association.

Bennett, D.S. (1994). Depression among children with chronic medical problems: A meta-analysis. *Journal of Pediatric Psychology, 19*(2), 149–169.

Branden, N. (1969). *The psychology of self-esteem.* New York: Bantam.

Breslau, N. (1985). Psychiatric disorder in children with physical disabilities. *Journal of the American Academy of Child Psychiatry, 24,* 87–94.

Brown, S.E. (1995). I was born (in a hospital bed)—when I was 31 years old. *Disability & Society, 10*(1), 103–110.

Cadman, D., Boyle, M., Szatmari, P., & Offord, D.R. (1987). Chronic illness, disability, and mental and social well-being: Findings of the Ontario child health study. *Pediatrics, 79,* 805–813.

Compas, B.E. (1987). Coping with stress during childhood and adolescence. *Psychological Bulletin, 101*(3), 393–403.

Coopersmith, S. (1967). *The antecedents of self-esteem.* San Francisco: W.H. Freeman.

Cummings, E.M., & Davies, P. (1994). *Children and marital conflict: The impact of family dispute and resolution.* New York: Guilford Press.

Drotar, D., & Bush, M. (1985). Mental health issues and services. In N. Hobbs & J.M. Perrin (Eds.), *Issues in the care of children with chronic illness* (pp. 827–863). San Francisco: Jossey-Bass.

Dubrow, E.F., Schmidt, D., McBride, J., Edwards, S., & Merk, F.L. (1993). Teaching children to cope with stressful experiences: Initial implementation and evaluation of a primary prevention program. *Journal of Clinical Child Psychology, 22,* 428–440.

Dyson, L., Edgar, E., & Crnic, K. (1989). Psychological predictors of adjustment by siblings of developmentally disabled children. *American Journal on Mental Retardation, 94*(3), 292–302.

Eiser, C. (1990). Psychological effects of chronic disease. *Journal of Child Psychology and Psychiatry, 31,* 85–98.

Ferguson, P.M., & Asch, A. (1989). Lessons from life: Personal and parental perspectives on school, childhood, and disability. In D. Biklen, D. Ferguson, & A. Ford (Eds.), *Schooling and disability* (pp. 108–140). Chicago: University of Chicago Press.

Field, S., & Hoffman, A. (1994). Development of a model for self-determination. *Career Development for Exceptional Individuals, 17*(2), 159–169.

Folkman, S., & Lazarus, R.S. (1980). An analysis of coping in a middle-aged community sample. *Journal of Health and Social Behavior, 21,* 219–239.

Garmezy, N. (1991). Resilience in children's adaptation to negative life events and stressed environments. *Pediatric Annals, 20*(9), 459–466.

Garrison, W.T., & McQuiston, S. (1989). Chronic illness during childhood and adolescence: Psychological aspects. *Developmental Clinical Psychology and Psychiatry: Vol. 10.* Newbury Park, CA: Sage Publications.

Gortmaker, S.L., Walker, D.K., Weitzman, M., & Sobol, A.M. (1990). Chronic conditions, socioeconomic risks, and behavioral problems in children and adolescents. *Pediatrics, 85*(3), 267–276.

Grolnick, W.S., & Ryan, R.M. (1989). Parent styles associated with children's self-regulation and competence in school. *Journal of Educational Psychology, 81*(2), 143–154.

Hahn, H. (1985, January-February). Disability policy and the problem of discrimination. *American Behavioral Scientist, 28*(3), 293–318.

Harper, D.C. (1991). Paradigms for investigating rehabilitation and adaptation to childhood disability and chronic illness. *Journal of Pediatric Psychology, 16,* 533–542.

Harter, S. (1985). *The self-perception profile for children: Revision of the perceived competence scale for children.* Unpublished manual, University of Denver, CO.

Harter, S. (1990). Causes, correlates, and the functional role of global self-worth: A life-span perspective. In R.J. Sternberg & J. Kolligan, Jr. (Eds.), *Competence considered* (pp. 67–97). New Haven: Yale University Press.

Harter, S. (1993). Causes and consequences of low self-esteem in children and adolescents. In R. Baumeister (Ed.), *Self-esteem: The puzzle of low self-regard* (pp. 87–111). New York: Plenum.

Henderson, P.A., Kelbey, T.J., & Engebretson, K.M. (1992). Effects of a stress-control program on children's locus of control, self-concept, and coping behavior. *The School Counselor, 40,* 125–130.

Hernandez, D.J. (1995). *America's children: Resources from family, government, and the economy.* New York: Russell Sage Foundation.

Heyman, W. (1990). The self-perception of a learning disability and its relationship to academic self-concept and self-esteem. *Journal of Learning Disabilities, 23*(8), 472–475.

Ireys, H.T., Werthamer-Larrsson, L.A., Kolodner, K.B., & Gross, S. (1994). Mental health of young adults with chronic illness: The mediating effect of perceived impact. *Journal of Pediatric Psychology, 19*(2), 205–222.

James, W. (1980). *Principles of psychology.* New York: Holt, Rinehart & Winston.

Jones, M.L., & Ulicny, G.R. (1986). The independent living perspective: Applications to services for adults with developmental disabilities. In J.A. Summers (Ed.), *The right to grow up: An introduction to adults with developmental disabilities* (pp. 227–244). Baltimore: Paul H. Brookes Publishing Co.

Jung, J. (1994). *Under the influence: Alcohol and human behavior.* Pacific Grove, CA: Brooks/Cole.

Kaplan, H., Martin, S., & Johnson, R. (1986). Self-rejection and the explanation of deviance: Specification of the structure among latent constructs. *American Journal of Sociology, 92,* 384–441.

Lazarus, R.S., & Folkman, S. (1984). *Stress, appraisal, and coping.* New York: Springer-Verlag.

Magill, J., & Hurlbut, N. (1986). The self-esteem of adolescents with cerebral palsy. *The American Journal of Occupational Therapy, 40*(6), 402–407.

Mattsson, A. (1972). Long-term physical illness in childhood: A challenge to psychosocial adaptation. *Pediatrics, 50,* 801–811.

Maccoby, E.E., & Martin, J.A. (1983). Socialization in the context of the family: Parent-child interaction. In E.M. Hetherington (Ed.), *Handbook of child psychology.* Vol. 4 (4th ed., pp. 1–101). New York: John Wiley & Sons.

McArarney, E.R. (1985). Social maturation: A challenge for handicapped and chronically ill adolescents. *Journal of Adolescent Health Care, 6,* 90–101.

McLanahan, S., & Sandefur, G. (1994). *Growing up with a single parent: What hurts, what helps.* Cambridge, MA: Harvard University Press.

Mink, I.T. (1986). Classification of families with mentally retarded children. In J. Gallagher & P. Vietze (Eds.), *Families of handicapped persons: Research, programs, and policy issues* (pp. 25–43). Baltimore: Paul H. Brookes Publishing Co.

Mink, I.R., Nihira, K., & Meyers, C.E. (1983). Taxonomy of family life styles: I. Homes with TMR children.*American Journal of Mental Deficiency, 87,* 484–497.

Moos, R.H., & Moos, B.S. (1991). *Family Environment Scale manual.* Palo Alto, CA: Consulting Psychologists Press.

Mruk, C. (1995). *Self-esteem: Research, theory, and practice.* New York: Springer-Verlag.

Olson, A.L., Johansen, S.G., Powers, L.E., Pope, J.B., & Klein, R.B. (1993). Cognitive coping strategies of children with chronic illness. *Journal of Developmental and Behavioral Pediatrics, 14*(4), 217–223.

Orr, D.P., Weller, S.C., Satterwhite, B., & Pless, I.B. (1984). Psychosocial implications of chronic illness in adolescence. *Journal of Pediatrics, 104,* 152–157.

Pantell, R.H., Lewis, C., & Sharp, L. (1989). Improving outcomes in asthmatic patients: Results of a randomized trial. *American Journal of Diseases in Children, 143,* 433.

Pless, I.B., & Roghmann, K.J. (1971). Chronic illness and its consequences: Observations based on three epidemiologic survey. *Journal of Pediatrics, 79,* 351–359.

Pope, A.W., McHale, S.M., & Craighead, W.E. (1988). *Self-esteem enhancement with children and adolescents.* Elmsford, NY: Pergamon Press.

Powers, L.E. (1995). Family and consumer parent activism in disability policy. In G.H.S. Singer, L.E. Powers, & A. Olson (Eds.), *Redefining family support: Innovations in public–private partnerships* (pp. 413–434). Baltimore: Paul H. Brookes Publishing Co.

Powers, L.E., Sowers, J., & Stevens, T. (1995). An exploratory randomized study of the impact of mentoring on the self-efficacy and community-based knowledge of adolescents with physical challenges. *Journal of Rehabilitation, 61*(1), 33–41.

Powers, L.E., Turner, A., Wilson, R., Matuskewski, J., Ellison, R., & Rein, C. (1995). *A controlled field-test of the efficacy of a multi-component model for promoting adolescent self-determination.* Lebanon, NH: Dartmouth Medical School.

Prout, H.T., Marcal, S.D., & Marcal, D.C. (1992). A meta-analysis of self-reported personality characteristics of children and adolescents with learning disabilities. *Journal of Psychoeducational Assessment, 10,* 59–64.

Rosenberg, M. (1965). *Society and the adolescent self-image.* Princeton, NJ: Princeton University Press.

Santelli, B., Turnbull, A.P., Lerner, E., & Marquis, J. (1993). Parent to parent programs: A unique form of mutual support for families of persons with disabilities. In G.H.S. Singer & L.E. Powers (Eds.), *Families, disability, and empowerment: Active coping skills and strategies for family interventions* (pp. 27–66). Baltimore: Paul H. Brookes Publishing Co.

Schoenherr, S.J., Brown, R.T., Baldwin, K., & Kaslow, N.J. (1992). Attributional styles and psychopathology in pediatric chronic-illness groups. *Journal of Clinical Child Psychology, 21,* 380–387.

Seligman, M.E.P. (1990). *Learned optimism.* New York: Pocket Books.

Shannon, F.T., Fergusson, D.M., & Dimond, M.E. (1984). Early hospital admissions and subsequent behavior problems in 6 year olds. *Archives of Disabled Children, 59,* 815–819.

Shapiro, J.P. (1993). *No pity: People with disabilities forging a new civil rights movement.* New York: Times Books.

Singer, G.H.S., & Powers, L.E. (Eds.). (1993). *Families, disability, and empowerment: Active coping skills and strategies for family interventions.* Baltimore: Paul H. Brookes Publishing Co.

Sinnema, G. (1991). Resilience among children with special health-care needs and among their families. *Pediatric Annals, 20*(9), 483–486.

Stein, R.E.K., & Jessop, D.J. (1989). What diagnosis does not tell: The case for a noncategorical approach to chronic illness in childhood. *Social Science Medicine, 29,* 769–778.

Timberlake, E.M. (1985). Self-concept protection by children with physical differences. *Child and Adolescent Social Work Journal, 2,* 232–246.

Turnbull, A.P., Patterson, J.M., Behr, S.K., Murphy, D.L., Marquis, J.G., & Blue-Banning, M.J. (Eds.). (1993). *Cognitive coping, families, and disability.* Baltimore: Paul H. Brookes Publishing Co.

Ward, M.J. (1988). The many facets of self-determination. *National Information Center for Children and Youth with Handicaps: Transition Summary, 5,* 2–3.

Wehmeyer, M.L. (1992). Self-determination and the education of students with mental retardation. *Education and Training in Mental Retardation, 27,* 302–314.

Wehmeyer, M.L., Kelchner, K., & Richards, S. (in press). Individuals and environmental factors related to the self-determination of adults with mental retardation. *Journal of Vocational Rehabilitation.*

Wells, E.L., & Marwell, G. (1976). *Self-esteem: Its conceptualization and measurement.* Beverly Hills: Sage Publications.

Wells, R.D., & Schwebel, A.I. (1987). Chronically ill children and their mothers: Predictors of resilience and vulnerability to hospitalization and surgical stress. *Journal of Developmental and Behavioral Pediatrics, 8,* 83–89.

Werner, E.E., & Smith, R.S. (1992). *Overcoming the odds: High risk children from birth to adulthood.* Ithaca, NY: Cornell University.

Williams, P., & Shoultz, B. (1984). *We can speak for ourselves.* Bloomington: Indiana University Press.

Zeltzer, L., Kellerman, J., Ellenberg, L., Dash, J., & Rigler, D. (1980). Psychological effects of illness in adolescence. II: Impact of illness in adolescents—crucial issues and copying styles. *Journal of Pediatrics, 97,* 132–138.

Zetlin, A.G., Turner, J.L., & Winick, L. (1986). Socialization effects on the adult adaption of mildly retarded persons living in the community. In S. Landsman-Dwyer & P.M. Vietze (Eds.), *Impact of residential settings on behavior.* Baltimore: University Park Press.

Zola, I.K. (1991). Bringing our bodies and ourselves back in: Reflections on a past, present, and future "medical sociology." *Journal of Health and Social Behavior, 32*(3), 1–16.

You Get Proud by Practicing

Laura Hershey

If you are not proud
for who you are, for what you say, for how you look;
if every time you stop
to think of yourself, you do not see yourself glowing
with golden light; do not, therefore, give up on yourself.
You can
get proud.

You do not need
a better body, a purer spirit, or a Ph.D.
to be proud.
You do not need
a lot of money, a handsome boyfriend, or a nice car.
You do not need to be able to walk, or see, or hear,
or use big complicated words,
or do any of the things that you just can't do
to be proud. A caseworker
cannot make you proud,
or a doctor.
You only need
more practice.
You get proud
by practicing.

There are many many ways to get proud.
You can try riding a horse, or skiing on one leg,
or playing guitar,
and do well or not so well,
and be glad you tried
either way.
You can show
something you've made
to someone you respect
and be happy with it no matter
what they say.
You can say
what you think, though you know
other people do not think the same way, and you can
keep saying it, even if they tell you
you are crazy.
You can add your voice
all night to the voices
of a hundred and fifty others
in a circle
around a jail house
where your brothers and sisters are being held
for blocking buses with no lift,
or you can be one of the ones
inside the jail house,
knowing of the circle outside.

You can speak your love
to a friend
without fear.
You can find someone
who will listen to you
without judging you or doubting you or being
afraid of you
and let you hear yourself perhaps
for the first time.
These are all ways
of getting proud.
None of them
are easy, but all of them
are possible. You can do all of these things,
or just one of them again and again.
You get proud
by practicing.

Power makes you proud, and power
comes in many fine forms
supple and rich as butterfly wings.
It is music

when you practice opening your mouth
and liking what you hear
because it is the sound of your own
true voice
It is sunlight
when you practice seeing
strength and beauty in everyone
including yourself.
It is dance
when you practice knowing
that what you do
and the way you do it
is the right way for you
and can't be called wrong.
All these hold
more power than weapons or money
or lies.
All these practices bring power, and power
makes you proud.
You get proud
by practicing.

Remember, you weren't the one
who made you ashamed,
but you are the one
who can make you proud.
Just practice,
practice until you get proud, and once you are proud,
keep practicing so you won't forget.
You get proud
by practicing.

2

Mastering the Developmental Challenges of Childhood and Adolescence

Sara N. Burchard

Studies since the 1960s have identified major developmental tasks and accomplishments that, powered by species-specific genetic programs, play out within the social context of human environments. These normative behaviors and competencies have been mapped as developmental progressions (Bee, 1992; Piaget, 1970; Sroufe, 1979; Tanner, Whitehouse, & Takaishi, 1966). These progressions show the powerful engine of biomaturation in the development of basic sensory, motor, linguistic, and cognitive competencies and social relatedness, which develop in almost any human social environment.

Studies have also shown that social context has a tremendous impact on the resolution of early developmental tasks and that this resolution lays the groundwork for adjustment and competence in later life. Early experience affects later development by providing a basic model for future social relationships. This manner of viewing oneself in relation to others is derived from the primary relationships experienced within the family (Lyons-Ruth & Zeanah, 1993; Rutter & Rutter, 1993). Early experiences also enable the development of basic physical, language, and cognitive (intellectual) com-

I wish to acknowledge the contribution made to this chapter by Janet Bramley, Naseem Choudhury, Susan Culbert, Kelly Hale, Brandy Smith, and Al Vecchione of the graduate program in psychology at the University of Vermont, whose seminar presentations and thoughtful discussion of issues related to development and disability were stimulating and helpful in conceptualizing this chapter; and to Kelly Allen, whose secretarial support was invaluable.

petencies. These competencies are the foundation for the child's formation of her or his own view of self and world, through which the child interprets future events and her or his own competence (Flavell, 1992).

The importance of early experience for later development is partly due to the surprising continuity of important environmental factors that contribute to support or to undermine the mastery of developmental tasks (Sameroff, 1993). For example, a family's values and practices, manner of coping with stressors, social milieu, and economic situation remain fairly consistent over time for many families. Environmental continuity reinforces the particular view of self that the child has been building, the view of who the child is and how he or she is seen and evaluated by others. The child uses this model to interpret and respond to the world. This process, in turn, contributes to further continuity in development (Dodge, 1983; Flavell, 1992).

Recent large-scale studies and studies following children over a period of many years have begun to provide information on *risk factors* as well as *protective factors* for successfully navigating developmental challenges. This research identifies having a disability as potentially constituting a risk factor (Cadman, Boyle, Szatmari, & Offord, 1987; Rutter, 1989; Werner, 1987). Other recent research emphasizes that having a challenge, including having the challenge of a disability, may strengthen development. When disability is present, individual and family functioning is not essentially different from that of comparable persons or families who do not experience disability (Dyson, 1993; Garrison & McQuiston, 1989; Thompson, Gil, Burbach, Keith, & Kinney, 1993). Sameroff, a prominent author and researcher, points out that all development takes place in the context of meeting and responding to challenges. Challenges are the impetus for development and adaptation for all children (Sameroff, 1993).

This chapter presents information on the typical course of child and adolescent development and explores the challenges that this developmental progression typically poses for individuals and their families, including children with disabilities and chronic conditions. The chapter examines the major age-related tasks and challenges that confront children from birth to early adulthood and identifies risk and protective factors that affect developmental outcomes. A knowledge of these factors can provide insight into opportunities for mastering the challenges faced by those with disabilities as well as by anyone undergoing development.

OVERVIEW OF DEVELOPMENT IN CHILDHOOD

Age is a convenient variable for examining developmental tasks, progressions, and accomplishments. Complex biologically based behaviors develop with age and express our phylogenetic heritage as human beings—for example, characteristic fine and gross motor abilities, language, recognition of self, thinking and problem solving, capacity to enjoy and create art and music, and capacity and need for social relationships. Age also correlates with social expectations and social institutions, which pose additional developmental challenges for adaptation and performance (e.g., timing of school entry, demands for academic mastery, timing of work force entry, range of work force options).

Development is in the context of our success in negotiating the tasks that are set before us by our culture and our biology (Erikson, 1963). Human development, driven by the engine of biological programs (e.g., learning to grab, to walk, to talk) tempered by individual constitutions (e.g., temperaments, biological rhythms, abilities, disabilities) is assisted, directed, and modulated by particular social and environmental experiences we meet and directed by the age-related and performance expectations of our families and culture.

The fundamental accomplishments of child and adolescent development, however, are social: to develop and enjoy interpersonal relationships and to live, work, and play among other people in normative settings (Burchard, 1991, in press; Burchard, Gordon, & Pine, 1990; Burchard, Hasazi, Gordon, & Yoe, 1991; Erikson, 1963). While this may be an oversimplification of the complexity of human needs and achievements, a lack of meaningful social relations and social supports is often cited as one of the major barriers to adjustment and meaningful community and personal participation for persons with disabilities (Wolfensberger, 1991), as it is also for those without identifiable disabilities (Werner & Smith, 1982). The fundamental role of the social nature and social needs in human development cannot be overstated (Adler, 1948; Rutter & Rutter, 1993). The drive for inclusion and participation may be partially driven by demands for equal rights, but it also reflects the natural desire to be part of the social context of one's own community. Other areas of human development provide keys to the building of successful social skills and for social adjustment. The development of skills that provide the foundation for being interpersonally successful, living among others with the behavior and understanding expected for one's age, and making and having friendships and ultimately forming intimate relationships depends in important ways upon the prior development of cognitive, motor, and communication skills.

Cognition (thinking, reasoning, understanding) is critical for the development of social relatedness. Through cognition, a child organizes experiences and assigns meaning to them: that is, understands the actions, intentions, and meanings of the social behaviors of other people. This cognitive organization is the basis for understanding, approaching, and interacting with other people and for developing relationships with them. Cognitive development is fundamental to the development of problem solving and coping skills. These skills can provide the basis for successfully meeting later developmental challenges to self, autonomy, and interpersonal relatedness. At the same time, language is important if not essential for social communication as well as for the full development of cognitive skills. For example, studies with infants with hearing impairment have shown that these infants need to live in an environment with a gestural language to fully develop their cognitive skills later in life (Liben, 1978).

Personal development, the other side of social development, entails the development of a concept of self and of self-esteem. This development is generated by the independent self-direction and self-care that developing motor skills enable—as well as by cognitive development. The development of a concept of self is based on a search for similarities with other people and is generated as a person perceives how other people typically respond to her (e.g., with delight or with frustration, by responding to one's needs or by ignoring them) and eventually by social comparison processes (Anastasiow, 1986). The development of a sense of self is forged within the context of what a person can do, what responses that brings forth from others, and how these abilities compare to those in the social comparison group. This process leads to self-esteem—one's self-perceived skills and abilities and place in the world. Those skills that a person believes she or he has in areas she or he perceives as valuable (e.g., sports, music, friendships) are the basis for self-esteem (Harter, 1983).

The drive for autonomy, growth, and competence is another characteristic drive propelling human development (Erikson, 1963). Autonomy is also a highly desired personal outcome (Burchard, in press; Burchard et al., 1990, 1991) and the culturally expected developmental outcome of adulthood. Autonomy and self-determination are important in our culture and have significant ramifications for the development of the self.

The major tasks, challenges, and accomplishments in normative development can be organized under the headings of cognition, autonomy, self, and social development (see Table 1). The tasks and accomplishments associated with each developmental period are described, and risks and protective factors are presented. These elements are examined to identify responses that bolster development and can be applied by individuals or families with disabilities as they traverse the same developmental periods across childhood and adolescence to adulthood.

INFANCY (BIRTH TO 18 MONTHS)

Infancy is a period of biologically programmed development. Given the presence of a human social environment, the characteristically human skills of grasping and manipulation, independent locomotion, beginning language, and cognition emerge. These behaviors develop within a wide variety of human environments and cultures (Bee, 1992).

In infancy a child is busy practicing skills, using her body and getting to know her abilities as fast as they come "on line." The infant kicks; grabs; puts her hand to her mouth continuously, with and without objects; and practices making sounds, babbling, and sometimes shrieking for the joy of making it happen. This is a period of great discovery and repeated practice (see Table 1).

Cognitively, an infant is learning about the world through his actions on it and the effects of his actions. He is not actively engaged in "thinking" about things (Piaget, 1970), but he learns he has an effect on the physical and the social world. This early sense of an active role is the basis of the developing concept of self.

During this period the infant also learns about his relationship with and his effect upon caregivers as well as upon objects in the environment. During the first months of infancy, the infant's main task is to develop the capacity to regulate himself and his basic physiological processes. Basic patterns of eating, sleeping, fussing, quieting, and responding to soothing build the basis for a satisfying reciprocal relationship with significant people in his environment, especially his parents. This is the time when parents and infant begin to get to know each other, an especially important time for parents (Lyons-Ruth & Zeanah, 1993).

The major social accomplishment during this stage is *attachment*. Research suggests that babies prefer to look at objects that look like eyes in a face and that they focus at the distance of breast to face, focus on a caregiver's face, prefer women's voices, respond to cuddling, and quiet to caregiving (Bee, 1992). During this period, attachment to specific people develops as the infant begins to recognize familiar people through all senses and begins to retain information over a longer period of time. Between 6 and 8 months of age, the baby develops *object permanence*—the cognitive capacity for recognizing, remembering, and pursuing objects. Preference for specific caregivers also emerges, and with new mobility, the infant can crawl toward preferred people and protest their leaving. This process greatly reinforces the caregiving adult's feelings of competence and of being needed by the baby. By the end of the first year, strong attachments are usually formed. Whether the attachment is positive, ambivalent, or conflicted is believed to be a function of the infant–caregiver interactions over the preceding year, the degree of "fit" and mutual responsivity (Sroufe, 1988). This attachment becomes a model for later relationships with people. The quality of attach-

Table 1. Tasks and challenges of development by stage and area for infancy, childhood, and adolescence

Stage	Cognition	Autonomy/competence	Self/self-esteem	Social development/ interpersonal relationships
INFANCY *Tasks: Develop secure attachment, basic sensorimotor skills, independent mobility, differentiation of self from other*				
Birth to 1½ years Trust/mistrust Sensorimotor intelligence	Object permanence Cause/effect (primitive) Learning to make things happen Imitation First representation First single words	Discovers and practices emerging sensory, motor, and vocal skills Independent mobility	Controls smile/cry/laugh Practices activities of sensorimotor self and language on environment	Attachment: Establishes preference for person(s); uses as safe base for exploration and social referencing Stranger fear/separation anxiety
EARLY CHILDHOOD *Tasks: Master basic language and gross and fine motor skills, develop physical self-care independence and self-control*				
2–3 years Autonomy/shame Preoperational intelligence	Internal representation 2-word, then 4-word sentences Delayed imitation Attempt to do everything for self Burst of language development Pretend play Spoken sentences	Mastery of the object world Exploration "No," "Me do," "No help" Initiative ("I can do it alone") Active imitation of people/activities Feed, dress, toilet self	Has schema of self: "like me" in size, gender, age Uses physical aggression to obtain own way	Parallel play Interactive skills: turn-taking, associative play Primitive empathy Attachment to parents when child under stress Response to external control of impulses Modeling/imitation of social roles

(continued)

33

Table 1. (continued)

Stage	Cognition	Autonomy/competence	Self/self-esteem	Social development/ interpersonal relationships
4–6 years Initiative/guilt Theory of mind	Theory of Mind: appearance/reality, fantasy/reality distinction Perspective/others think differently Classification by single attribute Understanding of social roles Language elaborated Conservation of number Simple jokes Focus on single external attribute Reliance on salient sensory dimension One-thing-at-a-time thinking	Self-control Dresses self Rides trike/climbs ladders Uses most fine/gross motor skills Buttons, zippers, uses crayons/pencils Mastery of self-care skills Mastery of spoken language	Has categorical self based on physical attributes and physical abilities Sex role identification Gender understood Has sense of self through social interactions Self a conglomerate of non-integrated skills, attributes Emerging self-esteem	Individual friendships Some self-control/other verbal control Understanding of social roles Social drama play Cooperative play Group play Preference for own gender Prosocial behavior Friends seen as those who play with child Peer social skills: control aggression, reciprocity, "joining in" vs. controlling, modulation of self-assertion Reading of social cues
CHILDHOOD	*Tasks: Build friendships, basic academic skills, self-schema, and self-esteem; establish sense of self, social understanding, sense of accomplishment, and security. Needed for success: physical adeptness, academic success, social competence*			
6–12 years Industry/inferiority Operational thinking	Conservation: weight, mass, volume Considers two dimensions of change at same time Internalized thinking Mental operations Rehearsal and memory strategies Problem solving Metacognition Inductive logic	Attainment and refinement of all gross and fine motor skills Ability to ride bike/skip School competence: reads, writes, does basic math School adjustment: structure, routine, expectations, performance Athletic competence	Builds sense of self based on reactions of others Support by peers and parents Social comparison Self-esteem established, high/low Integrated self: value based on parent and peer values of self Sex role stereotype (with same sex) Self-evaluation	Enduring friendship formation Mastering and following valued norms of social behavior, modulating self-assertion, reciprocity, cooperation Popular child: is fun; has humor; reads social cues; sees other points of view; is physically, academically, and socially competent; is attractive Play by rules/change rules with consensus; team play

ADOLESCENCE		Tasks: Develop advanced, abstract thinking and apply to self, social relations, and place in world; develop peer relations, intimacy, and individuation from clique, parents; prepare for vocation and independence		
12–14 years Group identity/alienation	Beginning of formal operations Deductive logic Systematic analysis	Identification with peers/cliques Potential for conflict with parents	Early: drop in self-esteem, changing body, change in school settings Body image concern Weak sense of individual identity Need for validation from peers/cannot be different Definition of self with more inner qualities	Social understanding (fairness) More coordinated peer activity Selects friends based on looks; like activities; same age, gender, and ethnicity Friends seen to have traits Loyal friendships/same-sex cliques Beginning heterosexual interests
15–18 years Individual identity/identity confusion Formal operational thinking	Consolidated formal operations (for some) Hypothetical thinking Thinking in abstract principles Projection into future Generating and exploring hypotheses to make decisions Increased multidimensional, abstract thinking Self-reflective thinking	Identity formation Vocational/future role selection Independence/drives car Part-time work Sorting out identity and goals Clear identity for some Questioning beliefs from family, religion, values Peak performance of athletic skills	Friendships as source of self-worth, security, confidence, information Rise in self-esteem Search for identity Integrated image of self as unique; abstract concept of self; attitudes, values, beliefs, expectations	Stable intimate friends/self-disclosure, emotional support More time with friends Easily influenced by friends Interest and exploration of sexuality and intimacy Seeks intimate relationships Increased emotional autonomy from parents May begin to have sex, use drugs
18–22 years		Leaves home for school or work Independent decision making Autonomy in relation to parents		

ment is a singularly strong message for the infant. Erikson (1963) characterizes this as a period during which the infant develops a basic sense of trust or mistrust in the world.

The establishment of a secure attachment is an extremely important accomplishment for several reasons. It provides a safe base and confidence, facilitating exploration and autonomy rather than fostering uncertainty, dependence, and insecurity. Secure attachment also ensures a social support upon which the child relies during stress in future years (Rutter & Rutter, 1993).

Research has shown that the existence of a secure caregiver–infant attachment within the first 18 months presages greater social competence and successful interaction with peers at ages 3 and 4 and greater social competence at ages 9 and 10 and even at young adulthood (Sroufe, 1988). Conflicted attachments are related to shallow social contacts and friendships and eventually with difficulty in establishing significant relationships with others as adults. Infants and children who have been reared in their early years in congregate settings or settings with no permanent caregivers experience cognitive as well as social developmental problems (Hunt, 1979; Tizard & Hodges, 1978). Children separated from their families due to extensive and frequent hospitalization during the first and second years of life also experience problems of adjustment (Rutter & Rutter, 1993). Parents need continuous and frequent contact with their infant and an opportunity to develop confidence in caring for their infant. This connection is the basis of mutually responsive, secure attachment (Minde, 1993).

Mutually satisfying social relationships and social competence are essential for participating in the world of work, family, and leisure as an adult. Although the impact of early experience may be changeable later, a child's environment (e.g., personalities and methods of caregiving adults, socioeconomic status, attitudes, values, cultural traditions) is generally stable over time (Sameroff, 1993), even more stable than an individual child's characteristics. Social relations in infancy and childhood often do presage social adjustment in later life.

The beginnings of using symbols to represent objects and activities also appears near the end of infancy. The infant plays, practices deferred imitation (acting out things seen before), uses gestures, and begins to use speech to communicate wants and intentions. The child shows interest in other infants. Some assertive behavior ("it's mine") and parallel and associative play with other infants emerge.

At-Risk Infants

Research has shown that infants who are not mature at birth; who have experienced some prenatal or perinatal stress (e.g., low birth weight); or for whom a sensory, physical, or developmental disability is identified are not prepared physically to efficiently elicit caregiving (Lyons-Ruth & Zeanah, 1993; Minde, 1993). Their functioning may be irregular, and caregiving may not be quieting for them. Responsiveness to their caregiver may not be predictable or be what the caregiver expects (e.g., babies with visual impairments quiet to the caregiver's presence rather than wiggle all over and make noises like other babies), and this unexpected response can be interpreted by a parent as rejection or lack of interest (Fraiberg, 1977). These babies are at risk for further developmental and social problems, as are those with difficult (overreactive or underreactive) temperaments (Thomas, Chess, & Birch, 1968). Early intervention may be warranted to apprise parents of expected reactions or lack of reaction from their infant. Parents may need to learn appropriate compensation so that they and the infant can develop a mutual and strong positive attachment rather than feelings of inadequacy, guilt, or rejection. Interventions aimed at educating parents to "read" and respond to their infant have resulted in normative outcomes for infants (Crockenberg, 1981; Lyons-Ruth & Zeanah, 1993).

Infants at risk also include those who, for reasons of their disability or the structure of their environmental situation, 1) do not receive responsive care, social interaction, and social stimulation from a caregiving adult; 2) do not receive stimulation for the development of pragmatic communication; and 3) do not experience organization, structure, and predictability in their lives (Anastasiow, 1986; Werner, 1987). The importance of having a responsive social environment that includes language stimulation as a social tool, opportunities for manipulation and exploration of objects and places, responsive caregiving, social stimulation, and play has been demonstrated repeatedly. The lack of these conditions during infancy and early childhood leads to delayed cognitive and language development and to less than optimal social development (Hunt, 1979; Tizard & Hodges, 1978; Werner, 1987).

Infants need to experience a language environment to learn the use and social nature of language, regardless of their sensory status (e.g., whether a child has hearing impairment or not). A social system that responds to and provides clear signals for the infant and toddler (Liben, 1978) is essential for later cognitive and academic competence as well as for language and social development. Special stimulation and substitute language (e.g., gestures, sign, pictures) may be required in situations where there are disabilities, such as when a child is hearing impaired or when oral language is delayed due to physical or cognitive challenges.

The importance of continuity of caregiving between 6 months and 3 years is especially important. The infant knows and remembers persons upon whom she or he relies for security and for having needs met, but does not yet have the language and cognitive capacity to understand disruptions in primary relationships. Recurrent hospitalizations or other forms of instability in family structure are risk factors for social adjustment (Rutter & Rutter, 1993).

Protective Factors

Protective factors include all factors that promote maximum responsiveness of warm, nurturing adult caregivers who provide consistent care and social and language stimulation. This responsiveness promotes infant trust, positive attachment, and cognitive growth. Protective factors are seen in a child who has an easy disposition (e.g., adaptable, predictable, self-regulating), who responds to caregiving, who elicits caregiving, or whose temperament matches that of the caregiver (Thomas et al., 1968). The infant's ability to draw out and reinforce caregiving in the adult promotes adult confidence. An active, healthy infant who is good-natured, likes and responds positively to people, attempts to do things for himself or herself, and achieves developmental milestones is buffered from environmental stresses and disorganization. These characteristics often lead to the successful resolution of developmental challenges by drawing out and reinforcing the attention and caregiving support available in the environment (Benard, 1992; Werner, 1987).

Protective factors in the family and environment that promote successful development are healthy, untroubled parents; first-child status; small family or spacing of several years between children; and availability of a consistent caregiver (Werner, 1987). These factors enable caregivers to have sufficient time and energy to provide nurturing, responsiveness, and much-needed attention to the infant during the first year. Other factors that promote these conditions are additional primary caregivers, emotional and social support for the family, and access to special services (Crockenberg, 1981; Werner, 1987). Reducing separations between caregivers and an infant and reducing the numbers of transitory major caregivers (e.g., reducing the number of hospitalizations, providing rooming-in for family members when hospitalizations are necessary, reducing the numbers of personnel the infant relies upon) are protective practices (Garrison & McQuiston, 1989). Providing support and techniques to parents so that they are responsive to their infant encourages development and increases their confidence in parenting (Fraiberg, 1977; Infant Health and Development Program [IHDP], 1990; Minde, 1993). Anything that reduces family stress and discord and supports the availability, confidence, and responsiveness of caregivers is a protective factor.

EARLY CHILDHOOD (AGES 2–6)

Early childhood is considered to be the period of development between ages 2 and 6 years. The major tasks and accomplishments of early childhood include the mastery of language and of gross and fine motor skills. These accomplishments, in turn, are the foundation for the development of autonomy, personal independence, and social interaction seen during this time. Mastery of physical self-care and the development of self-control and social play are tasks of this period. Early childhood falls into two general periods, ages 2–4 years being characterized by impulsive self-assertion and ages 4–6 years being characterized by the moderation of initiative by greater interpersonal understanding and peer relations (Erikson, 1963).

Autonomy (Ages 2–4)

The age of 2–4 years has been labeled *Autonomy vs. Shame* (Erikson, 1963). This is a time of extreme self-assertion, enabled by new motor independence that allows exploration. "No help," "me do," and "no" are heard with great frequency. The child observes and acts out roles, learning by trying everything and getting into everything. The child is preoccupied with imitating the actions of others and attempts to do everything for himself or herself—undressing, dressing, and bathing. The child recognizes himself or herself as independent from others and attempts to control and tease adults. Language is further developed to communicate wants and needs. The child finds other children interesting. The beginnings of dominance, empathy, guilt, knowledge of right from wrong, helping, and nurturing younger children are seen in this stage.

During this period, thinking and knowing become more internal and symbolic (Piaget, 1970), and representation by images, words, and thoughts becomes possible. However, cognitive skills are dominated by the world the child sees around her or him. The child focuses on one dominant sensory aspect of an event. The child is "caught" by highly visible observations, such as of changes, and the child assimilates these observations to be used at a later time. Cognitively, the child is creating categories, including categories for her- or himself, and seeking similarities. The child recognizes her or his own gender and self and labels her- or himself by concrete observable physical dimensions.

Throughout this time, continuity of responsive caregiving by significant family members remains critical for the development of social confidence and attachment. However, this is also the period of great achievements in motor and language development. These developments propel the child toward greater independence and self-assertion, laying the groundwork for a sense of self. Increased physical independence coupled with the urge for autonomy and self-assertion raises issues of social control and conflict with family and social institutions. Toilet training, recognizing limits, and developing language as a means of control are central tasks during this period. Restrictions and the beginnings of verbal control lead to the beginnings of self-control.

The young child's social development is exemplified by the quality of play. During the third and fourth year, the child's repertoire expands to include play alongside other children and then to more interactive play. Associative play emerges (e.g., sharing of toys in an uncoordinated fashion, turn-taking, and some cooperative play). Play is a major context for incorporating motor skills, a growing awareness of social role, and give and take in relationships.

Initiative (Ages 4–6)

The major developmental changes encountered between 4 and 6 years are the emergence of a "Theory of Mind" (Flavell, 1992); beginning friendships; and developing self-control, self-reliance, and a set of activities and skills that define the self (Sroufe & Rutter, 1984). Oral language is mastered and peer relations further developed through play. Parallel and associative play gives way to more organized, cooperative play with rules and sociodrama. The child achieves independence in self-care and can organize activities around a goal. He or she is more assertive and aggressive, while also learning more self-control.

The child is now able to perceive the difference between appearance and reality and can understand that others may see things differently and have a reaction different from his or her own. For example, the child knows that a person who puts on a gorilla suit has not been transformed into a gorilla, and the child also knows that if an individual didn't see the person put on the costume, he or she might think it really was a gorilla. This is a very important cognitive achievement necessary for the development of essential social skills—reading social cues and seeing others' points of view (Flavell, 1992).

The development of friendships, another important achievement that begins during this period, requires recognizing and responding to peer needs or at least modulating one's own behavior. Friendships, in turn, are the context for learning social skills—communication, cooperation, group entry, and conflict resolution. Friendships provide information about the self and others and about how to do things and provide emotional and cognitive resources.

A child's cognitive level and cognitive model may affect the character of her or his play and peer relations. Theorists maintain that the child's knowledge reflects what he or she chooses to see and how he or she chooses to interpret it (Flavell, 1992). The child begins making attributions that can help him or her build and reinforce either positive or negative actions and social interactions. If a child has built negative interpretations due to having many negative interactions, neutral peer overtures may be interpreted as hostile or threatening, and then the child may react aggressively (Dodge, 1983). The child helps to create continuity in his or her own environment by the cognitive models and interpretations built through interactions with others.

The child describes and thinks of her- or himself in terms of concrete skills and specific activities that she or he has or does not have. Still captured by the external appearance of activities, people, and events (Piaget, 1970), the child sees herself as a girl or himself as a boy who can ride a bike well, swim, or take her or his bath. By the end of this developmental stage, the child is likely to have developed either high or low self-esteem (Harter, 1983).

Risks

By the end of early childhood, the child has generally mastered the biologically pro-grammed basics of motor, communication, self-care, and elementary cognitive skills (still lacking problem solving and abstract reasoning). The genetic programs are pretty well fulfilled except for physical and sexual maturation. The extent to which language and cognition are elaborated and the extent of development of social skills (turn-taking, sharing, social roles, self-control) and self-esteem have been highly influenced, howev-er, by the social experiences of the child.

The risk factors in the social environment include those identified at the end of the preceding period: disorganization and discontinuity in the family environment; lack of significant, positive, and responsive adult caregiving from one or a few persons with whom the child has a major attachment; and lack of opportunities for interactive and useful social communication. In addition, these environmental risk factors now emerge: restricted opportunities for exploration and mastery of the physical environ-ment and inappropriate socialization experiences (highly punitive or highly permis-sive). Problems in these areas have been shown to adversely affect the child's mastery of developmental tasks during this period (Baumrind, 1971, 1993). The child who does not have the opportunity to explore and develop autonomy and physical motor compe-tence in activities of daily living may not develop a positive view of self, personal autonomy, or sense of competence. The child experiencing inappropriate socialization is at great risk for future social maladjustment.

The child who is at risk due to developmental challenges, excessive motor behav-ior (e.g., characterized by others as hyperactive and/or inattentive), or lack of structure in the environment may elicit erratic and highly punitive caregiving responses. If high-ly punitive physical punishments or rejection are used as forms of control or as a reac-tion to a child's autonomy demands and assertion, the child may develop self-control and cognitive problems (Sroufe & Rutter, 1984; Werner, 1987) and may later have low academic achievement and low self-esteem (Patterson, DeBaryshe, & Ramsey, 1989). Highly active children or children who have difficulty meeting the expectations of their caregivers may experience physical punishment or excessive or erratic forms of control that impede the child's social and personal development.

Protective Factors

Children who are outgoing, social, easy to get along with, adaptable, and autonomous and who master self-care and developmental tasks appear to thrive despite multiple environmental risk factors in their lives (Werner, 1987). However, environments can buffer children who have personal risk factors. We know that significant risk factors in low birth weight infants and in infants with prenatal or perinatal problems can be over-come by a healthy, safe, loving, and stimulating environment with responsible adults who provide opportunities for exploration as well as structure and limits (IHDP, 1990; Lyons-Ruth & Zeanah, 1993; Werner & Smith, 1982). These factors are essential for all children. Protective environments during early childhood are also those in which the primary caregivers provide organization and structure, have expectations for social and self-control (Baumrind, 1993), and offer opportunities for social interactions with oth-ers. Self-control and cooperation with others become the foundation for successful development in future stages (Anastasiow, 1986). Another protective factor that begins to emerge during this period is the opportunity to develop a meaningful responsible role within the family (Benard, 1992).

Implications for children with disabilities and their families point to the need for early intervention and special services to assist them with ways to compensate for specific disabilities, to be confident in their caregiving, and to receive the support that they need to provide a responsive, caring, and mutually reinforcing environment. Creating opportunities for autonomy and mastery of the self and the physical environment is especially important when there are physical, sensory, and cognitive challenges. It may be necessary to make creative modifications in clothing, home environments, and toys; to use adaptive equipment; and especially to encourage and facilitate attempts at autonomy. Effective social interaction is essential to enhance social and cognitive development and understanding of the self and others. Opportunities for peer interactions to facilitate acquisition of social skills and appropriate self-control can help meet some of the challenges of this stage of development. In addition, caregivers assist the child's development by defining a meaningful role for the child within the family (e.g., adapting household tasks so that the child can participate in or be responsible for some routine daily living task), providing the child with high expectations, and providing the structure and expectations for the child to develop self-control.

CHILDHOOD (AGES 6–12)

During this developmental period, there are major and significant shifts in tasks and challenges that are defined in large part by that significant social institution, the school. Academic and athletic skills emerge, and friends, self-awareness, and self-esteem become important. The child is expected to achieve academic competence (e.g., learn to read, write, and work with numbers), develop social relations with peers, form a sense of identity, and develop positive self-esteem. The latter two expectations are greatly affected by the success achieved with the others, social relations, academic success, and physical abilities (athletic prowess). Developing competence in social, academic, and physical skills are important factors in the continued positive development of self and self-esteem.

Cognitively, thinking is now mobile. The child can think about more than one thing at a time; can shift back and forth between one perspective and another; and can think about multiple attributes of things, people, and relationships. The child begins to consider intention in actions rather than simply the actual outcome or the authority-given rule (e.g., why someone broke the window—accident or anger—rather than simply that she broke the window). The child is not so bound by immediate observed changes or perceptual features of events, objects, and relationships and can think in ways that contradict her immediate impressions. He or she realizes that rules can be changed if all players agree and that games are social contracts. These cognitive accomplishments enable the child to think about and appreciate others' points of view and to recognize social cues, and they set the stage for developing friendships on bases other than shared space or shared activities.

Children's understanding and thinking about friendships parallels their cognitive development. In early childhood, friends are "people I play with," people who happen to be there. By the beginning of middle childhood, friends are peers "who help me." Then, between ages 8 and 10, friends are people who cooperate, who have the same likes and dislikes—people "who like me, and whom I like." Reciprocity of actions, helping, and interests become important (Selman, 1980).

The development of social skills also relies on the greater mobility of thinking that occurs during this stage. The child can put himself more readily in another's shoes and recognizes reciprocity of thoughts and feelings; and by the end of this stage, the child begins to identify and think in terms of psychological states. The child looks at intentions rather than actions and more clearly appreciates that others may feel differently from he or she does about events.

Friendship development is a critical task during this stage. The child spends a great deal more time with peers from this time on, into adulthood. Peers become more and more important for their role in facilitating or impeding successful developmental task resolution in this and future stages. During this period, children begin making best friends. Friendships formed during this period often last throughout adolescence and into adulthood, some for a lifetime (Bee, 1992). Friendships provide one important source of social support during this and all later stages, and they supply important information for the model of self the child develops and for self-esteem (Duck, 1973).

Children who have not made friendships and who are lonely are at risk as they approach the challenges of this and later stages. For many, loneliness persists over a very long time (Renshaw & Brown, 1993). Even at this early age, a lack of friendships, either due to social withdrawal or to a lack of self-control and insufficient modulation of self-assertion with peers, presages significant developmental problems. Where modulation of assertiveness is an issue, a lack of friends can lead to problems in achievement as well as in social relatedness and self-esteem (Eron, 1987; Rutter, 1989). Lack of peer social success or relatedness at age 8 has been identified as a clear signal for concern with regard to the successful negotiation of the developmental tasks of childhood.

How are friends made during childhood? Children continue to seek out others who are "like me," a tendency observed very early in development. They tend to choose as friends peers who are similar in age, gender, interests, activities, and backgrounds. As a result, they often select friends from the same social class, ethnicity, and religious group. Children also seek out other children who are physically attractive and have competencies in valued areas—sports, academics, or other pursuits (Bee, 1992).

How do children join new groups? Successfully socialized children watch what others are doing and then begin to join in and follow the patterns of play already established. They modulate their behavior to match that of other children. Unsuccessfully socialized children barge in and attempt to take over groups or do not enter at all. Self-assertion and aggression are behaviors that lead to general rejection by peers and inhibit the development of friendships (Dodge, 1983; Patterson et al., 1989).

Socially successful children have social skills—they read social cues, share, see another's point of view, and control self-assertion and aggression. They have the physical, motor, and personality factors that allow participating in social play, having fun, and having a sense of humor (Masten, 1986).

During this period, the model of self is elaborated based on social and cultural standards of appearance and on who is like me, who I am like, and who I want to be with. This process leads to gender segregation of friends and play and the selection of friends identified as similar physically as well as in interests and values. The sense of self is built through social interactions with family and now with peers and teachers, incorporating their values, rules, and attitudes to guide behavior. Success or failure— doing valued activities in school work, relationships, sports—contributes to the development of a sense of self and of self-esteem (Harter, 1983).

Children choose environments and experiences consistent with their own view of themselves. They also interpret experiences and social feedback within their model of themselves, which can result in self-fulfilling prophecies. For example, a child who has developed aggressive responses to social interactions may interpret ambiguous social situations as threats to which he or she then reacts aggressively (Dodge & Frame, 1982). Children who have received positive social responses from others believe people like them, and they reach out to people for help when they need it and get the help they need (Werner & Smith, 1982). The quality of transactions with others is incorporated into the child's model of self and becomes the way the child interprets interactions with others, a process that creates a bias in perception. The formation of self and the interpretation of events based upon that model add to the continuity of environmental factors in development as the child seeks out situations, environments, and people that continue to reinforce his or her existing models of self.

Perceived competence is the basis for the sense of self and for self-esteem. Competence includes competence at physical (admired) activities, social relationships (popularity), academic success (admired by peers), or special talents. If there is no large discrepancy between perceived and valued competence (Harter, 1983), a child has positive self-esteem. Positive self-esteem will likely lead to socially valued work habits (Anastasiow, 1986). By age 7, a child's feelings of positive or negative self-esteem are already evident (Harter, 1983).

Risks/Additional Challenges

Children at risk are those who are unsuccessful in developing peer relations and in meeting academic challenges. They are children who have difficulty mastering the initial literacy demands of our culture, who are considered aggressive, or who are not socially successful. Children who are lonely or considered aggressive are often ostracized, further threatening their self-esteem (Eron, 1987). Research strongly supports a directional relationship from reduced self-control to peer rejection; then to poor school achievement; and finally to conduct disorder, delinquency, rejection, and low self-esteem (Patterson et al., 1989). Children at risk show these danger signals for unsuccessful resolution of the tasks and challenges of childhood and later stages of development. These danger signals may actually be evidence of the unsuccessful resolution of the cognitive, social, or autonomy challenges of earlier stages of development.

Poor social skills seem to be the most important correlate of unsuccessful social adjustment. Many children who have labels such as attention-deficit/hyperactivity disorder, conduct disorder, or learning disabilities show poor social skills as well as social rejection and academic difficulties. Labels in and of themselves may constitute a risk factor, as they affect teachers' perceptions and expectations of the child as well as those of the child him- or herself lowering performance and achievement expectations and then performance (Gibbon, 1981). This process may help perpetuate behavior that creates a self-fulfilling prophecy (Dodge, 1983).

Protective Factors

Protective factors that the child possesses at this stage are seen in the successful child—a child who is intelligent, a social mediator who has social problem-solving skills and empathy, is physically able, is physically attractive, and has friends. The successful child can distance him- or herself from circumstances that he or she cannot control, such as family alcoholism (Benard, 1992). The model of self is positive and autonomous. The child has an internal locus of control and high expectations for him- or herself, and high motivation to achieve (Benard, 1992; Werner, 1987). Children who have special interests and hobbies; are able to take care of themselves; are literate; desire to improve themselves; have close peer friends; have a shared sense of values; and live in homes with structure, rules, and warm supervision (Baumrind, 1971; Werner, 1987) are those who are resilient in the face of multiple risk factors or challenges.

Protective environments provide the child with valued roles and meaningful participation. These environments include schools that provide a nurturing relationship with an adult, offer valued roles for the child, and have high expectations for the child's performance (Benard, 1992) and also homes that exemplify similar characteristics. These homes offer meaningful roles for the child and convey high expectations and maturity demands as well as provide nurturance and respectful relations with the child (Baumrind, 1971). Engagement in meaningful, constructive activities is highly associated with life satisfaction, well-being, and high self-esteem (Diener, 1984; Maton, 1990). A child who has social skills and some competencies her parents and peers value, who shares interests and activities with a peer group, and who has a meaningful role at school and home is in a strong position to master developmental challenges despite other risk factors.

Implications for children with disabilities include the need to provide opportunities to develop some strengths, interests, and activities, especially those valued by the child because they reflect parental and peer values. Social skills should be enhanced—learning empathy for others and learning to read social cues and to respond to situations with problem-solving strategies. Many schools and prevention programs (prevention of antisocial, aggressive behavior; drug abuse; depression; and promotion of positive mental health and social adjustment) have integrated social skills training and problem solving into their curricula based upon the methods of Shure and Spivack (1982) and others (Goldstein, 1988). Encouraging hobbies and special interests and strengthening special competencies are normative avenues to success in this stage. Children select friends on the basis of similar looks, interests, and activities; therefore, children at risk because of developmental, physical, or sensory challenges can benefit from developing skills and interests that allow them to befriend others through some activity in which they can participate cooperatively. Providing meaningful, instrumental roles at home and in school, including tutoring or assisting others, also supports and encourages the qualities that are evident in resilient children.

Factors associated with success at this stage are some combination of physical adeptness, academic success, social competence, and friends. Support in any of these areas can enhance the mastery of developmental challenges. As delineated by Benard (1992) in her thorough review of the factors leading to healthy resolution of developmental challenges, the operating dynamics are to bond, to belong, to have power and control, and to contribute. The first three dynamics are evident and important from birth and throughout development. The latter dynamic, having a meaningful role in a group, emerges at the end of early childhood and continues throughout life.

ADOLESCENCE TO ADULTHOOD

Tasks of adolescence are to integrate the physiological and emotional changes precipitated by puberty into a new identity: to incorporate sexuality and body image into self-image; to rebuild self-esteem, which often plunges in early adolescence (Bee, 1992); to develop an identity; and to prepare to separate from family (Erikson, 1963). The major issues of adolescence in normative development include body image concerns and a weak sense of individual identity. Youth are easily influenced by their peer group, spend even more time with friends, seek intimate friendships and emotional autonomy from parents, and may begin sexual relationships and use alcohol and other drugs. By the end of adolescence, children prepare to leave home. Here, with even greater intensity and importance, peer groups and friendships are the sine qua non of development.

Adolescence falls into two major periods: ages 12–14 years and ages 15–18 years. The first period is characterized by the forming of cliques with an extreme dependence on peer approval, and the later period is characterized by movement toward individual identity (Bee, 1992). Preparation for adult roles and economic independence extend for longer periods, as few in today's culture are able to complete individuation and enter the world of work and independent living by the age of 18. The tasks, challenges, and principles are the same, however, even if the period of dependency upon families and of developing vocational goals, securing economic independence, and establishing a primary relationship outside the family extends over a longer period, often into the 20s.

Early Adolescence (Ages 12–14)

The period between 12 and 14 years is characterized by a need for a new validation of self. This is a period of decreased self-esteem and uncertainty, produced by significant body changes associated with puberty and physical maturation and with movement into the middle or high school. Self-esteem decline is thought to be a function of changes in the school environment and increased academic demands as well as a function of biological changes and the accompanying self-consciousness. This is the period of cliques. Youth cannot be different from others in dress, behavior, preferences, or interests. Cliques provide security and support (Bee, 1992). Puberty, too soon? Not soon enough? The timing of puberty can produce additional challenges for some youth, and the peer group tends to be the validation for the self. Friendships produce the sense of self-worth, security, interpersonal confidence, socioemotional adjustment, information, and support that are so badly needed (Duck, 1973). Friends are mutually supportive and share similar interests (Selman, 1980). Friendships are developed by engaging in self-disclosure about the intimate and personal details of the youth's inner and outer life.

Late Adolescence (Ages 15–18)

The second stage of adolescence, ages 15–18, is a time when children adapt to puberty, achieve adult sexual identity, search for a future occupational role, and prepare for independence. Cognitive development is complete, and hypothetical imagining can take place (Piaget, 1970). Youths can begin to understand and contemplate mortality; they can plan ahead and look behind. This level of cognitive development is the foundation for much of the questioning and reorganization of identity that frequently takes place during the latter part of adolescence. Hormonal and neural developmental changes of childhood and adolescence are complete. Self-esteem rises.

Friendships are typically concerned with reciprocity, loyalty, and emotional sharing. Avenues for making and keeping friendships are through self-disclosure and empathy. Friendships are more stable. There is an increased need for autonomy from family. This autonomy can produce conflict, although conflict is not universal. Families that have developed mutual trust, mutual responsibility, and established rules may not encounter conflict around issues of adolescent autonomy (Baumrind, 1993; Bee, 1992).

The drive for autonomy and assumption of adult roles leads to sexual activity for large numbers of adolescents. Movement into socially defined roles of work and independence may begin later, and the assumption of roles for creating a family with children is shifted well beyond the onset of biological drives and capabilities, to the end of the 20s for many people. The normal age for work and financial independence, marriage, and family has moved substantially later, affected by economics and training needs, whereas sexual activity may begin at a younger age because of earlier physical maturation. Adolescent sexual activity is both encouraged and discouraged by conflicting cultural messages. During this period a youth must face and resolve the issues of how or whether to be sexual, how to be accepted, and how to separate from his or her family as an individual.

Risks

With the attainment of full cognitive capacity, the biological changes of puberty, and the social pressures for reaching adulthood, affective disorders such as depression and anxiety affect some youth. It is not known whether additional stressors in adolescence precipitate these disorders or whether factors related to cognitive development have a greater influence. The increased personal awareness of possibilities and limitations (cognitive development) and the increased social comparison that occur during adolescence may contribute to the incidence of these affective disorders. Some youths may experience fewer social supports, there may be age-related genetic vulnerabilities (Rutter & Rutter, 1993), or these factors may combine to exacerbate the challenges of this developmental period. Home and schools that lack structure and supervision, make few maturity demands, and fail to provide the adolescent with responsible roles for participation are associated with increased developmental risks, especially during adolescence (Baumrind, 1993; Benard, 1992; Werner, 1987).

Youths at risk include those who cannot self-disclose to others to form a basis for friendship—boys are at greater risk than girls (Maccoby, 1990)—or who do not share activities, interests, and events as a basis for friendship; boys, and now girls, can compensate by participating in team sports (Zetlin & Murtaugh, 1988). Lonely people have decreased self-esteem, rate others negatively, and can create their own models for perpetuating their isolation (Clegg & Standen, 1991).

Protective Factors

Protections at this stage are similar to those identified in earlier developmental periods. These factors include having a person as a confidante and for emotional support and having rules and structure and high expectations for oneself that reflect the regard of significant people in one's life at home, at school, and among friends. Having a meaningful role in the home, school, social group, and community is an important way to successfully meet the significant challenges of adolescence (Benard, 1992). Having the skills—cognitive, physical, and social—upon which to build further skills, interests, and self-esteem are ways to meet the demands of approaching adulthood. Among these, however, social skills are most important (Bradley & Meredith, 1991; Zetlin & Murtaugh, 1988); essential skills include sharing mutual interests and activities, using self-disclosure as an entry to friendship, and using problem-solving skills as a means to developing and maintaining friendships. Social problem solving in situations at school, work, and home and in the community are crucial in enabling adolescents to overcome risk factors and enter the adult world able to work, love, and play well (Werner & Smith, 1982).

CONCLUSIONS

A child is born to learn, to explore, to experiment, to communicate, and to form a model of self, others, and the world. The quality of transactions with other people, especially caregivers (birth to 5 years); caregivers, friends, and teachers (6–11 years); and best friend, friends, and parents (12–18 years) provide validation to the child of who she is. Relationships outside the family develop based upon the cultivation of skills (academic, physical, social, personal), activities, and interests. If the developmental challenges of earlier stages are successfully resolved, the child reaches biological maturity in late adolescence with a sense of self-worth and dignity and prepared to meet the adult challenges of work, love, family, and community (Erikson, 1963). To achieve these goals, the child needs social support; acceptance; positive feedback from family, friends, and neighbors; opportunities to develop interests and friendships; and meaningful roles in family, school, and community (Benard, 1992).

Risks and stresses are a part of living, and disabilities are potential risk factors, as are many other factors (e.g., family structure, life events, lifestyle, economic conditions, cultural context, living conditions, social conditions). Risk factors in these areas do not predict outcome. Outcome is affected by the model the child creates for him- or herself and the child's interpretation of events (the child's cognitive theory), the history of interactions experienced with significant others, and protective factors (e.g., social support, belonging, skills, and life roles). Some challenge is healthy and produces growth, but excessive challenge can be debilitating (Rutter & Rutter, 1993).

Three major themes emerge. The first is the importance of social skills, which lead to positive outcomes for the child (e.g., self-esteem, friendships, participation). The second theme is autonomy—having opportunities and expectations for independence and success, self-mastery, and competence in valued areas. These opportunities and expectations must be expressed and facilitated by the family, school, and community as well as by the individual. Autonomy is also a vehicle to self-esteem as well as to friendships and participation. The third theme is participation—having opportunities and skills to engage in valued and meaningful roles throughout each developmental period. These three themes all contribute to the essential goal: the establishment of friendships, close relationships, and interdependence with other people.

Risk or Challenge

For children who encounter stressful or challenging conditions, factors related to the individual child's characteristics, to family relationships, and to conditions outside the family can either exacerbate or buffer the response to stressors (Hetherington, 1989; Werner, 1987). Stressful conditions such as instability within the family; unemployment; absence (physical or psychological) of a major caregiver; divorce; chronic poverty; or erratic, unstructured, inconsistent, unresponsive, or punitive caregiving can be detrimental to the developing child. Any of these conditions, however, if not compounded, can constitute a challenge or opportunity for the child (Rutter, 1989). If the child has personal protective factors and other forms of support within the family and community, he or she is more likely to meet these environmental stressors and to grow from them. The child who has one or a few continuing, reliable, strong, positive relationships with a nurturing adult and who is able to reach out to people and obtain positive responses is more likely to interpret events in a positive way and does not blame her- or himself for the stressors. This child is more able to turn risks into challenge and growth.

If family stress provides the child with opportunities to take on more responsibility and to assume an important function in the family, as daughters often do when the mother is working or single or if the family structure is changing through divorce (Hetherington, 1989), the stress may promote positive growth for the child rather than becoming a barrier. Because poor health can be a risk factor for a child, it is important for children with health conditions to develop positive social skills, positive cognitive models for interpreting events and interactions, and responsible roles within their families.

Factors related to family relationships and family structure are important for children at risk. The number and spacing of children (i.e., the density of caregiving needs with respect to numbers of adult caregivers available) and the continuity, availability, and responsiveness of adult caregivers within the immediate or extended family all have a key role in the child's success in meeting developmental challenges. Structure, routine, high expectations for a child's performance, and the providing of an important role for the child in the family are also important factors.

Factors outside the family (e.g., availability of health care and services, employment, financial support, alternate caregivers) can also buffer the effects of developmental challenges and stressors (Hetherington, 1989; IHDP, 1990; Rutter, 1989; Werner & Smith, 1982). Access to services that provide information, support, and assistance for caregiving can assist families and children to successfully resolve early challenges. Support for caregivers in developing positive expectations; appropriate bonding; and environmental, social, and linguistic stimulation also promotes positive developmental outcomes (Anastasiow, 1986; Lyons-Ruth & Zeanah, 1993). Supports that provide encouragement for allowing exploration and promoting appropriate nutrition and health care help to compensate for challenges such as difficult temperament, physiological immaturity, and disability. Availability of social supports for parents, an extended caregiving network, and respite support all contribute to promoting the child's developmental progress in the face of challenges (Werner, 1987).

When families have high expectations for their children and provide responsibility training through rules and roles for their children, children are likely to be socially competent and well adjusted (Baumrind, 1993; Benard, 1992; Werner, 1987). Access to schools that provide the same qualities (e.g., structure, high expectations, opportunities for a meaningful role and success) also assist the child and the family to successfully navigate developmental challenges (Hetherington, 1989; Maton, 1990).

Developmental challenges increase with age, perhaps especially for children with disabilities. The younger child is supported by the responsive family environment, and the demands of play groups and day care peers are low. Peer social inclusion can be a reality (Gottlieb, 1990). With increasing age, however, factors outside the family become more important. Peers and peer activities are a major source of learning and development, and factors related to school activities and competencies and activities in the community have more direct effects. As Hetherington (1989) cogently described using data from longitudinal studies of divorce, the timing of significant stressors interacts in important ways for a child in relation to developmental status at the time and to the child's gender. Boys are at greater risk for difficulties meeting developmental and other challenges. As a result of socialization, fathers and sons are less able to reach out for social support when they need it (Maccoby, 1990). They are less able to use self-disclosure and to seek emotional support.

Risk also increases as the number of stresses and challenges increases. While social support from family members, friends, teachers, and others contributes to meeting stress and challenge, Hetherington's research (1989) shows that social support buffers stressful conditions for parents and children only in moderately stressful situations. When stress conditions are too great or intense, people do not use support effectively. Other research shows that families that experience chronic concurrent risk conditions (e.g., poverty, unstable family configuration) often have little social support available outside the family and are often isolated (Waller & Dumas, 1987).

What Are the Lessons?

The suggestions summarized in the following list can help increase the probability that a child will navigate developmental challenges successfully and convert challenges into opportunities for growth.

1. *Change the meaning of risk to challenge.* The cognitive model through which the child, the child's family, and the community view the tasks of the child with a disability is very important in terms of the child's meeting and benefiting from developmental challenges. Encouraging children to define their disabilities as manageable challenges can promote self-competence and success.

2. *Reduce exposure to excessive risk conditions, such as overcrowding and multiple stressors, as much as possible.* Support services for the child and family have an important role in this area. Risk reduction increases the ability of a child and the child's family to navigate each developmental period successfully.

3. *Focus on building competencies and strengths.* A child is admired for her or his skills, special interests, or knowledge. Special interests and knowledge can be shared with other people, becoming a vehicle for socialization as well as positive self-esteem. Supporting the child's strengths and interests and helping to build special areas of competence contributes to esteem building. Self-esteem is affected by the respect, opportunities, and social messages the child receives from the family and the community. Families and professionals should be encouraged to notice and point out a child's strengths.

4. *Increase opportunities for personal mastery and independence.* Activities and interests again provide ways to build friendships and self-esteem. People in the family and community may limit the child with disabilities rather than provide challenges and opportunities. It is essential that children be provided with incremental opportunities to try new activities and experiences in which there is reasonable expectation for success.

5. *Provide positive expectations.* Although this has become a truism in the field of disabilities, the message must be repeated and emphasized. Reasonable high expectations help increase a child's opportunities and performance in areas critical to development for all children, and a lack of expectations limits a child. The provision of opportunities to persons with developmental disabilities has often been the key to greater independence, community participation, and personal satisfaction (Burchard, in press).

6. *Provide and support instrumental, meaningful roles for the child within the family, school, and community.* Tasks and environmental constraints can be modified and, where necessary, partial participation encouraged.

7. *Support and encourage friendship building.* Friends become increasingly important as children develop. It is extremely important to encourage activities, opportunities, and interests that can allow access to peer groups and relationships and to promote the acquisition of social skills for entering and maintaining friendships.

All people need to be active participants in the world and to receive social and emotional support from others. This need to belong is the biggest challenge for all people, with or without disabilities. Having and using social problem-solving skills has been shown to be more important than intellectual level or age in predicting social adjustment (Healey & Masterpasqua, 1992). Many people learn social problem solving and empathy training from their social environments while growing up, but many schools and prevention programs (i.e., programs designed to reduce high-risk behaviors such as drug abuse, aggressive and antisocial behavior, and sexual promiscuity and to prevent depression and abuse) also provide training in these important areas (Goldstein, 1988; Shure & Spivack, 1982). The use of such curricula could bolster any child's competence in social skills.

Friendships depend upon physical proximity, age, gender, shared interests, shared activities, and shared perceptions. A child gains access to peer activities and relationships by being able to observe other children, by asking them questions about what they are doing, by listening, by paralleling their activity, and by joining in with what others are doing. It is important to encourage skills and to set up these opportunities. As children grow into middle childhood and adolescence, self-disclosure and sharing of personal feelings, desires, and needs is another important aspect of developing and maintaining friendships. Being able to talk about activities and events of mutual interest to other children is an important avenue to increasing social contacts. Children should be encouraged or taught how to communicate in this way.

The child who is able to elicit positive responses from the environment and who can actively reach out to people, especially peers during childhood and adolescence, has an advantage in meeting developmental challenges. Experiences and opportunities that support the child in developing these social skills will help the child meet challenges and overcome risk.

Ultimately, the developmental accomplishments and resolutions of age-related tasks is the result of complex interactions among the person, his or her experiences, and his or her perception of the meaning of these events (Flavell, 1992). The development of the individual's perception or model for interpreting those interactions has been shown to have important ramifications for social and personal outcomes (Dodge, 1983; Hetherington, 1989; Sameroff, 1993). Development is accomplished by accommodating and adapting in the face of challenges, among which disability is one. The extent to which a child is supported to effectively respond to developmental challenges will promote his or her progression toward self-competence and personal fulfillment.

REFERENCES

Adler, A. (1948). *Studies in analytical psychology.* New York: Norton.

Anastasiow, A. (1986). *Development and disability: A psychological analysis for special educators.* Baltimore: Paul H. Brookes Publishing Co.

Baumrind, D. (1971). Current patterns of parental authority. *Developmental Psychology Monograph, 4*(1, part 2).

Baumrind, D. (1993). The average expectable environment is not good enough: A response to Scarr. *Child Development, 64,* 1299–1317.

Bee, H. (1992). *The developing child.* New York: Harper Collins.

Benard, B. (1992). Fostering resiliency in kids: Protective factors in the family, school, and community. *Prevention Forum, 12*(3), 1–16.

Bradley, L.J., & Meredith, R.C. (1991). Interpersonal development: A study with children classified as educable mentally retarded. *Education and Training in Mental Retardation, 26,* 130–141.

Burchard, S.N. (in press). Normalization and residential services: The Vermont Studies. In Flynn, R.J. & LeMay, R. (Eds.) *Twenty-five years of normalization and social role valorization: Looking back, looking ahead.* Ottawa, Ontario, Canada: University of Ottawa Press.

Burchard, S.N., Gordon, L.G., & Pine, J. (1990). Manager competence, program normalization, and client satisfaction in group homes. *Education and Training in Mental Retardation, 25,* 277–285.

Burchard, S.N., Hasazi, J.E., Gordon, L.R., & Yoe, J. (1991). A comparison of lifestyle and adjustment in three community residential alternatives. *Research in Developmental Disabilities, 12,* 127–142.

Cadman, D., Boyle, M., Szatmari, P., & Offord, D. (1987). Chronic illness, disability, and mental and social well-being: Findings of the Ontario child health study. *Pediatrics, 79,* 805–834.

Clegg, J.A., & Standen, P.J. (1991). Friendship among adults who have developmental disabilities. *American Journal of Mental Retardation, 95,* 663–671.

Crockenberg, S.B. (1981). Infant irritability, mother responsiveness, and social support influences on the security of infant-mother attachment. *Child Development, 52,* 857–865.

Diener, E. (1984). Subjective well-being. *Psychological Bulletin, 95,* 542–575.

Dodge, K.A. (1983). Behavioral antecedents of peer social status. *Child Development, 54,* 1386–1399.

Dodge, K.A., & Frame, C.L. (1982). Social cognitive biases and deficits in aggressive boys. *Child Development, 53,* 620–635.

Duck, S.W. (1973). *Personal relationships and personal constructs: A study of friendship formation.* New York: John Wiley & Sons.

Dyson, L. (1993). Response to the presence of a child with disabilities: Parental stress and family functioning over time. *American Journal of Mental Retardation, 98,* 207–218.

Erikson, E. (1963). *Childhood and society* (2nd ed.). New York: W.W. Norton.

Eron, L.D. (1987). The development of aggressive behavior from the perspective of a developing behaviorism. *American Psychologist, 42,* 435–442.

Flavell, J.H. (1992). Cognitive development: Past, present, and future. *Developmental Psychology, 28,* 998–1005.

Fraiberg, S. (1977). *Insights from the blind.* New York: Basic Books.

Garrison, W.T., & McQuiston, S. (1989). *Developmental clinical psychology and psychiatry: Vol. 19. Chronic illness during childhood and adolescence.* Newbury Park: Sage Publications.

Gibbon, F.X. (1981). The social psychology of mental retardation: What's in a label? In J. Brehm, S.M. Kassin, & F.X. Gibbon (Eds.), *Developmental social psychology* (pp. 249–270). New York: Oxford.

Goldstein, A.P. (1988). *The Prepare Curriculum: Teaching prosocial competencies.* Champaign, IL: Research Press.

Gottlieb, J. (1990). Mainstreaming and quality education. *American Journal of Mental Retardation, 95,* 16–17.

Harter, S. (1983). Developmental perspectives on the self-system. In E.M. Hetherington (Ed.), *Handbook of child psychology: Vol. 4. Socialization, personality, and social development:* (pp. 275–386). New York: John Wiley & Sons.

Healey, K., & Masterpasqua, F. (1992). Interpersonal cognitive problem solving among children with mild mental retardation. *American Journal of Mental Retardation, 96*(12), 367–372.

Hetherington, E.M. (1989). Coping with family transitions: Winners, losers, and survivors. *Child Development, 60,* 1–14.

Hunt, J.M. (1979). Psychological development: Early experience. *Annual Review of Psychology, 30,* 130–146.

Infant Health and Development Program (IHDP). (1990). Enhancing the outcomes of low-birth-weight, premature infants: A multisite, randomized trial. *Journal of the American Medical Association, 262,* 3035–3042.

Liben, L.S. (1978). The development of deaf children: An overview of issues. In L.S. Liben (Ed.), *Deaf children: Developmental perspectives* (pp. 3–20). New York: Academic Press.

Lyons-Ruth, K., & Zeanah, C.H., Jr. (1993). The family context of infant mental health: I. Affective development in the primary caregiving relationship. In C.H. Zeanah, Jr. (Ed.), *Handbook of infant mental health* (pp. 14–37). New York: Guilford Press.

Maccoby, E.E. (1990). Gender and relationships: A developmental account. *American Psychologist, 45,* 513–520.

Masten, A. (1986). Humor and competence in school-aged children. *Child Development, 57,* 461–473.

Maton, K. (1990). Meaningful involvement in instrumental activity and well-being: Studies of older adolescents and at risk urban teenagers. *American Journal of Community Psychology, 18*(2), 297–320.

Minde, K. (1993). Prematurity and serious medical illness in infancy: Implications for development and intervention. In C.H. Zeanah, Jr. (Ed.), *Handbook of infant mental health* (pp. 87–105). New York: Guilford Press.

Patterson, G.R., DeBaryshe, B.D., & Ramsey, E. (1989). A developmental perspective on antisocial behavior. *American Psychologist, 44*(2), 329–335.

Piaget, J. (1970). Piaget's theory. In P.H. Mussen (Ed.), *Carmichael's manual of child psychology: Vol. 1.* (3rd ed., pp. 703–732). New York: John Wiley & Sons.

Renshaw, P.D., & Brown, P.J. (1993). Loneliness in middle childhood: Concurrent and longitudinal predictors. *Child Development, 64,* 1271–1284.

Rutter, M. (1989). Isle of Wight revisited: Twenty-five years of child psychiatric epidemiology. *Journal of the American Academy of Child and Adolescent Psychiatry, 28,* 633–653.

Rutter, M., & Rutter, M. (1993). *Developing minds: Challenge and continuity across the life span.* New York: Basic Books.

Sameroff, A. (1993). Models of development and developmental risk. In C.H. Zeanah, Jr. (Ed.), *Handbook of infant mental health* (pp. 3–13). New York: Guilford Press.

Selman, R.L. (1980). *The growth of interpersonal understanding.* New York: Academic Press.

Shure, M., & Spivack, G. (1982). Interpersonal problem-solving in young children: A cognitive approach to prevention. *American Journal of Community Psychology, 10*(3), 341–356.

Sroufe, L.A. (1979). Emotional development in infancy. In J. Osofsky (Ed.) *Handbook of infancy* (pp. 462–516). New York: John Wiley & Sons.

Sroufe, L.A. (1988). The role of infant-caregiver attachment in development. In J. Belsky & T. Nezworski (Eds.), *Clinical implications of attachment* (pp. 18–40). Hillsdale, NJ: Lawrence Erlbaum Associates.

Sroufe, L.A., & Rutter, M. (1984). Salient developmental issues. *Child Development, 55,* 2.

Tanner, J.M., Whitehouse, R.H., & Takaishi, M. (1966). Standards from birth to maturity for height, weight, height velocity and weight velocity: British children, 1965. *Archives of Disease in Childhood, 41,* 454–471, 613–635.

Thomas, A., Chess, S., & Birch, H.G. (1968). *Temperament and behavior disorders in children.* New York: New York University Press.

Thompson, R.J., Jr., Gil, K.M., Burbach, D.J., Keith, B.R., & Kinney, T.R. (1993). Role of child and maternal processes in the psychological adjustment of children with sickle cell disease. *Journal of Consulting and Clinical Psychology, 61,* 468–474.

Tizard, B., & Hodges, J. (1978). The effect of early institutional rearing on the development of eight-year-old children. *Journal of Child Psychology and Psychiatry, 19,* 99–118.

Waller, R.G., & Dumas, J.E. (1987). Stimulus class determinants of mother-child coercive interchanges in multidistressed families: Assessment and intervention. In J. Burchard & S. Burchard (Eds.), *Prevention of delinquent behavior* (pp. 190–219). Newbury Park, CA: Sage Publications.

Werner, E. (1987). Vulnerability and resiliency in children at risk for delinquency (and other mental health problems): A longitudinal study from birth to young adulthood. In J. Burchard & S. Burchard (Eds.), *Prevention of delinquent behavior* (pp. 16–43). Newbury Park, CA: Sage Publications.

Werner, E.E., & Smith, R.S. (1982). *Vulnerable, but invincible: A longitudinal study of resilient children and youth.* New York: McGraw-Hill.

Wolfensberger, W. (1991). Reflections on a lifetime in human services and mental retardation. *Mental Retardation, 29*(1), 1–15.

Zetlin, A.G., & Murtaugh, M. (1988). Friendship patterns of mildly learning handicapped and nonhandicapped high school students. *American Journal of Mental Deficiency, 92,* 447–454.

Coping in Children and Adolescents

Patterns, Influences, Interventions, and Implications

Wendy Kliewer

In the course of growing up, all children face situations that require coping. Common situations that elicit coping responses include teasing by the schoolyard bully, schoolwork that is too difficult, rejection by friends or peers, illness or death of pets, and exposure to conflicts between parents or other trusted adults. This chapter first reviews what we know about the natural course of development of children's coping competencies. The chapter then considers factors that influence children's coping, including factors intrinsic to the child, elements of the social environment, and features of the coping context. An overview of prevention programs designed to promote competence in children without special needs is provided. Finally, this chapter briefly discusses the implications of our knowledge of children's coping and of interventions for promoting coping efficacy among children with ongoing health conditions and disability.

THE COURSE OF CHILDREN'S COPING

According to Lazarus and Folkman (1984), a state of stress is created when individuals feel and think that their own resources are inadequate to handle the situations confronting them. This state of stress then elicits coping responses, which are merely what people do to manage stressful situations. Coping can involve many different types of activities, including trying to address the source of the problem, thinking about the situation differently, handling the emotions produced by the situation, or avoiding the situation entirely. As Lazarus and Folkman (1984) note, some coping strategies may be helpful, whereas others may have deleterious effects. They also note that coping is a *process,* and therefore can change over time. People may use a variety of coping methods to handle a problem as it unfolds. The complexity of coping is evident if we examine what children do in response to events that are stressful for them.

> Jessica, 10 years old, had a disturbing situation developing with several girls in her class at school. A group of Jessica's friends had formed a clique and had decided to systematically exclude her from all of their social interactions, including playing at recess and parties and sleepovers outside of school. Initially Jessica was so upset about the situation she did nothing but cry and avoid her classmates. The situation became worse, and Jessica then talked to her mother about potential ways of handling the problem. Together they thought about various solutions to the problem and the implications of each course of action Jessica could take. Jessica decided to talk to the ringleader of this group of girls in an attempt to make peace and regain favor with her peers. In this case, the strategy was successful, and Jessica was again included in the girls' activities.

The situation described above illustrates several points about coping. First, when situations occur that are highly arousing emotionally, often the most adaptive course to take initially is to avoid the situation and vent one's emotions (Kliewer, 1991). Once a person's emotions are somewhat under control, thinking through potential solutions and their consequences is beneficial. This strategy is referred to in the literature as planning, cognitive decision making, and active cognitive coping, and it is part of a larger group of strategies known as problem-focused or active coping. Problem-focused coping strategies involve dealing with the source of the stressful situation, whereas emotion-focused strategies concern managing one's affective responses to the situation. In general, children and adults who use problem-focused or active strategies to manage stress are also less depressed and anxious, display fewer behavioral problems, and have higher self-esteem (Armistead et al., 1990; Ayers, 1991; Compas, Malcarne, & Fondacaro, 1988; Ebata & Moos, 1991; Glyshaw, Cohen, & Towbes, 1989; Sandler, Tein, & West, 1994).

In addition to avoidance, venting of emotions, and cognitive decision-making coping strategies, direct problem solving is illustrated in the example of Jessica. Also termed active behavioral coping, direct problem solving is a common coping strategy and typically involves doing something concrete about the source of the stress. Direct problem solving is not always the best coping strategy to use, however. In general, it has been argued that strategies that attempt to change the source of the problem work best for situations that are changeable or controllable and are often ineffective for situations that cannot be altered (Folkman, 1984; Roth & Cohen, 1986). A number of studies have found this to be the case (Forsythe & Compas, 1987; Vitaliano, DeWolfe, Maiuro, Russo, & Katon, 1990). Presumably, with maturity we become better judges of which situations can be changed. Individuals of all ages can err in their judgments about which problems can be changed and which are immutable, and this can affect the effectiveness of coping efforts.

Over time, children and adolescents develop a repertoire of coping responses they can draw on in times of stress. Developmental and clinical research has shown that as children mature, their use of problem-focused strategies remains stable, but their use of emotion-focused strategies increases (Compas, Worsham, & Ey, 1992). Additionally, the effectiveness of cognitive coping strategies increases with age (Wilson, Hoffner, & Cantor, 1987). For example, a 7-year-old and a 12-year-old may exert similar amounts of effort to try to change a problem, but a 12-year-old is more likely than a 7-year-old to think about the situation in different ways or to control his or her emotional response to the situation. Furthermore, when 12-year-olds use cognitive strategies (e.g., focusing on the positive in a situation), these work more effectively than when younger children use these strategies.

These developmental trends in the use and effectiveness of cognitive and emotion-focused coping strategies are likely the result of several factors. First, with maturation, children may become better judges of which problems are changeable and which are not. Thus, as children understand that not all problems can be fixed, their energies are appropriately refocused on their affective responses to the situation.

Second, as children develop the ability to take the perspective of others and see situations from a nonegocentric viewpoint, they can consider more effectively the impact their behavior will have on others and can see positive as well as negative aspects of situations. Although forms of egocentrism persist throughout life, developmental research has shown that qualitative shifts in the ability of children to see the perspectives of others occur between the ages of 5 and 7. Children as young as age 2 or 3 do know that other people experience things differently from themselves, but figuring out *what* the other person sees or experiences comes later. Toddlers may, for example, change their speech or voice for a younger or older companion, yet still confuse their thoughts with those of others. By age 4 or 5, children have developed complex rules for figuring out what other people experience and have learned that other people have access to different information than they themselves may have (Flavell, 1985; Flavell, Green, & Flavell, 1990; Guralnick & Paul-Brown, 1984). At the beginning of middle childhood (age 6 or 7), children develop the ability to "step into another person's shoes," seeing situations from perspectives other than their own. By adolescence (age 12), children are able to view situations impartially, though they may not choose to do so (Selman, 1980). The shift away from an egocentric orientation results in improved communication and the development of empathic understanding (Harter, 1983; Shantz, 1983), which in turn is related to emotion-focused coping.

A third potential reason emotion-focused strategies increase with age and become more effective involves the concomitant shift in thinking about relationships (Selman & Selman, 1979). Most 12-year-olds, for example, are concerned about commitment and intimacy in their friendships, often demanding exclusivity. In contrast, most 7-year-olds are focused on having friends to do things with, and psychological dimensions of relationships with friends are not considered. A 16-year-old recognizes the complexity of relationships with friends, respecting both the needs for dependency and autonomy. These varied perspectives co-occur with cognitive development in other domains of the child's life and can influence the extent to which cognitive coping strategies are used in stressful situations, particularly those involving close relationships.

Fourth, over time there is an increase in the number of different coping models and coping behaviors to which children are exposed. Vicarious learning is one of the main ways children acquire behavior patterns (Bandura, 1977). It stands to reason that increased exposure to coping models is related to expanded coping repertoires and therefore to increased use of emotion-focused coping. Emotion-focused strategies are varied and complex and may require a certain level of cognitive sophistication to process. This fact may help explain developmental increases in the use of emotion-focused strategies.

In sum, with maturation, children's coping repertoires become more varied, and children use cognitive and emotion-focused coping strategies to a greater extent. These trends are paralleled by shifts in perspective-taking ability, shifts in perceptions of social relationships, and increased exposure to adults and peers.

INFLUENCES ON CHILDREN'S COPING CHOICES

As the preceding review demonstrates, natural developmental shifts in children's coping behavior occur over time. However, biological maturity is not the only influence shaping children's coping. At least three sets of factors affect a child's decision to use a particular coping strategy at a given time. These factors include individual qualities, social environmental qualities, and contextual qualities.

Individual Influences on Coping

In addition to gender, qualities of the child that affect coping behavior include personality traits such as "Type A" behavior; temperamental qualities such as impulsivity, approach-avoidance orientations, and arousability; established beliefs about the world, such as locus of control, pessimistic explanatory style, and hope; coping preferences, such as monitoring and blunting; and social competence.

A number of studies utilizing different methodologies and children of different ages have found that girls report doing more coping than boys. For example, girls report using more active coping strategies such as thinking about the situation in different ways, planning what they are going to do to solve the problem, taking direct action (Kliewer, Fearnow, & Miller, 1994), and using self-reliance (Patterson & McCubbin, 1987) and positive self-statements such as "I can do this" (Brown, O'Keefe, Sanders, & Baker, 1986) as compared with boys. The most consistent gender difference emerges in the area of social support (Kliewer, Fearnow, & Miller, 1994; Patterson & McCubbin, 1987; Wertlieb, Weigel, & Feldstein, 1987). Girls report seeking social support to cope more frequently than boys. This is not surprising, given the fact that girls' relationships are more intimate, dyadic, and self-disclosing than are boys' relationships (Belle, 1989). Girls also report being more receptive to social support in times of stress (Belle, 1987). In addition to overall gender differences in the use of social support, there may be gender differences in the *types* of social support sought. Kliewer, Lepore, Broquet, and Zuba (1990) found, for example, that elementary school–age boys sought more instrumental support (i.e., assistance in solving a practical problem) from a telephone help line, while girls sought more informational and emotional support (e.g., advice, encouragement, enhancement of self-worth).

Research has documented links between a child's temperament—the innate disposition to interact with the world in particular ways—and his or her coping. Dimensions of temperament include distractability, activity level, sociability, emotionality, general mood, flexibility, and approach-avoidance orientation. Lavigne, Nolan, and McLone (1988) found that young children (ages 3–8) who were not easily distractible also scored high on the ability to cope with their internal feelings. These children also showed fewer behavior problems. Young children who have the ability to focus also do a good job of monitoring and regulating their feelings associated with stressful events. In a large study, Ebata and Moos (1994) found that adolescents who were high on the activity and sociability dimensions of temperament also approached problems actively. Adolescents who scored high on the emotionality-distress dimension of temperament coped by avoiding dealing with their problems. Temperament has also been linked to social support. Children who reported having an approach (versus avoidance) orientation toward life and also reported being flexible had mothers who indicated that high levels of family support were available to their child (Wertlieb, Weigel, & Feldstein, 1989). Given these data, it is likely that Jessica, in the earlier example, was relatively flexible in her approach to new situations and also had more of an approach (vs. avoidance) orientation toward new things.

Locus of control is associated with children's coping, but results are equivocal. Some studies have found that children with an internal locus of control (i.e., believe they have control over events that happen to them) use more avoidant strategies (Blanchard-Fields & Irion, 1988; Kliewer, 1991), whereas other studies have linked an internal locus of control with more active coping attempts (LaMontagne, 1984). These conflicting results might be explained by differences in the types of stress situations children reported.

Although a number of studies exist with adults, the relationship between hope and coping is just beginning to be examined in children. In a study of 39 children and adolescents with sickle-cell disease, Lewis and Kliewer (in press) found that children with the lowest levels of anxiety reported having high levels of hope *and* using high levels of active, support, or distraction coping.

Regarding coping preferences, research has shown that children who are "monitors"—that is, who prefer to receive information in a stressful situation—also report seeking more social support than do children who do not have this preference. Children, particularly boys, who are "blunters"—that is, who prefer to remain in the dark about the details of a stressful situation—use avoidance coping strategies to a greater extent than do children without this proclivity (Kliewer, 1991).

Finally, although evidence is limited, children rated as socially competent by their teachers seem to use more avoidance coping (Kliewer, 1991) and fewer problem behaviors (Fabes & Eisenberg, 1992; Garmezy, 1989; Kliewer, 1991) as compared with their less competent peers. The finding linking competence with *greater* use of avoidance coping may seem counterintuitive at first. However, a closer look at the data shows that many of the problems facing children are uncontrollable. In uncontrollable situations, avoidance may be adaptive, at least initially. If Jessica, in the earlier example, had been faced with a problem that was completely beyond her control, active attempts to change the situation would probably not be adaptive and could lead to frustration.

Brian, age 12, had a fairly close relationship with his parents and older brother and was well-liked by his classmates. Like his father, Brian has a very problem-focused approach to life. Over the years, Brian has watched his father "take the bull by the horns" when a problem needed attention. Since he began school, Brian has welcomed opportunities to learn new material. He generally prefers to get all the information he can about a situation before trying to solve it, and he typically believes that most things that happen to him are under his control. In the transition from fifth grade into middle school, Brian began to have prob-

(continued)

lems with his schoolwork in areas where he had not had difficulty previously. These problems disturbed him greatly.

Consistent with research on individual influences on coping behavior, Brian took a very direct approach in addressing this problem. He first tried to figure out why he was having so much difficulty, and then he spoke to his parents and teacher about it. His teacher suggested an alternative way of studying the material, which Brian then tried. Brian's schoolwork improved a little, but he continued to struggle and is still trying different strategies to deal with this problem.

Brian's story illustrates that a child's personality, preferences, beliefs about the world, and competencies affect the choice of coping strategies. Parents and other adults who interact with children should be aware of these influences on coping activity.

Social Environmental Influences on Coping

Social environmental influences that affect children's coping include parental instruction (coaching) regarding coping choices; modeling by parents and other important people in the child's social network; quality of the parent–child relationship and interaction patterns in the home, neighborhood, and community; and norms regarding culturally appropriate coping behaviors.

Research on the influence of parental coaching on children's coping is just beginning, with most work emanating from the pediatric psychology literature. Blount et al. (1992) found that when parents were trained to coach their children to use distraction when undergoing routine immunizations, the children used more distraction coping as compared with no-treatment controls. Similarly, children whose parents provided them with information about a dental procedure adjusted better as compared with children who were not provided information (Bailey, Talbot, & Taylor, 1973). In studies in which parents are not put into the role of coach, child behaviors are also linked to maternal behavior. Bush, Melamed, Greenbaum, and Sheras (1986) found, for example, that when children were about to undergo a medical procedure, they were more likely to actively explore their environment when their mothers provided them with information about the impending procedure. More recent work with nonpediatric populations has shown that maternal coping suggestions are linked to child reports of coping, but that this relationship varies by gender of the child (Kliewer, Fearnow, & Miller, 1994). Boys, but not girls, report coping with everyday problems in a manner consistent with their mother's coping suggestions. These data indicate that children do attend to parental directives and suggestions regarding coping strategies—at least some of the time. More research is needed to understand the conditions under which parents' coping suggestions are related to children's coping.

The role of modeling in shaping children's behavior in general is well documented (see Bandura, 1977), but we know little about how parental modeling might influence the types of coping strategies children adopt to handle problems. There is some evidence for parent–child similarities in Type A behavior (Matthews, Stoney, Rakaczky, & Jamison, 1986; Weidner, Sexton, Matarazzo, & Pereira, 1988) and in attributional style (Seligman & Peterson, 1986), both of which theoretically influence the use of coping strategies in specific situations. There is also emerging evidence that children model their parents' specific ways of handling stressful situations. In a study of children with sickle-cell disease, Gil, Williams, Thompson, and Kinney (1991) found that parents who used passive adherence to cope with pain (followed the doctor's orders without questioning) had children who also used passive adherence coping. In another study of children with sickle-cell disease, Kliewer and Lewis (1995) found that parents who did not cope by thinking about situations in a positive way had children who reported using avoidance coping. The influence of parental modeling is also seen when we look at how children cope with everyday problems. In a study that included over 150 fathers and nearly 300 mothers, fathers who reported using religion to cope (primarily prayer) had children who reported that they used social support—turned to others for help—when faced with everyday stressors. Mothers in this study who reported coping by looking at the situation more positively had children who reported using more active coping (direct problem solving, thinking about solutions, and reframing the situation more positively), social support coping, and distraction coping (Kliewer, Fearnow, & Miller, 1994). These data suggest that how parents approach life as well as manage their own stress affects the coping strategies children use in particular situations. In the example given earlier, we can see how Brian modeled his father's approach to problem solving as he dealt with his own concerns about ineffective school performance.

In addition to coaching and modeling, the quality of the parent–child relationship and patterns of family interaction affect children's use of coping strategies. Attachment theory suggests that children with secure, warm, and accepting relations with their parents will have an active approach toward problem solving, while children with less secure relations with caregivers or who feel disengaged from parents will be more avoidant in their coping strategies. Several studies have borne out this point. Shell and Roosa (1991) found that in nonalcoholic families, elementary school–age children who felt accepted by their mothers used more support-seeking coping. Mothers who had very negative moods had children who coped by avoiding their problems. In the Kliewer, Fearnow, and Miller (1994) study, children who felt accepted by their mothers reported more active and support-seeking coping and less avoidance coping. Research assessing relations between family cohesion and coping have also supported this perspective. Alcohol use by adolescents has been associated with more conflicted and less cohesive family environments (Baer, Garmezy, McLaughlin, Pokorny, & Wernick, 1987) and with low parental warmth and high parental hostility (Johnson & Pandina, 1991). Hanson et al. (1989) found that low family cohesion was related to higher use of avoidance coping by adolescents with diabetes. Family cohesion was associated with less self-blame by adolescents (Stern & Zevon, 1990) and greater use of active coping strategies by children with sickle-cell disease (Kliewer & Lewis, 1995). These data point to the importance of the family climate and the child's perceptions of their relationship with their parents in affecting coping strategies. Again, as the example of Brian illustrates, children who feel that their parents love them and accept them as they are are more likely to make active attempts to cope with problems rather than run away from difficult situations.

Finally, resources in a child's neighborhood and community, as well as cultural norms regarding the appropriateness of particular coping behaviors, shape children's coping choices. Use of social support in particular may be affected by the size and location of a child's support network. Contact with adults outside of the family, whether in the neighborhood (Bryant, 1985) or from organized activities (e.g., church attendance, clubs) (Tietjen, 1989), is related to use of support. Furthermore, norms for giving and receiving support differ across cultures (Weisner, 1989) and affect the types of supportive exchanges in which children engage.

Contextual Influences on Coping

The context of the stressful situation is a third factor affecting children's coping. Contextual factors include the amount of control a child perceives he or she has or actually does have over the situation or the consequences of the situation; the predictability, frequency, and duration of the situation; the life domain in which the event occurred (e.g., family, academic, peer); and the meaning of the stressful event for the child.

Most of the work on contextual factors has focused on control. As noted earlier, situations perceived as controllable engender more active coping responses, and these responses are generally effective. Conversely, situations perceived as uncontrollable tend to produce emotion-focused responses, which are also effective in these situations. Several types of control have been examined in the literature, including control over the cause of an event and control over the outcome. In general, appraisals of control over the outcome of the event (e.g., I can improve this situation) are more strongly associated with coping than are appraisals of control over the occurrence of the event (e.g., I caused this to happen). For example, in a longitudinal study of predictors of coping (Ebata & Moos, 1994), adolescents who felt they had some control over how the situation would turn out also used more approach coping. They tried to understand the stressor and mentally prepare for it, they thought about the situation more positively, and they took steps to try to solve the problem. Whether or not adolescents thought they caused the problem to begin with had little bearing on how they coped with it.

Fewer studies have examined other dimensions of a situation (e.g., predictability, frequency, duration) for their relevance to coping behaviors. One exception is a study by Gamble (1994), who examined the contributions of control appraisals; event frequency, duration, and meaningfulness; and concerns about the self and others to the coping efforts of young adolescents and young adults. She found that among young adolescents, after accounting for the influence of control appraisals, events that were longer in duration evoked more expression of emotion and aggressive behaviors to cope. For young adults, events of shorter duration were related to more independent coping, which involved keeping feelings to oneself and dealing with problems by oneself.

In the 1990s, researchers have become interested in the meaning stressful situations have for children. Interest in the meaning of events is based on the supposition that to understand why children cope as they do, we must understand the situational context, including the goals, motivations, and history underlying the situation. One attempt to address meaning is to evaluate the types of threat produced by the stressful event. For example, several researchers have begun to ask children about the concerns or stake they have in a given stressful circumstance (Gamble, 1994; Sheets, Sandler, & West, in press). Gamble (1994) assessed concerns/stakes by having participants in her study indicate the extent to which they were worried about their own or others' feelings in the stressful situation. For young adolescents, concerns about themselves were associated with less emotive/aggressive coping (less expression of feelings and aggression) and more problem-solving and support-seeking coping. Concerns about others were associated with more emotive/aggressive coping and with more social support coping.

In their work with children of divorce, Sheets et al. (in press) identified six types of threat appraisals children make regarding divorce-related events. These appraisals can be further grouped into threats to the self, threats involving harm to others, and material loss. Sheets et al. have shown that these threat appraisals are stable over time and predict symptoms of depression and anxiety 5 months later. Children with high levels of threat appraisals also experience high levels of depressive and anxious symptoms.

Building on the work of Sheets et al. (in press), Kliewer, Pinson, et al. (1994) identified 10 sources of threat in their content analysis of children's descriptions of everyday problems. They found that types of threat appraisals were specific to types of events (e.g., conflict, loss) and to event domains (e.g., peer, parent). For example, concerns about unfairness, physical harm to oneself, negative evaluation by others, and disappointment in the behavior of loved ones were mentioned more often in conflict events as compared with events that did not involve conflict. Greater levels of threat activated more coping of all types. More work is needed to understand what factors influence children's threat appraisals.

In summary, there is evidence the demands of a particular stressful event influence how a child responds in that situation. It is unclear, however, whether individual differences in the child, features of the social environment, or particular situational demands are more influential in shaping coping. It is likely that these broad influences interact to influence coping in any given situation. More work is needed to understand how these broad influences collectively shape the coping behaviors children exhibit.

COPING PREVENTION AND INTERVENTION PROGRAMS

A number of programs have been developed to teach children how to cope effectively with a wide range of stressful events. Some programs have been developed for children who have experienced specific stressors, such as parental death or divorce, living with an alcoholic parent, or being diagnosed with a chronic physical illness or condition. Other programs have been designed to apply to a broad range of stressful circumstances, such a living in poverty, moving to a new home or school, or being "different." The logic of these broader programs is that primary preventive interventions can "provide young children with skills and competencies that enhance their ability to cope, and help them to develop a sense of efficacy that becomes part of their future adaptive resources" (Cowen, Hightower, Pedro-Carroll, & Work, 1990, p. 154).

Many coping programs with a prevention focus are school-based. In terms of curricula, common program elements that run through many of the coping programs include 1) a focus on social problem-solving skills (SPS), 2) anger management training, 3) training in appropriate expression of feelings, 4) a focus on developing adequate social support, and 5) enhancement of self-efficacy. Most of the existing school-based coping programs attempt to change individuals by enhancing their coping skills rather than by changing features of their environment (Compas, Phares, & Ledoux, 1989). In this vein, these broad coping programs are less likely to involve the family system as part of their programs. However, for interventions with specific problems, such as divorce, family involvement greatly enhances program effectiveness. The number of sessions in each coping program varies, but generally at least nine sessions are included. Some programs run the entire school year.

Social Problem-Solving Skills

Most training in social problem solving is highly structured. For example, Weissberg, Gesten, Liebenstein, Doherty-Schmid, and Hutton (1980) developed a 42-lesson, 143-page manual offering a systematic approach to solving interpersonal problems. The manual includes exercises using small-group role play, videotape modeling, cartoon workbooks, and class discussion (Weissberg et al., 1981). In Weissberg's program, as well as in other coping programs that emphasize SPS skills (e.g., Elias et al., 1986), children are taught a specific set of steps and skills that will improve the quality of their coping responses in stressful situations. The steps involved in SPS training include 1) heightened awareness of a child's own feelings and of the feelings of others in problem situations; 2) problem definition (what is the problem?); 3) goal definition (what does the child want in the situation?); 4) generation of alternative solutions and the consequences associated with those solutions; 5) selection and implementation of one solution; 6) evaluation of the effectiveness of the solution that was attempted; and 7) implementation of a new solution, if necessary. An implicit part of SPS skills training is the idea that children will develop positive beliefs about their ability to overcome obstacles.

Dubrow, Schmidt, McBride, Edwards, and Merk (1993) included training in problem solving as part of a 13-week, school-based primary prevention program targeted at fourth graders. In the fall, 44 children received the intervention, and another 44 received the intervention in the spring. In evaluating the effectiveness of the program, children receiving the immediate and the delayed intervention were compared. Problem solving was assessed by asking students to generate solutions to a series of five stressful situations. The number and effectiveness of the solutions were independently rated by people blind to the treatment condition of the student. After the completion of the fall term, children who received the program showed significant improvements in their problem-solving skills relative to children who had not yet received the program.

Elias et al. (1986) evaluated the effectiveness of a year-long SPS skills training program for elementary school students by testing students upon entry into middle school. Students who received no training, a half year of training, or a full year of training in the year prior to entering middle school were compared on the severity of stressors faced and on SPS skills. Children who received the full year of training had fewer and less intense problems in the middle school as compared with children who received no training.

Weissberg et al.'s (1981) evaluation of the effectiveness of a 42-lesson SPS training program with 563 second through fourth graders revealed a number of significant outcomes. Relative to children who did not receive training, children who received the training program improved more in the solutions they offered to problem situations and in their self-confidence about handling interpersonal problems. Teacher ratings indicated that children receiving the program showed higher levels of competence and lower levels of behavior problems as compared with children in the control group who did not receive the program.

Evaluations of SPS skills training programs show that children *do* learn SPS skills. However, links are weak between the actual SPS skills children possess and their level of adjustment. Intervention researchers have suggested that SPS skills training programs are important nonetheless because of their potential to enhance children's self-efficacy around problem solving. More work is needed to identify components of SPS skills training that are related to competence and behavioral adjustment.

Anger Management Training

Anger management is a common component of coping programs, though it is rarely evaluated. Children are taught to identify appropriate and inappropriate ways of handling anger and then to practice appropriate anger expression. In one coping program directed toward inner-city third graders (Henderson, Kelbey, & Engebretson, 1992), part of the evaluation involved an assessment of appropriate and inappropriate coping strategies. Use of aggression was considered an inappropriate strategy. Students who received the intervention, compared with students who did not, reported significantly more appropriate coping strategies after the intervention.

Expressing Feelings and Developing Social Support

Additional common components of coping programs include teaching children that expressing emotions in a positive way is valuable, as is seeking assistance from those people who provide the child with the feeling that he or she is valued. In evaluating their coping program, Dubrow et al. (1993) assessed changes in children's social support network size, but there were no effects of the coping intervention on this measure. The most appropriate test of this component of coping interventions is an evaluation of the number of times a child seeks social support and the effectiveness of those interactions. Unfortunately, this information is not routinely available.

Enhancing Self-Efficacy

A final common goal of many coping programs is to increase children's self-efficacy beliefs—that is, beliefs in their competence and ability to solve problems effectively. This is ideally accomplished by giving children concrete skills in coping and problem solving and also providing the opportunity to practice these skills. A number of programs have reported gains in self-efficacy as a result of exposure to training. Dubrow et al. (1993) reported enhanced self-efficacy in children's ability to implement positive coping strategies, and Henderson et al. (1992) reported gains in locus of control and self-concept following exposure to their intervention.

Summary

Evaluations of coping interventions for children suggest that training in coping and SPS skills works to enhance coping and feelings of self-efficacy. Less is known about the effectiveness of other program components, such as anger management, emotional expression, and social support seeking. Most evaluations of coping programs are short-term. In addition to more complete evaluations, long-term assessments of the effectiveness of school-based programs would make it possible to identify if and when "booster" interventions are needed.

IMPLICATIONS FOR CHILDREN WITH ONGOING HEALTH CONDITIONS AND DISABILITY

Children with ongoing health conditions or disability have the same need to learn effective coping as do children without these conditions. Having an ongoing illness or disability adds a layer of coping challenges to the everyday stresses associated with being a child or adolescent. From our knowledge of influences on children's coping and from results of coping interventions, we can draw several implications for children with special needs.

First, each child is unique and has unique ways of managing stressful events. Parents and others working with children should be aware that stable personality traits influence how children will respond to stressful situations. Knowing how a child sees the world and typically interacts with others can help parents or caregivers guide the child's behavior in ways that are consonant with the child's personality. For example, children who have high activity levels might be encouraged to channel that energy into thinking about and planning ways of handling difficulties that arise. Children who tend to be shy might be encouraged to develop special relationships with one or two adults who could provide them with emotional support in times of stress. For a child who is "slow-to-warm" to new situations, parents might give the latitude to feel comfortable with the situation before encouraging him or her to jump in and tackle the problem right away. Of course, some situations require immediate action, and matching the child's personality to the way a situation is handled is not always possible.

Second, children model their parents' behavior. Both general attitudes toward life and specific coping behaviors are modeled. If children are to become effective at coping, it is a step in the right direction to model appropriate coping as adults or to teach parents to cope effectively. The most overt behaviors parents display are typically the behaviors that will be modeled most readily. Is the objective to have children who control their anger and other emotional responses? Who seek social support when upset? Who talk about their concerns rather than bottling them up inside? Who seek solutions to problems rather than giving up? If so, then these are the behaviors parents should exhibit and reinforce.

There are several ways to help parents model appropriate coping in the family. Support networks might be developed for parents—perhaps in the form of support groups—where parents would have the opportunity to express their feelings about the challenges in their lives, gain emotional support from others in similar circumstances, and share ideas about practical solutions to challenges. Training in problem solving and emotion management might be offered to parents, and this service could be considered normative for families rather than as being suited only for ineffective parents. Though it is sometimes assumed that adults know how to problem-solve and how to handle anger and disappointment, this is often not the case. Specific training in these areas, as well as in basic parenting skills, could assist parents in modeling effective coping behavior.

Third, acceptance by parents and a warm and supportive household engender adaptive coping behaviors. Living environments characterized by cohesion and acceptance rather than by discord and rejection provide children with the security they need to face difficult challenges. A basic suggestion that might begin to help families create cohesive households is to communicate to parents how important the emotional tone of the house is to a child's development. From there, families could be encouraged to begin building family routines and traditions (special meals, family time in the evenings, weekly outings) that are fun and promote a spirit of family togetherness and interest.

Fourth, SPS skills can be taught, and this training does improve the quality of coping children exhibit. Training in SPS skills seems desirable for children with special needs. The secondary gain from SPS skills training is enhanced self-efficacy, also a desirable quality. One of the most important SPS skills for children with chronic conditions is recognizing which problems can be changed and which are immutable. For problems that cannot be changed, which are likely to occur in the lives of youth with chronic conditions, cognitive restructuring is a critical skill. Cognitive restructuring involves learning to think about the situation in a more positive way by minimizing the negative aspects of it or highlighting the potential benefits. This skill has been successfully taught to children of divorced families and is related to better psychological adjustment (I.N. Sandler, personal communication, March 29, 1995).

Fifth, most coping interventions are taught in a group format. Although not generally evaluated, one effect of a group format is to "normalize" the problems and experiences children encounter. This effect might be particularly beneficial for children with challenges that exceed those normally experienced by children. Groups could be constructed to include children with and without ongoing conditions or could comprise only children with ongoing conditions. An advantage of groups with a cross-section of children is that the children see that all children have problems and challenges to deal with, and there are similarities and differences in the problems children face. An advantage of groups comprising only children with ongoing conditions may be that there is greater identification with children in the group and thus more opportunity to foster social support among group members.

CONCLUSIONS

Children face a variety of stressful challenges in the course of growing up. As children mature, their use of cognitive and emotion-focused strategies increases, and the cognitive strategies they use become more effective. Stable individual differences, qualities of the social environment, and demands of the specific context all interact to influence coping behavior. Parents' behavior and the family environment are particularly important influences on coping.

Prevention programs have been developed to teach children how to cope effectively with a wide range of stressful events. Many of these programs are school based, utilize a group format, and teach a variety of skills including social problem solving and anger management. There is reason to believe that children with ongoing conditions or disability can benefit from similar prevention programs and that parents may also benefit from coping and parenting training.

REFERENCES

Armistead, L., McCombs, A., Forehand, R., Wierson, M., Long, N., & Fauber, R. (1990). Coping with divorce: A study of young adolescents. *Journal of Clinical Child Psychology, 19,* 79–84.

Ayers, T.S. (1991). *A dispositional and situational assessment of children's coping: Testing alternative theoretic models.* Unpublished doctoral dissertation. Arizona State University, Tempe, AZ.

Baer, P.E., Garmezy, L.B., McLaughlin, R.J., Pokorny, A.D., & Wernick, M.J. (1987). Stress, coping, family context, and adolescent alcohol use. *Journal of Behavioral Medicine, 10,* 449–466.

Bailey, P.M., Talbot, A., & Taylor, P.P. (1973). A comparison of maternal anxiety levels with anxiety levels manifested in the child dental patient. *Journal of Dentistry for Children, 40,* 277–284.

Bandura, A. (1977). *Social learning theory.* Englewood Cliffs, NJ: Prentice Hall.

Belle, D. (1987). Gender differences in the social moderators of stress. In R.C. Barnett, L. Biener, & G.K. Baruch (Eds.), *Gender and stress* (pp. 257–277). New York: The Free Press.

Belle, D. (1989). Gender differences in children's social networks and social supports. In D. Belle (Ed.), *Children's social networks and social supports* (pp. 173–188). New York: John Wiley & Sons.

Blanchard-Fields, F., & Irion, J.C. (1988). The relation between locus of control and coping in two contexts: Age as a moderator variable. *Psychology and Aging, 3,* 197–203.

Blount, R.L., Bachanas, P.J., Powers, S.W., Cotter, M.C., Franklin, A., Chaplin, W., Mayfield, J., Henderson, M., & Blount, S.D. (1992). Training children to cope and parents to coach them during routine immunizations: Effects on child, parent, and staff behaviors. *Behavior Therapy, 23,* 689–705.

Brown, J.M., O'Keefe, J., Sanders, S.H., & Baker, B. (1986). Developmental changes in children's cognition to stressful and painful situations. *Journal of Pediatric Psychology, 11,* 343–357.

Bryant, B.K. (1985). The neighborhood walk: Sources of support in middle childhood. *Monographs of the Society for Research in Child Development, 50* (No. 210). Chicago: University of Chicago Press.

Bush, J.P., Melamed, B.G., Greenbaum, P.E., & Sheras, P.L. (1986). Mother-child patterns of coping with anticipatory medical stress. *Health Psychology, 5,* 137–157.

Compas, B.E., Malcarne, V.L., & Fondacaro, K.M. (1988). Coping with stressful events in older children and young adolescents. *Journal of Consulting and Clinical Psychology, 56,* 405–411.

Compas, B.E., Phares, V., & Ledoux, N. (1989). Stress and coping preventive interventions for children and adolescents. In L.A. Bond & B.E. Compas (Eds.), *Primary prevention and promotion in the schools* (pp. 319–340). Beverly Hills, CA: Sage Publications.

Compas, B.E., Worsham, N.L., & Ey, S. (1992). Conceptual and developmental issues in children's coping with stress. In A.M. LaGreca, L.J. Siegel, J.L. Wallander, & C.E. Walker (Eds.), *Stress and coping in child health* (pp. 7–24). New York: Guilford Press.

Cowen, E.L., Hightower, A.D., Pedro-Carroll, J., & Work, W.C. (1990). School-based models for primary prevention programming with children. In R.P. Lorion (Ed.), *Protecting the children: Strategies for optimizing emotional and behavioral development* (pp. 133–160). New York: Haworth Press.

Dubrow, E.F., Schmidt, D., McBride, J., Edwards, S., & Merk, F.L. (1993). Teaching children to cope with stressful experiences: Initial implementation and evaluation of a primary prevention program. *Journal of Clinical Child Psychology, 22,* 428–440.

Ebata, A.T., & Moos, R.H. (1991). Coping and adjustment in distressed and healthy adolescents. *Journal of Applied Developmental Psychology, 12,* 33–54.

Ebata, A.T., & Moos, R.H. (1994). Personal, situational, and contextual correlates of coping in adolescence. *Journal of Research of Adolescence, 4,* 99–125.

Elias, M.J., Gara, M., Ubriaco, M., Rothbaum, P.A., Clabby, J.F., & Schuyler, T. (1986). Impact of a preventive social problem solving intervention on children's coping with middle-school stressors. *American Journal of Community Psychology, 14,* 259–275.

Fabes, R.A., & Eisenberg, N. (1992). Young children's coping with interpersonal anger. *Child Development, 63,* 116–128.

Flavell, J.H. (1985). *Cognitive development* (2nd ed.). Englewood Cliffs, NJ: Prentice Hall.

Flavell, J.H., Green, F.L., & Flavell, E.R. (1990). Developmental changes in young children's knowledge about the mind. *Cognitive Development, 5,* 1–27.

Folkman, S. (1984). Personal control and stress and coping processes: A theoretical analysis. *Journal of Personality and Social Psychology, 46,* 839–852.

Forsythe, C.J., & Compas, B.E. (1987). Interaction of cognitive appraisals of stressful events and coping: Testing the goodness of fit hypothesis. *Cognitive Therapy and Research, 11,* 473–485.

Gamble, W.C. (1994). Perceptions and controllability and other stressor event characteristics as determinants of coping among young adolescents and young adults. *Journal of Youth and Adolescence, 23,* 65–84.

Garmezy, N. (1989). The role of competence in the study of children and adolescents under stress. In B. Schneider, G. Attili, J. Nadel, & R. Weissberg (Eds)., *Social competence in developmental perspective* (pp. 25–40). London: Kluwer Academic Publishers.

Gil, K.M., Williams, D.A., Thompson, R.J., & Kinney, T.R. (1991). Sickle cell disease in children and adolescents: The relation of child and parent pain coping strategies to adjustment. *Journal of Pediatric Psychology, 16,* 643–663.

Glyshaw, K., Cohen, L.H., & Towbes, L.C. (1989). Coping strategies and psychological distress: Prospective analyses of early and middle adolescents. *American Journal of Community Psychology, 17,* 607–623.

Guralnick, M.J., & Paul-Brown, D. (1984). Communicative adjustments during behavior-request episodes among children at different developmental levels. *Child Development, 55,* 911–919.

Hanson, C.L., Cigrang, J.A., Harris, M.A., Carle, D.L., Relyea, G., & Burghen, G.A. (1989). Coping styles in youths with insulin-dependent diabetes mellitus. *Journal of Consulting and Clinical Psychology, 57,* 644–651.

Harter, S. (1983). Developmental perspectives on the self-system. In E.M. Hetherington (Ed.), *Handbook of child psychology: Vol. 4. Socialization, personality, and social development.* (4th ed., pp. 275–385). New York: John Wiley & Sons.

Henderson, P.A., Kelbey, T.J., & Engebretson, K.M. (1992). Effects of a stress-control program on children's locus of control, self-concept, & coping behavior. *The School Counselor, 40,* 125–130.

Johnson, V., & Pandina, R.J. (1991). Effects of the family environment on adolescent substance use, delinquency, and coping styles. *American Journal of Drug and Alcohol Abuse, 17,* 71–88.

Kliewer, W. (1991). Coping in middle childhood: Relations to competence, Type A behavior, monitoring, blunting, and locus of control. *Developmental Psychology, 27,* 689–697.

Kliewer, W., Fearnow, M.D., & Miller, P.A. (1994). *Models of coping socialization in middle childhood: Tests of maternal and paternal influences.* Manuscript submitted for publication.

Kliewer, W., Lepore, S.J., Broquet, A., & Zuba, L. (1990). Developmental and gender differences in anonymous support-seeking: Analysis of data from a community help line for children. *American Journal of Community Psychology, 18,* 333–339.

Kliewer, W., & Lewis, H. (1995). Family influences on coping processes in children and adolescents with sickle cell disease. *Journal of Pediatric Psychology, 20,* 511–525.

Kliewer, W., Pinson, S., Wood, H.K., Nicholson, M., McLaughlin, J., Palumbo, M., Schmid, M., Ampey, G., Sweet, M.C., McDonald, R., Frazee, T., & Fearnow, M.D. (1994). *Children's threat appraisals in response to everyday stressors: The role of affect, control, and event type.* Manuscript submitted for publication.

LaMontagne, L.L. (1984). Children's locus of control beliefs as predictors of preoperative coping behavior. *Nursing Research, 33,* 76–85.

Lavigne, J.V., Nolan, D., & McLone, D.G. (1988). Temperament, coping, and psychological adjustment in young children with myelomeningocele. *Journal of Pediatric Psychology, 13,* 363–378.

Lazarus, R.S., & Folkman, S. (1984). *Stress, appraisal, and coping.* New York: Springer-Verlag.

Lewis, H.A., & Kliewer, W. (in press). Hoping, coping, and psychological and physical adjustment among children with sickle cell disease: Test of mediator and moderator models. *Journal of Pediatric Psychology.*

Matthews, K.A., Stoney, C.M., Rakaczky, C.J., & Jamison, W. (1986). Family characteristics and school achievements of Type A children. *Health Psychology, 5,* 453–467.

Patterson, J.M., & McCubbin, J.I. (1987). Adolescent coping style and behaviors: Conceptualization and measurement. *Journal of Adolescence, 10,* 163–186.

Roth, S., & Cohen, L.J. (1986). Approach, avoidance, and coping with stress. *American Psychologist, 41,* 813–819.

Sandler, I.N., Tein, J.Y., & West, S.G. (1994). Coping, stress, and psychological symptoms of children of divorce: A cross-sectional and longitudinal study. *Child Development, 65,* 1744–1763.

Seligman, M.E.P., & Peterson, C. (1986). A learned helplessness perspective on childhood depression: Theory and research. In M. Rutter, C.E. Izard, & P.B. Read (Eds.), *Depression in young people: Developmental and clinical perspectives* (pp. 223–249). New York: Guilford Press.

Selman, R. (1980). *The growth of interpersonal understanding.* New York: Academic Press.

Selman, R.L., & Selman, A.P. (1979). Children's ideas about friendship: A new theory. *Psychology Today, 13,* 71–80.

Shantz, C.V. (1983). Social cognition. In J.H. Flavell & E.M. Markman (Eds.), *Handbook of child psychology: Vol. 3. Cognitive development* (pp. 495–555). New York: John Wiley & Sons.

Sheets, V., Sandler, I., & West, S.G. (in press). Negative appraisals of stressful events by preadolescent children of divorce. *Child Development.*

Shell, R.M., & Roosa, M.W. (1991, November). *Family influences on children's coping as a function of parental alcoholism status.* Paper presented at the 53rd annual conference of the National Council on Family Relations, Denver.

Stern, M., & Zevon, M.A. (1990). Stress, coping, and family environment: The adolescent's response to naturally occurring stressors. *Journal of Adolescent Research, 5,* 290–305.

Tietjen, A.M. (1989). The ecology of children's social support networks. In D. Belle (Ed.), *Children's social networks and social supports* (pp. 37–69). New York: John Wiley & Sons.

Vitaliano, P.P., DeWolfe, D.J., Maiuro, R.D., Russo, J., & Katon, W. (1990). Appraised changeability of a stressor as a modifier of the relationship between coping and depression: A test of the hypothesis of fit. *Journal of Personality and Social Psychology, 59,* 582–592.

Weidner, G., Sexton, G., Matarazzo, J.D., & Pereira, C. (1988). Type A behavior in children, adolescents, and their parents. *Developmental Psychology, 24,* 118–121.

Weisner, T.S. (1989). Cultural and universal aspects of social support for children: Evidence from the Abaluyia of Kenya. In D. Belle (Ed.), *Children's social networks and social supports* (pp. 70–90). New York: John Wiley & Sons.

Weissberg, R.P., Gesten, E.L., Liebenstein, N.L., Doherty–Schmid, K., & Hutton, H. (1980). *The Rochester social problem-solving (SPS) program: A training manual for teachers of 2nd-4th grader children.* Rochester, NY: University of Rochester.

Weissberg, R.P., Gesten, E.L., Carnrike, C.L., Toro, P.A., Rapkin, B.D., Davidson, E., & Cowen, E.L. (1981). Social problem-solving skills training: A competence-building intervention with second-to fourth-grade children. *American Journal of Community Psychology, 9,* 411–423.

Wertlieb, D., Weigel, C., & Feldstein, M. (1987). Measuring children's coping. *American Journal of Orthopsychiatry, 57,* 548–560.

Wertlieb, D., Weigel, C., & Feldstein, M. (1989). Stressful experiences, temperament, and social support: Impact on children's behavior symptoms. *Journal of Applied Developmental Psychology, 10,* 487–503.

Wilson, B.J., Hoffner, C., & Cantor, J. (1987). Children's perceptions of the effectiveness of techniques to reduce fear from mass media. *Journal of Applied Developmental Psychology, 8,* 39–52.

Reflections on Competence

Perspectives of Successful Adults

Laurie E. Powers,
George H.S. Singer, and Bonnie Todis

High self-esteem appears to be associated with positive childhood experiences and successful, independent function in adulthood (Harter, 1981). Children's perceptions of their competence are typically more predictive of their actual achievement and behavior than are objective measures of their capabilities (Phillips & Zimmerman, 1990). Parents, teachers, and peers clearly play critical roles in influencing children's perceptions of self-worth. Children's beliefs about others' appraisals of their competence are particularly important in shaping their self-perceptions (Marsh, Barnes, & Hocevar, 1985).

Global judgments of self-worth also are based upon a child's evaluation of how competently he or she performs in domains considered important. Children with high self-worth are able to discount the importance of their weaknesses while accentuating the importance of their strengths (Harter, 1986). These findings suggest that children's sense of self-worth is ideally promoted through support from significant others that encourages children to value their personal strengths and to minimize the importance of those domains that highlight personal difficulty.

The preparation of this chapter was supported, in part, by Grant No. H023T80013-90 from the U.S. Department of Education, Office of Special Education Programs (OSEP). The opinions expressed herein are exclusively those of the authors, and no official endorsement by OSEP should be inferred.

Middle childhood is typically marked by the emergence of perceptions of global self-worth (Harter, 1990). This is a period of dramatic development for most children, particularly in the achievement and social domains. Self-perceptions of competence tend to become more discriminating during middle childhood: Children become increasingly sensitive to their perceived capabilities in different life domains, to how their capabilities compare with those of others in their social group, and to the appraisals of significant others.

Middle childhood can be a particularly difficult period for children who experience disabilities and ongoing health conditions. Their navigation of typical developmental milestones may be complicated by physical, learning, emotional, and interpersonal barriers. Such barriers may place them at increased risk for functional challenge and impaired perceptions of self-worth, while also negatively affecting the development and communication of positive appraisals of competence by significant others in their lives (Garrison & McQuiston, 1989; King, Shultz, Steel, Gilpin, & Cathers, 1993).

Considerable attention has focused on documenting the influence of both family and disability on the development of low child self-esteem. Much of our current understanding has been derived from cross-sectional, quantitative analysis of familial and impairment-related correlates of low self-esteem during childhood and childhood predictors of low adult self-esteem. Comparatively less is known about specific child and familial factors and strategies that promote the emergence and maintenance of high levels of self-esteem among children with disabilities.

Growing interest in understanding the nature and emergence of resilience has catalyzed a shift toward focusing on the development of high self-esteem and on using qualitative methods to extract richness and detail regarding the specific events and strategies that promote high levels of self-esteem (Phillips & Zimmerman, 1990; Werner & Smith, 1992). It is clear that much can be gained through documenting the experiences of resilient individuals and their perceptions of factors important to their development of self-worth and personal competence.

This chapter summarizes the qualitative recollections of key middle childhood experiences of successful adults with significant physical disabilities. The discussion focuses on exploring the emergence of self-perceptions of competence and the impact of familial and social factors on the development and maintenance of self-worth.

APPROACH

Participants

Interviews were conducted with 14 adults who experienced significant physical disability during childhood and were currently living successful adult lives. The demographic characteristics of the respondents are presented in Table 1. A broad recruitment effort to identify adults with high self-worth yielded 10 male and 4 female respondents. Although the disproportionate number of successful male participants nominated may be coincidental, it is unfortunately also consistent with findings suggesting that females are more likely than males to experience low self-esteem and that females with disability typically exhibit lower levels of self-worth than their male counterparts (Magill & Hurlbut, 1986).

Participants experienced a wide range of physical disabilities, including polio, neuromuscular disease, cerebral palsy, and blindness. During their middle childhood

Table 1. Characteristics of respondents

Pseudonym	Age	Disability	Childhood severity[a]	Vocation
Mary	32	Spinal muscular atrophy	1	Psychologist
Joe	31	Post polio	2	Researcher
Susan	52	Cerebral palsy	3	Attorney
Jack	34	Muscular dystrophy	2	Counselor
Tim	38	Post polio	1	Teacher
Dick	37	Post polio	1	Mental health worker
Steve	37	Cerebral palsy	3	State administrator
Mark	47	Cerebral palsy	3	Disability advocate
Amy	40	Blindness	2	Teacher
Peter	39	Post polio	2	Teacher
Jeff	38	Cerebral palsy	3	Teacher
Sara	33	Cerebral palsy	3	Teacher
Eric	38	Muscular dystrophy	3	Attorney
Andy	26	Cerebral palsy	3	Disability advocate

[a]1, Ambulatory with assistance of walker or crutches, no upper body involvement; 2, manual wheelchair user, mild upper body involvement or speech or vision impairment; 3, power wheelchair user, significant upper body involvement and speech impairment.

years, most participants reported experiencing disabilities that significantly limited their lower and upper body functions. Eleven of the participants used wheelchairs, and three used crutches or bracing. Four of the respondents experienced significant speech impairment.

All of the participants were active in some type of paid or unpaid vocation. Two respondents indicated that they elected to engage in volunteer activities because paid employment would compromise their eligibility for funding for personal assistant services. Twelve of the participants were college graduates and were employed in a variety of occupations. The participants' ages ranged from 26 to 52, with the majority in their 30s. Eleven of the participants were married or otherwise involved in long-term relationships, and six of the participants were parents.

Procedure

Participants were recruited through independent living centers, universities, and informal outreach in the disability community. Referral sources were asked to identify adults with physical disabilities who were living independently, were employed or active in an unpaid vocation, and who conveyed positive self-perceptions. Initial contacts with nominees were made by referral sources. All nominees expressed interest in participating in the study and were subsequently contacted by the first author. Participants were told that the purpose of the study was to investigate the key childhood experiences of people with disabilities who grew up to be successful adults with positive self-perceptions. An informed consent was signed by each participant.

To obtain additional validation of participants' current levels of self-worth, each participant was also asked to complete a Rosenberg Self-Esteem Scale (RSE) (Rosenberg, 1979). The RSE is a 10-item Guttman Scale that asks general questions related to attitude toward self, perceptions of worthiness, success, and self-respect. The RSE has been widely used to measure global self-esteem, and it possesses high levels of internal consistency and construct validity (Rosenberg, 1979). Using the Guttman scoring procedure described by Rosenberg, all participants were categorized as having positive self-esteem.

A 2- to 4-hour interview was conducted with each participant. An interview protocol was designed to guide the discussion. The protocol included broad questions regarding participants' family demographics, personal and family morale, caregiving routines, school experiences, perception of disability, and supportive relationships. Each participant was encouraged to direct the focus of his or her interview, and follow-up questions were individually formulated to clarify and elaborate upon issues and stories described by participants. Participants were encouraged to share specific recollections of people and events they believed to be key to their later success and development of high self-esteem. Although the interviews focused on exploring participant recollections of their middle childhood years, several participants also described key adolescent experiences.

Interviews were recorded on tape and transcribed verbatim. Transcripts were then organized and analyzed using Ethnograph (Seidel, Kjolseth, & Seymour, 1985) to detect key factors and themes underlying the emergence and promotion of self-worth among the respondents.

CONTEXTUAL FACTORS

This section discusses the impact of key childhood contextual factors on respondents' lives. These contextual factors include residential life, family climate, and community involvement.

Residential Life

Three of the respondents lived in institutional settings during extended periods of their childhood. They indicated that institutionalization was a negative experience that constricted their expressions of self-determination and their family relationships. Mark, a 47-year-old man with severe cerebral palsy who was institutionalized at age 13 and discharged in his 30s, recalled his experience:

> My mother couldn't handle me and people told [her] about Fairview....I didn't know it at the time, but my mom had cancer....I remember the day I went there. I didn't like it. I hated it and I told mom they have really stupid rules.

The most salient memories of institutionalization for Mark related to the enforcement of rules that limited his personal freedom. Much of Mark's personal pride was derived from his resistance to these rules:

> The food was babies' food. I wasn't no fool, don't feed me slop. So one day, I got all my friends together, we all went on a hunger strike. For one whole day, we didn't go in and eat....They called a psychiatrist to talk to me....I told her flat out, "You come, you look and see what we have to eat and you find out why."...When I was at home, I would go in and ask my mother if I could do this, and she said, "Son, you have a mind of your own. Use your own mind. Use your own judgment. If you thinks it's okay, okay,"...and my dad said, "If you want something, you got to fight for it."

Throughout his institutionalization, Mark maintained contact with his family, and the encouragement his parents provided to him was critical in bolstering Mark's certainty and perseverance in resisting the conditions with which he was faced. Following discharge, Mark supported another resident, who would later become his wife, to advocate for her release. Mark continues to be active in the independent living movement.

Joe, a 31-year-old researcher with post polio, recalled that institutional rules forced a separation between him and his family that was not overcome until after he was discharged. Although his parents visited him regularly in the rehabilitation center, he was not permitted to spend time at home with his family.

> From the time I was until 4 until I was 9, I lived in a rehab center....an old mansion they converted for long-term physical therapy for people with polio and some other disabilities....The rules of the place were you weren't allowed to go home because the kids who went home didn't want to go back....When I went home it was like getting to know my family all over again in a way.

Amy, a 40-year-old teacher with blindness, recalled her mother's commitment to maintaining regular contact and parenting responsibilities during Amy's and her twin's years in a residential school for children with blindness:

> We got the best treatment of anybody in the school because we would go home every single weekend....I remember one thing that really sticks out is that mother refused to have our clothes washed by the method used for the other kids, which was to send them over to the state prison. She would take our clothes home every weekend and dinner would be there when we got home...mashed potatoes and meat loaf, string beans, I can just remember it, and apple pie. And she'd wear her buns off all weekend and then wash and iron all our clothes.

Institutionalization was clearly a negative experience for Mark, Joe, and Amy. Although they wished they had not been institutionalized, they expressed empathy for their parents' caregiving dilemmas. They were bolstered by ongoing parental support that communicated both their continued "belonging" to their families and their parents' commitments to their well-being.

Family Climate

Family composition, economic status, emotional climate, and stressors were all noted as significant factors in respondents' childhood experiences. Twelve of the respondents were reared in two-parent households by their parents of origin, and one respondent was raised by his mother and stepfather. The majority of these respondents reported that their mothers assumed primary responsibility for their daily care. Four respondents specifically noted that their fathers were actively involved in their daily physical care; however, all 13 indicated that other parenting responsibilities were jointly assumed by their mothers and fathers. Only Amy was reared solely by her mother after her parents' divorce when she was 8. However, much of the responsibility for Amy's daily care was assumed by a housekeeper and nanny, whom Amy described as a very supportive adult in her life:

> I remember her just being there from night to day, I mean she was always there...she owned her own home and went home at night...but she cooked and cleaned and ah...took care of us. She always smelled like good food and, ah cleaning solution and starch... She was just, she was very safe. And um, you know, she was always correcting us, "Stand up straight!" and "Don't pick your nose!" or whatever, but she always loved me. She was always singing, singing in the kitchen...all I had to do was listen and I could find her. She was a bus rider and so when we'd go places with her during the day, we'd go on the bus. And so, it was with her that I learned how to ride the bus, which has been a real important skill....There was a sense of pride, that it was okay to get on a bus.

There was general agreement among the respondents that having a stable family life was important for their development. This belief was expressed by Jack, a 34-year-old counselor with muscular dystrophy:

I think having a stable family with no substance abuse or any problems or divorce or any-thing like that was a positive thing on my side. You know, they gave me some securities.

Eleven of the respondents characterized their families as "middle class," citing home and automobile ownership and comfortable lifestyles as key indicators of their family's economic status. A few of the respondents indicated that their families experienced intermittent periods of economic stress that had a negative effect on family morale. According to Andy, a 26-year-old disability advocate with cerebral palsy,

Sometimes it [family morale] was good and sometimes it wasn't....My dad was out of work for a couple of months; it happened about every two 2 when the mill would close....My mom and dad would fight sometimes.

Although several of the respondents reported that their families experienced inter-mittent conflict, most indicated that they were reared in predominantly nurturing envi-ronments. As described by Peter, a 39-year-old teacher with post polio,

My mother and I had a real rapport. I can remember even at a young age: sitting down and just kind of sharing things. You know, talking about life in general. Uh, birth, death, you name it....I kind of always viewed her as having a real, kind of clear picture of how the world works. So she was a good resource that way, when there was confusion or whatev-er...she was always very open to sharing those sorts of things.

Respondents suggested that being reared in stable, nurturing families was impor-tant for their development of high self-esteem and their subsequent life success. How-ever, four of the respondents are testimony to the fact that the presence of family stressors does not always present an insurmountable obstacle to later life success. One respondent recalled much family discord during her childhood, two respondents reported that their parents abused alcohol, and one respondent reported that she was sexually abused by her older brother. Steve, a 37-year-old state administrator with cere-bral palsy, described the impact that his mother's alcohol abuse had on his care and their relationship:

There was this stretch of time for one summer that my mother took an active role in thera-py, and, again, the alcohol somewhat interfered with that...even though I remember the doctor's orders saying, "Make sure you get, two or three times a day, this exercise done," I was fortunate if it got done once a day...the best time to do any interactive thing with my mother was in the morning. She often worked at night and, when she didn't work at night, she wasn't sober anyway.

It is interesting to note that three of these respondents reported seeking out and benefiting from counseling later in life to process their responses to their family prob-lems. Their childhood family experiences were clearly painful; however, each noted specific action they had taken in adulthood to minimize their negative impacts.

Community Involvement

Respondents emphasized the importance of living in a cohesive community, for both their family well-being and their own social development. Several of the respondents reported that their neighborhoods provided ample opportunity for them to socialize with other children in addition to providing social support for their parents. As described by Tim, a 38-year-old teacher with post polio who grew up in New York City,

One of the nice things about where I grew up, it was an apartment house that was 13 stories and there were six families on each floor...it was just a ton of people having babies, so there were millions of kids my age. The elementary school was right across the street from my house and, in those days, you went home for lunch....it was really a neighborhood school. On the corner of the street that we lived was a park and then a golf course off the park where we would go sleigh riding in the winter….a lot of young families and their parents were socially involved with a lot of families….my parents were involved with other people, I was involved with other people, which was really nice….It was…a real sense of security for me to participate in that neighborhood and really know everybody.

A similar cohesive neighborhood climate was described by Dick, a 37-year-old mental health worker who, like Peter, also experienced post polio:

We were a real active neighborhood. Oh boy, we played regular sports—baseball, football, not much basketball. We played games like red rover and steal the bacon….I remember sweating and being pretty dirty and enjoying that, a lot of running around….It was a real fun neighborhood.

Susan, a 52-year-old attorney with cerebral palsy who grew up in a rural town in the Northwest, described the inclusive environment of her church:

I was included in everything in Sunday School. In the evenings we were always having plays…we would practice and perform for the church on stage. It was never questioned that I would have a part.

Parental Advocacy   Although community and neighborhood inclusion sometimes occurred spontaneously, most respondents reported that their inclusion was promoted through specific advocacy and accommodation efforts of their parents. Like many of the respondents, Peter's ability to participate in Boy Scouts became a reality as a result of his parent's advocacy:

I was real active in Boy Scouts, Cub Scouts. I went on a 25-mile hike; in fact I was one of the first handicapped Eagle Boy Scouts in the United States. Again, that was the thing that my parents had to fight for, to get some requirements changed and adjusted.

INCLUSIVE EDUCATION

Thirteen of the respondents indicated that they participated in inclusive schooling during some part of their childhood. Four were educated exclusively in typical classes, and the remaining nine went from segregated to typical education during their middle childhood. Only Mark attended exclusively self-contained classes for children with disabilities. The high percentage of respondents educated in inclusive settings is remarkable, given that all but one were schooled prior to the passage of the Education for All Handicapped Children Act, PL 94-142.This finding supports contemporary assertions that access to inclusive education is critical for successful development and life achievement. Comments by Jeff, a 38-year-old teacher with cerebral palsy, highlight the respondents' perceptions regarding the importance of inclusive education:

At school, in my special ed classes, I was on the top of the heap. I was one of the few kids in the class who could talk reasonably well…I could write….I was ambulatory and many of them weren't. So physically, in that small little environment I was the cream of the crop and I liked that…but it wasn't realistic. You put me in any other environment I was right at the bottom….It didn't prepare me at all for what was to eventually happen to me.

Respondents uniformly indicated that segregated education provided them with illusory perceptions of competence that were subsequently deflated. They also indicated that educational segregation accentuated their perceptions and the perceptions of others regarding their differences. According to Jack, a 34-year-old counselor with muscular dystrophy,

I liked to play with the neighborhood kids and I didn't see myself as real different until 8 or 9….Part of it was I had to go back to doing physical therapy. I think in fourth grade they started. They had gym and we all had to change suits. Plus, my parents wanted me to go to this physical therapy things and they would send me during gym class. So they'd send me to this other school on the other side of town. I just felt crummy because I'd go to this school on the other side of town and it was partly for kids with disabilities, partly a regular school. I remember going over there and the kids laughed at me. It was normal kids laughing at me. I don't think I ever told them I was going. I felt really ashamed about it so I didn't want to feel different from them.

The movement of respondents from segregated to inclusive educational environments was catalyzed by a variety of circumstances. In several cases, parents' advocacy forced the change. Peter's parents actively advocated for his transfer to his neighborhood school:

They had to fight with the schools when they went to enroll me. They were talking Easter Seals School and my parents said, "No, he will go to public school." My folks had to dig in their heels.

Eric, a 38-year-old attorney with muscular dystrophy, described how his transfer to inclusive schooling was also catalyzed by his mother's advocacy:

My mother identified, at that point, that if something didn't change in our lives, we were going to end up institutionalized. I think that she was assisted in that determination by a physical therapist....My mom, at that point, said, "Okay I want Eric referred out," and they did. We were real lucky in that there was only one elementary school and it happened to be our neighborhood elementary school.

In some instances, students with primarily physical challenges regularly went through transition into typical classes during junior high or high school. In a few other instances, teachers and other school advocates catalyzed their transition. Following Joe's discharge from the rehabilitation hospital, he was enrolled in a segregated classroom with a particularly creative teacher:

When I went home, I was immediately enrolled in what was called "the Sunshine Class"...Actually there were two classes: one was for physically dependent kids and the other class was for kids with mental retardation. The woman who taught the other class left and the district decided not to fill her job...so everybody got dumped into [my] class. My teacher was pretty overwhelmed trying to deal with all of us...so she farmed us out...those of us who were the best and the brightest...she would seat us into regular classrooms. I got integrated by the force of her design....Not only was she trying to relieve pressure on herself, but she also believed that there were some of us that had no need to be there. By the end of the year, she went to the principal and said that some of us really didn't need to be in her class, we'd been doing those classes...she got us mainstreamed that way.

Although participation in inclusive education was clearly valued by all of the respondents, Jack did express some regret over his total lack of access to support from peers with disabilities:

Being in school with other kids...it was probably good for me in a way that I was determined to work toward the standards other people were working toward....and I think as much pain as there was, I wouldn't have done it any other way. I would have just wanted more support. And maybe get to know some others that had disabilities somewhere.

Jack's comment suggests that some children with disabilities may benefit from participation in typical educational experiences in conjunction with other opportunities to share experiences with others who experience similar challenges.

MEDICAL CARE

All of the respondents had extensive interaction with doctors and hospitals during their childhood. Each participated in regular medical visits, and most had a number of surgeries. Virtually all of the respondents characterized their experiences with medical providers as negative. As expressed by Eric,

> I can remember, sure I guess, whenever we would need a new chair, we had to go to what they call "clinic." At these clinics, you got to be the freak of the hour. They would come in and they showed incoming; "This is what one of the freaks looks like"...I really resented that kind of behavior that I had to put up with at that place....I didn't like it at all.

Respondents' comments suggested that their negative perceptions of their medical experiences were primarily associated both with having their challenges highlighted in a depersonalized, stigmatizing fashion and with lacking personal control in medical decision making. Although recalling their experiences as negative, many of the respondents also reported that they derived self-confidence from assuming control over their medical decision making. Mary, a 32-year-old psychologist with spinal muscular atrophy, remembered:

> Basically life was normal from December until June. In May I would go to the doctors....The doctor would have decided to do surgery; within a week after the ending of school I would enter the hospital. I would be in the hospital for 2 weeks to 3 months...It went on that way for maybe 9 years...When I was 16, the doctor said that I should have spinal fusion and I would be in a body cast for several months. That was the first time that my mother let me decide what I wanted to do and, because I had just had a friend commit suicide after returning to school from the same surgery, I said "no." It was one of the best decisions I ever made and marked the beginning of my taking control of my medical life.

FAMILY THEMES

Active Temperaments

The relative impact of nature and nurture on the development of self-esteem is a complex, perhaps unresolvable issue. Eleven of the respondents in this study reported that they had self-determined, independent, and sometimes feisty personalities throughout life. Mark made this point:

> I'm a go-getter....I love to work. I like to be busy...I told myself to push. If they tell me I can't do it, I still do it. If you say you can't do it, you won't be doing anything at all.

Some respondents suggested that they were self-determined despite the attempts of others to limit them. As expressed by Mary,

> I was definitely a person who was strong-headed and when I got something on my mind I wanted to do, I did it until I found out from experience that I could do it or I couldn't do it. I wanted to ride a bike for years and it took me 3 or 4 times of cracking my head open and needing stitches before I finally conceded that I couldn't ride a bike. Well, actually I never did concede it because my feeling was that if somebody had taught me instead of just ignoring the fact that I was going to go out and try it anyway, I may have succeeded.

Respondents' recollections of their expressions of self-determination sometimes included active rebellion. As expressed by Joe:

> I had to push the limits for a while. You know, if I wanted to go down to the park and play with the other kids, maybe I wasn't supposed to even cross the street, but I'd go. I'd just say, "Well, everybody else gets to go, why not me?"

Most respondents indicated that they were independent in spirit and, although their desires were not always actively supported by their parents, their independence efforts were typically not resisted. Dick commented on this point:

> I remember my mom saying, "Now you know you're going to need to find a job where you can do things in an office because you're not going to be able to do physical things."

Maybe that was the biggest push of all for me to do physical things 'cause they said I wasn't going to be able to....They never tried to keep me off my horses or stop me from doing physical stuff...They didn't stand in the way....but the desire was with me.

Many respondents recalled that their parents reacted to their independence efforts in two primary ways. First, respondents' parents encouraged their independence and were available to provide support, when desired by their children. Susan described her father's support:

My dad was kind and understanding. He never put me down. He never told me I was stupid, or crazy, or couldn't do it...he just sort of accepted how I was....If I would ask for help, he would certainly give me help, but he would just let me struggle a little bit longer [than mom]. He wouldn't jump in and say, "Let me help you."

Second, when respondents' efforts were not successful, their parents typically did not emphasize their difficulties. Sarah, now a teacher, remembered her parents' response to her struggles with cerebral palsy:

I was very determined and I was stubborn...I had to do everything myself, they encouraged that...If it didn't work out, it was no big deal.

Those respondents who did not describe themselves as intrinsically self-determined recalled an interplay between their parents' mixed inhibition and encouragement of their independence and their own ambivalent responses to opportunities to express their competence. This interplay is evident in Jack's description of his reticent progression toward independence:

My mother did a lot for me, both my parents...I learned how to clothe myself when I was 13, but I could have a lot earlier. They were doing things for me that I could do myself at an earlier age....It made me feel a little awkward with other kids who could do those things....They [my parents] got me the bike. I wouldn't get on it. I just got real nervous. But, then [in the 7th grade] I just got on it and started riding. I just wasn't ready for it when they got it....It seems to me I was physically ready to do it, but maybe I wasn't psychologically ready to do it.

Jack's comments point out the challenges for parents and children in defining and optimally facilitating self-determination "readiness." Most respondents suggested that their parents were able to recognize and encourage their sometimes subtle assertions for greater independence without either pushing them or holding them back.

Typical Perceptions

Respondents generally reported that their positive self-regard was strongly linked to their being perceived as typical children. As expressed by Susan:

I wanted to grow up and be an attorney and I guess I saw myself as normal. I didn't see myself as handicapped and I think this is what made me...what kept me going.

Eric believed that this typical treatment was facilitated by the lack of attention to disability during his childhood:

I was real lucky that I didn't grow up in an era where people do have to come to grips with being anything...I didn't have to. I just had the free rein of childhood when the only thing you had to worry about was being where the action was...If I had to face them earlier, I think I could have developed some of the problems that I was fortunate enough not to develop.

Respondents indicated they were regarded as typical children who experienced challenges, in contrast to being "disabled children." Their participation in typical childhood activities was valued independent of their performance, as Dick recalled:

It just kind of happened at such a young age that I don't even remember thinking much differently, just grew up adapting. My parents didn't hide my disability a whole lot. They let me ride horses and I got thrown from horses. Played football, was in track. I didn't excel in any of them but I was in them. I think it had a real positive impact. I guess I just didn't look at it as disability.

Respondents also recalled that their parents conveyed ongoing confidence in their management capacities, which helped to deemphasize their attributions of disability. Mark made this point:

I didn't think too much about it [having a disability]...I just did know that it's harder for me to do things....I remember my dad said, "If it seems harder, you will find a way to do it...there's a way and you can do it." He beat that in my head.

The majority of respondents reported that they benefited from their parents' regard for them as typical children. However, Jeff indicated that his father's intense focus on promoting his physical capabilities highlighted Jeff's perceptions of his differences from others and impeded Jeff's self-acceptance:

My father would take time off from his job to come to the school and observe my therapy, take notes, and when he would be home, he would do the same thing....He was obsessive about it....Every weekend, if the weather was nice, my father would take me on long walks of a couple miles duration, and he just felt that the more walking I would do, the better I would become....He was constantly pushing me....He never really took the time to recognize me for what I am....We never really had a chance to interact...going to special ed. programs from the time I was about 3 years old....I watched the kids in the streets doing those things [playing] and I wished I could do those things and I knew I couldn't....Gradually, I remember believing that I was not a complete person...and I would never be able to become a whole human being. My father, at the same time as I had this image of myself, he was pushing, always pushing for me to be better...to be as normal as possible. Yet I couldn't reconcile what he wanted and what I would feel.

Jeff's story suggests that the promotion of children's self-regard involves balancing efforts to promote their capabilities with unconditional acceptance.

Communication About Disability Respondents uniformly reported that they benefited from their parents' willingness to acknowledge and support their management of specific disability-related challenges. For example, the impact of Dick's disability was acknowledged by his parents as was his management skill:

Oh, [vacations] they were a lot of fun. Oh, you know, I remember we have films of it, and I remember some of the films of them [parents] helping me climb up hills or go up a lot of steps. The last time we watched them, Mom said something like, "Well, I remember you got real tired doing that, but you did real well."

Interestingly, most respondents recalled that their parents did not initiate conversations about disability unrelated to their discussion of specific issues. Tim recalled this:

They never really talked about it. Basically, when it [polio] hit, we did what we needed to do. That's what we would talk about. It was more the mechanics of doing the thing as opposed to any consciousness or dealing with what happened.

Generally, respondents indicated that their parents limiting their communication about disability minimized their self-perceptions of difference. Sara suggested that her parents' lack of communication with her about disability was reflective of their adjustment:

My parents made me think that it was okay. The secret was I'm sure that they didn't talk about it and they got over having me disabled.

Two respondents expressed regret regarding their parents' lack of general communication with them. Mary and Jack indicated that their family's lack of openness made it difficult for them to ask questions about their disabilities and express their concerns. Jack suggested that his parents' silence may have reflected their lack of adjustment:

> They just talked about whether I should get physical therapy or that kind of thing. But never any real discussions about it. I think it was a problem for me because they didn't open up about it. Because maybe they weren't sure about their feelings in dealing with a disabled child. Because there were not any support groups or anything for them really....They were always nice to me and respected me. I never felt like I was made different, except that they did some things for me and protected me in a way....They could have made me be more independent and it helps to just talk about your feelings.

Typical Expectations for Behavior

Parents' typical perceptions of their children were reflected in their typical expectations for their children's assumption of family responsibilities and in their children's nonpreferential treatment and involvement in typical leisure activities.

Family Responsibilities   Most of the respondents recalled that they assumed typical family responsibilities, such as chores and oversight of siblings. Peter recalled that he was assigned chores that were appropriately matched to his physical capabilities:

> I had chores along with the rest of my siblings. I think some of those were adjusted where my older brother especially would be out there mowing the lawn, trimming hedges, moving shrubs, bushes. I'd tended to stay in the house and learn to cook, clean, do the laundry...just because it was more feasible. They [my parents] were always very set about that, reminding me periodically, "Don't expect anything special. There are some things you'll just have to do differently."

Many of the respondents reflected on their participation in family chores with enthusiasm and pride. Mark, who experienced severe cerebral palsy that substantially restricted his mobility, recalled this:

> My dad made [me] a little kiddy car. I would help my dad stack wood, mow the lawn, stuff like that....they asked my younger brother and he wouldn't do it...couldn't keep me out of the wood pile. I stacked it with my dad. I did it with one hand.

In addition to chores, a few of the respondents recalled assuming responsibility for caring for their younger siblings, as Eric reported:

> In some ways we did some fathering for my younger brother and I think I strongly played in that role for my younger brother.

Nonpreferential Treatment   Respondents reported that they generally were treated no differently than were their brothers and sisters. As described by Dick,

> It seemed pretty normal in that my oldest brother got most of the stuff. Being the middle son with three boys, the middle son was the one that kind of observed and saw what not to do because of the stuff my older brother got into. My younger brother was the cute little boy that was known to be the last in the family, so they treated him like the youngest and he got away with a lot more than my older brother and I did. That seemed pretty normal in that way.

Joe suggested that the interplay of his parents' somewhat different expectations for his independence facilitated their adoption of appropriate expectations for his participation in family responsibilities:

> I remember most clearly that I wasn't treated any differently, that I was aware of, than my brothers. We were all expected to follow the same rules, participate in the chores of the

house and do the same kinds of things....My mother had a natural tendency, I think because I had a disability, to be a little overprotective of me and a little more concerned. My father, on the other hand, was of the opinion that he wasn't going to treat me any different than he did my brothers and expected that to be the mode of operation around the house. So there was a balance that I think was struck.

Leisure Participation Respondents recalled their satisfaction in participating in normative leisure activities. Tim reported that he participated in sports with his dad and brother:

I was basically able to participate in most activities that my family did. My dad enjoyed sports and he and I would participate in sports. Having an older brother was helpful because he was involved also and enjoyed sports.

Susan recalled that her father actively supported her participation in 4-H:

I developed my own head of Holstein cattle for 4-H and I started just with a little old Guernsey steer....As time went on, I bought more with my earnings. My dad made me a box so I could put my curling iron in and my curling comb and my blanket. I was involved in all aspects [of 4-H]...cooking, sewing, livestock, and health.

Focus on Strengths

In conjunction with recalling their parents having typical perceptions and expectations for them, respondents reported that their parents and teachers consistently highlighted their disability-related and non–disability-related strengths. Tim recalled his experience with daily exercises:

My mother would do those pushing exercises with me, she'd put me on the kitchen table after breakfast....Every now and then she'd let me push with my good leg so I could show how strong I was, which was kind of neat. I think in her own way she was showing me there was a lot I could do, even through the therapies, which were really, at times it was real frustrating.

Many of the respondents learned to value their academic capabilities as a result of assistance and encouragement provided by their teachers. Eric described the support he received in reading:

I appreciated the fact that she [my teacher] helped me learn how to read. Reading was a real, for me, a real power thing because it was obviously one thing that I could do as well as anyone else in the world.

Peter recalled that being a strong reader provided balance to his physical challenges:

I was an early reader, I think probably showed some kind of real talent and gift in things at an early age and so I ran with that. It's okay if I'm not up to par in the rest of it because I'm a smart guy...it was something I could be proud of.

Respondents also described the respect they received from peers for their accomplishments. As Sara reported,

Other people told me I was smart. I remember that. It made me feel better. The kids asked me questions and the students copied my papers.

Amy echoed Sara's comments as she recalled her pride in being an accomplished swimmer:

Swimming was something I could do well...I just took great delight in waving to the neighborhood kids and diving in...and I knew I could outswim anyone in the pool and so that was a real source of pride that I was a good swimmer.

Accommodation to Challenge

Respondents recalled numerous examples of creative accommodations identified by family members, teachers, peers, and themselves to maximize their participation in typical activities. Mobility aides were obvious forms of accommodation provided to most respondents. Jeff described the impact of using crutches on his quality of life:

> I started wearing crutches which I probably should have worn all along....They gave me the mobility, the security that I needed....For the first time I could walk down the street without anyone around me....I could start using the buses and that, more than anything, along with the friends I made in high school, changed my life.

Parents and siblings often provided critical accommodations. Amy recalled her brother's accommodation to her visual impairment:

> I can remember my oldest brother really being sensitive about tuning in the TV with the highest amount of contrast so I could see it better if I wanted to watch TV. If my older brother was giving me a hard time for getting in the way of the picture, he would mediate...he would jockey us around so we could both see.

Parents also helped respondents to identify accommodations they could use. For example, Andy's mother helped him identify ways he could get assistance from others:

> When I was a kid my mom said, "When you talk to somebody and when you want somebody to help you, first make eye contact and it will work."

Andy has used this method throughout his life to direct his personal assistants.

Essential accommodations were also made by educators. Steve recalled an academic accommodation that reduced his stress and facilitated his performance:

> Even though I was slow at writing, the situation under which I learned to write was one in which speed was not encouraged, so I didn't feel pressed from a competitive standpoint. I actually learned how to make my letters in both a cursive and printed way that was really legible....If they wanted us to write something, they'd say, "Okay, here's an assignment. Write an essay on your favorite subject and get it in to us in 3 days." That put it in a framework where a person could concentrate on doing it right and doing it in a way that didn't put a lot of stress on them.

Accommodations were helpful in "leveling the playing field" for respondents and facilitating their perceptions of self-competence. Dick recalled that being assigned to strong sports teams reduced his focus on having a challenge and provided him with opportunities to experience success:

> As long as I wasn't reminded of it by being held back, I didn't have to look at it....I think there was a tendency to put me on the stronger teams, maybe to help balance the teams out. But they had the bigger guys protecting me.

Peter described the creative approach his peers used to facilitate his participation in baseball:

> We had a rule when we played baseball that if a fly ball were to come down, if I could even touch it with my crutch in the air...that's a fly pop-out. Their reasoning was, "Well, if you could touch it, then if you didn't have crutches, you would have been able to catch it"...I don't think I ever felt that different, there were always these adjustments.

Accommodations provided to respondents sometimes required additional efforts and resources from adults. Tim recalled that his parents provided him with numerous pairs of replacement orthopedic shoes to enable him to participate in sports:

There was this game in the city that you play, it's called "Skully."…I was able to play it pretty good, but what it meant was me crawling around on the ground….But I couldn't wear sneakers or anything, so I was wearing my orthopedic shoes…they weren't made for people to be active. When I was dragging, I used to put a hole in the tip of the shoe and I was going through shoes very quickly. I remember that was a concern to my parents, but I didn't get into trouble because of it. Looking upon it later in life, I think they were really glad that I was active, even though it was upsetting to them to see those shoes get worn out. I'm sure it was expensive to them, but they didn't make an issue of it.

Dick's parents alleviated his concerns about their spending scarce resources for an air conditioner by emphasizing the benefit for the entire family:

They tolerated life in the humidity until I had my first operation. That's when they got the air conditioner to make me more comfortable. We all benefited from that so they said it was kind of neat.

Unhelpful Accommodations As Peter implied, accommodations were helpful for respondents when they were made naturally and did not appear to highlight their differences. Peter illustrated this distinction in his description of an incident in which a well-meaning adult offered an accommodation that left Peter feeling stigmatized:

I was probably 8 or 9 and they were going to have a sack race. Suddenly, the guy announces lo and behold we don't have enough sacks…so he was wondering could we change the contest to who could go the farthest on foot on crutches….He was like playing too far and I felt very embarrassed….Like, don't load the contest.

Respondents also highlighted the importance of their understanding the reasons for and benefits of accommodations that were made. Because he was not informed, Tim recalled misinterpreting an accommodation as punishment:

I remember when they had fire drills [at school]. I wasn't allowed to participate. I was sent to the principal's office…because I guess I would have been an obstacle on the stairway. I remember sitting in the principal's office thinking I was in trouble. Whenever you got sent to the principal's office, it wasn't for anything good, so I really felt every time…like I was in trouble….I don't really remember anybody taking any time to explain.

Likewise, Joe reported that being forced to use what was perceived by others to be a more normalizing mobility aide made his life an unnecessary struggle:

I was forced to use crutches and braces. That was a very slow, arduous thing for me to walk around [in]…but in those days, walking was always preferable to a chair. There were times when I was just exhausted and I wanted to go see a TV show and it was going to take me 20 minutes to walk down to the TV room. I could have been there in 5 minutes in a wheelchair.

Autonomy

Respondents emphasized their expression of autonomy as a critical factor affecting their development of self-esteem. Their comments focused on opportunities for choice making, independence and achievement, risk taking, and assertiveness.

Choice Making Respondents recalled being permitted to make a variety of choices, from incidental decisions such as what clothes to wear to major medical decisions. Susan described her parents' willingness to allow her to select her school clothes:

I've always been a very independent individual, and from the point I could—even before a lot of kids—my parents were letting me make my own decisions. For example, I can remember in grade school going with my father….We'd go shopping for school clothes.

Rather than him buying my school clothes, well he would pay for them of course, but I would pick them out. I would have absolutely total say in what I wore.

Susan's capacity for informed decision making was fully developed and respected by her parents when it came to important medical decisions later in childhood:

When I was 16, the choice to have my leg amputated was totally mine. My parents had no say in that whatsoever.

Andy's parents also permitted him to make critical medical decisions:

Back then, they really didn't know about cerebral palsy and the doctors did tests on people. But mom listened to me when I said "no." I was happy she did that because, like one time, they said that my leg was...they wanted to straighten it out so I could walk easier. A couple of my friends had it done. One day I was playing with one of them...I was on my knees, they couldn't get up on their knees because they had their tendons cut. I saw that and the doctors told my mom that if they cut my tendons, I could walk and I said, "No way!"

Achievement Respondents recalled that their parents and teachers encouraged their expression of independence and achievement. Eric described his mother's approach to his achievement:

I think I was a fairly hard-working little kid. Even at playing I worked hard....My achievement was real important to my mother. She just maybe said to me that was what was expected and I think when I achieved things she was very encouraging...she took a lot of pride, as I did, in achievement.

Educators also provided respondents with important encouragement for achievement. Steve described the remarkable devotion of his teachers as they supported his desire for school achievement:

Three weeks after I started eighth grade regular school in a mainstream setting, the teachers ran me though a battery of tests and discovered that I had between a third- and fourth-grade education. I had three specific teachers who were willing to work with me after school. I worked 16 hours a day either at school or at home....Even though I was doing different assignments than most of my peers for the first third of the year, my teacher never drew special attention to it in a way that would embarrass me....By the end of the school year, I had actually finished eighth grade...that's an example of my being a very determined person.

Rather than promoting achievement in specified areas, respondents indicated that adults encouraged them to excel in domains that matched their interests and skills. Amy described her experience:

I just dreaded school....I just can't remember anything fun about school...but I was real tenacious with the Campfire [Campfire Girls] you know, I really stuck with it and I really liked that group.

Sometimes adults provided specific opportunities for respondents to achieve or experience independence. Sara indicated that her mother provided opportunities for her to adapt to being at home alone:

In grade school I was very curious but I was afraid to be left alone, and they would encourage me to stay alone while they ran errands and stuff.

While supporting respondents toward achievement, adults emphasized their capacities and minimized the importance of their challenges. Dick recalled with fondness the encouragement he received from a teacher:

I remember one teacher, she was encouraging me to go out for football. I can remember her saying "We have other kids that have had things happen to them—broken legs, broken arms—that played too, so you can play." Never did quite get that together, but it was that she had confidence in me.

Adults also provided instrumental support to promote respondents' success. Amy recalled that her mother arranged for her to have a tutor:

Mother recognized the fact that we needed hands on or we wouldn't get it....So she hired, or arranged for, or whatever, this one gal to come down who I became very close with. She was like an older sister...she would really work with me, really be patient, and uh, you know, I can just hear her saying a hundred times, "I know you can do this" and "It's okay." I didn't feel like she would go, "Come on, come on!...Geez, you're taking a long time!" She was very insistent, very patient, very nurturing.

Steve recounted the support he received from his father and grandfather to participate in fishing, although the rest of his family thought that it was beyond his capabilities:

With family types of things, there was very seldom, unless my father took the initiative to do it, the opportunity to go out and do things socially with my cousins. The assumption was made that I was either too fragile or something else by the rest of the family. There wasn't a clear understanding of what my disability was and what that meant....My father was the rare exception to that...my grandfather was on my dad's side. He loved to sturgeon fish. And so, as a kid 10, 11, 12 years old, he would literally do as my dad had done—put me up on his back and carry me piggyback down to the river. My father and my grandfather were the only two that were really accepting and open to that kind of thing at all.

Respondents reported that it was sometimes difficult or emotionally painful for adults to promote their independence and achievement. Peter shared a story of his mother's patience and willingness to tolerate negative judgments of neighbors as she encouraged him to learn to stand up independently:

When I was around 4 and I was using two leg braces, a hip brace, a back corset, and crutches to get around, they [my parents] had kind of taken a tact with my falling down, "You need to learn to get up because sooner or later you'll fall down somewhere where there isn't anybody there." So they really kind of encouraged me to learn how to do that 'cause I really needed to learn how to get up. They weren't off the wall with it, you know. If I'd fall down, given a few minutes of trying, if I weren't making it, "Well, would you like some help now?"...One day, I fell down in front of the house and just struggled for a number of minutes, you know, and they said, "Do you want help?" and I said, "By gosh, no, I'm gonna do it this time," and just kind of set my mind, "This is it. I'm gonna figure this out." Well, it took 20 minutes, which they said was very agonizing for them to watch. It was also very agonizing for a neighbor who called the police on them saying, "A poor crippled child has fallen down and the parents are sitting on the front porch and they won't even help him up." Luckily, the policeman who showed up at our house was a family friend and my folks explained what was going on....The one part that I do distinctively remember was them asking, "Do you need help now?" and me going, "No, no, I'm gonna do it this time...and I figured out how to get the crutches positioned just right, move at the right moment, and I managed to get up....It felt like a real major triumph.

Risk Taking Risk-taking behavior was recalled by virtually all of the respondents and cited as an important factor for both their development of autonomy and their understanding of their capabilities. Risk taking was also a source of pride for many of the respondents. Tim recalled his pride in testing his jumping skills:

I guess I was pretty active because we used to take pride in putting our fingerprints on high parts of the wall in our house, which was kind of a measure of how high I could jump...and then I had about 3 concussions when I was a kid, 'cause we had these wooden floors which my mother loved to polish....I was pretty good at going, not real good at stopping.

Although Tim took many risks, he did not recall that his parents challenged his behavior unless he was deliberately destructive to himself or others:

> My parents never took issue with what I could and couldn't do. If I was going to get to the top of the hill, I was going to get to the top of the hill. I don't ever remember him saying to me, "You can't do that." If I jumped down steps and broke my brace, they never yelled, unless I took it off and threw it at someone's head or chased someone to do damage to myself.

Respondents recalled engaging in three major variations of risk taking. The first involved performing mildly dangerous activities without a parent's permission. Dick described his mother's reaction after she observed him engage in risky behavior following surgery:

> I remember once I had an operation and one of my older friends brought me up on a bridge and pushed me down it. My mom wasn't real happy about that, but I wanted to do it. I hit a hole...and tipped over...it was a lot of fun, so I did it. I remember, my mom just happened to walk out and see the whole thing. I remember her walking towards us and I said, "She's really mad, I can tell by looking at her....She just kinda took the wheelchair and rolled me in and I was grounded. However you ground somebody in a wheelchair, I don't know, but [laughs] I was grounded for a period of time.

Mary also recalled her insistence with her parents that she be allowed to take risks. They did not encourage her risk taking and responded negatively to her failures:

> I can remember insisting that my parents let me do what all the other kids were doing and not treat me like a baby. I can remember fighting about that. Not that they held me back, but what they would do is not tell me that I could do something but leave it up to my own risk taking....If I was successful, they didn't tell me that I shouldn't have done it. But if I wasn't successful, they'd tell me that I shouldn't have done it.

The second variation of risk taking involved respondents performing dangerous activities with their parents' knowledge but not necessarily their encouragement. Peter described one of his risky experiences:

> One day I announced, "I want to try to learn how to ride a bike." My mother said, "You can't ride a bike." I said, "You said I could do anything I wanted to try." I remember her shaking her head, looking at my father and going, "You go out there because I can't watch this." So, I got on the bike in the driveway...he propped my feet up onto the wheels, and my right being a little bit better than my left, I remember trying to pedal with the one foot. And pretty much I did until I got to level ground and then, "Crash!" I'm getting some bruises and cuts...."Yeah, you're right, I can't do that." That wasn't fun and I didn't want to do it again. They laughed, just the whole concept of, it's like, "We tried to tell you this and you had to throw yourself on the cement to learn it." I think that's maybe another key element of our family life—humor. My mother was supplied with bandages and Mercurochrome or whatever they needed.

Although Peter's parents did not prefer that he attempt bike riding, his recollection suggests that they were willing to respect his need to find out whether he could ride, and they attempted to minimize the danger in his adventure. Equally important, they did not punish or criticize him when he was unsuccessful. Peter also recalled that his mother was usually nearby but seldom intrusive:

> She didn't make herself known, but she was always not more than 10 steps away...if suddenly brakes squealed on the street out front, you could almost bet she'd be the first one on the street. She was always kind of aware of who we were with or what we were doing and yet not poking in.

The third variation of risk taking recalled by respondents involved specific parental facilitation. For example, Andy's mother gave him specific assistance to extend his range in the neighborhood:

I had a walker and I wanted to walk down the block to the corner and back. My mom let me and my dad was uneasy about it. One day I did it and one of the neighbors saw me on the corner and she picked me up and took me home. I tried to tell her that it was okay and that it was okay with my mom, but the neighbor didn't believe me. I started crying and mom said it was okay. The next time I did it, I had her write me a note saying that it was okay....When I was a little kid, I didn't want to go outside, but my mom put me out [laughs].

Assertiveness   Respondents reported that they were assertive children and their parents actively supported their attempts. Steve recalled efforts he and his father made to improve conditions at his school:

We were doing social studies and I raised my hand to answer....I found myself being quite competitive and wanting to accomplish every day as a kind of measurement of my own accomplishment and self-esteem and stuff. The teacher said, "You might as well put your hand down 'cause I'm not going to call on you"...this was after I had my hand up for probably 5 minutes or so. Well, I went home that night and I told my dad what happened and my dad was absolutely livid....He said, "Dammit, I'm not paying taxes for you to go to school and not get the educational opportunities that you deserve and have a right to."...There was a very heated meeting between my dad and the principal of the school, the therapists—amazingly enough, I started getting more individualized attention as a result of that uproar. I also started to notice my peers were starting to get more direct attention....By the time I graduated from high school, not only did I finish in the top 5th of my class of 405 graduates, but I scored more points in competitive speech than anybody in the history of the school.

Steve's recollection suggests that he was positively influenced by his father's assertiveness on his behalf. His father's behavior subsequently helped to promote Steve's expression of assertiveness:

I and about five other people took it on ourselves to challenge the school district to come up with money to build the ramp...to make the cafeteria accessible to us, as disabled students, so that we weren't in that segregated setting again.

Friendship

Friendship with typical peers was unanimously cited by respondents as a critical factor in their development of competence. Steve's comments highlight the importance of friendship:

I can't stress it enough when I say that the key thing that helped me to recognize the need to compete with myself and challenge the opportunities that I had was the exposure that I had, even though it was on a relatively limited basis, to my able-bodied peers.

Friendships with typical peers facilitated respondents' adopting of a typical self-image that included being both "different" and "normal." Jeff recalled realizing that all of his peers felt different in some way:

We came to the topic of do girls like us...everyone of them, I viewed them as popular, very confident...and everyone of them stated something about their personality or their looks that made them feel that they weren't attractive, that they weren't likable. I just listened to them and I remember walking away feeling that's no different than I feel about myself. The only difference is that mine's more obvious and I can't hide it while they can....That point was the first time in my life that I realized and started thinking that I'm like everyone else.

Several respondents emphasized their pride in participating in all activities with their peers. Eric recalls engaging in entirely inclusive friendship activities:

I don't think there was ever any segregation between what they did and what I did. Whatever they were doing, I did, and whatever I was doing, they did. They went to play baseball, I went and watched baseball. They, you know, went to shoplift, I went to shoplift. They looked at girlie magazines, I looked at girlie magazines....I usually hung out with kids a couple of years older.

Establishing friends was difficult for many of the respondents, particularly those with severe disabilities. Often respondents recalled making friends with peers whose experiences and interests complimented their own. For instance, Jack developed an important friendship with a peer who was both different from and similar to Jack:

> I think my first semester of 11th grade I did find this one kid who was totally different from me, a football player, not intellectual really and he had a lot of family problems. He kind of took to me and we became friends...'cause he didn't have a lot either and I met some of his friends and they weren't really mainstreamed types but they accepted me....Just having one or two friends to do something with, that really helped me feel good, not quite so alone.

Respondents recalled that maintaining relationships required proactive efforts on their parts both to make their peers comfortable with their disabilities and to fit in. Andy recalled that he used humor and familiarity to help his friends feel at ease with his disability:

> I had a ball [in typical school] because I knew how to joke....I'd do everything they'd do. When we'd go out to play, I'd go with them. At first they were afraid of me getting hurt, but after they'd see me fall down a couple of times, they got over that.

Several respondents reported that they deliberately acted out in order to fit in with their peer group. Tim recalled his efforts to get into trouble after his academic excellence was highlighted:

> When I was 13, I remember the teacher pulled me out as model student and that was my social fall-down. So, through junior high school I kind of played down and actually went out of my way to get into trouble sometimes.

Parents were critical forces in promoting the friendships of their children. In some cases, respondents' development of friendships was facilitated through opportunities to interact with other children with whom their parents related. For example, Mary made friends in association with her mother's babysitting:

> She [my mother] babysat at what ended up being my best friend's house. They had seven children and she babysat and actually that's how I met my best friend when I was young. I would go there and that was real close to home.

In several cases, respondents reported that their parent actively promoted the visits of other children to their homes. Peter recalled his home was a social center in the neighborhood:

> Our house tended to be, in the neighborhood, kind of the visitor center. My folks, both of them, but my mother particularly, felt strongly that, as much as it would make her crazy to have all the neighbors in the house, she liked it....Kids would tend to gravitate towards our house because she was friendly and because you could get snacks and you could play in the living room and there was no plastic on the furniture.

Joe described similar efforts made by his parents to encourage children to visit their home:

> Our house would be the center of activity a lot. My parents made sure there were lots of [games and] things like that so that kids would want to come over and hang out.

Coping with Social Rejection

Social stigma and rejection were major obstacles for respondents in establishing friendships. Joe recalled his surprise and disappointment at the reaction of typical peers to his disability:

> Then I was truly mainstreamed...that's the first time it really hit me that I was "different." 'Cause when I got there, other students reacted to me very differently than I would have expected....I remember people staring a lot...talking about me but not with me and not approaching me....I remember asking the teacher, "Why?" She said, "Well, because you're in a wheelchair and they've never seen that."...It didn't have a great positive effect on the way I felt about myself at the time. I was bummed out that it [making friends] was going to be harder than it seemed like it should be.

Respondents indicated that their abilities to manage social rejection substantially enhanced their self-confidence and social success. They reported using a variety of strategies to manage rejection. Several respondents used cognitive reframing to interpret their social rejection as indicative of their peers' maladjustment. Dick felt sad for those peers who teased him:

> There were kids that picked on me when I first went to school. I really felt sorry for those guys. It was like..."What's wrong with them? Why would they want to pick on a person like me? I'm a nice guy." I remember once a girlfriend said, "Doesn't this make you angry?" and I said, "No, it makes me real sad because there's no reason for this to be happening and they must be miserable."

Dick also recalled that there were peers in his environment who spontaneously organized to protect the more vulnerable children:

> There were those kids that bothered me and then there were those kids that protected. They were a little bit older and a little bit smarter kids that would watch out for that sort of thing...sort of like defenders of the playground....The bigger kids just coming in and going, "Hey, let's cool it."

Jeff reported having a similar experience in which peers spontaneously organized to protect him:

> All of a sudden my problems ceased...they formed a little protection gang around me. Anyone who looked cross-eyed at me or started saying something, they would take them around the corner and they told me afterwards that either they'd try to verbally tell him what was going on...or they'd physically beat the heck out of them. I was shocked at what happened but at the same time, I was grateful for it.

Other respondents recalled creative steps they took to protect themselves from bullies. For example, Andy got a dog:

> When I was a kid, about 8, I got my first trike and I liked to ride it but sometimes kids would come up to me and tip me over and I was stuck. After a while, I got tired of riding ....I got my dog. I would tie my dog on my trike and they didn't bother me 'cause my dog was there.

Several of the respondents indicated that their parents were able to help them to manage teasing, either by assisting respondents to identify strategies they could use or by intervening on their behalf. It was very difficult for Jack to share his distress with his parents; however, they were able to help:

> I had trouble taking the teasing and people just devastated me. I guess I didn't really have a strong sense of who I was, being that young and getting teased. It made me feel like I wasn't any good. By eighth and ninth grade...those were the worst times. I knew when people were teasing me. I couldn't tell my parents, feeling like, "Well, they expect me to

just bear it." I assumed that's what everyone expected of me....That was my fate or whatever....Well, I started talking to them. I just said one day, "I've been really depressed...the kids make fun of me." They were kind of surprised. It just didn't occur to them and they were uncomfortable with it. They just were supportive....They helped me at school getting in to a counselor.

Although this strategy was not advocated by adults, several respondents recalled with pride the benefits of fighting against bullies. Steve's recollection highlights his satisfaction in defending himself:

This guy...wasn't watching where he was going and walked right smack into me. He said, "Move out of my way, you retard, m---f---r." I didn't take too kindly to that....I said, "What did you say?" He repeated it again, I moved closer, he backed up. Well, about 10 feet behind him was this wall and on about the fourth time I had him repeat it....He realized that I was setting him up 'cause he was only about a foot and a half away from the wall. He swung and I partially blocked his punch and he caught me right across the bridge of my nose. Even though it hurt, I hit him twice right up into the rib cage with my fist and brought him down to my level. Once I did that, I took my elbow and hit him right square in the back of the neck and said, "Okay, you son of a bitch, if you want more, get up. If you don't, stay down." Then I went away. Everybody was out on the playground and I'm in a wheelchair....It was amazing how people started asking me to do things like spend lunch periods with them.

Unfortunately, many changes have occurred in our social and cultural life since the childhood of these respondents. In particular, the rapidly increasing presence of weapons in our schools has made this management technique more dangerous and less useful than it was 30 years ago.

Benefactors

The final major factor respondents cited as important for their development of personal competence was support provided by adult benefactors. Twelve of the 14 respondents remembered having benefactors who facilitated their success and development of positive self-images during childhood. Several benefactors were parents and grandparents; approximately half were teachers. Joe recalled the efforts made by a teacher to promote his access to inclusive education:

I thought she [teacher] was one of the greatest people I ever met. You think back on your life with some crucial incidents where you say, "Gee, if this had happened just a little different, my life could have been very different." She's one of those people. I remember that she would call my mother and my father and talk to them about me, saying that she didn't think that it was necessary for me to be in that class and that perhaps they might want to help in the process of getting me out. She told me on several occasions that I was very bright and that the other teachers had said that I was doing very well....She was very diabolical...she wanted to get us out of there. It turned out my birthday was the same day as the principal of the school. On the principal's birthday, she'd pack up a card for me and send me down there to give the card to the principal, you know, on behalf of our class. I'd always think she was trying to get me some exposure with the principal. She'd say, "Maybe you don't want to do this, but it would be good for you. It's gonna help."

Susan described a similar experience in which her teacher made sure she could socialize with other children on the playground:

I recall that my parents would take me to school and carry me in and sit me down at my desk. My teacher would carry me outside for recess and carry me outside for the lunch hour. It was nice....She was very adamant that I be included in things. She would carry me outside at recess to be with the kids.

Although benefactors were usually remembered as providing specific, additional instrumental support within the context of their regular activities, a few instances were recalled in which adults took a more expanded role in respondents' lives. For example, Andy remembered his teachers going beyond their traditional roles:

> I had real good teachers. They gave more time to me. We'd go out after school, we'd eat pizza, go to the movies, over to their house and watch TV and work there, at their house....I feel like they gave me a push to let me do a lot of things on my own: to try stuff. And [if it didn't work] they'd tell me it's okay, but challenge me to figure it out. They'd say they knew I could do it. They treated me like anybody else. They didn't make a big deal out of it if I couldn't do something.

Andy's teachers clearly took a special interest in him that helped him to feel capable and supported.

Most respondents recalled their experiences with benefactors who did not experience disabilities. However, Jack remembered a transformational relationship he had with a teacher who had a disability:

> He was a huge man. Physically, he was about 6 feet tall and he had shoulders, just an immense figure, and he wore these full leg braces, and he had these crutches on both sides, and I was just in awe of him....He was the first person that I had met who was disabled and he was up, he was my teacher. He was a significant person. Through him I realized, I saw someone who was like me who had made it.

Clearly, this relationship positively influenced Jack's belief in his capacity for success as a person with disability.

CONCLUSIONS

Respondents shared many insightful recollections and comments related to factors that supported and impeded their development of high self-esteem and personal competence. Themes identified through this study warrant further investigation; however, several preliminary conclusions can be drawn. In general, respondents' comments suggested that they were supported by opportunities for inclusion, typical expectations and advocacy from adults, deemphasis of their differences in conjunction with access to disability-related accommodations, promotion of their autonomy and friendships, management of social rejection, and help from benefactors. In contrast, their progress was thwarted by segregation, atypical treatment that highlighted their differences, inappropriate accommodations, restriction of opportunities for independence, social isolation, and social rejection.

The nature of respondents' descriptions of their childhood experiences is very similar to the descriptions of resilient adults from impoverished environments described by Werner and Smith (1992). Like the children followed by Werner and Smith, respondents in this study were generally intelligent, perservering children with outgoing personalities and access to supportive adults. They were able to use their capacities and supports to creatively manage their difficulties and achieve typical goals. Additional study of other resilient populations would be helpful in order to better understand the specific impact of these factors. In particular, qualitative study of people who demonstrate resilience despite experiencing cognitive challenges or social isolation would be informative.

Perhaps the most important finding from this study is that children with challenges—if nurtured, treated typically, and provided with necessary accommodations and supports—will most likely grow up to be successful and self-competent adults.

Although children with challenges require respect for and attention to their uniqueness, the essence of their capacities, desires, and needs varies little from those of children without disabilities. This sentiment was eloquently expressed by Eric as he reflected on his parenting a son without disability:

> I think whatever other kids want is probably what most handicapped kids want. There are a lot of handicapped children who are taught that they are going to be real different, therefore they are different....I was lucky, I grew up in a family that didn't make a deal out of the thing, so it remains a healthy way to live and let go....It's the same thing I do with my son. I want my son to get good strokes for achievement and I want him to know that he's got high expectations from me. That doesn't have anything to do with being handicapped, it just has to do with being a kid.

REFERENCES

Education for All Handicapped Children Act of 1975, PL 94-142. (August 23, 1975). Title 20, U.S.C. 1401 et seq: *U.S. Statutes at Large, 89,* 773–796.

Garrison, W.T., & McQuiston, S. (1989). *Chronic illness during childhood and adolescence: Psychological aspects.* Newbury Park, CA: Sage Publications.

Harter, S. (1981). A model of mastery motivation in children: Individual differences and developmental change. In W.A. Collins (Ed.), *Minnesota symposium on child psychology* (Vol. 14, pp. 215–255). Hillsdale, NJ: Lawrence Erlbaum Associates.

Harter, S. (1986). Cognitive-developmental processes in the integration of concepts about emotions and the self. *Social Cognition, 4,* 119–151.

Harter, S. (1990). Causes, correlates, and the functional role of global self-worth: A life-span perspective. In R.J. Sternberg & J. Kolligian, Jr. (Eds.), *Competence considered* (pp. 67–97). New Haven: Yale University Press.

King, G.A., Shultz, I.Z., Steel, K., Gilpin, M., & Cathers, T. (1993). Self-evaluation and self-concept of adolescents with physical disabilities. *The American Journal of Occupational Therapy, 47*(2), 132–140.

Magill, J., & Hurlburt, N. (1986). The self-esteem of adolescents with cerebral palsy. *The American Journal of Occupational Therapy, 40*(6), 402–407.

Marsh, H.W., Barnes, J., & Hocevar, D. (1985). Self-other agreement on multidimensional self-concept ratings: Factor analysis and multitrait-multimethod analysis. *Journal of Personality and Social Psychology, 49,* 1360–1377.

Phillips, D.A., & Zimmerman, M. (1990). The developmental course of perceived competence and incompetence among competent children. In R.J. Sternberg & J. Kolligian, Jr. (Eds.), *Competence considered* (pp. 41–66). New Haven: Yale University Press.

Rosenberg, M. (1979). *Conceiving the self.* New York: Basic Books.

Seidel, J.V., Kjolseth, R., & Seymour, E. (1985). *The ethnograph.* Littleton, CO: Qualis Research Associates.

Werner, E.E., & Smith, R.S. (1992). *Overcoming the odds: High risk children from birth to adulthood.* Ithaca, NY: Cornell University.

A Conversation
with Cerebral Palsy

Jill Allen

Dedicated to my teacher, Ms. V.,
for her support and encouragement of my talent

Well, cerebral palsy—
Do you mind if I call you CP for short?—
You've been with me for fourteen years:
My constant companion.

I accept that you are with me,
Yet I resist you.
I ignore you most of the time, CP.
I hope you don't mind.

But if I devoted every waking hour to you,
I'd be miserable
And get nowhere in life.

True, you do cause me stress and pain,
But I know it does no good
To lay the blame directly on you.

You couldn't leave me
Even if you tried.

But sometimes I can't help it, CP.

Why do you cause me so much grief?
Because of *you,*
My privacy is invaded!
Because of *you,*
I've had countless operations!
Look what I have to put up with
Because of *you,* cerebral palsy!

I wouldn't mind so much if you'd let me do the
Personal care for myself, *but ...*

Why am *I,*
Of all people,
Stuck with you?!

It's *not fair!*
Oh, well.
That's the way it's gotta be.

Anyway, most of the time
You're just a nuisance, *but ...*

I'll never let you get me down, CP!
You hear me?
Never!!!

I must thank you, though, CP.
If it wasn't for you,
I wouldn't be me.

Because of you,
I am more determined than ever
To make something of myself:
To *succeed.*

Through you, I learned
Self-advocacy.
I don't think I
Would be as assertive without you.

Having you has made me more attuned
To the hardships
Other minorities face
In our society.

Thank you.

I *hate* it when people pity me
Because of you:
Staring,
Offering trinkets.

There's a lot of fear
And ignorance out there, CP.
Let's work together
To dispel it:

To show the populace that *I*
Have power over *you*,
Not the other way around!

My poem underscores two crucial points with regard to teens with disabilities taking charge of their lives. First, in order for them to be independent, they *must not* let their disabilities take too much control of their actions! If this happens, the teens may start to view themselves as "disabled teens" not as "teens with disabilities." There is a fundamental difference between these terms. We are *people* first!

Second, the teen's disability shouldn't be treated as an obstacle that has to be overcome. Instead, it should be viewed merely as something to be dealt with. If seen as something insurmountable, then the disability is always cast in a negative light. This hurts the outlook of the person with the condition. The disability needs to viewed realistically.

If this poem can make one person think differently, I'll be satisfied.

A Developmental Perspective on Stress Appraisal

How Children Understand What Is at Stake During Stress

Kathleen Mongan Thies

Of all children and adolescents, 10%–15% face the challenges of health conditions (e.g., asthma, diabetes, arthritis, cancer) as a routine part of their everyday lives (Gortmaker, 1985). These children also deal with the usual challenges of growing up, such as establishing relationships with peers, developing a sense of self-competence, and planning for the future. Pediatric psychologists have suggested that how children appraise and cope with stress associated with ongoing health conditions may enable them to resist the negative consequences that can be associated with such adversity (Wallander & Varni, 1992).

Many studies have described the types of stresses these children experience (e.g., Bossert, 1994; Delamater, 1992; MacLean, Perrin, Gortmaker, & Pierre, 1992) and which personal and social variables are associated with the presence or absence of behavioral problems (Lavigne & Faier-Routman, 1993). Furthermore, psychologists and pediatricians have called for research that explains rather than describes clinical phenomena (Shonkoff, 1993; Wallander, 1992). Research with this clinical population needs to be driven by hypotheses based on theoretical models that explain the relationships being studied.

The transactional model of stress developed by Lazarus and Folkman (1984) is most often cited in research on stress, appraisal, and coping. They define stress as a relationship between a person and the environment that is appraised by the person as taxing limited resources or threatening well-being. A stressful person–environment relationship is mediated by cognitive appraisal of stress and coping. Cognitive appraisal is an evaluative process through which the person determines the personal relevance of the stressor. This appraisal is referred to as a *process* because the term implies that person–environment transactions are subject to change. The term *cognitive* serves to distinguish the transactional model of stress from noncognitive models, such as those generated by drive reduction and stimulus–response theories.

The transactional model of stress was developed by Lazarus and Folkman after extensive research with adults. Its application to children and adolescents would benefit from an interpretation based on developmental theory and research. The major reason for the need to rethink the transactional model of stress from a developmental perspective is its emphasis on cognitive processes as stress-mediating factors. The fundamental bias of the model is that cognition is the primary processor of experience (Lazarus, 1982, 1984)—that is, the idea that cognition gives structure and meaning to experience.

Many years of research have identified that children undergo predictable changes in their cognitive structures as they mature into adolescence. For example, cognitive changes have accounted for similarities and differences in how children understand themselves (Harter, 1983, 1986, 1988), peer relationships (Selman & Schultz, 1991), and illness (Bibace & Walsh, 1981) over the course of normative development. As a result, children's relationship with their environment changes as they mature cognitively. How they understand everyday stressful experiences should undergo predictable changes as they mature as well.

The use of theoretical models that account for normative developmental changes is of particular importance in the study of children and adolescents with health conditions. Developmental theory acknowledges that children with health problems are fundamentally normal children growing up under abnormal circumstances (Patterson & Geber, 1991). Unfortunately, there has been much speculation about the degree of psychological adjustment versus maladjustment in this population (Lavigne & Faier-Routman, 1992). A developmental approach may help to put this debate into perspective. Rather than examine the relationship between quantity of stress and psychological dysfunction, developmental theory can explain qualitative differences and similarities in how children and adolescents understand illness-related stress in the first place. In addition, a reliance on cognitive-developmental theory means that qualitative differences and similarities in understanding stress can be explained as a function of normative levels of development rather than simply described as a function of age or disease characteristics.

The purpose of this chapter is to discuss a study (Thies, 1994a, 1994b) in which cognitive-developmental theory was used to analyze how children and adolescents appraise the everyday stresses related to growing up with an ongoing health condition. This chapter includes an explanation of the developmental progression of stress appraisal in children and adolescents. The implications of this progression for identifying strategies that can help to promote competence in dealing with stress is also discussed.

A DEVELOPMENTAL ANALYSIS OF STRESS APPRAISAL

How individuals appraise stress is considered to be a cognitive process (Lazarus & Folkman, 1984). Therefore, the hypothesis of this study was that the ways in which children and adolescents structure and find meaning in stressful experiences is a function of their cognitive development. The focus was not on *what* experiences children found to be stressful, threatening, or challenging. Instead the focus was on *how* they structured, organized, and understood those experiences. If how children appraise—or organize—stress determines what it means to them and how they will cope with it (Rutter, 1981; Wallander & Varni, 1992), then it is important to examine how appraisal of stress works in children.

It was expected that the organization of stressful experiences would be qualitatively different at different levels of cognitive development, like, for example, concrete versus abstract thinking. Interventions with chronically stressed children would begin at the developmental level consistent with the child's appraisal, regardless of whether or not that level was typical for the child's age group or was deemed appropriate by adult health care professionals. In other words, when interventions designed to promote effective coping begin with the child's understanding of stressful experiences, efforts to support the development of personal competence will likely be more fruitful.

The Category System for Cognitive Appraisal of Stress

The study identified three aspects, or categories, of cognitive appraisal of stress for children and adolescents. These categories were interpreted as addressing 1) what children and adolescents consider to be at stake for them during a stressful experience, 2) the reasons they give for why they behave as they do during a stressful episode, and 3) how they use emotion words to describe their feelings during a stressful episode. These three categories were derived from research on the transactional model of stress developed by Folkman and Lazarus and their colleagues (Folkman & Lazarus, 1985; Folkman, Lazarus, Dunkel-Schetter, DeLongis, & Gruen, 1986; Folkman, Lazarus, Gruen, & DeLongis, 1986).

For example, a child or adolescent subject might report feeling angry and upset in an incident in which health problems made it difficult for the child to participate fully in peer group activities. Consequently, the child either left the scene or stayed. The specific situation might vary from one subject to another; but what was at stake typically involved the subject's self-concept and relationships with others, although the meaning of self and other is qualitatively different at different levels of development. Similarly, the reasons that different subjects would give for staying or leaving would reflect qualitative differences as well.

Cognitive-developmental theory was used to create two category systems that would reflect qualitative differences for 1) how children determine what is at stake for them during stress and 2) the reasons that they give for their behavior. Category systems describe and explain a predictable developmental order in the structure and organization of subjects' responses to selected questions about their experiences (Fischer & Silvern, 1985; Walsh & Bibace, 1991). In the study, the two category systems were statistically validated using empirical data from structured interviews with 79 children and adolescents. In addition, a checklist of 28 emotion words such as *angry, sad, frustrated, calm,* and *quiet* was used to capture the feelings that children reported they had experienced during a stressful incident.

The category system for how children and adolescents determine what is at stake during stress represented the children's concept of themselves and their relationships with other people, especially peers. Children with health conditions spend most of their time at school, at home, and with friends, not in health care settings such as the hospital or clinic. Unfortunately, even normal environments can be at odds with the special needs of children with health conditions. To use the terms of the transactional model of stress, the relationship between children with health conditions and their environments is likely to be appraised by those children as taxing their resources and as not meeting their normative developmental needs.

Fortunately, normative issues related to self-concept, competence, and peer relationships have begun to receive more attention as fundamental to the development of children and adolescents with health conditions (Hanson et al., 1990; LaGreca, 1990; Noll, LeRoy, Bukowski, Rogosch, & Kulkarni, 1991; Patterson & Geber, 1991; Perrin, Ramsey, & Sandler, 1987; Pless & Pinkerton, 1975; Spirito, DeLawyer, & Stark, 1991; Wallander & Varni, 1992). Researchers have identified predictable changes in how children think of themselves and their relationships with others based on normative changes in cognitive development (Damon & Hart, 1986; Harter, 1983, 1986, 1988; Horn & Hasbrook, 1987; Montemayor & Eisen, 1977; Selman, 1980; Selman & Schultz, 1991). For example, self-concept becomes more integrated as children become more self-evaluative with maturity. Similarly, more mature children and adolescents integrate the points of view of other people in their understanding of situations. The predictable order of these changes served as the basis for categorizing responses.

Interviews with Children About Stressful Experiences

The study included 79 children and adolescents, boys and girls, in three age groups: ages 8–9, 11–12, and 14–17. Their diagnoses included diabetes, asthma, cystic fibrosis, and juvenile rheumatoid arthritis. The children were recruited from outpatient clinics and from camps for children with diabetes in Massachusetts and New Hampshire. Although the sample included children and adolescents from a variety of social, economic, and ethnic backgrounds, the majority of those interviewed were white and middle class. They were asked to describe a situation of their own choosing that had been "hard" for them because of their illness. Virtually every situation they described involved school, friends, sports, or recreation; some adolescents discussed their jobs. These situations tended to reflect everyday events, such as eating lunch in the cafeteria, playing basketball, going on school field trips, and spending time with friends.

These mundane events are not typically found on the stressful event inventories (e.g., the Life Events Checklist by Johnson & McCutcheon, 1980) that researchers use to make inferences about the relationship between stress and psychological adjustment in children and adolescents with health conditions (e.g., Delamater, 1992; MacLean et al., 1992; Wallander & Varni, 1992); nor do the everyday events reported by the children in the study under discussion represent the medical stressors, such as venipuncture or other procedures, that have been the focus of some stress-related research (e.g., Bossert, 1994; Dahlquist, 1992; Delamater, 1992). The significance of the reported events is that they were ordinary. The implication is that children and adolescents with ongoing health conditions experience stress on a daily basis going about the very activities that provide the backdrop for normative development.

After reporting a stressful episode of their own choosing, the children were shown a list of positive and negative emotion words, which they rated on a Likert scale from "1: didn't feel that way" to "4: really felt that way a lot!" To determine what was at stake, they finished a sentence for each word that described how they felt: "I felt really angry because _____ ." For example, a child might say, "because I wanted the cookie."

Next, the children were asked, "What do you wish happened instead?" This question proved to be the single most valuable question to ask during the study. Every child who was interviewed could readily identify, often in detail, the nonstressful scenario that was the preferred alternative for the one that was hard. The alternative scenario got to the heart of what was at stake. For example, a child might report an incident in which he or she could not fully participate with peers. A younger child might say "I wish I could play with them," whereas a more mature child might report "I wish I wasn't different."

Finally, the children and adolescents were asked why they behaved as they did to resolve the situation: "I did that because _____ ." For example, a child might report, "I didn't say anything because I didn't want to get in trouble" or "because I'm not the kind of person who talks back to teachers. It's not right."

Throughout the interviews, the clinical method of Piaget (1930) was employed. In this method, the interviewer continues to ask clarifying questions until all avenues related to the topic have been exhausted. For example, "If you weren't different, what would happen instead?" The purpose is to elicit responses that are as complete as possible from each child so that the quality of the response as a whole can be studied.

What follows is an explanation of the developmental levels of response that formed the category system for identifying what was at stake during stressful episodes. The levels represent the modal response for each age group. More important, they form a predictable sequence of development that makes sense theoretically apart from descriptions based on age. A brief explanation of the reasons that children gave for their behavior is also provided.

What Is at Stake for Children Ages 8–9

The modal level of response among the 8- to 9-year-olds was the concrete/unilateral level for appraising what is at stake. *Concrete* thinkers attend to events that are immediate and observable and for which a logical sequence of cause and effect can be identified, even if that sequence is inaccurate (Laurendeau & Pinard, 1962). A concrete relationship with the social environment is *unilateral* or one-way in that it tends to be organized around external physical events with themes of competition and dominance (Selman & Schultz, 1991). One person wins and one person loses. Nobody wants to lose.

Self-concept is differentiated into domains of competence and tends to emphasize "doing things," such as playing games with friends or making things (Damon & Hart, 1986; Harter, 1983). Being good at something fits into a concept of self that is structured to incorporate "good" and relegate the "not good" to external forces (Harter, 1985). Children can state reasons for both internal feelings and external behaviors, but they are not self-reflective (Harter, 1986). Other people are also recognized as having feelings, but their point of view is not taken into consideration; the primary concern is with one's own preferences (Selman & Schultz, 1991). To not get one's own way is "not fair." If things go wrong, it is someone else's fault.

Consequently, the appraisal of concrete/unilateral thinkers has two organizing characteristics. First, there is an appreciation for the logical rules that govern social behavior and the management of the medical regimen. The rules are usually set by external agents of authority, such as adults, or by the demands of the illness itself.

Second, external events and other people are seen as the agents or cause of stress. That is, the stressor comes *from* the environment *to* the subject as a one-way press. The subject "has to" do something unpleasant, is prevented from doing something pleasant, or has something "done to" him or her. The child wants other people to change their behavior because they are in the wrong.

"Doing things that I want to do" is at stake. Some typical responses for what is at stake at the concrete/unilateral level of development include the following:

"I was angry 'cause I couldn't have the cookie. I wish I could have it. It's no fair!"
"I was frustrated 'cause I had to rest and I didn't want to 'cause I wanted to go out and play with my friends."

It is important to note that the children do not say that they felt left out. Rather, they wanted to do what they could not do.

"I was upset because they were teasing me. I wanted them to stop. They should be nice." [What would be "nice?"] "They would play with me."

Teasing is consistent with a unilateral relationship with the social environment in that there is competition for one party to dominate the other.

The most common types of stressful events for the group of 8- to 9-year-olds were "having to" stop playing to comply with the medical regimen (testing blood glucose, using inhalers); being teased by classmates about health problems; and, among the children with diabetes, not eating sweets when peers were doing so. The experiences of Michael, an engaging 9-year-old sports enthusiast with diabetes, and Rebecca, a shy, slender 9-year-old girl with multiple health problems and several pets, were typical of the children who were concrete/unilateral thinkers in appraising what was at stake.

Michael said that he "had to" stop playing with his friends because he "had to" go in to check his blood glucose level. The level was high, and his mother told him he "had to" rest until it came down. Michael complained, "I couldn't go out to play with my friends. Not fair!" He argued with his mother and was subsequently banished to his room because of his attitude and bad language.

What Michael wanted to have happen instead was for "my [blood sugar to be] regular so I could go outside and play." When asked what helped him to feel better about this hard situation, he replied, "I forgot about it." [How?] "Go to sleep and the next morning you're playing again, it's easy." In other words, Michael wanted to play, he was not allowed to play, and playing ultimately made him feel better.

Michael complied with his mother's commands and went to his room because "she told me to and I was in enough trouble already." His answer is consistent with reasons for behavior that represent an external orientation to the environment and an appreciation for the fact that trouble with authority figures—or with illness—is the logical consequence of breaking the rules (Ryan & Connell, 1989). Externalized reasons for behavior represented the modal level of response for the children at age 8–9 years.

For Rebecca, it was hard being teased by classmates who thought, incorrectly, that she was blind. Her eyes were often swollen and reddened from congenital herpes, and she rode the bus for students with disabilities to school. Rebecca was angry and upset, saying, "People make fun of me and I don't do anything to them. I wanted them to stop." She felt better when some friends "who are nice and never make fun of me" invited her to play with them at recess.

What Rebecca did next was interesting. Consistent with the theme of dominance central to teasing, she told the teacher about the offending classmates. Her reason, like that of Michael when he complied with his mother's order, demonstrated an appreciation for rules, the consequences of breaking them, and the role that authority figures play in enforcing them: "I thought the teacher would do something about it like tell the principal and they would get suspended or something but they never do." In other words, if they hurt me, I want to hurt them back.

Michael and Rebecca both appraised stress as coming *from* the environment *to* them as a unilateral press. Stress was imposed on Michael by his mother, who was enforcing the rules of diabetes management. For Rebecca, stress was imposed by classmates who wanted to dominate her by "putting her down." Neither Michael nor Rebecca sought to understand the position of the other people involved in these situations, nor did they reflect on the effect of their own behavior on the evolution of the situations.

For both children, doing what they wanted to do was at stake: to play with friends without any unpleasant interference. In both cases, playing with friends ultimately made them feel better. Playing with peers is the central task relevant to self-concept and to competence in the social domain at this level of development (Harter, 1982; Hartup, 1983; Selman & Schultz, 1991). In other words, what was at stake for Michael and Rebecca was within normative developmental parameters, even if the health conditions that triggered the stressful situations in question were not.

The organization of the appraisal, with its emphasis on "doing things" and the role of external unilateral forces, should provide clues regarding stress management in this age group. Concrete thinkers are not emotionally introspective, although they know how they feel. Helping them get in touch with their feelings would not be appropriate. Instead they need guidelines regarding how to behave—that is, what to do—in specific stressful situations. The implications for intervention are discussed later in this chapter.

What Is at Stake for Children Ages 11–12

The modal level of response among the 11- to 12-year-olds in the study was the transitional/reciprocal level of development for appraising what is at stake. *Transitional* thinkers are primarily concrete thinkers in that they continue to think in terms of sequential cause and effect, but the beginning of abstract reasoning processes can also be observed (Laurendeau & Pinard, 1962). The relationship with the social environment is reciprocal or two-way (Selman & Schultz, 1991).

Reciprocity—the ability to take a second-person perspective—broadens the organization of the appraisal and determines the meaning of the event. When you can see things from someone else's point of view, you know that he or she can see things from yours. You explain your side of things to the other person, expecting that he or she will then understand and accept you. When the other person doesn't accept you, you are unpleasantly surprised and want to understand the reasons for his or her behavior.

Transitional/reciprocal children are self-reflective and self-evaluative, taking into account how "good" they are in comparison to their peers, especially peers who are perceived by the group as competent and popular (Harter, 1983, 1985). Children at this level want to integrate different domains of personal competence into one whole self-concept. Self-reflection adds depth to the appraisal process as children become aware of inner conflict. For example, "I'm not as athletic as my friend Joe even though I wish I could be, but I am really good in math even if everybody else hates it. But that's okay, you know?"

Certain themes are the hallmarks of reciprocal thinking and self-reflection. Stressors are experienced as violations of trust, understanding, and acceptance. Children feel left out, different, and painfully self-conscious. Being left out hurts because it is understood as intentional behavior on the part of other people. Being different or not as good or as popular as peers causes self-doubt about one's general competence and social standing.

In terms of health needs, children wrestle with decisions about what to do or not do, given conflicting information and competing interests in a social setting. They recognize that adults expect them to be more responsible for making decisions in health-related matters. Children don't want to fail in meeting these expectations, but they also don't want to make the wrong decisions.

"Being competent" and "being accepted as normal" are at stake. Typical responses at the transitional/reciprocal level of development for what is at stake include the following:

> "I was angry because he knew what he was saying about me wasn't true but he was saying it anyway. I wanted to know why."
> "Nobody else has to go in there and stick themselves with a needle. I think that they think that I'm weird."
> "I just want to be treated like a regular person, because I am."
> "I wish that I went to the party and no one asked me if I could have candy so I didn't have to make all these decisions. If you feel fine you don't know if you should have it or not. If you feel shaky, you think you should have it. It's based on how you feel."

The situations related by Jonas, Adam, and Maria are typical of children at the transitional/reciprocal level of development. The most common situations involved birthday parties and sleepovers, field trips and classroom parties, sports, and spending time with the families of friends. Teachers and other adults also played a major role among children at this level of development.

Jonas, a bright and thoughtful sixth grader who loves to read and has bronchiolitus obliterans, was playing basketball at recess when he had trouble breathing and called time out to use his inhalers. The game went on without him, and Jonas walked away to play alone on the monkey bars and to use his inhalers. "I wanted to show everybody that I'm good even though it was hot out. They knew I was good but they don't want to keep wasting time-outs for me. It's all about winning I guess. If I was normal I would want to win too....I would do all these sports....I'm a normal kid with bad lungs it seems like."

Jonas could reflect on the idea that being normal like everyone else was at stake for him. He also understood the situation from his friends' point of view. He could see that winning was important to them and that they didn't want to change the rules just for him. Despite the fact that Jonas could take his friends' point of view into account and that he was motivated by their approval when he joined the game in the first place, he did not try to persuade them to see his point of view in return. He did not argue a case for why the rules regarding time-outs could be bent during recess so that he could resume playing after using his inhalers.

Instead, he walked away because "I needed [my inhaler]. It helps my lungs get more oxygen." Jonas's reasons were consistent with a desire to follow the rules of schoolyard basketball and of his health condition. Like the 8- to 9-year-olds, the modal level of response among the 11- to 12-year-olds was an external orientation to someone else's rules and the negative consequences of breaking them (Ryan & Connell, 1989). However, what ultimately helped Jonas to feel better about this stressful situation was a good grade that he received on a spelling test after recess. "It tells me that I'm good at something else too, besides one event."

Jonas wants to compensate for a lack of competence in one domain (sports) with competence in another (academics). First, however, he has to decide how important sports, or more specifically winning, is for him. In addition, like most of the 11- to 12-year-olds in the study, Jonas's understanding of a situation and the reasons he gives for his behavior seem to represent two different developmental levels. He can differentiate between points of view and reflect on who he is and what he values, but he does not persuade others to change or to understand. Jonas has not yet integrated how he understands himself, his friends, and the stressful situation with his behavior in response to stress.

For Adam, a polite and reserved 12-year-old boy with diabetes, the ability to understand the situation from his teacher's point of view underscored his distress. He must ask permission from his teacher to go to the nurse's office when he feels that his blood glucose level is low. The teacher "doesn't really believe me that I'm having reactions. He thinks that I'm using them for an excuse to get out of his class. He says 'Are you really having a reaction?' It's the way he says it and he looks kind of mad. I wish he'd trust me. It just feels better [to have teachers trust you]. I wish I was a better student. If I was a better student he might believe me. He probably thinks the same of me that I think of him. I just think he thinks I'm weird."

Adam says nothing in response to the teacher's comments because "You shouldn't talk back to teachers. It's just good manners." Adam falls back on the safety of the rules for socially acceptable behavior to guide his behavior during a stressful encounter. He is reluctant to persuade his teacher to understand his situation.

What is at stake is a matter of trust between Adam and the teacher whose cooperation he needs in order to attend to his diabetes and whose esteem he wants in order to feel like a competent and trustworthy person. Adam recognized that his lack of competence in one domain (academics) affected his teacher's opinion of him in another (diabetes management). The two domains added up to an unacceptable whole. Adam reported that he felt better when he could talk with the school nurse, who "is nice... [she] always believes me." Adam is fortunate to have earned her trust.

Maria, a talented 13-year-old pianist with cystic fibrosis, is the final example of children at the transitional/reciprocal level of understanding what is at stake. "We had to run laps around the track and I could only run one time around and I started breathing heavy. The teacher asked me if I was okay and I said yeah because I hate being picked out of the group. But he said, 'Why don't you stop?' And all the other kids were like, 'No fair. How come she gets to stop and we have to keep running?' So he explained it to them and they said, 'You're lucky. You don't have to run. I wish I was like you.' And I told them I don't breathe that great and no they don't want to be like me. I mean they wouldn't want to have it either....I want them to accept me for what I am because I can't change....I told them so they can understand why I cough. Some friends understand but some don't."

Both Maria and her teacher explained to her classmates why she was short of breath in hopes of promoting understanding and acceptance. Instead Maria felt that the explanations singled her out. Maria reported that she eventually felt better when the class walked back into the school and "they started talking to me and forgot about it....when they accepted me again." She also said that she found solace in prayer—an aspect of development that is often ignored in studies of children—and also in academic achievement. "All I really care about is school. I get A's. School is gonna get me somewhere."

The reason that Maria gave for why she stopped running around the track was "the teacher told me to and I was out of breath. I can't help it if he tells me to stop." Like 9-year-olds Michael and Rebecca, and her agemates Jonas and Adam, Maria is relying on the rules imposed by the illness and by authority figures to guide her behavior during a stressful situation.

Consistent with this transitional period of development, however, she experienced some inner conflict about her competence in making decisions on her own behalf. When asked what she wanted to have happen instead, she could not decide: "I think he should have let me try to make it around the track if I wanted to...I think I could have made it but umm I don't know." [You'd rather decide?] "Well, when I can't breathe he lets me stop." [Is this his decision or your decision?] "Well, if he really thinks I have to stop then I have to stop....I wish he had just let me walk around. So they wouldn't be going 'oh you're so lucky' and stuff like that."

In all three situations, the normative abilities to take a second-person perspective and to be self-reflective provide the underlying structure for understanding the stressful situations. What is at stake is a sense of competence across domains, trust, group membership, and normalcy. The need for approval, acceptance, and understanding and the distress that comes from within for not measuring up in the eyes of others and in one's own eyes shape the meaning of these situations.

The implications for stress management and support for the reciprocal thinker are more complex than for the concrete thinker. The organization of the appraisal is broader socially and deeper intrapersonally. Whereas interventions with 8- to 9-year-old concrete thinkers should focus on specific behaviors, interventions with reciprocal thinkers can begin to emphasize *understanding* behavior, one's own behavior as well as that of others.

What Is at Stake for Children Ages 14–17

The modal level of response for the children at age 14–17 years was the abstract/mutual level of development for what is at stake. *Abstract* thinkers can weigh several pieces of information at once, making and remaking different combinations of possible alternative solutions to problems. This process is often referred to as "hypothesis testing." Cause and effect is understood in terms of systems of interacting causes and effects rather than as a linear sequence (Laurendeau & Pinard, 1962).

The relationship with the social environment is characterized by *mutuality* (Selman & Schultz, 1991). The critical advance is the third-person perspective, the ability to step outside of the self and watch the self and other people interact as part of a larger ongoing system of relationships. Adolescents want to coordinate many perspectives at once in order to establish a balance among all of the parties and their own competing and conflicting needs. Adolescents can state that relationships are at stake. There is a desire to take care of relationships and still maintain one's social image and self-respect all at the same time.

Adolescents at this level are introspective, aware of being aware (Harter, 1983, 1985). There is an emphasis on layers of the psychological self and on matters of personal importance, like thoughts, hopes, and personal standards for behavior, including the need for personal control. Consequently stress can be an entirely internal experience, and the subject may identify that what is hard is "just thinking about it."

Certain themes highlight these conceptual changes. First, the process of appraising stress now takes into account the full realm of possibilities, not just the actual events that have occurred. A future orientation is also apparent as adolescents worry about events that might happen and as the potentially serious implications of the person's illness begin to hit home.

Second, responsibility for one's own health is a major challenge when the task of being healthy is perceived as being far more complex than just following a set of rules. Adolescents understand that the context in which they assume responsibility plays a role in the management of their health care needs. For example, at school and at work, adolescents learn to either accommodate their needs to a schedule devised by adults or to negotiate that schedule with the adults in charge. In relationships with friends, management of health care needs builds on mutuality. Adolescents must meet their needs in ways that do not jeopardize friendships. This requires a level of skill and maturity that may be difficult to achieve without assistance. Finally, mutual understanding between friends builds on reciprocal understanding. Adolescents want other people to understand not just the demands of the illness but also the *experience* of the illness and the effect that experience has had on shaping the adolescent's personality and relationships.

"Being myself" and "working it out with you" are at stake. Only adolescents at the abstract/mutual level of development for what is at stake could understand and answer the question "What is at stake for you?" It is an abstract question, as were the answers:

"My health."
"Freedom."
"Peace of mind."
"Taking control."

Other typical responses included the following:

"I was upset because I had to explain to him what was wrong with my leg. It also added more pressure to get to know him and just another factor to throw in. Starting a relationship is hard, to have to explain this [arthritis] is real hard. I wanted him to see that. I'm not the disease but the disease is part of me."

"I feel angry 'cause taking more control [of diabetes] is harder than I thought....It's a whole new step, kind of growing up."

"I felt guilty that I couldn't eat the cookie for him [teacher]. If you baked your kids cookies they would want to eat them to make you happy. And I couldn't have it for him."

"I felt guilty that I had to stop the game [to treat symptoms]. They didn't mind, but I wanted my friends to have a good time."

Common situations among adolescents included what to tell boyfriends/girlfriends, employers, and colleges about the illness, not letting down one's friends or teammates, and "just thinking about" the implications of the illness for future wellbeing. Sarah, a 15-year-old honors student with diabetes, was very articulate. Her interview represents a unique opportunity for observing the developmental structures that underlie a mature level of development. Sarah's story was not unusual among those of her peers, and it contained many of the major themes relevant to this developmental period.

Sarah and a group of friends had planned to spend the whole day at a major amusement park near her home. Unfortunately, the security personnel confiscated her glucose monitor, insulin, and needles and accused her of bringing drugs into the park. She showed them her medic alert bracelet, but they said they had never heard of diabetes. She offered to leave her supplies at the first aid office and said she would use them there in the presence of security personnel, "even though it wouldn't make me feel as independent." The security guards implied she was a troublemaker. Sarah called her parents, but only after she managed to handle the situation fairly well herself.

Sarah's initial reaction was panic: "I thought that they would send me to jail and it's going to go on my record. Then I realized I had a real reason [to carry medical supplies]." She immediately differentiated what was unrealistic from what was realistic—diabetes is not a crime—and became angry: "I felt like I was being discriminated against because I had a medical problem and I couldn't help it. This was the first time I think I've not been able to do something [because of my diabetes]. They wouldn't let me in and I wanted to go in. I wasn't doing anything wrong."

At this point, Sarah sounded like 9-year-old Michael, who was discussed earlier. He was angry because he was prevented from playing with his friends by his high blood glucose level and by his mother. Sarah was appraising the situation as an external, unilateral stressor; the guards were imposing rules upon her, preventing her from doing what she wanted to do. Her reasons for complying with the guards echoed the same externally oriented theme: "I don't like getting into trouble or disagreeing with an authoritative figure."

But then Sarah "kind of looked at it from their [the guards'] point of view. I bet there are some people that do that [sneak in drugs]. I guess they have no way to know that. Four kids walking in with needles? But we walked in and smiled and I don't think that they would think that I was doing anything wrong." She pointed out that looking at the situation from the point of view of the security guards helped her to calm down and feel less frustrated. She also began to wonder about how her friends would see the situation. "My friends finally realized that diabetes wasn't such a big deal and it was still normal...and I thought that if they saw that I was really panicking they would be like, 'Maybe she's been lying to us.' "

Sarah could appraise the situation reciprocally. She took the point of view of the guards and of her friends. She then was able to integrate several issues into a more mature and complex appraisal process: the guards had a job to do; it was good that they did it because it protected good kids like her; her friends were upset; her friends would get the wrong idea about how limiting her diabetes is; she would ruin their fun if they had to leave or if she panicked; she had always figured her way out of things before, and she could again.

Finally, Sarah was able to step outside of herself and take a third-person perspective (Selman & Schultz, 1991). She observed how she was behaving in the situation and compared her public performance with her inner turmoil: "On the inside I was all upset but on the outside I was just trying to play it cool." In the process of integrating this information about her experience—"pulling herself together"—she called on a mature source of motivation: "I didn't want to get everyone else all worried and think it was a big deal. I knew I'd figure something out. I knew I would be okay even if it was upsetting. I wasn't biting anybody's head off and I was going along with the guards. I felt in control."

Sarah kept her cool when she might easily have responded otherwise. She had high personal standards for her own behavior: "I get really concerned when other people are upset and something's not right. I try to do the best I can at everything." Being in control of her own behavior and taking care of the people around her are important to her. Personal standards for behavior represent a mature level of development consistent with an internal source of motivation (Ryan & Connell, 1989). Internalized reasons for behavior like Sarah's were the modal level of response for the group of 14- to 17-year-olds in the study on how children appraise stress.

Sarah is a wonderful example of the theory that development does not proceed through sequential stages. Rather, it builds on what came before, evolving through hierarchies, becoming more complex, internalized, and integrated with maturity (Sameroff, 1989; Werner, 1948). Less mature levels of development continue to be operative in more mature individuals (Zigler & Glick, 1986), potentially giving them more flexibility for meeting stressful demands.

CLINICAL IMPLICATIONS OF WHAT IS AT STAKE

The responses of the children and adolescents to inquiries about what was hard for them demonstrated a predictable developmental order in how they appraised what was at stake for them. Developmental theory accounted for the similarities and differences in the organization and quality of children's responses in such a way that what was typical at each developmental level could be readily identified. Without that theoretical base, clinical interpretations of how children understand illness-related stress would be subject to the personal and often atheoretical biases of the doctors, nurses, and teachers who work with children and adolescents with chronic health conditions.

An atheoretical approach leads to a deficit model in education and pediatric practice. In a deficit model, the key question is quantitative: What don't children know and how can we get them to know more earlier? In a developmentally based approach, the question is qualitative: How do children understand what they already know?

The level of development at which a child is already functioning may or may not be the level of development typical for that child's age group, but it is the level at which interventions *must* begin. By understanding how a predictable order of development works, clinicians and teachers can understand what is normative within certain developmental levels of how children understand stress and what is not normative. It might help these adults to recognize what is immature or potentially troublesome and to structure the child's environment in order to promote normative competence across several domains of development.

The concrete/unilateral level of development for what is at stake is characterized by concrete thinking, a unilateral relationship with the environment, and a self that is differentiated into separate domains of competence. Michael and Rebecca, described earlier, are examples of this developmental level.

Michael's experience showed how children with special health care needs must develop competence in the usual domains of childhood, such as peer relationships, at the same time that they learn the rules of managing their health needs. The fact that Michael appraises his medical regimen as an imposition on his playtime is consistent with his developmental level and does not represent a problem in the "pathological" sense. With that in mind, the adults in his environment can help him to structure his time so that he can play and still test his blood glucose levels, subsequently learning to "be good at" both.

For Rebecca, being teased about something that cannot be changed required that she change either the situation or her response to the teasing. Rebecca tried to change the situation when she "told" on her classmates. Her expectation that the teacher should intervene is normative at this developmental level. One wishes that Rebecca's teacher had done so, as is required of her role as an enforcer of the socially acceptable rules for behavior. Teasing may be normative behavior at this level, but it hurts people and is wrong.

Developmentally, Rebecca is not yet self-reflective enough to manage the internal distress that the teasing causes. She needs concrete rules for what to say and what to do when children tease her. She would benefit from efforts to promote her competence within the normative contexts of childhood, such as playing with her peers, and being good at school work, hobbies, and other activities. "Doing things" is at stake.

At the transitional/reciprocal level of development, reciprocal thinking and self-reflection underscored the distress experienced by Jonas, Adam, and Maria. They understood that how they saw themselves was at odds with how the people in their environment saw them. Jonas was sorting out how important winning at athletics was to him in comparison to his peers. Adam wanted to prove himself trustworthy. Maria wanted to be understood and accepted. All three could contrast and compare different areas of competence, trying to compensate for a lack of competence in one area (e.g., sports) with a show of competence in another (e.g., academics).

Many of the children and young adolescents in the study at this level of development maintained that teachers did not trust their ability to make decisions. Teachers were seen to be either overly protective (constantly asking children if they were okay), insensitive to the implications of the illness for peer group acceptance (referring to the illness in front of peers without the child's permission), or suspicious that the child used the illness as an excuse to be relieved of academic responsibilities. Teachers would probably disagree with this picture of them, but that is how the children saw it.

Teachers who work with children and adolescents need some guidance regarding the demands of specific health conditions and the normative developmental needs of the children who have them. The issue of who needs to know what about the illness is of importance at all levels of development, but it is particularly important when children feel different or self-conscious and when a sense of personal competence and being accepted are at stake.

The implications at the abstract/mutual level of development are more complicated. In the study on how children appraise stress, virtually all of the adolescents ages 14–17 had demonstrated abstract thinking on an independent measure of cognitive development. However, not all of them understood what was at stake at the abstract/mutual level of development that was typical of their age group. Several demonstrated the transitional/reciprocal level of development, and a few were concrete. The latter could be identified readily as "immature." Similarly, many gave reasons for their behavior that reflected someone else's rules and not their own personal standards. At the same time, no children ages 8–9 demonstrated the mature levels of abstract/mutual development and internal standards for behavior, as would be expected.

In other words, age does not guarantee maturity, although a mature understanding of what is at stake is associated with abstract thinking. The ability to think abstractly does not mean that adolescents will appraise stress in abstract terms or that they will see themselves in mutual relationships. Being capable of setting personal standards for one's own behavior does not mean that a person will do so. In addition, it may be normal for adolescent abstract thinkers to want to try out their own rules, but sometimes the rules they develop don't work very well in society at large.

Adolescents begin to spend more time in society, away from the environments that conscientious parents and teachers have helped structure for them. The society is not designed to accommodate chronic health conditions, as the example of Sarah demonstrated. Adolescents who appreciate their place in a larger network of people want to fit into that network, even if the network doesn't fit them. They must meet all of the usual challenges of coming to maturity, including sexuality and preparing for future work and educational opportunities.

At the same time, they are called upon to educate the very people whose cooperation they need to meet these goals. They often must explain their health conditions and their needs to new teachers and classmates, employers and co-workers, girlfriends and boyfriends, and college admissions officers. They don't always know how to ask for accommodation when they need it. They may also be reluctant to ask because becoming more independent is their index of maturity.

Thus, the normative developmental goals of adolescence may be at odds with the accommodations that an ongoing health condition may require. Finding a balance between competing needs is stressful when being who you are and working things out with the people around you are at stake. Adolescence is probably the most difficult period of development for children with health conditions.

The implications for stress management among adolescents reflect the complexity of the developmental period. Because age does not guarantee maturity, many adolescents do not organize stress in terms consistent with abstract thinking and mutuality on a regular basis across all situations. Consequently, the expectation of parents and teachers that adolescents "act their age"—that is, exhibit a level of maturity that adolescents are working to attain—fails to acknowledge the level of development at which an adolescent is already functioning. Parents and teachers may fail to supply the behavioral and emotional support and structure needed for developing maturity in the first place.

Interventions under these circumstances must address an issue central to theories of developmental psychology. That is, if the hallmarks of maturity are integration, complexity, and internalizing, what has to happen in terms of the individual's relationship with the environment for the person to become mature? If earlier levels of development are differentiated and then integrated into later and more mature levels, then earlier interventions can be integrated into those that support maturity as well.

Adolescents with health conditions may need concrete suggestions from parents and teachers about what to say and to do under certain circumstances—for example, when applying for a first job or negotiating terms for making up work missed during illness-related absences in high school. They need to develop insight into their own behavior and how it affects others in the safety of trusting relationships with adults and peers. In addition, to paraphrase the renowned psychologist Eric Erikson (1968), adolescents with health conditions need enough freedom to make their own rules and learn from their mistakes, but they also need enough structure to help show them what rules they are choosing and to ensure that mistakes do not jeopardize their future.

CONCLUSIONS

In a review of the literature on vulnerability and resilience in children, Luthar and Zigler (1991) urged researchers to develop separate measures of coping and cognitive appraisal. If cognitive appraisal predicted coping behaviors, and if coping was so crucial to adjustment, it was important to understand the process of how children appraised stress. The study discussed in this chapter represents an initial attempt to develop a separate measure of cognitive appraisal in a chronically stressed population. The fact that it was done from a developmental perspective gives the analysis theoretical validity.

Eleanor Maccoby (1983) hypothesized that "it is unlikely that there is any linear increase or decrease with age in vulnerability to stress" (p. 219). Instead, stress is a potentially destabilizing experience at any age, rendering individuals vulnerable to the risk of disorder at the level of development at which they are already functioning. The children and adolescents from the study provided meaningful examples of how each child felt stressed based on his or her level of development. It was each child's interpretation of the situation that mattered, not his or her relative age.

This analysis of one facet of stress processing provides some insight into how children and adolescents understand stressful situations. It is only one piece in a much larger puzzle and demonstrates that future research on children and stress can and must be developmentally based.

REFERENCES

Bibace, R., & Walsh, M.E. (1981). Development of children's concepts of illness. In R. Bibace & M.E. Walsh (Eds.), *New directions for child development: Children's concepts of health, illness, and bodily functions* (pp. 31–48). San Francisco: Jossey-Bass.

Bossert, E. (1994). Stress appraisals of hospitalized school-age children. *Children's Health Care, 23*(1), 33–49.

Dahlquist, L. (1992). Coping with aversive medical treatments. In A. LaGreca, L. Siegel, J. Wallander, & C. Walker (Eds.), *Stress and coping in child health* (pp. 345–376). New York: Guilford Press.

Damon, W., & Hart, D. (1986). Stability and change in children's self-understanding. *Social Cognition, 4*(2), 102–118.

Delamater, A. (1992). Stress, coping, and metabolic control among youngsters with diabetes. In A. LaGreca, L. Siegel, J. Wallander, & C. Walker (Eds.), *Stress and coping in child health* (pp. 191–211). New York: Guilford Press.

Erikson, E. (1968). *Identity: Youth and crisis.* New York: Norton.

Fischer, K., & Silvern, L. (1985). Stages and individual differences in cognitive development. *Annual Review of Psychology, 36,* 613–648.

Folkman, S., & Lazarus, R. (1985). If it changes, it must be a process: Study of emotion and coping during three stages of a college examination. *Journal of Personality and Social Psychology, 48*(1), 150–170.

Folkman, S., Lazarus, R., Dunkel-Schetter, C., DeLongis, A., & Greun, R. (1986). Dynamics of a stressful encounter. *Journal of Personality and Social Psychology, 50*(5), 992–1003.

Folkman, S., Lazarus, R., Gruen, R., & DeLongis, A. (1986). Appraisal, coping, health status, and psychological symptoms. *Journal of Personality and Social Psychology, 50*(3), 571–579.

Gortmaker, S. (1985). Demography of chronic childhood diseases. In N. Hobbs & J. Perrin (Eds.), *Issues in the care of children with chronic illness* (pp. 135–154). San Francisco: Jossey-Bass.

Hanson, C., Rodrigue, J., Henggeler, S., Harris, M., Klesges, R., & Carle, D. (1990). The perceived self-competence of adolescents with insulin-dependent diabetes mellitus: Deficit or strength? *Journal of Pediatric Psychology, 15*(5), 605–618.

Harter, S. (1982). The perceived competence scale for children. *Child Development, 53,* 87–97.

Harter, S. (1983). Developmental perspectives on the self-system. In P.H. Mussen (Series Ed.) & E.M. Hetherington (Vol. Ed.), *Handbook of child psychology: Vol. 4. Socialization, personality, and social development* (4th ed., pp. 275–386). New York: John Wiley & Sons.

Harter, S. (1985). Competence as a dimension of self-evaluation: Toward a comprehensive model of self-worth. In R. Leahy (Ed.), *The development of the self.* New York: Academic Press.

Harter, S. (1986). Cognitive developmental processes in the integration of concepts about emotions and the self. *Social Cognition, 4*(2), 119–151.

Harter, S. (1988). Developmental and dynamic changes in the nature of the self concept: Implications for child psychotherapy. In S. Shirk (Ed.), *Cognitive development and child psychotherapy.* New York: Plenum.

Hartup, W. (1983). Peer relations. In P.H. Mussen (Series Ed.) & E.M. Hetherington (Vol. Ed.), *Handbook of child psychology: Vol. 4. Socialization, personality, and social development* (4th ed., pp. 103–196). New York: John Wiley & Sons.

Horn, T., & Hasbrook, D. (1987). Psychological characteristics and the criteria children use for self-evaluation. *Journal of Sport Psychology, 9,* 208–221.

Johnson, J., & McCutcheon, S. (1980). Assessing life stress in older children and adolescents: Preliminary findings with the Life Events Checklist. In I. Sarason & C. Spielberger (Eds.), *Stress and anxiety* (Vol. 7, pp. 111–125). Washington, DC: Hemisphere.

LaGreca, A. (1990). Social consequences of pediatric conditions: Fertile area for future investigation and intervention. *Journal of Pediatric Psychology, 15*(3), 285–307.

Laurendeau, M., & Pinard, A. (1962). *Causal thinking in the child.* New York: International Universities Press.

Lavigne, J., & Faier-Routman, J. (1992). Psychological adjustment to pediatric physical disorders: A meta-analytic review. *Journal of Pediatric Psychology, 17*(2), 133–158.

Lavigne, J., & Faier-Routman, J. (1993). Correlates of psychological adjustment to pediatric physical disorders: A meta-analytic review and comparison with existing models. *Developmental and Behavioral Pediatrics, 14*(2), 117–123.

Lazarus, R. (1982). Thoughts on the relation between emotion and cognition. *American Psychologist, 37*(9), 1019–1024.

Lazarus, R. (1984). On the primacy of cognition. *American Psychologist, 39*(2), 124–129.

Lazarus, R., & Folkman. (1984). *Stress, coping, and appraisal.* New York: Springer-Verlag.

Luthar, S., & Zigler, E. (1991). Vulnerability and competence: A review of research on resilience in childhood. *American Journal of Orthopsychiatry, 61*(1), 6–22.

Maccoby, E. (1983). Social-emotional development and response to stressors. In N. Garmezy & M. Rutter (Eds.), *Stress, coping, and development in children* (pp. 217–234). New York: McGraw-Hill.

MacLean, W., Perrin, J., Gortmaker, S., & Pierre, C. (1992). Psychological adjustment of children with asthma: Effects of illness severity and recent stressful life events. *Journal of Pediatric Psychology, 17*(2), 159–171.

Montemayor, R., & Eisen, M. (1977). The development of self-conceptions from childhood to adolescence. *Developmental Psychology, 13,* 314–319.

Noll, R., LeRoy, S., Bukowski, W., Rogosch, F., & Kulkarni, R. (1991). Peer relationships and adjustment in children with cancer. *Journal of Pediatric Psychology, 16*(3), 307–326.

Patterson, J., & Geber, G. (1991). Preventing mental health problems in children with chronic illness or disability. *Children's Health Care, 20*(3), 150–161.

Perrin, E., Ramsey, B., & Sandler, H. (1987). Competent kids: Children and adolescents with a chronic illness. *Child Care, Health, and Development, 13,* 13–32.

Piaget, J. (1930). *The child's conceptions of physical causality.* London: Kegan Paul.

Pless, I., & Pinkerton, P. (1975). *Chronic childhood disorder: Promoting patterns of adjustment.* Chicago: Yearbook Medical Publishers.

Rutter, M. (1981). Stress, coping, and development: Some issues and some questions. *Journal of Child Psychology and Psychiatry, 22,* 323–356.

Ryan, R.M., & Connell, J.P. (1989). Perceived locus of causality and internalization: Examining reasons for acting in two domains. *Journal of Personality and Social Psychology, 57*(5), 749–761.

Sameroff, A. (1989). Commentary: General systems and regulation of development. In M. Gunnar & E. Thelen (Eds.), *Systems and development: The Minnesota symposia on child psychology: Vol. 22* (pp. 219–235). Minneapolis: University of Minnesota Press.

Selman, R. (1980). *The growth of interpersonal understanding.* New York: Academic Press.

Selman, R., & Schultz, L. (1991). *Making a friend in youth.* Chicago: The University of Chicago Press.

Shonkoff, J. (1993). Reflections on an emerging academic discipline: The prolonged gestation of developmental and behavioral pediatrics. *Journal of Developmental and Behavioral Pediatrics, 14*(6), 409–412.

Spirito, A., DeLawyer, D., & Stark, L. (1991). Peer relations and social adjustment of chronically ill children and adolescents. *Clinical Psychology Review, 11,* 539–564.

Thies, K. (1994a). *A developmental analysis of cognitive appraisal of stress in chronically ill children.* Unpublished doctoral dissertation, Boston College.

Thies, K. (1994b, April). *Cognitive appraisal of stress in children and adolescents with chronic health conditions.* Paper presented at the North Coast Regional Pediatric Psychology Conference, Cincinnati.

Wallander, J. (1992). Theory-driven research in pediatric psychology: A little bit on why and how. *Journal of Pediatric Psychology, 117*(5), 521–536.

Wallander, J., & Varni, J. (1992). Adjustment in children with chronic physical disorders: Programmatic research on a disability-stress-coping model. In A. LaGreca, L. Siegel, J. Wallander, & C. Walker (Eds.), *Stress and coping in child health* (pp. 279–298). New York: Guilford Press.

Walsh, M., & Bibace, R. (1991). Children's conceptions of AIDS: A developmental analysis. *Journal of Pediatric Psychology, 16*(3), 273–285.

Werner, H. (1948). *Comparative psychology of mental development.* New York: Science Editions.

Zigler, E., & Glick, M. (1986). *A developmental approach to adult psychopathology.* New York: John Wiley & Sons.

6

Self-Determination for Youth with Significant Cognitive Disabilities

From Theory to Practice

Michael Wehmeyer

Many people presume that the presence of a significant cognitive or intellectual impairment precludes, a priori, an individual from becoming competent. The terms *self-determined* and *severe disability* are usually viewed as mutually incompatible. The presence of a significant cognitive disability is more likely to evoke assumptions of incompetent decision making, need for protection or legal guardianship, and vulnerability than of competency, effective decision making, goal setting, and independence. The educational, psychological, and rehabilitation literature has virtually ignored self-determination as a factor in school and adult success for individuals with disabilities. Even when this topic has been addressed for people with disabilities, there has been limited discussion about its applicability to people with severe disabilities, and discussion has focused almost exclusively on the rights and capabilities of individuals with significant cognitive impairments to make choices and express preferences. While choice making is one critical component, self-determination goes beyond simply expressing preferences or making choices.

Does the presence of a significant cognitive disability, like mental retardation or autism, necessarily preclude self-determination and competence? This chapter offers a definitional framework for evaluating self-determined behavior and proposes that, although many people with severe disabilities do not act in a self-determined manner, the presence of a significant cognitive disability is not, in and of itself, sufficient to explain this outcome. Instead we must examine the environments in which people with significant disabilities live, work and play, and we must consider others' interactions with and expectations for this group and explore practices that have an impact on the opportunity for people with significant disabilities to become self-determined individuals.

WHAT IS SELF-DETERMINATION?

In its earliest conceptualization, self-determination referred to the inherent *right* of individuals with disabilities to assume control of and make choices that have an impact on their lives (Nirje, 1972). Individuals with disabilities emphasized this interpretation as they demanded fairness and equal access. In the eyes of many, particularly those Americans who have experienced a disability and the subsequent discrimination associated with that experience, self-determination means empowerment—the right to assume control of one's life. As fundamentally important, however, as it is to understand the essential relationship between self-determination and empowerment, it is inadequate to conceptualize self-determination strictly as a right. Individuals have an inherent right to the opportunity to *be* self-determined; the right for free association, freedom of speech and expression, equal employment opportunity, equal protection and due process, and freedom from cruel and unusual punishment; the right to marry, procreate, and raise children; the right to vote; the right to freedom of religious expression; and the right to privacy. Without these basic civil rights, it is not possible to be fully self-determined. For many people with disabilities, becoming self-determined requires access to these basic rights.

How is self-determination best conceptualized, given that access to such rights constitutes a prerequisite for being fully self-determined and that self-determination must ultimately reflect the empowerment of the individual? Self-determination has been defined as "acting as the primary causal agent in one's life and making choices and decisions regarding one's quality of life, free from undue external influence or interference" (Wehmeyer, 1992a, pp. 305). Self-determined behavior is associated with specific attitudes and abilities learned across the life span and associated primarily with achieving adulthood and fulfilling adult roles. Within this framework, self-determination is conceptualized in terms of characteristics of the individual's actions and, subsequently, in terms of the frequency and consistency of actions that are self-determined. An individual is self-determined if his or her actions reflect four essential characteristics: 1) autonomy, 2) self-regulation, 3) psychological empowerment, and 4) self-realization. Individuals who consistently display or engage in self-determined behaviors can be construed as being self-determined, where self-determined is used to describe a dispositional characteristic. Dispositional characteristics involve the organization of psychological and physiological elements such that an individual's behavior in different situations will be similar.

Central to this definition is the idea that self-determined individuals are the causal agents in their lives. Causal agency implies that the person makes things happen in his or her life. However, because one's mere physical presence or the exhibition of behaviors that are exclusively autonomic and self-governing (e.g., seizure activity) or primarily noncommunicative or a response to an organism's internal state (e.g., a neonate's cry of hunger, certain stereotyped behaviors in children with disabilities) can likewise result in changes in the person's immediate environment, it is necessary to consider the individual's intent in order to assess causality. An agent is a person through which power is exerted or an end is achieved. As opposed to merely associating an individual's action with an outcome, causal agency requires that the action is purposeful and is performed to achieve a given outcome. Self-determined actions are not always and not necessarily intentional, however, as many actions that can be seen as self-determined may not be the result of conscious decision making each time.

To be the primary causal agent in his or her own life, an individual must show these four essential elements of self-determined behavior: autonomy, self-regulation, and a psychologically empowered and self-realizing initiation and response to events. An event that is not characterized by all of these elements cannot be considered self-determined. An individual is truly self-determined when his or her actions show all of these qualities predictably and consistently.

An action can be seen as reflecting autonomy if the individual is acting 1) according to his or her own preferences, interests, and abilities; and 2) independently, free from undue external influence or interference. The word *autonomy* derives from the Greek *auto* (self) and *nomos* (rule) (Haworth, 1986). Autonomous individuals have the capacity to indicate preferences, make choices based upon these preferences, and initiate action based upon these selections. This ability includes acting on the basis of personal beliefs and values, thoughts and emotions, and likes and dislikes instead of exclusively on social norms or individual and group pressure. Lewis and Taymans (1992) defined autonomy as

> a complex concept which involves emotional separations from parents, the development of a sense of personal control over one's life, the establishment of a personal value system, and the ability to execute behavioral tasks which are needed in the adult world. (p. 37)

Acting independently, or being independent, does not imply that one acts separately from all other people. Human beings are not completely autonomous but are interdependent; a person's life intermingles with the lives of many others, seen and unseen. Autonomous actions reflect interdependence of individuals with other people, including families, friends and acquaintances, and others with whom a person interacts on a daily basis. This healthy interdependence suggests why self-determined actions are defined as being free from *undue* external influence or interference (Wehmeyer, 1992a). In a culturally, socioeconomically, and ethnically diverse society, any conceptualization of self-determination must recognize and be able to account for wide normal variations in self-determination due to cultural and societal factors. For all people, choices are frequently constrained and rarely represent optimal options. In short, self-determination does not reflect a complete lack of influence or even interference from others but instead reflects decisions made without undue interference or influence. The term *undue* remains purposely subjective, because what may be perceived by one individual to be an acceptable level of influence may appear to another as unacceptable.

Self-regulation can be seen as

> a complex response system that enables individuals to examine their environments and their repertoires of responses for coping with those environments to make decisions about how to act, to act, to evaluate the desirability of the outcomes of the action, and to revise their plans as necessary. (Whitman, 1990, p. 349)

To show dynamic self-regulation, individuals must make decisions concerning what skills to use in which situation; examine the task at hand and their strategic repertoire; and formulate, enact, and evaluate a plan of action, with revisions, if necessary. Self-regulation differs from automatic processing in that it requires focused attention and continuous decision making among alternative responses (Whitman, 1990). Self-regulation includes the skills of self-monitoring (observation of one's social and physical environment and one's own actions); self-evaluation (making judgments about the acceptability of one's own behavior through comparing information about what one is doing with what one ought to be doing); and, based upon the outcome of this self-evaluation, self-reinforcement.

Certain skills and proficiencies enable a person to become the primary causal agent and to make choices about his or her quality of life. These "core" skills are a part of most interventions to promote self-determination, and they include the ability to make choices and decisions; to identify alternatives, recognize consequences, and locate resources to act upon decisions; to identify and solve problems; to set realistic, achievable goals; and to organize. To promote the development of personal efficacy and self-awareness, individuals must learn to recognize and identify physical and psychological needs and to understand how these needs are met and how they influence actions. Acting autonomously involves not only knowing your own needs, beliefs, and values, but also understanding and accepting individual differences in beliefs and priorities and recognizing that others have rights and that citizenship has responsibilities. Autonomous individuals are not free from external influences; and an understanding of authority and appropriate behaviors and the ability to manage one's emotions or desires to deal with frustrating or stressful experiences are aspects of self-determination. Self-advocacy and communication skills are often cited as skills essential to self-determination. These include learning about civil rights and responsibilities, communicating assertively at appropriate times, and developing listening and leadership skills.

Personal perceptions and beliefs about oneself and one's environment affect the degree to which a person is capable of becoming the primary causal agent in his or her life. Individuals who are self-determined believe that they have the capacity to influence outcomes in their environment. This belief emerges from perceptions of control and efficacy that, according to Zimmerman (1990), reflect "psychological empowerment" (p. 73). Zimmerman defines psychological empowerment as consisting of the various dimensions of perceived control, including the cognitive (personal efficacy), personality (locus of control), and motivational domains. The components contributing to development of a perception of psychological empowerment include 1) self-efficacy, a sense of personal mastery over one's environment and the expectation that one can successfully execute behavior(s) required to produce a specific outcome or outcomes; 2) outcome expectancy, an individual's estimation that a specific behavior will lead to a predetermined outcome; and 3) locus of control, the degree to which a person perceives contingency relationships between personal actions and outcomes. Locus of control encompasses how an individual views reinforcement in his or her life, as primarily the consequence of one's own actions or as the result of outside forces such as luck, fate, or powerful others.

Additionally, the actions of self-determined individuals reflect a comprehensive and reasonably accurate knowledge of one's strengths and limitations and a conscious, purposeful intent to use this knowledge and understanding in day-to-day situations. This self-realization forms through experience with and interpretation of one's environment and is influenced by evaluations of significant others and by reinforcements and attributions of one's own behavior.

Causal agency is framed here within the concept of quality of life because acting in a self-determined manner is a quality of life issue. Being self-determined is a valued outcome for most adults in our society. As with self-determination, a consideration of quality of life focuses attention on both subjective and objective indicators. Dalkey (1972) stated that

> quality of life is related not just to the environment and to the external circumstances of an individual's life, but whether these factors constitute a major share of an individual's well being, or whether they are dominated by factors such as a sense of achievement, love and affection, perceived freedom and so on. (p. 9)

An individual's quality of life is determined across settings, environments, and opportunities; and virtually all choices and decisions contribute to an individual's quality of life. Viewing causal agency within a quality-of-life framework allows for consideration of a diversity of activities and behaviors relating to both major decisions that occur infrequently (buying a house, making medical decisions) and those decisions that are less consequential but more frequent, such as what to wear or eat or how to spend one's free time.

Evidence to Support the Framework

To test this definitional framework, Wehmeyer, Kelchner, and Richards (in press-a, in press-b) conducted a study of adults with mental retardation to determine their relative self-determination status and the relationship between this status and the hypothesized essential elements (autonomy, self-regulation, perceptions of psychological empowerment, and self-knowledge/realization). Interviews with 408 adults with mental retardation yielded responses to a survey instrument constructed to identify the degree to which individuals acted in a self-determined manner. Respondents were assigned to one of two groups, high self-determination or low self-determination, based on these responses. This survey instrument (described in Wehmeyer et al., in press-b) asked participants to answer a series of questions exploring the individuals' behaviors in six principal domains: 1) home and family living, 2) employment, 3) recreation and leisure, 4) transportation, 5) money management, and 6) personal leadership. Questions were designed to elicit information on the amount of choice and control individuals had in each of these areas or the degree to which the individual acted in a manner reflecting self-determination.

Participants also completed a series of assessments designed to determine their autonomy, self-regulation, psychological empowerment, and self-realization. Autonomy was measured using two scales, the Autonomous Functioning Checklist (Sigafoos, Feinstein, Damond, & Reiss, 1988) and the Life Choices Survey (Kishi, Teelucksingh, Zollers, Park-Lee, & Meyer, 1988). Self-regulation was measured using the Means End Problem-Solving scale, a measure of interpersonal cognitive problem solving (Platt & Spivack, 1989), and a second scale measuring assertiveness. Psychological empowerment was measured using a widely adopted locus of control scale (the adult version of the Nowicki-Strickland Internal-External Scale; Nowicki & Duke, 1974) and additional measures of social self-efficacy and outcome expectancy. Self-knowledge was assessed using an indicator of self-awareness (short version of the Personal Orientation Inventory), general self-esteem, and domain-specific self-concepts.

Comparisons between groups based on self-determination status found that adults who exhibited more self-determined behaviors were significantly more autonomous (on both measures of autonomy), were more effective social problem solvers, were more assertive and self-aware, and held significantly more adaptive perceptions of control, self-efficacy, outcome expectancy, and self-esteem (Wehmeyer et al., in press-a). With the exception of certain domain-specific self-concepts, there were significant differences between groups in all areas related to the definitional framework presented.

DEVELOPMENT OF SELF-DETERMINATION

Self-determination develops based on learning experiences across the life span and is associated primarily with achieving adulthood and fulfilling adult roles. Full self-determination is primarily an adult outcome principally because in most societies, children and, perhaps to a lesser degree, adolescents are by their status as minors not allowed to be or fully capable of being self-determined. In this concept, self-determination is viewed not as a characteristic achieved by a select few but as normally distributed. The definitional framework also supports the idea that there is significant variation in and between individuals and that people can be described as partially or fully self-determined based on the performance of self-determined behaviors across contexts and time. Self-determination must be examined in reference to the individual, considering his or her potential and abilities and the constraints imposed by environmental factors. Behavioral expressions of self-determination vary greatly across settings, individuals, and age ranges; and certain perceptions contributing to self-determination likewise vary according to context. St. Peter, Field, and Hoffman (1992) ascribe the principal of reciprocal causation to self-determination. This principle suggests that behaviors of self-determination are also expressions of self-determination. Behaviors of self-determination are in turn causal in ascribing self-determination to oneself and as such reflect both outcome and etiology.

This framework proposes that the essential characteristics of self-determination are, independent of one another, necessary but are not sufficient for self-determination. Age, opportunity, and circumstances may moderate the degree to which any of the components are present; and the relative self-determination expressed by an individual will likely vary, sometimes over time and sometimes across environments.

The essential characteristics of self-determination emerge from the development or acquisition of several interrelated component elements, some of which follow characteristic developmental pathways as described in the child development literature. A model of the development of self-determination can be described in relation to the developmental pathways of these component elements. This development is necessarily contingent upon and concurrent with development in cognitive, social, and linguistic domains. Interventions to enhance self-determination must reflect these characteristics. However, unlike physical development, where there are fixed "endpoints" to the developmental process, many aspects of self-determination have no such endpoint and may continue to develop over an individual's life span.

Prerequisites to the Expression of Self-Determination

Newborns do not enter the world self-determined, but instead, through learning across multiple environments, become adults who may be self-determined. Although self-determination is not by definition contingent upon specific levels of intelligence, there are prerequisites to self-determination without which individuals cannot or will not become self-determined. These contingencies are primarily cognitively based and must be present along with the opportunities necessary to fully develop and express self-determination. Inadequate opportunities in this area may suppress or hinder development; and for many people with signicicant cognitive disabilities, the lack of such opportunities may mean they will not be self-determined. However, some people overcome the same lack of opportunities to become self-determined. As such, opportunities that are important for the eventual expression of self-determination can be seen as critical to but not prerequisite for its development.

At the most fundamental level, a person who is self-determined must first develop and possess a sense of self, an awareness of oneself as possessing an identity that is unique and distinct from others and is stable over time. These qualities emerge in early childhood in at least a rudimentary form by 2–3 years of age (Damon, 1983; Lewis & Brooks-Gunn, 1979).

As described in this chapter, self-determined behavior is largely intentional and purposeful; Whitman (1990) concurs that self-regulated behavior is intentional. Certainly most of the activities associated with self-determination are intentional and planned, although this does not mean that behaviors are self-determined only if they result from conscious thought and decision making each time. Many behaviors or actions that reflect our preferences and choices are self-regulated but are not necessarily consciously controlled. Learning and experience allows us to act intentionally without necessarily being conscious of that intent. The prerequisite for this kind of action involves the development of rudimentary metarepresentational capabilities.

If a sense of self is important to the expression of self-determined behavior, so too is a sense of other. However, this sense of other refers to more than simply an understanding of the existence of others separate from oneself. In addition to the sense of self, one must be able to understand a theory of others, their actions, reactions, and thought processes; these are metarepresentative capabilities. Representations refer to internal, symbolic systems that depict or represent aspects of the external world (Oatley, 1978). Representations have been alternatively referred to as schemas or personal theories. Metarepresentation refers to thinking about others' representation of the external world.

This process can occur on a very simple level, but it is critical to self-determination. The development of metarepresentative abilities is related to the appearance of numerous cognitive abilities, including the differentiation of self and others, object permanence, and certain symbolic representational capabilities. Metarepresentation involves diverse cognitive processes, including social cognition (cognition about people and knowledge of self, others, and social relationships), role and perspective taking (the ability to take another person's point of view), and metacognitive abilities. Premack and Woodruff (1978) described the ability to conceive of mental states (e.g., knowing what others know, want, or feel) as a "theory of mind."

Metarepresentative abilities are particularly important if an individual is to be self-regulating. Self-regulation requires that the individual adjust his or her behavior according to both the actions and the expected actions of others. To accomplish this, one must have a theory, however rudimentary, about how another person will react in a given situation and must be able to plan current and future actions and events based upon this prediction. Although the process seems complicated, people do this on a regular basis. The way in which a person greets another depends on an understanding of him or her and on the prediction of the other person's response. If someone has recently won the lottery, we may predict that a boisterous greeting will be well received and proceed accordingly. If, however, we know that that same individual has recently lost a job or experienced poor health, our greeting will be moderated to reflect our prediction of the individual's current state of mind. Likewise, problem solving and decision making require, in most cases, the ability to represent others' thoughts, emotions, and reactions (Wehmeyer & Kelchner, 1994).

Development of Component Elements of Self-Determination

The essential characteristics of self-determination probably emerge contingent on the development of various component elements that are, in turn, based on learning experiences across the life span. It is useful to chart the developmental pathways of these component elements to ensure more effective intervention, but it may be worth addressing a topic of concern to many educators when they reference typical development as important for instruction. Many special educators believe that a developmental model of intervention perpetuates the use of chronological age–inappropriate activities and limits the acquisition of more functional skills. This belief is based on the misapplication of the developmental approach to the acquisition of certain cognitive and academic skills that has resulted in circumstances where adolescents with more significant cognitive disabilities spend their days engaged in inappropriate, childlike activities. This proposed model of the development of self-determination as a springboard for intervention does not advocate a strict adherence to mental ages and chronological age–inappropriate activities. Instead, it is proposed that only by describing the normative development of self-determination does it become possible to define chronological age–appropriate instruction.

There is a tendency to view self-determination in terms of successful, productive behaviors. However, self-determined behaviors are not always successful, and the outcomes of self-determined actions are not always positive. Self-determination is just one component of self-competence, with the development of coping strategies and self-esteem as additional components for adult success and self-sufficiency. It is one thing to be the causal agent in one's life, and it is yet another to be successful at that endeavor!

Nonetheless, it is tempting for many people to define self-determination by specific behaviors that are often affiliated with it. This view has limited utility because any behavior can be "self-determined." For example, skills related to self-advocacy or assertiveness are frequently cited among self-determination skills. However, behaviors that are not self-advocating or not assertive can also be self-determined behaviors (Wehmeyer & Berkobien, 1991). Many people who are self-determined do indeed stand up for their own rights; these same people may choose not to stand up for their rights if actively advocating for their own personal rights would have negative consequences for someone else. The behavior reflects self-determination in both situations, despite the differences.

A number of component elements are integral to the emergence of self-determination. These are not definitionally tied to self-determination, but are instead antecedents to the expression of this characteristic. This list is not intended to be exhaustive, but these component elements seem particularly important: 1) choice making; 2) decision making; 3) problem solving; 4) goal setting and attainment; 5) self-observation, evaluation, and reinforcement; 6) internal locus of control; 7) positive attributions of efficacy and outcome expectancy; 8) self-awareness; and 9) self-knowledge. Each component has a unique developmental pathway that, to greater or lesser degrees, has been described by research. Doll, Sands, Wehmeyer, and Palmer (1996) have described the development of these component elements as they pertain to the development of self-determined behavior.

SIGNIFICANT COGNITIVE DISABILITY AND SELF-DETERMINATION

Cognitive impairments that impede an individual's rate of learning, ability to generalize, and development in learning, memory, and language have an impact on his or her relative self-determination, but do not preclude the development of component elements of self-determination. People with significant cognitive disabilities experience limits in the number and complexity of skills they acquire that are important to becoming fully self-determined. Self-regulation skills, social cognitive problem solving, and other such skills require the use of metacognitive strategies. Limited cognitive social problem-solving skills, often combined with limited communicative abilities, pose real hurdles to decision making. However, behavioral and adaptive technologies can remove or mitigate many of the barriers imposed by cognitive impairments. An individual's cognitive and intellectual impairment may be so significant as to preclude the development of skills for self-determination, but these circumstances seem to be the great exception and not the rule, even among people with significant cognitive disabilities.

Given adequate supports, opportunities to experience control by having one's preferences honored, chances to learn to make choices, reasonable accommodations, and the opportunity to learn skills related to self-determination, *it is possible that a person with a significant cognitive disability can become not only self-determined, but fully self-determined.* Fredericks (1988) related the efforts of his son, Tim, to attain the rank of Eagle Scout in Troop 161 in Philomath, Oregon. Tim, who has Down syndrome, was included in the activities of the regular scout troop instead of participating in a "special scouting" program. In order to achieve this rank, scouts must carry out a community service project. Tim's desire was to communicate to other students what the experience of having a significant cognitive disability meant to him. He sought and gained approval to conduct his Eagle Scout project giving speeches at school campuses in the local district. Because Tim has difficulty writing and reading, he prepared his speech with the help of his family. Tim dictated what he wanted to say to a family member, who printed his words. Tim then copied the dictated words in his own script. Tim's father comments that "Tim's dictation over the years has become quite fluent, and he does not tolerate any editing of his ideas. He occasionally tolerates a suggested word or phrase change" (p. 8).

After the speech was finished, Tim prepared to present his project. His original intent was to speak at a few schools, but in the end he presented his speech at 27 schools to a total audience of more than 2,500 people. This is the speech Tim gave:

> My name is Tim Fredericks. I am handicapped because I have Down syndrome. I was born with Down syndrome. Down syndrome people have an extra chromosome. Nobody knows why we have this extra chromosome. All of you have forty-six chromosomes. I have forty-seven. Would any of you like my extra chromosome? I would be glad to give it to you if I could.
>
> I would like to tell you what it is like to be retarded. I am doing this so that you might be able to understand people like me. School is a good place to learn, but I don't really like to go to school. I am a slow learner. I have a hard time spelling. Some of your teachers tell me that you have a hard time spelling, and you don't have my problem. I have trouble reading. Everyone tells me that I read about the fifth grade level. I hate to write letters and to write in my diary because it is hard for me to write. After I graduate from school, I hope to live in an apartment with a good friend. I also hope to have two or three part-time jobs. I have two now that I get paid for. I work at Ark Animal Hospital every morning for two hours. I have to be there at 7:15. I work at Vandehey's Cabinet Shop three afternoons a week. I have been working now for more than a year at both jobs.

I do chores at home. I have to take care of the animals, twelve chickens, three cats, a dog, three goldfish and a horse. That's a lot of mouths to feed.

I also help my Dad cut wood. I take care of my own room, and I help my Mom vacuum. She says I do a better job than she does. And she is right!

I love music, but I like hard rock best, but my Mom doesn't.

I have a hard time explaining how I feel, but I feel the same way you do.

The hardest thing for me is when people make fun of me or ignore me. For instance, I went to a dance a few weeks ago, and no girl would dance with me. Can you imagine how you would feel if that happened to you? Well, I feel the same way.

Kids on the bus used to make fun of me. That used to make me mad.

I have a girlfriend, but she goes to a different school than I do. I don't get to see her too often. She is handicapped too. I have other handicapped friends, but my best friends are Chris and Mark Weaver. They have been my friends for five years. I think they really like me, and I like them.

I feel good when people talk to me or are friendly to me. That's one of the things I like about Boy Scouts. The boys accept me as I am. They know I am handicapped, but it doesn't make any difference. I am a scout just like them. It takes me longer, and I have to work a little harder to get my merit badges, but I get them done.

That is one of the reasons I am here. I am trying to be an Eagle Scout. I only have three more merit badges to go. My Eagle Scout project was to tell you about myself. I hope I have done that. I want to thank the principal, the staff, and the students for letting me come to talk to you.

If anyone would like to ask any questions, I'll try to answer them, but if I can't my Dad is here, and he can help me. (Fredericks, 1988, pp. 8–9)

There seems no question that Tim's actions are self-determined. He acts autonomously, is self-regulated, and acts based on an understanding of himself and a belief that he can make an impact. The content of his speech suggests that Tim is self-determined in many other areas of his life.

This is not to suggest that most individuals with significant cognitive and intellectual disabilities are able to take *full* control of decisions that have an impact on their lives. It seems evident that many people with significant intellectual impairments need considerable support in financial and medical decision making, social interactions, and many other domains. However, causal agency does not imply absolute control over decisions. For example, people with significant physical disabilities may rely on a personal care attendant to perform specific actions that they cannot accomplish themselves because of their disabling condition. As long as the personal care attendant is acting based on the preferences and instructions of the person with the disability, the person can be seen as self-determined. The same can be true for people with cognitive disabilities. Tim's family provided the support he needed to overcome the barriers to acting in a self-determined way, simply by the process of dictation and transcription.

Such accommodations may be quite extensive for some individuals with severe disabilities. In 1992, The Arc awarded its national Bill Sackter Award to William Crane, of Minneapolis, Minnesota. The Sackter award recognizes a person with mental retardation who has become an achieving, integrated member of society after having left an institutional setting. Bill Crane lived at the Faribault State Hospital in Minnesota for 20 years. Bill experienced significant challenges in his efforts to improve his life. He was born with cerebral palsy, was labeled as having severe mental retardation, and was deaf. He lacked a systematic means of communication. He exhibited behaviors that were deemed too disruptive for the community. Bill was even denied access to a sheltered workshop because of the severity of his disability and his behaviors. According to the nomination form, his psychological report described him as functioning in the severe to moderate range, having no survival skills, and needing constant supervision.

Bill was powerless because the system that was designed to serve his needs instead controlled his life.

The accommodation to overcome these barriers came in the form of legislation and advocacy. Christine Boswell, at the time the Executive Director of the local chapter of The Arc, became Bill's advocate. Bill and Christine forged a working relationship and then a friendship. Christine took the time to listen to Bill, to decipher what he was trying to communicate, and finally to begin to advocate on his behalf. He gained the opportunity to move into the community. He learned some basic sign language. He worked with his advocate to get access to employment, first sheltered and then supported. Bill's contribution to this process was simple but essential. He simply never gave up. He never gave up hope. He never gave up expressing his preferences. He never gave up trying to explain what he wanted to anyone who would listen.

The nominating form of the Sackter Award chronicled the achievements of a man who lives a self-determined life. Bill works 30 hours per week as a clerk in a Minneapolis nonprofit agency with the support he needs. He has received commendations from his employer as a valued employee. He lives independently in a supported living home in a suburban neighborhood. He has two roommates whom he selected. He interviewed the support service personnel who were then scheduled to come into their home on a daily basis. He enjoys mountain camping, whitewater river rafting, hockey, and visiting friends and relatives. He was reunited with his mother after 15 years and travels to visit her when he can make room in his schedule. Bill cooks with a microwave, shops, and is responsible for his own self-care needs.

The final sentence in Bill's nomination form states that "IQ labels have been disregarded as irrelevant to Bill's potential and capabilities." Bill's accommodations went beyond a personal care attendant or a technological device. Without system changes in the form of legislation and changing perspectives on how to provide services, and without strong advocacy, it is probable that Bill would have been unable to overcome his barriers. However, as all of those who spoke during the award ceremony acknowledged, there was never any doubt as to who the causal agent in this process was—it was Bill.

For many with significant cognitive disabilities, the person's family is the catalyst for change and the primary impetus for providing accommodations. Turnbull and Turnbull elegantly illustrate the important role the family plays in self-determination (see Chapter 10). A person may be self-determined even if the individual providing assistance is a family member instead of a personal care attendant. However, it is sometimes difficult for a family member to change his or her relationship with the individual to become a neutral accommodation. Some such relationships may become overly controlling, may be dominated by a parent or sibling, and may create dependency. The same is often true for teacher–student relationships. Most people with significant cognitive disabilities have had very limited opportunities to experience choice and control in their lives and have grown up in environments that foster dependency, from the home to the school to the sheltered workshop. Many people with significant cognitive disabilities lack not only the skills and attitudes to become self-determined, but also the opportunities to do so and, consequently, the understanding or motivation to overcome these barriers and assume greater control.

These barriers are too often insurmountable for people with significant cognitive disabilities, and they are perceived as incompetent and in need of protection. If an individual tries to exert an influence on his or her life, the result may be even greater segregation and isolation. Individual preferences are treated as problem behaviors and subjected to modification. Too frequently the reliance on family for support toward independence becomes yet another dependency-creating relationship that is dominated as much by the needs of the supporter as the needs of the individual. The teacher's need for structure and control in the classroom take precedence over the student's need to take control over learning and educational decision making. Staff needs based on time constraints overwhelm individual needs to maximally participate in daily activities. Family needs for protection and safety eventually win out over the risk taking and exploration needed to develop independence and autonomy.

The greatest threats to self-determination for people with significant cognitive disabilities are external. Through behavioral interventions and adaptive technologies, however, people with significant cognitive impairments can learn skills that enable them to become at least partially autonomous and self-regulating. Combined with the efforts of families, friends, and professionals who act for the individual based upon his or her preferences, wants, needs, abilities, interests and choices, this effort to provide interventions should enable people with significant disabilities to be self-determined.

HOW SELF-DETERMINED ARE PEOPLE WITH SIGNIFICANT COGNITIVE DISABILITIES?

Given that people with cognitive disabilities can become self-determined, it is useful to evaluate self-determination in people with cognitive impairments. It has been difficult to evaluate this outcome, at least partly because very few researchers cared to ask; and definitional inadequacies limited investigation. To evaluate the degree to which individuals with cognitive disabilities are self-determined, one must piece together findings from school follow-up/follow-along studies regarding outcomes as adults; studies comparing peers with and without disabilities on certain relevant social-psychological measures (e.g., locus of control, self-concept); and the few studies that have evaluated opportunities for students and adults with cognitive disabilities to make daily choices.

For most adults, employment or engagement in meaningful activities constitutes an important aspect of their perceptions of control and of self. Holding a job is essential for financial security and autonomy and contributes to the degree to which one perceives oneself and is perceived by others as being an adult. Employment outcomes for young adults with disabilities are not as positive as most would desire. Chadsey-Rusch, Rusch, and O'Reilly (1991) reviewed the research on employment, residential, and social outcomes of youth transitioning from school to adulthood. Most studies found that special education students had employment outcomes much worse than their peers without disabilities, with under 40% of students employed full-time and with most of them underemployed. Wagner et al. (1991) reported that only 20% of youth with mental retardation and 37% with learning disabilities were employed full-time.

Employment status can be an ambiguous indicator of self-determination. A person may be unemployed though self-determined or, as is more likely, employed but not experiencing significant control or choice. The data of Wagner et al. included sheltered environments as an employment option, yet there is evidence that sheltered settings limit control and that individuals in such settings have lower perceptions of quality of life (Gersten, Crowell, & Bellamy, 1986; Inge, Banks, Wehman, Hill, & Shafer, 1988; Schalock, 1990). To the extent that many youth with significant disabilities have few employment options outside of sheltered workshops, one has to consider the impact of this variable on self-determination.

Several investigations have compared individuals in sheltered and competitive work environments. Schalock, Keith, Hoffman, and Karan (1989) found significantly higher scores on a quality of life index for individuals employed in competitive or supported settings versus sheltered environments. Sinnot-Oswald, Gliner, and Spencer (1991) reported that individuals in supported employment scored higher on a quality of life indicator than did peers in sheltered employment. Wehmeyer (1994a) found significant differences between locus of control scores for adults with cognitive disabilities, with individuals who were unemployed or working in a sheltered setting perceiving themselves as having less control than did peers in competitive settings.

Wehmeyer (1992b) surveyed adults with cognitive disabilities in self-advocacy groups about employment status, job preference, and amount of choice in career decisions. Of 254 respondents, a large percentage (87.5%) were employed. Most of these people (95%) indicated that they were satisfied with their jobs. However, only 37% of those employed listed a job equivalent to their current one as their preferred job. Of those indicating job preferences, 73% were able to list the abilities necessary for those jobs. Although individuals in this sample were older (mean age, 36 years) and had been in the work force for several years, only 8% reported that they had found their current job themselves. Essentially, these adults wanted other jobs and knew what was necessary to perform such work, but were waiting for someone else to locate the job.

Other outcome indicators support the assumption that individuals with severe cognitive disabilities experience limited self-determination. Wehmeyer and Metzler (1995) analyzed the data from the National Consumer Survey (NCS), a survey of Americans with disabilities that evaluates their satisfaction with their lives, for nearly 5,000 people with mental retardation. Only 6.3% indicated they had a choice in where they currently lived, 9.4% said they had selected their roommates, and 11.3% indicated they had selected where they worked or their daytime activities. These figures are low not only when compared with adults without disabilities, but also when compared with people with noncognitive disabilities. For example, of 10,000 adults with disabilities other than mental retardation, 15.3% indicated that they chose where they live. For people with mental retardation, the opportunity to exert control over their lives was a function of the relative importance of the activity. Thus, 56.3% of the respondents indicated that they determined what clothes they wore (which still leaves more than 40% who do not have control even over that aspect of daily life!), while only 17.6% indicated they provided unassisted consent for medication. While it may be prudent to request assistance in making decisions such as consent for medication for individuals with cognitive disabilities, 56.7% indicated that they had absolutely no control in the process.

Several other outcomes from this survey provide evidence of the need to address self-determination for people with significant cognitive disabilities. Only 5.8% of the respondents indicated that they owned their home, and only 4.5% indicated that they were currently married or had ever been married (or lived with someone). For the sample with noncognitive disabilities, 12% were or had been married. Among adult Americans without disabilities, 58% are married or live with someone and 20% are separated or divorced. Several other studies provide information regarding opportunities for choice. Kishi et al. (1988) determined that adults with mental retardation had significantly fewer opportunities than did their peers without disabilities to make choices regarding daily activities, such as what or where to eat or how to spend their time.

The environment in which one lives affects how much choice one has on a daily basis. Pierce, Luckasson, and Smith (1990) found that there were significant differences between settings where a person lived (group home vs. mini-homes) in the extent to which staff members selected activities during unstructured time. People living in group homes spent more time in activities selected by staff than did peers living in smaller, less structured homes. Lord and Pedlar (1991) found that individuals who had moved from an institution to group homes exercised some choice about things such as menu planning and leisure activities, but

> more often were at best invited or at worse told to do something. Some staff members saw the residents as having choice in their lives because they could choose ways of filling free time in an evening. (p. 217)

Wehmeyer et al. (in press-a) found that relative self-determination varied according to the individual's living arrangement (independent, semi-independent, congregate setting), with people living in the more restrictive environments showing less self-determination.

The degree to which an individual perceives himself or herself as having control over outcomes and reinforcers (e.g., internal control orientation) has been correlated with positive life outcomes, and the lack of this perception has been related to negative outcomes. Dudley-Marling, Snider, and Tarver (1982) reviewed the literature on locus of control and learning disabilities and concluded that these students were more externally oriented when compared with children without disabilities. Wehmeyer (1993a) found that students with learning disabilities were more externally oriented than expected based on findings from peers without disabilities and that females with learning disabilities were significantly more oriented externally than males. Similar investigation for students with mental retardation has been limited, but research suggests that these individuals are also more likely to perceive control as external, or outcomes controlled by others, fate, or chance. In their review, Mercer and Snell (1977) determined that four of five studies surveyed attributed more external orientations (thus maladaptive) to students with mental retardation than to peers without disabilities. Wehmeyer (1994b) found that adolescents with mental retardation held less adaptive perceptions of control and efficacy than did peers with learning disabilities or no disability. Research has also found that adolescents with mental retardation evidenced perceptual and psychological barriers to effective career decision making that included external locus of control and low efficacy expectations (Wehmeyer, 1993b).

IMPLICATIONS FOR INTERVENTION AND PRACTICE

Children and adolescents become self-determined adults through opportunities and experiences leading to success; through constructive experiences with failure; through opportunities to explore, take risks, and learn from their consequences; and by watching adults take control and make decisions. They learn by participating in decisions, making choices, and experiencing control at home, at school, and elsewhere. Self-determination emerges when children and adolescents perceive themselves as effective, worthy individuals who can engage in actions that affect outcomes in their lives. Students become self-determined by learning specific skills such as problem solving, learning to identify consequences, and identifying alternatives.

Clearly there are important roles for both educational and home environments in promoting self-determination. In this area, there is an overwhelming need for parent and professional collaboration. Sinclair and Christenson (1992) emphasized that child development does not occur in a single environment and without influence from multiple sources:

Children learn, grow and develop both at home and at school. There is no clear cut boundary between home and school experiences for children and youth, rather, there is a mutually influencing quality between experiences in these two settings. (p. 12)

One of the values of describing a model of the development of self-determination is that in so doing one highlights areas of critical need for instruction and intervention across all environments. In self-determination, those areas are clearly the component elements described earlier. Schools and families must work together to ensure adequate learning environments and experiences to promote these elements.

What Is the Role of Education in This Process?

Achieving the outcome of self-determination for students, with and without disabilities, through the educational system will be as complex and difficult as are comparable efforts to ensure that school leavers with disabilities are employed or involved in their communities. It has become increasingly obvious that an educational program that adequately promotes self-determination will not consist only of unilateral efforts to change curriculum, create peer mentor programs, or structure environments. Instead, an effective educational emphasis to promote self-determination will encompass a host of alterations and adaptations as well as parallel emphasis in the student's home and community. Appropriate, functionally derived curriculum, environments that enhance opportunities to experience choice and to express preferences, interactions with peers without disabilities, access to adult role models, experiences with success, and control in decision making all contribute to the eventuality that a student will become self-determined. In addition, it is clear that educational efforts to promote self-determination must span the student's learning experience.

Educators play a critical role in the development of self-determination. The need to structure the classroom to meet educational, behavioral, and administrative requirements may result in an environment promoting dependence and limiting choice and decision making. Teacher recognition of the importance of skills related to self-determination may be the critical first step in the promotion of self-determination. Educators can help students learn how to obtain resources; communicate preferences; set realistic, achievable goals; plan and manage time; identify and solve problems; develop self-advocacy skills; and make choices.

In addition to the instruction in such skills, the methods and strategies teachers adopt can facilitate the acquisition and utilization of self-determination skills. Instructional models such as role-playing are effective methodologies for promoting autonomy and self-determination. Instructional techniques such as relaxation training, metacognitive instruction, and brainstorming are typically underutilized with students receiving special education services.

Skills development goes hand-in-hand with the promotion of attitudes and perceptions critical to becoming self-determined. To enhance motivation and encourage self-determination, teachers should provide activities that optimally challenge the student. Educators can promote autonomy by supporting the initiation of activities and allowing choice. Of particular concern here is the control orientation of the teacher. Students with cognitive disabilities need to learn that they are causal agents for their own lives, and excessive external control is detrimental to this effort. Students need to be provided opportunities to express preferences and make choices and then to experience the outcomes. Efforts have focused on the individualized education program (IEP) process as a key element in this process. Students can learn to assume more control and responsibility in their IEP, identifying and prioritizing goals or objectives and taking a leadership role in the IEP or transition planning meeting.

What can educators do to promote expectations of personal competence and efficacy? Generally, successes raise efficacy expectations. However, even within the experience of failure, the perception of progress can lead to efficacy expectations. A primary means of perceiving success or progress is through verbal feedback or reinforcement. Positive feedback can be administered in a context and in a way that is noncontrolling but honest. Students also need to be provided with reasons for the performance of activities. Teachers must plan ongoing opportunities for students to make choices.

Finally, the educational process must empower the student and his or her family members to become an active part of the educational planning process and must enable students to invest in their own futures by taking advantage of educational opportunities. Federal law now requires that student preferences and interests be a part of the transition planning procedure. Educational personnel must not only reach out to involve parents, siblings, and students; they must also attempt to shift real control to these team members. Educational practices that take away the student's perception of control only alienate students further from the process and limit self-determination. Perhaps the most flagrant violations in this regard involve the assessment process. Special education has been built on a deficits identification process in which professionals diagnose problems through testing and assessment procedures that rarely try to involve the student as a contributing member and in fact often require that the student remain unaware of the intention of the test. We must move beyond this model to actively involve students and family members in the educational process.

It is important to remember, however, that transferring control and responsibility to students requires instruction, structure, and support. Teachers, administrators, parents, related-services personnel, and the student must work together to optimize opportunities for self-determination.

Although many skill areas related to self-determination are more applicable to older students or students with mild disabilities, self-determination is not the sole domain of secondary education or suitable only for students with minimal support needs. Making choices, expressing preferences, and having self-awareness and confidence involve lifelong experiences and instruction, independent of level of disability. Instruction should be tied to normative developmental courses for children's understanding of causality and of self-concepts and self-awareness. The elementary years should offer experiences conducive to these achievements, and this experience is then helpful in adolescence, a critical period for the development of many skills related to self-determination. Adolescents without disabilities begin to question authority, rely upon peers for opinions and advice, and generally move toward becoming self-determined individuals. Students with cognitive disabilities need to be enabled to do likewise.

What Is the Family's Role in Self-Determination?

A family is a system with a set of objectives and rules and interdependent relationships. The birth of a child within a family represents a significant change, the degree of which varies according to the nature of the family. Just as the operation of each family system varies, the reaction to the birth of a child with a disability also varies. One of the most important needs of most families who have a child with severe cognitive impairment is to maintain the normal functions of the family as closely as possible.

As family members move toward acceptance, they may maintain attitudes that are barriers to self-determination. One such barrier is viewing the disability as a problem; this may convey a message to the child that he or she is the problem and that the child and the disability are indistinguishable. Ward (1988) defines two of these barriers as overprotection and "the belief that a child with a disability has too many problems to be burdened with expectations of self-determination." Overprotection is "seen as the opposite of self-determination" (p. 3). Other elements that hinder the development of self-determination include architectural barriers, transportation problems, and a lack of sufficient attendant care; financial barriers may also occur.

Families may assist members with a disability first by accepting the child as a valued member of the family and then by embracing the importance of the concept and development of self-determination. They can structure environments to ensure opportunities for choices. While children with mild disabilities may develop self-determination through self-advocacy and leadership roles, children with more severe disabilities may use nonverbal cues to indicate choices and preferences (Guess & Siegel-Causey, 1985).

Ward (1988) suggests that families be open about the disability, avoid demeaning and negative terms like *hardship* and *burden,* not attempt to hide the disability, avoid comparisons with others, and stress positive coping strategies. As early as possible, parents should involve the child in the meetings and conferences that relate to the child's well-being.

CONCLUSIONS

Despite widely held assumptions to the contrary, people with significant cognitive disabilities can be competent, self-determined individuals. The fact that this is not the case for many people with such disabilities makes it even more important to focus on promoting self-determination. The first steps in this process will revolve around changing not the individual, but instead altering the environments in which that person lives, works, and plays and altering the way others interact with them and perceive them. To achieve this end, people with cognitive disabilities must be included in all communities, educational, vocational, and social; receive the supports they need from people around them; and be afforded the basic rights that come with the belief that all people are worthy of respect and dignity.

REFERENCES

Chadsey-Rusch, J., Rusch, F., & O'Reilly, M.F. (1991). Transition from school to integrated communities. *Remedial and Special Education, 12,* 23–33.

Dalkey, N.C. (1972). *Studies in the quality of life: Delphi and decision-making.* Lexington, MA: Lexington Books.

Damon, W. (1983). *Social and personality development: Infancy through adolescence.* New York: Norton.

Doll, E., Sands, D.J., Wehmeyer, M.L., & Palmer, S. (1996). The development and acquisition of self-determined behavior. In D.J. Sands & M.L. Wehmeyer (Eds.), *Self-determination across the life span: Independence and choice for people with disabilities* (pp. 65–90). Baltimore: Paul H. Brookes Publishing Co.

Dudley-Marling, C.C., Snider, V., & Tarver, S.G. (1982). Locus of control and learning disabilities: A review and discussion. *Perceptual and Motor Skills, 54,* 503–514.

Fredericks, B. (1988). Tim becomes an Eagle Scout. *National Information Center for Children and Youth with Handicaps: Transition Summary, 5,* 8–9.

Gersten, R., Crowell, F., & Bellamy, T. (1986). Spill-over effects: Impact of vocational training on the lives of severely mentally retarded clients. *American Journal of Mental Deficiency, 90,* 501–506.

Guess, D., & Siegel-Causey, E. (1985). Behavioral control and education of severely handicapped students: Who's doing what to whom? And why? In D. Bricker & J. Filler (Eds.),

Severe mental retardation: From theory to practice (pp. 230–244). Reston, VA: Council for Exceptional Children.

Haworth, L. (1986). *Autonomy: An essay in philosophical psychology and ethics.* New Haven, CT: Yale University Press.

Inge, K.J., Banks, D., Wehman, P., Hill, J., & Shafer, M.S. (1988). Quality of life for individuals who are labeled mentally retarded: Evaluating competitive employment versus sheltered workshop employment. *Education and Training in Mental Retardation, 23,* 97–104.

Kishi, G., Teelucksingh, B., Zollers, N., Park-Lee, S., & Meyer, L. (1988). Daily decision-making in community residences: A social comparison of adults with and without mental retardation. *American Journal on Mental Retardation, 92,* 430–435.

Lewis M., & Brooks-Gunn, J. (1979). *Social cognition and the acquisition of self.* New York: Plenum.

Lewis, K., & Taymans, J.M. (1992). An examination of autonomous functioning skills of adolescents with learning disabilities. *Career Development for Exceptional Individuals, 15,* 37–46.

Lord, J., & Pedlar, A. (1991). Life in the community: Four years after the closure of an institution. *Mental Retardation, 29,* 213–221.

Mercer, C.D., & Snell, M.E. (1977). *Learning theory research in mental retardation: Implications for teaching.* Columbus, OH: Charles E. Merrill.

Nirje, B. (1972). The right to self-determination. In W. Wolfensberger (Ed.), *Normalization* (pp. 176–200). Ottawa, Ontario, Canada: National Institute on Mental Retardation.

Nowicki, S., & Duke, M.P. (1974). A locus of control scale for non-college as well as college adults. *Journal of Personality Assessment, 38,* 136–137.

Oatley, K. (1978). *Perceptions and representations: The theoretical bases of brain research and psychology.* London: Methuen.

Pierce, T.B., Luckasson, R., & Smith, D.D. (1990). Surveying unstructured time of adults with mental retardation living in two community settings: A search for normalization. *Exceptionality, 1,* 123–134.

Platt, J., & Spivack, G. (1989). *The MEPS procedure manual.* Philadelphia: Department of Mental Health Services, Hahnemann University.

Premack, D., & Woodruff, G. (1978). Does the chimpanzee have a theory of mind? *Behaviour and Brain Sciences, 1,* 516–526.

Schalock, R.L. (1990). Attempts to conceptualize and measure quality of life. In R.L. Schalock (Ed.), *Quality of life: Perspectives and issues* (pp. 141–148). Washington, DC: American Association on Mental Retardation.

Schalock, R.L., Keith, K.D., Hoffman, K., & Karan, O.C. (1989). Quality of life: Its measurement and use. *Mental Retardation, 27,* 25–31.

Sigafoos, A.D., Feinstein, C.B., Damond, M., & Reiss, D. (1988). The measurement of behavioral autonomy in adolescence: The Autonomous Functioning Checklist. *Adolescent Psychiatry, 15,* 433–462.

Sinclair, M.F., & Christenson, S.L. (1992). Home-school collaboration: A building block of empowerment. *IMPACT Feature Issue on Family Empowerment, 5*(2), 12–13.

Sinnott-Oswald, M., Gliner, J.A., & Spencer, K.C. (1991). Supported and sheltered employment: Quality of life issues among workers with disabilities. *Education and Training in Mental Retardation, 26,* 388–397.

St. Peter, S., Field, S., & Hoffman, A. (1992). *Self-determination: A literature review and synthesis.* Detroit, MI: Wayne State University, Developmental Disabilities Institute.

Wagner, M., Newman, L., D'Amico, R., Jay, E.D., Butler-Nalin, P., Marder, C., & Cox, R. (1991). *The first comprehensive report from the national longitudinal transition study of special education students.* Menlo Park, CA: SRI International.

Ward, M.J. (1988). The many facets of self-determination. *National Information Center for Children and Youth with Handicaps: Transition Summary, 5,* 2–3.

Wehmeyer, M.L. (1992a). Self-determination and the education of students with mental retardation. *Education and Training in Mental Retardation, 27,* 303–314.

Wehmeyer, M.L. (1992b). Self-determination: Critical skills for outcome-oriented transition services. *The Journal for Vocational Special Needs Education, 15,* 3–7.

Wehmeyer, M.L. (1993a). Gender differences in locus of control scores for students with learning disabilities. *Perceptual and Motor Skills, 77,* 359–366.

Wehmeyer, M.L. (1993b). Perceptual and psychological factors in career decision-making of adolescents with and without cognitive disabilities. *Career Development for Exceptional Individuals, 16,* 135–146.

Wehmeyer, M.L. (1994a). Employment status and perceptions of control of adults with cognitive and developmental disabilities. *Research in Developmental Disabilities, 15,* 119–131.

Wehmeyer, M.L. (1994b). Perceptions of self-determination and psychological empowerment of adolescents with mental retardation. *Education and Training in Mental Retardation, 29,* 9–21.

Wehmeyer, M.L., & Berkobien, R. (1991). Self-determination and self-advocacy: A case of mistaken identity. *TASH Newsletter, 17*(7), 4.

Wehmeyer, M.L., & Kelchner, K. (1994). Interpersonal cognitive problem-solving skills of individuals with mental retardation. *Education and Training in Mental Retardation and Developmental Disabilities, 29,* 265–278.

Wehmeyer, M.L., Kelchner, K., & Richards, S. (in press-a). Essential characteristics of self-determined behavior of individuals with mental retardation and developmental disabilities. *American Journal of Mental Retardation.*

Wehmeyer, M.L., Kelchner, K., & Richards, S. (in press-b). Individual and environmental factors related to the self-determination of adults with mental retardation. *Journal of Vocational Rehabilitation.*

Wehmeyer, M.L., & Metzler, C.A. (1995). How self-determined are people with mental retardation? The National Consumer Survey. *Mental Retardation, 33,* 111–119.

Whitman, T.L. (1990). Self-regulation and mental retardation. *American Journal on Mental Retardation, 94,* 347–362.

Zimmerman, M.A. (1990). Toward a theory of learned hopefulness: A structural model analysis of participation and empowerment. *Journal of Research in Personality, 24,* 71–86.

7

Self-Esteem and Learning Disabilities

An Exploration of Theories of the Self

Bridget Smith-Horn and George H.S. Singer

Powers, Singer, and Sowers (see Chapter 1) have cogently argued that self-esteem, coping, and self-determination have an impact on self-competence. In this chapter we focus on the first of these factors, self-esteem, which has a long and controversial history in psychology and education. Despite this rocky history, which has led some researchers to conclude that self-esteem is too vague and unmeasurable to yield any useful or consistent research results (Wylie, 1974), self-esteem persists as a focus for new studies and is a highly popular target for intervention in education and psychology (Mruk, 1995). In this chapter we concern ourselves with self-esteem in middle school children with learning disabilities. We use the findings from a comprehensive quantitative and qualitative study of 20 children with learning disabilities as a basis for discussing some of the key issues related to self-esteem.

The preparation of this chapter was supported, in part, by Grant No. H023T80013-90 from the U.S. Department of Education, Office of Special Education Programs (OSEP). The opinions expressed herein are exclusively those of the authors, and no official endorsement by OSEP should be inferred.

DOES SELF-ESTEEM MATTER?

Why bother with self-esteem in regard to children with disabilities? Is self-esteem important, or should parents, teachers, and psychologists devote their energies to other more important targets for intervention? Anyone who lectures on self-esteem to audiences of teachers or parents encounters the belief that self-esteem somehow should be at the core of the mission of special education. If we were to consider this common view of the importance of self-esteem in terms of statistics, we would expect to find high correlations between self-esteem and major life outcomes such as job success, mental health, and well-being; but the literature on self-esteem rarely offers clear, unequivocal findings. More often than not, the correlations between scores on common self-esteem measures and other outcomes are low. Smelser (1989) summed up the literature by noting that the most consistent finding is that associations between self-esteem and expected consequences are mixed, insignificant, or absent. In the 1970s, Wylie filled two large volumes with reviews of the literature on self-esteem and came to the conclusion that researchers should abandon the topic because it simply did not yield any consistent or useful findings (Wylie, 1974). Despite the thumbs-down reviews, thousands of studies have been produced since these reviews were published; and dozens of new interventions for children and adults have been developed. New popular books on self-esteem appear frequently.

Whenever there is a big gap between what people commonly believe and what research indicates, there are at least two major possibilities: common sense is flawed, or the research is flawed. Both errors have happened before in social science and in the beliefs of the general public. People are not very good at accurately estimating the risks of getting a disease like AIDS as compared with the risk of being injured in a car accident or getting hit by lightning. Researchers believed for several years that people who are grieving go through a series of emotional stages on their way to a resolution of grief, but research has gradually rejected this idea. It has been found that some people have relatively little reaction to loss, whereas up to a third of widows may never resolve their grief and may never or may only rarely experience the presumed stages. Is the idea that self-esteem matters for children with disabilities one of these two kinds of mistakes? Or, more basically, is the idea that self-esteem matters in life a mistaken view?

FAILURE EXPERIENCES AND SELF-ESTEEM

The general muddle in this line of research has prompted some social scientists to come up with new ways of thinking about self-esteem and new ways of testing its importance. These more recent lines of work converge around the importance of failure experiences and negative feedback in respect to self-evaluation. Initial findings from this approach have yielded clearer findings than has previous work. Brown and colleagues have published an elegant set of studies regarding the impact of self-esteem on the way people respond to failure (see, e.g., Brown & Smart, 1991). They used experimental situations to compare how college students with normal and low self-esteem respond to failure at tasks. Both groups of students were given the same set of tasks to perform. Some of the problems were designed to be unsolvable to ensure that the students would inevitably encounter failure. After failing, they were then offered the choice of doing an easy task or trying again at a more difficult one. The students with low self-esteem consistently avoided the hard task once they experienced failure, whereas the students with high self-esteem tried again with the more difficult tasks. Thus, a teacher could sort a room full of young adults into those who would or would not evaluate themselves low on a common measure of self-esteem; and the teacher could then predict fairly well how these two groups of people would respond to a failure experience.

Brown et al. also tested the impact of failure experience on the way that people with low or high self-esteem present themselves to others after experiencing a failure. In this experiment, young adults were again given tasks that resulted in failure. A second student was then introduced to the first and was given the same hard tasks. The students with high self-esteem tried to help the newcomer with the task, even though they had just failed at it; whereas the students with low self-esteem did not try to help and again avoided involvement with something that had led to failure. Low self-esteem was linked to social withdrawal when failure was involved.

Other researchers have also focused on the importance of dealing with failure experiences in understanding self-esteem. Bednar, Wells, and Peterson (1989) approached the issue from a clinical perspective. He argues that low self-esteem is a common underlying problem in most psychological problems. A recent review of the literature supports Bednar's point; Skager and Kerst (1989) concluded that "There is no doubt that self-esteem is central in the consciousness of the troubled human being. Psychotherapists report that those who seek help typically suffer from low self-esteem" (p. 250). Bednar goes on to build the case that the key to a positive sense of self-esteem is active coping with negative experiences. He believes that avoidance of failure situations or negative information about the self results in low self-esteem whereas active efforts to learn from failure or to grapple with negative feedback enable people to develop a realistic and positive sense of self-worth.

Bednar and his colleagues attribute particular importance to the way people process negative feedback. They argue that negative feedback from the social environment is both commonplace and inevitable. If a person perceives these negative inputs rather than filtering them out and then actively evaluates and deals with the negative information, they argue that he or she is more likely to develop an internally consistent and honest positive sense of self-worth. By contrast, if a person copes with negative feedback through avoidance or ineffective tactics, he or she is more likely to put up a false front and then, in time, to disbelieve his or her own mask.

One particular effort to manage or avoid negative judgment from others involves efforts to please others:

> If people continually present themselves to others in ways that are artificially designed to be pleasing, then any interpersonal feedback about their pleasing qualities will be a reflection of the facade they have presented rather than the enduring qualities of the personality. (Bednar et al., 1989, p. 102)

They go on to assert that avoidance strengthens people's beliefs that they cannot handle threatening information. Avoidance does not provide an opportunity for learning new or adaptive response patterns by actively trying, and thus it contributes to a sense of disconnection between one's effort and outcomes. Bednar's view of self-esteem is consistent with Brown's experimental findings that people with low self-esteem do not persist in the face of failure and make efforts to avoid further failure.

This theory suggests a different tactic for improving a student's sense of self-worth. An educational application of Bednar's approach to the self would focus on the situations that provide negative and threatening feedback to children, and, rather than shielding them from these experiences, it would arm them with strategies for preventing these experiences or realistically dealing with them when they occur. This theory would then emphasize the importance of teaching children academic and social skills that help them prevent failure, but would also help teach them ways to grapple with and learn from failure experiences. Bednar and colleagues (1989) believe that self-esteem is improved the most when people face situations that they normally avoid and make realistic efforts to cope with them:

> We submit, then, that a sense of self-appreciation is primarily a reflection of one's tendency to choose coping over avoidance when faced with conflicts that involve fear and anxiety. It is, secondarily, a reflection of the way one is perceived by others. (p. 118)

If it is true that self-esteem is particularly important in regard to our relationship with failure or negative feedback, then we can begin to see why educators and parents are so commonly concerned about self-esteem in children with disability. By definition, disability involves unusual difficulty in accomplishing tasks, whether academic or social, in typical ways. This is not to say that people with disabilities do not or cannot accomplish goals when provided alternative means or supports, but simply that without accommodations many normal tasks are unusually difficult.

Children with learning disabilities encounter a major mismatch between their skills and the behavioral and academic expectations at school. In order to acquire the label *learning disabled*, they must fall dramatically behind their classmates in a major academic subject. On their way to attaining the label and placement in special education programs, by definition they experience repeated failure. It is therefore reasonable to assume that many children with learning disabilities suffer damage to their self-esteem and are at risk of developing a negative sense of themselves. The answer to the question "Why be concerned about self-esteem in children with disabilities?" is that self-esteem is intimately linked to how people cope with failure and negative feedback; and children with disabilities, given our imperfect world, must inevitably deal with a stiff dose of failure and negative social feedback.

Teachers are involved each day in creating the climate in which children spend approximately one fourth of their waking lives. Studies of school and teacher effectiveness have demonstrated that teachers and schools have a major impact on how students learn, behave, and feel about themselves (Good, 1979; Levine & Orenstein, 1993; Rosenshine, 1978). Landry and Edeburn (1974) found that as children become older and progress through the grades, they often develop poorer self-esteem and negative attitudes toward school.

SELF-ESTEEM IN ADOLESCENTS WITH LEARNING DISABILITIES

The development of self-esteem is particularly difficult with the transition into adolescence. Mental, physical, emotional, and social developmental changes are compounded by environmental changes that students confront as they move from elementary into middle or junior high schools. Simmons, Rosenberg, and Rosenberg (1973) found a decrease in self-esteem between the ages of 12 and 13 and hypothesized that the shift to junior high school was the primary factor responsible. These findings were reinforced by Connell (1981) and Harter and Connell (1982), who discovered that the scores on a scale of perceived competence dropped during the first year of junior high school. Similarly Powers, Singer, and Todis (see Chapter 4) found that adults with physical disabilities recounted that early adolescence was an unusually difficult time when they were forced to cope with social rejection and stigma. Bednar et al. (1989) insisted that the sheer number of threatening evaluation experiences in school may make the institution as powerful a force in shaping self-esteem as the parents. These developmental and environmental changes put demands on the adolescent that can cause heightened self-consciousness, an instable self-image, and lowered self-esteem. This is particularly true of at-risk students with learning disabilities. Hargreaves (1982) found that many schools do not treat students at lower academic levels with dignity and that students respond by rejecting the schooling process.

Young adolescent students with learning disabilities are a population at risk for low self-esteem and a limited sense of self-determination. In our work with these students, we have noted that adolescents with seemingly high self-esteem appeared to view school positively and see the resource room as exactly that—a "resource" room where they could develop the skills necessary to perform at grade level. They also interacted positively with peers and teachers. Students with learning disabilities seemed to have a low general self-concept as well as low self-concept in particular subject areas. Associated with low self-esteem appeared to be other problems such as procrastination, blaming others, or insisting they didn't care about the consequences of negative school behavior. Many of these students with learning disabilities entered a cycle of failure that led to their dropping out of school mentally and emotionally while they still attended physically. These students often became dropouts during the high school years. But are these informal impressions correct?

Is it true that children with learning disabilities experience lower self-esteem than do children without learning disabilities? Once again we encounter some of the puzzles about self-esteem research that we discussed earlier. We would expect to find clear, strong associations between learning disabilities and low self-esteem, but these relationships often do not show up in individual studies and appear consistent only when many small studies are combined to paint a more general picture. It is widely believed that children with learning disabilities suffer negative psychological effects from their disability (Prout, Marcal, & Marcal, 1992). Teachers and clinicians have described the stigma that adheres to many children who fall drastically behind in academic work, and educators have recommended that the self-concept of the child with learning disabilities should be a focal point for educational interventions (Levine & Orenstein, 1993). When looked at one at a time, however, research studies on self-esteem and other self-reported psychological states have been equivocal regarding whether these children do indeed suffer from a damaged sense of self. Zigmond and Thornton (1988) reviewed studies comparing adolescents with and without learning disabilities on general measures of self-concept. They found that most studies did not arrive at statistically significant differences between the two groups. This kind of literature review would make us think that we are chasing a mirage and that the common sense idea that children who have serious difficulty in school have lower self-esteem is not true. Again we encounter the two major possibilities: Common sense is wrong, or the research is flawed.

A study by Prout et al. (1992) suggests that the problem may be more with the research than with common sense. Prout et al. clarify these findings by using meta-analytic methods, a way of determining the size of the difference between the two groups of children. Traditional statistical comparisons can hide a condition that is in fact present in a group if the number of subjects in the studies is small or if the condition is weak. One way to deal with this problem is to use statistical methods that allow the researcher to combine many studies and examine the strength of a condition with much larger numbers. Prout et al. (1992) reviewed 51 comparisons of students with and without learning disabilities ages 6–20. They found that when all of these studies were considered together, so that the total number of students was 1,202, children with learning disabilities did evaluate themselves lower in self-esteem than did children without disabilities. The size of the effect was .65, considered a moderate effect size, meaning that there is a consistent trend in the direction of low self-esteem for students with learning disabilities. The children also rated themselves more negatively on measures of locus of control and anxiety. An effect size of .65 indicates that there is a difference between the two groups of children on measures of self-esteem, but that there are also many children with learning disabilities who do not have low self-esteem.

ASSESSING SELF-ESTEEM AND ITS MEASUREMENT

If teachers and psychologists commonly believe that children with learning disabilities have low self-esteem, what accounts for the fact that many of these children do not seem to rate themselves in ways that are consistent with adult observations? There are at least two possible answers to this question: We don't know how to measure self-esteem, or teachers and psychologists are not accurate in judging how children with disabilities evaluate themselves. We set out to answer this question with a quantitative and qualitative study of children with learning disabilities in a middle school. We also wanted to learn whether there was a correlation between direct observations of children's interactions with teachers and peers and their self-esteem. Finally, we wanted to know whether we would find the relationship that Brown and Smart (1991) and Bednar et al. (1989) predicted between how children react to failure and their self-esteem.

The subjects for this study consisted of 20 middle school students with learning disabilities, 10 girls and 10 boys, from four middle schools in a single school district in the Pacific Northwest. The students were Caucasian, except for one African American student and one Native American student.

The school district is located in a town of approximately 40,000 people, many of whom are blue collar workers in the logging and wood products industry. At the time of the study the town was recovering from a recession and facing mill closures and employment cutbacks. As a consequence, many of the study group lived in poverty.

The 20 students in the study group were chosen from the population of students with mild learning disabilities, as determined by their individualized education program (IEP) status. Much of the data in the study were obtained by observing and interviewing these students. Of the 20 students, 10 were identified by their teachers as having high self-esteem and 10 as having low self-esteem.

The study also gathered data from the teaching staff: five resource room teachers, one resource room aide, and one regular language arts classroom teacher. These people will be referred to here as teachers.

It was also necessary to gather data from the students' classmates because they make up a vital part of the students' social network, and their interactions with the student are thought to be key determinants of the self-esteem of the study group students.

The research was conducted to learn why some children with disabilities grow up to be happy, well-adjusted adults while many others are passive, unmotivated, and unwilling to take advantage of vocational opportunities and community resources which are increasingly available to them.

The study collected a variety of behavioral data to use as a basis for interviews with the 20 students. This approach is important because, historically, self-esteem research has been restricted by the lack of suitable methods of assessment, especially with young children. Prior research has relied heavily upon behavioral observations made by others when the investigation of self-concept necessarily depends on self-report.

In contrast to earlier research that has relied solely on observation, this study combined data collection strategies of observation and interviewing. These strategies allowed students to report the content of their perceptions that referred directly to the subjective experiences that comprise self-concept itself. The first author gathered observational data from the 20 students, their teachers, and their peers in selected behavioral and environmental areas that appear to be related to the development of student self-esteem. We used this observational data in interviews with these students and the teachers in order to search for relationships between the observations and the ways in which students and teachers reported the student's self-esteem.

TEACHER UNDERSTANDING OF
SELF-ESTEEM OF STUDENTS WITH LEARNING DISABILITIES

We asked middle-school teachers of students with learning disabilities to rate their students on several behavioral dimensions that are believed to underlie how middle school–age children evaluate themselves (Harter, 1990). In order to investigate differences between teachers' evaluations and the children's self-evaluations, we used two measures that have a virtually complete overlap in content. The children were asked to complete the Self-Perception Profile for Children (Harter, 1985), a 32-item questionnaire that asks children to rate themselves on the dimensions of behavioral conduct, physical appearance, social acceptance, athletic competence, scholastic competence, and global self-worth. We also asked resource room teachers who had primary responsibility for these 20 children to rate them on the same dimensions using a parallel measure by Harter (1985), the Teacher's Rating of Child's Actual Behavior.

True to the pattern in the literature, the teachers rated the children as below the midpoint on the measure, indicating that they generally rated the children low in the areas that are thought to contribute to a child's self-concept. By contrast, the children rated themselves at above the midpoint, indicating that they did not have the low self-esteem that their school difficulties might lead us to believe. Furthermore, there were only low correlations between the teacher's ratings and the children's ratings on all of the domains except behavioral conduct, where students and teachers concurred. In order to find out why the teachers and the children have these different perceptions, the first author interviewed the children and their teachers about each of the domains on the Self-Perception Profile for Children Inventory. A close look at these qualitative findings helps paint a picture of the differences between what teachers perceive and what children perceive. They also offer vivid insights into how these children think about themselves.

CLARIFICATION OF TEACHER–STUDENT
DIFFERENCES THROUGH INTERVIEW DATA

The interview data often helped to explain otherwise confusing and inconsistent findings in the quantitative data. The examples here illustrate the different interpretations made by students and teachers in rating students' self-esteem. On the Social Acceptance subscale, for example, one student interpreted the term *friend* to mean neighborhood friends in a town where he used to live. The student used a completely different reference group to gauge his social standing than did the teacher. Another student referred to his age-mate relatives as his best friends. In both instances, the teachers who evaluated the students' self-esteem referred to resource room classmates when discussing these students' friends. In these instances, the children and the teachers had very different points of reference. The children thought about positive relationships outside of school, connections that were out of the teachers' view.

Quality was also an issue. One student thought having friends meant having 15 or 20 and rated himself lower than the teacher did. To another student, having two friends meant he had friends. The number did not matter to other students. Some thought having friends meant that they had to have popular, athletic, or smart children as friends. In these examples, the teachers and children had differing standards about what the term *friend* meant when they answered questions about how good the child was at making friends.

Another important disparity occurred between the student and teacher responses in their choice of a comparison group for the Scholastic Competence subscale. The students' frame of reference was often regular mainstreamed students and/or the requirements of regular mainstream classes, whereas the teachers' frame of reference was the students' resource room peers and/or the resource class requirements.

The students often tended to base their responses on a specific experience, whereas the teachers used a general evaluation based upon observations of several experiences. For example, one student said he was pleased with himself because he can jump, another because she can babysit well. In contrast, the teachers had a more general perspective of the students' year-long competence in the school setting. Some of the teachers based their judgments on 3 years of student–teacher interaction.

Some students gave socially acceptable answers that did not coincide with their behavior. For example, one boy said that when people say or do something hurtful, he goes to them and says, "That wasn't nice," or "That wasn't called for." The first author had observed him in four physically aggressive confrontations and several negative verbal exchanges during one lunch period, calling into question the veracity of the child's report.

Another source of the disparity in ratings seemed to derive from the way some students fantasized that they were more socially competent than others thought them to be. For example, one student claimed to have enough friends and said that no one had ever said or done anything to hurt him. His teacher said, however, that he had a lot of difficulty with peers: "He is seen as not attractive to peers. He is overweight, has acne, and visible tooth decay. He does not take care of himself. He wears old shoes, his clothes are not always clean, and he does not smell good. He is not seen as a cool kid and others will often give him a hard time, calling him 'scuz ball.'" In this case the child's self-evaluation appeared to be defensive, perhaps a kind of protection against a reality that he otherwise would feel helpless to change.

Students often demonstrated an inconsistency between their test responses and their subsequent comments. For example, two students who had indicated in the written test that they had only limited difficulty in making friends went on to say, "Nobody likes me" and "No one wants to see my side."

Finally, students' verbal ability clearly influenced how they interpreted and responded to the test items. An example of one student's confused and convoluted comments occurred in response to a question about having friends. He indicated that it was sort of true that he had a lot of friends, but then commented, "I don't have a lot, but I don't really have very many. I don't have a few but I have a lot."

Social acceptance was a very sensitive area for students to rate and discuss. Students tended to be inconsistent, rating themselves higher than their own comments would suggest. A student and teacher both responded that it was "sort of true" that the student had difficulty making friends, and the student commented, "It's quite a bit hard to make friends. No one ever listens to me and they don't understand. I don't know why, and the way I look sometimes—they don't want to see what kind of person I am. So I can't really make that many friends."

A teacher indicated that it was "really true," and her student "sort of true," that the student had difficulty making friends; and yet the student commented, "It is always hard to make friends. I wish I had a lot more friends, cooler kids. I wish kids that were good at sports and smart would be my friends." For this student, the issue was his inability to make friends with the high-status children.

Another area of student and teacher difference in perspective resulted from students' fantasy or difficulty in discerning ideal self-image from real self. A teacher indicated that a student had some difficulty in making friends, but the student indicated that she made friends easily: "There are so many girls I love for friends. I'd say around twenty." But school observations suggested that she was essentially alone or interacting minimally on the periphery of a group and had friends as long as she had candy to share. It appeared that she used the word "friends" to mean acquaintances and confused her wish for friends with the reality of their friendship.

The following example illustrates how very differently a student and his teacher interpreted the question. The teacher rated difficulty in making friends as "really true," and the student rated ease with making friends as "really true," saying "Right now I have only two. I can live with only two. This is the longest I've ever kept a friend before I had to move. We moved three times last year. Sometimes there are also two girls that are my friends if they are interested in playing around." For this child, his criteria for what made up friendship appeared to be different from the teacher's.

One teacher indicated that it was "sort of true" that a student wasn't very good when it came to sports, adding "I am not familiar at all with this child's sports, games, or activities." However, the student rated himself as doing really well at all kinds of sports, saying, "I'm best at playing softball, soccer, basketball, and Nintendo. I ride my skateboard good and jump my bike good and I can [bike] ride down Big Mama and Dynamite Hills real good." He used his out-of-school physical activities in judging himself, whereas the teacher had limited access even to his school athletic experience. Thus, sometimes teachers were asked to rate domains for which not only did they have different information from what was relevant to the children, but they also did not have much information at all to serve as the basis of a judgment.

Another teacher indicated that it was "sort of true" that the student was unable to play as well as others of his age at sports, whereas the student thought it "sort of true" that he was better than others of his age at sports, commenting that he long jumps and high jumps on the track team.

A third teacher indicated that it was "sort of true" that the student was not very good at sports. Conversely, the student felt that it was "really true" that he could do very well at all kinds of sports, saying, "My favorite sport is baseball and my favorite position is batting." Once again, the teacher and student were making ratings based upon different degrees of knowledge of a sport. They do not have the same frame of reference.

In summary, it appears that one reason the literature finds only moderate correlations between how teachers and other adults believe children with learning disabilities feel about their self-worth and the children's own ratings of self-esteem is that children and teachers do not have the same referents in mind when they make evaluations. The children take into account their whole experience in school and outside of school, whereas the teachers have a more narrow frame of reference. Furthermore, the children often seem to use protective self-evaluative strategies that may serve to filter out some of the failure that they often experience in school.

RELATIONSHIP BETWEEN TEACHER EVALUATIONS AND CHILDREN SELF-EVALUATIONS OF OBSERVABLE ACADEMIC BEHAVIOR

Our finding that children and teachers are not talking about the same thing when they estimate children's competence of self-esteem measures is bolstered by another one of our findings. The one area where teachers and students concurred concerned the child's behavioral conduct. As part of our quantitative study, we gathered data on the percentage of time that children were engaged in academic work. We thought that this measure of on-task behavior would be a good general indicator of the child's behavioral conduct in the classroom. We found that for the students who had the most difficulty with behavioral conduct that there was a high degree of agreement between the teacher's ratings, the child's self-evaluation, and our direct observations.

The two students who had the lowest percentage of academic engaged time, 38.4% and 49.9%, were both given consistently low behavioral ratings on the test items. The teacher interviews reinforced these findings. For example, one teacher described the student with 38.4% academic engaged time as

> A kid that needs to take the time to get himself centered and sometimes he can't do that with the groups. His social skills are not there....He does not know what is appropriate about making contact with other children. Very gross types of behavior—things from picking his nose to taking his shoes off. He has poor hygiene and flaunts the poor hygiene for attention and he does not seem to care that the attention is negative....He passes gas a lot and giggles, thinking it is funny. So that makes it hard for kids to like him and while he is doing this, he is also hitting, hands on, not real violent, but he has. There are things in his records where he has hit kids (stabbed a kid) with a screwdriver in shop this year, so he has that explosive streak.

A different teacher described the student who was academically engaged 49.9% of the time as a student who

> Does not like to do his work. He is so distractible that it is hard for him to do his work. If there are distractions in the room, that is what he focuses on....You usually have to go to him (instead of him raising his hand). He requires reinforcement and follow through because he won't stay on task unless you get to him several times....He is one of my most frustrating students. His on task is so low. He is so distractible. He can be so defiant and so angry....He shows a lot of classical L.D. behavior—leaving things, misplacing things (coat). When he loses something, he will just interrupt the whole class in the middle of instruction to look for it. He has a lot of confusion—time confusion and space confusion combined with other severe behavior problems. Some improvement in being less rude, more polite to teachers and students. Gets so little done that no academic improvement has shown.

The teachers' ratings of the student behavioral conduct correlated significantly ($r = 0.52$, $p = .009$) with the percentage of time the students were engaged in positive interaction during instruction. This relationship was especially evident in the students who had the highest percentage of positive interaction.

Representative teachers commented regarding the four students who were observed in positive interaction 86% of the time and above. The first student was described as "good at making sure her work is done" and as having "a sense of humor and caring." The second student was said to be

A great girl....rarely has a missing assignment....kid with high self-esteem, yet she is a low performer in some cases. She is a success story....In order to stay out of the resource room, she has picked herself up.

The third student was described as

Conscientious since the first of the year....Has a good sense of humor....draws pictures for the teacher and likes the teacher's written comments....Pretty compliant....Into the academic part of it more than most of my students and wants to have good grades. Works hard whenever....Is very organized and likes being ready.

The fourth student was also spoken of highly:

She has gotten a 90% for the last four weeks on getting her homework in and being on time.

Representative teacher comments about two students who scored lower in positive social interaction and who were both on behavior modification programs also underscore the high correlation between teacher and student ratings. One student was described behaviorally as having difficulty in these areas:

Following directions, doing the work quickly, without comment, positive or negative....chit-chatting with himself. He does not realize how much he affects others.

The other student was said to be

on a daily program with me where she can earn a chance award for being to class on time and having her work done. Until I set this program up, we were in a constant you don't have this, you don't have this....She denies any wrong doing or correction....[She does] things that require the least amount of effort. I don't think she really knows "try hard."

As mentioned earlier, the teachers and the students concurred about their behavioral conduct more than on any other dimension measured by the self-esteem instrument. The children's rating of their own behavioral conduct and the teachers' ratings correlated at a moderate to high level ($r = .63$, $p < .05$). This was the only significant correlation between teacher and student ratings on the Harter instrument. Based upon our observations of children during academic work, it appears that both students and teachers are referring to behavioral conduct that involves learning tasks in the classroom as their main indicator of how well they meet behavioral expectations at school. It appears that when children and teachers are asked to rate the students' behavioral conduct, both groups have the same referent in mind: the way the child behaves during academic instruction.

PEER RELATIONSHIPS AND CHILDREN'S SELF-ESTEEM

One prominent theory of self-esteem emphasizes the role of evaluations by significant others as the source of self-evaluation. Scholars such as Cooley (1902), Mead (1934), Allport (1961), Adler (1979), and Bandura (1986) followed this traditional approach, emphasizing social and interpersonal learning. These scholars stressed the importance of the level of acceptance in the social environment and the role of significant others in determining one's self-esteem. They described self-concept in terms of "the looking glass self"; that is, they posited that self-concept was based upon internalization of evaluations from others. Mead in particular emphasized the importance of significant others, those people who are the most important source of feedback about the self. Because middle school children are extremely concerned about peer relationships, this group of self-concept theories would predict that children's self-esteem in middle school would be strongly related to the way they are treated by their same-age peers. In contrast, other theorists (Bednar et al., 1989; Harter, 1988; James, 1890; May, 1983; Rogers, 1951) did not consider psychological factors external to the individual as an adequate basis for understanding the development of self-esteem and believed a broader conceptual foundation that included an internal evaluation was necessary.

In order to test the Cooley–Mead theory of self-esteem in regard to middle school–age children with learning disabilities, we examined the relationship between the children's self-evaluations and their observed interactions with other children on the playground as well as the way that other children rated them using sociometric ratings. The self-assessment again used the Harter Self-Perception Profile for Children. Direct observations of children at lunch hour were collected with the Peer Social Behavior Observation System, an interval coding measure that rates children according to whether they are engaged with peers or not and whether the interaction is positive or negative. The system yields two scores, a percentage of total intervals in which interaction is observed and a percentage of intervals in which those interactions are positive or negative. In order to measure peer acceptance, we used a standard sociometric rating procedure in which children were asked to nominate the three people they most prefer. The number of nominations was counted for each of the target children with learning disabilities. The peer group that we used for collecting sociometric ratings was determined by where the child spent the greatest percentage of his or her school day. Thus, 18 children were evaluated by peers in the resource room, and 2 were evaluated by typical class peers.

The direct observations of interactions did not yield any strong correlations among self-ratings of social competence or self-esteem of the children with learning disabilities. A moderately high correlation of $r = 0.49$ ($p = .05$) was found between the way children rated themselves on the Harter Social Acceptance subscale and peer sociometric ratings. Thus, peer ratings were a better indicator of how children rated themselves for social competence than were the direct observational data. It is likely that our direct observations did not sample enough of the children's interactions to paint a full picture of their social world. However, ratings by peers did correlate with self-evaluations of social competence, suggesting that the children with learning disabilities evaluated themselves in a way consistent with the reflected self-perceptions of self-esteem.

The direct observations of the children's social interactions at lunch correlated moderately with the teachers' rating of children's behavioral conduct. Once again, these findings suggest that teachers base their judgments on observation of children's behavior in the settings where they have access to the children. The teachers' ratings of children's physical appearance also correlated significantly ($r = .51$, $p < .05$) with peer sociometric ratings. Appearance has an important impact on peer relationships, and it seems that the teachers were aware of which children met or did not meet the local cultural standards for attractiveness.

Again these findings were further substantiated in the qualitative interview data. About the four students who interacted positively with the peers 86% of the time or more, the teachers who rated the students made the following comments. One teacher said,

> She seems to have quite a few friends. There are the usual girl fights. 'I hate you' on one day and 'I love you' the next....She has a peer group that she runs with....She runs with girls that are not in the resource room and tends to act rather normal. She feels best about herself at school as a result of having friends and being out in the halls and socializing.

Another teacher noted how one of the high-scoring children was very involved in the social world of her peers and how, despite difficulties in interaction, she maintained a friendship with a high-status peer:

[She has] sixth grade-itis. Girl fights, verbal abuse. Doesn't feel as smart and tries to snow them into thinking she is....Her best friend is a talented and gifted student so they work together.

A third student was described as follows:

In class she prefers to work alone but socializes on the way into class....I have never seen kids act negatively toward her.

The teacher commented about the fourth child:

She has friends....She was in the track meet yesterday with the regular sixth graders. That was important to her....She is so social.

On the other end of the continuum, the two students who were observed interacting positively with peers only 37% of the time or less were described in an opposite light by the teachers. A student who scored 37% was described this way by his teacher:

[He] needs to take the time to get himself centered and sometimes he can't do that with the group. Usually, he will follow the directions. Sometimes he is not ready, so I tell him to take his test to "time out" and when he can take it with the group to come out....He does not have very many friends at all, only one boy, and the last time I had a conversation with them, they were on the outs. If he has a friend, he tends to overpower the friend. He is so outside the group of what is going on, not belonging...not having friends...not made to feel a part of....

A student who scored 24% on positive social action was described by her teacher as having a tough time with peers:

She doesn't have friends in the resource group. She has higher social skills but uses them in a negative way....I think she wishes someone would come back to the table [and work] with her but they don't.

These teachers were perceptive about children's peer interactions for those students in particular who had either very high or very low levels of engagement with peers. The teachers also had some sense of how peers rated their students for social acceptance.

The pattern of interrelationships among peer interaction, peer acceptance, and self-evaluation suggests that the looking glass theory of self-esteem does describe an important part of how children with learning disabilities evaluate themselves. These findings suggest that interventions aimed at improving social acceptance of children could be useful in improving self-esteem in children with learning disabilities.

TEACHERS' TREATMENT OF CHILDREN WITH DISABILITIES AND CHILDREN'S SELF-ESTEEM

A further test of the Cooley–Mead theory of self-esteem would examine the relationship between how teachers interact with children and how these children rate themselves. In order to directly measure teacher behavior, we used the Adapted Direct Instruction Observation System (ADIOS) (Englert & Sugai, 1981). ADIOS is a direct-observation coding system in which an observer codes the interactions between a teacher and a single student during instructional sessions. It measures the percentage of time that the teacher engages the child in direct teaching through giving information, asking questions, and providing feedback. It also measures the student's accuracy in answering questions. The measure yields classroom "climate" scores, the percentage of time in which the teacher engages positively with the student (climate 1), the percentage of time in which the teacher gives positive feedback (climate 2), and the percentage of time in which the teacher gives negative feedback or reprimands (climate 3). The Cooley–Mead theory of self-concept would predict a positive correlation between the first two classroom climates and a negative correlation with the negative climate. Our findings generally supported this prediction. We found modest positive correlations between how the children rated themselves and the amount of positively toned direct instruction they received from their teachers (climate 1). For example, children's global self-worth correlated at a level of $r = .29$ with percentage of intervals of positive direct instruction. Furthermore, negative interactions with teachers (climate 3) correlated negatively with the children's self-evaluations. For example, the children's total score on the Self-Perception Profile for Children correlated at $r = -.34$ with percentage of time in climate 3, the climate marked by negative teacher behavior. Children's global self-worth correlated at $r = -.47$ with negative teacher interactions. These findings suggest that the way teachers relate to their students with learning disabilities is associated with children's self-esteem.

COPING WITH FAILURE OR DIFFICULTY AND SELF-ESTEEM

We were particularly interested in exploring the relevance of the Bednar theory of self-esteem to children with learning disabilities. As discussed earlier, children with disabilities must cope with some task failure and negative social interactions directly related to their differences. Bednar's theory suggests that students' ways of coping with these experiences is central to their self-concept. In order to explore this issue, the first author administered a coping questionnaire to the teachers and interviewed teachers and children about how the students cope with difficult school experiences.

Teachers completed Zeitlin's Coping Inventory Measure of Adaptive Behavior, a 48-item rating scale designed to evaluate how children cope with self and with the environment. We found high positive correlations between the teachers' ratings of children's coping and the teachers' estimations of children's competence in areas related to self-esteem ($r = .73$, $p < .05$). Because it is unclear that the Coping Inventory effectively measures how children specifically deal with threatening failure experiences, we designed a six-item interview questionnaire that the first author administered to teachers and children. We asked how the children coped with the following situations: 1) a class assignment is too difficult, 2) the student cannot read something, 3) the student cannot do a homework assignment, 4) a classmate says or does something that is hurtful, 5) the teacher seems unfair, and 6) classmates ignore overtures of friendships. The students' self reports generally concurred with the teachers' reports of how children coped with negative experiences. Furthermore, there was a clear pattern of association between ineffective coping responses and low self-esteem. The qualitative data give the clearest sense of this relationship.

The following selected comments from students and teachers indicate the flavor of these student–teacher responses. The first set of paired student–teacher comments comes from students and their teachers who agreed that the student has good coping skills.

How does the student cope when the class assignment is not understood?
Student: I just ask for help [from the mainstreamed classroom teacher] or bring it to my resource room teacher. I understand the teacher but, okay, it is not like you are normal and you know that, okay, I can do it. I'll have an A and straight, like that. It is not like that. Okay, they don't give enough information and all that, just like the resource room [teacher] does. For science and social studies, she gives more information and details, so I understand and the normal teachers don't.
Her teacher: I've seen her pout a couple of times, but I'm not even sure she would understand that she didn't understand. Usually I think she gives it her best shot. She might, if she doesn't understand, ask for help.
How does the student cope when the teacher seems unfair?
Student: Usually wait till I get home, go to my room, and think things over, start explaining to myself if it is fair or not fair, and I can usually live with it. If it hasn't gotten into the drastic category yet, try to work it out.
Her teacher: Doesn't seem to think teachers unfair...pretty compliant.

The second set of paired student–teacher comments comes from students and their teachers who agreed that the student has poor coping skills.

How does the student cope when the class assignment is not understood?
Student: I get mad, then I get a referral slip, then I get in trouble. [Interviewer says, "Say that again."] First I get mad, then I get frustrated, then I hit my desk, then I get kicked out of the room. [Interviewer asks, "Is that because the assignment is too hard?"] Yeah.
His teacher: He will throw his pencil or paper on the floor, say, "I can't do it. You are going too fast." Mostly, he does not take responsibility for his actions. He can stomp out of the room. He has only tossed a chair or desk once, but it was not at anybody, that kind of tantrum. Or he will pound on a table in time-out, make noises, sing, or peek around the time-out corner. I have a pretty good group that can ignore him most days.
How does the student cope when he or she can't do the assigned homework?
Student: I don't do it, nope.
His teacher: Not too much help at home. He pretty much does it. He may not do it, but it is not because he doesn't understand. He loses it or he doesn't have a structured time to do it, where you sit down and work.

The interviews revealed that sometimes children did not accurately report how they dealt with negative experiences. Bednar's theory would suggest that these kinds of avoidant or unrealistic responses are also likely to be associated with low self-esteem. Generally, the teachers evaluated these children as being less skilled than the children presented themselves to be:

How does the student cope when the class assignment is not understood?
Student: I stop and set back and relax for 2 or 3 minutes, then I go back to work.
Her teacher: She will get into stomping her feet or just staying away from school. Her attendance has been absolutely terrible. Teachers, friends, and mom are manipulated.

IMPLICATIONS OF FINDINGS FOR SCHOOL PRACTICES

Cooley's looking glass model, which emphasized internalized social feedback, suggests that one way to raise children's self-esteem would be to treat them with positive regard and create circumstances in which significant others would value them. This approach would stress improving the social climate at school.

Bednar's theory of self-esteem would suggest that teachers should teach children specific coping strategies for dealing with situations that are threatening to the self. The strategies would include effective social problem solving as well as ways of thinking about negative feedback. These coping skills would be added to the academic skills that are taught in effective resource room or consulting teacher models. Of course, these approaches are mutually compatible, and an effective school program for students with learning disabilities should not only teach skills and strategies but also create a positive social climate.

We began by analyzing the differences between how children with learning disabilities think of themselves and how their teachers evaluate them. We suggested that one of the reasons for generally low correlations between children's self-esteem and other variables is that we do not measure it very well. Children often have different referents in mind than do teachers when we ask them about friendship, athletic competence, and other important areas of their life. Perhaps the most important implication from this finding is that in our efforts to help children with disabilities to develop a positive sense of self-esteem, we need to work with their goals and experiences and adapt our interventions to make them meaningful in their lives as they experience them, not as others assume.

REFERENCES

Adler, A. (1979). *Superiority and social interest.* New York: Norton.

Allport, G.W. (1961). *Pattern and growth in personality.* New York: Holt, Rinehart & Winston.

Bandura, A. (1986). *Social foundation of thought and action: A social cognitive theory.* Englewood Cliffs, NJ: Prentice Hall.

Bednar, R.L., Wells, M.G., & Peterson, S.R. (1989). *Self-esteem: Paradoxes and innovations in clinical theory and practice.* Washington, DC: American Psychological Association.

Brown, J.D., & Smart, S.A. (1991). The self and social conduct: Linking self-representations to prosocial behaviors. *Journal of Personality and Social Psychology, 60*(3), 368–375.

Cooley, C.H. (1902). *Human nature and the social order.* New York: Scribner's.

Connell, J.P. (1981). *A model of the relationships among children's self-related cognitions, affects and academic achievement.* Unpublished doctoral dissertation, University of Denver, CO.

Good, T.L. (1979). Teacher effectiveness in the elementary school. *Journal of Teacher Education, 30*(2), 52–64.

Hargreaves, D. (1982). *The challenge for the comprehensive school.* London: Routledge and Kegan Paul.

Harter, S. (1985). *The self-perception profile for children: Revision of the perceived competence scale for children.* Unpublished manual. University of Denver, CO.

Harter, S. (1988). *The self-perception profile for adolescence.* Unpublished manual. University of Denver, CO.

Harter, S. (1990). Issues in the assessment of the self-concept of children and adolescents. In A. LaGreca (Ed.), *Childhood assessment: Through the eyes of a child* (pp. 1–42). Newton, MA: Allyn & Bacon.

Harter, S., & Connell, J. (1982). A comparison of alternative models of the relationships between academic achievement and children's perceptions of competence, control, and motivational orientation. In J. Nicholls (Ed.), *The development of achievement-related cognition and behaviors* (pp. 72–84). Greenwich, CT: JAI Press.

Harter, S., & Pike, R. (1984). The pictorial scale of perceived competence and social acceptance for young children. *Child Development, 55*(6), 1969–1982.

James, W. (1890). *Principles of psychology.* New York: Holt.

Landry, R., & Edeburn, C. (1974, April). *Teacher self-concept and student self-concept.* Paper presented at the American Educational Research Association Convention, Chicago.

Levine, D.V., & Orenstein, A.C. (1993). School effectiveness and national reform. *Journal of Teacher Education, 44,* 335–345.

May, R. (1983). *The discovery of being.* New York: Norton.

Mead, G.H. (1934). *Mind, self, and society.* Chicago: University of Chicago Press.

Mruk, C. (1995). *Self-esteem: Research, theory, and practice.* New York: Springer-Verlag.

Prout, H.T., Marcal, S.D., & Marcal, D.C. (1992). A meta-analysis of self-reported personality characteristics of children and adolescents with learning disabilities. *Journal of Psychoeducational Assessment, 10,* 59–64.

Rogers, C.R. (1951). *Client-centered therapy: Its current practice, implications, and theory.* Boston: Houghton Mifflin.

Rosenshine, B. (1978, March). *Instructional principles in direct instruction.* Paper presented at the annual meeting of the American Educational Research Association, Toronto.

Skager, R., & Kerst, E. (1989). Alcohol and drug use and self-esteem: A psychological perspective. In A.M. Mecca, N.J. Smelser, & J. Vasconcellos (Eds.), *The social importance of self-esteem* (pp. 248–293). Berkeley: University of California Press.

Smelser, N.J. (1989). Self-esteem and social problems: An introduction. In A.M. Mecca, N.J. Smelser, & J. Vasconcellos (Eds.), *The social importance of self-esteem* (pp. 294–326). Berkeley: University of California Press.

Wylie, R. (1974). *The self-concept: Vol. I.* Lincoln: University of Nebraska Press.

Zeitlin, S. (no date). *Coping Inventory: A measure of adaptive behavior.* Bensenville, IL: Scholastic Testing Service.

Zigmond, N., & Thornton, H.S. (1988). Learning disabilities in adolescents and adults. In K.A. Kavale (Ed.), *Learning disabilities: State of the art and practice.* Boston: College Hill Press.

II

CONTEXTUAL FACTORS

8

The Interrelationship of Education and Self-Esteem

Jan Nisbet

Do the things that you can do and learn the things that you can't do. When you learn the things that you can't do, it then becomes the things you can do. (Jason Kingsley, *Count us in,* 1994, p. 180)

It was the issue of stigma, education, and self-esteem that ultimately influenced the Supreme Court in *Brown v. Board of Education.* In this key case, the NAACP successfully argued that the forced segregation of black children negatively affected their self-esteem, and that damage to self-esteem ultimately had a negative effect on their ability to learn. The Supreme Court's ruling in *Brown v. Board of Education* that "separate is not equal" stemmed in part from certain assumptions about the negative effects of segregation on children's self-esteem. Before this ruling, Watson (1947) published a review of research regarding effective relations among different ethnic groups. He concluded that conditions that promoted effective interactions were 1) positive interdependence, 2) equal status contact, 3) social norms favoring equalitarian cross-ethnic contact, 4) perceived attributes of groups that contradict prevailing stereotypes, and 5) contact that promotes interactions on a personal as well as a task level. These conditions continue to provide the basis for educational methods such as cooperative learning.

In the field of special education, debate continues about the effect of segregation on self-esteem. In some cities, separate high schools for African American adolescents have been proposed as one method to reduce the high dropout rate fostering a sense of identification and providing access to positive role models. Another example includes separate math classes for girls to counteract declining interest in math and lower self-esteem relative to boys. Similar arguments support separate schools for students with deafness and/or blindness (Shapiro, 1993). The disability rights movement has argued that the deliberate coalescing of people with disabilities can assist in the development of community, identification, and ultimately self-esteem. In particular, some members of the Deaf community argue that a separate linguistic culture requires a separate education (Thomas & Chees, 1989). Members of the disability community, including consumers, families, advocates, and educators, are clear, however, that forced segregation based on discrimination is unacceptable. However, the ideology behind the support for segregated environments that does exist is similar to a secessionist ideology. Goffman (1963) reflected on this situation:

> When the ultimate political objective is to remove stigma from the differentness, the individual may find that his very efforts can politicize his own life, rendering it even more different from the normal life initially denied him even though the next generation of his fellows may greatly profit from his effort by being accepted. (p. 141)

> It constantly challenges those who represent the stigmatized, urging these professionals to present a coherent politics of identity, allowing them to be quick to see the "inauthentic" aspects of other recommended programs but slow indeed to see that there may be no "authentic" solution at all. (p. 124)

As the field of education continually questions the appropriateness of inclusive environments (Fuchs & Fuchs, 1994), it turns to inadequately researched social constructs for arguments. However, research conducted in the 1950s and 1960s is clear. Children with disabilities had significantly lower levels of peer acceptance, self-concept, and other indicators associated with self-esteem (Gottleib & Leyser, 1982; Hallahan & Kauffman, 1981; Kauffman & Kauffman 1981). These findings should not lead to the assumption that peer acceptance is unlikely; research that systematically examines both changes in placement and changes in curriculum and classroom organization and expectations is virtually absent. In fact, very little useful insight can be drawn or even interpreted from the body of research that exists.

The field continues to struggle with many of the basic yet essential questions about education in a time of inclusive education, desegregation of educational services, and heterogeneous classes. How can the educational system assist students with disabilities to develop positive self-esteem? What is the impact of the inclusive education on the self-esteem of students with disabilities? Are there curricular options that support the development of student self-esteem? What can families and communities do to assist in the development of self-esteem of children and youth with disabilities?

DEFINITIONS AND MEASURES OF SELF-ESTEEM

The presence or lack of self-esteem, the judgment about one's own worth, and the sense of how well-liked and competent a person feels as expressed in his or her voice, posture, gestures, and performance (Coopersmith, 1967) has been correlated with educational success and failure. Efforts to improve self-esteem have focused on assisting students to achieve challenging goals, gain the respect of others, and engage in favorable comparison with others (Putnam, 1993).

Historically, self-esteem has been viewed as a human construct influenced by biological, family, and educational factors. Numerous studies have compared children with disabilities to those without disabilities (e.g., Heyman, 1990). Although the results vary, overall studies report lower self-esteem among children with disabilities. The strength of the influence of each of these factors has been subject to numerous studies and hypotheses. There is considerable disagreement in the literature as to the meaning of the term *self-esteem*. Many view it as a measurement of self-concept, a better researched variable; others refer to it as self-efficacy or mastery learning (Todis, Irvin, Singer, & Yovanoff, 1993). In any case, the interest in self-esteem stems from the understanding of its relationship to achievement, identity, and personal self-fulfillment. Wylie (1979) argued that "the widespread occurrence of null or weak findings in studies of self-esteem might be explained by the methodological inadequacies inherent in existing self-esteem scales" (p. 690). Furthermore, Damon and Hart (1982) argued that the existing instruments for measuring self-concept and self-esteem in children and adolescents are "gravely in error" as they do not account for developmental changes and the evolving nature of self-understanding. Research indicates that self-concept is lower in children with disabilities than in their peers without disabilities and that their lower self-concept can be improved (Fitts 1972; Friedman, Rogers, & Gettys, 1975; Long, Ziller, & Bankes, 1970; Marasciallo, 1969; Milligan, 1995; Semmel & Snell, 1979; Wylie, 1979).

Jahoda (1958) argued that self-esteem was a critical index of mental health. Higher self-esteem has been linked to happiness, satisfaction; lower self-esteem has been linked to depression, anxiety, and maladjustment (Damon, 1983). In a study conducted by Harter and Pike (1984) children were shown pictures that were designed to tap into one of four domains thought to be important to self-esteem: 1) cognitive competence, 2) physical competence, 3) peer acceptance, and 4) maternal acceptance. Children ultimately evaluated their own self-worth in two categories: competence and acceptance (Cole & Cole, 1993).

FACTORS THAT INFLUENCE SELF-ESTEEM

Parental styles of child rearing have also been linked with self-esteem. Parents of boys who scored high on self-esteem measures used a mixture of firm control, promotion of high standards of behavior, encouragement of independence, and willingness to reason with their children (Baumrind, 1989). Other studies (e.g., Coopersmith, 1967) support Baumrind's findings on the interaction between child rearing and self-esteem. Through the mid-1990s, no studies have successfully measured the differential effect on self-esteem of child-rearing and educational practices.

Much of the research establishes the need to examine different concerns associated with different developmental ages. For example, development from childhood to middle childhood (ages 6–12) is compounded by the growing influences of peers and the experiences of comparing, mediating, and ultimately reconsidering oneself. During adolescence, self-esteem is often correlated with attractiveness, followed by peer acceptance. Research on self-esteem and gender (Gilligan, 1982; Offer, Ostrov, Howard, & Atkinson, 1988; Simmons & Blyth, 1987) supports the notion that at certain points in their lives girls seem to have lower self-esteem than boys. Entry into junior high is associated with lower self-esteem for both sexes (Simmons & Blyth, 1987). This finding may be related to the change in status that results from being the oldest in elementary school and the youngest in junior high or middle school. Harter (1983) summarized the research and argued that the data suggest that the key to high self-esteem is the feeling, transmitted in large part by the family, that one has some ability to control one's own future by controlling both oneself and one's environment (Cole & Cole, 1993).

The interpretation of self-identity by others may ultimately have an effect on one's self-esteem. Goffman (1963) used the term *personal identity* to describe positive marks or identity pegs and the unique combination of life history items that comes to be attached to the individual with the help of these pegs for his or her identity. Furthermore, Goffman remarked that biography attached to documented identity can place clear limitations on the way in which an individual can choose to present him- or herself. This recognition of the importance that records or biography play in the development of self-identity is supported by those who are wary of the constant passing of judgmental educational and evaluative data among teachers and related personnel. The process of ensuring successful transitions from one learning environment to another may in fact only reinforce negative stereotypes and ultimately create low expectations. Bogdan and Taylor (1982) reflected on Edgerton's (1967) assumption that the incompetence in people with mental retardation is stigmatizing—that is, destructive to their self-esteem. They documented how professional assumptions have been mistaken and were ultimately harmful to two individuals who spent significant portions of their lives institutionalized.

The vast majority of research relating to students with disabilities and self-esteem and self-concept is inextricably linked to the context of community, school, classroom, and instruction. Few studies actually detail the instructional environment and its possible impact on student's sense of personal value. It can be argued that self-concept is area specific, situation specific, and multidimensional in nature. It would be naive to suggest that any one strategy or any one model can address the complexity of human behavior and perception. Too much is influenced by factors over which schools have little control. However, educators too often do not understand the impact their practices, philosophies, and interventions have on student self-esteem.

SCHOOLS, TEACHING, AND SELF-ESTEEM

Teachers and other professionals may unintentionally contribute to lower self-esteem in children. This effect is sometimes referred to as prophecy communication. There is an interaction between one's ability to achieve and the conscious or unconscious evaluation of that achievement. This phenomenon, the Pygmalion effect described by Rosenthal and Jacobson (1968) and applied to the healing professions, is clear about the difficulties associated with documenting prophecy communication. They argue that

> perhaps it is appropriate to stress the unintentional aspect of the self-fulfilling prophecy since in several of the experiments described, the examiners and experimenters tried hard to avoid having their prophecies affect their subjects' performance.

Equally troubling was the finding in one study that, when children on the "slow track" gained intellectually as measured by an IQ test, the less favorably they were regarded by their teachers in almost every respect. This has been described as one concrete measure of stigma. Rosenthal and Jacobson (1968) found that

> for those children whose educability is in doubt there is a label. They are the educationally, or culturally, or socioeconomically, deprived children and, as things stand now, they appear not to be able to learn as do those who are more advantaged. The advantaged and disadvantaged differ in parental income, in parental values, in scores on various tests of achievement and ability, and often in skin color and other phenotypic expressions of genetic heritage. Quite inseparable from these differences between the advantaged and disadvantaged are the differences in their teachers' expectations for what they can achieve in school. There are no experiments to show that a change in pupils' skin color will lead to improved intellectual performance. There is, however, the experiment in this book to show that changes in teacher expectations can lead to improved intellectual performance. (p. 181)

Clearly, teachers' attitudes and their professional preparation must be closely evaluated to ensure that there is understanding and acknowledgment of the concept of stigma, personal values, and assumptions about children and their families.

Numerous researchers have explored the relationship between stigma and self-concept. Does society's and the educational system's stigmatization of an individual necessarily result in reduced self-esteem? As Maslow (1979) suggested, is a sense of belonging in schools and classrooms a prerequisite for self-esteem and achievement? No one seems to know unequivocally. The research investigating these themes is also problematic, unclear, and often superficial. However, the topic is worth exploring, even if it only addresses some commonly held beliefs that educational environment is a determinant of self-esteem. For example, a participant in a national educational conference commented that, in her state, children were not placed in inclusive classrooms because it ruined their self-esteem. When asked why that was true, she said that the competitive nature of the classroom and chiding from peers contributed to problems with self-esteem. This example captures the lack of consensus in understanding of the interrelationships between instructional setting, teaching style and curriculum, teacher attitudes, self-concept, and family and community involvement.

EDUCATIONAL INTERVENTIONS AND SELF-ESTEEM

Cooperative instruction or learning (Johnson & Johnson, 1989) is one educational method that has purported to have positive effects on student achievement and self-esteem. Johnson and Johnson (1983) presented a theoretical formulation and meta-analysis of research related to interdependence and interpersonal attraction among heterogeneous and homogeneous individuals. They found that increases in self-esteem were correlated with decreases in prejudice. They further concluded that "self-esteem explains some of the relationship between cooperation and interpersonal attraction among heterogeneous individuals" (p. 24) and that the impact of positive peer evaluations may be especially powerful for individuals with a history of failure (Turnure & Zigler, 1958). Through meta-analysis, Johnson and Johnson (1983) also found that 1) the more positive the pattern of interaction among students and the more students facilitate each other's goal achievement, the greater the resulting interpersonal attraction; 2) the greater one's conviction that others are encouraging, supporting, and accepting of one's efforts to achieve, the greater the interpersonal attraction; 3) the more accurate one's perspective taking, the greater one's empathy with, understanding of, and altruism for others, which results in greater interpersonal attraction; 4) the more realistic, dynamic, and differentiated one's perceptions of others are the more one likes and identifies with them; 5) the higher one's self-esteem, the less one's prejudices against and the higher one's liking of others; 6) the greater one's academic success, the more one likes those who have contributed to and facilitated that success; and 7) the more one expects future interaction to be positive and productive, the more one likes others. These findings, combined with the finding of higher academic success in cooperative learning situations, reinforces the notions of success and peer acceptance.

In a review of 60 studies, Putnam (1993) found that "positive achievement outcomes were most likely to occur when the conditions of positive interdependence and individual accountability were ensured" (p. 25). Johnson and Johnson (1989) conducted a research review on cooperative, individualistic, and competitive learning as they related to self-esteem. Meta-analysis techniques on 77 studies revealed that 53% favored cooperative learning, whereas less than 1% favored competition. The average student involved in cooperative learning has three fifths of a standard deviation higher than the average competitive learner and two fifths higher than the average person working independently (Putnam, 1993).

McPhail (1993) compared the subjective experiences of adolescents with learning disabilities with those of their low-achieving and typically achieving peers. Students with learning disabilities reported feeling more positive and active than either of the other groups during school hours, whereas after school there were no differences. Szivos-Bach (1993) measured the relationships among social comparisons, stigma, and self-esteem. Students who perceived the most stigma had the lowest self-esteem and the lowest ideals. They also felt the least likely to fulfill their aspirations. Students with low self-esteem also viewed themselves in a negative light and had "impoverished interpersonal relationships." Mainstreaming was not correlated with lower self-esteem and feeling more stigmatized. Clever, Bear, and Juvonen (1992) examined perception of global self-worth in 35 students with learning disabilities, 122 typically achieving students, and 27 low-achieving students in a full-time integrated setting. There were no differences in global self-worth among the student groups. Bear, Clever, and Proctor (1991) also studied 339 third graders and found that students with learning disabilities in integrated classes had lower self-worth than their peers without disabilities, but also that integration may have a positive effect on the self-worth of boys without disabilities in integrated settings.

Intervention research conducted by Lewis (1992) described how one teacher used techniques that included giving praise and appropriate commenting in a writer's workshop classroom as a method to build self-esteem for students with learning disabilities. Growth in self-esteem was a by-product of the growth in writing skills during the 9 months of instruction. Through a group counseling program that stressed student strengths and challenged their erroneous belief systems, 10 upper elementary students demonstrated significant improvements between pretest and posttest ratings in self concept and self-esteem. Barretti (1993) reported on a community college course for students with learning disabilities. The program involved 24 hours of instruction on understanding one's disability, finding strategies necessary to compensate for disability. dealing with frustration and self-esteem, and examining alternatives to college. The program exceeded all expectations by increasing both academic and social competence.

In a study of 87 children between the ages of 9 and 11, Heyman (1990) found that self-perception of one's learning disability as modifiable and nonstigmatizing was related positively to self-concept and self-esteem and that each of these relationships remained significant when controlling for sex, ethnicity, age, reading, math achievement, self-contained versus mainstreamed setting, and age of diagnosis. In a 2-year longitudinal study of 25 children with learning disabilities, Kershner (1990) found that self-concept predicted patterns of successful achievement, whereas IQ has no relationship with the student's learning ability. He argues for consideration of low self-concept as a possible primary cause of academic underachievement. Likewise, Price (1989) reported on a study of the self-concept of 56 high school juniors and seniors with learning disabilities by means of analysis of empirical data and staff observation. She found that the majority of participants scored in the average range of self-esteem and appeared to have levels of self-esteem similar to those of students without learning disabilities.

Murtaugh (1988) suggested that, for students who were likely not to be high achievers, an alternative path to achievement and self-esteem for many people might be *nonacademic* activities outside of school. Some of the research on adventure learning supports this notion. Perske (1972) argued that conservative approaches to risk taking often followed with adolescents and adults with disabilities may in fact be counterproductive to their emotional and social development. The theoretical benefits of outdoor experiences for children with behavior disorders have been presented by Apter (1977), Hughes and Dudley (1973), and Shea (1977). Blanchard (1993) and Maizell (1988) used adventure-based therapy and a ropes course as an intervention with adolescent psychiatric in-patients and court-involved adolescents, respectively. Significant results were found in the areas of self-esteem and improved interpersonal behavior. In another study of boys labeled as having behavior disorders, Langsner and Anderson (1987) participated in an alternative curriculum that included outdoor education, camping, and leadership training. Seventeen boys between the ages of 9 and 13 were randomly assigned to the treatment group. The authors found nonsignificant changes and explained the results as partly due to small sample size. The results, however, were consistent with the effect of Rigothi's (1974) outdoor education program for children with behavior disorders.

Families cannot be left out of the equation when children's self-esteem and achievement are examined. Singer and Irvin (1988) conducted a 4-year research project to test Harter's (1981) model on mastery motivation and its relationship to high self-esteem and verified the importance of environmental variables on the development of self-esteem finding that families, the students themselves, schools, and communities all played an interactive role. Additionally, they found that the children of parents who held high, appropriate standards for the child's behavior, firmly enforced these standards, encouraged the child's independence and individuality, openly communicated, and recognized the rights of parents and children had higher scores on self-esteem measures. Several other factors have also been found to be critical to high self-esteem, including 1) making choices, 2) having personal and household responsibilities, 3) participating in leisure activities, 4) engaging in peer interactions, 5) practicing assertiveness, 6) learning to cope with difficult situations, 7) accepting the consequences of one's actions, and 8) having parental advocates who teach self-advocacy skills (Irvin & Todis, 1992; Singer & Powers, 1993).

Research supporting Singer and Irvin's (1988) work has also been conducted by Morvits and Motta (1992) with children in grades 3–6. They examined the children's perception of parental acceptance and the relationship of this perception to self-esteem among 31 self-contained students with learning disabilities, 35 resource room students, 30 general class students, and 30 general class students requiring the compensatory education remedial program. Students' perceptions of both maternal and paternal acceptance was significantly correlated with the students' self-esteem. As one might expect, students in regular classrooms who did not require remedial instruction had higher self-esteem than the other groups. The research on student self-esteem is clear. How students perceive themselves is embedded in how families, schools, and communities value and educate their children and youth. Too often we have blamed the individual and his or her peers, rather than recognizing the context for the development and nurturance of self-esteem.

STRATEGIES LIKELY TO IMPROVE STUDENT SELF-ESTEEM

School is not a pleasant place for all children (Cole & Cole, 1993). In fact, school practices such as homogenous groupings, tracking, self-contained education, and standardized measures of performance have contributed to alienation and underachievement for some students. However, few schools recognize the negative effects of their practices. Without some form of intervention, some students may proceed down a path inadvertently designed to lower their self-esteem. What needs to change? Strategies that appear to be associated with higher levels of self-esteem and learning include restructured and inclusive educational practices, friendship and peer support, family involvement, and mastery learning.

School restructuring and reform is attempting to address some of these issues. The restructuring movement has its foundation in concerns about the educational and post-educational performance of typical students, students who are at risk because of their race or culture, and students with mild disabilities (Brookover et al., 1982; Gartner & Lipsky, 1987; Sizer, 1992). Students graduating from high school need a different set of knowledge and skills from those graduating just a few decades ago if they are to be contributing members of a global community whose economy is dependent upon workers who can understand and synthesize information and work collaboratively with others to identify and solve problems (Goals 2000: Educate America Act of 1994). For schools to adequately provide students with that knowledge, more than a curricular facelift is needed. A total reexamination of desired student outcomes, including self-esteem, must take place along with a critical look at the structure of schools. This educational restructuring, whether it is called "effective schooling," "essential schooling," or simply "educational reform," has been characterized by a number of ideas and principles including, but not limited to, the following: 1) curriculum driven by a small set of desired student outcomes, 2) teacher empowerment, 3) site-based management, 4) active involvement of students in the learning process, 5) increased reliance on collaboration among staff, 6) use of coaching as the dominant pedagogy, 7) use of nontraditional evaluation processes, and 8) individualization in teaching methods based on students' learning styles and needs (Pugach & Johnson, 1989; Sizer, 1992; Thousand & Villa, 1992; West, l990).

RATIONALE FOR SCHOOL RESTRUCTURING THROUGH INCLUSION

Inclusion means that students with disabilities are fully included in general education classes in their neighborhood schools and that individualized supports are available in those classrooms so that all students can learn. This model blends the values and strategies of the regular education initiative (Will, 1984) and the integration initiative of the 1980s, which has typically focused on students with severe disabilities. Inclusion has been justified on the basis of several rationales, including civil rights, enhanced academic outcomes, a belief that schools should reflect a pluralistic society, potential for the development of social relationships, benefits to typical children, and preparation for optimum functioning in integrated adult communities (Biklen, 1985; Brinker & Thorpe, 1984; *Brown v. Board of Education,* Brown et al., 1988; Brown, Nietupski, & Hamre-Nietupski, 1976; Halvorsen & Sailor, 1990; *PARC v. Commonwealth of Pennsylvania,* 1971; Voeltz, Johnson, & McQuarter, 1983). Some individuals who support a new system of education such as inclusion contend that the continuation of two separate systems is in fact counterproductive to the values and desired outcomes of this new system; they recommend the merger of special and general education into a unified system of quality education for all students (Gartner & Lipsky, 1987; Stainback & Stainback, 1984; Stainback, Stainback, & Bunch, 1989; Wang, Reynolds, & Walberg, 1986).

The inclusive education model is based on the following beliefs: 1) children who have disabilities are full human beings whose presence enriches our schools; 2) people with disabilities don't need to be "fixed" before they are allowed to participate in the mainstream of school and community life; 3) support systems should be provided by the most natural, available person in the environment; and 4) changes in the educational system that will facilitate the inclusion of children with the most challenges coincide with changes that will benefit all children (Gartner & Lipsky, 1987; Rowe, 1989; Strully & Strully, 1985; Thousand & Villa, 1989).

Much has been written on restructuring American schools, and many schools throughout the country have embraced this new thinking and developed innovative approaches to educating students. The quality of education in schools is on the rise; however, it is important that school reform efforts improve the quality of education for students with and without disabilities. Given the link between achievement and self-esteem, reform will have to include attention to both. Unfortunately, not all of these approaches recognize and include students with significant disabilities; therefore, it is essential that advocates of inclusive education continue their efforts to ensure that all systems change and restructuring efforts result in schools that truly are for *all* students.

Including students with disabilities into general education classes and neighborhood schools creates an atmosphere that respects and values the diversity of all learners. Valuing diversity reflects the notion that all students are respected members of their communities. The sense of belonging has been linked with peer acceptance and higher measures of self-esteem. Students with and without disabilities learn to accept the strengths and needs of others, as well as the strengths and needs within themselves. The general classroom community becomes a place where all can freely offer support and all can freely receive it, a place where doing something a bit differently is valued and respected, and a place where the diversity of our human community is accepted and even celebrated.

The challenge of introducing and sustaining inclusive education is greatest when classroom teachers use approaches that rely primarily on homogeneous ability groups, oral instructions, and the use of only one or two formats (written reports or multiple choice tests) for demonstrating what has been learned. Inclusive education tends to be most successful when teachers use instructional practices that are effective for heterogeneous groups of students. Certainly the *type* of instruction should not prevent students with disabilities from being members of general classrooms. However, it is wise for classroom teachers to learn about teaching strategies that enhance the learning of all students, regardless of ability.

Many schools have reconsidered the curriculum guides being used in classrooms. Some schools have decided to rewrite grade-level curricula taking into account innovative approaches such as the *Reading and Writing Process* (Hansen, Newkirk, & Graves, 1985; Hansen, 1987) and *Cooperative Learning* (Johnson & Johnson, 1983, 1989). Secondary schools have instituted internships, mentorships, and community service opportunities for all students. Students with and without disabilities benefit when schools work to incorporate new strategies into the classroom and school minimally creating an environment where self-esteem can flourish. Because much of the research that supports these strategies is based in valuing diverse learning communities and improving student self-esteem, schools that employ these strategies find great success when teaching students with disabilities in regular classrooms. Any school district developing a systems change plan is wise to strongly encourage teachers to gain greater comfort with these teaching strategies. Plans may include training and peer mentor-ships for teachers and community information sessions.

Inside and outside of both general and special education, educators are raising questions about what constitutes good teaching. Most agree that good teaching happens when teachers recognize that all students are unique, capable learners and value this diversity in their classrooms. Classroom teachers realize it is not effective to teach a class of 30 students using only one instructional methodology. They realize that all students learn differently, and they take advantage of a variety of teaching styles and approaches. Good education happens when teachers focus on building the gifts and strengths of all students, rather than on fixing the deficits and disabilities.

PEER SUPPORT AND FRIENDSHIP

Few people would deny how important friendship is to achieving a full and satisfying life. Asher and Gottman (1981) studied 200 children in grades 3–6 and found that rejected children were the most lonely group and that this group differed significantly from other groups. Educators realize that friends play a large part in students' lives both in and out of school. Schools are beginning to recognize friendship as an educational issue, given the impact it has on self-esteem and on developing a full and satisfying life long after graduation.

As classrooms welcome students of all abilities and disabilities, it is important that schools teach the values of accepting differences, honoring individual contributions, fostering interdependence, and nurturing friendships. Classrooms and schools are places where friendships can be cultivated so that they grow beyond the school day. Teachers can become friendship facilitators for students where this is necessary. Parents can be encouraged to value friendships after school, on weekends, and in the summer. A collaboration between school and home can ensure that students have meaningful relationships both in and out of school. A systems change support plan should include ways in which friendships can be facilitated. Plans may include train-ing in both values and strategies for teachers, parents, and students and may include friendship as an educational goal in the school district's philosophy.

The development of friendships among students with and without disabilities can be nurtured when students participate together in class and school activities. It is important that the student with disabilities be viewed by classmates and teachers as a *true* member of the general education class. If this student spends some, but not all, of the day in the general education class (with the remainder of his or her time in special education settings or disability-specific community-based instruction), it is likely that he or she will be viewed by peers simply as a visitor, not a member of the class com-munity. When the child is seen as a visitor, it is less likely that equitable relationships will develop. Peer acceptance will be lower, and, as the research suggests, self-esteem may be lower.

With their day-to-day practices and beliefs, educators and administrators in inclu-sive schools can promote the development of friendships among students. Schools that clearly value the unique abilities and contributions of all students through heteroge-neous classes, diversity celebrations, cooperative learning groups, and people-first lan-guage actively promote students' appreciation of the similarities and differences in themselves and others. This appreciation can easily develop into genuine caring, not simply benevolence, among students, and real friendships are more likely to develop.

Because many students have become included late in their educational careers, the development of friendships may initially require structured opportunities and facilitation. For students who begin their education as full members of general education classes, this intervention or support may not be necessary.

PEER MODELS FOR LEARNING

In a review of 18 articles on peer tutoring, Byrd (1990) reported on successful models that were positively correlated with student self-esteem. Similar peer-related positive interventions have been reported by Guidon (1993). Learning from the people around us is a common way of gaining information and developing new skills. Young children in play groups and preschools learn new words and problem-solving skills from one another. Children in elementary school classes and on the playground learn the newest games and the latest jokes. Adolescents turn to their peers to determine what clothes are "in" and to learn what is "cool" in music. Even adults watch their dinner partners to determine which fork to use with which course. The old sayings "when in doubt, look about" or "when in Rome, do as the Romans do" apply as much to children and teenagers as they do to adults.

When students with disabilities are separated from their typical peers, they are denied the basic opportunity provided to all other students—the opportunity to learn what is expected of someone their age. No matter how skilled or experienced, a special education teacher cannot teach a 14-year-old student how to be a teenager. A physical therapist cannot teach a student the latest dance steps. A speech pathologist cannot teach a student the latest slang. These are things that can be learned only when students interact with others their own age. The learning of these commonly valued behaviors assists in peer acceptance, which is related to self-esteem.

By including students with disabilities in general education, all students are afforded the opportunity to benefit from peer models and support. By working together, students observe the ways in which other students are successful and model these behaviors. A student who has difficulty communicating can learn effective strategies by being with students who use language all day long. A student who needs to learn to stay on task should be surrounded by other students working diligently at their lessons. A student with goals in reading can work side-by-side with other readers. At times, all students may find their best teachers are among their peers.

FAMILY INVOLVEMENT

Parents must be recognized as full and equal members of their child's education team. Teachers, assistants, and principals may change over time, but only parents have the perspective of knowing their child's past, present, and future dreams. As a school district begins to provide quality inclusive education for all students, it must evaluate the way in which parents participate in the school, class, and team process and must develop strategies to encourage their participation to the fullest extent.

Welcoming parents' involvement in their child's education may require many changes in practice. Addressing parental priorities in the individualized education program (IEP) process may represent a change in the school district's policy. Including parents in policy forums may require a change in the way the school district makes decisions. Encouraging all parents to become members of schoolwide parent organizations can provide opportunities for parents of children with and without disabilities to develop common visions and goals. Opening classroom doors to all parents can support both parents and teachers in achieving their desired outcomes for all students. Unfortunately, too many families are faced with a 15-year-old child who cannot read, feels a sense of failure, has low self-esteem, and appears to be increasingly alienated from their schools and families. These families beg for help, become frustrated with the superficial answers, and seek alternatives that are all too often segregated and expensive. All of this division is unnecessary. We share the burden in making schools places where all children can achieve, have friends, have high self-esteem, and have a vision of the future.

CONCLUSIONS

In the end, it is the school, family, and community that raise the child. Each has a responsibility

> to provide a sense of meaning, belonging, and purpose in our lives, as well as a framework of values. People need to have something to believe in and live for, to feel they are part of a community and a valued member of society, a sense of relatedness and connectedness to the world and the universe in which they exist. (Eckersly, 1993, p. 4)

Our schools, classrooms, homes, and neighborhoods must convey this message in the ways they are structured, in the ways that children are included and taught, and in the ways we evaluate our successes and failures.

REFERENCES

Apter, S.J. (1977). Applications of ecological theory: Toward a community special education model. *Exceptional Children, 43,* 366–373.

Asher, S.R., & Gottman, J.M. (1981). *The development of children's friendships: Cambridge studies in social and emotional development.* Cambridge: Cambridge University Press.

Barretti, M.R. (1993). *Increasing the success of learning disabled high school students in their transition to the community college through the use of support services.* Fort Lauderdale, FL: Nova University.

Baumrind, D. (1989). Rearing competent children. In W. Damon (Ed.), *Child development today and tomorrow.* San Francisco: Jossey-Bass.

Bear, G., Clever, A., & Proctor, A.W. (1991). Self-perceptions of non-handicapped children and children with learning disabilities in integrated classes. *Journal of Special Education, 24*(4), 409–426.

Biklen, D. (1985). *Achieving the complete school: Strategies for effective mainstreaming.* New York: Teachers College Press.

Blanchard, K.H. (1993). Situational leadership. In R.A. Ritvo, A.H. Litwin, & L. Butler (Eds.), *Managing in the age of change: Essential skills to manage today's diverse workforce* (pp. 14–34). New York: Irwin Professional Publishing.

Bogdan, R., & Taylor, S. (1982). *Inside out: The social meaning of mental retardation.* Toronto: University of Toronto Press.

Brinker, R.P., & Thorpe, M.E. (1984). Integration of severely handicapped students and the proportion of IEP objectives achieved. *Exceptional Children, 51*(2), 168–175.

Brookover, W., Beamer, L., Efthim, H., Hathaway, L., Miller, J., & Tornatsky, L. (1982). *Creating effective schools: An in-service program for enhancing school learning climate and achievement.* Holmes Beach, FL: Learning Publications.

Brown v. Board of Education, 347 U.S. 483, 493 (District 1954).

Brown, L., Long, E., Udvari, S., Davis, L., VanDeventer, P., Ahlren, C., Johnson, F., Gruenewald, L., & Jorgensen, J. (1988). The home school: Why students with severe intellectual disabilities must attend the schools of their brothers, sisters, friends, and neighbors. *Journal of The Association for Persons with Severe Handicaps, 14*(1), 1–11.

Brown, L., Nietupski, J.A., & Hamre-Nietupski, S. (1976). *Madison's alternatives for zero inclusion: Papers and programs related to public school services for secondary age severely handicapped students* (Vol. VI, Part 1). Washington, DC: Bureau of Education for the Handicapped.

Byrd, D. (1990). Peer tutoring with the learning disabled: A critical analysis. *Journal of Educational Research, 84*(2), 115–118.

Clever, A., Bear, G., & Juvonen, J. (1992). Discrepancies between competence and importance in self-perceptions of children in integrated classes. *Journal of Special Education, 26*(2), 125–138.

Cole, M., & Cole, S. (1993). *The development of children.* New York: Scientific American Books.

Coopersmith, S. (1967). *The antecedents of self-esteem.* New York: W.H. Freeman.

Damon, W. (1983). *Social and personality development: Infancy through adolescence.* New York: W.W. Norton.

Damon, W., & Hart, D. (1982). The development of self-understanding from infancy through adolescence. *Child Development, 53*(4), 841–865.

Dornsbusch, S., Ritter, P., Liederman, P., Roberts, D., & Fraleigh, M. (1987). The relation of parenting style to adolescent school performance. *Child Development, 58*, 1244–1257.

Eckersly. (1993). Unpublished manuscript, University of New Hampshire, Durham.

Edgerton, R.B. (1967). *The cloak of competence: Stigma in the lives of the mentally retarded.* Berkeley: University of California Press.

Fitts, W.H. (1972). The self-esteem, perceived performance, and choice on causal attributions. *Journal of Personality and Social Psychology, 16*, 311–315.

Friedman, S., Rogers, P., & Gettys, J. (1975). Project Re-Ed: Increase in self-esteem as measured by the Coopersmith inventory. *Perceptual and Motor Skills, 40*, 165–166.

Fuchs, D., & Fuchs, L.S. (1994). Inclusive schools movement and the radicalization of special education reform. *Exceptional Children, 60*, 294-309.

Gartner, A., & Lipsky, D. (1987). Beyond special education: Toward a quality svstem for all students. *Harvard Educational Review, 57*, 367–395.

Gilligan, C. (1982). *In a different voice.* Cambridge, MA: Harvard University Press.

Goals 2000: Educate America Act of 1994, PL 103-227. (March, 1997). Title 20. U.S.C. 5801, *U.S. Statutes at Large, 108*, 125–280.

Goffman, E. (1963). *Stigma: Notes on the management of spoiled identity.* Englewood Cliffs, NJ: Prentice Hall.

Gottleib, J., & Leyser, Y. (1982). Friendships between mentally retarded and nonretarded children. In S.R. Asher & J.M. Gottman (Eds.), *The development of children's friendships* (pp. 150–181). New York: Cambridge University Press.

Guidon, G. (1993). *Enhancing the self-concept and self-esteem of upper elementary grade students with learning disabilities through counseling, modeling, reverse-role tutoring, and parent and teacher education.* Fort Lauderdale, FL: Nova University.

Hallahan, D.P., & Kauffman, J.M. (1976). *Introduction to learning disabilities: A psycho-behavioral approach.* Englewood Cliffs, NJ: Prentice Hall.

Hallahan, D., & Kauffman, J. (1981). Special education/learning disabilities. In J.M. Kaufmann & D.P. Kaufmann (Eds.), *Handbook of special education* (pp. 141–164). Englewood Cliffs, NJ: Prentice Hall.

Halvorsen, A., & Sailor, W. (1990). Integration of students with severe and profound disabilities: A review of research. In R. Gaylord-Ross (Ed.), *Issues and research in special education* (pp. 110–172). New York: Teachers College Press.

Hamre-Nietupski, S., Krajewski, L., Nietupski, J., Ostercamp, D., Sensor, K., & Opheim, B. (1976). Parent/professional partnerships in advocacy: Developing integrated options with resistive systems. *Journal of The Association for Persons with Severe Handicaps, 13*, 251–259.

Hansen, J. (1987). Each belongs. In M. Forest (Ed.), *More education/integration* (pp. 95–100). Downsview, Ontario, Canada: G. Allan Roeher Institute.

Hansen, J., Newkirk, T., & Graves, D. (1985). *Breaking ground: Teachers relate reading and writing in the elementary school.* Portsmouth, NH: Heinemann.

Harter, S. (1981). A model of mastery motivation in children: Individual differences and developmental change. In S. Collins (Ed.), *Minnesota symposium on child psychology: Vol. 14* (pp. 21–255). Hillsdale, NJ: Lawrence Erlbaum Associates.

Harter, S. (1983). Development perspectives on the self-system. In P.M. Mussen (Ed.), *Handbook of child psychology: Vol. 4. Socialization, personality and social development.* New York: John Wiley & Sons.

Harter, S., & Pike, R. (1984). The pictorial scale of perceived competence and social acceptance for young children. *Child Development, 55,* 1969–1982.

Heyman, W.B. (1990). The self-perception of a learning disability and its relationship to academic self-concept and self-esteem. *Journal of Learning Disabilities, 23*(8), 472, 475.

Hughes, A.H., & Dudley, H.K. (1973). An old idea for a new problem: Camping as a treatment for the emotionally disturbed in our state hospitals. *Adolescence, 8,* 43–50.

Irvin, L.K., & Todis, B.J. (1992). *School-based factors related to development of self-esteem in children with physical/neuromotor disabilities.* Unpublished research proposal submitted to U.S. Department of Education.

Jahoda, M. (1958). *Current concepts of positive mental health.* New York: Basic Books.

Johnson, D.W., & Johnson, R.T. (1983). Interdependence and interpersonal attraction among heterogeneous and homogenous individuals: A theoretical formulation and a meta-analysis of the research. *Review of Education, 53*(1), 5–54.

Johnson, D.W., & Johnson, R.T. (1989). *Cooperation and competition: Theory and research.* Edina, MN: Interactions Books.

Kauffman, J.M., & Kauffman, D.P. (Eds.). (1981). *Handbook of special education.* Englewood Cliffs, NJ: Prentice Hall.

Kershner, J.R. (1990). Self-concept and IQ as predictors of remedial success in children with learning disabilities. *Journal of Learning Disabilities, 23*(6), 368–374.

Kingsley, J., & Levitz, M. (1994). *Count us in.* New York: Harcourt Brace & Co.

Langsner, S.J., & Anderson, S.C. (1987). Outdoor challenge education & self esteem & locus of control of children with behavior disorders. *Adapted Physical Activity Quarterly,* pp. 236–246.

Lewis, M. (1992). The writing workshop approach with learning disabled students to build self-esteem, one teacher's experience. *Reading and Writing Quarterly, 8*(3), 275, 286.

Long, B.H., Ziller, R.C., & Bankes, J. (1970). Self other orientations of institutionalized behavior problem adolescents. *Journal of Consulting and Clinical Psychology, 34,* 43–47.

Maizell, R.S. (1988). *Adventure-based counseling as a therapeutic intervention with court-involved adolescents.* Dissertation Abstracts International, 50/06-B, 2628. (University Microfilms No. AAD89-21901).

Marasciallo, O.L. (1969). The self-perception of deviate boys in special public school classes and its relationship to their achievement and adjustment. *Dissertation Abstracts, 30*(4-B), 1901.

Maslow, A.H. (1979). *The jounals of A.H. Maslow.* Monterey, CA: Brooks/Cole Publishing Co.

McPhail, J.C. (1993). Adolescents with learning disabilities: A comparative life-stream interpretation. *Journal of Learning Disabilities, 26*(9), 617–629.

Milligan, B. (1995, Spring). Preventing disability and building self-esteem: Vinland programs for Native American youth. *What's working* (p. 2). Minneapolis: University of Minnesota.

Morvits, E., & Motta, R.W. (1992). Predictors of self-esteem: The roles of parent child perceptions, achievement and class placement. *Journal of Learning Disabilities, 25*(1), 72–80.

Murtaugh, M. (1988). Achievement outside of the classroom: The role of nonacademic activities in the lives of high school students. *Anthropology and Education Quarterly, 19*(4), 382–395.

Offer, D., Ostrov, E., Howard, K.I., & Atkinson, R. (1988). *The teenage world: Adolescents' self-image in ten countries.* New York: Plenum Press.

PARC v. Commonwealth of Pennsylvania (1971). 343F Supp 279.

Perske, R. (1972). The dignity of risk and the mentally retarded. *Mental Retardation, 19*(1) 24–26.

Price, L. (1989). *Self-esteem levels of learning disabled adolscents and adults.* Unpublished report. (ERIC Clearinghouse document EC232603.) Minneapolis: University of Minnesota.

Pugach, M.C., & Johnson, L.J. (1989). The challenge of implementing collaboration between general and special education. *Exceptional Children, 56,* 232–235.

Putnam, J. (Ed.). (1993). *Cooperative learning and strategies for inclusion.* Baltimore: Paul H. Brookes Publishing Co.

Rigothi, A. (1974). *A residential school's outdoor education program for emotionally handicapped adolescents.* Final project report of the Rinecliff Union Free School District, Holy Cross Campus, New York State Education Department, Albany.

Rosenthal, R., & Jacobson, L. (1968). *Pygmalion in the classroom: Teacher expectations and pupils' intellectual development.* New York: Holt, Rinehart & Winston.

Rowe, L. (1989, May). *A description of the Johnson City, New York, school district.* Paper presented at the meeting of the New Hampshire Special Education Administrators. Concord, New Hampshire.

Semmel, M., & Snell, M. (1979). Social acceptance and self-concept of handicapped pupils in mainstreamed environments. *Education Unlimited, 1,* 65–68.

Shapiro, J.P. (1993). *No pity: People with disabilities forging a new civil rights movement* (1st ed.). New York: Time Books.

Shea, T. (1977). *Camping for special children.* St. Louis: C.V. Mosby.

Simmons R.G., & Blyth, D.A. (1987). *Moving into adolescence: The impact of pubertal change in school context.* New York: A. de Gruyter.

Singer, G.S., & Irvin, L.K. (1988). *Development of positive self-perceptions and mastery orientation in children with multiple disabilities.* (Contract No. H023T80013 between U.S. Department of Education and Oregon Research Institute, 1988–1991). Eugene: Oregon Research Institute.

Singer, G.H.S., & Powers, L. (Eds.). (1993). *Families, disability, and empowerment: Active coping skills and strategies for family interventions.* Baltimore: Paul H. Brookes Publishing Co.

Sizer, T. (1992). *Horace's school: Redesigning the American high school.* Boston: Houghton Mifflin.

Stainback, W., & Stainback, S. (1984). A rationale for the merger of special and regular education. *Exceptional Children, 51*(2), 102–111.

Stainback, W., Stainback, S., & Bunch, G. (1989). A rationale for the merger of regular and special education. In S. Stainback, W. Stainback, & M. Forest (Eds.), *Educating all students in the mainstream of regular education* (pp. 15–28). Baltimore: Paul H. Brookes Publishing Co.

Strully J., & Strully, C. (1985). Friendship and our children, *Journal of The Association for Persons with Severe Handicaps, 10,* 224–227.

Szivos-Bach, S.E. (1993) Social comparisons, stigma, and mainstreaming: The self-esteem of young adults with a mild mental handicap. *Mental-Handicap Research, 6*(3), 217–236.

Thomas, A., & Chees, S. (1989). Temperament and personality. In G.A. Kohnstamm, J.E. Bates, & M.K. Rothbart (Eds.), *Temperament in childhood.* New York: Wiley.

Thousand, J.S., & Villa, R. (1989). Enhancing success in heterogeneous schools. In S. Stainback, W. Stainback, & M. Forest (Eds.), *Educating all students in the mainstream of regular education* (pp. 15–28). Baltimore: Paul H. Brookes Publishing Co.

Thousand, J., & Villa, R. (1992). Collaborative teams: A powerful tool in school restructuring. In R.A. Villa, J.S. Thousand, W. Stainback, & S. Stainback (Eds.), *Restructuring for caring and effective education: An administrative guide to creating heterogeneous schools* (pp. 73–108). Baltimore: Paul H. Brookes Publishing Co.

Todis, B., Irvin, L.K., Singer, G.H.S., & Yovanoff, P. (1993). The self-esteem parent program: Quantitative and qualitative evaluation of a cognitive-behavioral intervention. In G.H.S. Singer & L.E. Powers (Eds.), *Families, disability, and empowerment: Active coping skills and strategies for family interventions* (pp. 203–229). Baltimore: Paul H. Brookes Publishing Co.

Turnure, J., & Zigler, E. (1958). Outer-directedness in the problem solving of normal and retarded students. *Journal of Abnormal and Social Psychology, 57,* 379–388.

Voeltz, L., Johnson, R., & McQuarter, R. (1983). *The integration of school-aged children and youth with severe disabilities: A comprehensive bibliography and a selective review of research and program development needs to address discrepancies in state of the art.* Minneapolis: Minnesota Consortium Institute.

Wang, M.C., Reynolds, M.C., & Walberg, H.J. (1986). Rethinking special education. *Educational Leadership, 44,* 26–31.

Watson, G. (1947). *Action for unity.* New York: Harper & Row.

West, F. (1990). Educational collaboration in the restructuring of schools. *Journal of Educational and Psychological Consultation, 1*(1), 23–40.

Will, M. (1984). *Supported employment services: An OSERS position paper.* Washington, DC: U.S. Department of Education.

Wolfensberger, W., & Thomas, S. (1983). *Program analysis of service system's implementation of normalization goals (PASSING)* (2nd ed.) Toronto: National Institute on Mental Retardation.

Wylie, R.C. (1979). *The self concept: Theory and research on selected topics: Vol. 2.*, (Rev. ed.) Lincoln: University of Nebraska Press.

Increasing the Ability
of Educators to Support
Youth Self-Determination

Sharon Field and Alan Hoffman

Self-determination is a critical life skill to be developed and promoted for youth in schools. Self-determination can be defined as "the ability to identify and achieve goals based on a foundation of knowing and valuing oneself" (Field & Hoffman, 1994a, p. 164). Every intention, decision, and action of an individual both reflects and affects his or her level of self-determination. Self-determination has a significant impact on school success and on post-school adjustment.

Self-determination is promoted or discouraged by environmental variables (e.g., opportunities for choice making, attitudes of others, supports in the environment) and by the knowledge, beliefs, and skills of the individual (e.g., awareness of one's strengths and weaknesses, valuing of the self, and planning and communication skills). Educators' efforts to build environmental opportunities and supports for self-determination and to strengthen student skills that further self-determination are important in meeting the individual needs of students.

Increased self-determination during the school years can maximize successful school achievement and experiences. There is substantial evidence to support the claim that students who are involved in the planning and implementation of their edu-

Funding to support the development of this chapter was partially provided by Grant Nos. H158K00036 and H023J20004 from the U.S. Department of Education, Office of Special Education and Rehabilitative Services (OSERS), awarded to Wayne State University. Opinions expressed herein do not necessarily reflect those of OSERS.

cational programs are more successful in those programs than those who are uninvolved. For example, research indicates that students who participate in choosing school activities are more persistent and perform better in those activities than students who are not involved in the decision-making process (e.g., Koestner, Ryan, Bernieri, & Holt, 1984; Swann & Pittman, 1977, as cited by Wehmeyer, 1992). In addition to promoting greater success in school activities, equipping youth with skills and knowledge to pursue self-determination throughout their lives is one of the most important functional life skills that can be taught in school. The notion of self-determination is important to most groups in our culture. It is commonly believed that people should begin to acquire self-determination knowledge and skills in childhood and should continue to acquire knowledge and proficiency in skills as they mature. However, these skills are usually acquired, if they are acquired at all, through incidental learning both in and out of school. Instruction and support for self-determination is an important component of a school program that promotes the life skills needed to meet typical adult independent living expectations.

Adolescence, the time during which youngsters define and clarify their individuality and uniqueness (Erickson, 1975), is a critical phase in the development of self-determination knowledge and skills. One developmental task of adolescence is to develop identity and acquire the skills to express that identity in the home, school, and community. Although the acquisition of skills and knowledge that promote self-determination is a lifelong process, adolescence is clearly a critical time for developing these skills.

The degree to which one is self-determined is greatly affected by one's interactions with others. Interviews conducted with adults with and without disabilities who were employed and living in the community found that the expectations and influence of others was the most frequently cited barrier to self-determination (Field & Hoffman, 1994b). Support from others, in the form of encouraging choice and acceptance of the resulting consequences, also emerged as an important factor that promotes self-determination.

Educators play an especially significant role in the lives of youth with disabilities and their families. Educators promote or hinder self-determination through the ways in which they interact with students, through the school environments they help to create, and through the instruction and type of support they provide on a daily basis.

This chapter discusses ways in which educators can enhance self-determination through student skill building and environmental interventions. The chapter also considers the supports needed by educators to enable them to provide students with increased opportunities to become more self-determined.

A MODEL FOR SELF-DETERMINATION

The strategies suggested for educators in this chapter are derived from the model of self-determination proposed by Field and Hoffman (1994a) (see Figure 1). A modification of the four-step process described by Gordon (1977) was used to develop the model over a 3-year research effort. The model development process included input gathered from observations of students, interviews with youth and adults, and opinions from three state and one national panel of experts (Field & Hoffman, 1994a).

The model delineates five major components related to the individual's knowledge, beliefs, and skills that promote self-determination: know yourself, value yourself, plan, act, and experience outcomes and learn. The first two components (know

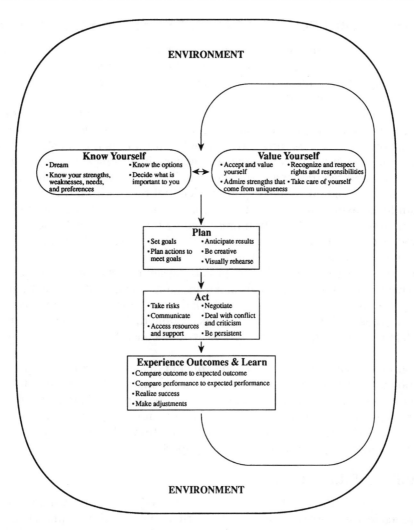

Figure 1.   Model for self-determination. (From Field, S., & Hoffman, A. [1994a]. Development of a model for self-determination, *Career Development for Exceptional Individuals, 17*[2], 165; Copyright © 1994 by CDEI; reprinted by permission.)

yourself and value yourself) describe internal processes that provide a foundation for acting in a self-determined manner. The next two components (plan and act) identify skills needed to act on this foundation. A person must have both the internal awareness and the ability to act on this internal foundation to be self-determined. To be self-determined, one must know and value oneself and possess skills to seek what one desires. The final component in this self-determination model is to experience outcomes and learn. This step includes both celebrating successes and reviewing efforts and outcomes to make adjustments that will enhance future efforts.

Environmental variables have a major effect on self-determination. The environment may either support (e.g., by providing students choice in class projects) or obstruct (e.g., by overprotecting youngsters by teachers or parents) the development of self-determination. Teachers must be aware of environmental factors in the classroom and school and of the effect these factors have on students' attempts to develop self-determination.

THE EDUCATOR'S ROLE IN SUPPORTING SELF-DETERMINATION

The educator's role in supporting student self-determination is wide-ranging. This role includes creating an environment conducive to student expression of self-determination as well as helping students acquire knowledge and skills that will assist them in becoming more self-determined.

A basic tenet of self-determination is that people with disabilities have the right to make choices about issues and about the priority of those issues in their lives. Self-determination, therefore, requires a fundamental shift in the relationship between the individual, his or her family, and service providers, including educators. Encouraging self-determination requires that experience and self-knowledge be viewed as having validity and value equal to that of knowledge that results from training and study. Thus, students' expressions about their strengths and weaknesses should receive as much attention as does information presented by the school psychologist or teacher. This process discredits neither party, and it creates a role shift from a more authoritative to a more collaborative relationship.

The role of the service provider in promoting self-determination is to provide specialized expertise to help individuals make decisions about matters important to them. Service providers must listen to people whom they serve and understand and acknowledge their needs, feelings, and attitudes (Deci, Connell, & Ryan, 1989). A commitment to self-determination requires educators to assume consultative, facilitative roles with students.

A philosophical commitment to the concept of self-determination provides the foundation for creating school environments that support and foster self-determination. The specific ways in which that commitment can be expressed are organized into the following types of educational strategies and interventions: 1) the quality and availability of role models, 2) curricula in self-determination, 3) opportunities for choice, 4) communication patterns, and 5) student supports.

Availability of Role Models

Modeling is one of the most powerful instructional strategies available (Bandura, 1986). Much learning takes place through informal role modeling. Although educational research is replete with studies that demonstrate the effectiveness of modeling as an instructional strategy, one has only to watch a young toddler telling the family dog "no, no" as she has been told "no, no" by her parents to be convinced of the potency of modeling as an instructional strategy.

Teachers who model self-determination for their students enhance the vicarious learning of skills and appreciation of rewards associated with self-determination. If a teacher demonstrates a sense of direction and responsibility, the possibility and benefits of adopting an internal locus of control is conveyed to students. If a teacher communicates to students either a helpless or an authoritarian orientation, a sense of powerlessness is communicated to students. Lessons learned vicariously through the role modeling process are more powerful, meaningful, and enduring than any direct instructional intervention, with the exception of applied learning (Bandura, 1986).

Teachers who are effective models of self-determination share their goals and plans with students and demonstrate their actions to achieve those goals. The more teachers can become conscious of their efforts to be self-determined and the more they allow students to observe those efforts, the more potent is the resulting vicarious learning for the students.

Providing students with the opportunity to have access to role models with characteristics similar to theirs enhances the role model's effectiveness. Similarity in characteristics such as gender, ethnicity, socioeconomic status, and age make the lessons learned from the role model more applicable and realistic for the student. Former students who are close in age to a student can often provide especially good role models. Teachers, staff, parents, and community members also provide good resources for potential role models.

Mentor programs, in which students are paired with adults in the school or the community or with other students with a specific experience, provide an excellent modeling resource to promote the acquisition of self-determination knowledge and skills. For example, in the field testing of the *Steps to Self-Determination* curriculum (Field & Hoffman, in press), peers who completed the curriculum in the previous year served as mentors for students beginning the curriculum. Teachers reported that the peer mentors were highly effective in supporting students in the curriculum.

Many mentor programs have a vocational focus that provides students the opportunity to learn work habits, attitudes, and skills from their mentors. A self-determination component could be added to these mentoring experiences to help students become more aware of how self-determination knowledge and skills helped their mentors achieve success in their careers. Providing students with interview questions to ask the mentor or helping students make deductions from observing the mentor's habits and behavior are ways in which the mentor experience could be structured to promote self-determination.

Peer tutoring and cooperative learning interventions also provide an excellent opportunity for students to benefit from observing their peers' self-determination knowledge and skills. Substantial research supports the effectiveness of peer tutoring and cooperative learning strategies (Johnson & Johnson, 1986; Johnson, Johnson, Holubec, & Roy, 1984; Johnson, Johnson, & Maruyama, 1983). These interventions provide an opportunity for students to learn from the modeling of other students. When using peer tutoring or cooperative learning strategies, teachers can help ensure that the modeling experience provided by peers is positive by 1) attending to the way in which students are paired or combined into groups, 2) structuring the task carefully to focus on positive outcomes and the strengths of each student, and 3) providing support to students in the group as needed.

Self-Determination Curricula

The increased emphasis on self-determination has resulted in the development of curricula specifically designed to help students acquire skills and knowledge that will help them become more self-determined. Providing students with instruction in skills to assume greater control over their lives will give them tools they need to seize opportunities to make choices and decisions. The following curricula specifically promote self-determination.

Life Centered Career Education (LCCE) (Brolin, 1991) is a functional skills curriculum that delineates three basic life domains: daily living skills, occupational guidance and preparation, and personal–social skills. Through a collaborative effort between The Arc and the developers of the LCCE curriculum, the LCCE curriculum was examined for its appropriateness in promoting self-determination skills. First, a model curriculum for self-determination encompassing four domain areas was identified (Wehmeyer, 1992). It was hypothesized that if students moved through these domain areas sequentially they would become more self-determined. The four domain areas were 1) self-awareness, 2) self-confidence, 3) choice and decision-making skills, and 4) goal attainment behaviors. Next, the project staff examined the LCCE curriculum to determine the competencies and subcompetencies that related to these domains. This examination resulted in the identification of four LCCE competencies that most clearly contribute to self-determination (i.e., No. 10, achieving self-awareness, No. 11, acquiring self-confidence, No. 15, making adequate decisions, and No. 14, achieving independence). The relevant lesson plan for these competency areas in the curriculum were reviewed and, when necessary, strengthened for their use in promoting self-determination. In addition, a section was added to the LCCE curriculum on ways to support student self-determination when using the curriculum.

The purpose of the *Project PARTnership Core Course* (Harris & McKinney, 1993) is to promote self-determination through participation in the arts. There are 20–40 sessions in the *PARTnership Core Course,* with 3 to 4 sessions devoted to instruction in each arts modality (i.e., visual arts, creative movement and dance, music, drama, creative writing). Within this curriculum, the purpose of participation in arts activities is to give students opportunities to 1) establish a goal and a plan to accomplish it, 2) make choices, 3) work independently, 4) initiate plans, and 5) self-evaluate. While specific arts activities are delineated in this curriculum, the model established for promoting self-determination through the arts can be used with a wide range of arts activities. Students are given the opportunity to learn art skills, acquire and use self-determination skills, and express how they feel or what they think about something that is important to them.

Steps to Self-Determination (Field & Hoffman, 1996) is based on the Field and Hoffman model (1994a) of self-determination described earlier in this chapter. Each of the 17 sessions in the curriculum focuses on specific components of the self-determination model. Actively setting and working toward goals is a major emphasis in the curriculum and is central to most of the homework students complete between class sessions. The curriculum was designed to be used with students with and without disabilities in a variety of scheduling arrangements (e.g., as part of an existing course, as a separate class, as an extracurricular activity). Teachers are encouraged to participate in the curriculum as co-learners with the students, thus providing role models for the students and creating a collaborative classroom climate. Parents or other significant persons in the students' lives also participate in the curriculum to support students' efforts. Field test results indicated that participation in the curriculum had a significant positive effect on students' knowledge of self-determination concepts and on behaviors associated with self-determination (Hoffman & Field, 1994).

The *TAKE CHARGE Model* (Powers, 1993) is a student-directed approach for promoting self-determination. The centerpiece of the model is a self-help guide for youth that provides step-by-step strategies for dreaming about the future, identifying and accomplishing personal goals, and building partnerships with others. Youth are provided with individual or classroom-based facilitation or coaching to promote their progress. Additionally, youth participate in self-selected community activities with mentors who have similar challenges and interests. Their parents are also provided with strategies they can use to promote self-determination of their sons and daughters.

Opportunities for Choice

Self-determination is promoted or hindered by specific beliefs, knowledge, and skills of the individual, but it is also affected by the opportunities for choice that are available in the environment. The opportunities for choice available in the school environment affect the degree to which a student can choose to use and benefit from acquired self-determination knowledge and skills. Using self-determination skills helps students develop and refine those skills. Therefore, the availability or lack of availability of opportunities for students to practice their self-determination skills affects the competency level students achieve with these skills. If schools maximize the opportunities available for students to make choices and to identify and work toward their goals, they are helping students experience increased levels of self-determination as well as helping them develop skills that promote self-determination.

A classroom environment that has a strong teacher control orientation provides few opportunities for student self-determination or for the development of self-determination skills. According to Wehmeyer (1992), classroom environments too often promote dependence and limit choice and decision-making opportunities as a result of the perceived need to structure classrooms to meet anticipated educational, behavior management, and administrative expectations.

Providing opportunities for student choice does not negate the importance of an orderly classroom climate. The difference is in *how* the orderly classroom climate is achieved. A climate that promotes self-determination provides for order and structure by providing many opportunities for students to make choices *and* to experience the consequences of those choices rather than by reducing the number of available options. For example, providing students with choices about how they will demonstrate subject mastery, such as selecting an oral report, written report, project, or video project does not cause a disorderly classroom. Furthermore, setting up a behavior management system that encourages students to control their behavior by experiencing the natural consequences of their actions can effectively provide for both an orderly classroom climate and self-determination at the same time.

Choices are always associated with some degree of risk. Providing opportunities for choice means that educators must support and encourage students in taking risks. While some protection from risk is expected and necessary in schools, overprotection decreases the opportunities for students to learn to exercise control over their lives.

Overprotection, protecting someone who is seen as having a weakness, actually protects the more powerful person from some imagined and predicted terrible result (e.g., feeling hurt, failing, being sad). Overprotection is frequently seen as a barrier to self-determination, particularly for individuals with disabilities. According to Ward (1991), overprotection opposes self-determination.

One way that overprotection can be minimized is to help individuals learn how to assume a protective role for themselves. For example, as part of this instruction, individuals who are developing self-determination skills should receive skill development in anticipating consequences of actions (Field & Hoffman, in press). They can then make determinations to act, to modify their planned actions, or to change their plans.

It is important that opportunities for choice be provided about "smaller" daily decisions (e.g., where to sit, what to eat, which task to work on first, which topic to use for a report) as well as "larger," less frequent decisions (e.g., individualized education program [IEP] goals, course selection, vocational choices). If a student does not have the experience or skill needed to make a decision, support should be provided to assist the student in the decision-making process, rather than limiting the student's opportunities for choice. The amount of support provided to a student in making decisions should be geared toward the amount of experience that the student has in a given area and the magnitude of the potential consequences of the decision.

An important area of decision making in schools where students should be provided with opportunities for choice is the educational planning and transition planning processes. The Individuals with Disabilities Education Act of 1990 (IDEA), PL 101-476, mandates provisions that require student involvement in the transition planning process. This legislation requires that "the coordinated set of activities [for transition services] shall be based upon the individual student's needs, taking into account the student's preferences and interests" (Section 602 [a] [19]). IDEA also requires that students be included as participants in their transition planning meetings.

Although the importance of student involvement in transition planning is recognized in the IDEA legislation, preliminary research has found that students often have little meaningful involvement in the development of their transition plans. A study conducted by Field, Hoffman, and Sawilowsky (1994) found that students with disabilities experience low levels of involvement in the development of the transition planning components of their IEPs. The respondents were 41 students from two high schools in the Midwest. The students, all of whom were eligible for special education services, had diverse disability classifications and included students who were in low-incidence disability groups. Of the respondents, 71% said they had attended their last IEP meeting. However, 56% of the students said they had not been told the purpose of the meeting, 63% said they had not been told things to think about before the meeting, and 76% said they had not prepared for the meeting. Of the students, 64% said that what they would do after graduation was not discussed at the IEP meeting. Only 41% of the students said that they helped set the goals that were included in their IEPs.

The IEP and transition planning processes are key decision-making points that have an impact on a student's educational program and on the level of success that the student will experience after graduation. The student should play a central role in this process. This is an important component of the school program in which students should be provided with opportunities for choice. Two programs have recently been developed specifically to help students prepare to take an active role in the educational and transition planning processes. The *Self-Directed IEP* (Martin & Marshall, 1993) is targeted to help students develop the knowledge and skills that will give them a stronger voice in the IEP process. The *Self-Directed IEP* curriculum includes lesson plans and videos that help students become comfortable and familiar with the IEP process, make decisions about input they would like to provide to the process, and develop skills to lead and actively participate in the planning process.

The *I PLAN* model (Van Reusen & Bos, 1990) is focused on helping students communicate in planning conferences. The technique is centered on the following five-step strategy:

I   Inventory your strengths, weaknesses you need to improve, goals and interests, and choices for learning.
P   Provide your inventory information.
L   Listen and respond.
A   Ask questions.
N   Name your goals.

Students are provided with instruction in the strategy in small groups. They use the acronym *I PLAN* to remember the five steps in the strategy. Like the *Self-Directed IEP* intervention, the *I PLAN* strategy helps students prepare for and assert themselves in the educational planning process.

Communication Patterns

The climate in which student expressions and behaviors are responded to is an important part of the school environment that either encourages or hinders self-determination.

Responses by important others to a student's actions affect the student's level of encouragement to express himself or herself, initiate actions, and take risks. In a school that promotes self-determination, it is clearly communicated through words and action that outcomes are not all predetermined and that control and responsibility are shared by students, parents, faculty, and staff. For example, in a school that supports self-determination, students' opinions regarding schoolwide policy decisions will be solicited and seriously considered in the decision-making process.

Behavioral Strategies Reinforcement techniques that foster motivation, self-esteem, and creativity and encourage internal rather than external locus of control are recommended to promote self-determination. Self-esteem, a critical element of self-determination, can be encouraged with behavioral strategies that reward desired behaviors through positive reinforcement rather than extinguishing negative behaviors through the use of punishment. As self-determination implies, the goals and the means to those goals are determined by the individual. It is recommended that, while teachers should not interfere with naturally occurring reinforcers and consequences, they should emphasize reinforcement of behaviors that help students reach their own goals.

Reinforcement techniques should also promote appropriate student experimentation and risk taking. It may be appropriate to reinforce close approximations of desired behaviors, depending on the starting level for each student. New and creative attempts at a task should also be rewarded, even if those attempts do not immediately lead to the desired result. For example, in successive attempts, a student who is learning how to complete a job application form may demonstrate increased understanding of the content that is supposed to be included in each section of the form, even though he or she makes errors in spelling or punctuation. It is important in such an instance to reinforce the creative, although misspelled, attempts at inserting the appropriate responses on the form. It is also important to provide constructive feedback that will allow the student to correct the spelling errors.

Excessive use of teacher-controlled behavioral techniques tends to decrease motivation. For example, Koestner et al. (1984) examined the role of teacher versus student control on motivation and engagement in activities. They set up three conditions. In the first condition, children were offered a reinforcer for painting pictures (contingent reinforcement). In the second condition, children were not told before they painted pictures that they would be reinforced, but they received reinforcement for painting the pictures upon completion of the activity. In the third condition, no external reinforcement for painting pictures was provided. When students were given the opportunity to paint pictures at a later time, the group that had earlier been given contingent reinforcement drew significantly fewer pictures than did either of the other two groups. While reinforcement can be useful in helping students acquire and maintain behaviors, it is important to consider the potential negative consequences of contingent reinforcement on internal motivation.

Listening One of the most important responses that affects self-determination is the degree to which a student feels listened to and understood. We listen carefully to information that we think is important. Feeling listened to and understood is empowering to the individual. It represents the importance given to both the person and to his or her thoughts by another person who is valued. Over a period of time, the effect of being listened to and understood communicates being valued, having importance, and living or working in a safe and trusting atmosphere. Furthermore, feeling listened to and understood prepares a student to hear and accept, although not necessarily agree with, another's reactions to his or her statements. This feedback helps students clarify their thoughts and feelings. The more clear and confident students can be about their beliefs and desires, the greater the likelihood that they will be able to identify and achieve goals that are meaningful to them.

Active listening is a technique that can help communicate to students that their expressions are important (Pietrofesa, Hoffman, & Splete, 1984). Active listening also helps students clarify their thoughts, ideas, and plans. Field and Hoffman (1996) summarize from the communication literature, the following steps in active listening:

1. Listen carefully as another speaks.
2. Ask clarifying questions to seek additional information about what was said.
3. Tell the individual what you heard.

In active listening, it is important not to ask questions or to make any statements that challenge the speaker's right to his or her opinion. The speaker then has an opportunity to correct any misunderstanding in communication and to feel understood. The purpose of active listening is to ensure that one is really understanding what another is saying, not to make personal judgments about what was said. Alternative opinions should be expressed only after the communication is clarified and confirmed.

By using active listening techniques, school personnel can communicate to students that their expressions are valued and important. In addition, good communication skills, including listening skills, have been identified as an important skill for self-determination (Field & Hoffman, 1994a). By using active listening techniques, school staff can model a skill that enhances the attainment of self-determination.

Humor   Another communication skill that has been associated with promoting self-determination is the appropriate use of humor. In research leading to the development of the Field and Hoffman self-determination model, humor was consistently and insistently identified by consumer advisory groups as both a useful communication tool and a helpful device to deflect conflict and criticism when barriers are encountered in the pursuit of goals. Using humor can decrease anxiety, anger, and other emotions that accompany conflict, permitting the participants to avoid "getting stuck" in the emotion.

By appropriately acknowledging, soliciting, and using humor in interactions with students, school staff can model and encourage an important communication and coping strategy. For example, when teaching a session on passive, assertive, and aggressive styles of communication, a teacher role-played each of the communication styles. Using a light-hearted manner, she exaggerated each style using a situation that was a commonly understood potential source of conflict in the classroom (i.e., not completing an assignment). The exaggerated examples were humorous to the students and created an enjoyable, memorable lesson.

Win-Win Negotiation   Win-win negotiation styles have been identified as an important component of self-determination (Field & Hoffman, 1996). Negotiation can be modeled and demonstrated through day-to-day interaction and response to student conflicts. In win-win negotiations, the purpose of negotiation is to find solutions to problems or conflicts that allow both people to "win" something they want. They win enough to satisfy their needs, but not necessarily enough to satisfy all of their wants. Field and Hoffman (in press) summarize from pertinent communication and social skills literature the following steps in win-win negotiation:

1. Ask the other person to say what he or she thinks and how he or she feels about the issue. Use active listening to make sure you are understanding the other person's point of view.

2. Use assertive communication and "I" statements; tell how you think and feel about the issue.
3. Each person thinks about ways to solve the problem so that both people "win."
4. Both people state ideas for solving the problem.
5. Find a solution that is agreeable to both people, select it, and make plans to implement it.

Certainly not all issues are negotiable, and it is not recommended that these negotiation techniques be used each time a conflict arises. However, when multiple appropriate solutions to a conflict between a student and a staff member or between the student and any other individual (e.g., another student, a tutor, a co-worker) are potentially available, win-win negotiation strategies can often help identify solutions that increase, rather than decrease, self-determination.

Student Supports

Providing self-determination instruction and opportunities for choice may be insufficient as interventions to promote self-determination in students. Specific supports aimed at helping students engage in behaviors to increase their self-determination may be helpful. Support can include providing students with information, allowing students to reflect on and verbalize their plans, "walking through" the steps of the decision-making process, listening and providing feedback, asking questions, helping to identify alternatives, identifying steps in the negotiation process, and identifying appropriate responses to the consequences of actions. In a school where self-determination is a goal for students, the roles of teachers and other school personnel become more consultative in nature; and school staff provide information and support to students as needed.

In addition to the supports identified above, it is important that any accommodations or supports that a student needs to appropriately deal with a disability (e.g., interpreters, hearing aids, communication devices) be provided. The lack of these basic accommodations and supports for a student's disability will have a significant negative impact on the student's ability to be self-determined.

As stated earlier, the amount and type of support a student needs will vary depending on the student's prior experience, type of disability, personal beliefs, knowledge and skill level, and the type and level of decision that must be made. For example, a student who has a high level of self-awareness and has made course selections many times may need little support making decisions about his or her school schedule but may need extensive support in setting vocational or postsecondary education goals. Likewise, a student who has a clear sense of career direction may have little experience or skill in choosing leisure activities. In order to determine the level of support that is helpful to a student, it is important to know the student well and to involve the student in identifying the type of support that would be most beneficial.

PREPARING EDUCATORS
TO SUPPORT STUDENT SELF-DETERMINATION

Like students, teachers need both an environment that encourages self-determination and specific instructional efforts and supports to increase their self-determination. If school personnel are to promote self-determination for students, they must be encouraged to be self-determined. Furthermore, staff must be provided with instruction and support on how to deliver curriculum and provide an environment that encourages self-determination for their students.

For teachers to become more self-determined, they need to be provided with the same type of instruction and environmental qualities recommended for students. While the type of instruction and environment recommended for students and staff are similar, the unique needs of school staff should be considered when the principles of self-determination are applied to their work roles. The major areas that need to be addressed to support greater self-determination for teachers are the same as for students: 1) the availability and quality of role models, 2) curricular issues, 3) opportunities for choice, 4) communication patterns, and 5) availability of supports. Specific suggestions for supporting staff within each of these five areas related to promoting self-determination are discussed in this section.

Availability and Quality of Role Models for Staff

Role models are available to school staff throughout the school, district, and community. The quality of those models for promoting self-determination is influenced by the workplace climate and by the opportunities for choice available in the work environment. The quality of role models is also affected by the degree to which self-determination for students and staff is stressed in the school. It is important to remember that students provide models for staff, just as staff provide models for students. Self-determination will be either strengthened or weakened in a school based on the types of models (e.g., self-determined, authoritarian, passive) to which students and teachers are exposed.

Although the types of role models provided by staff, students, and administrators throughout the school are important, the role modeling provided by those in leadership positions (e.g., the principal, student body president, superintendent, union steward, department chairs) is especially important. Individuals in these positions often have a high level of visibility in the organization through their roles in supervision, leadership, and coordination of activities. The models they provide related to self-determination are likely to have a strong impact on the degree to which staff are able to learn vicariously about self-determination. If the superintendent has supported the self-determination of the principal in involving teachers and students in the governance of the school, the principal is more likely to support a teacher in being self-determined in experimenting with a new teaching technique that gives students more choice in a classroom.

One strategy that has been used successfully to help teachers promote self-determination for staff and students through modeling is co-teaching. Co-teaching was used in field-testing of *Steps to Self-Determination* curriculum (Field & Hoffman, 1996). Teachers who were new to the curriculum were paired with teachers who had previously taught the curriculum. In addition, special education teachers, general education teachers, counselors, and psychologists were paired to deliver the curriculum. This strategy provided an opportunity for less-experienced teachers to have mentors and to observe more experienced role models promoting self-determination. It also provided an opportunity for staff with different roles to learn from each other through modeling. For example, teachers learned group process skills from psychologists and counselors; and psychologists and counselors developed skills in instructional delivery by observing teachers.

Consultants and trainers who interact with faculty are also a part of the modeling process. Models for living in a self-determined manner and encouraging self-determination in students can be observed through participating in workshops and conferences as well as through video and audio formats. For example, *The Self-Directed IEP* (Martin & Marshall, 1993) includes a video of a student demonstrating his leadership and of staff demonstrating support in an IEP meeting. Although the primary audience for these materials is students, the video also provides an excellent model for teachers and parents.

It is important to remember that short-term interventions will not have the same potency as models that are available on a daily basis. Therefore, if short-term or intermittent interventions that use modeling are undertaken, it will be important to use this strategy to build effective models that are available in the environment on a daily basis. For example, if a workshop is provided for staff using a motivational consultant who models self-determination, it will be important to capitalize on the experience of the workshop by providing follow-up that encourages self-determined behavior on a daily basis within the school.

Staff Curricular Issues

The concept of self-determination is a relatively new concept in schools. School staff need to have an opportunity to examine the concept of self-determination and what will lead to greater self-determination for themselves and their students. The curriculum for staff in-service and preservice training must address awareness of self-determination concepts as well as specific strategies for promoting self-determination in the school.

In-service training that takes a comprehensive approach (i.e., that helps staff increase their own self-determination as well as that of their students and that looks at schoolwide strategies as well as specific techniques or curricula) will be most successful. Furthermore, in-service training should be connected to the daily, ongoing activities within the school. Although one-time workshops can help acquaint staff with self-determination concepts and strategies, training with multiple sessions and opportunities for application between sessions or training that is combined with ongoing consultation or technical assistance will have greater impact.

An outcome of the Skills and Knowledge for Self-Determination project (Field & Hoffman, 1994b) was to identify in-service training needs for implementing the *Steps to Self-Determination* curriculum. The primary staff development needs identified for successful implementation of the curriculum included the following:

- Introduction to the concept of self-determination and understanding of the self-determination model upon which the curriculum is based
- Awareness of the curriculum "cornerstones" and strategies to apply the cornerstones throughout the curriculum
- Understanding of the overall scope and sequence of the curriculum
- An opportunity to address how self-determination will be infused into existing curriculum efforts

Awareness of the curriculum cornerstones was identified as an especially important area of need for in-service training. The 10 cornerstones provide the foundation for the curriculum and are infused throughout the lessons (Hoffman & Field, 1994):

1. Establishing a co-learner role for teachers
2. Emphasizing modeling as an instructional strategy
3. Using cooperative learning techniques
4. Using experiential learning strategies

5. Promoting integrated or inclusive environments
6. Obtaining support from family and friends
7. Fostering an open, accepting classroom environment
8. Incorporating interdisciplinary teaching
9. Appropriately using humor
10. Capitalizing on teachable moments

In-service training to promote self-determination should include support to staff for infusing self-determination throughout the curriculum. For example, legislation related to self-determination should be included in courses that deal with students' rights and responsibilities. Curriculum that promotes self-determination should be taught in appropriate courses (e.g., Career English, Career Planning, Health), and strategies that are consistent with self-determination concepts (e.g., provisions of choice and skills, win-win negotiation, listening) should be included in the instruction of appropriate subjects. In-service for staff should address how to most successfully infuse self-determination knowledge and skills throughout the curriculum.

In addition, self-determination should be modeled and practiced for students in personnel preparation programs. Preservice programs need to help students prepare for the more consultative and less authoritarian roles consistent with self-determination. Preservice students should be encouraged to listen to the needs of the youth whom they are preparing to serve. Furthermore, coursework and field experiences must provide ample opportunity for students to interact with and listen to individuals with disabilities and other potential recipients of their services (e.g., family members) about their needs. Guest speakers and panels can provide one vehicle for this process.

Personnel preparation programs should also promote self-determination for students in their programs. It is difficult to expect future teachers, administrators, and related-services personnel to promote self-determination if they feel disempowered. Personnel preparation programs should examine their course- and fieldwork requirements, advising practices, instructional techniques, and methods of evaluation to determine if current practices promote or discourage student self-determination and make modifications as needed.

Opportunities for Choice

Just as students need ample opportunities for choice to exercise self-determination knowledge and skills, so do teachers and other school personnel. If school staff work in an authoritarian, hierarchically structured workplace, it will be very difficult for them to experience being self-determined or to encourage self-determination in their students. A school that emphasizes shared decision making and collaboration among students, parents, community members, teachers, administrators, and other staff provides an atmosphere that is conducive to promoting self-determination among staff and students. Many of the school improvement models embodied in the school reform movement have such a collaborative emphasis.

Another factor that affects the ability of staff to support self-determination is the level of control they have over the curriculum. If the curriculum is already filled with rigidly structured requirements, it will be difficult for staff to address knowledge and skills that lead to self-determination. Although self-determination should be infused into existing curriculum and not taught only as an isolated subject, there needs to be some flexibility in the curriculum to introduce instruction in the basic knowledge and skills specific to self-determination, such as self-awareness, goal setting, anticipating consequences, assertive communication, and reviewing outcomes.

In addition to providing instruction in basic self-determination skills, there needs to be adequate flexibility in the curriculum to infuse the application of self-determination concepts and skills into existing subject matter. For example, students in English can read biographies of successful people and discuss the factors that contributed to and hindered being self-determined. Government class could focus on the Constitution and its preservation of citizen self-determination, while history class could elaborate on the contribution of self-determination to the founding of the country.

A related factor that affects the ability of staff to be self-determined and to promote self-determination is the degree of bureaucratization in the school. In complex bureaucracies there are often few opportunities for choice and little incentive for risk taking and creativity. Both of these factors greatly affect self-determination. Bureaucratization is often the result of overregulation by state, federal, and local government and is usually more extensive in larger school systems. The higher the degree to which school district staff find ways to comply with regulations while minimizing the number of rules and forms needing completion, the more likely they are to develop a school climate that supports self-determination. If an impact can be made on the governing and legislative bodies to develop fewer, more meaningful regulations, another step will have been taken to encourage self-determination in the schools.

Communication Patterns

The type of communication established in a school affects the degree to which students and staff feel encouraged to express themselves, initiate actions, and take risks. For staff, it is important to look at the following areas when examining how a school's communication patterns can best encourage self-determination.

Type of Supervision A collaborative approach to supervision and performance review establishes an expectation of self-determination. Employees should be active participants in establishing goals, performance indicators, supports, and activities that will help them attain their goals. If employees are active participants in their evaluation process, it is more likely that they will encourage students to be active participants in their educational process.

Organizational Structure Open communication lines between all school community members (e.g., students, parents, staff) helps to promote self-determination. The climate emphasized in the school (e.g., level and type of structure, encouragement to take risks, types of reporting lines) has a strong effect on the type of communication that occurs in a school. For example, if an organization is too rigidly structured, individuals will not feel that it is safe to express divergent opinions or take risks; if it is too loosely structured, they may have difficulty identifying boundaries and knowing when communication is valued and useful and when it is not.

Reinforcement Patterns The reinforcement patterns that exist in a school are part of the communication pattern within the school. The reinforcement pattern has an important impact on the level of encouragement staff receive for being self-determined and for promoting self-determination with students. If the staff's primary motivation is to avoid criticism or punishment for mistakes rather than seek rewards for exemplary work, it is unlikely that they will develop or maintain the necessary risk-taking behaviors and creativity to promote self-determination. It is also important that acknowledgment and value be associated with or communicated regarding a variety of accomplishments that are identified by staff as important. Reinforcement patterns should encourage individuals to develop and seek their own goals, not just respond to an externally driven contingent reward system. In other words, it is important that the same reinforcement patterns recommended for supporting student self-determination are available to staff.

Staff Supports

The supervisory process offers an excellent opportunity to provide support for self-determination. If a collaborative approach is taken to performance appraisal, supervisors can assume a coaching role to assist staff in achieving goals that are mutually identified. Coaching activities should be mutually identified and agreed upon by staff and their supervisors. These coaching activities can include identifying resources, asking questions, providing information, listening, and providing feedback. This collaborative coaching approach to supervision can help staff experience increased levels of self-determination as well as provide models for staff for taking on more consultative, facilitative roles with students.

SUMMARY

The ability of staff to encourage and support self-determination in students is dependent upon the staff members' self-determination and the support available to them. Like students, teachers need an environment that encourages self-determination in order to flourish. Environments that encourage and support self-determination provide quality role models, appropriate curriculum, opportunities for choice, open and positive communication patterns, and ongoing supports. These environments help individuals develop knowledge and skills that lead to self-determination, and they provide opportunities and appropriate reinforcements for using those skills.

To be most effective in encouraging and supporting self-determination in students, school staff need specific training and support for applying principles of self-determination within the school environment. This training and support should build on and be coordinated with efforts to support staff self-determination and should include activities such as in-service training, technical assistance, consultation, coaching, and team teaching.

The most successful self-determination efforts will be those that are schoolwide and that promote greater self-determination for all members of the school community. Although this approach to increasing self-determination requires significant effort, the potential rewards are also highly significant.

REFERENCES

Bandura, A. (1986). *Social foundations of thought and action: A social cognitive theory.* Englewood Cliffs, NJ: Prentice Hall.

Brolin, D.E. (1991). *Life centered career education.* Reston, VA: Council for Exceptional Children.

Deci, E., Connell, J., & Ryan, R. (1989). Self-determination in a work organization. *Journal of Applied Psychology, 74*(4), 580–590.

Erickson, E.H. (1975). *Life history and the historical moment.* New York: Norton.

Field, S., & Hoffman, A. (1996). *Steps to self-determination.* Austin, TX: PRO-ED.

Field, S., & Hoffman, A. (1994a). Development of a model for self-determination. *Career Development for Exceptional Individuals, 17*(2), 159–169.

Field, S., & Hoffman, A. (1994b). *Skills and knowledge for self-determination: Final report.* Detroit, MI: Wayne State University.

Field, S., Hoffman, A., & Sawilowsky, S. (1994). *Student participation in the IEP/transition planning process.* Unpublished manuscript.

Gordon, R.L. (1977). *Unidimensional scaling of social variables: Concepts and procedures.* New York: Free Press.

Harris, C., & McKinney, D. (1993). *Project PARTnership: Instructional kit.* Washington, DC: USA Educational Services.

Hoffman, A., & Field, S. (1994). Promoting self-determination through effective curriculum development. *Intervention in School and Clinic, 30*(3), 134–141.

Individuals with Disabilities Education Act of 1990 (IDEA), PL 101-476. (October 30, 1990). Title 20, U.S.C. 1400 et seq: *U.S. Statutes at Large, 104,* 1103–1151.

Johnson, D.W., & Johnson, R.T. (1986). Mainstreaming and cooperative learning strategies. *Exceptional Children, 52*(6), 553–561.

Johnson, D., Johnson, R., Holubec, E., & Roy, P. (1984). *Circles of learning.* Alexandria, VA: Association for Supervision and Curriculum Development.

Johnson, D.W., Johnson, R.T., & Maruyama, G. (1983). Interdependence and interpersonal attraction among heterogeneous and homogeneous individuals: A theoretical formulation and meta-analysis of the research. *Review of Educational Research, 53*(1), 5–54.

Koestner, R., Ryan, R.M., Bernieri, F., & Holt, K. (1984). The effects of controlling versus informational limit-setting styles on children's intrinsic motivation and creativity. *Journal of Personality, 52,* 233–248.

Martin, J., & Marshall, L. (1993). *The self-directed IEP.* Colorado Springs: University of Colorado.

Pietrofesa, J., Hoffman, A., & Splete, H. (1984). *Counseling: An introduction.* Boston: Houghton Mifflin.

Powers, L.E. (1993). Promoting adolescent independence and self-determination. *Family-Centered Care Network, 10*(4), 1, 15–16.

Van Reusen, A.K., & Bos, C. (1990). IPLAN: Helping students communicate in planning conferences. *Teaching Exceptional Children, 23,* 30–32.

Ward, M.J. (1991). Self-determination revisited: Going beyond expectations. In *National Information Center for Children and Youth With Handicaps: Transition Summary, 7,* 2–4, 12.

Wehmeyer, M.L. (1992). Self-determination and the education of students with mental retardation. *Education and Training in Mental Retardation, 27,* 302–314.

Wehmeyer, M. (in press). Promoting self-determination using the LCCE. In D. Brolin, *Life Centered Career Education* (pp. 1–16). Reston, VA: Council for Exceptional Children.

Helping Tom Learn
to Do for Himself...with Help

Jeanne Matuszewski

The question "What are some of the things you do that you believe help Tom become more self-determined?" didn't seem very difficult. After all, we get up in the morning, do what needs to be done during the day, and go to bed at night...just like everyone else! Everyone in our family has ideas about what they like to do and want to do and are pretty good in following through with their plans...just like their friends! It's a fairly regular routine of school, work, and play...shouldn't be too difficult to describe. "You just do it!"

My response "You just do it!", while accurate in how I initially felt about the question and perhaps accurate in that the things one does for self and others do become routine, is truly misleading because there is much involved in getting to the "doing it" phase.

I had so many thoughts about where to begin this essay, and it took some time to sort these out. I began by thinking what "self-determined" would look like for Tom: He would be able to engage in some type of occupation, he would possess social skills and participate in a variety of social activities, he would be able to live independently and manage his personal life, and he would be supported in assuming responsibility for all of this. Because these are the same goals that I have for his brother and sister, I realized that any explanation I was going to find to the initial question was not going to relate only to Tom but also to my other children.

I realized in preparing to write that if I were to focus on Tom and begin with his birth, I would be describing agony. When Tom was born, I heard not "It's a boy," but rather "Who's the pediatrician?" There were what seemed like hundreds of people telling us things that we as parents were supposed to remember in order to make very serious decisions. A nurse in the emergency room lifted the blanket that covered my face when the ambulance brought me in. She said, "Oh, you came in with that baby," and tossed the blanket back down over my face. The doctor compared the care and cost of medical services for my son to the upkeep of an expensive foreign automobile. I experienced a sense of total loneliness as we waited for the surgeons to tell us if our son had survived surgery.

While all those memories do haunt me, and while some of my actions are based on those events, I believe that my parenting techniques are primarily rooted not in this agony but rather in my own desire to enjoy my children. In trying to find answers, I spent many hours thinking about my childhood and my experiences within my family as I was growing up. I came to the realization that part of the answer to "What are some of the things you do to help Tom become more self-determined?" is found in who I am as a person and how I respond to different situations.

I am one of the older siblings in a large family. We grew up with both parents in our home. Our maternal grandparents lived close by and visited frequently, and our paternal grandparents visited from the opposite coast during the summer. We also had aunts and uncles close by and very much involved in our lives.

There were so many of us that it really wasn't necessary to go out and meet new friends, but there was frequently so much noise in our house and yard that we were encouraged to take our bikes and meet a friend at the park for a picnic lunch or go to the city pool for the afternoon and see who was there. As a parent I now believe that my mother was truly looking for some quiet moments and that in addressing her need she also provided us an opportunity to learn to meet our needs. Because we walked to and from school, we were allowed to stay and help in our classrooms or to walk to a friend's home and stay for an hour or so before going home. We were not encouraged to do things that cost money, such as going to the movies or buying the latest record album, as the money that was available had to feed and clothe many people. We were, however, encouraged to be creative, resourceful, and responsible.

As we got older and got our driver's licenses, we were also expected to take on more responsibilities. Errands that needed to be done became the responsibility of the teenage drivers and frequently the youngest children were taken along for these excursions. We were rewarded for accepting these responsibilities by being allowed to take the car (and the younger siblings!) to the beach or to a favorite desert location.

My grandparents, aunts, and uncles also played significant roles during my youth. We had many family gatherings for special occasions as well as "Bean Supper" together every Saturday night. There were many rituals associated with these gatherings and, as I look back upon these occasions, I recall a sense of working together to arrive at common goals. My grandfather was not influenced by any belief that boys and girls should be treated differently (as many were at that time), and as we spent time together, he taught me to do many things traditionally done by men.

When I was in elementary school I had a wonderful teacher whose husband died unexpectedly. I do not know the details of his death; however, I still recall a sense of secrecy surrounding it. This is reinforced when I remember her reaction to hearing some of my classmates discuss a newspaper article about his death. She was always a kind, warm, soft-spoken person, but on this occasion she was very upset. I remember her furrowed brow and her red face as she yelled, "Do you believe everything you hear? Do you believe everything you read? You *have* to learn to think for *yourself.*" I remember being frightened by this outburst and not understanding it. I remember feeling badly for this woman who had lost her husband, but I have remembered what she had said and I now recognize that I liked being given a type of "back-door" permission, from a person I respected, to think for myself.

I hope that my children will remember, as I have, some of the events, both positive and negative, that have occurred during their childhoods. I hope that they will be able to take those memories and use them to shape their adult lives. There are no assurances, however, that anything I have done or not done will help my children become more self-determined and that in itself is another difficult part of this process.

Before having children, I had never given parenting much thought. My techniques were a blend, modeled after those of my mother, grandmother, aunt, and newly acquired friends who brought techniques from their own families with them.

Modeling worked while I had two children, but then I had a third child—a child with a disability who challenged all of my abilities. My mother, grandmother, aunts, and friends had never had a child with a disability, and I had no one to model, no one to talk with. How was he going to be able to do the same types of things that his brother and sister did? How was I supposed to discipline Tom? What would he do while his brother and sister participated on sports teams? With all of his medical needs, were we ever going to be able to take him on a trip?

I recognized that we had a unique individual in a unique family with a unique set of circumstances. But also what I had was a child who could talk and laugh and enjoy life—a person who could learn, who could play and work, and who had the ability to live a live of his own choosing. It was my responsibility to help him accomplish this, just as it was my responsibility to do the same for his brother and sister. In this respect he was not unique.

I accepted the professionals' recommendations to read everything they presented to me. I gathered pamphlets and booklets and kept them by the bedside. I took the dusty parenting books off the shelves and opened them up one more time, and I went to "support" group meetings to meet other parents "just like" me. This didn't seem to be getting us anywhere as I was exhausted and crabby! While I wanted to learn more and I wanted to meet and talk with other parents, what I really wanted to do was have some fun with my children, to enjoy their childhoods, and that wasn't happening.

One strategy that has worked for me has been to do just what my elementary school teacher told me to do so many years ago: think for myself. I did begin to think about what made sense and what did not, and I incorporated what felt comfortable and began to eliminate things that just did not make sense.

Even though our lives were a little different from those of our friends and relatives, one thing that did make sense was to continue to have rules and to expect that everyone be responsible for honoring them. While I try to keep them simple (e.g., be polite and respectful of others, call home if there is a change in your plans, write down all phone messages), I also allow for some flexibility from child to child and situation to situation (e.g., not all children have to eat all their vegetables every day!). Tom is, at times, treated differently because of his needs, but the same rules apply to him as to the other children.

I thought I was being equally fair to my children in expecting them to do household chores until the day my older son Ken told me it wasn't fair that he always had to set the table and his brother never had to help. I explained that I hadn't yet figured out a way for Tom to carry things to the table and that if he could find a solution, Tom would be helping him set the table. "Tom's Table Setter" won Ken a monetary prize in a local "contraption invention" contest, and Tom is now helping to set the table! He also enjoys complaining about it, something that he would not have experienced had it not been for his brother's frustration!

As we began to do more of this type of problem solving in order to include Tom, we began to talk more about things we wanted to do and how we were going to go about doing them. Something important that quickly emerged from this process was the realization that, similar to my parents' expectation that the older children would perform more responsible tasks, I expect each person in our family to be responsible for something. While other children his age may be carrying groceries in from the car, a task he cannot do, one of Tom's responsibilities is to put groceries away.

Expecting responsibility from the children has also involved identifying for myself what is important for them to learn and what is not. They both know how to administer Tom's medications should he need them when they are alone with him, and they know that they should call 911 if they feel they have an emergency. They can all prepare a simple meal or snack as well as clean up after themselves. When it is important to them, they will make their beds—in the meantime, I just close the bedroom doors!

In addition to accepting responsibilities, the children participate in the planning of many activities. I have found that as I ask the children to contribute toward the planning, it has been important that I accept their contributions. I cannot ask "What do you think might work?" if I am not willing to accept and incorporate their contributions.

Tom has many food allergies, and finding food for him while we are out doing errands or taking a trip is sometimes a challenge. Although we do now carry a cooler with us, we also found it helpful to have "emergency" nonperishable food in the car at all times. Originally meant to address Tom's needs, this quickly changed into meeting everyone's needs. When it is time to refill the container, the children accompany me to the grocery store, take their own cart, and do their own shopping. While I don't always agree with their choices, I recognize that this has become a good experience for them. They have become very adept at reading labels and making decisions about what they want in the container. I will continue to build on this by having them plan a budget and make the purchases themselves.

Tom is expected to participate in decision making when appropriate. We began with simple decisions such as what type of vegetable to eat. As we move on to more complex decisions, discussions with Tom are more lengthy than those with his siblings, but that does not deter me from including him in this process.

Because of his complex medical issues, I believe it is important for Tom to be included in all discussions and decisions about his care. While he is not comfortable talking with all doctors, he is able to explain some of his concerns to me, and we are able to have a discussion about how to present his concerns to doctors and other providers. During our rides home from visits, we frequently have talks about how things went. Tom also cooperatively wears a necklace identifying his medical problems and understands the importance of this.

Now that Tom is part of the school community as well as the health community, I find that I continue to use the same techniques of including Tom in discussions and decisions, expecting that he will abide by the rules, and expecting that he will be given and will accept responsibility. He has begun to attend meetings at school (parent–teacher meetings, placement meetings, IEP meetings), and I will encourage him to participate actively in planning his future.

I believe that, as a person, I will find that I always want to read, to listen, to explore, and to think for myself. As a parent, I believe that I will continue to encourage my children to also read, listen, explore, and think for themselves. I will also try to model assertive behaviors and encourage my children to help identify people in their community with whom they can work and play. I hope that I also remember to kiss my children goodnight, no matter where in this world they are.

10

Self-Determination within a Culturally Responsive Family Systems Perspective

Balancing the Family Mobile

Ann P. Turnbull
and H. Rutherford Turnbull, III

> In a mobile, all the pieces, no matter what size or shape, can be grouped together and balanced by shortening or lengthening the strings attached, or rearranging the distance between the pieces. So it is with a family. None of the family members is identical to any other; they are all different and at different levels of growth. As in a mobile, you can't arrange one without thinking of the other. (Satir, 1972, pp. 119–120)

In this chapter, we highlight basic concepts of a family systems perspective and self-determination; describe four components of a family systems framework; and, within each component, raise pertinent issues related to self-determination. We supplement our discussion of self-determination by incorporating family perspectives identified through a qualitative study on transition that we previously conducted with parents of adolescents and adults with disabilities from Argentina, Uruguay, and Brazil (Turnbull & Turnbull, 1987). We will use the term *Latin American parents* to refer to parents from Argentina, Uruguay, and Brazil who participated in this study. Although we used this collective term, it is important to recognize that there are differences in perspectives among parents within and across Latin American countries. The parental perspectives that we discuss cannot be assumed to generalize to all families from Latin America or to all Latino families within the United States, particularly not to those whose families have been in the United States for a number of generations. We caution against any assumption that there is a single Latino perspective.

BASIC CONCEPTS

Undergirding our discussion throughout the chapter are basic concepts of a family systems perspective and of self-determination.

Family Systems Perspective

Bertalanffy (1975), a biologist, defined a system as a "set[s] of elements standing in interrelation among themselves and with the environment" (p. 159). The core assumption of general systems theory is that the system must be understood as a whole rather than analyzed in its component parts and that the wholeness of the system is greater than the sum of its individual parts.

Although there was emerging literature over the last few decades within family sociology and family therapy concerning how families actually operate as a system (Broderick & Smith, 1979), a systems view of families was not incorporated into the disability field until the early 1980s. Many researchers contributed to that effort. The original framework that we proposed for a family systems orientation to families of children with disabilities is shown in Figure 1 (Turnbull & Turnbull, 1990). The following four major components are part of this framework.

Family characteristics consist of the descriptive elements of the family in terms of the almost countless ways that families vary. Specific types of variation include the characteristics of the disability, characteristics of the family, personal characteristics, and special challenges. Within a systems framework, family characteristics are the *input* into the family interaction. For example, a family's cultural traditions and beliefs provide input or shape the nature of the interactions between husband and wife, parents and children, brothers and sisters, and nuclear and extended family members. Thus, family characteristics significantly determine the nature of that interaction.

Family interaction refers to the roles, relationships, rules, and nature of communication that occur among the subsystems of family members on a daily and weekly basis. Within a systems framework, family interaction is the *process* of how the family operates and thus how it meets its individual and collective family needs, which is the output of the system.

Family functions represent the different categories of needs for which families generally assume responsibility. Within a systems framework, carrying out family functions is the *output* of family interaction. Many people would describe meeting family functions as the ultimate purpose of families.

Family life cycle represents the *sequence* of developmental and nondevelopmental changes that affect families. Within a systems perspective, these changes continually alter family characteristics, family interaction, and family functions.

A major trend within the disability field over the last 10 years has been a pervading and increasing influence of family-centered practices. Allen and Petr (1996) have comprehensively reviewed literature on family-centered practices across a number of disciplines and have developed the following synthesized definition:

> Family-centered service delivery, across disciplines and settings, views the family as the unit of attention, and organizes assistance in a collaborative fashion and in accordance with each individual family's wishes, strengths, and needs. (p. 64)

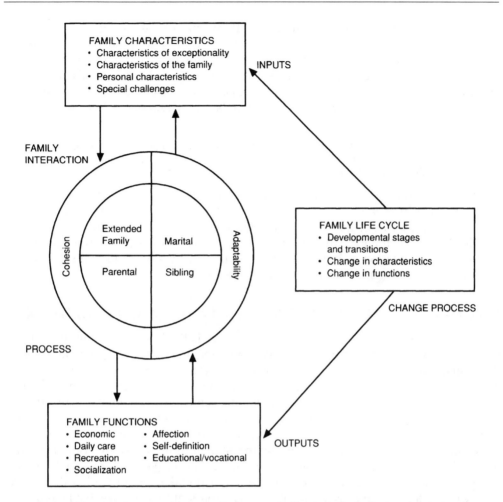

Figure 1. Family systems conceptual framework. (From Turnbull, A.P., & Turnbull, H.R. [1990]. *Families, professionals, and exceptionality: A special partnership* [2nd ed., p. 18]. Columbus, OH: Charles E. Merrill; reprinted by permission.)

The key characteristics of this definition are as follows: A focus on the family as the unit of attention, family–professional collaboration, family choice, emphasis on family strengths, family-identified needs, individualized services, family-sensitive information sharing processes, a focus on normalization principles, and the creation of a user-friendly service delivery system (Allen & Petr, 1996).

Returning to the analogy of the mobile, a family-centered approach rooted in family systems theory recognizes that the consideration of only one string jeopardizes the balance of the entire mobile. Alternatively, a family systems orientation approaches the mobile by considering the balance of all of the strings and respecting the reverberating impact that every individual string has on the whole.

Self-Determination

Although definitions of self-determination vary, for the purposes of this chapter, we adopt the definition of Wehmeyer (also see Chapter 6): "acting as the primary causal agent in one's life and making choices and decisions regarding one's quality of life, free from undue external influence or interference" (Wehmeyer, 1992a, p. 305).

Because Wehmeyer does such an excellent job of explicating this definition in Chapter 6, we will not repeat it here. We do want to highlight one concept, however, which is being a primary causal agent. Wehmeyer explains that causal agent "implies that it is the person who makes or causes things to happen in his or her life" (p. 116). Wehmeyer suggests that being a primary causal agent in one's life translates into acting autonomously. He also cites Lewis and Taymans (1992), who define autonomy as

> a complex concept which involves emotional separations from parents, the development of a sense of personal control over one's life, the establishment of a personal value system, and the ability to execute behavioral tasks which are needed in the adult world. (p. 37)

Returning to the mobile analogy, the concept of being a causal agent acting in an autonomous fashion can be likened to focusing almost exclusively on lengthening the mobile's string without necessarily taking into account the balance of the entire mobile. Thus, in comparing the definitions of a family systems orientation and a self-determining orientation as it is being implemented within the field of disability, the need for a reconciling framework becomes apparent.

SELF-DETERMINATION WITHIN A FAMILY SYSTEMS FRAMEWORK

Figure 1, which we have already briefly described, is the basis of our family systems analysis. As we describe a family systems orientation, we will comment about some of the strengths and weaknesses of self-determination intervention programs. For the sake of brevity, we make collective comments about all self-determination programs without thoroughly describing the differences among some of the programs. Typically, we make the assumption that the majority of self-determination approaches give primary emphasis to the individual with the disability in terms of increasing that individual's autonomy. This approach is consistent with the definition offered by Wehmeyer that emphasizes acting as a primary causal agent in one's life. We do recognize, however, that some self-determination approaches (a minority) take a family rather than a primarily individualistic approach; therefore, it is important to recognize that heterogeneity does exist.

Family Characteristics

The four subcategories of family characteristics illustrated in Figure 1 include characteristics of the disability, characteristics of the family, personal characteristics, and special challenges.

Characteristics of the Disability   Disabilities vary greatly in terms of nature of the disability, level of severity, age of onset, and concomitant strengths and needs. Whether a person has a physical or cognitive disability will affect family relationships and family functions in different ways. Obviously, severe physical limitations increase the need for ongoing support for mobility, whereas cognitive delays have significant impact on communication and decision making.

In addition to these more typical types of environmental impacts, the characteristics of the disability affect the evolving nature of self-determination. Given the taxonomy of self-determination needs described by Wehmeyer (see Chapter 6), one must consider the likelihood of full and partial development for people with severe and profound cognitive disabilities. The term "severe disabilities" is used so freely in our field, often without operational meaning, that it is often impossible to discern exactly what it means in terms of self-determination for people with severe and profound mental retardation. We are reminded of Elizabeth Boggs' (1985) description of her son, David, whom she describes as having profound mental retardation:

> David is now thirty-two. He does not understand instructions, let alone any conversation which might enable him to anticipate what is going to happen....David likes to eat, rock in a rocking chair, swing in a playground swing, ride in an automobile, and get into water, whether it be a shower or swimming pool. (p. 47)

David will not be able "to act as the primary causal agent" in his life as defined by Wehmeyer. This level of disability supports the need to consider ways in which people with more significant cognitive limitations can be given opportunities to express their preferences through a broad range of nonverbal means and also to consider options for partial participation in self-determination decision making. Boggs questions some of the current emphasis on normalization and self-determination for people with profound mental retardation:

> There are some parents who like the idea of normalization (Wolfensberger, 1972) because it is useful in glossing over the realities of difference. I sometimes think there are professionals who like it for the same reason....In a recent large meeting a well-known superintendent who runs a facility in which there are residents like David remarked that they had recently placed a number of profoundly retarded adults in the community, and that when these profoundly retarded adults were asked whether they would like to return to the institution, they all said no. I am sure that the adults to whom he referred were successfully placed, and I do not doubt their capacity nor the lack of coercion in their response. However, if people who could make such a conceptual choice, who could understand the question and express an answer are called profoundly retarded, then we need some new term for those who cannot do any of these things. (pp. 48–50)

In work being done on self-determination, it is essential that policy makers and program developers 1) be mindful of the cognitive requirements for various skills and the kinds of supports that are needed for people who truly do experience profound mental retardation and 2) distinguish those people whose cognitive limitations are not as pervasive from those people with developmental disabilities who have quite advanced cognitive disabilities. Glossing over the differences is not in the best interest of people with disabilities, their families, the programs that serve them, or society in general. Thus, it is impossible to understand a family's vision and concerns about self-determination without also considering carefully the characteristics of the disability and the supports and services available to maximize how individuals with severe and profound disabilities are able to function.

Characteristics of the Family   Families vary in many ways, including size and form, cultural background, socioeconomic status, and geographical location. Something that may seem as simple as size and form may have a substantial impact on self-determination. For example, a family that has only one child who is a teenager, who has autism, and who engages in challenging behavior may have quite different perspectives on the nature of self-determination when compared with a family with eight children, the youngest of whom is an adolescent (with the same characteristics of autism and challenging behavior) whose older brothers and sisters have been extremely assertive and even rebellious in their insistence in establishing their own autonomy from an early age.

Research and demonstration programs on family support and on the development of self-determination have not taken cultural background and socioeconomic status sufficiently into account to understand their systemic influences on development. In fact, we conjecture that self-determination itself is largely rooted in the cultural values of middle- and upper-middle-class Anglo American professionals and families.

We present here excerpts from our qualitative study with Latin American families to highlight that the values associated with self-determination are incongruent with the predominant values they articulated. (This incongruence does not apply just to self-determination but also applies to other initiatives within the disability field related to promoting independence, supported living, and supported employment.)

In our conversations with Latin American families, a dominant theme was their emphasis on the centrality of the family. Although we described the concept of family-centered practice earlier in the chapter, Latin American parents and professionals very much emphasize the family as the "center of society," "the source of society," and "a union and team" and as a culturally and generationally transmitted "ethic."

As parents and professionals described the Latin American family, they emphasized over and over that three dominant values are held by the family: family unity and permanence, interdependence, and protectiveness.

Unity and Permanence   The value of unity and permanence was manifest in numerous comments from Latin American parents. When asked how they would respond to the possibility that their children, upon attaining the age of majority, would move out of their parents' home and establish homes of their own while they continue their education or work, one said without hesitation, "It would be a tragedy. A shame would fall on our family. We cannot contemplate it."

These families explained that the Latin American tradition is that the family remains a tightknit and permanent unit. Its members continue to live in the parental home even after they become adults. When they marry, they may still continue to live in the parental home, in part because the tradition accommodates the two families in a single home.

Many parents and professionals confirmed these judgments. It is informative to have their exact words, because direct quotations not only inform but also express the spirit that reveals the tradition of family unity and permanence:

> "There is a relationship between parents and children that never breaks."
> "We never separate from our children. We never cut the cord."
> "It is against the family for the children to live alone as adults."
> "Young married couples live at their parents' home; it is Latino tradition."
> "Families live in the same house...always has been that way."

Even after sons and daughters marry, establish their own families, and move out of the parents' home, there still are activities that evidence the value attached to family unity and permanence:

> "We get together every week...we are passionate, committed to each other."
> "There is always much celebration within the family. We rejoice in being with each other, in being together."
> "We telephone each other often."
> "We always go to our parents' house for Sunday dinner."
> "There are strong physical ties...we live close together."

Interdependence   The value of unity and permanence is a means to make another value possible, which is interdependence. Unity and permanence make it possible for family members to help each other and to depend on each other for help. Again, the direct quotations express not only the substance but also the emotion of interdependence:

> "We all help each other because we all live together."
> "We all help pay for each other's services."
> "The family is a service vocation on behalf of the member with a disability."

"Family interdependence is the soundest possible way of support for each member."
"Children and parents all desire interdependence."

Protectiveness   Again, family unity and permanence and family interdependence are not only ultimate but also instrumental values. They are instrumental in that they enable and encourage families to be highly protective of each other and particularly of members with disabilities. Direct quotations reveal not only the fact of protectiveness but also the intensity with which it is valued:

"Families are protective, even overprotective; but they treat the disabled and nondisabled child alike in that respect."
"Families take too much care of the child with a disability. They even call adults by the term *mia nino* [my new one, my baby]."
"Children are always children. They do not go their own way, as a rule."
"The adult child is pampered [by his parents]."
"Parents are overpossessive of their children."
"It is difficult for parents to face the fact that children are not children forever."
"Parents can't forgive a child for moving away...for not letting the grandparents see their grandchildren."

An analysis of these values related to unity and permanence, interdependence, and protectiveness suggests potential conflicts with the values of self-determination. This should not be overinterpreted to suggest that Latin American families do not under any circumstances support self-determination, but it is critically important to recognize that self-determination itself is a cultural value and that it is more consistent with the Anglo American culture (Hanson, 1992) than with the Latin American culture.

Table 1 compares and contrasts the values of Latino cultures with the Anglo American values. It is not difficult to note which culture is most consistent with the values of self-determination.

Families who share a value system with the values characterizing self-determination will likely be far more supportive and more eager to embrace this disability policy and intervention direction. Unfortunately, our experience suggests that when families

Table 1.   Contrasting beliefs, values, and practices

Latino cultures	Mainstream culture
Collective orientation	Individual orientation
Interdependence	Independence
Collective, group identity	Individual identity
Cooperation	Competition
Saving face	Being direct
Relaxed with time	Time sensitive
Emphasis on interpersonal relations	Emphasis on task orientation
Spiritual/magical belief orientation	Rational/empirical orientation
More recent agrarian influence	More urbanized/industrialized mode
Tendency toward more patriarchal family structure	Tendency toward more democratic family structure
More relaxed with child development	Strong expectations for child development
More overt respect for the elderly	Less value/respect toward the elderly
Extended family systems more pronounced	Nuclear family systems more pronounced

From Zuniga, M.E. (1992). Families with Latino roots. In E.W. Lynch & M.J. Hanson (Eds.), *Developing cross-cultural competence: A guide for working with young children and their families* (p. 176). Baltimore: Paul H. Brookes Publishing Co.; reprinted by permission.

representing diverse cultures act on their own values—unity and permanence, interdependence, and protectiveness—they are sometimes criticized by culturally dominant professionals as not acting in the best interest of their son or daughter. A key issue for a family systems understanding of self-determination is not only the acknowledgment, but indeed the respect, of culturally diverse family values and the ability to analyze the issues associated with self-determination from myriad cultural perspectives.

Clearly there are situations in which the parents, perhaps representing their culture more strongly, may differ from the values of the adolescent with a disability in terms of his or her desire for self-determination. Thus, conflicts of interest can occur within families in terms of how values are acknowledged and acted upon. All of these issues make it essential for professionals working with self-determination intervention to have a finely honed understanding of family dynamics, cultural responsiveness, and strategies for supporting families where there are such internal conflicts of interest. For professionals who are from a different culture than the families whom they are serving, linking with mentors and community guides from the families' culture can be extremely helpful in learning culturally responsive ways to ascertain each family's and adolescent's vision and to provide services and supports that are respectful.

Personal Characteristics   Although family units have specific characteristics such as cultural values, each member within the family (just like each string on the mobile) has specific and idiosyncratic characteristics that influence how a family functions. Some of these individual characteristics include mental health, physical health, and individual coping styles. For example, parents who face challenges associated with long-term mental illness or with illnesses such as cancer or lupus will need to devote time and resources to their individual circumstances.

Additionally, members within families may have idiosyncratic coping styles; yet in some situations, these coping styles converge to a collective family coping style. Olson and his associates (Olson et al., 1983) specified five categories of coping styles:

- Passive appraisal—Ignoring a problem and hoping that it will go away
- Reframing—Changing the way one thinks about a problem in order to solve it and/or to make it seem less stressful
- Spiritual support—Deriving comfort in guidance from one's spiritual beliefs
- Social support—Receiving practical and emotional assistance from family and friends
- Professional support—Receiving assistance from professionals and human services agencies

All of these coping strategies can be used to model self-determination for children and youth with disabilities, and the degree to which family members effectively demonstrate these coping strategies influences the self-determining learning opportunities that are provided to children and youth. One of the coping strategies, passive appraisal, often gets in the way of self-determination development by ignoring the need for children and youth with disabilities to learn decision-making skills and to develop the sense of self-esteem that contributes effectively to decision making. Thus, family coping styles can be resources or barriers to self-determination.

Special Challenges   In the social and economic complexity of the mid-1990s, it is increasingly apparent that many families face tremendous challenges in terms of dealing with the effects of poverty, isolation, and abuse. Our discussion here will focus on abuse.

Many researchers agree that demographic characteristics placing children with a disability at risk of maltreatment are the same as those for children without a disability:

parents who are unmarried, poorly educated, and not regularly employed; and neighborhoods with low resources, high stress, and frequent episodes of violence (Benedict, White, Wulff, & Hall, 1990; Garbarino & Kostelny, 1992). Societal practices may increase vulnerability to abuse for children with disabilities. For example, residential placement and segregated classrooms for children and youth with a disability increase the risk of abuse and neglect (Baladerian, 1993; Sobsey, 1994). Child abuse is understood as a cause of disabilities (Baladerian, 1991; Garbarino & Kostelny, 1992) as well as a possible consequence of a disability. Some studies have found that children with a disability are at greater risk of abuse and neglect than are children without a disability (Sobsey & Varnhagen, 1991). Other studies report no increased risk for students with disabilities (Garbarino, Brookhouser, & Authier, 1987).

The issue of abuse and neglect of children with disabilities has been largely unaddressed within the disability field. Perhaps because of the need to move away from the view of families as dysfunctional and pathological, family strengths has been the focus of the last decade. Certainly this emphasis needs to continue, but likewise there is a compelling need within the field to address the particular issues of abuse and neglect associated with disability. One of the special implications for self-determination is teaching children and youth about the indicators of abuse and ways to report abusive situations that they may be experiencing. This is a particularly difficult issue, given the dual vulnerability of youth and disability.

Family Interaction

Family characteristics provide the input into family interaction, as illustrated in Figure 1. Family interaction is the process of how the family operates in terms of its subsystems and the cohesion and adaptability within which subsystem roles are carried out.

A defining feature of a family systems orientation is its emphasis on the interrelationships of the family subsystems. Subsystems within the family include marital, parental, sibling, and extended family (see Figure 1). A systems orientation recognizes the simultaneous, competing, and sometimes conflicting interests among the subsystems and seeks to identify those; however, a systems orientation is primarily focused on how the various subsystems converge at the systems level in creating a "whole that is greater than the sum of the parts" (Whitechurch & Constantine, 1993).

Recognition of and even respect for subsystems are fundamental considerations in terms of analyzing the nature of self-determination for an individual with a disability. Within the field of self-determination research and its application, the intertwining of individual self-determination with every other family member has not been taken into sufficient account. This is a fundamental problem given the nature of how systems operate:

> Because components in a system are *interdependent,* are held together in a system, behaviors of the components exhibit *mutual influence,* meaning that what happens with one component generally effects [sic] every other component. In families, this means that each family member's behavior affects every other family member. (Whitechurch & Constantine, 1993, p. 332)

The nature of this interdependence and the age at which the adolescent or adult is not as intertwined with the family again is highly dependent on cultural traditions and beliefs.

One way to think about the interaction circle shown in Figure 1 is to think of the mobile. Any change in the mobile's shape (i.e., in the self-determination of the individual with a disability) reconfigures the whole mobile (i.e., the whole family) into a different constellation. Furthermore, any change in other members' roles and relationships likewise influences the degree and nature of the self-determination of the child or youth with a disability. Concentrating on self-determination without taking the family interaction into account might be likened to substantially lengthening one string of a mobile without taking the other strings into account.

Of the four subsystems noted in Figure 1, the parental and sibling subsystems are the focus of our discussion, but our concentration should not be interpreted as an intention to ignore the marital or extended family subsystems, which are critical to the development of self-determination.

Parental Subsystem In terms of the parental subsystem, the earlier quotes from Latin American families suggest cultural values regarding the role of parents in the raising of their children not just during childhood and adolescence, but also throughout the adult years. Cultural expectations regarding timing, especially in terms of when it is appropriate for children and youth to separate from the family and set up their own household, greatly influences how the parental subsystem is carried out. Although extended parenthood is clearly evident from the Latin American traditions, many Anglo American families also share this perspective. Krauss and Seltzer (1993) reported on their longitudinal data for almost 400 aging parents among whom the average age of the mother was 67 years and the average age of the son or daughter was 34 years. Data suggest that the mothers who had been involved in long-term caregiving compared very favorably in family well-being with their age peers who had not had long-term caregiving responsibilities. The authors suggested that one explanation may be that

> the mother may be deriving benefit from her relationship with her adult child with retardation. Many mothers feel that they have a continued purpose in life derived from their ongoing active parenting role. Other women in our sample feel that they have high self-esteem because they successfully met the challenge of rearing a child with a disability. For any one or a combination of these reasons, the mothers in our sample currently are, on balance, a well-functioning group with aging women who appear to have weathered the nonnormative storm of having a child with retardation and of rearing him or her well into adulthood....despite decades of care provision, they retain a vitality and commitment to caregiving. (pp. 60–61)

It is critical to realize that some of the assumptions of self-determination in terms of the individual with a disability making the transition to an independent adult lifestyle may run contrary to the preferences of parents. Although there is often the assumption among the professionals in this field that long-term caregiving is a burden for parents, Krauss and Seltzer suggest that there are positive outcomes for some parents. Thus, in self-determination planning and intervention, it is wise to gain the perspective of parents on their preferences as well as the perspectives of the youth or adult with a disability and to seek to create "win-win" situations to the greatest degree possible. Strategies for creating win-win situations include ensuring that the visions and preferences of parents and adolescents are identified and that any conflicts are addressed through compromises that have the potential of satisfying both parties. For example, in one situation in which an elderly father preferred that his middle-age adult daughter with a disability continue to live in his family home and assist him in maintaining the household, the daughter negotiated her need for autonomy by getting a job during the day, taking some courses at a community college in the evening, and spending weekends and vacations with friends and siblings.

Many successful strategies have been developed to help people in varying family situations mediate different needs and preferences, and these same mediation strategies can be useful within self-determination programs. When such win-win situations are not possible, supporting the self-determination of the adolescent or the adult will likely be more successful when parental needs can also be respected. For example, in the situation just discussed, if the adult with the disability believes that it is necessary for her to establish her own residence, the self-determination program might assist her father in locating other live-in companions so that his needs are met and ultimately he does not place pressure on his daughter or make her feel guilty for her decision. We address this issue in more detail in the later section of the chapter focusing on life span changes.

Sibling Subsystem   There has been increasing interest in the disability field since the mid-1980s concerning the role of siblings in the lives of children and youth with disabilities and the impact on them of having a brother or sister with a disability (Powell & Gallagher, 1993; Stoneman & Berman, 1993). The literature on sibling issues has not, however, explicitly addressed the role of brothers and sisters in supporting self-determination.

Because many brothers and sisters are also dealing with similar autonomy issues at approximately the same time within the family life span, brothers and sisters could be an extremely valuable resource in providing support, communication facilitation with parents and other adults, and opportunities for more independent decision making. An important consideration for research and demonstration is to identify the perspectives of children and youth with disabilities regarding the roles that their brothers and sisters might play in supporting them and also to identify the perspectives of siblings regarding the benefits and drawbacks of their involvement as self-determination role models. This may be particularly important for individuals with severe and profound cognitive disabilities, given the fact that siblings often are the persons who provide long-term support after parents die (Seltzer, Begun, Seltzer, & Krauss, 1991).

Cohesion and Adaptability   A close examination of Figure 1 reveals that there are four quadrants representing the four family subsystems, but there is a circle around these quadrants that contains the terms *cohesion* and *adaptability*. Cohesion and adaptability are the rules of interaction within the family system (Olson, Russell, & Sprenkle, 1980). These rules substantially affect the boundaries between the subsystems and the boundaries between the family and the environments in which it operates. The concept of boundary is fundamental within a family systems approach because boundaries determine the permeability and impermeability of the family regarding change, support, and intervention of any kind (Whitechurch & Constantine, 1993). In many systems, rules and boundaries maintain a state of homeostasis or resistance to change. This resistance becomes a fundamental issue to recognize and address effectively if one seeks to promote self-determination in any of the family members, especially when there are strong societal influences for dependency.

Family *cohesion* represents the continuum of close emotional bonding that members have with each other, as well as the level of autonomy individuals experience within the family system (Olson et al., 1980). On one end of the continuum is a high level of disengagement, and on the other end is a high level of enmeshment. In disengagement, families have rigid subsystem boundaries; relationships are often characterized by spending a great deal of time apart, having few activities or relationships in common, and generally having a highly individualistic lifestyle. Disengagement is characterized by each family member "doing my own thing."

In contrast with disengagement, enmeshment occurs when the boundaries between subsystems become blurred and when family interactions are characterized by overinvolvement and overprotection. Families who might be described as being highly enmeshed typically spend all of their time together, do not have separate space to pursue their own interests, and think of themselves as one collective group rather than as a group of individuals.

In reflecting on the cohesion continuum, it is critically important to consider the definition of self-determination and its fundamental concepts. As discussed earlier in the chapter, self-determination suggests that a person acts as his or her primary causal agent, meaning that the person acts autonomously. We earlier cited a definition of autonomy as

> a complex concept which involves emotional separations from parents, the development of a sense of personal control over one's life, the establishment of personal value system, and the ability to execute behavioral tasks which are needed in the adult world. (Lewis & Taymans, 1992, p. 37)

From a family systems perspective, the key is that not all families believe such autonomy is consistent with an appropriate level of cohesion. When service providers and/or individuals with developmental disabilities do not take into account the rules and roles related to the family's cohesion continuum, the balance of the family mobile can be jeopardized. Obviously, some families fully concur with the values of self-determination and promote autonomy for all family members on a consistent basis. An important cultural consideration is that although it is normative for adolescents and young adults to push family limits and rules to achieve greater autonomy within some cultures, it is not *always* culturally typical to do so.

Thus, one of the most important places for self-determination intervention to start is in listening to families about their own cohesion rules and in attempting to work within those rules to the fullest extent possible. It is also important for service providers to avoid interpreting all family decisions as specifically related to the disability. Sometimes service providers may be concerned that the family does not encourage autonomy for the individual with a disability, and they attribute that to the family's overprotectiveness because of the disability. On the contrary, many families do not promote the autonomy of any of their members; and they interact with the member with a disability in a way that is consistent with all of their family interactions.

Adaptability refers to the ability of the family to change in response to a particular situational or developmental demand or expectation (Olson et al., 1980). Adaptability also exists on a continuum, with one end being characterized by an extremely high degree of control and structure and the other end being characterized by everchanging rules and expectations. With an extremely high degree of control and structure, there might be such rigidity that changes, such as those associated with the development of self-determination, cannot be manifest because the family will not tolerate different roles and decision-making styles. However, everchanging rules, as characterized by the other end of the continuum, create special challenges within families because the rules change so fast that it is impossible to know what to expect.

Given that cohesion and adaptability both exist on a continuum, family theorists suggest that optimal family functioning occurs when there is a balance in the approximate middle of the continuum. The point at which balance is considered appropriate, however, is very much determined by cultural values. We illustrate this point by considering a Latin American family perspective on transition from high school to adulthood (Turnbull & Turnbull, 1987).

Many Latin American families are cohesive and reluctant to have any of their members, particularly adolescents with a disability, separate from the family unit.

Families are typically interdependent and inclined by reason of long cultural tradition to be self-reliant and to regard themselves as the most certain source of assistance in accommodating the adolescent. They are protective and typically continue to embrace the adolescent, both literally and figuratively, to prevent or minimize the risks inherent in adulthood; and they often consider the out-of-home placement of the adolescent or adult and indeed of any members as anathema. Quotes from our qualitative study with Latin American families highlight their perspectives on the appropriate level of cohesion and adaptability:

> As one professional remarked, "Transition is a challenge to the values of the family. It is contrary to our…traditions."
> Another professional noted, "There are conflicted goals in transition. Parents and professionals tend to train the child to be as independent as possible; certainly that is the goal. But parents still delay the child's adolescence, adulthood, and independence. But they do this for all of their children; only with the disabled child, it is more of a problem."
> One parent commented, "Our dream? The growth of our child and family, health, happiness, but all near the family. Work and recreation, independently. But we want to grow with our children."

As noted, the Latin American tradition is for the adolescent to remain at home as an adult; it is contrary to the tradition—"not normal"—for the adolescent to leave home. Accordingly, the adult child with a disability is accommodated at home across the child's life span:

> "Prolonged childhood? Of course! It is crazy for the child to leave home."
> "It would be a pity…just terrible…for any of our children to leave home. We [parents] would just die…we can't bear the thought."

In this cultural context, the child with a disability is expected to live with the parents or other family always. The ideal is for the child to live at the home of a relative, preferably a sibling, after the parents die. Families report that there is no problem with the adult with a disability living at home; institutionalization is rare.

Professionals working in self-determination programs might be particularly tempted to interpret these family values as "wrong," but instead they should recognize that the appropriate level of cohesion and adaptability within family subsystems and within the overall family system is culturally determined. This is why the component of family characteristics (e.g., cultural values) is conceptualized as the input into the family interaction process. One cannot understand family interaction without taking into account all of the factors discussed previously related to family characteristics. Each of those characteristics has a pervasive impact on how the family operates in terms of cohesion and adaptability.

One of the major contributors of a family systems understanding to successful self-determination development is for professionals and families to have a much keener understanding of how cohesion and adaptability operate within an individual family. The development of self-determination often creates a jarring impact to the homeostatic cohesion and adaptability rules. It would be extremely helpful for people working on self-determination to collaborate with family systems specialists in devising interventions that are respectful and supportive of the family's cohesion and adaptability roles and relationships. Rather than encountering frustration when families are apparently blocking the self-determination of their son or daughter, family systems supports could be responsive in supporting families to make the interactional changes they choose, changes that are appropriate for them within their cultural traditions and in light of the subsystem relationships and boundaries.

A family systems orientation is likely to produce far more successful self-determination outcomes than what often happens, in the analogy of the chapter's opening quote, when one string in the mobile is substantially lengthened without regard for the mobile's balance. The important point here is that individual strings can be lengthened (individuals with disabilities can gain greater autonomy) by taking into account the perspectives, concerns, and visions of other family members. In fact, lengthening one string of the mobile may create a new balance that is far more satisfactory for the families in the long run. Thus, family change can be viewed as a catalyst of other family changes that will ultimately enhance family well-being.

Family Functions

Now that we have discussed the input to the system—family characteristics—and the process within which the system operates—family interaction, it is appropriate to consider the output of family process, which is meeting the individual and collective needs of families (Caplan, 1976; Leslie, 1979). The fundamental purpose of families in our society is the uniting of individual effort in order to meet the individual and collective needs of the unit. Within a family systems framework, seven broad categories of family functions include economic, daily care, recreation, socialization, affection, self-definition, and educational/vocational (Turnbull & Turnbull, 1990).

Economic Needs   The economic impact of disability very much depends upon the particular characteristics of the disabling condition, the availability of informal supports, and the family's geographic location. Costs also must be considered in terms of the actual dollar costs as well as costs of having available child care so that parents can pursue employment. Knoll (1992) conducted a combined survey and interview study with 92 families of individuals with disabilities in eight states. He reported data indicating the percentage of families who identified specific impacts as follows:

- Major increase in household expenses—56.5%
- Someone gave up a job—50%
- Someone did not pursue employment—43.5%
- Someone did not pursue further education—37.0%
- Someone refused a transfer or promotion—21.7%
- Job change for better medical coverage—7.6% (Knoll, 1992, p. 33)

Furthermore, economic needs of families must be addressed in terms of the financial resources that they accrue through both employment insurance and governmental supports. One of the major issues in some self-determination demonstration programs is supporting adolescents to identify career preferences and to obtain critical employment experience as precursors to the transition to full-time employment as adults. There are many issues for families related to the opportunities for adolescents and adults with disabilities to have paid employment. There are economic advantages in terms of having the individual contribute to his or her economic support as well as possibly to the economic support of other family members. Critical issues that must be addressed include the family's potential loss of economic resources when their son or daughter moves out of the family home, no longer receives government benefits, or sets up a household in such a way that the money that they earn supports them and their newly established household unit rather than the nuclear family unit. An analysis of the potential economic benefits and drawbacks for families and the support of families in their effort to avoid economical penalties as a result of their son's or daughter's self-determination will likely bring more successful self-determination outcomes.

The conventional wisdom within the disability community in the United States is to encourage supported living for adults with significant cognitive disabilities. Given that the vast majority of economic resources are invested in residential and community formal residential and adult services systems, supported living often requires that the adult with the disability and his or her family generate additional economic resources. As self-determination opportunities flourish and as adolescents and adults choose a variety of alternatives, it is essential that federal and state funding streams and tax policy keep up with these changes so that the family will at least not be penalized financially.

Daily Care Needs   One of the roles of families has been to attend to the daily care needs of their members with disabilities, often over their entire life span. Knoll (1992) also reported that 54.3% of the children were described as having "extensive" overall daily care needs. Types of daily care needs that were reported to require most extensive assistance were movement in the community, medical monitoring, bathing, and grooming.

One of the issues in the development of self-determination is the ability to carry out the daily care requirements more independently rather than rely on parents for this role. For people with cognitive limitations, this often means learning to do the task oneself; people with physical disabilities are increasingly using personal assistance services. Many personal assistance services are not available or are not adapted for people with cognitive disabilities. Sometimes an issue for service providers working on self-determination is the expectation for families to teach more independent functioning around the home. A critical issue for families is the sheer time demands that many face and the multiple responsibilities of meeting the needs of the members within other family subsystems. A family systems orientation examines the needs and preferences of all family members and does not place exclusive emphasis on supporting the development of any one family member—including the development of self-determination for the individual with a disability. Consider this example:

> A mother has agreed to work with her teenage daughter with cognitive limitations on getting up to an alarm clock and taking a shower without assistance. Incorporating instruction in this routine triples the time involved, as compared with the mother's taking a more instrumental role. Thus, rather than getting her daughter up at 7:00 A.M. in order to get to school by 8:20 A.M., she must make sure that her daughter's alarm clock is set at 5:30 A.M.so that there is time not only for instruction but also for the daughter to proceed through the morning routine at a much slower pace. While the mother is overseeing the intervention program with her daughter, her three other children prepare their own breakfast with the help of their father, who assists them in accomplishing all of their tasks. The father cleans the kitchen and the siblings proceed to school, often without having an opportunity to interact with their mother or older sister and generally feeling overlooked and a bit resentful. The mother is frazzled and frustrated by the time she gets to work and experiences disconcerting conflict about whether it is in the best interest of her family for her adolescent daughter to develop these independent living skills at the expense of other family members' needs.

Self-determination and promoting independence in daily care needs will be far more successful when service providers take into account the multiple and competing responsibilities of family life. A major support needed by families is to have people come into the home to provide this type of instruction so that the family interaction is not so disrupted. Families can learn to be assertive in stating their preferences of what they are and are not able to do. Likewise, it is critically important for the adolescent with a disability to express preferences about how he or she would most like to learn daily care skills.

Recreation Needs   Families of children and youth with disabilities have reported limitations in opportunities for family recreation because of the presence of challenges that result from the disability (Knoll, 1992; Lonsdale, 1978). One of the issues that might be a part of self-determination programs is the identification of recreational preferences of the individual with a disability and also of other family members. By identifying shared interests that might be pursued collectively as well as individual interests that might allow each person to "do his or her own thing," a more cohesive balance in recreational opportunities can be found. State-of-the-art leisure and recreation programs need to merge with self-determination programs in ensuring that optimal opportunities are being provided in this important area of family functioning.

Socialization Needs   It can be particularly challenging for families to facilitate the social relationships of their children and youth with disabilities, given that many families report a strong sense of isolation themselves. Knoll (1992) reported that 30.4% of the families in his sample indicated they felt somewhat isolated in their communities and neighborhoods, and 13% indicated that they felt very isolated:

> In almost every case, the families indicated a sense of being the outsider. This feeling of isolation coupled with the time demands associated with the care of their children leaves little energy or motivation for connecting with their communities. In some instances, neighbors were actively hostile. (p. 38)

An important support for families would be for schools and other formal services to be more proactive in facilitating friendships and community connections (Amado, 1993; Falvey, Forest, Pearpoint, & Rosenberg, 1994).

Affection Needs   The private and public display of affection is determined very much by one's cultural values. For example, Latin American families describe themselves as very affectionate:

> "When we feel affection, we show it."
> "It is natural to touch and kiss our friends."

This same public display of affection would be considered awkward in some other cultures. Thus, each family needs to define its roles, relationships, and rules in terms of the display of affection.

There are many issues that families face in terms of expressing affection within the various family subsystems. One of the most critical roles for families is to provide a nurturing environment for meeting physical intimacy needs as well as the need for unconditional love from others. Although there has traditionally been a strong influence, particularly within the early intervention field, supporting the involvement of parents as teachers of their children with disabilities, there can be a conflict of interest for the parent between the role of therapist and the providing of unconditional love and acceptance. This potential conflict is illustrated in a quote by Sondra Diamond (1981), an adult with a physical disability who describes the interaction with her mother when she was a child:

> Something happens in a parent when relating to his disabled child; he forgets that they're a kid first. I use to think about that a lot when I was a kid. I would be off in a euphoric state, drawing or coloring or cutting out paper dolls, and as often as not the activity would be turned into an occupational therapy. "You're not holding the scissors right," "Sit up straight so your curvature doesn't get worse." That era was ended when I finally let loose a long and exhaustive tirade. "I'm just a kid! You can't therapize me all the time! I get enough therapy in school every day! I don't think about my handicap all the time like you do!" (p. 30)

As parents are increasingly encouraged to be teachers of self-determination within the home and community settings, the potential conflict with the expression of affection must always be considered.

Sexuality is another critically important area in terms of the development of adolescents with disabilities. Issues of sexuality often pose tremendous conflicts for families, particularly families of females who may fear sexual exploitation (Gardner, 1986). Furthermore, adolescents' inappropriate sexual activity can place major restrictions on their opportunities. Often there is a double standard, and the options for expressing sexuality are much narrower for a person with a disability than for his or her counterparts who do not have a disability.

As with other issues that we discussed, views on the appropriateness of sex education and sexual behavior by children and adolescents with disabilities are determined by cultural values. From our qualitative study with Latin American families, some of their perspectives on this subject are as follows:

> "Sex is a taboo."
> "Sex is terrible to families."
> "Families cannot face their children's sexuality."
> "Families have a paralyzing fear about sex in their children."

Self-Definition Needs　It is perplexing that there has been such a limited emphasis within the family literature on the roles and contributions of family members in supporting children with disabilities to develop self-esteem and a positive self-concept. Paradoxically, there has been more emphasis in the literature on preparing siblings and classmates without disabilities to understand disability issues than on preparing the child with a disability to have insight about the disabling condition and his or her particular strengths and needs. Related to self-determination, Ward (1991) emphasizes the danger of having family members convey to a child with a disability that he or she is a problem and that the disability is the overriding consideration.

Families need support from the earliest years in developing a positive view of disability themselves and in knowing how to thwart stigmatizing influences. For example, Carmen and Alfredo Ramirez, parents of Danny, a 12-year-old with Down syndrome, described their first experience in the hospital when they went to the nursery to look at Danny just after they were given his diagnosis. A well-intentioned, but unfortunately misinformed, nurse asked them, "Do you want your son at the window where everybody can see him or do you want him away from all the other babies, where nobody can see him?"

When families encounter such stigmatizing experiences from the earliest days of their baby's life, they obviously need support in knowing how to counteract them and in developing their own positive sense of their child's wholeness. From such a vantage point, they are in the best position to convey that same sense of unconditional love and respect to their child and to other family members. The importance of parental influence in self-definition is described by Harilyn Rousso (1984), an adult with cerebral palsy, as follows:

> My mother was quite concerned about the awkwardness of my walk—which she feared would subject me to endless teasing and rejection. To some extent it did. She made numerous attempts over the years of my childhood to have me go for physical therapy and to practice walking more "normally" at home. I vehemently refused all of her efforts. She cannot understand why I wouldn't walk straight. Now I realize why. My disability, with my different walk and talk and my involuntary movements, having been with me all of my life, was part of me, part of my identity. With these disability features, I felt complete and

whole. My mother's attempt to change my walk, strange as it may seem, felt like an assault of myself, an incomplete acceptance of all of me, an attempt to make me over. I fought it because I wanted to be accepted and appreciated as I was. (p. 9)

Because self-determination is so inextricably linked to self-esteem, a critical element of self-determination development from the earliest years is supporting parents and significant others to reframe the meaning of disability. Vohs (1993) challenges all professionals and families interested in self-determination and particularly the enhancement of self-definition:

There is a need to begin to explore the unknown, almost taboo arena of human relationships and the impact of difference. How do we shift these attitudes? How do we help families gain the tools they need to tell (and believe) a different story about disability and empower and ennoble themselves at the same time? How do we learn to speak differently about disability in such a way that our speaking will cause new social structures to take the place of the ones we have now? How do we all learn to tell the kind of stories that will help ameliorate differences and allow for a sense of belongingness? What would it take to equip professionals-in-training with a sense that learning to speak differently about disability is part of their job? (p. 65)

Educational/Vocational Needs   The involvement of families in educational decision making has been their most prominent role since the passage of the Education for All Handicapped Children Act of 1975. Educational involvement and decision making has been characterized primarily as involvement in developing individualized education programs (IEPs), giving consent for initial evaluation and placement, and receiving written notification of changes in program planning. A careful analysis of research on the roles of parents in educational decision making has generally revealed more a passive than an active approach (Lynch & Stein, 1982; Turnbull & Turnbull, 1990). Promising models have developed to enhance the contributions of families in IEP decision making (Turnbull & Turnbull, 1990).

Some of the most exciting developments within IEP participation have primarily targeted students in preparing them to be more effective advocates, particularly around transition issues. Van Reusen and Bos (1994) have developed a training model for high school students with learning disabilities and their parents. Their five-step strategy begins with the students and parents identifying and listing their perceptions of the student's learning strengths, weaknesses, goals, and interests, and preferences. Once inventory sheets are completed, these four steps follow:

P—Provide inventory information during the IEP conference.
A—Ask questions.
R—Respond to questions.
S—Summarize the IEP goals. (p. 469)

Students and parents were taught to negotiate a partnership by determining which goals were held in common and which goals could be attributed to either the student or parent. Research results based on a comparison of students who went through these procedures versus students who received only an informational lecture/discussion on IEP roles indicated that students who had received the systematic instruction provided more goals and information during the conference and provided more information on learning and career goals. They contributed three times as much information on learning strengths. Interestingly, several parents also reported that their adolescents had used the strategies they had learned for the IEP conference in interviewing for jobs and for postsecondary school admission. An essential direction for self-determination training is to prepare parents and students to collaborate with each other and with other members of the planning team in terms of educational and vocational decision making.

Family Life Span

The pervading theme of family life span is change, but the amount of change that a family finds suitable is tied very much to the family's sense of cohesion and adaptability. Families at one end of the continuum of adaptability may resist change at all costs, and families on the other end of that continuum may seek to implement every new idea and to have constant change and upheaval. Again, in terms of cohesion and adaptability, the key concept for system functioning is maintaining a balanced level.

In our discussion of family characteristics, family interactions, and family functions, we have attempted to some extent to take a snapshot of family life. Such a snapshot can be deceiving in the sense that families are constantly in some state of flux and change. Rather than a snapshot, family life can be described much better in terms of a motion picture in the sense that experiences of the moment are constantly influencing how the future will be played out (Turnbull & Turnbull, 1990).

Life span theorists have characterized developmental and nondevelopmental changes. Developmental changes are those that are typically associated with life span stages and the transitions between stages. Nondevelopmental changes focus on single, distinct occurrences that are not tied to typical growth and evolution from one life span stage to another. Our discussion of life span changes focuses on developmental stages, developmental transitions, and nondevelopmental changes.

Developmental Stages Developmental stages can be visualized as a series of relatively level plateaus in which family roles and responsibilities (family interaction) and family needs (family functions) are carried out in similar ways. Although there are many different conceptualizations of stages ranging from just a few to as many as 24 different stages (Carter & McGoldrick, 1980), typical conceptualizations of life span stages include birth and early childhood, school-age years, adolescence, post-parental years, couple years, and aging (Turnbull & Turnbull, 1990).

Developmental stages are typically defined in terms of the age of the oldest child (Hill & Rodgers, 1969), based on the assumption that as the older child advances, families have to change their roles and responsibilities to account for emerging autonomy and individual functioning. This fundamental assumption of developmental stages is rooted in an Anglo American tradition:

> In illustration, Latino families find it acceptable for preteens to sit on the mother's lap. Preschoolers who drink from a baby bottle may not be admonished. Moreover, it is normal in these families for members to sit close to one another and to have direct physical contact regardless of age. Anglo professionals might view this closeness as symbiotic behavior and unacceptable. (Zuniga, 1992, p. 164).

In terms of family cohesion, a fairly typical Anglo American family pattern is for there to be closer bonding with members as infants and a general pattern of "letting go" as adolescents and young adulthood stages are reached. As we have already discussed in terms of Latin American families, the pattern for this same stage is often different. Thus, the roles, relationships, and functions typical of stages are influenced not only by the age of the children but also by one's cultural heritage.

Families who have a member with severe cognitive disabilities face the increasing discrepancy between chronological age and developmental competence, including decision-making competence. Particular challenges within families can occur at times when younger siblings overtake the developmental competence of the older brother or sister and thus have some role reversals in the biological birth order (Breslau, 1982). Another issue for many families with children and youth with severe cognitive disabilities is decreased experience with life span "punctuation marks" such as obtaining a driver's license, participating in religious confirmation, going to bars at age 21, voting, participating in the military, marrying, and having children (Turnbull, Summers, & Brotherson, 1986). The absence of these environmental indicators of increasing autonomy can decrease the adaptability of family interaction by reinforcing rigidity rather than change.

Developmental Transitions   Within a life span perspective, developmental transitions are the periods between the relatively stable plateau stages and are characterized by change and discontinuity. In terms of life span theory, transitions have been classified as normal because transitional events and changes are "*ubiquitous* (they occur to most families), *expectable* (families can anticipate their occurrence at certain points in the family life cycle), and *short-term* (not chronic)" (McCubbin et al., 1980, pp. 860–868). Transitions can involve changes in family characteristics, the composition of the family subsystems, levels of cohesion and adaptability, and the method with which family functions are carried out.

Within the disability field, often the term *transition* is used to refer almost exclusively to the movement of students with disabilities from high school to adulthood. This is particularly true within the self-determination literature that primarily focuses on adolescents. Families experience transitions at every life span stage. By the time the family member with a disability reaches the end of adolescence, the family has already had a number of successes and failures with transitional experiences.

Another important consideration is the emphasis that families place on future planning. Future planning, like so many other aspects of family life, is strongly influenced by cultural traditions. In our qualitative study with Latin American families (Turnbull & Turnbull, 1987), families described a general trend of not seriously planning for transition:

> "Parents don't think about the future."
> "Families tend to take life a day at a time."

That is not to say, however, that they do not worry about the future. For many parents, the main concern is "What happens after I die?" Yet that concern is powerfully mitigated by the Latin American family traditions and values of unity and permanence, interdependence, and protectiveness—traditions and values that enable parents to assume that the family will care for the child:

> "When I die, my family will take over."
> "The family cares for its own."

Because of these traditions, values, and expectations, and because there is a strong tendency to maintain adolescents and adults at home, transition planning is delayed and transition itself is postponed, usually until the parents' death. Indeed, the time when families begin to plan for transition is calculated to be soon enough before the parents' death (expecting a normal life) that a new residence and a new informal support system can be put into place, but not so soon as to result in a "premature" move out of the parents' home.

A major issue in terms of self-determination training is that a great deal of emphasis related to self-determination is placed on planning for the future. This aspect of the adolescent's planning must be done within the context of family roles, relationships, and cultural traditions if the delicate balance of the mobile is to be maintained.

The issue can frequently arise that the adolescent wants to create a different future and the family wants to maintain the status quo. In situations such as this, a strategy such as that of Van Reusen and Bos (1994) described earlier might be used to support students and parents to negotiate a partnership for determining which goals they hold in common and which goals are potentially conflictual. Support for negotiating and mediating the similarities and differences can help all parties have their preferences and priorities recognized and addressed through compromise decision making. (It is important to recognize, however, that compromise decision making can conflict with cultural values.)

Nondevelopmental Changes Families encounter many changes that are not related to age or stage. A parent may lose a job, and the economic resources of the family may be seriously curtailed. A parent may become ill and have an extended hospitalization that disrupts family interaction. The family may relocate from one community to another, and the formal and informal support system must change across all family functions.

Many of the same skills for planning for transition from high school to adulthood apply when families are planning transitions from one community to another or from one family lifestyle to another. A fundamental need of many families is learning to change within the rules of adaptability and cohesion that they have established for how their family interacts.

A second implication is that as children and youth with disabilities exercise self-determination, often they make decisions that create not only changes for themselves but also changes that reverberate among all family members within the family system. Skills that are taught and used by children and youth to enhance their well-being can unintentionally create stress and difficulty for other family members. Thus, it is essential that people working in self-determination programs be savvy in terms of the intentional and unintentional consequences of self-determination on creating change throughout the family system. For example, an adolescent might be introduced to a full range of supported living options and decide that she wants to have an apartment of her own and some day to be able to buy a house of her own. This desire may create major financial burdens for the parents in trying to come up with the money not only for rent, but also for daily living expenses and for personal care assistance. If they are not able to generate financial resources and if no resources are available through formal support programs in their community or state, disappointment and even anger could be created in the relationship between the adolescent and her parents that might have long-term consequences. If the parents take all of their possible resources and invest them in making the vision come true for their daughter, her brothers and sisters may be resentful of the potential loss of economic support for themselves. Although this example may seem extreme, it illustrates that there can be a domino effect in the consequences of self-determination that is not immediately apparent in simply trying to support adolescents to be more informed about what their potential options might be. Again, as stated earlier, it is important for federal and state funding sources to be directed toward the priority choices of adolescents and their families so that economic barriers can be minimized.

CONCLUSIONS

Family Characteristics

Based on our discussion of family characteristics, it is clear that all families have idiosyncratic features that shape the particular way that the family interacts and the way that they carry out their functions. A fundamental consideration in working on self-determination with families is the assumption that because all families vary, the approach with each family must be as individualized, like the approach with each student. Having a prototypical "ideal family" in mind and judging all families against that prototype is a strategy that brings only frustration and failure. A key for success is not only recognizing family diversity, but indeed honoring it and taking it fully into account when designing self-determination training, supports, and services.

Culture has a permeating impact on one's view of what is appropriate for a family. A clear need within the self-determination literature and for future research is to recognize that self-determination is itself a cultural value and to take into account the similarities and differences that the self-determination values have with the family traditions representing the full range of different cultures. Self-determination has primarily been conceived within an Anglo American culture by Anglo American professionals and families and has been supported by Office of Special Education and Rehabilitative Services (OSERS)–funded projects that have been and still are directed largely by Anglo American professionals. Ironically, it is possible to be paternalistic and oppressive toward some cultural traditions and some families in an attempt to support their autonomy and independence. We must understand that danger and seek to avoid it.

Realizing the diversity within family characteristics concomitantly means recognizing that all families have strengths, although families can differ widely from each other. An important starting point for supporting the self-determination of the adolescent is to identify and build on family strengths in seeking to actualize the adolescent's opportunities.

Family Interaction

A keen knowledge of family subsystems as well as family rules (cohesion and adaptability) can increase the likelihood that self-determination support will be functional and successful. A key concept of family interactions is that there are multiple and competing priorities, responsibilities, and resources within the family system. The self-determination of the individual with a disability can best be supported by taking into account the needs and strengths of other individuals and other subsystems. In essence, for the individual with a disability to gain more power and autonomy within the family, usually some other family member will lose power or that power will need to be redefined. Thus, negotiating the shifts in decision making can help ensure that shifts are made successfully and securely.

When working with individuals and families, it is extremely helpful to have a sense of the family's place along the continuum of cohesion and adaptability. By reflecting consideration for the closeness and distance of family boundaries (cohesion) and the abilities of families to make changes (adaptability), self-determination supports and services can be far more responsive. Again, we must be highly mindful of the impact that cultural traditions have on cohesion and adaptability and must refrain from making judgments, implicitly or explicitly, concerning "universals" of how families should optimally operate.

Family Functions

The way that family functions are carried out depends to a large extent on the input of family characteristics and on the process of family interaction. Given the seven different areas of family functions, one of the most essential themes is the time, resources, and energy required to attend to all of these functions simultaneously for all family members. Sometimes service providers within the disability field take an individual rather than a family systems perspective and wonder why parents are not investing more time, resources, and energy in the individual with a disability, especially related to the development of self-determination skills. The family mobile has many strings that must be balanced simultaneously. When unbalanced emphasis is given to one string, it throws off the balance of the entire mobile.

Self-determination training and support is most successful when there is respect and appreciation for families' multiple responsibilities and for efficient ways of lengthening one member's string on their family mobile—the need to teach self-determination skills. Families often need support in learning how to incorporate this effort into their ongoing routines and activities because for many families there are simply no unclaimed minutes of the day or night. Additionally, there is the need for family support services to aid families in carrying out some of these routine functions so that they will have time to focus on self-determination. Finally, many family members would prefer not to be the major teachers of critical skill development but to maintain the role of family nurturer and provider and to have assistance from others in teaching critical skills.

Family Life Span

In terms of the overall impact of considering the family life span, one of the most pervasive trends is that families encounter the most stress when there is a pile-up of change. Encouraging the self-determination of children and youth with disabilities will likely be most difficult for families when they are encountering myriad change; thus, the timing of intervention and particularly of family expectations in supporting self-determination might be established around the "periods of calm," avoiding significant developmental and nondevelopmental transitional periods.

It is impossible, however, to totally eschew self-determination issues during transitional periods. Since these are times of greatest change, families especially need support and adolescents with disabilities have their greatest opportunity for self-determining input when these periods of change occur. For example, when a student is graduating from high school, there are numerous opportunities for self-determination in terms of job, living, transportation, and community participation options. Given a life span perspective, professionals working in self-determination should be especially mindful of the stress that all individuals experience around transition and attempt to minimize this stress to the greatest possible degree. They should also be mindful of the strong pull on many families to "take a day at a time" to minimize this stress overload; thus, urging families to plan for the future may be pulling the coping foundation out from under them. Timing, responsive supports and services, and nonjudgmental and trusting communication are all advantageous in minimizing these types of problems.

As you provide self-determination supports and services to individuals with disabilities currently and in the future, we urge you to purchase a mobile and hang it in a place where you see it frequently. As you reflect upon the mobile's balance, we hope it will be a symbol and continual reminder that self-determination development will likely be far more successful when supports and services foster balance in the functioning of family life.

Balanced functioning in family life, however, does not mean that the visions, preferences, strengths, and needs of the individual with a disability should be neglected.

Those needs are essential and should not be overlooked in an attempt to be responsive to the perspectives of all family members. Ultimately, the approach that we are recommending seeks to emphasize the importance of shared negotiations between the individual with a disability and other family members so that desirable outcomes can be achieved for *all* stakeholders. We strongly believe that the family can be the greatest resource of the individual with a disability and that the role of services and supports is to foster the reciprocal support and long-term stability that family members can provide each other.

REFERENCES

Allen, R.I., & Petr, C.G. (1996). Towards developing standards and measurements for family-centered practice in family support programs. In G. Singer, L. Powers, & A. Olson (Eds.), *Redefining family support: Innovations in public–private partnerships* (pp. 57–86). Baltimore: Paul H. Brookes Publishing Co.

Amado, A.N. (Ed.). (1993). *Friendships and community connections between people with and without developmental disabilities.* Baltimore: Paul H. Brookes Publishing Co.

Baladerian, N. (1991). *Abuse causes disability.* Culver City, CA: Spectrum Institute.

Baladerian, N. (1993). *Abuse of children and adults with disabilities: A prevention and intervention guidebook for parents and other advocates.* Culver City, CA: Spectrum Institute.

Benedict, M.I., White, R.B., Wulff, L.M., & Hall, B.J. (1990). Reported maltreatment in children with multiple disabilities. *Child Abuse and Neglect, 14,* 207–217.

Bertalanffy, L. von. (1975). General system theory. In B.D. Ruben & J.Y. Kim (Eds.), *General systems theory and human communication* (pp. 6–20). Rochelle Park, NJ: Hayden.

Boggs, E.M. (1985). Who's putting whose head in the sand? (Or in the clouds as the case may be). In H.R. Turnbull III & A.P. Turnbull (Eds.), *Parents speak out: Then and now* (pp. 39–63). New York: Macmillan.

Breslau, N. (1982). Siblings of disabled children: Birth order and age-spacing effects. *Journal of Abnormal Child Psychology, 10*(1), 85–96.

Broderick, C., & Smith, J. (1979). The general systems approach to the family. In W.R. Burr, R. Hill, F.I. Nye, & I.L. Reiss (Eds.), *Contemporary theories about the family* (Vol. 2, pp. 112–129). New York: Free Press.

Caplan, G. (1976). The family as a support system. In G. Caplan & M. Killiliea (Eds.), *Support systems and mutual help: Multidisciplinary explorations* (pp. 19–36). New York: Grune & Stratton.

Carter, E.A., & McGoldrick, M. (Eds.). (1980). *The family life cycle: A framework for family therapy.* New York: Gardner Press.

Diamond, S. (1981). Growing up with parents of a handicapped child: A handicapped person's perspective. In J.L. Paul (Ed.), *Understanding and working with parents of children with special needs* (pp. 23–50). New York: Holt, Rinehart & Winston.

Education for All Handicapped Children Act of 1975, PL 94-142. (August 23, 1977). Title 20, U.S.C. 1401 et seq: *U.S. Statutes at Large, 89,* 773–796.

Falvey, M.A., Forest, M., Pearpoint, J., & Rosenberg, R.L. (1994). Building connections. In J.S. Thousand, R.A. Villa, and A.I. Nevin (Eds.), *Creativity and collaborative learning: A practical guide to empowering students and teachers* (pp. 347–368). Baltimore: Paul H. Brookes Publishing Co.

Garbarino, J., Brookhouser, P.E., & Authier, K.J. (1987). *Special children, special risks.* Hawthorne, NY: De Gruyter.

Garbarino, J., & Kostelny, K. (1992). *Neighborhood-based programs.* Manuscript prepared for the U.S. Advisory Board on Child Abuse and Neglect. Chicago: Erikson Institute.

Gardner, N.E.S. (1986). Sexuality. In J.A. Summers (Ed.), *The right to grow up: An introduction to adults with developmental disabilities* (pp. 45–66). Baltimore: Paul H. Brookes Publishing Co.

Hanson, M.J. (1992). Families with Anglo-European roots. In E.W. Lynch & M.J. Hanson (Eds.), *Developing cross-cultural competence: A guide for working with young children and their families* (pp. 65–87). Baltimore: Paul H. Brookes Publishing Co.

Hill, R., & Rodgers, R.H. (1969). The developmental approach. In H.T. Christensen (Ed.), *Handbook of marriage and the family* (pp. 171–211). Chicago: Rand McNally & Co.

Knoll, J. (1992). Being a family: The family experience of raising a child with a disability or chronic illness. In V.J. Bradley, J. Knoll, J.M., & Agosta (Eds.), *Emerging issues in family support* (9–56). Washington, DC: American Association for Mental Retardation.

Krauss, M.W., & Seltzer, M.M. (1993). Current well-being and future plans of older care giving mothers. *The Irish Journal of Psychology, 14*(1), 48–63.

Leslie, G.R. (1979). The nature of the family. In G.R. Leslie (Ed.), *The family in social context* (4th ed., pp. 3–23). New York: Oxford University Press.

Lewis, K., & Taymans, J.M. (1992). An examination of autonomous functioning skills of adolescents with learning disabilities. *Career Development for Exceptional Individuals, 15,* 37–46.

Lonsdale, G. (1978). Family life with a handicapped child: The parents speak. *Child: Care, Health and Development, 4,* 99–120.

Lynch, E.W., & Stein, R. (1982). Perspectives on parent participation in special education. *Exceptional Education Quarterly, 3*(2), 56–63.

Lynch, E., & Stein, R. (1987). Parent participation by ethnicity: A comparison of Hispanic, Black, and Anglo Families. *Exceptional Children, 54*(2), 105–111.

McCubbin, H.I., Joy, C.B., Cauble, A.E., Comeau, J.K., Patterson, J.M., & Needle, R.H. (1980). Family stress and coping: A decade review. *Journal of Marriage and the Family, 42*(4), 855–871.

Olson, D.H., McCubbin, H.I., Barnes, H., Larson, A., Muxen, M., & Wilson, M. (1983). *Families: What makes them work.* Beverly Hills, CA: Sage Publications.

Olson, D.H., Russell, C.S., & Spenkle, D.H. (1980). Circumplex model of marital and family systems: II. Empirical studies and clinical intervention. In J.P. Vincent (Ed.), *Advances in family intervention assessment and theory* (Vol. 1, pp. 129–179). Greenwich, CT: JAI Press.

Powell, T.H., & Gallagher, P.A. (1993). *Brothers and sisters: A special part of exceptional families* (2nd ed.). Baltimore: Paul H. Brookes Publishing Co.

Rousso, H. (1984). Fostering healthy self-esteem. *Exceptional Parent, 8*(14), 9–14.

Satir, V. (1972). *Peoplemaking.* Palo Alto, CA: Science and Behavior Books.

Seltzer, G.B., Begun, A., Seltzer, M.M., & Krauss, M.W. (1991). Adults with mental retardation and their aging mothers: Impacts of siblings. *Family Relations, 40,* 310–317.

Sobsey, D. (1994). *Violence and abuse in the lives of people with disabilities: The end of silent acceptance?* Baltimore: Paul H. Brookes Publishing Co.

Sobsey, D., & Varnhagen, C. (1991). Sexual abuse, assault, and exploitation of Canadians with disabilities. In C. Bagley (Ed.), *Child sexual abuse: Critical perspectives on prevention, intervention, and treatment.* Toronto: Wall and Emerson.

Stoneman, Z., & Berman, P.W. (Eds.). (1993). *The effects of mental retardation, disability, and illness on sibling relationships: Research issues and challenges.* Baltimore: Paul H. Brookes Publishing Co.

Turnbull, A.P., Summers, J.A., & Brotherson, M.J. (1986). Family life cycle: Theoretical and empirical implications and future directions for families with mentally retarded members. In J.J. Gallagher & P.M. Vietze (Eds.), *Families of handicapped persons: Research, programs, and policy issues* (pp. 45–65). Baltimore: Paul H. Brookes Publishing Co.

Turnbull, A.P., & Turnbull, H.R. (1990). *Families, professionals, and exceptionality: A special partnership* (2nd ed.). Columbus, OH: Charles E. Merrill.

Turnbull, H.R., & Turnbull, A.P. (1987). *The Latin American family and public policy in the United States: Informal support and transition into adulthood* (Report P-2). Lawrence, KS: Beach Center on Families and Disability.

Van Reusen, A.K., & Bos, C.S. (1990). IPLAN: Helping students communicate in planning conferences. *Teaching Exceptional Children, 22*(4), 30–32.

Van Reusen, A.K., & Bos, C.S. (1994). Facilitating student participation in individualized education programs through motivation strategy instruction. *Exceptional Children, 60*(5), 466–475.

Vohs, J. (1993). On belonging: A place to stand, a gift to give. In A.P. Turnbull, J.M. Patterson, S.K. Behr, D.L. Murphy, J.G. Marquis, & M.J. Blue-Banning (Eds.), *Cognitive coping, families, & disability* (pp. 51–66). Baltimore: Paul H. Brookes Publishing Co.

Ward, M.J. (1991). Self-determination revisited: Going beyond expectations. In *NICHY Transition Summary: Options after high school for persons with disabilities, 7,* 2–7.

Wehmeyer, M.L. (1992a). Self-determination and the education of students with mental retardation. *Education and Training in Mental Retardation, 27,* 303–314.

Wehmeyer, M.L. (1992b). Self-determination: Critical skills for outcome-oriented transition services. *Journal for Vocational Special Needs Education, 15*, 3–7.

Whitechurch, G.G., & Constantine, L.L. (1993). Systems theory. In P.J. Boss, W.J. Doherty, R. LaRossa, W.R. Schumm, & S.K. Steinmetz (Eds.), *Sourcebook of family theories and methods: A contextual approach* (pp. 325–352). New York: Plenum.

Wolfensberger, W. (1972). *The principle of normalization in human services.* Toronto: National Institute on Mental Retardation.

Zuniga, M.E. (1992). Families with Latino roots. In E.W. Lynch & M.J. Hanson (Eds.), *Developing cross-cultural competence: A guide for working with young children and their families* (pp. 151–179). Baltimore: Paul H. Brookes Publishing Co.

How Children with Ongoing Illness Cope with Negative Social Interaction

A Qualitative Study

George H.S. Singer

Social life with peers is one of the most important facets of a child's world. In the early 1990s, studies of how older children and adolescents experience stressful events have provided evidence in support of this common sense assertion. In a study of 232 sixth graders, Kanner, Feldman, Weinberger, and Ford (1991) asked children about events that made them feel good (uplifts) and events that made them unhappy (hassles). Children were asked to indicate if an event had happened in the last month and how often it made them feel happy or unhappy when it happened. The most important uplifting events are listed in Table 1, which shows the events, the percentage of children who experienced them in the last month, and the percentage who said the event made them feel good when it happened.

In Table 1, a potency score of 86% means that 86% of the children who experienced the event in the last month felt that it made them happy. Out of 25 items that included performance in schoolwork and sports as well as family relations, the social experiences listed in Table 1 were rated among the most potent. Similarly, when older children are asked about the events that made them feel bad in the past month, they also ranked negative social interactions among the most potent of hassles. Table 2 pre-

Table 1. Events perceived as positive (uplifting events)

Item	Occurrence (%)	Potency (%)
You had a good time playing with friends.	93	89
You had fun joking with the kids at school.	83	77
Your friends wanted you to be on their team.	81	86
You made a new friend.	68	76

Adapted from Kanner et al. (1991).

sents the items that the children responded to as hassles and the potency of the experience; that is, the percentage of children who said that the event made them feel unhappy when it occurred.

IMPACT OF ONGOING CONDITIONS

Like their typical peers, children with ongoing illness and disability have to deal with social hassles. Because their illness may accentuate behavioral or physical differences from others, they may experience social hassles that are linked specifically to their condition. Whereas a typical child might be teased for dropping a fly ball in a baseball game, a child with a disability might be teased for needing to go to the bathroom more often than his peers or for walking with a limp. A qualitative study by Powers, Singer, and Todis (see Chapter 4) suggests that these kinds of negative social interactions remain prominent in the memories of adults with disabilities, who describe the way that they handled negative social events in childhood and adolescence as important determinants of their self-esteem as adults.

Powers et al. interviewed 14 successful adults who happened to be people with visible physical disabilities that require special equipment and other accommodations. All 14 were living independent lives and described themselves as reasonably happy and successful. Powers et al. were interested in gaining insights from these people about what factors in their childhood experience helped them develop a strong positive sense of self-esteem and the belief that they could succeed. The investigators were surprised that every one of these individuals, unprompted, brought up childhood experiences in which they encountered rejection, teasing, or exclusion from activities. In most cases they remembered coping with these negative social events in ways that were important to them later. For example, one young man told this story:

> One thing really sticks out [about memories from the early school years]. During playtime, Bill, who was a tough kid, he and I got into a fight. He spit in my face and called me Hoppalong Cassidy or something. I tried to chase him, fell down and broke my good leg.

Table 2. Events perceived as negative (hassles)

Item	Occurrence (%)	Potency (%)
Your brothers and sisters bugged you.	73	51
Kids at school teased you.	61	51
When the kids were picking teams, you were one of the last ones chosen.	39	62
You got into a fight with another kid.	35	51
Your best friend didn't want to be your best friend any more.	30	64

Adapted from Kanner et al. (1991).

I remember missing a bunch of school...my mother had to take me out in a baby carriage so I could go outside. Well, I didn't like being 7 years old and in a baby carriage.

When I told my mom I didn't like it she said something like it wasn't [the other child's] fault that I was in that baby carriage, it was my own. I couldn't act like a baby if someone called me a name because there's lots of name-calling with little kids and she was saying that I had to learn not to let it get to me.

As soon as I got out of that cast, I jumped on that kid and we had a major fight...and that was the end of that. Nobody really got hurt but I made my point. I guess I was saying to my mother that there were some things...some things I would not put up with....And this was a big deal because when there's bullies, they pretty much rule, you know, at that grade level.

Another accomplished young man recalled how he felt when he was 9 years old:

From my personal frame of reference I didn't think of myself as any different than anyone else. Even at that age. And it was really sort of a, a surprise and shock to me that people would relate to me differently.

Several of the interviewees mentioned this theme. They did not think of themselves as different from others during their early childhood. The awareness that they were somehow different arose from experiences of being treated differently by other children and adults in later childhood. Often the first awareness of difference arose as a result of teasing or insensitivity from others.

Another one of the adults interviewed by Powers et al. described vividly the impact of unwanted attention from strangers:

Right near our house was a park named Echo Park, and we used to go there...to play. On one side there were old men listening to a baseball game and playing checkers. On the other side was women with their curlers, talking about whatever they want to talk about and the kids would be playing throughout the playground area. One day my mother calls to me, and I got up in the middle of the playground and I started walking toward her. And you must understand at that time I didn't wear crutches, and I walked with my hands up in the air to maintain my balance, and I walked tippy-toed. Like a ballerina.

I remember that time all of a sudden many of the men stopped playing checkers and started looking at me. I remember kids who ran up to their mothers and would be pulling on their skirts, pointing to me, asking "Why, what's going on? Why is he walking that way?" Some of the older kids just stopped and just laughed.

...that particular incident started me thinking and realizing how different I am and...until that time I wasn't consciously aware of the difference. [How old were you?] I was either 7 or 8...what was significant with that event was I started being conscious of people being aware of that difference, and I started to be aware of their reactions to me and I didn't like it.

The awareness of being different was precipitated by scorn. Most of the interviewees reported dealing with similar experiences and spoke of a variety of ways in which they learned to cope with negative social interactions. Because negative social experiences were, in retrospect, important milestones for these adults, we wondered how children who are currently dealing with childhood disability or chronic illness would describe their responses to negative social interactions.

QUALITATIVE ACCOUNTS OF NEGATIVE SOCIAL INTERACTIONS

Interviews were conducted at summer camps, one camp for children with juvenile arthritis, and another for children with diabetes. The campers ranged in age from 8 to 15 years. A description of the study and a request for informed consent was mailed to parents of all campers prior to the beginning of summer camp. The parents of 15 children with juvenile arthritis gave consent, and all the children participated in small group interviews. A total of 19 children with diabetes attended focus group sessions. The group meetings lasted 1 hour each and were held outdoors near the dining halls of the camps. First, the young people were asked if they were ever teased because they had arthritis or diabetes. They were asked to take turns speaking to allow easier audio-taping of the session. When children mentioned a teasing incident, they were asked to explain where it happened, what was said or done to them, how they felt, how they reacted, and if they got help from anyone regarding the incident.

Although initially children were asked to talk about teasing, it quickly became apparent that, from their point of view, teasing was part of a larger class of negative social interactions that centered around their illness, its symptoms, or its management procedures. The source of the teasing or ridicule was important to the children. They experienced a difference, for example, between being ridiculed by a stranger and teased by a brother or sister. Different types of social aggression required different coping strategies. A response to a physical attack was different from a response to insensitivity from an adult. The children reported using different coping strategies that included ignoring, getting help from others, educating, confronting, cognitive coping, and aggression. Because coping is always embedded in a particular circumstance, the following discussion presents examples of the *sources* and types of negative social interactions that children reported and the *ways in which they coped.* Coping and its implications for supporting children with chronic illness in public schools are then discussed.

Unwanted Attention and Insensitivity

One category of negative social events was *unwanted attention/insensitivity.* The source of undesirable attention was usually adults rather than other children. One high school–age male who had diabetes described how a teacher at school, also a diabetic, was overly interested in comparing notes about their condition:

> At first I thought it was kind of cool, I mean he would stop me in the hall and ask me what my count was…I would tell him and then he'd tell me his…it got old real fast, he's always stopping me, every time he sees me and that can be a lot of times in a single day.

The student's tone suggested that he found the repetitiveness of the questions to be forced and he felt uncomfortable, although this was a relatively minor annoyance. Sometimes the unwanted attention was extremely embarrassing. One teenager with juvenile arthritis described how a sixth-grade teacher told his classmates that he had arthritis without obtaining the student's permission:

> She told everybody in my whole class about my life and everything. Like what happened to me and everything. I got sick and tired of it, I just walked off and got a new room. I got a new teacher. My mom had a big argument with her too. I made my mom have them put me in a different class.

This teenager coped with the embarrassment of having his condition revealed without his permission by seeking help from his parent.

Some of the campers reported that they encountered insensitivity from adults at school regarding changes in the normal rules or routines for management of their illness. For example, one high school student with diabetes described how he sometimes had to urinate more often than is typical for other students. In one class he raised his hand and asked for permission to go to the bathroom. The teacher told him to wait, and he said he could not wait. In frustration, the teacher told him that if he could not wait, he could just "Go in the corner back there." The student responded defiantly by taking the teacher literally. He walked to the corner in the back of the room and began to open his fly. When the teacher asked what he was doing, he replied, "I'm doing what you told me to do." She then told him to go to the bathroom. The student recalled this incident with a tone of bitterness toward the teacher, but also with pride in recounting his defiance. I asked if the teacher knew he was diabetic. According to the student, she knew about his illness but did not understand that some days he needed to go to the bathroom more often.

Another form of adult insensitivity consisted of adults trying to enforce illness management routines on older students who believed themselves capable of monitoring and treating their conditions themselves. One teenager recounted an incident in which he made a deliberate decision to eat some ice cream in order to raise his blood sugar level. The principal saw him eating an ice cream cone and ordered him to throw it away. According to the student, the principal then told him he was suspended. The student handled this situation by going to the school nurse and telling her what had happened. In this case, having an adult who understood his condition and was willing to be an ally was important. She explained to the principal that he could eat dairy products on some occasions and that the student was good at monitoring and controlling his own blood sugar level, and the principal rescinded the school suspension. Later this same young man said that, during the first 6 months after his diagnosis, he refused to go along with the diabetic diet and his blood sugar level rose so high that he had to be hospitalized. After that incident, he became more compliant with the treatment regime and was frustrated that the principal lacked confidence in his ability to manage his illness. Other teenagers reported a similar frustration. One said, "I've been taking care of myself for years. So why don't they believe me that I know what I need?" At the conclusion of one of the group interviews at the camp for children with diabetes, one of the older students said, "Tell them they should believe us when we say what we need."

The children who had visible disabilities explained that they had to deal with two other types of adult insensitivity. In situations with unfamiliar adults, people would often stare at them. Another kind of uncomfortable social attention consisted of unwanted assistance or unwanted offers of assistance from adults:

> People aren't making fun of you or imitating you or that kind of thing but it's more people staring or trying to help you with something that you don't need help with.
>
> I: [What do you do when people stare?]
>
> I don't really care 'cause I think that they just, I just ignore them 'cause they have a problem if they can't deal with it that I'm in a chair. I mean it's not like I'm totally different. I mean, I'm in a chair and I have arthritis, but, I mean, inside I'm like everybody else. About the stare and stuff, I usually stare back at them.
>
> [Does that work to make them stop staring?]
>
> Yeah. Usually they smile after. Like I'll look them straight in the eye and they'll end up smiling or something. Or I give them a dirty look. Especially when I'm in the wheelchair, I feel like I'm gonna run them over but I don't 'cause I know I couldn't.

These coping strategies involved subtle assertive behavior, such as staring back, or not so subtle assertiveness: "I give them a dirty look." She also reported using a cognitive coping strategy when she said, "I just ignore them 'cause they have a problem." The ability to attribute the problem to the other person appeared to be an important form of protection for several of the children.

Ridicule from Strangers

People on the periphery of children's social networks can sometimes be a source of negative social interactions. Ridicule from strangers can be a powerful vehicle for communicating a sense of difference and stigma to children. The young people with diabetes and juvenile arthritis also talked about the way that strangers or children who were not friends teased or ridiculed them. A teenager with diabetes reported this:

> I was riding the bus and this girl behind me said, "Don't get near him, he's a dia-beat, it's contagious." So I reached over and did this [he touches the interviewer on the shoulder in a deliberate, almost forceful fashion similar to the way children tag one another in playing tag or touch football]. And I said to her, "Well then, now you've got it."

Upon hearing this story, other children in the group nodded their heads or stated agreement that they had also been called "dia-beats" or had other children treat them as if they had a contagious disease, a common form of childhood cruelty among peers. A common playground taunt is to say a child has "cooties [lice]." The contagious person is viewed as one who should be held at a distance, is potentially dangerous, and, by a primitive logic, is even unclean. The statement that any young person should be shunned is a form of verbal aggression. In this case, the boy responded ironically by pretending he was contagious and "gave" the illness to the teaser. The children indicated that educating others about their illness was one way to prevent this kind of teasing, because diabetes is not a contagious illness.

Children with visible symptoms of juvenile arthritis reported more negative encounters with strangers or classmates who were not friends than did children with no visible symptoms. One teenage boy recounted an incident at the beach involving other teenagers who were strangers:

> And another time with a person who didn't know who I was, I was at the beach and these people were walking behind me and they were imitating my limp and I knew that they weren't, that they didn't have a limp. So I confronted them and asked them what their problem was and they pretty much said that they don't have a problem…it was a long time ago…I'm not sure exactly what he said, but they pretty much just left.

Imitating the movements of the youth with a disability was a form of active ridicule. Again, the boy chose to deal with the situation actively and assertively. By confronting the strangers, he changed the interaction and probably shamed them into stopping.

Several children reported having troubles with others whom they described as bullies. Sometimes the children would explain why the bully was so hostile:

> And so one day I had a biopsy day and I came back after missing a couple of days of school because of it and…there was somebody that was in my class who's short and he's short for his age and he's just, he is mean. He's an s.o.b. And he was imitating me and then he was laughing at me so I said, "Here, you take my shoes and I'll take yours. You take my place." He never spoke to me again about that.

The bully was somebody who was nasty to others and this hostility was described as a trait: "he is mean." The child also attributed the meanness to the other boy's embarrassment over being short for his age. The children implied that other schoolmates also had trouble with bullies and that the aggression was not completely unexpected.

Some children reported that they were physically attacked by bullies. Two teenage boys with diabetes reported that they got into physical fights with other aggressive students.

Ridicule from Friends and Siblings

In the shifting relationships that characterize childhood, even normally supportive peers could occasionally resort to teasing or ridicule. Juvenile arthritis is characterized by periods of relative remission interspersed with flare-ups, times when movement is painful. A task such as opening a door is easy for a child on one day, and the next day the same task might be impossible. When flare-ups occur, these children need to be excused from some tasks. The children do not appear different on good days than on flare-up days, making it difficult for others to tell the difference:

> A couple of times in school, the teacher will say I don't have to do work at the blackboard because there's too much writing on the board. And they [classmates] will say [sarcastic tone] "Oh great. She doesn't have to write so why do we have to write?"
>
> [Kind of as if you're deliberately trying to get out of it?]
>
> Yes.

The children with arthritis needed to manage their illness by monitoring the kind and amount of their activities. At times they had to cut activities short, and others made negative comments:

> We live right next to a school yard so a lot of times there is baseball games...and sometimes I don't feel up to it...I just don't feel like running or something and they'll say, "Oh yeah, you're a quitter." ...I try to play as long as I can, but sometimes I can't.
>
> [Because of your arthritis?]
>
> Yeah.

Learning to persist when tired or to work even when uncomfortable is a common part of socialization. Children enforce norms of trying hard or working hard by calling others "slackers" or "quitters" when others stop early. For the child with ongoing illness, however, stopping because of discomfort is a mark of self-control in the same way that persisting can be for a child without disabilities; but others may not perceive this strength:

> Even your friends make fun of you in a joking way sometimes. Like in gym class. They want to know why you don't go in gym and stuff. Even your friends do it sometimes.

Children reported that being unfairly criticized in this way was a common challenge at home. Home life for children usually involves chores and activities that are not considered fun. The norm of working or doing something that is required but not very enjoyable is taught in many homes as part of working together as a family. Because illness sometimes involves being excused from activities, the children with ongoing illness reported that their brothers and sisters occasionally got angry or accused them of faking when they did not do a chore or said they were too ill to go to church. Some of the children reported that illness-imposed dependency set the stage for some negative interactions among siblings. For example, one child with juvenile arthritis who uses a wheelchair shared a room with her twin sister. To keep their 2½-year-old brother from getting into their things, they had a latch on the inside of their bedroom door. The latch was placed high enough to be out of the brother's reach. Unfortunately, it was also out of reach for the girl in the wheelchair:

> My sister and I will lock our doors and stuff and she bugs me because every time I'm in the room and I'm busy doing something I tell her to pop the lock....When I ask her to open the door for me she turns around and tells me to pop it, even though she knows I can't reach where it is.

[She won't do it?]

Yeah…my mom and dad have to yell at her.

[That works?]

It works all right.

As Kanner et al. (1991) indicated, negative interactions between siblings are commonplace in typical families, even in homes where children are normally cooperative. The added dimension of disability appears to focus some of this normal rivalry around illness symptoms and limitations. This child made it clear that her sister was normally very supportive and helpful and that conflicts such as the one over the door latch were infrequent but irritating. When these conflicts arose, she coped with them by enlisting her parents' help.

Social Rejection or Exclusion

Some of the children reported that they encountered a subtler kind of social interaction that involved exclusion from activities. Two boys related that they were often chosen last when teams were picked for playground sports, the implicit message being that they were not as desirable as teammates because of limitations imposed by their illness. Other children described different ways that they were excluded from activities. A teenage girl who uses a wheelchair told this story:

> My cousins are 14 and 11…we used to always play together. Now, I just went to a birthday party and both of them, I was talking to them and all of a sudden they walked up and stopped and we were going to go in the other room to ask the adults if we could go swimming and they both came out and they said, "Well, we're going to the arcade. See you later," and they left. And then half the time when they come over to the house they won't even come in and say hi to me because, I don't know why….When we were little we played all the time together.

I speculated that when the cousins reached the middle school years, they did not want to be seen with a child who used a wheelchair. Having numerous scars from surgery and using a wheelchair made this child seem an undesirable companion to her cousins during these early teen years.

COPING STRATEGIES

The majority of children appeared to adapt to these negative social experiences. With a few exceptions, most reported the problems as if they were of lesser significance than the positive parts of their social world. It was evident that they had learned strategies for defending themselves and for changing the social situation when possible. In the following discussion, these ways of responding to the negative social behavior of others are presented more thoroughly.

Ignoring and Cognitive Coping

Ignoring and cognitive coping were commonly mentioned together as ways of dealing with teasing or unwanted attention. Ignoring was mentioned more often by girls than boys and more often by older than younger students. One girl explained that there were different kinds of ignoring. She used "regular ignoring" when she acted as if she did not hear the unkind words or did not see the unwanted attention. On some occasions she used "the total and complete ignore," in which she did not make eye contact, respond, or in even the slightest way acknowledge the presence of the teaser. She illustrated how she does the "total ignore" by looking down, freezing her facial features into a mask of indifference, and sitting perfectly still. She said that this form of ignoring was powerful as a way to get the aggressor to stop.

Adults commonly advised the children to use ignoring as a way to handle social aggression. One teenage girl told the story of how she responded to a child who used to be a friend but developed a hostile attitude toward her:

> I had a friend when I was little and in school. I was in fourth grade or something. So we were like really good friends and she liked to push me around and stuff. And then…last year she started hating my guts.…I felt so bad 'cause I thought, "What did I do wrong?" She just loved it.…She got high off it or something. So then I told my parents; they just said to ignore her. So I think I like started ignoring her and she hated that.

When parents counseled their children to ignore, they seemed to imply that the problem would go away easily. In fact, for some aggressive children like the hostile girl in this incident, being ignored increases their hostility. In this example, the student went on to say that her former friend eventually hit her and a physical fight developed. Ignoring was not uniformly effective.

The children who reported using ignoring as a strategy usually had a rationale for the other's behavior and for their own decision to ignore. One older child said,

> if you just ignore people when they tease you, most of the time they just leave you alone because they are only doing it to get, to entertain themselves.

This child's tone of voice implied an understanding that people who try to upset others as a sport are themselves very limited.

When children talked about ignoring, they generally meant that they did not respond to provocation. They remained silent or acted as if they had not heard a taunt. Some of the children seemed to have a different but related meaning when they spoke of ignoring:

> Kids at school would imitate my limp and you know I didn't like it any. They knew it. But…I didn't make a point to ignore them. I didn't say, "I'm going to ignore you" or anything. I just walked right on and thought about it later.…the thought that kept me going was "Well, I'd like to see them in my position." Just thinking about that just kept me going.…

> The kids, they also bother me. You know, they think, some of them, you know, accuse me of faking. Because I have off days and I have good days and I don't know until I wake up what it's going to be.

> [What do you do when you are accused of faking?]

> Once again, I just press on. Picture them in the same position and press on.

For this young man, ignoring not only had the passive connotation of not rising to the bait, but it also had an active sense of persisting in the face of opposition.

Cognitive Coping

Several children explained that when they ignored unwanted attention or teasing, they used ways of thinking about the other person that helped them keep the experience at a distance or helped them maintain a positive view of themselves in the face of hostility. These internal strategies consisted of adopting an attitude or of covertly telling oneself a statement that helped to buffer the adverse nature of the interaction. Children were asked, "Was there anything you told yourself or anything that you did inside your mind that helped you deal with that situation [a negative social encounter]?" The 8- to 10-year-old children rarely reported using such covert strategies. However, most of the older children had developed ways of internally responding to social aggression or unwanted attention in order to reduce its painful impact.

One of the most elaborate strategies that children reported involved covertly telling themselves that the other person would not be able to do well if the tables were turned and he or she had the illness. Sometimes they made this strategy overt by speaking to the person teasing them. One teenager described earlier told his assailant, "Here—you take my shoes and I'll take yours, and we'll see how you handle it." Other children reported making similar statements to themselves when teased, saying to themselves, "I'd like to see you try to deal with the things I have to manage." This kind of internal monologue has at least two important elements. First, there is an implicit sense that the children know they have to cope with something that is difficult and that they are proud of how they handle the challenge of living with a chronic illness. They seem to see themselves as people who handle adversity well, a quality often associated with high self-esteem in the literature on children's development. Second, children compare themselves to the person teasing them in a way that puts the aggressor in an unfavorable light. When children think "I'd like to see him in my shoes," they are implicitly asserting that the other person would not be able to cope as well or, alternatively, that the other would know how unpleasant it is to be the recipient of teasing.

Cognitive coping strategies were clearly efficacious for some children. One child described the sense of satisfaction that her inner monologue gave her:

> I just ignore them. Then later on when I'm thinking about it, I'll think about an awesome comeback I could have used. But it's like too late to use it....
>
> And I like to replay it in my mind—me saying it to them....I just laugh and stuff.
>
> [Does it make you feel better to think about those things you wished you had said?]
>
> Yeah. A lot.

Educating Others

The question of whether or not to tell the class as a group about their illness was mentioned by several of the children. In general the children wanted to have control over the decision to tell the class, and some expressed resentment when the teacher did not get their consent prior to informing the others. The reluctance that some children expressed was stated clearly by a middle school student with juvenile arthritis:

> I wouldn't choose to do it. Like to get up in front of everyone 'cause I really don't like telling them that I have arthritis. But it's kind of obvious something is wrong with me because I'm in a chair. So I think that it would be easier if I could walk. I think if I could just walk I wouldn't tell any...like I would tell my friends or something and that's all I would tell. I don't want it to be, you know I wouldn't want it to be obvious—"Oh, I have arthritis, hello." But I'm in a chair so it's like—[other children often ask] 'What's wrong with you?' So I just figure, well I might as well get it over with.

This young woman was indicating that she did not want to present herself first as a person with arthritis but rather as simply another person.

Educating others about their condition was a common strategy that children used to reduce misunderstanding and to circumvent unwanted attention. A few children had worked out ways of informing their classmates in a way that was comfortable, although it involved some feelings of embarrassment. One young woman described her decision to make presentations to her classmates about her arthritis:

> Usually every year before when school starts I get in front of the whole class...whatever grade it is and I just, like, it's kind of embarrassing sometimes, but I have to do it because

> then everybody knows I have arthritis. I tell them about it and like what it is and like all the operations I've had and like what it involves and stuff...when I was younger they used to tease me a lot. [They'd say] that my bones were so fragile that if somebody touched me or something I'd break...I talked to my mom and dad about it and like said "you know you need to do something about this" and then I figured out that [I would tell the class].

This teenager seemed to be saying that by taking the lead in informing her classmates, she could head off misunderstandings and unwanted questions. She also went to her parents to talk about the problem of teasing. They did not give her specific advice about what to do, but rather gave the problem back to her to develop a solution.

Positive Identity as a Coping Measure

Many of the children expressed the implicit belief that their disability or illness was peripheral to their identity. Several children with diabetes communicated that they thought it was silly for people to tease them for something as distant from their true selves as having a problem with blood sugar levels. One teenage girl with arthritis expressed it this way:

> I just ignore them cause they have a problem if they can't deal with it that I'm in a chair [wheelchair]. I mean, it's not like I'm totally, totally different. I mean I'm in a chair and I have arthritis but, I mean, inside I'm like everybody else.

This child, like most of the other interviewees, did not experience herself as different from others or as stigmatized. Having a sense of identity that is fundamentally the same as that of other people, regardless of the disability or illness, placed the locus of the problem in the other: "they have a problem" rather than "I am the problem." Having a positive sense of self appears to be more than the use of a strategy. It suggests that many of the children have developed an identity that serves as a bulwark against mistreatment. This identity is most likely the result of years of cumulative experience in basic relationships in which the children have been treated as complete, normal persons who have peripheral differences but are not "totally, totally different." One child explained that she no longer needs to think that she is basically the same as everyone else because "I guess I just know it so I don't even bother to think of that."

Assertiveness and Counteraggression

Roughly one fourth of the interviewees described dealing with social hostility with varying degrees of assertiveness that ranged from staring back at a person who stared at them to physically attacking the person. Counterattacks included replying with ridicule, threatening to get the help of an older sibling who could beat up the hostile person, and threatening aggression. Several of the boys and two of the girls described themselves as more reactive and more likely to reciprocate aggression than to ignore it. It was not clear whether actual fights were common or whether simply the possibility of calling on friends who could beat up another child was sufficient as a way to terminate another child's hostile behavior. Friends could also be called on to prevent fights, as one teenage boy with diabetes explained:

> My friends know I've got a real bad temper...so if somebody says something about my diabetes, they'll hold onto me to keep me from pounding the kid.

In describing the way his friends restrain him, this young man showed that he was a tough kid who would not put up with nonsense from others and that he had friends with whom he shared a sense of solidarity. By almost getting into a fight, he saved face by appearing forceful; but by having friends restrain him, he also did not have to come to blows.

Using Allies

With the exception of one or two children, all of the interviewees said that adults sometimes helped them deal with negative social interactions. Supportive adults were often
parents, nurses, teachers, and guidance counselors. It was evident from the children's
reports that most benefited from the thoughtfulness of supportive adults. For example,
an 8-year-old girl with diabetes told how her school nurse encouraged her to bring a
friend along when she went to the nurse's office for blood testing or an insulin shot. Her
friends viewed it as a special activity to go along with her, and they sometimes compet-
ed for the job. The nurse made activities that might otherwise seem mysterious and
possibly stigmatizing into more normal routine events. As described earlier, several of
the children were encouraged by their classroom teachers to talk about their illness in
front of the class. The way that the informing process was planned was important to
the children. They wanted to have a say in whether and how their classmates would be
told, as one teenage boy explained:

> My teacher last year was, she was so great. She told people [about the illness] and I didn't
> really like that. So finally I told her [I want to do the talking] and then she let me do the
> talking. What I wanted to do.

A number of students with diabetes described how they were invited by their teachers
to help give lessons about diabetes during health class. One older student described
how his teacher viewed him as the "class expert" on nutrition and blood sugar. Teachers also were allies in helping to stop repeated aggression from bullies. One girl
described how she went to her teacher with a complaint about a boy who repeatedly
antagonized her:

> I told the teacher...after the teacher talked to him he never even walked up to me and said
> hi ever again. I don't know what the teacher said to him.

Most of the children reported that their parents were important sources of support
when difficulties occurred with other children. The most common advice from parents
was to ignore unwanted attention or teasing. Parents also helped by meeting with
school teachers and suggesting ways to educate the class about diabetes or arthritis. As
mentioned earlier, it was very important to the children that parents and teachers
obtain their consent before informing others about their condition. The children also
relied on parents to solve disputes with siblings, as is the case with sibling disputes
when ongoing illness is not involved.

The extent to which parents gave advice seemed to differ widely. Two teenagers
described how they went to their parents to report problems with classmates, and their
parents told them they would need to find ways to handle the problem by themselves.
In both cases the students did generate some strategies. At least in part, the parents'
hands-off attitude represented the parents' faith that their children could find ways to
fend for themselves.

Most of the children also listed friends and siblings as allies. Brothers and sisters
could be both sources of unpleasant interactions as well as supporters in dealing with
hostility. For example, one child described the way one sibling frequently accused her
of faking symptoms and her other sibling defended her:

> My sister...she's older, she's seventeen. If I can't do something [because of illness symp-
> toms], she'll think I'm faking....my sister hates to go to church, and if my mom says...I
> don't have to go, she'll say I'm just faking it to get out of going to church. She says that a
> lot. If we have to go somewhere we don't want to go, she always says that.

[What do you do when she says that?]

I usually ignore her. But my brother...he stands up for me....he just tells her off.

Older brothers and sisters were also allies at school. Younger children described how they could ask their older siblings to protect them from bullies or teasers.

The children also relied on friends as allies. One girl described the way other children with disabilities were a source of support:

I'm pretty lucky because there are two other...kids with arthritis besides me. And there is a kid with spina bifida. And I mean all I have to do is tell them that somebody's threatening me and stuff and she, the girl with arthritis...will get all their friends and beat them up.

Friends and siblings helped the children put the behavior of teasers or bullies into perspective or helped them to discount it. When I asked one child what she did when a bully ridiculed her, she replied that she told her friends:

[What did they say?]

They said he was a jerk.

[Did that make you feel better to hear that they thought he was a jerk?]

Yes.

By high school, being a part of a friendly group served as a major buffer against hostile social interactions. The high school students reported that they rarely encountered teasing or social rejection due to their illness in high school because they spent most of their free time with groups of other students who were their friends. One teenage girl explained that by the time she got to high school, she knew there were certain groups of students she should avoid. If she stayed away from these hostile groups and stayed with her friends, she did not have negative social interactions related to her illness. Problems of exclusion from social activities and problems with dating were more important for the older students.

Poorly Protected Children

Two children in these groups did not seem to have much social support or an effective coping repertoire. I found myself worrying about how these children would fare. The following excerpt from an interview with a 14-year-old with arthritis illustrates her unsupportive environment:

Some people actually kick you. Hurt you....I get back at him. He don't like it. I make fun of him.

[Does that work? Does he stop?]

No.

[Have you ever gotten any help from anybody about it.?]

Nope.

[Have you ever thought of talking to the teacher about being teased?]

No. 'Cause they'd go and spread rumors.

[You don't think they would be able to help you?]

No. 'Cause they said that they'd go tell another teacher and then that teacher will go and tell another teacher.

[Do you mean the teacher would not respect your privacy?]

Yeah.

[Do you ever ask your brother or sister for help?]

No, 'cause he's a jerk.

[Will your mother or father ever help you with that?]

Well, my mother says that she really can't do nothing about it.

The literature on childhood ongoing illness suggests that children with ongoing illnesses are at higher than normal risk of developing serious emotional problems, and this teenager may be a likely candidate for such problems because she did not seem to have reliable allies or effective coping strategies.

Combined Strategies

The children's narratives have been deliberately fragmented here into categories, but this presentation may not adequately convey that children used a combination of coping strategies. The children often employed two or three coping strategies and had more than one ally. Children described coping with some incidents by using several strategies in a fluent seamless fashion: ignoring, cognitive coping, telling friends, and talking to an adult. This use of multiple strategies seemed to be common.

IMPLICATIONS FOR TEACHERS AND PARENTS

Before suggesting what these results might imply for parents and teachers, the limitations of the study should be acknowledged. The children in this study were all from one region of the United States, and all came from English-speaking families of European origin. While no data on the socioeconomic status of the children were available, it appeared that most were from middle- and upper-income homes. The interviews were conducted in groups, were relatively brief, and focused specifically on teasing. While the children responded to questions with comments about negative social interactions in general, their responses could not be placed definitively in a broader context.

This study is useful as an initial exploration of a topic that appears to be very important to children. The following suggestions are offered with the hope that they will be the subject of further research:

1. Parents and teachers should expect that children with ongoing medical conditions are likely to encounter unwanted attention and some outright hostility from peers.
2. Educating other children about the illness or disability can reduce misunderstandings, such as the fear that diabetes is contagious.
3. Supportive adults are important resources to these children.
4. Children benefit from knowing a variety of coping strategies to use in different situations to meet the varying challenges of hostile encounters.
5. Children are interested in hearing from one another how others have coped with negative social situations. Discussion groups and support groups are likely to be good forums for teaching children how to cope with negative social situations.
6. Older children are capable of using relatively subtle cognitive strategies. These methods of coping can be modeled and taught.

7. Before adults inform others about the child's condition, the child should be consulted about how and where to inform. Children are easily embarrassed by unwanted disclosure of their condition.

8. A sense of being a normal person who is not essentially different from others serves as a protection against hostility.

9. If parents counsel children to turn the other cheek, they should also show that they have an understanding of the norms that prevail among the children's peers in regard to fighting and physical aggression.

10. Adults who are involved with children with ongoing illness should be particularly concerned to identify and try to help children who do not have allies at home or among peers and who do not appear to have adequate coping skills.

REFERENCE

Kanner, A.D., Feldman, S.S., Weinberger, D.A., & Ford, M.E. (1991). Uplifts, hassles, and adaptational outcomes in early adolescents. In A. Monat & R.S. Lazarus, *Stress and coping: An anthology* (3rd ed., pp. 158–182). New York: Columbia University Press.

12

A Qualitative Study
of a Mentor Intervention
with Children Who
Have Multiple Disabilities

Bonnie Todis, Laurie E. Powers,
Larry Irvin, and George H.S. Singer

Children with physical and multiple disabilities are confronted with significant challenges to their development of self-competence and independence. Functional limitations may restrict child engagement in age-appropriate activities (Garrison & McQuiston, 1989; Stopford, 1987), and architectural and attitudinal barriers exclude them from opportunities to participate in inclusive environments (Scherer, 1988). Children with disabilities and their parents often lack access to demonstrations of independent living options and information about later life challenges and strategies to overcome them (Espinosa & Shearer, 1986). As a result of these restrictions, many children with physical disabilities do not achieve their potential for independence and self-competence. Parents also have difficulty establishing realistic perceptions of their children's current and future capabilities and optimally promoting their development of self-competence.

One approach that holds promise for enhancing the independence and self-competence of children and the perceptions of their parents is relationships with successful adult role models or mentors. Parents are the first mentors for most children. Teachers often provide the next level of mentoring for school-age children. As children move through adolescence, adults from the community often fill this role. For children with physical disabilities, adults with similar levels of disability could be appropriate mentors.

Mentor relationships are typically founded on shared experience between mentor and protege. Mentors share their expertise and enthusiasm, demonstrate methods to achieve goals and overcome barriers, and provide encouragement and guidance to aspiring proteges. Mentors also provide a protected relationship in which learning and experimentation can occur and potential skills can be developed (Boston, 1976).

Mentoring is a popular approach for promoting the functional competence, knowledge, self-confidence, and motivation of youth with disabilities (Rhodes, 1994). Access to role models is considered significant for the development of self-esteem, positive views of disability, and living skills for youth with disabilities (Fredericks, 1988; Jones & Ulicny, 1986; Rousso, 1988). Participation of adolescents with physical challenges and their mentors in community activities has been shown to enhance child knowledge of independent living options, child self-efficacy, and parent perceptions of child capabilities (Powers, Sowers, & Stevens, 1993).

Although preliminary evidence suggests that mentoring experiences are important for adolescents and their parents, it is unclear whether mentoring experiences provided to younger children will enhance their independence and self-competence and associated perceptions of their parents. As with other interventions to promote the transition of young adults with disabilities to adulthood (Szymanski, Turner, & Hershenson, 1992; Wehmeyer, 1992), introduction of mentor interventions during the middle school or late elementary years might increase the impact of the intervention by providing models for early goal setting and providing additional time to practice skills before leaving the school setting. However, a variety of factors related to age and stage of development might contribute to making mentor interventions more effective for adolescents than for younger children. These factors include normative adolescent interest in independence and skills for independent living, greater awareness of the effects of disability, and increased engagement in social comparison.

Furthermore, although mentoring has been shown to affect parent perceptions of adolescent competence, it is unclear whether mentoring has any effect on actual parenting practices. This issue is important given evidence that the self-competence of children with disabilities is influenced by parenting practices as well as parent attitudes (Baumrind, 1966; Todis, Irvin, Singer, & Yovanoff, 1993). Specific parenting practices that have positive effects on the competence and self-esteem of children with disabilities include providing opportunities to make choices, participate in normative leisure activities, and interact with peers; holding children responsible for age-appropriate self-care and household tasks; modeling assertive behavior and encouraging children to be assertive; encouraging children to develop positive coping behaviors to deal with disappointment, failure, and social rejection; and providing effective advocacy until children develop self-advocacy skills (Todis et al., 1993).

This chapter describes a qualitative study that evaluated the impact of exposure to adults with physical disabilities on elementary-age children with physical disabilities and their parents. We investigated whether pairing children with adult mentors with similar disabilities would have positive effects on the children's self-competence and views of disability. We also examined what effect such an intervention might have on the attitudes and practices of their parents. Our approach was descriptive and exploratory, rather than explanatory (Yin, 1989), and sought to identify promising applications for mentor interventions and topics for further research, rather than establish causal relationships among variables or describing a theoretical model for the intervention.

METHODOLOGY

Rationale for Qualitative, Case Study Approach

Several factors contributed to the decision to employ an exploratory, descriptive, case study approach for this study. These factors included the absence of previous research with this age group, the small number of subjects available, the heterogeneity of the sample, and the complexity of the intervention. In addition, qualitative research methodology was indicated because the difficulty of anticipating the likely outcomes of the study presented a major obstacle to using a quantitative design. To document change in all behaviors and attitudes that might be affected by the intervention would have required a large array of pre- and postintervention measures, especially since unanticipated positive outcomes have been frequently noted anecdotally by participants in adolescent mentor projects (Powers et al., 1993). Furthermore, the effects of the intervention might be subtle and not easily demonstrated quantitatively, yet have substantial impact over time on factors related to desired child outcomes. A qualitative research design avoided the problem of prematurely narrowing the field of inquiry (Bauman & Adair, 1992) and thereby missing these subtle, unanticipated effects.

Qualitative methodology also permitted access to the perspectives of the children as well as to those of their parents and mentors. It is difficult to obtain reliable responses from children with disabilities on questionnaires or through structured interviews, especially when they have limited ability to communicate verbally (Sigelman, Budd, Spanhel, & Schoenrock, 1981). The combined techniques of participant observation and informal, recursive interviewing help overcome such reliability issues as acquiescence and avoidance, which were evident in the interviews with the children in this study. These techniques permit the researcher to compare respondents' behavior during participant observations with their reported responses to the intervention activities and to resolve inconsistencies through further interviews and observations (Edgerton, 1984; Sigelman et al., 1981; Stainback & Stainback, 1984).We also had access to child comments to family members about the intervention via interviews and informal conversations with parents. An additional benefit of the qualitative design was that it provided detailed information to increase the effectiveness and improve the efficiency of future mentor interventions with this age group. Such information could be used, for example, to identify points at which facilitation by research staff is helpful; to determine optimal amounts of interaction among child, mentor, and parent; and to suggest optimal duration of formal intervention.

We present the findings in the form of descriptive case studies in order to provide as much detail as possible. Detailed information about the participants, the intervention, and the perceived outcomes facilitates tentative assessments of relationships among variables that might produce differential outcomes. Such information can be used both by practitioners with an interest in implementing a mentor intervention with a similar population and by researchers attempting to identify promising lines of inquiry.

Recruitment of Child Participants

Children were recruited through local school districts. District personnel distributed information about the project to parents of children between the ages of 8 and 12 who had significant physical disabilities and who had no cognitive disabilities or had mild cognitive disabilities. Three parents responded by returning Consent to Contact forms. Project personnel met individually with each parent who responded to explain the project in detail and to obtain informed consent to participate from parents and children.

The participants included Hope and Darla, two 11-year-old girls with quadriplegic cerebral palsy, and David, a 9-year-old boy with muscular dystrophy.

Recruitment of Mentors

Two female mentors, Betty and Joan, were recruited through a local independent living program. Betty had participated previously in an adolescent mentor project. Joan was acquainted with Betty and had expressed an interest in being involved in a mentor project. The third mentor, Mikhail, was recruited through the local Muscular Dystrophy Association. The two adults who had not previously been mentors completed an application form and interview. The application included employment history and character references. The interview was designed to assess mentors' personal interaction styles, attitudes toward disability, and ability to handle emergencies or difficult social situations. Mentors who would be using their own vehicles to transport children for some of the activities provided information on auto liability insurance and their driving records. They signed photo permission forms and informed the project coordinator of any type of assistance that might be required for certain activities. Mentors were each paid $100 for their training and coaching time. Mentor–child pairs were formed on the basis of gender, similarity of disability, and shared interests.

Mentor Training

A manual describing project procedures and activities was designed for this project (Powers, Stevens, & Sowers, 1992). Project staff met individually with mentors to go over the manual, discuss their role, and suggest general approaches to the planned activities. The mentors were asked to provide a model of a positive, active person who happens to have a disability similar to that of the child. Mentors were encouraged to talk openly about their disabilities, to reinforce the child's positive outlook and response to challenges, to model strategies for overcoming obstacles, to describe ways his or her parents and other adults had provided support, and to provide information about topics associated with project activities.

With each mentor, project staff discussed issues and topics that might come up in each activity. Mentors were encouraged to use any barriers that might be encountered during activities as opportunities to model strategies for dealing with challenges. The issues, topics, and strategies were also listed in the manual provided to each mentor.

In each activity, mentors were asked to emphasize some key themes: disability is a challenge, not a tragedy; parents help children learn how to overcome the challenges; and children with disabilities need to do the same activities and have the same responsibilities as other children their age.

Field Researcher Selection and Training

Each mentor pair was assigned a field researcher who would accompany them on all activities and attend all mentor–parent meetings. The field researchers were recruited from the departments of anthropology and sociology at the local university, where they had received training in the qualitative research techniques of participant observation and unstructured interviewing. In addition, they attended a 4-hour training session to learn procedures specific to this project (e.g., observing mentor–child interactions as unobtrusively as possible and preparing field notes in a standard format). Field researchers were also instructed to take a passive role and to assist in providing personal assistance to mentors and children only when requested.

Field researchers attended biweekly meetings with project staff throughout the data collection period to discuss such topics as practical issues arising in the field;

maintenance of a balance between participant and observer roles; and emerging patterns and themes in the relationships among mentors, parents, and children.

Initial Meeting

Project staff facilitated initial meetings of the mentor, child, parents, and field researcher. The purpose of the meeting was to make introductions, establish positive rapport, explain the field researcher's role, discuss possible activities, and decide on a first activity. At this meeting, parents signed release forms including a medical release with information about the child's medications, doctor, and dentist; an attendant permission form; a travel release for public and private transportation; and a photo permission form. Parents were asked to attend at least one activity—the visit to the mentor's home—and were encouraged to attend as many other activities as they wished.

Activities

Mentor pairs were to participate in six specified categories of activities: a visit to the mentor's home, a shopping trip, a bus ride, an adapted recreation activity of choice, an activity in an area with accessibility barriers, and a meal at a restaurant. These categories were selected because they provided maximal in-situ opportunities for children, mentors, and parents to interact around various disability-related issues. In addition, each pair was asked to select two other activities, one of which was novel to the child, for a total of eight activities. In practice, some of the activities were combined in a single outing, such as going shopping and going out to eat or dealing with accessibility barriers in the context of another activity.

Activities took place in the late spring and, for two mentor pairs, throughout the summer. One mentor pair participated in one informal and nine formal activities; one pair, in which the mentor lived about 200 miles from the child, completed eight activities; and the third pair completed six activities before the child left to spend the summer with her mother in another state.

Project staff helped schedule each activity once it was decided upon and made arrangements for transportation for each activity. The project provided $20 toward the cost of each activity and reimbursed parents and mentors for mileage if their own vehicles were used.

Mentor–Parent Meeting

Three months into the project, mentors and parents attended a meeting facilitated by project staff. Field researchers also attended and prepared field notes of their observations and impressions. The purpose of the meeting was to provide adult participants with an opportunity to discuss their experiences in the project, their perceptions of the children's capabilities, their hopes for the children's future, obstacles to the children's achievement of their hopes, and strategies to overcome the obstacles. Parents and mentors were then to meet individually to discuss goals for remaining activities. However, the discussion, which centered on the experience of being the parent of a child with a disability, was animated and highly personal and the group chose to continue the discussion rather than meeting in small groups.

Data Collection

Interviews Field researchers conducted preintervention interviews with each mentor and child and with the mother of each child. Protocols were prepared to ensure that the same broad topics were addressed, but the interviews were conducted in an unstructured manner so interviewees could discuss these topics in as much detail as they wished and could raise additional topics. Parents were asked to talk about their families, their children and the nature of their physical challenges, family activities, expectations for the future of the child with disabilities, adult friends of the family who have disabilities, and expectations and concerns related to the mentor project.

Mentors were asked to talk about their current living and work situations, leisure activities, and social support systems. They were also asked to talk about their childhood experiences, including family and peer relationships, schooling, and activities. Their interview protocol also included questions about how they achieved their present independence, about factors that help them maintain their independence, and about their expectations and concerns about the project.

Children were asked to talk about their families, friends, and favorite activities. They were also asked what they thought their lives would be like when they were adults and whether they knew any adults who had disabilities. They were asked what they thought the project would be like; what they were looking forward to; and what, if anything, they had concerns about.

Mentors, parents, and children were also interviewed individually after the intervention. Each was asked to discuss their overall impressions of the project, the most successful and least successful aspects of the project, and suggestions for improving this type of intervention. Mentors and parents were asked for their impressions of the effect of the intervention on the children.

Interviews were audiotaped and transcribed verbatim. Field researchers reviewed the transcripts of the child interviews to fill in sections unclear to the transcriber.

Participant Observations   Field researchers took no notes during activities. Immediately after each activity, however, they prepared detailed field notes describing events, interactions, and settings. Field notes also included, in a separate section, field researchers' impressions regarding participants' affect and relationship and questions or emerging themes to be examined in future observations or interviews.

Project Log   Project staff telephoned mentors and parents before each activity to schedule and plan and after each activity to debrief. Staff kept a descriptive log of these conversations as well as records of transportation and other arrangements.

Triangulation of Data Sources   Child interview responses were short and often hard to interpret. (One child responded "I don't know" to almost all of the interview questions.) We therefore attempted to answer questions regarding child expectations of and responses to the intervention through close observation of child behavior and affect during observations. Parent reports of child comments about the mentor and activities and reports of behavior change following the intervention were also used to supplement child interviews.

Qualitative Data Analysis

Coding   All interview transcripts and log entries were coded by topic using the constant comparative method (Glaser & Strauss, 1967; Lincoln & Guba, 1985). As each incident or interview comment was coded, it was compared to all other coded data to determine if the new material was an example of something already labeled or required a new category. This constant comparison generated thinking about theoretical properties of the categories, which were recorded in memos and discussed among project staff.

Not surprisingly, code categories emerging from interviews corresponded closely to topics included in the interview protocols. Special note was taken of additional topics raised by interviewees in interviews, during observations, and in telephone conversations recorded in the log, as indicators of categories that participants considered important. Incidents and interactions observed during activities were also coded descriptively, sometimes contributing to previously coded categories, sometimes requiring new code categories.

Approximately 50 code words were used, related to the description of participants, activities, design of the intervention, and impact of the intervention. Code categories included *behavior, safety, disability awareness, parent participation, independence, accessibility, parenting practices,* and *observer role.*

Memos describing the "rules" for inclusion in each code category were prepared by the first author and distributed to the project coordinator and field observers. The memos were discussed and revised at project meetings. Previously coded segments were reexamined to see if they fit the revised categories. In some cases, subcategories were required to accommodate data; in other cases, the category definitions were again revised to accommodate all segments.

Case Study Analysis   Because the perspectives of the different participants in the intervention (child, parent, and mentor) were of interest, the first author constructed a role-ordered matrix (Miles & Huberman, 1994). Several broad categories formed the columns of the matrix: salient characteristics of the individual, future expectations (parent and child), expectations of the intervention, positive features of the intervention, critique of the intervention, and outcomes of the intervention. Categories entered on the matrix were selected because they 1) represented important themes emerging from the data; 2) contributed to the development of case studies of the individual interventions; and 3) were directly related to the research questions: What effects, if any, did the mentor intervention have on child and parent behaviors and attitudes?

A computer program for the analysis of text-based data, *The Ethnograph* (Seidel, Knolseth, & Seymour, 1988), was used to search the interview, log, and observation data and retrieve coded segments in these categories. The first author entered in each cell a brief summary of the data for each category for each participant. In constructing the summary, we used the decision rule suggested by Miles and Huberman (1994): The statement must be supported by data and not internally contradicted. A log was compiled of coded data segments supporting each statement on the matrix.

In some cases, statements made in interviews were contradicted by observed behavior. The discrepancy was noted and the data were searched again to better understand the factors contributing to the apparent contradiction. Tentative theories were formed that were then checked against new data, often in the form of responses to direct questions by participants about the source of the discrepancy. The process continued until an explanation was produced that was satisfactory to participants and project personnel. For example, one parent talked in the initial interviews about her high expectations for her child's future independence. However, observations revealed parenting practices that fostered the child's dependence. Subsequent conversations and observations indicated that the source of the discrepancy was a lack of awareness of the impact of early childhood experiences on attitudes and skills related to independence and self-determination.

Cross-Case Analysis   The role-ordered matrix highlighted similarities and differences among parents, mentors and children, their individual interventions, and the intervention outcomes. To analyze how these differences and similarities interacted to produce differential effects and perceptions about the intervention, the first author constructed a causal network for each case. Initially, the factors from the role-ordered matrix were used to construct the network. Two other factors were added: logistics (scheduling, transportation, and other logistical details of the intervention activities) and intervention focus (types of activities, information, and interactions that characterized the individual interventions).

The Ethnograph was used to search for coded segments in the new categories. In constructing the causal networks, closely related factors were clustered together. Arrows were drawn between factors using the decision rule: There must be at least one incident in the data supporting the relationship and no contradicting evidence (Miles & Huberman, 1994).

Based on this analysis, case studies were prepared, describing the salient features of each mentor pair's activities and interactions, the perspectives of mentor and parent before and after the intervention, and factors contributing to differential outcomes of the intervention. The case studies were sent to the participants for their review, providing an opportunity to give us feedback on our interpretations of their experiences.

The case studies are presented in the Results section. The Discussion section describes our analysis of the interaction of factors that influenced the outcomes of the intervention for each child and implications for further mentor intervention research.

CASE STUDY 1: HOPE AND BETTY

Participants

Hope is a tall, attractive 11-year-old girl who looks and acts more mature than her age. She has severe spastic athetoid quadriplegia. Speech is difficult for her, but people who know her have little trouble understanding her. At the time of the intervention, Hope was in fifth grade in a regular classroom with a full-time assistant and approaching the transition to middle school. Feeling socially isolated in her elementary school, she was looking forward to this transition as an opportunity to meet some new friends and to become more independent.

Hope lives with her mother, Patty, and her younger brother and sister. Patty, a special education teacher, is a well-informed, effective advocate for Hope in the school and social services network. She has also been involved with Hope in a number of research and service projects designed to promote independence and inclusion. Patty has a long-range goal of independence for Hope, but currently, as a full-time professional and the single parent of a child with severe disabilities and active young twins, her focus is meeting day-to-day schedules and caregiving demands.

The mentor, Betty, is in her 50s and developed rheumatoid arthritis as a young adult. Like Hope, she uses a motorized wheelchair and has limited use of her arms and hands. Betty is active in disability rights and awareness organizations. She writes and directs plays and performs occasionally as a comedian using material with a disability focus. Betty participated in two previous adolescent mentor projects that mentor, parents, and children all found successful, and she has maintained some contact with the children. Hope and her family were acquainted with one of these children and her family and were aware of the positive outcomes and ongoing positive relationship.

Expectations

Hope had relatively high expectations for the project. She wanted the mentor to influence her peers to be more accepting of her. She also had as a model an older friend who is very self-assured and assertive who had the same mentor. She may have expected to gain similar confidence from the intervention.

Hope's mother's expectations of the project were relatively low. Patty regarded the Mentor Project as an opportunity for Hope and herself to "see independence in a disabled person," but indicated that this seemed like a remote goal for Hope: "I can't even envision…I don't think Hope can envision, because I can't envision it. And so maybe it will be something that opens our eyes." In other discussions, Patty made it clear that her expectations of research interventions in general were low: "[research projects] are all fine and dandy, but then they come to a screeching halt and there's nothing left to take over."

Betty had high expectations for the intervention, and they got higher as she got to know Hope. Recognizing Hope's intelligence, maturity, and sensitivity, she wanted to influence Hope to be more aware of her preferences for how she should be treated and how her environment should be arranged and to be more assertive about making her wishes known.

Intervention

Activities   Hope and Betty participated in 10 activities over a 5-month period. Betty saw their early activities, which focused on Hope's interests—going to a movie, swimming, and shopping at a mall—as a chance to get to know Hope and to decide what her own role should be as mentor. Hope and her teacher asked Betty to come to school to read to Hope's class the children's books she had written that dealt with the issue of how to interact with children who have disabilities.

Later activities focused on Betty and her involvement in the local community of people with disabilities: a visit to Betty's home; observation of an audio recording session at which actors and actress, both with and without disabilities, produced books on tape for individuals with visual impairments; and a potluck dinner sponsored by Mobility International USA to host a group of visitors with disabilities from the former Soviet Union. As an unscheduled event, Betty also attended Hope's fifth-grade graduation ceremony. In the early activities, for which she set the agenda, Hope participated fully. In the later, more adult-focused activities, Hope appeared to be "taking it all in," involved as an observer rather than a participant.

Logistics   Although alternative transportation arrangements were available, Patty and Hope's father provided the transportation for all but one activity. (In that case Patty had a last minute conflict and asked the observer to drive Hope in the family van.) This transportation arrangement sometimes cut into Hope's time with her mentor, and Hope was not exposed to transportation options as other children were.

In spite of the fact that Patty was present at the beginning and end of most events, her opportunities to interact with Betty were minimal. Even at the parent–mentor meeting, there was no time for her to talk privately with Betty about their impressions of Hope and about how to maximize the potential impact of the project.

Postintervention Impressions

Hope enjoyed Betty's attention, and she was interested in many things she observed during the activities, but her high expectations for the mentor intervention were not met. Although Betty validated Hope's assessment of the social rejection she perceived at school, peer acceptance was not impacted by Betty's visit. Nor did she exhibit or report gains in self-confidence.

At the conclusion of the project, Patty commented that it would have been helpful if Hope's mentor had had cerebral palsy. This suggested that she, and perhaps Hope, found it difficult to draw comparisons between Betty's independent living arrangements and possible arrangements for Hope in the future because of the incongruity of their disabling conditions. Patty also reported that Hope told her she wished she could have a younger mentor.

Patty thought that Betty was a "nice person to have as a role model" and that Hope "learned a lot" by observing and interacting with Betty. Patty was not specific about what Hope may have learned. Patty neither reported nor exhibited changes in parenting practices or in expectations for Hope's future.

The logistics of the intervention were important for Patty. She felt that scheduling the activities within a 5-month period had the advantage of providing consistency of contact between Hope and Betty and possibly had helped them establish their relationship. However, Patty said it was challenging to work the activities into her already busy schedule, and she sometimes felt pressure to come up with an activity, whether or not it was something both Betty and Hope wanted to do.

Betty seemed to view the formal project as a time to get to know Hope with both the constraints and the supports that the project provided. She felt that the most effective mentoring would take place after the project was completed, when she had a chance to meet with Hope informally and talk to her about social interaction, mobility issues, management of assistance, and other topics that had come up during activities.

Betty was frustrated that the project design did not provide time to talk at length with Hope about these issues. Because Betty felt that there was much she could offer and little time to do so, she found herself "lecturing, but in a nice way" to impart important information. The pressure Betty felt to be a teacher as well as a friend may have contributed to Hope's statement that she would have liked a "younger" mentor.

CASE STUDY 2: DAVID AND MIKHAIL

Participants

David is an active 9-year-old boy, big for his age, with reddish hair and freckles. He has muscular dystrophy (MD), which was diagnosed at age 6. He attends a special education program in a public school and uses a motorized wheelchair independently. David looks forward all year to attending MD camp, where a group of counselors called the Hounds lead younger campers in pranks, practical jokes, and other outrageous adolescent activities.

David is the youngest of four children. His father, Wayne, covers several states in his work as a salesman and is frequently away from home. David's mother Kay is a full-time homemaker and is responsible for most of David's assistance needs. In fact, family members often anticipate David's needs and do things for him without being asked. David's main contacts with adults outside his family have occurred at church, at school, and at Easter Seals camp. His mother commented in the initial meeting that, except for school and camp, he had been away from her only once, for a few hours.

Mikhail, David's mentor, is a 37-year-old graphic artist with a dystrophy-like condition. The progress of his disease is much slower than that of other types of dystrophy. In fact, Mikhail's condition was not diagnosed until he was 21. Mikhail can walk short distances. He drives a van and uses a scooter for mobility and can load and unload the scooter independently. He lives in a small city about 200 miles from David's home. His interests include process work in psychology, sailing, water skiing, travel, and activities with a men's group and with his girlfriend and her two children.

Expectations

Kay said that initially David "wasn't thrilled" about the project because he thought it was going to be like therapy. However, when he learned that the project would be based on activities of his choice, David may have used his camp experiences as a basis for his expectations for activities with his mentor. Clearly his primary interest was having fun. During the intervention, he often engaged in teasing or horseplay and usually would not comply with Mikhail's requests to stop until Mikhail "got tough" with him. His age and problems with maintaining attention, which Kay had mentioned in the initial meeting, probably contributed to this pattern.

At the time of the study, the family was planning to remodel the house to give David a room of his own and an accessible bathroom and to make other modifications to accommodate David's wheelchair. One of Kay's expectations for the intervention was that Mikhail could give her advice in this area. She was also hoping to learn more about David's disability, from the perspective of a person with a similar condition and about the lives of people with disabilities in general.

Mikhail's expectations for the project were personal and coincided with two of his interests at the time: process work and establishing a connection with the disability community. His goals for the project were therefore to develop relationships with David and his family, using this as an opportunity to reflect on his childhood experience of disability and to share with David and Kay some insights on the adult experience.

Intervention

For this triad, the intervention was characterized by high levels of activity for David and information for Kay.

Activities   Mikhail and David completed eight activities over a period of 5 months. The first activity was a visit by Mikhail to David's home. The pair also went on two shopping trips, received instruction from a city bus driver on using the lift, launched model rockets, went swimming, and visited the Country Fair, an annual 3-day gathering of counterculture craft vendors and entertainers. Because of the distance to Mikhail's home, arrangements were made for Kay and David to stay overnight. Mikhail gave them a detailed tour of his house, which he has remodeled extensively to be accessible and convenient and to accommodate his needs as his disease progresses. Mikhail and David prepared dinner together, watched a videotape with some of Mikhail's friends who were invited to meet Kay and David, and the next day explored the town in their wheelchairs.

During activities, David frequently asked the observer to provide assistance. Mikhail consistently stepped in to model how the task could be done from a wheelchair and to point out gently that David could do many things for himself. Usually David good-naturedly ignored these prompts. Mikhail also tried to point out accessibility features and to demonstrate how to overcome barriers to accessibility, but David seemed uninterested in or embarrassed by these attempts.

Logistics   Because Mikhail had to travel about 4 hours, activities needed to be planned when he had an entire day free. Kay attended all but two activities, and one of those was attended by David's father and brother, so David was unaccompanied by a family member for only one activity. Project staff arranged for a disability taxi service to transport Kay and David for most activities.

Kay seems to have been closely involved in the project both out of concern for David's safety and a need to feel involved and because she expected to learn a lot from Mikhail. When Kay was present, her conversations with Mikhail sometimes dominated the triad's interactions. When this occurred, David seemed bored and would sometimes act out to get the adults' attention.

Postintervention Impressions

Kay commented in her final interview, "I don't think [David] liked it when Mikhail was being parenting to him." However, on those occasions when Mikhail directly asked David to behave more appropriately, David responded by complying immediately. With Mikhail encouraging him and declining to do things for him, David also exhibited more independent behavior during activities than at home. However, these behavior changes did not generalize to other situations. Because of his immaturity and lack of attention to strategies and other types of instruction, the impact of the intervention on David seems to have been minimal.

Kay identified several ways in which the project had been beneficial to her personally: 1) She got access to a number of ideas to help with their remodeling project, 2) participation in the project expanded her knowledge of the disability community and of services available to persons with disabilities and their families, and 3) getting to know Mikhail broadened her personal perspective and experience.

At the mentor–parent meeting, David's parents seemed to derive support from talking with Hope's mother, mentors, and project staff about the frustration of trying to get appropriate educational services and about dealing with the knowledge that David's condition is progressive and terminal. At that meeting, Kay described an incident that occurred during the second activity when Mikhail, David, and Kay toured the downtown mall. Mikhail and David rode an elevator to the top of a parking garage and, when the elevator malfunctioned, drove their chairs back down. Although she gave no indication of distress at the time, Kay commented during the parent meeting that seeing David deal with this incident was important for her. She said at that moment she saw David not as a child with a disability who needed constant help from his parents, but as a boy who solved a problem with the help of a friend. Kay added that this experience made "the whole project worthwhile." Interestingly, during the final interview, Kay indicated that she did not remember the incident. The intervention had no discernible impact on her parenting practices or on her expectations for David.

For Mikhail, the interpersonal relationship with David was more important than being a role model or teaching strategies for independence:

> I don't know what he got out of it. It feels weird to say that, but I was involved in an interpersonal relationship with him. I was not there to think about what he might be getting from this. I mean, he may have learned some things about self-esteem. I hope he learned some things about using his wheelchair in public, things like that.

Mikhail had several recommendations for improving the intervention, mostly focused on fostering the relationships among mentor, child, and parent—his personal goal. He felt that more time should have been allotted for contact between mentor and parent apart from activities with the child. Because he felt that "this mentoring stuff is a two-way street," Mikhail would have liked to learn more about David's life, rather than just exposing David to his life, in order to focus on specific issues in ways that would be useful to David. Mikhail pointed out that a critical feature in the success of the visit to Mikhail's home was that David got to spend the night. This made it possible for David to enjoy the independence of taking a shower in Mikhail's accessible bathroom, meet Mikhail's friends, and "experience a full day in [Mikhail's] life," not just visit his house. Mikhail felt that the project should have had a formal conclusion, perhaps some sort of ceremony or party, whether or not the mentor pair planned to maintain contact.

CASE 3: DARLA AND JOAN

Participants

Darla is an 11-year-old girl with big brown eyes, dimples, and a pixie haircut. She, like Hope, has quadriplegic cerebral palsy. While Hope looks and acts older than her 11 years, Darla appears to be younger. Darla's use of her hands is limited, and her speech is difficult to understand, even for family members. Darla aids communication by spelling key words. She attends a self-contained special education classroom in a public school and participates in few community-based activities.

Darla's family consists of her father, her stepmother Meg, an older sister, and a younger sister. At the time of the intervention, their house was not accessible to her power chair because there was one outdoor step, and the family had no plans to install a ramp. In her manual wheelchair, which Darla used inside the house, she needed assistance to move from room to room. A parent took over driving when Darla was outside in her motorized chair if the terrain was even slightly rough or slanted. There had been some frightening experiences when Darla was learning to drive her chair, and Meg was reluctant to have them repeated.

Although Meg encouraged Darla to think in terms of being independent in adulthood, as in Hope's family, daily caregiving demands left little parental time and energy for thinking about how to increase Darla's current level of independent functioning.

Joan, Darla's mentor, is a middle-age woman who had polio as an infant. She has no upper body involvement but uses a motorized wheelchair. Like Betty, she is active in disability rights groups. She is a friend of Betty's and was pleased to be asked to participate in the mentor project, having observed how enjoyable Betty's experience with the adolescents had been.

Expectations

Many of Darla's responses to interview questions were "I don't know." However, a few responses, and her later response to the intervention, seemed to indicate that she hoped that the intervention would provide her with more choices for activities and more independence within activities.

Meg, like Patty, thought of the intervention as a way for her daughter to get to know an adult with disabilities, someone who would have an insider's perspective on disability issues that might be helpful to Darla. Meg had also noted that Darla seemed to be afraid of people in wheelchairs, and she hoped the intervention would help her overcome this.

Joan regarded the mentor program as an opportunity to share her knowledge about how to establish a successful, independent life as a person with a disability and to act as a role model. She hoped to give Darla an experience that she wished she had had as a child: a positive outlook on life with a disability.

Intervention

Activities   This mentor pair got off to a slow start because of scheduling difficulties. Darla also had to leave as soon as school was out to spend the summer with her mother in another state. As a result, the project was shortened and "telescoped" for this mentor pair: They completed six activities in 2 months.

The first three activities were visits to Joan's house and "rolls" through her neighborhood. Darla and Joan also attended an outdoor folk music festival on a university campus, and during another activity they went shopping.

In the first activity, Darla had a great deal of difficulty controlling her chair, and even in a parking lot she had trouble making turns or going in a straight line. Joan broke the tension by bumping into Darla's chair on purpose and getting her to laugh. Joan offered pointers, provided reassurance, and worked with Darla patiently when she repeatedly ran off the sidewalk and got stuck. Darla cheerfully persisted and was open to Joan's coaching. Joan also determined that the controls on Darla's chair had an unusual amount of play and that the chair had very little power. She assured Darla that her difficulties were caused by the chair, not by anything she was doing. In all subsequent activities, Darla chose to focus on practicing her driving skills with feedback and coaching from Joan. At the music festival, Darla chose to practice using the automatic door openers at the student union rather than listen to the music. During visits to Joan's house, Darla developed a favorite game: purposely getting her chair stuck in the grass in Joan's yard and practicing getting herself unstuck.

Meg accompanied the pair on the final visit to Joan's house. On a roll through the neighborhood, Meg commented repeatedly on how surprised she was that Darla was so far ahead of them. She reviewed for Joan a number of frightening driving experiences and expressed her concern for Darla's safety when driving unassisted. Joan told Meg how hard Darla had worked to manage her wheelchair more independently. She also related some of her own childhood and adult experiences related to mobility issues. As Meg and Joan talked, Darla went off ahead, as if to demonstrate her new driving ability and independence and perhaps to distance herself, literally, from Meg's descriptions of her past driving difficulties.

Logistics Darla rode the city bus with the field researcher for one activity and, for the others, arrived by the taxi service for persons with disabilities, unaccompanied by a parent or by the field researcher. Darla's father and Meg were unable to attend the mentor–parent meeting because they were out of town. At the initial meeting, Joan was frustrated by the difficulty in communicating with Darla. The problem was later exacerbated by Joan's tendency to ask a series of questions that could have different answers, making it difficult for Darla to convey which question she was responding to. The observer had a somewhat easier time understanding Darla's speech and sometimes interpreted for Joan, who felt that this interfered with her ability to get to know Darla.

Postintervention Impressions

Darla clearly enjoyed the independence the intervention afforded her. When her family drove by Joan's house during an early visit, she politely said, "Hi," and sent them on their way. She exerted a great deal of control over activities and made choices within activities. Her skill and confidence in driving her wheelchair improved greatly. In her final interview, Darla said that what she liked best about her mentor was that she had her own house, indicating perhaps that she was impressed by the degree of independence Joan had created for herself.

Meg reported changes in Darla's behavior that she attributed to the intervention. She indicated that Darla was taking more initiative in using her motorized wheelchair and that she was using it differently. Before the project Darla had used her chair only to get from place to place, but during the intervention she began to use it to explore her environment. She became more assertive about making her preferences known.

Meg said that observing these changes, which they attributed to the intervention, made the family aware that they had limited Darla's opportunities to drive her chair at home because of difficulties she had when the chair was new. Through the mentor project, Meg said that they realized that Darla needed to have more freedom to operate her chair in order to build skills and become more independent:

> I think from the standpoint of independence, it's important to be able to decide which room you're going to, without having to ask somebody to take you there. I think that...even though she's having problems with her chair we'll make a greater effort than we have for more use of the chair.

Darla's role in the family also shifted because of the intervention. Before the intervention, the family had made plans and fit Darla in as best they could. When she became more assertive about making her preferences known, the family began to consult with her before making plans.

Meg was pleased that Darla had Joan to give her feedback on using her chair, but did not seem to consider Joan as a model for how the family could help Darla problem-solve mobility challenges:

> If she had gotten on the grass, my tendency probably would have been to [take the controls to] help her get back on the sidewalk. Whereas, with the mentor, she would tell her the best way for her to approach getting off the grass without being in a situation where her

wheelchair may tip or something like that, or talk to her about "This wasn't a good idea," and "What are you going to do about it?" That kind of thing. And I think she needs that approach.

Joan was encouraged by the progress Darla made during their activities. She felt that the activities represented a positive start in broadening Darla's perspective, increasing her independence, and establishing their relationship. However, Joan found the structure of the project confining in several ways. Although her ability to communicate with Darla improved, she felt that the presence of the field researcher interfered with their interactions. She also felt that the project's list of recommended activities was too prescriptive. She looked forward to continuing her relationship with Darla beyond the structure of the project and having more latitude to choose activities spontaneously.

DISCUSSION

Because the project permitted a great deal of flexibility, child, mentor, and parent characteristics interacted to produce highly individual interventions for each of the three groups. Of the three child participants, only Darla exhibited behavior changes that were attributed by her parents to the intervention. Darla's mother, Meg, was the only parent participant who planned changes in her parenting practices as a result of Darla's changed behavior. Our data analysis revealed several factors that might account for the differential outcome of the intervention with the three groups of participants.

First, Darla was the only one of the three children whose mother and mentor both exerted a low degree of control throughout the intervention. While the mentor, Betty, selected the majority of the activities for Hope, and Kay both attended and dominated most of her son David's activities, both Joan and Meg allowed Darla to set the agenda for her activities. She chose to practice mobility skills, with Joan as her coach, and to experience independence from her family.

Second, the aims of the intervention—to promote independence and self-determination among children with disabilities by exposing them to mentors who exhibit those attributes—was highly salient to Darla, but less so to the other two children. Hope, who was already relatively integrated and independent, was more interested in the fine points of social integration than in gaining access to integrated environments. David, who was 2 years younger than the girls and rather immature for a 9-year-old, regarded the intervention primarily as entertainment. Of the three children, the intervention was best suited to Darla.

Third, differences among the three parents mirrored those of their children. Meg, Darla's mother, was open to the idea of independence for Darla, but relatively naive about how such independence is achieved. Meeting Joan and seeing Darla interact with her helped Meg understand that the attitudes and skills upon which independence is built can and should be developed in childhood. Hope's mother Patty, on the other hand, was already aware of the importance of social and educational integration for children with disabilities. The activities Hope participated in with Betty were of interest as examples of what Hope might expect as an adult, but a little removed from Patty's primary concerns for her middle-school–age daughter. Likewise, while David's mother Kay was interested in learning about the disabilities community and the independent living movement in particular, concerns about her son's health and the fact that he was so young—and the baby of the family at that—made the intervention more academic than practical for her.

It is somewhat remarkable that Meg identified so readily the factors in the intervention that contributed to Darla's new independence, particularly since she observed Darla and her mentor Joan together during only one activity and was not able to attend the mentor–parent meeting. She said that the family would work toward giving Darla independent mobility, a wider choice of activities, and more personal control. Possibly Meg had read or heard about these factors and their impact on child attitudes prior to the intervention, and Darla's striking response to them helped Meg understand their importance. It seems unlikely, however, that most parents, however impressed with the behavioral changes in their children, would be able to extrapolate the changes in parenting practices that would support those changes in the home. The mentors' feedback on how the intervention might be improved also reflected their personal characteristics and agendas. Mikhail had specific recommendations for improving the intervention, which reflected his focus on relationships. Betty would have liked more opportunities to pursue with Hope her views on assertiveness, an area in which she teaches classes for people with disabilities. Joan, who is fiercely independent, complained about the constraints imposed by the project. In fact, all three mentors felt that the structure imposed by the project was somewhat restrictive, even though none of the three groups followed a prescribed list of activities or met on a regular schedule. Interestingly, Betty and Joan planned to continue to see Hope and Darla, but neither of them did. This might indicate that the support of the project was helpful in scheduling, providing assistants and transportation, and motivating busy people to take on more activities.

RECOMMENDATIONS

The case study analysis suggests several ways to increase the effectiveness of a mentor intervention with 9- to 12-year-olds. First, such an intervention may be most effective with 11- to 14-year-olds who have had relatively little experience in integrated educational and community settings. For preadolescents who have had more opportunities to interact in integrated settings, a mentor intervention might be more salient when they are a couple of years older in order to focus on the details of independent living and vocational preparation (Powers, 1993). Children younger than 11, unless they are unusually mature, may see the intervention primarily as a fun series of outings.

Second, if a goal of the intervention is to have an impact on parent attitudes and practices, this should be made clear to parents and mentors. Preceding or concurrent with the mentor intervention, opportunities should be provided for parents to build awareness of their role in promoting children's self-esteem and to learn skills for enhancing child self-determination through daily activities, interactions, and parenting practices. A similar multipronged approach has been successfully demonstrated by Powers (1993) with adolescents and their parents. Singer, Irvin, Todis, Stevens, and Alvernaz (1992) have developed a curriculum for parents that includes support for making changes in parenting practices and instruction and practice in identifying and planning how to overcome barriers to accessibility and inclusion (Todis et al., 1993), which could be used in conjunction with the mentor intervention.

Based on our experience, we recommend that the parent education described here be provided apart from child–mentor activities to prevent parent involvement from interfering with the development of the child–mentor relationship. There should be sufficient contact between parent and mentor to ensure that parents are comfortable with the intervention and that they are involved enough to see mentors model behaviors and to see their children's interactions with an adult friend. Several steps can be taken to address the safety and security concerns of parents and to permit parents and mentors to share information without infringing upon activity time:

1. Hold the initial meeting with the mentor in the child's home, with all family members present. This both provides the parent an opportunity to learn more about the mentor and gives the mentor a sense of the child's daily routine.

2. Invite the parent to participate in the visit to the mentor's home.
3. Once the mentor pair has established a routine, invite the parent to go on a typical outing. This permits parents to observe how the mentor and child interact and handle both routine and challenging situations without interfering with the child–mentor relationship.
4. Schedule regular meetings for mentors and parents, individually or with other parents and mentors.
5. Invite mentors to attend parent intervention training meetings to provide insights on effective parenting practices for children with physical disabilities.

We recommend formalizing the approach to planning activities that the mentor pairs in this intervention eventually adopted—that is, let children take the lead in selecting activities, particularly the first several activities. As rapport is established between mentor and child, the mentor can suggest activities related to his or her interests. Although planning activities to model or discuss particular issues on the mentor's or the researcher's agenda is probably not efficacious for this age group, the case studies clearly indicated that at least one visit to the mentor's home should be included as part of the intervention and that an overnight visit should be considered.

We recommend extending the time of the intervention to at least 6 months, to 1 year if possible, and marking the end of the project with a party or ceremony. If mentor and child both want to continue past the project period, project staff should facilitate planning for transition to independent activities.

Based on our experience, we recommend that the project provide all transportation. Having transportation provided by the project or by the mentor allows the child to experience independence with a variety of public conveyances or to see the mentor use accommodations to drive a vehicle and permits the mentor pair to decide which activities to invite the parent to attend. In this project, parents were given the option of providing transportation to ensure that concerns about the child's safety would not be a barrier to the child's participation in activities. However, safety concerns would be better addressed by establishing rapport between the mentor and the parent as suggested. The support person, if needed, should have a minimal role and should receive direction from mentor or child. Support should be sufficient to reassure the parent that his or her involvement is not needed to facilitate transportation or personal care arrangements. There is a suggestion in the case studies that intervention effects may be enhanced if mentors and children are matched in terms of disability. However, this factor may be more salient for parents than for children.

Finally, we highly recommend additional research in this area. Given the huge number of variables operating within a child–parent–mentor triad, the complexity of the intervention, and the myriad outcomes (intended and unintended) that might result, many replications of this study would be required to identify predictable effects of a mentor intervention on parents and children. Current emphasis on fostering self-determination in children with disabilities (Ward, 1988; Wehmeyer, 1992) would argue for undertaking such studies as a promising, relatively inexpensive, enjoyable means of introducing children and their families to the world of successful adults with disabilities.

REFERENCES

Bauman, L.J., & Adair, E.G. (1992). The use of ethnographic interviewing to inform questionnaire construction. *Health Education Quarterly, 19,* 9–23.
Baumrind, D. (1966). Effects of authoritative parental control on child behavior. *Child Development, 37,* 887–907.

Boston, B.O. (1976). *The sorcerer's apprentice: A case study in the role of the mentor.* Reston, VA: Council for Exceptional Children.

Edgerton, R.B. (1984). Anthropology and mental retardation: Research approaches and opportunities. *Culture, Medicine, and Psychiatry, 8,* 25–48.

Espinosa, L., & Shearer, M. (1986). Family support in public school programs. In R.R. Fewell & P.F. Vadasy (Eds.), *Families of handicapped children: Needs and supports across the lifespan* (pp. 253–277). Austin, TX: PRO-ED.

Fredericks, B. (1988). *Tim becomes an Eagle Scout.* Transition Summary 5. Washington, DC: National Information Center for Children and Youth with Handicaps.

Garrison, W.T., & McQuiston, S. (1989). Chronic illness during childhood and adolescence: Psychological aspects. *Developmental clinical psychology and psychiatry, Vol. 19.* Newbury Park, CA: Sage Publications.

Glaser, B.G., & Strauss, A.L. (1967). *The discovery of grounded theory.* Chicago: Aldine.

Jones, M.L., & Ulicny, G.R. (1986). The independent living perspective: Applications to services for adults with developmental disabilities. In J.A. Summers (Ed.), *The right to grow up: An introduction to adults with developmental disabilities* (pp. 227–244). Baltimore: Paul H. Brookes Publishing Co.

Lincoln, Y.S., & Guba, E.G. (1985). *Naturalistic inquiry.* Newbury Park, CA: Sage Publications.

Miles, M.B., & Huberman, A.M. (1994). *Qualitative data analysis.* Thousand Oaks, CA: Sage Publications.

Powers, L.E. (1993). Promoting adolescent independence and self-determination. *Family-centered care network, Association for the Care of Chldren's Health, 10*(4).

Powers, L.E., Sowers, J., & Stevens, T. (1993). *An exploratory randomized study of the impact of mentoring on the self-efficacy and functional independence of adolescents with disabilities.* Eugene: Oregon Research Institute.

Powers, L.E., Stevens, T., & Sowers, J. (1992). *A manual for the implementation of community-based mentoring for adolescents with disabilities.* Eugene, OR: Oregon Research Institute.

Rhodes, J.E. (1994, Spring). Older and wiser: Mentoring relationships in childhood and adolescence. *Journal of Primary Prevention, 14*(3), 187–196.

Rousso, H. (1988). *Mentoring empowers! How to start a networking project of disabled women and girls in your community.* (Available from the Networking Project for Disabled Women and Girls, YWCA of the City of New York.)

Scherer, M.J. (1988). Assistive device utilization and quality-of-life in adults with spinal cord injuries or cerebral palsy. *Journal of Applied Rehabilitation Counseling, 19*(2), 21–30.

Seidel, J.V., Kjolbeth, R., & Seymour, E. (1988). *The Ethnograph.* Amherst, MA: Qualis Research Associates.

Sigelman, C.K., Budd, E.C., Spanhel, C.L., & Schoenrock, C.J. (1981). When in doubt, say yes: Acquiescence in interviews with mentally retarded persons. *Mental Retardation, 14,* 53–58.

Singer, G., Irving, L., Todis, B., Stevens, T., & Alvernac, T. (1992). *Something to grow on: Building self-esteem in children with disabilities.* Eugene: Oregon Research Institute.

Stainback, S., & Stainback, W. (1984). Methodological considerations in qualitative research. *JASH, 9,* 296–303.

Stopford, V. (1987). *Understanding disability: Causes, characteristics, and coping.* London: Edward Arnold.

Strauss, A., & Corbin, J. (1990). *Basics of qualitative research: Grounded theory procedures and techniques.* Newbury Park, CA: Sage Publications.

Szymanski, E.M., Turner, K.D., & Hershenson, D.B. (1992). Career development and work adjustment of persons with disabilities: Theoretical perspectives and implications for transition. In F.R. Rusch, L. Destefano, J. Chadsey-Rusch, L.A. Phelps, & E. Szymanski (Eds.), *Transition from school to adult life: Models, linkages, and policy* (pp. 391–406). Sycamore, IL: Sycamore Publishing Company.

Todis, B., Irvin, L.K., Singer, G.H.S., & Yovanoff, P. (1993). The self-esteem parent program: Quantitative and qualitative evaluation of a cognitive-behavioral intervention. In G.H.S. Singer & L.E. Powers (Eds.), *Families, disability, and empowerment: Active coping skills and strategies for family interventions* (pp. 203–229). Baltimore: Paul H. Brookes Publishing Co.

Wehmeyer, M. (1992). Self-determination and the education of students with mental retardation. *Education and Training in Mental Retardation, 27,* 302–314.

Yin, R.K. (1989). *Case study research: Design and methods.* Newbury Park, CA: Sage Publications.

Overcoming a Health Challenge

Jessie Skinner

I was 3 when I was first diagnosed with diabetes. My Mom gave me my shots until I was 8. The first few times I gave myself shots, it was scary! It got easier as I got older. I went to camp and everyone else was doing their own shots, so I decided to start doing it myself.

My diabetes is hard to control. I remember being in the hospital when I was in seventh grade because my blood sugar was high. Close to the end of seventh grade I changed doctors because I didn't feel comfortable adjusting my own insulin. My new doctor was really nice when my Mom was in the room; she'd always compliment me. But when my Mom left the room, she'd tell me, "You'd better start taking your insulin!" I'd tell her, "I *am* taking my insulin!" I never really felt that she believed me. Once when I was in the hospital, the same thing happened—my blood sugar was really high, but *they* were doing my shots for me. From that point on, she believed that I was doing my shots on a regular basis.

Once my doctor started believing me, we got closer and I could talk to her better. I wasn't afraid to tell her that I forgot my insulin on a day. Now she wants me to write some things down to help other kids with hard-to-control diabetes. One suggestion is for kids to always tell the truth about skipping their insulin. I learned that the hard way. One day I was mad at my Mom and I skipped my insulin, thinking that I was going to hurt her. The only one I hurt was myself. I got really sick and ended up in the hospital. Then I had to tell the truth.

If your doctors say that you're skipping your insulin and you're not, keep telling them that you aren't—sooner or later, they'll listen! Also, try to be involved in the decisions about your insulin. They tried to get me to four shots a day, but I told them I only wanted to do three. I would rather do the regular shots less often and the booster shots more often.

I think it's important for kids to learn to take care of their medical issues because it makes you more responsible and it helps you to better understand what you have. If you need help, don't be afraid to ask. For me, if my blood sugar is really high, my vision isn't very good. It's good to take a break once in awhile and let someone else do the shot, to make sure its the right dosage. I'll sometimes ask the nurse at school for help.

Another suggestion I have is in dealing with adults who don't understand. My softball coach found out that I had diabetes. This changed my relationship with her a whole lot. The positions that I was good at she no longer let me play. She put me in right field where no balls ever come. I think she was scared and didn't know anything about diabetes. I ended up talking to her and asking her what her problem was. Her response was, "Your diabetes." I asked her why she was holding me back, because it was something that I couldn't help. She told me that she didn't realize that she was treating me any differently than the other kids. Talking with her turned our relationship around. Now we're best friends. We even go skiing together! And now I play all the positions on my softball team.

When kids feel that they're being treated differently, I suggest they talk to the person and ask what's bothering him or her. Don't give up! I didn't, even though I wanted to give up. I now feel good that I didn't. I was so nervous when I approached my coach, because I thought she was going to kick me off the team. I'm afraid to tell other people that I have diabetes because I'm afraid they'll treat me differently. Even though I have a good relationship with my coach now, I still wonder if she looks at me differently.

Health professionals need to be honest with teens. For example, they need to help teens schedule their medications based on their own personal lifestyles. If a teen is a late sleeper on weekends, let her take her medications later on Friday evening, so she can sleep late the next day. Another suggestion is to believe in your patient. Help build a relationship with the person you're treating. If possible, provide a mentor for the teenager who had similar problems when she was her age, because it helps kids realize they're not the only ones who are going through problems.

Employers need to recognize people as individuals. If you find that an employee has a health challenge, DON'T treat him any differently than you would if he didn't have the challenge! My boss recently found out that I have diabetes. Since then, he's been driving me crazy by calling me to the front of the store every half hour to ask me if I'm feeling okay. If kids learn to be responsible for their medical care and other people listen to and respect what kids say they need and don't need, managing a health challenge will be a lot easier for everyone.

The Role of Medical Professionals in Supporting Children's Self-Competence

Ardis L. Olson and W. Carl Cooley

A quiet change in the roles of medical professionals caring for children has been occurring since about the 1970s. The Norman Rockwell image of pediatric care with a child passively and apprehensively awaiting a shot from the kindly but firm doctor has been replaced by physicians, nurses, and health educators more involved in teaching children and families to care for themselves. This change in the medical approach is seen most clearly in the treatment of ongoing health conditions in childhood and adolescence. In order to provide more effective care, medical professionals have promoted a broader approach to illness management. This chapter explores how this new approach supports the development of a child's sense of competence and enhances self-esteem. In addition, some of the specific strategies used by health professionals to support the child's participation in medical care are presented.

FACTORS PROMOTING A FOCUS ON SELF-COMPETENCE

As with many changes in health care delivery, a number of seemingly unrelated factors have been important in promoting child and family participation in medical management. First, there are more children with ongoing health conditions. Those children with the most serious conditions, such as cancer, spina bifida, and cystic fibrosis, are routinely surviving into adulthood. It is estimated that 15–20 million American children have some kind of ongoing health condition (Gortmaker & Sappenfield, 1984), of which 1–2 million have severe health conditions that require extensive daily care (Newacheck, Budetti, & McManus, 1984). More children are surviving the newborn period as a result of therapies for congenital heart disease and the complications of premature birth. Many of these children have conditions that require ongoing treatment. The development of new technologies that allow children to survive may leave them dependent on technological supports. New illnesses such as HIV/AIDS have also increased the childhood population with ongoing illnesses. Finally, children with mental retardation and severe medical disabilities are now less likely to be placed in institutions and are more typically living at home.

Second, the growing number of children with ongoing health conditions and the use of new technologies have changed patterns of hospital use by children. Children with ongoing illnesses account for a disproportionate share of hospitalizations. Initially, hospitalizations for these children were prolonged and expensive. For respirator-dependent children remaining in the hospital, a year of care may cost $300,000 or more. Thus, financial pressure to reduce the cost of care has been one force that has promoted new models of home care for children (Anderson, 1990; J.M. Perrin, Shayne, & Bloom, 1993).

Third, children who require mechanical supports to replace or supplement the function of their own organs now receive extensive home care services. Typically these technologies support respiration or nutrition. For a second group of children, major responsibility is placed on the child and family to perform nursing and therapeutic care at home. Although less technology is involved, these daily activities were formerly done by trained and paid personnel. For example, children with spina bifida require bladder catheterization four times per day, and children with cystic fibrosis require daily chest physiotherapy. A third group of children require extensive medications and monitoring of therapy by their families. Children with diabetes, in addition to giving insulin injections two or more times per day, now monitor blood glucose levels several times each day to modify their insulin dosage. Children with asthma measure their lung function and adjust medications based on the results. It is clear that medical caregiving responsibility for many ongoing conditions has been shifted toward the child and family. As families perform these functions, third-party payers are less willing to pay for inpatient admissions or even for outpatient services in the community. Efforts at cost containment were initiated to deal with lengthy hospitalizations; now families are expected by their insurance companies to provide home care.

Fourth, the consumer movement in health care has led to the demand for information to help patients make decisions and to participate more actively in their care. The force of consumerism has led families to the expectation of greater participation in the medical care of their children. In addition, there is the reward of having their child home sooner from the hospital or the promise of a healthier, more normal life for their child. As the child grows, it is expected that he or she will gradually assume responsibility for managing his or her own illness.

Fifth, changes in the provision of primary pediatric care have also set the stage for changes in the care of children with ongoing medical conditions. Pediatricians have emphasized the central role of parents in assisting their children to become independent and have promoted healthy self-care habits during well-child visits. Pediatricians have also been trained to incorporate more emphasis upon education and prevention into routine medical care (Task Force on Pediatric Education, 1978). Although the focus has often been on acute illness and well-child care, pediatricians now have the training to apply these principles to care of ongoing illness (McInerny, 1984).

Last, as more children survive with more complex care needs, the structure of pediatric specialty care has changed to support patient education and family support. Multidisciplinary care teams consisting of specialty physicians, nurse clinicians or practitioners, social workers, and other health professionals have become a common means of delivering care to this population. Early experiences at university-based clinics for diabetes provided models in which nurses and other professionals played a core role in providing education, support, and clinical care. The success of such models led to their extension into other conditions (e.g., cancer, spina bifida). In many states, Maternal and Child Health Title V programs also provide chronic illness nurse coordinators who coordinate care and provide education for families, children, and community care providers such as school nurses and primary health care personnel (Haas, Gray, & McConnell, 1992).

CHANGES IN MEDICAL APPROACH TO CHILDHOOD ONGOING MEDICAL CONDITIONS

Research Studies of Childhood Ongoing Illness and Competency

Research about childhood ongoing illnesses began to increase in the 1960s as more children began to survive. In this section, we explore the contribution to the medical literature by psychology, nursing, and pediatrics. In particular, we examine what have been the expectations in these disciplines about the family and child's competence.

Initial studies from the psychology literature were based on research with hospitalized and more severely involved populations. Small populations, often of children and their families coping with the terminal stage of illness, were typical of this early work. Case studies of children with ongoing illness served an important role of alerting the medical profession to the issues involved, but often presented severely dysfunctional situations emphasizing psychopathology. For many years, studies focused on populations of convenience; that is, children who were accessible to researchers in the hospital inpatient units and specialty clinics. A picture emerged in the 1970s and early 1980s of families under increased stress (Sabbath, 1984), high rates of divorce (Tew, Payne, & Laurence, 1974), and children with more psychopathology (Drotar, 1981). Because such study often used different measures of function and studied different ongoing health conditions, comparison of results and outcomes was difficult. Even in large medical centers, these studies were often limited by small numbers of children from each illness category and by a crosssectional instead of a longitudinal design. Although some studies pointed out that children with ongoing illness functioned well (Tavormina, Kastner, & Slater, 1976; Zeltzer, Kellerman, Ellenberg, Dash, & Rigler, 1980), most research was driven by hypotheses of pathology rather than by efforts to identify good coping strategies.

The nursing research literature provided a different perspective on childhood ongoing illness. Early reports contributed important information in a more qualitative format and focused on successful techniques of illness management. Within the specialty journals, nursing explored the developmental framework for educating patients with ongoing illnesses (Lipman, Difazio, Meers, & Thompson, 1989) and practical issues in providing care. The role of the school nurse in the care of an ongoing illness was described (Snyder, 1987). Since the mid-1970s, as doctorate-level nurses have contributed to the field, research methods have become more rigorous. Nursing studies have emphasized the family's role in care (Thomas, 1987).

During the 1980s, pediatric professionals developed a less biased approach to the issues of children with ongoing medical conditions. A noncategorical approach contended that all children with ongoing illnesses dealt with similar challenges and that ongoing illnesses should be grouped rather than separated by condition (Stein & Jessop, 1982). Although details of management may differ, researchers have contended that up to 80% of the issues are the same across ongoing illnesses (Stein, 1989). This generic approach permitted a broader look at how this population functioned and promoted the provision of more supportive health care to children across a variety of conditions (Stein & Jessop, 1984). Other researchers have examined positive aspects of function, family traits associated with effective coping (Garrison & McQuiston, 1989), and successful coping strategies used by children (Delamater, Kurtz, Bubb, White, & Santiago, 1987; Olson, Johansen, Pope, Klein, & Powers, 1993) as well as personality and temperament traits associated with good function (Lavigne, Nolan, & McLone, 1988; Perrin, Maclean, & Perrin, 1989; Perrin, Ramsey, & Sandler, 1987).

Later studies of long-term survivors of ongoing illness suggest that children experience less psychological pathology than previous investigators had found (Olson, Zug, & Boyle, 1993; Sawyer, Rice, Haskell, & Baghurst, 1989). Large population-based surveys with controls conducted in the late 1980s portrayed a different picture of childhood ongoing disease. Children showed only a modest increase in psychosocial problems. Difficulties in psychosocial adjustment were more likely to be present in those who also had physical or cognitive disabilities (Cadman et al., 1986). Large-scale surveys do not provide enough detail on functional status to determine if this result is associated with the disability or interaction between the disability and the environment. Children with ongoing medical conditions and their families are now regarded as capable and "normal," but facing certain additional stresses.

Innovative changes in medical care systems have begun to emphasize support of the family (Santelli, Turnbull, Lerner, & Marquis, 1993), better community care, the role of the family and child, and better coordination of care (MacQueen, 1986; Perrin, Shayne, & Bloom, 1993). We are entering a new stage in which research focuses on evaluating the effectiveness of these new approaches to supporting families and youth (Powers & Bauman, 1994) and the establishment of new systems that provide more comprehensive services (Singer et al., 1993).

Medical Care of Ongoing Childhood Conditions

As a result of the factors described earlier, there has been a substantial increase in the amount and type of home and community care expected for many ongoing illnesses. Current family and child home care expectations for major childhood ongoing diseases are detailed in this section. Specifically, models of home and community care provided by children and their parents are presented for diabetes, cystic fibrosis, hemophilia, spina bifida, asthma, and bronchopulmonary dysplasia.

Juvenile-Onset Diabetes   The management of juvenile-onset diabetes requires daily involvement of both child and family in disease management. Because so many complex principles of disease management as well as details of tasks need to be taught, diabetic education has become a large aspect of the health care of children with diabetes. Pediatric diabetic nurse specialists have a well-developed approach to teaching children to be competent with complex management tasks. Detailed guidelines about the tasks and information to be taught at each developmental stage are available, as well as extensive educational materials in the form of books, workbooks, games, and computer programs (Kohler, Hurwitz, & Milan, 1982). All visits to diabetic specialists involve reinforcement of educational topics and of child and family roles.

Initially parents, and later children, are educated about the role insulin plays in the body's functions, along with learning practical aspects of how to handle acute problems. Later, long-term complications and their prevention are discussed and incorporated into self-care plans. Successful control of diabetes demands rigorous attention to many details of daily life, including physical activity and dietary intake. Blood sugar testing occurs two to four times per day by fingerstick blood sampling. Insulin injections are done two times per day, but new research promoting tighter control encourages even more frequent insulin use (American Diabetes Association, 1993). With tighter control, hypoglycemic episodes are more common. The child and parent need to recognize the early symptoms of hypoglycemia as well as educate others (e.g., siblings, child care providers, teachers) about what to do.

Children become involved in diabetes management activities early, typically as soon as the diagnosis is made. By middle elementary school–age, they are testing their own blood daily and, a few years later, giving their own injections. Children (8–12 years old) have been shown to maintain good metabolic control while learning to become independent in their diabetes self-management (McNabb, Quinn, Murphy, Thorp, & Cook, 1994).

Cystic Fibrosis   Cystic fibrosis is another serious ongoing illness for which children and families have assumed a major role in management. Like diabetes, cystic fibrosis has a major impact on daily living. Optimal outcomes have been found with regular aerobic exercise, treatment of nutritional deficits, and home respiratory therapy, often with medications delivered by nebulizer equipment and frequent chest physiotherapy.

Children participate by adjusting their diet, taking large amounts of medication daily, and pursuing vigorous aerobic conditioning even though they may have less endurance than their peers. Frequent chest infections necessitate additional medications. Children with cystic fibrosis and their parents know that the promise of new treatments on the horizon requires the maintenance of the best possible lung function for the new treatments to be effective. Educational efforts focus on the child as an active partner in treatment regimes.

Hemophilia   The major change in the management of childhood hemophilia came with the recognition that early, intensive treatment of bleeding episodes prevented the development of arthritis and associated disability. When specialized intravenous treatment was required promptly, nurse clinicians on the specialty medical team became the primary contact with the families. Ambulatory intravenous treatment providing the missing blood clotting factors began to be performed by parents, who administered intravenous treatment. Numerous trips to the emergency room with active young children made parents very familiar with the technique. They recognized that long travel and waiting times could be avoided by performing the procedure themselves at home. Nursing educators and physicians developed specific protocols for parents, and later children, to learn these new skills.

During adolescence, children typically learn how to self-infuse and to make judgments regarding when they need treatment. Just as outcomes for these children appeared to be improving with these new methods, it became clear that children repeatedly given blood products from the mid-1970s to mid-1980s were likely to get HIV infection. Care for an entire cohort of children with hemophilia has been transformed into management of two ongoing illnesses. Without a cure for AIDS, the goals of care of hemophilia for this group change considerably. However, younger children with HIV-free blood products remain a group for which management still has more optimistic goals. Even so, for all concerned parents, the issues of HIV infection remain.

It is not uncommon for families to chose not to be tested for HIV or to keep results confidential because of their fears about the possible social sequelae in the community.

Spina Bifida (Myelomeningocele)   When new urological techniques were introduced to maintain normal kidney function, the management of spina bifida shifted to involve substantial daily tasks by the family. Because of paralysis associated with spinal cord dysfunction, children with spina bifida do not have normal bladder and bowel function. When the bladder is emptied on a regular basis, these children have been shown to have fewer kidney infections and less chronic kidney disease. Thus, since the 1980s it has become routine for parents to catheterize their child's bladder four or more times per day from infancy throughout childhood. School nurses and others become involved as children become older. By the middle of grade school, most children are performing this daily task themselves.

Usually nurses on a multidisciplinary specialty team play a major role in teaching families and children the skills needed for catheterization. Dividing the process into a series of tasks that the child gradually participates in is helpful. Videotapes have been helpful in providing the background, but individualized coaching is key. Daily medications are also needed to assist children in having better control of bladder and bowel. Although these new techniques offer substantial improvement in social acceptance, there still are occasional "accidents." It is difficult for young children to see the merit of persisting with catheterization when they often have to deal with ambulation aides as well. In optimal situations, parents and medical staff work together in helping children develop competencies in both social and self-care areas.

Bronchopulmonary Dysplasia   As more infants survive the respiratory diseases of prematurity, some children who required ventilator assistance have persistent lung damage known as bronchopulmonary dysplasia (BPD). BPD varies in its impact from requiring ongoing artificial ventilation at home to requiring the use of supplemental oxygen. Children with BPD may also need external nutritional support with feeding tubes and special formulas. As children grow older, the need for these extensive supports gradually diminishes. Preschool and older children may experience only asthmalike symptoms. Extensive efforts have taken place to provide home rather than hospital care. Professional daily home nursing care may be necessary initially. However, parents learn these extensive nursing skills as well and often provide a substantial portion of each day's care. Since the most extensive needs occur when these children are young, the parent, not the child, develops competency. However, some children continue with significant asthma and learn illness management skills when they are older.

Asthma   Asthma is the most common childhood ongoing illness and the most recent to involve children in substantial degrees of self-management. The development of inhaled forms of medication beginning in the mid-1980s has shifted management to the home setting. Either with equipment to nebulize medication or hand-held inhaler, treatment at home can be as effective as that given in the emergency room. Patient education programs have been developed that can teach parents and children specific steps to both prevent and treat asthma attacks (McNabb, Wilson-Pessano, Hughes, & Scamagus, 1987). These programs have resulted in fewer emergency room visits and school absences (Wigal, Creer, Kotses, & Lesis, 1990). School and camp programs have also provided additional opportunities in which children learn with other children and become more independent in managing their asthma.

Unfortunately, most children with asthma do not have access to camps and formal education programs. Involvement of children must occur in the primary physician's office to be most effective. Most primary care physicians do not have nurse educators, and these roles must be performed by physicians and office nurses. Patient education materials that clearly outline care plans have been made widely available to primary care physicians (National Heart, Lung and Blood Institute, 1991). Patient treatment choices are linked to symptoms using the concept of red, yellow, and green zones. The stoplight analogy makes this management plan appropriate for use by children as well.

In the ongoing illnesses reviewed, a key element is the provision of information and illness management education for parents and children. Specialty nurse clinicians and practitioners have provided excellent services. However, their teaching activities are time-consuming and are not well reimbursed by insurers. As a result, nurse clinicians are not widely available in all specialty programs. With health care financial reform, it is possible that the long-term cost savings of these nursing services will not be recognized. For the most common ongoing illnesses, other outreach efforts are needed to involve office nurses and school nurses in the education of children and their parents.

A note of caution must be raised about higher expectations for self-care and management by the parent or child. For many ongoing conditions, early hospital discharge has become the only option. Under financial pressure to discharge, home care planning cannot adapt well to individual family stresses such as mental illness, substance use, or poverty. A family with marginal personal and social resources may have a chaotic, crisis-oriented home environment and may not be able to respond to the expectations of health care providers to offer daily well-organized nursing services to their young child. Systems of care need to adjust expectations and provide more extensive support for these atypical situations.

ISSUES IN DEVELOPMENT OF SELF-COMPETENCY IN CHILDREN

Competence in Medical Versus Daily Life Settings

Competence in daily life and medical tasks are interrelated. Higher self-esteem in children or youth has been associated with better adherence to ongoing medication regimes. For example, adolescents with arthritis (Litt, Cuskey, & Rosenberg, 1982) with higher self-esteem had better blood levels of medication. Children with diabetes who either had high self-esteem or perceived themselves as capable in managing aspects of their illness (i.e., self-efficacy) demonstrated better disease control documented by hemoglobin A_1C levels (Delamater et al., 1987). Those who are perceived by their parents as more competent in daily life have been shown to have better control of their asthma (Perrin et al., 1989). The nature of the relationship between competency in managing illness and self-esteem is unclear. Does successful self-management of illness enhance children's self-esteem or are children with high self-esteem more able to approach the complex tasks required in managing illness? Unfortunately, most studies of self-esteem are cross-sectional and do not provide information about which aspect is causative.

Children's perceptions of themselves have been shown to change from one specific type of social and education intervention—the ongoing illness camp experience. Although many disease skills are taught, this setting also provides positive social experiences. Many children do not otherwise have the opportunity to interact with peers with similar ongoing conditions. Children with diabetes have been shown to develop a more internal sense of control that persists beyond the camp experience (Moffat & Pless, 1983). Children with juvenile arthritis develop higher self-esteem during the camp experience (Stefl, Shear, & Levinson, 1989).

Likewise, children participating with other children with epilepsy in a school-based education program about epilepsy perceived themselves as more socially competent afterwards (Lewis, 1989). A similar program of asthma education has shown positive health and social outcomes (Lewis, Racheleefsky, Lewis, de la Sota, & Kaplan, 1984). Children's perceptions of their capabilities are also related to the process of their chronic disease. Teens with high self-esteem were more likely to perceive the illness had less impact (Zeltzer et al., 1980). Although more studies are needed, the development of disease management skills in a socially supportive setting such as camps and school groups has clearly been shown to enhance self-esteem. Other social experiences that enhance the self-esteem of children and youth warrant continued investigation as well.

Child and Family Factors Affecting a Child's Participation in Care

The health professional who promotes the development of a child's active participation in his or her medical care considers a variety of factors when determining the role of the child. This section addresses aspects to be considered when developing an approach for the individual child and family.

Developmental Factors   The first issue is whether the tasks the child is being asked to perform are appropriate to the child's level of development. Does the child have the fine motor skills to perform this task? Children with physical disabilities may need careful assessment. It is also important that the child has the attention span to focus on the task. Is the child ready to handle the performance of the task on a daily basis? This issue is important. Children can technically perform tasks before they have the interest or motivation to continue to perform them on a daily basis. It is not uncommon to hear of a child called "lazy" by parents or school staff because he or she does not follow through with a self-catheterization or blood testing program. Children continue to need strong external rewards and motivators from the people near them to consistently perform these tasks. In grade school, many children do not yet have the internal control or abstract thinking to recognize the benefits of daily disease management. As they enter adolescence, their focus upon peer and social issues may cause disease management to take a back seat. As a result, even the most successful program of illness management at home requires continual support from professionals. Recognizing these ups and downs as normal will help prevent casting blame on a child or family when management deteriorates. It is important to consider these issues, explore the details of the problem with the child and family, and together generate new solutions that are practical and appropriate.

Some ongoing illnesses also affect children's cognitive function, either from the disease or secondary to the treatment. Up to 70% of children with epilepsy may have learning disabilities (Holdsworth & Whitmore, 1974). Children with spina bifida commonly have attention difficulties as well as specific learning disabilities that affect hand–eye coordination and organizational skills. Some conditions are associated with lower intellectual functioning that may require the professional to adapt expectations or modify tasks the child is asked to perform. However, children should remain involved to the greatest extent possible. Sometimes children with mental retardation are unnecessarily excluded from learning the simpler routines of self-care that they could indeed master.

Temperament Issues   The child's personality or temperament has been considered clinically in advising parents about their child's learning and behavioral styles

(Chess & Thomas, 1984). More recently, research is beginning to show that temperament has an important role in the outcomes of children with ongoing health conditions. Children with spina bifida with greater temperament difficulties have been shown to have more behavior problems (Lavigne et al., 1988). For children with orthopedic disabilities and seizures, temperament traits were key determinants of social competence, even more important than the intensity of their illness (Perrin et al., 1987).

Parental Attitudes   A child's approach to self-care is strongly related to his or her family's attitudes. Mothers' attitudes have been the most extensively studied. A mother's belief regarding whether health can be changed by one's own actions is important. Mothers give messages to children about whether the extra effort in daily management is worthwhile and whether there is time in the day for it, and the mother's belief about how much control one has over one's health has been shown to be a strong predictor of overall adjustment for children with epilepsy and a variety of orthopedic conditions (Perrin, Ayoub, & Willett, 1993). Mothers also convey to their children their attitudes toward physicians and how actively one should be involved in the medical visit. In a variety of adult ongoing illnesses, an active participation style has been shown to result in better medical outcomes (Greenfield & Ware, 1985). Parents with a passive approach to their medical care are likely to transmit this attitude to their children. In treatment of diabetes and childhood asthma, parents' specific efforts to model successful participation in the visit have been shown to improve medical outcomes (Pantell, Lewis, & Sharp, 1989).

Parental Involvement   Parents may vary in how involved they are in their child's care. Most parents try hard to maintain a balance between providing medical care to their child themselves and having the child participate. Some parents perceive early self-limited medical events in their child's life as a continuing threat. The child may be seen as excessively vulnerable, resulting in overprotection by parents. These parents may become overinvolved in their child's medical care and may be unwilling to transfer medical self-care to the child as he or she matures.

Often the parents of children with ongoing conditions both work, sometimes at multiple jobs. Parents are stressed with many demands. The child's initial ineptitude at self-care tasks may lead parents to feel that it is easier for them to perform the task. This is a common issue and one of the reasons that continued support and education are needed to allow the transfer of time-consuming self-care tasks from parent to child. Parents need to understand the long-term goals of child participation in self-care and should understand how it can help the child in terms of emotional growth. As parents find themselves too busy and overly stressed, some withdraw from these difficult issues. The underinvolved parent may allow other relatives to provide the help or leave the child responsible for complex tasks at a young age without adequate supervision. The daily help and support of the parent is needed for many medical regimes, and a lack of support may make it very difficult for the child to become competent or to ensure the best medical outcomes.

The family's energy may also be dissipated if there are other major emotional or social issues to contend with in addition to the child's needs. Ongoing illness or depression in the mother has been shown to have a strong impact on the child's functioning (Stein & Jessop, 1991). The chronic stress of alcoholism in the family or recurring financial crises leave the family unable to devote time and energy to the child's needs. Other community or school sources of support or stress may affect the child and family's ability to provide self-care. Health professionals need to assess these issues to ensure that they set realistic goals with the families and seek appropriate social services resources to deal with these other influences. Otherwise, careful planning for the child's needs may fail.

Some children seem to respond better to adversity than other children. Such children are felt to possess resilience to personal stresses. These children grow up to become well-functioning adults in situations in which poor outcomes would be expected. Long-term studies show several factors to be important to resilience in children. Inherent personality traits as well as the response from others in the environment seem to be key factors. These children consistently have a strong connection to another adult in the extended family or community (Masten & Garmezy, 1985).

This review of child and parental factors makes it clear that the health professional needs to assess the situation of each child and family when developing a plan for self-care by families and children. If this process is not done formally or informally and not incorporated into goals and expectations, professionals are likely to invest a great deal of effort in an approach that does not work for that family. Similarly, if self-care goals are not being met, one needs to stop and review these issues.

METHODS FOR DEVELOPING A CHILD'S COMPETENCE AND MEDICAL SELF-MANAGEMENT SKILLS

This section describes practical ways in which the health professional can enhance competence in daily medical care. It is grouped by the different settings and major issues: the medical encounter, teaching of self-care skills, hospitalization, referrals to other resources for information and support, and transition periods.

The Medical Encounter

Whether explicitly or not, clinicians establish certain parameters with the child and family about how they conduct medical visits. These expectations influence the kind of partnership that will develop among parent, child, and physician. It is helpful for all involved to discuss expectations about the professional's role and the role of parent and child in illness management. The format established for the visit is also important. At what age are the children seen alone for part of the visit? How much time is scheduled with the physician or others for learning skills or being educated about their condition?

The initial portion of the office visit provides a framework or agenda for the visit. It is helpful to determine the main concerns the parent and child or adolescent want dealt with in that visit. When the family first enters the room, specifically directing the initial conversation toward children or adolescents conveys their importance. This is also an opportunity to reduce children's anxiety by briefly talking about other happenings in their lives. Parents may not be comfortable at first with having the illness review begin with the child, but they can see why their consistent participation is important if long-term goals for the child's independent functioning are discussed. Involving the child in the discussion provides additional insight into how conflict about illness management issues are being handled by parent and child. Families have emphasized how important it is for them to have the clinician value their input and perspective on health care issues. Asking the parent and child to first suggest solutions to a care issue sometimes provides the clinician with novel approaches.

Parents may not know what expectations and activities are age-appropriate because they do not have older children or because they have altered their expectations in response to their child's illness. The provider needs to have a clear understanding of what are normal behaviors and achievements for each age group and, wherever possible, promote them for children with ongoing illnesses and disabilities. When explaining disease processes to children, educational efforts are more effective if clinicians understand at what ages children understand aspects of anatomy and body function and the concept of disease prevention. Some children with ongoing health conditions have advanced understanding of disease, whereas in others it is woefully lacking (Perrin & Gerrity, 1984). It is helpful to have an anticipatory approach when dealing with common issues found in management of a specific condition, rather than a reactive, problem-oriented approach.

Children need to be involved in all stages of the visit. It has been shown that physicians typically take some of the history from the child but direct all diagnosis and treatment information to the parent (Pantell et al., 1989). Involving the child and parent in shared decision making is an important step in self-management. Simply choosing a liquid or pill form of antibiotics is a task in which even preschool children can be included. For many patients, it will be novel to be asked to help develop the plan. If one starts with shared decisions about small issues, both family and physician become comfortable with this approach. This is particularly important when involving grade school children. Beginning with a small task or change in treatment in response to their input will encourage their further participation. It is important that the clinician remember to follow up on these aspects of care at the next visit. Although initial attempts to involve the family and child may not always succeed, gradual change often does occur. Changing communication in this manner among children with asthma, their families, and physicians has been shown to decrease school absences and improve medical outcomes (Pantell et al., 1989).

Teaching Self-Care Skills

Many chronic illnesses require that specific tasks be taught to parents and/or children. These vary from handling medical details such as self-catheterization in children with spina bifida, indwelling intravenous lines for children with chemotherapy, or special supplemental nutritional needs. In addition, children need to know the indications and techniques of treatments such as asthma medication inhalers or insulin injections. Many children need to develop the cognitive skills to assess how a situation needs to be handled differently because of their condition. For example, a child with cystic fibrosis knows certain activities may make him or her cough, and a child with diabetes needs to adjust diet based on variations in exercise. Children also need to learn the process of how to prevent or manage acute episodes if they occur.

These various medical self-care tasks require different approaches. First, it is important to assess each family's unique situation and consider the parent and child factors detailed earlier. A realistic plan must be developed by the health professionals involved, and an appropriate setting and amount of time must be provided for the patient or parent education process. Within the tremendous range of childhood ongoing illnesses, the plan may involve either hours of family training and involvement of an entire care team or review by an office nurse of issues and techniques at the beginning of the visit. Some acute situations demand a great deal of training in a brief time, but most chronic care teaching happens gradually over many contacts. For some ongoing conditions (e.g., asthma, epilepsy) a series of parent–child group sessions has been shown to be effective (Lewis, 1989; Wigal et al., 1990). The greatest number of educational options has been developed for asthma, where home study and individualized programs have been created (McNabb, Wilson-Pessano, & Jacobs, 1986; Rakos, Grodek & Mack, 1985).

Teaching technical skills and self-management requires consideration of the separate steps involved. A psychomotor skill procedure can be broken into smaller units and demonstrated, and the child can then practice each step to mastery. Many children are primarily visual learners and can get lost in a barrage of words with no chance to participate. In ongoing health conditions, the first step is to introduce descriptions of what one is doing and to involve the child in helping prepare for the procedure. Reviewing what has been done and giving the child or parent a chance to restate what has been learned is another important step that markedly improves later recall (Creer, Kotses, & Wigal, 1992). Positive reinforcement and subtle corrections are essential to maintain the child participation. When teaching the family and child aspects of medical decision making, additional skills need to be taught (Creer, Renne, & Chai, 1982).

Knowledge required to understand why one performs the skill must be conveyed at an age-appropriate level. The child then needs to learn to collect and record information monitoring his or her condition. The next stage is to process this information and pinpoint potential problems. From this process a variety of solutions are considered, and the patient learns to decide what to do. This effort leads to initiating treatment, changing an activity, or seeking more help. The process of effective education in childhood ongoing conditions is complex and requires attention to details to be successful. Nursing coordinators, other health educators, and public health and office nurses are important participants. Health providers need to seek out these resources and work together in order to achieve the often ambitious goals set in home care.

Hospitalization

When hospitalization is necessary in the care of childhood ongoing illness, it provides another opportunity to help children and parents become more competent. Recurrent treatments or surgery may require children to be hospitalized, and they are mentally alert and not feeling ill during much of the time. This opportunity to address important issues with parents and children is often missed. During the admissions process, the agenda of education and enhancing the child's self-competency can be included in the initial management plan. The professional can enlist the help of other professionals and use contacts with the family to review progress and set new goals on a wide variety of issues. This is a chance to hear more about the parent and child's perspective on coping with their condition than may be possible in the ambulatory setting.

A review of knowledge of disease and management, dietary issues, or learning self-care tasks is appropriate to this setting. For older children and adolescents, hospitalization provides opportunities to test approaches for active involvement in decision making. Participation in small decisions about care also helps these children feel less passive and cope with hospitalization. Trying these efforts in the hospital setting also allows staff to adapt their efforts and set realistic home goals for self-care. These issues need to be included along with medical issues in the discharge plan. This population needs advanced home care planning throughout hospitalization, rather than just prior to discharge. If the health professional considers hospitalization in the continuum of the child's care, there are many opportunities for the hospital experience to enhance children's competence.

Referrals to Other Resources

The health professional plays a key role for families and children in connecting them with other sources of information and support. Parents benefit from the practical knowledge and support available from other parents dealing with the same condition (Perrin et al., 1993). In many parts of the country, parent support groups exist either for specific conditions or generically at a community level. Many conditions have national organizations that connect parents and provide detailed knowledge on a specific disease. Through these contacts, parents, particularly parents with children with rare conditions, may become a source of important new information for their health care provider.

Peer experiences with children who deal with similar ongoing health conditions are also helpful for children. These vary from ongoing teen groups to weekend retreats and summer camp experiences. Some involve family members, and others are focused more on the child's needs. These opportunities all give the message that it is possible to have fun while being more independent in managing one's illness. Camps for diabetes, cancer, asthma, and arthritis have been shown to provide knowledge, improve medical outcomes, and enhance children's sense of control (Lebovitz, Ellis, & Skyler, 1978; Moffat & Pless, 1983; Stefl, Shear, & Levinson, 1989). Even patient education experiences can include peer experiences. Some chronic illness programs include parent and child support groups as part of the clinic visit. School-based courses for ongoing illnesses also allow children to understand that others in their peer group deal with the same issues they do.

Transitions

Health professionals can also play an important role helping with specific transitional periods that may be stressful in the child's life. The family and child with an ongoing condition may have more difficulty in three major transitions: entering school, entering adolescence, and entering the work force. The health care provider's understanding of these typical issues and resources available to address them can be very helpful. During the transition into school, the physician can help the family learn how to advocate effectively for their child's needs as well as provide the school with information and support (Perrin et al., 1993).

During the transition into adolescence, the professional's relationship with the child and family must slowly change. Gradually the prime contacts can be shifted to the adolescent and away from the parents. Phone follow-up with the teen as well as seeing the adolescent alone, at least for part of the visit, are important shifts. The health professional can play a crucial role in linking the needs of parent and teenager into a care plan with which both can be comfortable. Building on their long-term relationship, the clinician can be a major support to adolescents trying to become independent. These adolescents have to cope with all the issues healthy adolescents face, as well as with the limitations imposed on them by their illness. Because the physical care needs of teens with ongoing illnesses and disabilities may promote dependence, promoting independence needs to be an active focus of medical care. Early in a child's adolescence, clinicians may find marked deterioration in the teenager's effectiveness in illness management as other personal and social issues dominate the individual's life. It is difficult but important for care providers to remain nonjudgmental and supportive of adolescents when the adolescents neglect their care. It is also important to be aware that depression is more common in teenagers with ongoing health conditions coping with these typical issues of adolescence (McAnarney, 1985). With the support of parents and providers, most teenagers gradually are successful in returning to a responsible role in their health management. Later in adolescence, the provider can help them understand how their disease will progress in adulthood and what adult disease management services they will require. Health professionals, in addition, have a role in helping these teenagers gain access to social experiences that build their confidence as well as helping them find appropriate vocational guidance. Although adolescent transition services are lacking in many communities, there are a variety of youth support groups for those with ongoing health conditions, camps, and sometimes adult support groups that are possible.

CONCLUSIONS

Some of the most gratifying experiences for the health care professional can come from playing a role in enhancing children's self-competence. To see a family and child evolve from being overwhelmed by the disease and the demands of care to becoming confident active managers of care is one of the major rewards in caring for children with ongoing health conditions. Optimal medical care for children with these medical conditions now routinely includes illness self-care as a major component. This chapter has summarized the important issues clinicians need to consider when they work to enhance children's self-competence. Health professionals working together can be effective in providing this new type of medical care in which parents, children, and clinicians are active partners.

REFERENCES

American Diabetes Association. (1993). *Diabetes Care, 16,* 1517–1520.

Anderson, J.M. (1990). Home care management in chronic illness and the self-care movement: An analysis of ideologies and economic processes influencing policy decisions. *Advanced Nursing Science, 12,* 71–83.

Bauman, L. (1994, May). *Adolescent work skills and competence enhancement program.* Paper presented at the Ambulatory Pediatrics Association National Meeting, Seattle, WA.

Cadman, D., Boyle, M.H., Offord, D.R., Szatmari, P., Rae-Grant, N.I., Crawford, J., & Byles, J. (1986). Chronic illness and functional limitations in Ontario children: Findings of the Ontario Child Health Study. *Canadian Medical Association Journal, 135,* 761–767.

Chess, A., & Thomas, A. (1984). *Origins and evolution of behavior disorders.* New York: Brunner/Mazel.

Creer, T.L., Kotses, H., & Wigal, J.K. (1992). A second-generation model of asthma self-management. *Pediatric Asthma, Allergy and Immunology, 6,* 143–165.

Creer, T., Renne, C., & Chai, H. (1982). The application of behavioral techniques to childhood asthma. In D.C. Ruso & J.W. Varni (Eds.), *Behavioral pediatrics: Research and practice* (pp. 27–66). New York: Plenum.

Delamater, A.M., Kurtz, S.M., Bubb, J., White, N.H., & Santiago, J.V. (1987). Stress and coping in relation to metabolic control of adolescents with type 1 diabetes. *Journal of Developmental and Behavioral Pediatrics, 8,* 136–140.

Drotar, D. (1981). Psychological perspectives in chronic childhood illness. *Journal of Pediatric Psychology, 6,* 211–216.

Garrison, W.T., & McQuiston, S. (1989). *Chronic illness during childhood and adolescence: Psychological aspects.* Newbury Park, CA: Sage Publications.

Gortmaker, S., & Sappenfield, W. (1984). Chronic childhood disorders: Prevalence and impact. *Pediatric Clinics of North America, 31,* 3018.

Greenfield, S., & Ware, J., Jr. (1985). Expanding patient involvement in care: Effects on patient outcomes. *Annals of Internal Medicine, 102,* 520–528.

Haas, D.L., Gray, H.B., & McConnell, B. (1992). Parent/professional partnerships in caring for children with special health care needs. *Issues in Comprehensive Pediatric Nursing, 15,* 39–53.

Holdsworth, L., & Whitmore, K.A. (1974). Study of children with epilepsy attending ordinary schools: Their seizure patterns, progress and behavior in school. *Developments in Medical Child Neurology, 16,* 746–758.

Kohler, E., Hurwitz, L.S., & Milan, D. (1982). A developmentally staged curriculum for teaching self care to the child with insulin-dependent diabetes mellitus. *Diabetes Care, 5*(3), 300–304.

Lavigne, J.V., Nolan, D., & McClone, D.G. (1988). Temperament, coping and psychological adjustment in young children with myelomeningocoele. *Journal of Pediatric Psychology, 13,* 363–378.

Lebovitz, F.L., Ellis, G.J., & Skyler, J.S. (1978). Performance of technical skills of diabetes management: Increased independence after a camp experience. *Diabetes Care, 1,* 23–26.

Lewis, C.E., Racheleefsky, G., Lewis, M.A., de la Sota, A., & Kaplan, M. (1984). A randomized trial of ACT (asthma care training) for kids. *Pediatrics, 74,* 478–486.

Lewis, M.A. (1989). Randomized trial of a program to enhance the competencies of children with epilepsy. *Epilepsy, 31,* 101–109.

Lipman, T.H., Difazio, D.A., Meers, R.A., & Thompson, R.L. (1989). A developmental approach to diabetes in children: Birth through preschool, part 1. *Maternal and Child Health Nursing, 14,* 255–259.

Litt, I.F., Cuskey, W.R., & Rosenberg, A. (1982). Role of self-esteem and autonomy in determining medication compliance among adolescents with juvenile rheumatoid arthritis. *Pediatrics, 69,* 15–17.

MacQueen, J. (1986). *Iowa's mobile and regional clinics.* Iowa City: Iowa Department of Public Health.

Masten, A.S., & Garmezy, N. (1985). Risk, vulnerability, and protective factors in developmental psychopathology. In B.B. Lahey & A.E. Kasdin (Eds.), *Advances in Clinical Child Psychology* (Vol. 8, pp. 1–52). New York: Plenum.

McAnarney, E.R. (1985). A challenge for handicapped and chronically ill adolescents. *Journal of Adolescent Health Care, 6,* 90–101.

McInerny, T. (1984). Role of the general pediatrician in coordinating the care of children with chronic illness. *Pediatrics Clinics of North America, 31,* 199–210.

McNabb, W.L., Wilson-Pessano, S., Hughes, C., & Scamagas, P. (1987). Self-management education of children with asthma airways. *American Journal of Public Health, 75,* 1219–1220.

McNabb, W.L., Wilson-Pessano, S., & Jacobs, A. (1986). Critical self-management competencies for children with asthma. *Journal of Pediatric Psychology, 11,* 103–117.

McNabb, W.L., Quinn, M.T., Murphy, D.M., Thorp, F.K., & Cook, S. (1994). Increasing children's responsibility for diabetes self-care: The in control study. *The Diabetes Educator, 20,* 121–124.

Moffat, M.E., & Pless, I.B. (1983). Locus of control in juvenile diabetic campers: Changes during camp, and relationship to camp staff assessments. *Journal of Pediatrics, 103,* 146–150.

National Heart, Lung and Blood Institute. (1991). Guidelines for the diagnosis and management of asthma. In *National Asthma Education Program: Expert Panel Report.* Bethesda: U.S. Department of Health and Human Services.

Olson, A.L., Johansen, S., Pope, J., Klein, R.B., & Powers, L. (1993). Cognitive coping strategies of children with and without chronic illness. *Journal of Developmental and Behavioral Pediatrics, 14,* 217–223.

Olson, A.L., Zug, L., & Boyle, W. (1993). Overall function in rural childhood cancer survivors. *Clinical Pediatrics, 32,* 334–342.

Pantell, R.H., Lewis, C., & Sharp, L. (1989). Improving outcomes in asthmatic patients. *American Journal of Diseases of Children, 143,* 433.

Perrin, E.C., Ayoub, C.C., & Willett, J.B. (1993). In the eyes of the beholder: Family and maternal influences on perceptions of adjustment of children with a chronic illness. *Journal of Developmental and Behavioral Pediatrics, 14,* 94–105.

Perrin, E.C., & Gerrity, P.S. (1984). Development of children with a chronic illness. *Pediatric Clinics of North America, 31,* 19–32.

Perrin, E.C., Ramsey, B.K., & Sandler, H.M. (1987). Competent kids: Children and adolescents with a chronic illness. *Child-Care, Health and Development, 13,* 13–32.

Perrin, J.M., Maclean, W.E., & Perrin, E.C. (1989). Parent's perception of health status and psychological adjustment of children with asthma. *Pediatrics, 83,* 26–30.

Perrin, J.M., Shayne, M.W., & Bloom, S.R. (1993). *Home and community care for chronically ill children.* New York: Oxford University Press.

Rakos, R., Grodek, M., & Mack, K. (1985). The impact of a self-administered behavioral intervention program on pediatric asthma. *Journal of Psychosomatic Research, 29,* 101–108.

Sabbeth, B. (1984). Understanding the impact of chronic childhood illness on families. *Pediatric Clinics of North America, 31,* 47–57.

Santelli, B., Turnbull, A.P., Lerner, E., & Marquis, J. (1993). Parent-to-parent programs: A unique form of mutual support for families of persons with disabilities. In G.H.S. Singer & L.E. Powers (Eds.), *Families, disability, and empowerment: Active coping skills and strategies for family interventions* (pp. 27–57). Baltimore: Paul H. Brookes Publishing Co.

Sawyer, M.G., Rice, M., Haskell, C., & Baghurst, P. (1989). School performance and psychological adjustment of children treated for leukemia, a long term follow-up. *American Journal of Pediatric Hematological Oncology, 11,* 146–152.

Singer, G.H.S., Powers, L.E., Olson, A., & Cooley, C. (1993). *Partners in health.* Unpublished grant proposal funded by the Robert Wood Johnson Foundation. Hanover, NH: Dartmouth Medical School.

Snyder, A. (1987, January & February). The role of school personnel in caring for the child with diabetes. *School Nurse,* 9–17.

Stefl, M.E., Shear, E.S., & Levinson, J.E. (1989). Summer camps for juveniles with rheumatic disease. Do they make a difference? *Arthritis Care Research, 2,* 10–15.

Stein, R.E.K. (1989). *Caring for children with chronic illness: Issues and strategies.* New York: Springer-Verlag.

Stein, R.E.K., & Jessop, D.J. (1982). A noncategorical approach to childhood chronic illness. *Public Health Report, 97,* 354–362.

Stein, R.E.K., & Jessop, D.J. (1984). Does pediatric home care make a difference for children with chronic illness? Findings from the pediatric ambulatory care treatment study. *Pediatrics, 73,* 845–853.

Stein, R.E.K., & Jessop, D.J. (1991). Long-term mental health effects of a pediatric home care program. *Pediatrics, 88,* 90–96.

Task Force on Pediatric Education. (1978). *The future of pediatric education.* Evanston, IL: American Academy of Pediatrics.

Tavormina, J.B., Kastner, L.S., & Slater, P.M. (1976). Chronically ill children: A psychologically and emotionally deviant population? *Journal of Abnormal Child Psychology, 4,* 99–109.

Tew, B., Payne, H., & Laurence, K.M. (1974). Must a family with a handicapped child be a handicapped family? *Development in Medical Child Neurology, 16*(32), 95–98.

Thomas, R.B. (1987). Family adaptation to a child with a chronic condition. In M.H. Roxe & R.B. Thomas (Eds.), *Children with chronic conditions: Nursing in a family and community context.* Orlando, FL: Grune & Stratton.

Wigal, J.K., Creer, T.L., Kotses, H., & Lesis, P.D. (1990). A critique of 19 self-management programs for childhood asthma. Part I: The development and evaluation of the programs. *Pediatric Asthma and Allergy Immunology, 4,* 17–39.

Zeltzer, L., Kellerman, J., Ellenberg, L., Dash, J., & Rigler, D. (1980). Psychological effects of illness in adolescence. II. Impact of illness in adolescent–crucial issues and copying styles. *Journal of Pediatrics, 97,* 132–138.

III

INNOVATIVE PRACTICES

Teaching Self-Determination

Content and Process

Michael J. Ward and Paula D. Kohler

In 1988, the Office of Special Education and Rehabilitative Services (OSERS) began an initiative on self-determination to focus on systemwide activities to help people with disabilities have more input into the decisions that affect their lives. Although self-determination is not a new concept, the initiative was important because it applied principles associated with self-determination for other populations to those with disabilities. This initiative also stressed that the federal government wanted service providers to include consumers in the decision-making process.

In the preliminary stages of the OSERS initiative, Ward (1988) referred to self-determination as both "the attitudes which lead people to define goals for themselves and the ability to take the initiative to achieve those goals" (p. 2). Since then, the field has researched the concept of self-determination for people with disabilities and has expanded its definition to reflect emerging issues and trends. Wehmeyer (1992) defined the construct of self-determination as "the attitudes and abilities required to act as the primary causal agent in one's life and to make choices regarding one's actions free from undue external influence or interference" (p. 305).

The investigation of self-determination projects described in a portion of this chapter was sponsored in part by the Office of Special Education and Rehabilitative Services (OSERS), U.S. Department of Education, under a cooperative agreement (H158-T-00-1) with the University of Illinois. Opinions expressed herein do not necessarily reflect those of OSERS.

Based on his review of related motivation literature, Wehmeyer (1992) conceptualized self-determination as involving the constructs of autonomy, self-actualization, and self-regulation.

Schloss, Alper, and Jayne (1994) defined self-determination as "the ability to consider options and make appropriate choices regarding residential life, work, and leisure time" (p. 215). Stowitschek (1992) viewed self-determination as "a composite of traits which may vary according to the person and the level of application" (p. 3) and as comprising five major categories of skills: goal setting, self-advocacy, assertive pattern of responding, decision making, and interpersonal problem solving.

Consensus on a common definition of self-determination may not exist, because the ongoing research has not yet reached the boundaries of what is meant by self-determination, especially as it relates to people with disabilities. In general, the literature reflects the view that self-determination for people with disabilities is the same as self-determination for the population in general; yet the process of teaching self-determination skills to individuals with disabilities, and the supports they might need to practice self-determination, may be more extensive than for other individuals.

As recently as 1991, little information existed about self-determination for persons with disabilities, especially for youths. To some degree, it is likely that the increased interest in self-determination for persons with disabilities was an indirect result of the federal priority and specifically of the OSERS initiative. Common elements of the various definitions of self-determination that have emerged in recent years include attitudes and skills, goals, and choices relevant to decisions that affect a person's future.

SELF-DETERMINATION MODEL DEMONSTRATION PROJECTS

To promote the study of self-determination for youths with disabilities, the Secondary Education and Transitional Services for Youths with Disabilities Program of OSERS supported a competition to identify and teach skills necessary for self-determination. A total of 26 model demonstration projects were supported. An analysis of the applications for the projects awarded in the final years of the competition indicated that the review of the literature in those applications contained many more references specific to self-determination for persons with disabilities than were funded initially. Most of the initial applications extrapolated from social and behavioral psychology or from movements to empower other populations.

During the 4 years of the OSERS self-determination competition, projects focused on the identification of related skills, methods of instruction, and opportunities to practice self-determination. Specifically, a number of innovative approaches to teaching self-determination were developed by the model demonstration projects. Several projects employed a futures planning or person-centered planning process to teach strategies for achieving self-determined futures (e.g., University of Colorado at Colorado Springs, 1991; Wayne State University, 1990). Another model project (New Hats, Inc., 1992) supported youths with disabilities to actualize their dreams. A project for youths with physical disabilities and other health impairments (Hood Center for Family Support, 1992) developed a curriculum that considered aspects of self-determination unique to this population (e.g., managing attendants, leadership through augmented communication). Two projects (i.e., People First of Tennessee, Inc., 1991; People First of Washington, 1992) adapted "People First" strategies for the adolescent population; such strategies recognize and support people with developmental disabilities as full and capable citizens and assist members to exercise the full rights and responsibilities of citizenship and to participate in the decisions that affect their lives and the lives of others. Another project (Southern Illinois University, 1992) applied ethics and self-management skills training to promote self-determination among youths with emotional and behavioral disorders.

Projects also focused on self-determination as a process whereby students become actively involved in setting goals and making decisions (e.g., Family Resource Center on Disabilities, 1992; Portland State University, 1992; University of Colorado at Colorado Springs, 1991). Thus, many projects sought to create opportunities for students to exercise their newly attained self-determination skills. This process was facilitated in many cases informally through activities such as self-evaluation and goal setting and formally through individualized education program (IEP) planning and implementation.

A cursory review of the funded self-determination project proposals indicated that a more formal and structured analysis of project activities might provide insight into the emerging knowledge associated with teaching and facilitating self-determination for individuals with disabilities. Thus, an in-depth review of project proposals was undertaken. The purpose of this analysis was to identify specific practices and approaches related to teaching and applying self-determination. This inquiry focused on determining 1) what activities were initially proposed by the OSERS-funded model demonstration self-determination projects, 2) how these activities could be organized to facilitate further study, and 3) what specific strategies were projects using to implement the activities.

IDENTIFICATION OF SELF-DETERMINATION PRACTICES

The in-depth examination of funded model demonstration proposals focused on evaluation of two areas: proposed activities and project design. By gathering information in these two areas, it was expected that a picture would emerge showing what projects were proposing to do and showing the framework within which they would conduct their activities.

In all, 26 proposed "practices" were identified in the funded proposals. In general, these practices represented activities and processes that focused on facilitating self-determination skill development and on providing opportunities to practice self-determination. The practices were organized into four groups: self-determination skills curriculum, mentoring and modeling, community-based experiential learning and generalization across environments, and futures planning and student involvement in planning (see Table 1). *Self-determination skills* curriculum included specific skill content as well as methods of instruction. *Mentoring and modeling* included the use of peer and adult mentors and other strategies to deliver instruction and to structure project activities. *Community-based experiential learning and generalization across environments* pertained to community-based instruction and practices focused on the generalization of self-determination to environments outside of school. Finally, *futures planning and student involvement in planning* included practices in which students, and in some cases significant others, participated in actual goal setting, planning, and evaluation of their progress. Subsequent to the analysis of funded proposals, 22 key project personnel worked with the authors to identify implementation strategies associated with each of the 26 practices.

TEACHING SELF-DETERMINATION: CONTENT AND PROCESS

The number of activities and strategies identified across each of the four practice categories varied greatly. The greatest number of activities and strategies were identified in

Table 1. Practices related to promoting self-determination identified in funded project proposals

Category	Practices
Self-determination skills curriculum	Specific skill content • Self-advocacy • Life-centered career education • Ethics and self-management • Decision making and goal setting • Using community resources • Creativity and self-expression • Assertiveness and self-actualization • Empowerment and social independence Methods of instruction • Ecological assessment • Focus groups • Direct instruction • Participatory learning
Mentoring and modeling	• Matched pairs • Mentor forums • Modeling self-determined behavior • Role playing • Use of video for feedback
Community-based, experiential learning and generalization across environments	Community-based experiential learning • Community projects • Learning by doing • Support in actualizing dreams Generalization across environments • Changing roles of significant others from primary caregivers to consultants • Parent involvement • Teacher roles • Teacher follow-up • Cultural diversity • Expanding opportunities for practicing self-determination
Futures planning and student involvement in planning	• Group action planning • Group consciousness • Personal transition action plans • Student-directed IEP

the curriculum category and included subcategories related to specific skill content and methods of instruction. The lowest number of activities and strategies was identified for the categories of mentoring and modeling and of futures planning and student involvement. A description of practices within each category follows, including the activities and strategies identified by project personnel.

Self-Determination Skills Curriculum

Great diversity with respect to curricular issues existed across the projects. Using the preliminary list of curricular practices (see Table 1), project activities were examined with respect to specific skill content and methods of instruction. Within these areas, methods of curriculum development, specific skill content areas, instructional strategies, and assessment methods to evaluate changes in student skill levels were identified.

Method of Curriculum Development   Generally, curricula were developed from either a conceptual model or on an experiential basis. Projects that applied a conceptual model tended to infuse self-determination skill development and experiences into a preexisting curricular framework. Projects that took an experiential approach to identify curriculum content typically relied on program developers' past experiences with self-determined individuals with disabilities and/or surveys of the experiences of individuals with disabilities relevant to self-determination. In other cases, experiential and conceptual models were combined to produce the curriculum framework. Generally with this approach, a course to teach self-determination skills was developed and offered either on an elective or required basis. Through such a course, students typically identified their strengths and weaknesses, identified their ideal self and dreams, got feedback from others, learned decision making, and set personally meaningful goals.

Some projects empowered students to choose their own topics related to self-determination. For example, Full Citizenship, Inc. (1992) developed an elective course for high school students with developmental disabilities. Students participated in the development of the curriculum by deciding what they wanted to learn and in what sequence. In a program developed through Southern Illinois University (1992), the curriculum was based on a model of ethical decision making combined with assertiveness, communication skills, and self-management of behavior. Yet another project combined self-determination training with a lifelong learning model of career education. Through this program, The Arc (1990) interfaced self-determination concepts and skills with a preexisting widely adopted career education program.

Specific Skill Content   All 20 projects included in the analysis developed curricula that focused on developing specific skills associated with self-determination. Skill content across projects was diverse, but generally addressed one of three areas: problem solving, self-development, and self-advocacy and life skills. Content related to problem solving included individual and group decision making, clarification of stakeholders and their roles in decision making, and decision evaluation and team building. People First of Washington (1992) focused on skills that had been identified by individuals with disabilities as associated with their development of self-determined behaviors.

Self-development content included activities to enrich the individual and develop self-determination. Projects focused on interpersonal skills, assertiveness training, communication, and listening skills. On a more personal level, projects addressed such issues as self-talk, coping, self-management, and self-esteem and included activities to draw upon and activate one's creative potential. A Portland State University (1992) project included a focus on teaching high-functioning students with autism to communicate their need for facilitation and support.

The self-advocacy and life skills area included daily practice activities focused on specific living skills such as shopping in the community and directing one's own IEP staffing (e.g., Hood Center for Family Support, 1992; University of Colorado at Colorado Springs, 1991). Curricula also focused on skills related to networking and overcoming barriers in the community (e.g., Family Resource Center on Disabilities, 1992).

Instructional Strategies   The format and strategies utilized to deliver the self-determination curricula varied as greatly as the projects themselves. In general, the format consisted of individual or small-group activities; and curricula were delivered in both school-based and community-based settings. Projects utilized modeling, role play, and performance feedback via videotaping, with case studies or specific scenarios, to enhance skill instruction and review (e.g., Wayne State University, 1990). In teacher- or mentor-directed activities, instructors were often peers or adults with a disability (e.g., University of Minnesota, 1990). Other projects used self-generated activities such as self-folios (Portland State University, 1992) or a creative art project (Very Special Arts, 1990) to assist students in setting goals, evaluating options, and making decisions. The University of Washington (1992) provided simulated situations for students to learn and practice self-determination skills. For example, through these activities, students were taught appropriate responses to specific situations such as offers from strangers to take drugs and responding to a patronizing employer. Other projects engaged students in situations such as taking a teams adventure course (Portland State University, 1992), practicing life skills in the community (e.g., Wayne State University, 1990), and directing an IEP meeting (University of Colorado at Colorado Springs, 1991). Finally, the University of Hawaii (1991) focused specifically on providing instruction and experiences in integrated settings.

Assessment Strategies used to assess changes in student skill levels included the use of standardized instruments, behavioral records, authentic assessments, ecological assessment, and the use of Bloom's (1956) taxonomy to structure assessment tools. In one project, the Tennessee Self-Concept Scale (Fitts, 1965) was utilized to measure a respondent's perceptions of himself or herself before and after the project. Through the University of Washington (1992) project, participants recorded and charted their behavior; data pertaining to daily behaviors of attendance, tardiness, verbal and physical aggression, and frequency count of skills obtained through small group activities were used to determine the effectiveness of the curriculum.

Authentic assessment was utilized by students in the Irvine Unified School District (1991) and focused on individualized criteria for self-sufficiency in eight life areas. Students prepared a permanent product in the form of a portfolio that focused on the skills they developed through the curriculum to demonstrate they had met the individualized criteria.

Ecological assessment consisted of documenting the number of times students had the opportunity to exercise control over their lives in different environments (University of Minnesota, 1990). Increasing environmental opportunities to exercise such control were translated into self-determination goals for students.

Finally, Protection and Advocacy Systems (1990) applied Bloom's seven levels from the *Taxonomy of Educational Objectives* (1956) to structure assessment tools. Through this strategy, the project assessed knowledge and learning of individual students in diverse groups with respect to higher-level thought processes relevant to the self-determination skills addressed in the curriculum.

Mentoring and Modeling

Mentoring and modeling activities were used to deliver instruction and to provide students with role models who have successfully acquired self-determination skills. Mentors and role models are not new concepts and are based on relationships formed between two people to transfer knowledge, skills, and experiences from the expert to the novice. During the late 1960s, programs that provided role models for children of diverse cultures were established (Dodson, 1970; Hamilton & Hamilton, 1992). Recently, mentoring programs have been established for other at-risk groups.

Mentors have been ascribed several unique roles. Schein (1978) describes a mentor as a coach, a positive role model, a developer of talent, an opener of doors, a protector, and a sponsor. Mentoring can build skills, increase self-esteem, and indicate to young people that adults think they are worthy (William T. Grant Foundation Commission on Work, Family, and Citizenship, 1988). Mentors have also been linked to providing assistance in career decisions and understanding the world of work (Patton, 1985).

Practices associated with mentoring and modeling were components of about half of the projects. Across projects, persons who performed in these capacities were referred to as mentors, role models, and peers (not necessarily in age, but with similar disability conditions). In all cases, the mentor served as a role model and as an advocate in order to promote self-determination skill development. All projects provided mentors with training relevant to their roles and responsibilities and with goals related to developing self-determination skills in students. Generally, mentoring and modeling practices were applied through one or more of the following strategies: matched pairs, mentor forums, modeling self-determined behavior, role playing, and videotaped feedback.

Matched Pairs   The relationship between mentors and youths varied across projects. In some cases, students with disabilities were matched individually with mentors (e.g., National Center for Disability Services, 1991). Also, adults served as mentors (e.g., Prince George's Private Industry Council, Inc., 1990); in others, mentors included same-age peers (e.g., National Center for Disability Services, 1991). Most student–mentor matches involved a student and a mentor with a disability, although some mentors included individuals without disabilities. In one project, mentors were matched with parents of students (Family Resource Center on Disabilities,1992).

Across projects, students and their mentors participated in workshops, seminars, support groups, and field experiences. These activities were designed to provide students with information and develop skills in such areas as public transportation, use of assistive technology, career development and employment, postsecondary education and training, housing, identifying and gaining access to community service agencies, policy making, recreation and leisure, and use of media and mass communication systems. In many cases, students and mentors developed a plan to meet personal goals in these topic areas and then engaged in activities in which students applied self-determination skills in appropriate school and community settings. Interactions between mentors and students included social activities (e.g., parties, movies, sporting events), training related to disability issues, group activities focused on skills development, student visits to mentor workplaces, and mentor facilitation of family support sessions.

Most of the projects that involved mentors reported that the process of matching adults with students was more difficult than anticipated, especially when the goal was to identify mentors who have a disability. Projects indicated that the pool of such individuals who have the time, resources, and/or interest in participating was often very limited. To identify mentors, projects contacted local disability organizations and in some cases recruited mentors through the local media.

Mentor Forums   Periodically, groups of adult mentors with disabilities met informally with groups of students with disabilities to share experiences and coping strategies and to provide information about particular topics. One topic area focused on utilizing college students with disabilities as a means to introduce college-bound youths to college life (National Center for Disability Services, 1991). Mentor forums were held also to provide information about career development skills, such as job-seeking strategies and interviewing for a job (e.g., Prince George's Private Industry Council, Inc., 1990).

Modeling Self-Determined Behavior　　Teachers, students, and adults with disabilities served as role models for self-determined behavior. In some cases, teachers and students participated as co-learners through the curriculum (e.g., Wayne State University, 1990). Through this process, the relationship between students and teachers was redefined and modeling was promoted. Also, emphasis was placed on promoting interactions among teachers and students that emphasized student expression and teacher understanding of what students were communicating. In the Wayne State University (1990) project, teachers described how the plans and activities for achieving their classroom goals related to the self-determination process. In other cases, adults with disabilities shared personal experiences related to their development of self-determination (e.g., Family Resource Center on Disabilities, 1992; University of Minnesota, 1990). Finally, in some projects, fictional characters were used to model self-determination skills and behaviors (e.g., Wayne State University, 1990).

Role Playing　　Role playing was used by several projects to provide students opportunities to practice responding to specific situations or to initiate appropriate self-determining behavior. In one situation, students practiced and responded to passive, assertive, and aggressive communication (Southern Illinois University, 1992). Students also participated in role-play situations that required conflict resolution and negotiation skills.

Use of Videotapes　　Within the context of the self-determination curriculum developed by some projects, students created and produced videotapes for both instructional purposes and for evaluating learned behaviors (e.g., University of Colorado at Colorado Springs, 1991; Wayne State University, 1990). Videotapes were used to provide instruction by presenting modeled target behaviors and to present new information to students, teachers, and/or the public. Also through videotape media, teachers provided opportunities for students to view and evaluate their behavior in simulated or role-play situations. Across projects, videotape topics included conducting mock interviews, playing music, and depicting dreams. To increase public awareness, the Prince George's Private Industry Council, Inc. (1990), produced a videotape for distribution through the cable network that focused on advocacy and the personal futures planning process. The University of Colorado at Colorado Springs (1991) produced a videotape of a high school student directing his IEP meeting and used this videotape in the curriculum to prepare other students to do the same.

Community-Based Experiential Learning and Generalization Across Environments

Although most projects viewed self-determination as being applicable to all domains of a person's life, several projects included specific activities focused on promoting generalization to environments other than the immediate school environment (e.g., Family Resource Center on Disabilities, 1992; Hood Center for Family Support, 1992; Wayne State University, 1990). Toward this end, projects conducted community-based activities and focused on new or changed roles for teachers and parents. With respect to community-based learning, projects conducted activities in community settings, offered opportunities to learn by doing, and provided support to students in actualizing their dreams.

Community-Based Experiential Learning　　Community-based activities included field trips to community events such as musicals, plays, recitals, and art festivals (Very Special Arts, 1990). In conjunction with these trips, students also participated in performances or exhibits of their own at community art centers. The National Center for Disability Services (1991) developed school and business partnerships as a method for establishing in-school and community-based exploration related to employment. In this case, students participated in summer jobs and volunteer positions at partner businesses, company representatives visited schools to speak to students, and students participated in career shadowing with specific employees to learn about selected occupations.

The Family Resource Center on Disabilities (1992) used community-based explorations as the primary method to increase students' awareness of organizations and opportunities across a number of transition outcome areas. These students visited large employment sites (airport, large hotel, factory, mall, newspaper office, television studio), postsecondary education and training sites (community colleges, 4-year universities, vocational and adult training programs), housing sites with a particular focus on accessibility issues (commercial rental and purchase sites, subsidized housing facilities, independent living centers), and public agencies (rehabilitation, state board of education, mayor's office for employment and training).

In conjunction with community-based activities, students often participated directly in activities designed to let them learn by doing. Through the Very Special Arts (1990) project, students received and participated in demonstrations of various arts activities and then planned and implemented independently an arts activity with support from instructors or artists. Subsequently, students participated in special performances or exhibits. In another case, students established short-term and long-term goals through their curriculum; and between weekly classroom sessions, they took steps to achieve their goals in school, home, or community settings (Wayne State University, 1990).

Goal setting was the common topic as projects worked to support students to actualize their dreams. Through the Wayne State University (1990) curriculum, students examined their dreams for the future to discover common themes and to identify information these aspirations might reveal about what was important to them. Students then used this information to help develop short-term and long-term goals.

Generalization Across Environments   To facilitate the generalization of self-determined skills and behaviors to nonschool and postschool environments, several projects focused on changing the roles of significant others in the student's life from primary caregivers to consultants. Many projects recognized that self-determined behavior has not always been accepted by teachers and parents; thus, project activities focused also on helping others accept and promote student participation in goal setting, choice making, and problem solving. Through these activities, projects involved teachers and parents in new and unique roles or provided specific training focused on self-determination. Projects also structured activities to provide increased opportunities for students to practice their newly learned skills in different environments.

As mentioned previously, one project structured the curriculum in such a way that teachers became co-learners with the students (Wayne State University, 1990). In this case, teachers completed activities related to promoting self-determination and worked toward these goals along with the students. Curricular activities were structured to place an emphasis on student expression of their beliefs and opinions, while significant others (e.g., teachers, parents, other adults) focused on listening and understanding. Parents or another significant adult participated through the curriculum in the role of support person or consultant rather than caregiver.

The University of Minnesota (1990) project utilized mentors to cofacilitate parent workshops focused on parent awareness of their roles in facilitating self-determined behavior. In another case, Very Special Arts (1990) provided workshops for parents on the importance of building self-determination and self-expression and on identifying and providing effective motivation for students. Another project involved parents and students in pre-IEP conference workshops in order to address the issue of students taking control of and directing the IEP meeting (University of Colorado at Colorado Springs, 1991).

Finally, the Hood Center for Family Support (1992) provided a series of workshops for parents to improve their ability to provide support to their children. Materials and an orientation session provided parents with information regarding what students would learn through the project. Information and coaching activities pertaining to typical experiences of youths and parents were also provided. Furthermore. the project worked with families on such topics as strategies for dealing with family stress related to system burnout, parent–adolescent conflicts regarding independence, and other family crises. The project also provided parents with specific strategies for promoting self-determination, including encouraging choice and independence and developing friendships.

Futures Planning and Student Involvement in Planning

Clearly, the ability and opportunity to plan for one's future are central to self-determination. It is not surprising that most of the projects focused on developing skills related to goal setting and decision making and provided students with opportunities to practice these skills to plan for the future. Some projects developed curricula that focused on planning in general, whereas others focused specifically on transition planning and IEP development and then provided the opportunity for students to participate formally in the IEP process.

Futures Planning In many cases, students participated in specific curricular activities through which they identified goals, identified and selected options for achieving their goals, and then took action toward their goals through in-school and/or community-based activities (e.g., Portland State University, 1992; University of Colorado at Colorado Springs, 1991; Wayne State University, 1990). In several projects, students planned, made decisions, and took action with support from significant others (e.g., Hood Center for Family Support, 1992).

Full Citizenship, Inc. (1992), for example, established a group action planning process that focused on eight domains associated with daily living. Within each of the eight domains, students—in conjunction with their support group—selected options, developed goals and objectives, and took steps to achieve these goals. Membership of the support group varied from student to student and varied also for individual students across time. Group membership and members' roles at a particular time depended on the targeted domain and goals the student had selected to address. Potential members included the student's parent or parents, other family members, a job coach, teachers(s), adult service provider(s), a transition specialist, a behavior specialist, or a friend. Students participated in an elective course focused on self-determination that included instruction on the group planning process, goal setting, and decision making. Project staff trained parents as well, and subsequently staff served in a facilitator role for group meetings. The group planning process was dynamic and ongoing and was used to facilitate futures planning for short-term and long-term goals and objectives.

Involvement in the IEP Process In projects that focused on the IEP process, students identified their interests, life dreams, and vision for the future through structured activities (e.g., Family Resource Center on Disabilities, 1992; New Hats, Inc., 1992; University of Minnesota, 1990). Then they matched their preferences to available opportunities through activities that supported the discovery of conclusions about themselves and their environment.

Through one project, students utilized self-evaluation and evaluation by significant others to identify their skills and limits and then participated in curricular activities that would help them direct their IEP planning (University of Colorado at Colorado Springs, 1991). Students and family members participated in training about rights and responsibilities, communication with and access to service providers, advocacy and negotiation skills, and community resources. In addition, teachers were trained to facilitate student involvement by preparing students for educational planning sessions and were provided specific strategies for initiating student participation. Through the IEP planning process, students chose goals, activities, timelines, criteria for accomplishment, and persons to help support them in attainment of their goals. The students described the plan in their own words and, through planning activities, learned to break goals into achievable tasks, set standards for completion, identify support needs, discover their motivation for completing tasks, schedule tasks, and evaluate their performance. Students also conducted preplanning mini-meetings in community settings with significant others; scheduled and arranged the IEP meeting; and prepared for the meeting through role play, practice, videotaping and/or by watching an instructional videotape.

Students then directed the IEP meeting during which logistics, commitments, and timelines were finalized. Subsequently, students worked toward their IEP goals through activities planned into the daily schedule, decided on the methods for documenting progress and goal attainment, and developed a schedule for reviewing the process. Students credited themselves for progress on a regular basis and evaluated their outcomes. They learned to take responsibility for mistakes along the way and celebrated their achievements; when necessary and beneficial, the plan was changed. To evaluate the process of conducting their IEP meetings, students participated in post-IEP meeting discussions with teachers and peers. Through these experiences, students developed self-determination skills; interacted with significant others in planning for their future; established specific goals, activities, and timelines; conducted formal IEP meetings; and evaluated the process and their progress. In sum, students were directly involved in planning for their future.

IMPLICATIONS FOR SERVICE DELIVERY

It is recognized that developing self-determination skills in youths with disabilities is important (e.g., Schloss et al., 1994; Ward, 1988; Wehmeyer, 1992). In fact, some contend that developing self-determination in young people is the ultimate goal of education (Ward & Halloran, 1993). Furthermore, there is a legislative mandate to involve students with disabilities in their transition planning (e.g., Individuals with Disabilities Education Act of 1990 [IDEA], PL 101-476). Many school districts and service providers continue to struggle, however, with questions related to what self-determination is, what skills are needed to do it, how it can be taught, and how to include students in a process that has traditionally excluded them. Clearly, the 26 self-determination model demonstration projects have much to offer toward answering these questions.

Analysis of project activities indicated that projects developed curricula to teach students to evaluate their skills, recognize their limits, set goals, identify options, accept responsibility, communicate their preferences and needs, and monitor and evaluate their progress. The activities taught decision making, goal setting, self-awareness, and self-advocacy. To teach these skills, they used teachers, mentors, and parents to model self-determined behavior; involved students in role play and simulated situations; developed student portfolios; and used videotape media to instruct and to provide feedback. Furthermore, projects conducted numerous activities in community settings such as business and industrial sites, the public service sector, postsecondary education and training facilities, residential environments, and community art centers. To increase the capacity of others to recognize and promote self-determination, many projects trained teachers, parents, and other significant adults in students' lives. Finally, projects created opportunities for students to exercise their newly developed skills and, in some cases, formally positioned students as leaders in the IEP process.

All model demonstration projects in general are required to evaluate the model by using a variety of quantitative and qualitative analyses. With respect to their interventions, many of the self-determination projects measured changes in a number of dependent variables, including student skill levels, perceptions of significant others, student satisfaction, and opportunities to participate in decision making. Initial evaluation data from project final reports indicated that students who participated in project activities showed increased skills and behaviors associated with self-determination. For example, one project used a Solomon Four group design in a field test of the curriculum to measure self-determination knowledge and skill (Field, Hoffman, Sawilowsky, & St. Peter, 1994). Three assessment instruments were used to conduct the analysis: a cognitive multiple choice instrument, an observation checklist of behavioral correlates, and a measure of teachers' perceptions of students' self-determination. In general, findings indicated that for those students who participated in the curriculum, knowledge and skills related to self-determination improved significantly (Field et al., 1994). The Arc (1990) used knowledge battery tests associated with the Life Centered Career Education model (Brolin, 1989) to evaluate effectiveness of the self-determination curriculum. Findings indicated that students exhibited increased knowledge and awareness with respect to competencies associated with self-determination (e.g., achieving self-awareness, acquiring self-confidence) (Wehmeyer, 1994).

Preliminary information from other projects also indicated that positive outcomes occurred when students learned to make decisions, be assertive, and self-advocate. Anecdotal information indicated that the interventions developed by model demonstration projects made a positive impact on the youths who participated in them. Success stories have emerged about individuals who gained more control over their lives by avoiding trouble with the law, others who exhibited leadership and advocacy skills in community activities, and yet others who became contributing and participatory members of their families. Such stories serve to reinforce the notion that it is important to teach self-determination. The role, however, of the evaluation and research data is to indicate which of the strategies are most effective in doing so. As these data on project practices and strategies become available, the potential for the model demonstration projects to have an impact on practice should become even greater.

Historically, students with disabilities have achieved poorer postschool outcomes than have their peers without disabilities. Follow-up studies of special education graduates have indicated high rates of unemployment and underemployment (Hasazi, Gordon, & Roe, 1985; Mithaug, Horiuchi, & Fanning, 1985; Wagner, 1989; Wagner, D'Amico, Marder, Newman, & Blackorby, 1992). Wehmeyer (1992) proposed that one reason for poor quality of life after exiting high school is that students in special education lack self-determination skills and are infrequently afforded opportunities to experience self-determination. Educators must begin to take responsibility for giving students opportunities to experience self-determination. Van Reusen and Bos (1990) warned, "If special educators plan and carry out instructional activities without involving or considering the adolescent's perceptions and priorities, they may be minimizing the student's self-determination" (p. 30). We agree with Wehmeyer (1992) and hypothesize that self-determination, in conjunction with other independent living and employment skills, may well be a strong predictor of postschool success.

Involving students in their IEP development and meetings may be one critical step in facilitating self-determination. Martin, Marshall, and Maxson (1993) suggested that in order to facilitate environments in which students with disabilities are able to develop self-determination skills and apply those skills in their adult lives, the IEP process must be restructured to encourage active student participation and direction. Specifically, the practices implemented by the self-determination projects have direct implications for schools seeking to implement the mandates of IDEA that require educational agencies to include students in their transition planning and IEP development, take an outcome-oriented approach when developing educational programs, consider students' needs and preferences, and develop a coordinated set of activities in both classroom and community settings.

As schools evaluate their current practices in light of the legislative mandate, they may find that curricula similar to those developed by the self-determination projects are needed to prepare students to take responsibility and to assume active roles in the educational process—curricula that teach students to be proactive rather than inactive participants in learning and planning. Furthermore, schools may find that teachers, staff, and parents need training that will prepare them to promote self-determination rather than resist it. Most important, schools may find that they need to restructure educational planning and service delivery to allow opportunities for students to accept responsibility and to actively plan and learn, both in classrooms and in the community.

Also critical is for all professionals to subscribe to a belief supported by Ward and Halloran (1993) that self-determination is *the* ultimate goal of education. Although this concept was probably not considered by Brown and his colleagues (e.g., Brown, Nietupski, & Hamre-Nietupski, 1976) when presenting their theories related to "programming for the next environments" and "the criteria of ultimate functioning," the belief that schools must be responsible for producing individuals who are competent in many areas, including the area of self-determination, is certainly consistent with these theories.

It was hoped that the transition requirements of IDEA would compel teachers and others to focus on outcomes of youths with disabilities—outcomes associated with becoming adults, such as living and working in the community—the achievement of which may require specific services or training. We believe, however, that this outcome perspective continues to elude many, particularly some in middle and elementary school settings who appear to take a "Peter Pan" approach toward the education of young children and youths with disabilities; that is, an approach that assumes these children and youths will never grow up, so why bother teaching skills related to work or independent living, let alone self-determination? In other words, even though IDEA calls for an outcome approach for the development of education programs, many fail to believe that students with disabilities can and will make the transition into valued, typical adult roles. In some ways, it appears that rather than improve accountability of educators with respect to student outcomes, the transition-related mandates of IDEA may have limited accountability, as many educational agencies have developed ways to appear in compliance without changing their educational planning practices in any meaningful way. In essence, these agencies comply with the letter of the law, but not with the intent; and by so doing, they fail to address realistic, achievable postschool outcomes, particularly those associated with self-determination.

Consistent with our belief is the realization that youths with disabilities do not magically become responsible, self-sufficient adults upon reaching a certain age or exiting school. While this is probably true for most youths in general, youths *without* disabilities typically have greater opportunity and latitude for experimental behavior, opportunity and latitude often denied to youths *with* disabilities. It is not uncommon that within the same family, behavior considered unacceptable for the sibling with a disability is not only tolerated, but often expected, in other siblings. Whereas being truant from school might be considered a part of Jane's antisocial, emotionally disturbed label, parents may view the same act as Bob's typical adolescent acting-out behavior.

All youths need self-determination skills; it is imperative, however, that youths with disabilities receive *training* to develop these skills and that they have multiple opportunities to use the skills while still in school. Through self-determination skills training, youths with disabilities can experiment with typical adolescent behaviors such as risk taking and assertiveness (behaviors that many adults understandably find obnoxious). Because they learn skills such as decision making, goal setting, and responsibility as part of their self-determination development, adolescence could become a more positive experience for all involved.

In summary, self-determination skill development must be included in the educational process so that individuals with disabilities can define short-term and long-term goals for themselves and take initiative in achieving those goals. Furthermore, in looking toward the future we must ask ourselves, "What do we want for *all* people with disabilities?" The answers must include living as independently as possible, having friends and relationships with significant others, participating in community activities, and working in a gainful and satisfying job. An equally important answer is leadership skills—skills to continue the momentum of the disability rights movement so that the legislative intent of IDEA, Section 504 of the Rehabilitation Act of 1973, and the Americans with Disabilities Act of 1990 (ADA) is fully realized. Self-determination in and of itself is important, but self-determination that leads to meaningful postschool outcomes and the ability to improve the quality of life for all must be the focus of our efforts.

REFERENCES

Americans with Disabilities Act of 1990 (ADA), PL 101-336. (July 26, 1990). Title 42, U.S.C. 12101 et seq: *U.S. Statutes at Large, 104*, 327–378.

The Arc. (1990). *Self-determination curriculum project.* Arlington, TX: Author.

Bloom, E. (Ed.). (1956). *Taxonomy of educational objectives: Handbook 1, cognitive domain.* New York: McKay.

Brolin, D. (1989). *Life centered career education: A competency based approach.* Reston, VA: Council for Exceptional Children.

Brown, L., Nietupski, J., & Hamre-Nietupski, S. (1976). The criterion of ultimate functioning and public school services for severely handicapped students. In M.A. Thomas (Ed.), *Hey, don't forget about me: Education's investment in the severely, profoundly, and multiply handicapped* (pp. 197–209). Reston, VA: Council for Exceptional Children.

Dodson, D.W. (1970). Sociological perspectives on educational materials. In W.M. Lifton (Ed.), *Educating for tomorrow: The role of media, career development, and society* (pp. 12–30). New York: John Wiley & Sons.

Family Resource Center on Disabilities. (1992). *MAINROADS to self-determination.* Chicago: Author.

Field, S., Hoffman, A., Sawilowsky, S., & St. Peter, S. (1994). *Skills and knowledge for self-determination: Final report.* Detroit: Wayne State University.

Fitts, W.H. (1965). *Tennessee self-concept scale.* Los Angeles: Western Psychological Services.

Full Citizenship, Inc. (1992). *Self-determination through group action planning project.* Lawrence, KS: Author.

Hamilton, S.F., & Hamilton, M.A. (1992). Mentoring programs: Promise and paradox. *Phi Delta Kappan, 73,* 546–550.

Hasazi, S.B., Gordon, L.R., & Roe, C.A. (1985). Factors associated with the employment status of handicapped youth exiting high school from 1979 to 1983. *Exceptional Children, 51,* 455–469.

Hood Center for Family Support. (1992). *A student-directed model for the promotion of self-determination through skill facilitation and peer support.* Lebanon, NH: Dartmouth-Hitchcock Medical Center.

Individuals with Disabilities Education Act of 1990 (IDEA), PL 101-476. (October 30, 1990). Title 20, U.S.C. 1400 et seq: *U.S. Statutes at Large, 104,* 1103–1151.

Irvine Unified School District. (1991). *Independence through responsible choices.* Irvine, CA: Author.

Martin, J.E., Marshall, L.H., & Maxson, L.L. (1993). Transition policy: Infusing self-determination and self-advocacy into transition programs. *Career Development for Exceptional Individuals, 16,* 53–61.

Mithaug, D.E., Horiuchi, C.N., & Fanning, P.N. (1985). A report of the Colorado statewide follow-up survey of special education students. *Exceptional Children, 51,* 397–404.

National Center for Disability Services. (1991). *A demonstration project to identify and teach skills necessary for self-determination.* Albertson, NY: Author.

New Hats, Inc. (1992). *It's my life project.* Salt Lake City: Author.

Patton, S.L. (1985). *The mentor project: Involving handicapped employees in the transition of handicapped youth from school to work. Final report.* Waltham, MA: Russell and Associates, Inc. (ERIC Document Reproduction Service No. ED 280 249)

People First of Tennessee, Inc. (1991). *Consumers helping students toward self-determination.* Nashville: Author.

People First of Washington. (1992). *Self-determination training for secondary students.* Clarkston, WA: Author.

Portland State University. (1992). *Life-decisions strategies program.* Portland, OR: Author.

Prince George's Private Industry Council, Inc. (1990). *Self-determination program for transitioning youth in Prince George's County.* Landover, MD: Author.

Protection and Advocacy Systems. (1990). *Self-determination: The road to personal freedom.* Albuquerque: Author.

Rehabilitation Act of 1973, PL 93-112. (September 26, 1973). Title 29, U.S.C. 701 et seq: *U.S. Statutes at Large, 87,* 355–394.

Schein, E.H. (1978). *Career dynamics: Matching individual and organizational needs.* Reading, MA: Addison-Wesley.

Schloss, P.J., Alper, S., & Jayne, D. (1994). Self-determination for persons with disabilities: Choice, risk, and dignity. *Exceptional Children, 60,* 215–225.

Southern Illinois University. (1992). *Developing self-determination in youth with emotional behavior disorders through ethics and self management instruction.* Carbondale: Author.

Stowitschek, J. (1992). *Development of a model self-determination program and taxonomy for youth with moderate and severe disabilities (project proposal).* Seattle: University of Washington, Experimental Education Unit WJ-10.

University of Colorado at Colorado Springs. (1991). *Choice makers.* Colorado Springs: Author.

University of Hawaii. (1991). *Self-determination in integrated settings.* Honolulu: Author.

University of Minnesota. (1990). *Facilitating the self-determination of youths with disabilities.* Minneapolis: Author.

University of Washington. (1992). *Curriculum based self-determination project.* Seattle: Author.

Van Reusen, A.K., & Bos, C.S. (1990). I plan: Helping students communicate in planning conferences. *Teaching Exceptional Children, 22*(4), 30–32.

Very Special Arts. (1990). *Project PARTnership.* Washington, DC: Author.

Wagner, M. (1989). *Youth with disabilities during transition: An overview of descriptive findings from the National Longitudinal Transition Study.* Menlo Park, CA: SRI International.

Wagner, M., D'Amico, R., Marder, C., Newman, L., & Blackorby, J. (1992). *What happens next? Trends in postschool outcomes of youths with disabilities. The second comprehensive report from the National Longitudinal Transition Study of special education students.* Menlo Park, CA: SRI International.

Ward, M.J. (1988). The many facets of self-determination. *Transition Summary, 5,* 2–3. Washington, DC: National Information Center for Children and Youth with Handicaps.

Ward, M.J., & Halloran, W.D. (1993). Transition issues for the 1990s. *OSERS News in Print, VI*(1), 4–5.

Wayne State University. (1990). *Skills for self-determination.* Detroit: Author.

Wehmeyer, M.L. (1992). Self-determination and the education of students with mental retardation. *Education and Training in Mental Retardation, 27,* 302–314

Wehmeyer, M.L. (1994). *Self-determination curriculum project: Final report.* Arlington, TX: The Arc.

William T. Grant Foundation Commission on Work, Family, and Citizenship. (1988). *The forgotten half: Non-college youth in America.* Washington, DC: Author.

15

TAKE CHARGE

A Model for Promoting Self-Determination Among Adolescents with Challenges

Laurie E. Powers, Jo-Ann Sowers,
Alison Turner, Maggie Nesbitt,
Eric Knowles, and Robin Ellison

Adolescence is typically a time for expanding personal independence; preparing for employment, postsecondary education, and community living; and developing new relationships with peers and community members. Each of these activities is essential if youth are to prepare for their quickly emerging adult roles, responsibilities, and privileges. Successful transition from adolescent to young adult roles is, in many cases, a natural and self-perpetuating process that becomes increasingly important to most teenagers as they move closer to adulthood (Larson & Kleiber, 1993).

For adolescents with disabilities, however, this process is often not so natural. Physical, learning, emotional, and health disabilities pose challenges to teenagers' efforts to live their lives as typically and independently as their peers without disabili-

The preparation of this chapter was supported, in part, by Grant Nos. H086D90001 and H158K20006 awarded by the U.S. Department of Education, Office of Special Education and Rehabilitative Services (OSERS). The opinions expressed herein are exclusively those of the authors, and no official endorsement by OSERS should be inferred.

ties. Disability-related restrictions in mobility, speech, language, dexterity, vision, endurance, emotional regulation, and learning present major challenges to the success of youth with challenges (Goldenson, Dunham, & Dunham, 1978; Stopford, 1987). Many youth also experience health instability, requiring ongoing medical care and exposure to procedures that may be uncomfortable, disempowering, and incapacitating (Steinhausen, Schindler, & Stephan, 1983). To obtain assistance in performing daily activities, many youth with disabilities use support provided by others. However, they are typically passive recipients of such support (Ulicny, Adler, & Jones, 1988). The prevalence of architectural and communication barriers further exacerbates the dependence of youth with disabilities (Cruikshank, 1976; Scherer, 1988), as do negative societal and professional attitudes regarding their worth and potential for achievement (Edgerton, 1967; Fichten, 1988; Goffman, 1973).

Evidence suggests that some children with disabilities fail to develop the mastery motivation necessary to enable them to make choices and to attempt behaviors that will maximize their functional independence and self-confidence (Kleinhammer-Tramill, Tramill, Schrepel, & Davis, 1983; Lindemann, 1981; Robinson & Robinson, 1976). This result occurs as a function of protectiveness and the provision of unnecessary help (Cruikshank, 1976; Kessler, 1977; Powers & Sowers, 1994), reinforcement of passive behavior by teachers (see Chapter 9) and medical care providers (Lewis, Pantell, & Sharp, 1991), and through restricted access to successful role models with disabilities (Rousso, 1988) and peers (Mitchell, 1988) who could serve to reinforce self-confidence and effective strategies for coping with challenge. Additionally, teachers and other school personnel often lack the necessary skills to enhance the perceived competence, social skill development, and functional abilities of such students (Brown et al., 1979; Neistadt, 1986) or to have an impact on the expectations of their parents (Espinosa & Shearer, 1986). Simply put, many young people with significant disabilities are at risk to develop patterns of behavior that include passivity, expectations for failure, depressed affect, and resistance to new challenges (Jones & Ulicny, 1986; Lindemann, 1981).

The vast majority of efforts to promote the capabilities of youth with disabilities have focused on demonstrating strategies that professionals and parents can use to assist youth to become more independent. Only recently has our attention begun to shift toward investigating the potential link between assisting youth to learn *self-help* strategies to promote their self-competence and promoting their functional capabilities. Much of this work has been accomplished through federally funded initiatives to identify and demonstrate strategies that promote the self-determination of youth with disabilities (Brown, 1992).

Self-determination refers to personal attitudes and abilities that facilitate an individual's identification and pursuit of goals. The expression of self-determination is reflected in personal attitudes of empowerment, active participation in decision making, and self-directed action to achieve personally valued goals. Self-determined students identify goals and accomplish the functional requisites to achieve those goals. Professionals who promote the self-determination of youth assist them to learn and apply approaches for identifying and working toward goals. Youth who experience various levels of disability can express self-determination: Actively participating in career planning, demonstrating basic preferences through the activation of communication switches, or attempting new behaviors are all potential examples of self-determined behavior.

This chapter describes *TAKE CHARGE,* a supported self-help model to promote the self-determination and functional competence of adolescents who experience disabilities (Powers, Singer, & Sowers, 1992; Sowers & Powers, 1989). The model has been collaboratively implemented by school districts, independent living programs, and parent organizations in several states. The primary target population for the development of *TAKE CHARGE* has been youth with physical disabilities and ongoing health challenges, approximately 50% of whom also experience mild to moderate learning and cognitive challenges. Most recently, *TAKE CHARGE* has been implemented with adolescents with primary emotional and learning challenges and with inclusive groupings of youth with and without disabilities.

While most existing models to enhance adolescent independence and inclusion rest on either parent-directed support to the student or instructor-directed intervention, *TAKE CHARGE* has as its centerpiece student-directed participation in personally relevant activities in school, community, and home settings. Students learn that they are responsible for promoting their own independence and self-confidence, they are exposed to specific strategies to identify and achieve their personal goals, and they are provided with information and support necessary to ensure their success. This chapter describes the conceptual foundation for the *TAKE CHARGE* model, provides an overview of its major intervention components, and presents case illustrations of the experiences of three youth who participated in model implementation. We conclude with a discussion of the implications of *TAKE CHARGE* for the design and delivery of educational supports.

CONCEPTUAL FOUNDATIONS FOR *TAKE CHARGE*

TAKE CHARGE is designed to systematically promote self-determination and functional competence by reducing learned helplessness and promoting mastery motivation and self-efficacy expectations.

Learned Helplessness

Learned helplessness is an *acquired* behavioral disposition characterized by passivity, self-denigration, and internalization of devalued social status (Seligman, 1975). This disposition is induced through repeated failed attempts to affect the environment and it is perpetuated through permanent and pervasive negative self-attributions (Seligman, 1990). A child who experiences repeated failure is likely to avoid new challenges. Zeaman and House (1960) demonstrated the pervasive effect of failure in a study of adults with cognitive disabilities. Participants were initially presented with a task that they completed with ease. Subsequently, they were asked to complete an unsolvable problem. Following failure on this task, the easy task was reintroduced. Results indicated that participants had great difficulty completing the easy task following their failure experience. They demonstrated a tendency to react to failure by withdrawing and ceasing to try. Learned helplessness is associated with reduced autonomy and impaired problem solving (Luchow, Crowl, & Kahn, 1985; Margalit & Shulman, 1986; Peterson & Stunkard, 1989).

Many youth who experience disabilities are constantly confronted by difficult tasks, often have high potential for failure, and must exhibit perseverance to be successful (Allsop, 1980; Davis, Anderson, Linkowski, Berger, & Feinstein, 1985; Fielder, 1988). They are highly susceptible to developing learned helplessness unless they are provided with methods to enhance their success.

Learned helplessness is reinforced by environmental factors that encourage passivity by providing little opportunity for an individual to actively make choices and generate successful responses, by communicating expectations of noninvolvement or failure, or by reinforcing failure or not reinforcing striving (Houghton, Bronicki, & Guess, 1987; Hoy, 1986). Factors that promote learned helplessness include overprotection and economic, academic, or social deprivation. As a result of these influences, youth with disabilities may not learn the necessary skills to successfully interact with their environments and become disposed toward orientations of dependency and passivity. Such passivity, in association with restricted access to opportunities to learn and practice mastery skills, substantially reduces the ability of adolescents and young adults with disabilities to exercise the self-determination required to assess, use, and benefit from adult independent living, interpersonal, and vocational opportunities (Clark, Mack, & Pennington, 1988; Thomas et al., 1985).

Mastery Motivation

In contrast to learned helplessness, a model of mastery motivation proposed by Harter (1981) provides a framework for understanding how youth acquire a generalized positive disposition toward achievement and striving. Mastery motivation is characterized by perceived competence, self-esteem, maintenance of an internal locus of control, and internalization of goals and rewards. It is achieved through repeated attempts paired with reinforcement for successes. Youth who possess mastery motivation exhibit a demonstrated willingness to expend effort in domains that are historically associated with success. Such children try hard to achieve goals and often succeed more often than do children who lack such motivation (Clark, 1980). Parents and professionals who encourage mastery motivation set goals that are slightly beyond the present capabilities of a child; they do not require too little of the child and thereby reinforce passivity, nor do they demand too much and thereby set the stage for failure (Lindemann, 1981). As children mature, they are encouraged to set their own goals, to take acceptable risks, and to self-advocate (see Chapter 4).

Self-Efficacy Expectations

Bandura's theory of self-efficacy provides a detailed framework for understanding specific influences on the development of self-determination. According to Bandura (1977, 1986), behavior depends on both outcome expectations and personal efficacy expectations. Outcome expectations consist of beliefs about whether a particular behavior will lead to a particular consequence. Personal efficacy expectations refers to a person's expectation regarding his or her capability to realize a desired behavior in a specific context. Personal efficacy does not reflect a person's skills, but rather one's judgment of what one can do with whatever skills one possesses. This distinction is particularly salient for youth with challenges because it provides a mechanism whereby they can perceive themselves as competent regardless of their practical limitations. Youth who exhibit high levels of self-efficacy believe that they have the necessary capabilities to accomplish their goals and that they will achieve their goals if they exercise those capabilities. Youth with high levels of self-efficacy are more likely to make choices, attempt new behaviors, and persevere through difficult tasks than are youth with low self-efficacy (Bandura, 1977).

There is a growing body of evidence that self-efficacy beliefs are an important predictor of academic success (Graham & Harris, 1989), motivation (Schunk, 1989a, 1989b), and functional well-being (Dolce, 1987) for people with disabilities. Adolescents with high self-efficacy are also less likely to experience depression (Ehrenberg, Cox, & Koopman, 1991). As depicted in Figure 1, the following four specific sources have an impact on self-efficacy appraisals.

Enactive Attainment The most important source of self-efficacy information, enactive attainment, is derived from repeated performance accomplishments (Bandura, 1986). There is general agreement in the field regarding the importance of functional capabilities for enhancement of child autonomy and quality of life (Brown et al., 1979; Sowers, Rusch, Connis, & Cummings, 1980; Wehman, 1981; Wilcox & Bellamy, 1987). Individual capabilities are fostered through the creation of specific opportunities in which youth can experience success through achievement and successful management of challenge. Such opportunities are created by supporting students to engage in activities that they deem important and can successfully perform or participate in performing. Critical to creating success experiences for students is assisting them to identify and apply strategies to cope with obstacles that impede their progress: personal obstacles such as communication challenges, academic difficulties, limitations in mobility, or difficulties in emotional regulation and contextual barriers such as discrimination, lack or complexity of services, and disincentives to independence and self-direction.

Most important, opportunities must be available that maximize youth self-attribution of success. It is not sufficient to orchestrate enjoyable activities for youth or to

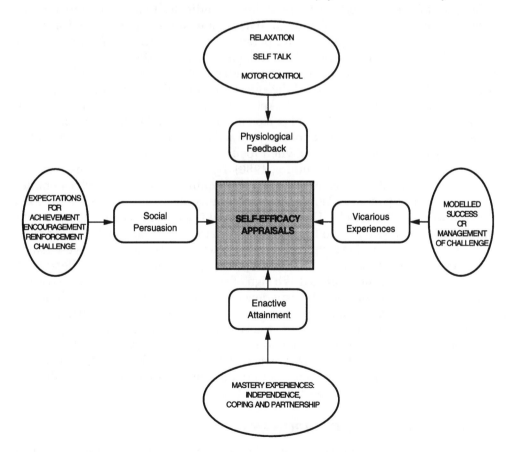

Figure 1.   Enhancing self-determination by promoting self-efficacy appraisals.

ensure their success by performing key activity elements for them. Rather, opportunities must be created for youth to exercise their own capabilities and to achieve outcomes they value. Ideally, such opportunities should facilitate youth self-help, provide only those supports necessary to give youth a reasonable chance for success, and highlight youth accomplishments (Arborelius & Bremberg, 1991; Hughes, Korinek, & Gorman, 1991).

Vicarious Experiences   Vicarious experiences are essential for the development of self-efficacy expectations, particularly in novel contexts with ambiguous task demands. Self-efficacy appraisals are bolstered by observing similar other's success and effective management of challenge. This type of learning typically occurs in the course of contact with peers and other members of the individual's informal social network (Fewell & Vadasy, 1986). The importance of peer support, for purposes of enhancing personal empowerment, social skill development, and quality of life is echoed across the field of education and is associated with both vicarious learning and enhancement of social support (Brown, 1992; Brown et al., 1979; Powers, Sowers, & Stevens, 1995). Role models are another source of vicarious learning. Through exposure to successful role models, students with challenges have an opportunity to learn and practice disability-related strategies for overcoming obstacles and develop personal identity and pride (Powers, Sowers, et al., 1995; Rousso, 1988).

Social Persuasion   Persuasion can take the form of encouragement, evaluative feedback, reinforcement, or challenge. Evidence indicates that youth who are reinforced for their attempts demonstrate motivation and success in learning (Brophy & Good, 1974; Lindemann, 1981). Social persuasion is particularly effective when it leads people to expend the increased effort required to successfully accomplish activities (Bandura, 1986). Children who are persuaded that they are capable of mastering tasks and challenges are likely to mobilize greater effort and are more likely to achieve success (Schunk, 1982). They are most likely to be influenced when they perceive that their persuader is credible by virtue of personal knowledge and skill and by experience in judging the requirements for performing the activity (Crundall & Foddy, 1981). Persuasion is believable and effective when focused on inspiring a person to achieve slightly beyond current levels (Bandura, 1986). By providing encouragement in conjunction with information about realistic activity requirements, parents, educators, and mentors may assist youth to identify and successfully strive toward short-term goals.

Physiological Feedback   Heightened arousal is associated with expectancy for failure and, consequently, with lowered self-efficacy (Bandura, 1986). For example, having shaking hands during a typing task may cause an individual to expect that he or she will be unable to type well. Those who perceive themselves to be ineffective are especially prone to misjudge arousal as a sign of coping deficiency. Such is the case for many students with disabilities who experience repeated failure and/or have disability-related impairments in physiologic or motor control (Sowers & Powers, 1991; Stopford, 1987). Experiences that reduce fear and arousal or stimulate change in self-appraisal of the reason for arousal are likely to increase self-efficacy (Bandura, 1986). Techniques such as relaxation training (Sowers & Powers, 1991) and positive self-talk can be used to both facilitate motor performance and to reduce negative self-attributions that can affect a student's self-efficacy expectations.

TAKE CHARGE MODEL COMPONENTS

Derived from the conceptual foundations of mastery motivation and self-efficacy theories and refined through the ongoing input of youth consumers, the *TAKE CHARGE* model is designed to promote adolescent development of self-determination through four primary components: skill facilitation, mentorship, peer support, and parent support.

Component 1: Skill Facilitation

Perhaps the most critical factor affecting an adolescent's self-determination is his or her skill development. At a basic level, self-determination can be most effectively understood as a series of skills that can be acquired and refined through opportunities for learning and applied practice. This conceptualization is in contrast to views of self-determination as a motivational variable intrinsic to the personalities of some resilient individuals and difficult to foster in those who do not possess an internal disposition toward self-direction. Although it is likely that there is some dispositional contribution to the emergence of self-determination (Werner & Smith, 1992), most agree that all youth can enhance their self-determination if provided with necessary skills and supports (Powers, 1993; Wehmeyer, 1993; also see Chapter 14).

The *TAKE CHARGE* model uses skill facilitation to assist youth in learning self-determination skills. Youth learn all skills in the context of applying them to identify and achieve personal goals. In an individualized approach, each youth participant is matched with a facilitator or coach who meets with the youth once or twice a week. Small groupings or classes of youth can also be coached by one or two facilitators with whom they meet regularly. Group facilitation is enhanced through delivery of *TAKE CHARGE* to heterogeneous groupings of adolescents of different ages, with and without disabilities. Facilitators may be educators, related services personnel, guidance counselors, instructional assistants, school nurses, staff or volunteers from community agencies, or any other individuals who are willing to commit to meeting with youth regularly for a period of 6–9 months. Facilitators are provided with a guide that describes the philosophy of *TAKE CHARGE,* strategies to promote youth learning and achievement and collaboration with parents and mentors, and methods for managing common implementation challenges (Powers, Wilson, Turner, & Rein, 1995).

There is general agreement that self-determination skills include goal setting, problem solving, assertiveness, coping with challenges, self-regulation, and management of helping partnerships (Clark et al., 1988; Powers & Sowers, 1994; Starke, 1987; Summers, 1986; Varela, 1986; also see Chapter 14). *TAKE CHARGE* introduces youth to the application of three major categories of skills: achievement, partnership, and coping. Skills are presented in a self-help guide that leads youth through the *TAKE CHARGE* process (Powers & Ellison, 1995). Skills are presented as generic strategies for taking charge of life, with each strategy presented as a small number of systematic steps. The major strategies in *TAKE CHARGE* are presented in Table 1. Youth are also provided with companion informational materials in adolescent-friendly formats. Companion materials provide basic information and tips about making and keeping friends, getting into college, getting a job, and living in the community.

Table 1.   Generic strategies in *TAKE CHARGE*

Achievement	Partnership	Coping
Dream	Schmooze	Think positive
Set goals	Be assertive	Focus on accomplishments
Problem solve	Negotiate	Manage frustration
Prepare	Manage help	Track and reward progress
Do it!		

Facilitators assist, encourage, and challenge youth to apply generic strategies to achieve their personal goals. Movement through *TAKE CHARGE* is self-directed: Adolescents are told that they are responsible for taking charge of their lives and they are challenged to take the lead. Although facilitators may provide instruction to assist youth to learn particular strategies, their major roles are as supportive coaches. They assist youth to review their self-help materials, cheer their progress, occasionally challenge them to take action, and make themselves available to help students to rehearse particular strategies (e.g., role-play negotiation of a goal with parents) or to perform particular activities necessary for goal achievement (e.g., call an agency on the student's behalf to obtain information).

Achievement Strategies   Youth proceed through five systematic strategies for identifying and achieving personal goals. Each strategy is composed of specific generic steps that youth can apply to enhance their success in present and future goal attainment.

Dream   The importance of identifying future dreams for enhancing both personal motivation and future planning is well recognized (Bolles, 1995; Pearpoint, O'Brien, & Forest, 1992). Youth begin the *TAKE CHARGE* process by creating general maps of what they want their lives to be like 5 years hence. Youth are invited to develop their dreams in four life domains: school/college, work, friendship and recreation, and daily living. Figure 2 presents general questions youth are encouraged to answer as they identify their dreams. They are challenged to think creatively, the primary purpose of dreaming being to awaken their hope and excitement about the future. Young adolescents typically dream about the life they want during high school, whereas older teenagers typically focus on life after high school. Some youth, particularly those exposed to economic and cultural deprivation, have difficulty acknowledging or exploring their dreams. It is essential that these youth be encouraged to risk developing dreams for a more hopeful future. It is also common for youth to develop far-reaching dreams that their parents or teachers may believe are inappropriate or unrealistic. However, the specific nature of a youth's dream is less important than the enthusiasm dreaming generates for goal achievement. Our experience also suggests that future dreams become more realistic as youth mature, learn about future life options, and have opportunities to work toward specific goals.

Set Goals   Goal setting may indeed be the most important skill for self-determination because it encompasses both the act and the pursuit of choice (Brotherson, Backus, Summers, & Turnbull, 1986; Gardner, 1986; Mitchell, 1988). Individuals typically choose goals that they value and are empowered through creating opportunities to achieve desired outcomes. They tend to infer high self-efficacy from success achieved through effort on tasks that are perceived to be difficult. In contrast, they infer low self-efficacy if they have to work hard to master easy tasks (de Vries, Dijkstra, & Kuhlman, 1988). As such, facilitators typically encourage youth to select moderately challenging goals with which they have a reasonable probability of success. Common goals for adolescents include learning to drive, exploring post–high school educational and vocational options, planning recreational activities, and developing friendships and romantic relationships (Clark et al., 1988).

Youth learn a three-step process for setting goals: 1) look at what you are doing now, 2) choose activities you want to do, and 3) decide exactly what activities you will do. The first step is accomplished by completing a self-assessment of activities typically performed by adolescents in one or two youth-selected domains described above. Youth self-assess whether they perform each activity and whether they would like to perform it more independently or more often. The second step is accomplished by hav-

My Dream

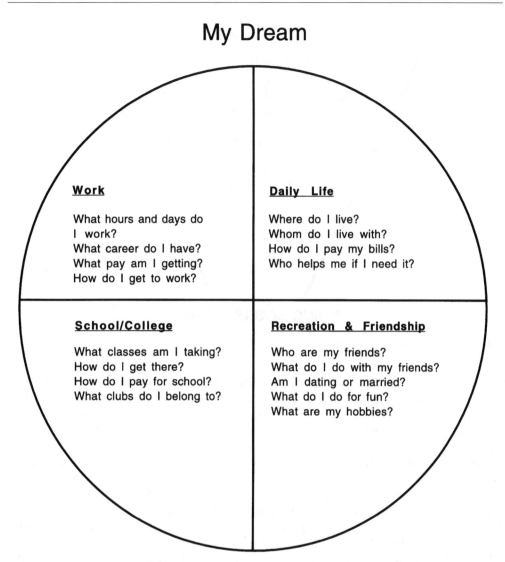

Work

What hours and days do
I work?
What career do I have?
What pay am I getting?
How do I get to work?

Daily Life

Where do I live?
Whom do I live with?
How do I pay my bills?
Who helps me if I need it?

School/College

What classes am I taking?
How do I get there?
How do I pay for school?
What clubs do I belong to?

Recreation & Friendship

Who are my friends?
What do I do with my friends?
Am I dating or married?
What do I do for fun?
What are my hobbies?

Figure 2.   Future-planning questions for youth.

ing youth select activity goals based on how important specific activity options are to
them, the extent to which activity goals are "the best place to start," and the likelihood
that adults in the teenagers' lives will support their choices. The final step is accomplished by narrowing each goal to even more specific activities that an adolescent can
accomplish in a brief period and, ideally, accomplish repeatedly. An example of goal
narrowing is shown in Figure 3.

Adolescents often experience difficulty in setting goals and require structure,
encouragement, and assistance. Typical problems include identifying goals that are too
broad, such as "making friends" or struggling with deciding exactly which goals to pick
when there are many options. Youth benefit from coaching to help them identify
options for narrowing their goals. For example, "making friends" may be narrowed to
"saying hi to other students in the hall at school, calling a friend on the phone, or having a party," depending on their interests and current level of friendship skill. Coaching youth to select goals may involve helping them gradually reduce their list of

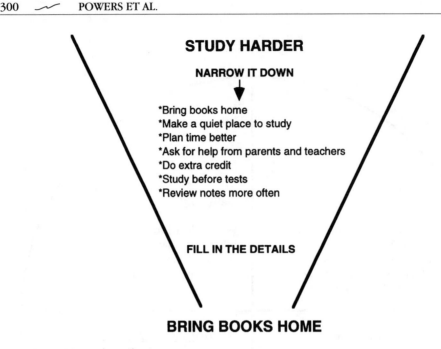

STUDY HARDER

NARROW IT DOWN

*Bring books home
*Make a quiet place to study
*Plan time better
*Ask for help from parents and teachers
*Do extra credit
*Study before tests
*Review notes more often

FILL IN THE DETAILS

BRING BOOKS HOME

Figure 3.　Activity goal specification strategy.

options to those activities youth and coaches agree are achievable and personally important. If necessary to maintain the youth's momentum, activities can be selected from this reduced list by a blind drawing or a coin flip. Ultimately, the specific activities selected are usually less important for building self-determination than is a youth's valuing and achieving whatever goal is picked.

Problem-Solve　Following goal selection, youth learn a simple three-step approach to problem solving ways to accomplish their goals. This process is presented in Table 2. First, youth identify the parts or subactivities that have to be accomplished by anyone to perform the activity. In effect, youth learn how to perform rudimentary task analysis. The second step of problem solving involves having youth identify exactly what will be hard for them in performing each step. Identifying these "hard parts" can be accomplished through abstract reasoning, by asking the opinions of others aware of the requirements of the activity and the youth's capabilities, or by actually trying each step. The final step involves youth using brainstorming to identify all sorts of new strategies to make each hard part easier and selecting the best strategy to try. Youth are encouraged to be creative and to solicit the ideas of others. Generally, the best strategy is the method that is feasible for a youth and maximizes his or her independence.

Problem solving is initially difficult for many adolescents. They often have a history of limited access to life experiences and information about the requirements of activities and solution options (McCarthy, 1986). Many youth with challenges also have a history of being provided with well-meaning assistance from others that inadvertently deprives them of opportunities to learn problem-solving skills. As a result, youth often need coaching to identify activity requirements and potential solutions. For example, it is common for youth to be able to identify approximately 20% of the activity requirements for achieving a goal during their initial attempts at problem solving. At this point, it is appropriate for facilitators to heavily praise youth for identifying those requirements while also providing youth with information about additional require-

Table 2. Problem-solving strategy

Name Jose   Date May 22   Activity Apply for a summer job

Parts	What is hard to do	New strategies
1. Go to the SuperSack.	Getting to the store.	1. Ask folks or friend for a ride. **2. Take the bus.** 3. Ride bike.
2. Ask for an application.	—	
3. Fill out the application.	Remembering information for the application.	**1. Write down information ahead of time and bring it with me.** 2. Take Mom along to fill it out for me. 3. Bring application home to fill it out.
4. Return the application.	—	
5. Wait 3–4 days.	Remembering to call.	1. Ask my parents to remind me. **2. Write it down on the calendar.** **3. Put up Take Charge reminder.**
6. Call the store.	—	
7. Ask if they have made any decisions about my application.	Knowing what to say.	1. Ask my friends. 2. Ask my teachers or parents. **3. Write out a script to use when I call.**

Note: Boldfaced entries indicate the strategy chosen.

ments. As a youth becomes more familiar with the processes, his or her facilitator can gradually increase expectations for the youth's problem-solving performance and fade the assistance he or she provides.

Prepare   The successful performance of most activities requires thorough preparation. After adolescents problem solve exactly how they will perform activities, they learn how to identify and carry out arrangements to execute their strategies. For example, parents may need to be asked if they can provide transportation to the movies on Friday night, or adaptive equipment may need to be ordered to enable a youth to use the phone to call a friend.

It is fairly common for youth to experience difficulty following through in their execution of preparation activities. This lack of follow-through is often misinterpreted as resistance or lack of motivation, with the typical adult response being to ask youth why they won't do specific preparation activities. Youth commonly respond by communicating that they don't care or that the activity is "dumb," thus supporting a motivational explanation for their resistance. Motivation may provide an accurate explanation in some cases. In many cases, however, lack of follow-through by youth is indicative of inadequate skills or support to effectively carry out preparation activities. Most teenagers are reluctant to admit that they don't know how to perform activities or that they need help. As such, it is usually not productive to push them for an explanation of their resistance. The most effective response typically involves coaching adolescents to further problem solve their preparation activities and to identify strategies and supports they can use to carry them out. Youth must be provided with adequate assistance to identify strategies for completing preparation activities that are within the scope of their current capabilities, and they must also receive support to accomplish preparation activities that they aren't able to perform independently. Otherwise, they are likely to experience preparation as a punishing experience that isn't worth their efforts and to give up working toward their goals.

Do it!   The final and most important accomplishment strategy in *TAKE CHARGE* involves executing one's game plan to successfully perform an activity. This is the time a youth applies for that job she identified, calls that friend, goes to a school club meeting, takes the city bus to shop, or begins to regularly do her math homework. It is through successful, self-attributed achievement of their goals that youth ultimately promote their self-determination. It is critical that youth gain experience in repeatedly achieving their goals and that faciliators provide coaching necessary to ensure youth have reasonable probabilities of success. Once youth experience their personal success, they often demonstrate increasing enthusiasm for working toward additional goals and become more resilient when faced with challenges (Seligman, 1990).

Partnership Strategies   In the context of learning to apply the achievement strategies outlined here, youth also learn and practice specific partnership development skills. Implicit within the *TAKE CHARGE* model is an assumption that we are all interdependent; thus, independence can be expressed either through independent action or by actively soliciting and managing assistance provided by others. Neither of these strategies is less valuable for independence than the other; however, independent action is considered the strategy of choice when feasible for the individual.

To promote their preparation for adult life, their abilities to advocate for needed services, and their personal empowerment, students with disabilities must learn to assume control for mobilizing and directing partnerships with others. *TAKE CHARGE* provides two types of opportunities for youth to learn strategies for partnership development. First, facilitators help youth learn to effectively manage the assistance they require to implement the achievement strategies in *TAKE CHARGE* by providing students with opportunities to solicit and direct the help that facilitators provide. Rather than directly offering assistance, facilitators help youth to identify their assistance needs and make themselves available as helping resources that youth must elect to use. Facilitator assistance is provided only with the knowledge and consent of youth. In addition to learning how to direct assistance from their facilitators, youth learn to apply several specific partnership promotion strategies to advance their goal achievement.

Schmooze   To schmooze is to "be friendly," "chat," or otherwise engage in positive conversation with others. Schmoozing helps to create an environment of positive interaction upon which more directive communication is conducted. Schmoozing is often utilized by skilled communicators. Most adolescents have difficulty schmoozing, particularly with adults with whom they wish to express their viewpoints and assert their independence. In the *TAKE CHARGE* model, youth are provided with opportunities to practice schmoozing in the context of sharing their dreams, goals, and game plans with adults who are important in their lives. Many youth prepare outlines or scripts for talking with specific adults and practice during rehearsals with their facilitators. Youth are encouraged to integrate a positive presentation of their desires and plans with expressions of appreciation for others' support and interest in others' lives and opinions.

Be Assertive   Assertiveness refers to the ability to express needs directly and to act with self-confidence (Des Jardins, 1986). Assertiveness training has been used widely with populations without disabilities and has been shown to be effective for individuals with disabilities (Granat, 1978; Heimberg, Montgomery, Madsen, & Heimberg, 1977). Skills such as establishing positive body language, communicating clearly, using stop-action communication techniques, and managing others' resistance are important components of assertiveness (Jakubowski & Lange, 1978). Many adolescents are motivated to behave assertively; however, they typically err toward passive or aggressive responses that fail to provide opportunities for them to demonstrate their competence or build positive rapport.

In the context of preparing to share their goals, youth learn to apply a three-step assertiveness strategy: 1) look others in the eye; 2) speak calmly and firmly; and 3) if others disagree, repeat what you want and explain your reason. After thorough preparation, most youth are able to positively and clearly communicate their goals and solicit support. Typically youth report that this experience has a positive impact on their self-confidence, and parents report that they are surprised and favorably impressed by the presentations of their sons and daughters.

Negotiate   Engagement in skillful win–win negotiation can be a fairly complex and demanding process (Fisher & Ury, 1981). However, possessing rudimentary negotiation skill is essential if one is to navigate the many systemic and interpersonal obstacles to goal achievement. *TAKE CHARGE* provides opportunities for adolescents to practice negotiation in the context of sharing goals and making arrangements with others as they prepare to do activities. Youth learn a three-step negotiation strategy: 1) listen to what others want, 2) decide what you can live with, and 3) compromise (find a solution both of you can accept). Our experience suggests that adolescents of diverse cognitive abilities can learn to enhance their negotiation skills. Critical for their success is an opportunity for advance consideration of acceptable alternatives and rehearsal of negotiation interactions.

Manage Help   Providing youth with systematic strategies to solicit and direct the assistance they receive is considered essential for their development of independence and perceptions of self-efficacy and for their abilities to supervise support providers as adults (Vash, 1981). Evidence in the independent living literature indicates that consumer-directed personal service assistance is associated with enhancement in consumer activity, quality of life, and consumer ability ratings (Conservation Company and Human Organization Science Institute, 1986). Youth who are able to direct their support through active participation and management are likely to both feel a sense of added control over their lives and to experience a higher quality of life (DeJong, 1979; Sailor, Gee, Goetz, & Graham, 1988; Ulicny & Jones, 1987).

For virtually all youth, successful performance of goal activities necessitates using assistance from others. *TAKE CHARGE* presents assistance management in three major classes: getting information (introduced as a method for learning about goal options), asking for a one-time favor (presented in the context of making activity preparation arrangements), and managing ongoing help (discussed in the context of performing activity goals). Youth learn to apply the same three-step strategy across each class of assistance management: 1) decide *what* you need, 2) pick *who* will help, and 3) tell them *how* to help. Youth then learn simple substeps in association with each strategy. For example, the substeps for "tell them *how* to help" are 1) communicate what you want done, 2) stop and correct them if they do something wrong, and 3) say "thank you" when they are done. Facilitators encourage youth who must rely intensively on support from others to focus most intensively on bolstering and practicing their assistance management skills. Youth also are encouraged to identify ways in which they may be able to assist others, promoting reciprocity and mutual support in their relationships.

Coping Strategies   There is growing acknowledgment that effective coping with personal challenges is critical for the development of self-esteem, self-confidence, and self-determination. Self-efficacy is fostered through mastery experiences involving both performance success and effective management of obstacles (Biran & Wilson, 1981). Evidence also suggests that self-esteem is positively influenced through successful coping with difficult experiences as well as through success experiences (Bednar, Wells, & Peterson, 1989).

TAKE CHARGE introduces youth to four specific coping skills considered essential for achievement and effective management of personal obstacles. These skills are presented in the context of youth progression through the five primary achievement strategies, with their introduction timed to coincide with the emergence of typical coping dilemmas encountered during goal pursuit.

Think Positive   There is a growing body of literature indicating that feedback such as self-talk is effective in assisting people to shape their own behavior (Dush, Hirt, & Schroeder, 1989). Positive self-talk, although an extremely valuable skill, is difficult for many youth to understand and to learn to modify. Youth are typically unaware that they engage in internal dialogue that influences how they respond to difficult situations. To promote their acquisition of this skill, *TAKE CHARGE* begins by initially asking youth to generate positive self-statements and then introduces youth to analyzing specific self-statements they make in association with events such as preparing for communication encounters with their parents and considering their success in achieving goals. Youth are encouraged to immunize themselves with positive affirmations and to refute pervasive negative self-statements. For example, if a teenager loses her temper and argues with her parent about a goal, she is encouraged to shift negative self-statements such as "I can't talk to people" to self-statements such as "I lost it with my mom...I will learn to keep it together better the next time."

Focus on Accomplishments Through self-monitoring of their own skillfulness, people have opportunities to observe their competence and, as a result, begin to view themselves as more competent (Dowrick, 1983). In turn, they actually begin to demonstrate higher levels of skill (Gonzales & Dowrick, 1983). Youth, like the rest of us, seldom attend to their accomplishments or positive experiences. *TAKE CHARGE* provides specific opportunities for adolescents to focus on and communicate their accomplishments. On a regular basis, youth are invited to list accomplishments they are proud of, and they are encouraged to boast a bit about their successes with their peers and adults. Although many youth initially regard noting their accomplishments as a "dumb" exercise, facilitators consistently report that youth demonstrate growing pride in their efforts and capabilities as they repeat this process. Learning to attend to personal accomplishments is considered an essential core skill for promoting self-attributions of competence.

Manage Frustration Striving to achieve personal goals is typically associated with experiences of situational mastery and failure. Youth skilled in the use of problem-focused and emotion-focused coping strategies are optimally prepared to effectively respond to obstacles (Compas, 1987). Problem-focused techniques such as problem solving are appropriate coping strategies in situations in which an obstacle can be overcome, whereas emotion-focused strategies are helpful in instances in which an outcome cannot be controlled (Folkman & Lazarus, 1980). Generally, coping responses that emphasize situational, depersonalized, and temporary interpretations of negative events are associated with heightened perseverance through failure and frustration (Seligman, 1990).

Frustration is a normal response in situations in which goals are not achieved quickly or adequately enough. Learning to productively manage frustration is important if youth are to avoid demoralization and maintain their momentum for goal attainment. *TAKE CHARGE* encourages youth to use emotion-focused and problem-focused methods to manage their frustration. As discussed above, they are encouraged to use positive self-talk to reframe failure as a temporary, situational event. They are also encouraged to depersonalize failures by attributing the problem to a flawed game plan rather than to personal failings. To the extent that youth learn to attribute failure to a flawed plan, they are able to respond by problem solving new strategies that will bolster their probability for future success.

Track and Reward Progress Tracking and rewarding one's progress toward goal attainment is a form of self-regulation. Self-regulation encompasses self-monitoring, self-evaluation, and self-reinforcement (Schunk, 1989a, 1989b). Self-regulation is associated with enhancement of personal empowerment, autonomy, and internal locus of control (Brigham, 1989; Williams & Long, 1979). These skills are critical for youth who are making the transition from controlled school environments into an adult world in which rules are often ambiguous and external reinforcement is rare. Self-regulation is also an important skill for promoting autonomy in situations in which others seek to exert influence or control.

The effectiveness of reinforcement methods for assisting people to accurately perform activities is also well substantiated (Bellamy, Horner, & Inman, 1979). Evidence indicates that the learned helplessness of adolescents with disabilities is exacerbated by noncontingent rewards (Kleinhammer-Tramill et al., 1983). Accurate self-monitoring, self-feedback, and contingent delivery of valued rewards by youth appear to provide an effective method to enhance self-determination.

TAKE CHARGE provides repeated opportunities for youth to monitor and reward their efforts and progress toward goal attainment. Youth are encouraged to identify and deliver personal rewards in association with acknowledgment of their accomplishments and efforts toward achieving their goals. Rewards range from asking parents to set up an allowance arrangement, to going to the movies, to sleeping in late on Saturday.

Component 2: Mentorship

Mentorship refers to a personal relationship between a mentor, or a role model who has achieved success in a particular area and who demonstrates personal commitment to supporting another less experienced person, and a protégé, or a person who desires to develop in that area and wants to learn from the mentor (Haensly & Parsons, 1993). Parents are the first mentors for most children. Teachers often provide the next level of mentoring for school-age children. As children move through adolescence and toward adulthood, adults from the community often assume this role.

Mentor relationships are typically founded on shared experience between mentor and protégé. Mentors share their expertise and enthusiasm, demonstrate methods to achieve goals and overcome barriers, and provide encouragement and guidance to aspiring protégés. Mentors also provide a protected relationship in which learning and experimentation can occur and potential skills can be developed (Boston, 1976).

It is clear that mentoring is a popular approach for promoting living skills, a positive view of disability, knowledge, self-confidence, and motivation of youth with disabilities (Fredericks, 1988; Jones & Ulicny, 1986; Rhodes, 1994). Evidence suggests that interaction with adult role models who experience disabilities enhances the disability-related knowledge and self-confidence of adolescents with disabilities and also enhances parent perceptions of the knowledge and capabilities of their children with disabilities (Powers, Sowers, et al., 1995).

Youth who participate in *TAKE CHARGE* are matched to successful adults of the same gender who experience similar challenges and share common interests. The *TAKE CHARGE* mentor program has typically been implemented by a local independent living program; however, mentor programs can be feasibly conducted by schools or other community organizations. Mentors are recruited through local colleges, independent living programs, disability-related organizations and support groups, and other community organizations. Adults selected to be mentors live independently, are employed or active in a volunteer vocation, demonstrate commitment to mentorship, and present a positive view of disability. Mentors participate in an 8-hour training program during which the purpose of mentoring and their roles and responsibilities are explained, instruction and role-play practice is provided related to positive communication strategies with adolescents and their parents; procedures for selecting, organizing, and implementing activities with youth are detailed; and common challenges for mentors and youth are problem-solved.

Mentors are introduced to their protégé and their protégé's parents during a visit to the protégé's home. During the visit, the mentor program coordinator reviews the purpose and structure of the program with the youth and parent and conducts a structured interview to ascertain the youth's needs while in the community. Specific procedures for handling any special needs are defined and recorded.

Protégés and their mentors participate in monthly community-based activities over a 6- to 9-month period. Mentors and their protégés complete a form that describes each planned activity and associated logistical arrangements. Youth are required to have their parents sign their activity forms and mail them to the mentor program coordinator. Although mentors and protégés are free to perform any activities they choose, they are encouraged to select activities that will provide opportunities for youth to learn about living successfully as an adult with disability. Participants are provided with a list of activity categories from which they might choose: 1) employment/continuing education, 2) recreation, 3) community resources, 4) independent living, 5) novel activities that youth are interested in trying, and 6) activities with the protégé's parent. For example, in the employment/continuing education category, youth may elect to visit their mentors' jobs, go to a job fair, request a meeting of their transition teams to discuss supports needed to find a job, visit a college, or arrange to meet with a person who is employed doing a job that interests the protégé.

Mentors and youth are contacted by the Mentor Program Coordinator following each activity. They debrief on the events of the prior activity and discuss preparation for the following activity. Mentors are assisted in anticipating opportunities to provide relevant information, addressing particular issues, modeling strategies within the context of upcoming activities, or trouble shooting any difficulties they are having in their interactions with youth or parents. Parents are also contacted regularly to solicit their perceptions and ideas regarding their children's mentoring experiences. This level of program support is essential to ensure successful mentoring experiences for youth, parents, and mentors.

Mentors are provided with a checklist of important themes to address with protégés and their parents at some point during their time together. Themes include encouraging the youth to ask questions about the mentor's challenge, sharing information about past experiences in coping with disability-related barriers, and emphasizing the importance of decision making, self-advocacy, responsible risk taking, and perseverance. Themes directed to parents include acknowledging and encouraging parent efforts to promote protégé transition to adult roles and pointing out protégé strengths and accomplishments observed during mentoring interactions.

Skill facilitation and mentorship activities can be creatively integrated to provide coordinated opportunities for youth to work toward goals or develop related partnership skills. For example, youth who identify community involvement goals such as riding the city bus may receive school-based coaching from their facilitators to develop their game plans while actually implementing their activities with support provided by their mentors. Likewise, a youth's mentor and facilitator may decide to jointly encourage the youth to give more thought to attending college or to practicing positive self-talk. The successful coordination of facilitator and mentor efforts requires ongoing communication and collaboration among the mentor, facilitator, and youth.

Component 3: Peer Support

Since the mid-1980s, much emphasis has been focused on the importance of promoting interaction between youth with and without disabilities. It is clear that the development of relationships among youth of diverse capabilities generally promotes the well-being of all participants (Bricker, 1978; Gaylord-Ross, Haring, Breen, & Pitts-Conway, 1984). However, as youth with disabilities become increasingly included in typical settings, it is important to acknowledge that they may have fewer opportunities to learn from and share support with their peers without disabilities about challenge-related issues such as getting around the community, explaining disability to peers and employers, identifying adaptations, self-advocacy, or managing personal assistant services.

Peer support among people with disabilities can be a powerful method to enhance self-determination, self-acceptance, and leadership (Jones & Ulicny, 1986; Williams & Shoultz, 1984). Intervention by a peer counselor with a disability can also significantly accelerate the transition to independent living for an individual with a disability (Saxton, 1983). Through interaction with their peers with disabilities, youth have opportunities to learn and practice self-determination and leadership skills, to share strategies for managing disability-related barriers, and to receive support for self-acceptance.

TAKE CHARGE provides individual and group peer support opportunities for youth with disabilities. The nature and content of these opportunities strongly reflect the preferences of youth participants and include workshops and individual support.

Workshops   Youth are invited to participate in workshops that provide information and support related to life options, disability-related resources, and self-advocacy strategies. Workshops also provide youth with ongoing opportunities to share successful strategies and to validate their personal challenges and accomplishments. Workshops are typically conducted by independent living program staff, and adult mentors are invited to participate. Typical workshop topics are presented in Table 3. Workshops are cofacilitated by staff and youth volunteers who present information, lead discussion groups or structured exercises, and participate in special events such as writing and performing a one-act play related to a particular workshop topic.

Individual Support   In addition to participating in peer support workshops, youth are encouraged to network with one another. Some youth choose to have telephone, face-to-face, or computer-based contact with one another, whereas others do not. Individual networking is facilitated through circulation of a phone list of youth participants, e-mail and computer bulletin boards, and informal assistance to help youth identify other youth with whom they might benefit from talking. For example, one teenager preparing for surgery was encouraged to contact, accept a phone call from, or meet with a peer who had experience with that surgery. The two teens elected to meet at a fast food restaurant and spent about an hour discussing what surgery might be like and possible strategies to get through it. Following this initial interaction, the teenagers maintained their contact by telephone.

Additional Approaches to Peer Support   Peer support opportunities can be creatively fostered by schools and community organizations utilizing a variety of approaches such as 1) integrating challenge-specific peer support into existing peer support programs, 2) establishing databases of youth who are interested in providing specific forms of support and matching these youth to youth requesting support, and 3) developing individual or group peer support opportunities to address specific populations or problems (e.g., support between underachieving girls and girls who have

Table 3.   Peer support conference topics

• Living with disability	• Community resources for independence
• Dating and marriage	• Managing help from others
• Friendship	• Building self-esteem and personal confidence
• Self-advocacy	• Recreation options
• Getting a job	• Negotiating with doctors
• Going to college	

overcome obstacles to achievement, support between youth recently exposed to violence and youth who have experience coping with violence, or support between middle school youth preparing for their transition to high school and high school students who successfully navigated their transition).

An outcome of implementing *TAKE CHARGE* in New Hampshire has been the establishment of a statewide peer support and community education program called Teens Coping (Calling on Peers for Independent Nonjudgmental Guidance). A student-directed network, Teens Coping matches youth who contact the program for support with teenagers experienced in the specific area in which support is requested (e.g., dealing with teasing). Experienced teens receive training in peer support and ongoing coaching from the program coordinator. In addition to providing individual support, Teens Coping members also conduct workshops and presentations for educators, parents, and medical providers. Typically, youth presenters share their perspectives about particular issues and suggest strategies parents and professionals can use to support adolescents.

Component 4: Parent Support

Parents generally agree that self-determination opportunities are very important for their children (Brotherson et al., 1988) and parents play critical roles in supporting their children's development of self-determination (Fewell & Vadasy, 1986; Turnbull & Turnbull, 1986; also see Chapter 4). Historically, many self-determination interventions have either neglected to integrate parent involvement or have focused on *instructing* parents in specific methods to promote the self-determination of their sons and daughters, evaluating parental support based upon compliance with prescribed recommendations (see Chapter 10). Such approaches have failed to acknowledge that parents generally know their children's strengths and challenges better than anyone and that the expression of self-determination by youth is typically negotiated between youth and parents within the context of individual family culture and circumstance.

Parents generally try their best to facilitate their son's and daughter's development of competence, and they are keenly aware of barriers to their efforts. Our experience suggests that parents often encounter four major obstacles as they attempt to promote their son's or daughter's self-determination. First, many parents are unclear about how much self-determination they should expect from their children. They may lack reference points about typical levels of self-determination expressed by youth who do not experience disabilities. If this information is available, parents may have difficulty translating it into appropriate expectations for their children with challenges. Second, parents may be uncertain about strategies they could effectively use to encourage their son's or daughter's development of self-determination. Their uncertainty may be based upon inadequate information regarding potential strategies or concerns about selecting strategies that are likely to promote their children's success and yet guard against threats to child safety if strategies are unsuccessful. Parents generally want to be reasonably sure that serious harm will not result from permitting their children to take certain risks. Third, some families may have different cultural meanings and expectations for their children's expression of self-determination. These families may find that their deviation from common Anglo American expectations may pose their greatest obstacle (see Chapter 10). A fourth obstacle for some families is the presence of multiple stressors that prevent parents from supporting the self-determination of their children. Such stressors may include poverty, unemployment, health problems, marital discord, or problems affecting other children in the family. Many parents of adolescents also experience stress and fatigue associated with years of struggling to advocate for their children with little support.

It is essential that self-determination models acknowledge, respect, and respond to parent perspectives regarding their desires, capabilities, and barriers to promoting the self-determination of their children. Methods that might be used to support parents include 1) acknowledging the many ways in which parents already successfully support their children (Summers, Behr, & Turnbull, 1989), 2) respecting family norms guiding child expression of self-determination (see Chapter 10), 3) offering technical assistance to help parents identify potential strategies they would like to use to promote the self-determination of their sons and daughters, 4) providing parents with information about the typical emergence of self-determination during adolescence and resources available to support their son's or daughter's optimal expression of self-determination (Sowers, 1989), 5) introducing parents to self-determined adults who experience challenges similar to those of their son or daughter (Powers, Sowers, et al., 1995), 6) supporting parents as they attempt to balance encouraging self-determination with providing a safety net for the autonomous activities of their children (Espinosa & Shearer, 1986), and 7) assisting parents as they manage family stressors that impede their capacities to support the well-being of family members (Singer & Irvin, 1989).

The *TAKE CHARGE* model focuses on promoting partnerships among youth, parents, and professionals aimed at facilitating the self-determination of youth. These partnerships emphasize collaboration, respect for family norms and preferences, flexibility, and parent-to-parent support. Three specific forms of support are offered to parents: information and technical assistance, written materials, and parent-to-parent contact.

Information and Technical Assistance Information and technical assistance can be offered to parents both by facilitators coaching youth through *TAKE CHARGE* and by staff or volunteers from collaborating parent support programs. Information and technical assistance are generally provided by facilitators to ensure that parents are kept informed of their son's or daughter's activities in *TAKE CHARGE,* and their input is solicited regarding methods that may be useful in promoting their children's skill development. Facilitators provide parents with monthly updates regarding their children's achievements, goals, and upcoming experiences in *TAKE CHARGE.* Updates may be provided through brief telephone conversations, positive messages left on answering machines, or personal notes. If an adolescent is likely to select a goal or strategy that the facilitator believes may be problematic for his or her parent, the facilitator coaches the youth to positively communicate and negotiate the choice with his or her parent. With the knowledge of the youth, the facilitator also contacts the parent to prepare him or her for the child's upcoming communication and to support the parent's role in defining acceptable parameters for the child's goals and activities. Facilitators generally try to assist parents and youth to identify win–win compromise solutions; however, they also emphasize with youth their responsibilities to function within parameters comfortable for their parents. Many youth may desire to push these limits, but they are encouraged to advocate for small steps that their parents will accept.

In conjunction with their regular check-ins with parents, facilitators or parent support staff provide opportunities for parents to identify their children's strengths and successes in promoting their children's positive self-attributions, decision making efforts, autonomous behavior, or effective management of challenges. Supporters may share progress they are observing in youth at school and ask parents to describe any progress they are observing at home. Parents are also encouraged to share their ideas about strategies they use successfully to promote their children's growing autonomy and self-confidence. Often these conversations focus on brainstorming between parents and support staff to identify strategies that have promise or are not likely to work. Given the busy lives of most parents, these discussions often provide some of the few opportunities for parents to consciously process their children's development and to receive acknowledgment for their efforts to support their children. Such conversations also provide support staff with opportunities to learn from parents.

Rather than exclusively focus on what parents do or could do to provide special support to their children with disabilities, parent support staff or volunteers try to validate that parents have a right to typical expectations for their children and do not have to center their lives around their adolescents with disabilities. During typical adolescence, it is common for parents to begin to plan for their lives after their children become more self-sufficient young adults. As parents dream about their personal plans for their future lives with less dependent children, their dreams may motivate their identification of additional expectations for their children's autonomy. For instance, a parent may dream of returning to college or work. With that dream in mind, the parent may become more keenly aware of the level of autonomous behavior required by his or her children to make feasible returning to college or work and raise her expectations accordingly.

Many parents of adolescents with disabilities receive little encouragement to identify future dreams independent of their children. As a result, they may miss typical developmental opportunities to use their dreams as a stimulus to formulate enhanced expectations for their children's autonomous behavior. Our experience suggests that many parents are invigorated by being encouraged to dream about their own lives, and this approach helps parents to more clearly identify the progression of independent behavior they will need from their children if the parents are to realize their family dreams. This approach can also be effective in assisting parents and youth to identify and advocate for community supports the son or daughter needs to achieve optimal levels of typical adult living.

Parent support organizations participating in *TAKE CHARGE* also are available to provide general family support. It is essential to recognize that families have many competing, interrelated demands, one of those being to promote the growing autonomy of their children. If families are not supported in addressing the needs they identify as most important, they will be unlikely to be interested in, or benefit from, other forms of support. As such, priorities for parent support in *TAKE CHARGE* may include providing information about community resources, helping parents gain access to financial resources and services, or providing crisis intervention. Regardless of the formal roles of staff, they must be willing and prepared to be flexible in assisting families to gain access to the supports that families identify as important.

Written Materials   Parents are provided with a parent guide that overviews three major topics using family-friendly language (Powers & Matuszewski, 1995). First, general information is provided about the normative emergence of self-determination among typical adolescents and the challenges that teenagers with disabilities and their parents sometimes face that may impede their progression along typical developmental paths. Second, the guide discusses strategies youth learn through *TAKE CHARGE* and provides menus of various methods parents might use to facilitate their son's or daughter's use of strategies. Parents are provided with written exercises they can complete to gain personal exposure to some of the strategies their children are learning. For instance, parents are invited to dream about their personal futures, set a short-term goal, and do some basic problem solving. Finally, the guide presents some common challenges families face in promoting the self-determination of their teenage children and provides some potential solutions. In addition to the parent guide, parents are individually provided with bulletins, publications, and information sheets that describe specific resources and strategies relevant to their unique needs and interests.

Parent-to-Parent Support   A parent-to-parent approach recognizes that parents provide the most empathetic, informed, and legitimate source of support to other parents (Santelli, Turnbull, Lerner, & Marquis, 1993). Although professionals have traditionally provided much parent support, there is growing recognition of the value of peer support among parents for facilitating parent knowledge, skill development, and empowerment. The rapid expansion of parent-to-parent programs throughout the United States is testimony to the emergence of mutual support as a major helping strategy.

TAKE CHARGE uses two major strategies to facilitate parent-to-parent support. First and foremost, model implementation is conducted in collaboration with local parent support organizations. Ideally, an arrangement is made with a parent program for a staff member or volunteer who has some personal experience in parenting adolescents with challenges to be available to parents of youth participating in *TAKE CHARGE*. Depending on individual family need, availability may translate into information and occasional telephone contacts, matching to supporting parents, or more intensified assistance. Because providing this type of support is already within the scope of most parent programs, many are willing to discuss ways they can work as partners with schools and independent living programs to provide integrated supports to youth and their parents.

A second type of parent-to-parent contact is provided through monthly parent workshops, typically conducted in association with peer support workshops for youth. Workshop topics are defined by parents, who are invited to identify issues they would like to learn about and discuss with other parents. Common workshop topics include options for adult life, advocacy, promoting teenager friendships, negotiating with teenagers, taking care of oneself, community resources for families, and transition planning. In some cases, parents, youths, and mentors may meet to share information or listen to a topic of mutual interest. After this activity, parents meet in separate groups for follow-up discussion. Workshops generally include presentation of information requested by parents, opportunity for parents to share their ideas and experiences, and discussion of methods parents might use to apply the information or strategies discussed. Parents are also encouraged to network with one another outside of the meetings. Telephone numbers are typically exchanged and parent support staff encourage parents dealing with common issues to contact one another.

TAKE CHARGE CASE ILLUSTRATIONS

This section provides case descriptions of the experiences of three youth and their parents who participated in *TAKE CHARGE*. These examples are provided to illustrate the integrated implementation and the impact of major model components.

Lee

Lee was a 17-year-old male who participated in *TAKE CHARGE* during his junior year in high school. Lee had spina bifida and mild mental retardation. He used a manual wheelchair and was fully included in his local high school with a modified curriculum. Lee required extensive assistance to accomplish his personal care, and his family was experiencing intense strain and discord associated with meeting Lee's ongoing care demands. Lee expressed much uncertainty and concern about the future, and his parents indicated that they might be forced to locate a residential placement for Lee if additional supports were not available to them.

Through *TAKE CHARGE,* Lee dreamed of eventually living independently, driving a car, and going to college. Lee realized that achieving these dreams would require him to assume greater responsibility for taking care of his personal needs. After self-assessment of his current capabilities, Lee identified two major goals: to make his bathroom accessible and to use the bathroom independently.

Lee problem-solved the requirements for adapting his bathroom and identified strategies he would use to locate a contractor, to identify the specific adaptations he required, and to obtain the funding. Lee benefited from step-by-step coaching in ways to identify and organize the strategies he would use. With systematic coaching and some *in situ* support from his facilitator, Lee completed various preparation tasks such as calling contractors, getting bids and working with his parents to prepare a list of required bathroom renovations. During the course of these activities, Lee's mother commented that he was already beginning to assume new responsibility for dressing and taking care of his personal belongings. She reported that Lee's demeanor had become more positive, and he was expressing satisfaction about doing more for himself.

Lee's parents were concurrently provided with support by a parent support coordinator from the local parent-to-parent program. The parent coordinator assisted Lee's parents in applying for and successfully obtaining additional services and financial assistance through the local developmental disabilities agency. In addition to agreeing to provide Lee with adult services support following graduation from high school, the agency identified funding to pay for Lee's bathroom modifications. Lee's parents were also provided with information about additional transition resources, and they took part in several workshops with other parents of youth participating in *TAKE CHARGE.*

Lee was matched to a young adult mentor who also had spina bifida, lived and worked independently, and drove a car. The two played basketball, visited the independent living center, and attended peer support workshops together. Lee, his mentor, and a same-age friend of Lee's also went out for video games and fast food. Lee's mentor suggested this activity after Lee reported that his friend resisted going out into the community with Lee because he was afraid Lee might have problems and his friend wouldn't know how to respond. During their community outing, Lee's mentor encouraged Lee and his friend to discuss the strategies Lee used to meet his needs in the community and the ways in which this friend might be called on to help. Lee's mentor provided the friend with reassurance that Lee was unlikely to have problems Lee himself could not manage, and, if he did, Lee would provide his friend with specific instructions regarding how to help. After this outing, Lee and his friend began going out into the community regularly.

Lee's bathroom was adapted according to his specifications. He successfully problem solved methods to accomplish all of his personal care activities in the bathroom. Because Lee no longer required his mother's assistance, she was able to return to work. Stress and conflict within Lee's family was significantly reduced. Lee's subsequent goals included conducting career planning, convening a transition planning team, and taking driver's education classes. Lee is currently taking driver's education, he has been accepted to college, and he plans to take courses part-time and work part-time after graduation from high school.

Lee also has joined a peer support program and he is providing support to a younger teenager with spina bifida and participating in community education efforts to promote understanding of the needs of adolescents with health challenges. Lee described his experience:

> Before *TAKE CHARGE* I depended on my mom and dad to help me with a lot of stuff. I felt like I depended on people, I felt like there was more I could do for myself, but I didn't do it. Now I do. I'm willing to try new things, more things than I would before, things that I never thought I'd try. I never thought I'd apply to college, and I've done that. I didn't use to think much about my future. Boy, has that changed. That feels good. Other people notice that I'm doing more, that I'm showing more responsibility.
>
> It felt great achieving my first goal. I knew after getting that first goal that I could definitely accomplish another goal. I was more confident about myself. Now I can figure out ways to do new things. If they are hard for me, I can figure out different ways to do them. A whole lot of things have changed, not just what I worked on; I'm playing pick-up basketball, I have more friends, and even a girlfriend. I feel better about myself, and I'm thinking bigger.

Mary

Mary was a 13-year-old girl who attended a seventh-grade classroom and lived with her mother, stepfather, and three siblings. She experienced severe cerebral palsy and learning challenges, had limited use of one hand, demonstrated a second-grade reading level, and had much difficulty understanding abstract concepts.

Through *TAKE CHARGE*, Mary targeted three primary goals. She wanted to be able to open the choir room door at school, have lunch with a friend, and go to the mall with a friend. Through problem solving, Mary realized she had difficulty grasping the choir room door and backing up her chair in the narrow hallway to open the door. She selected and ordered a rubber grip to place on the door knob. She also planned and conducted several practice sessions to learn how to navigate the hallway while holding the door. As Mary became more proficient, she no longer required the rubber grip.

Like many youth in *TAKE CHARGE,* Mary found her second goal, having lunch with a friend, complicated to achieve. During the course of problem solving, it became clear that Mary defined a friend as one particular student who was unavailable during lunch. Additionally, Mary acknowledged that she had never initiated even a hello to another student and felt very intimidated about talking with others. Through discussion with her facilitator, Mary decided to narrow her goal into some more minor interaction steps that she could work toward in preparation for eating lunch with someone. Mary began by practicing saying hello to other students in the hall. She then expanded her interaction to initiating a brief conversation. Finally, in conjunction with a choir field trip, Mary arranged to eat lunch with a group of other students. In selecting students to approach, Mary was encouraged to begin with students she liked and who appeared to need friends rather than focusing on the most popular students at school. By the end of the school year, Mary had eaten lunch on several occasions with students from her choir class.

During the spring, Mary problem-solved and carefully prepared to go shopping with a neighborhood friend at the mall. Mary asked her friend to go, arranged for transportation with her mother, and saved money for the trip. Mary's facilitator helped her conduct one practice visit to the mall, during which they problem-solved strategies Mary could use to drive her wheelchair, pay for items, and eat a snack. Mary successfully completed this goal and continues to frequent the mall.

Throughout the year, Mary also participated in activities with her mentor. Mary's mentor was a married woman with cerebral palsy. They went to the mall on several occasions, they practiced driving their wheelchairs in the community and reviewed safety strategies, and Mary and her mother visited her mentor's home. Through this experience, Mary became more hopeful about her potential for getting married when she was older, and her mother expressed increased confidence in Mary's safety in the community. Mary's mother was also provided with the parent guide and monthly update and with technical assistance telephone calls from Mary's facilitator.

While participating in *TAKE CHARGE,* Mary also decided to self-advocate with the staff who managed her swimming program. Mary did not like swimming because she had to wait too long to get her bus and she preferred to swim in inclusive classes. As a result of her passive protest, Mary had developed a reputation among the staff as "lazy," and they resisted making any changes to accommodate her. To address this problem, Mary requested that her facilitator help her write a letter that described her problems and potential solutions. Mary then organized a meeting with the pool staff during which she read her letter aloud. Mary requested an opportunity to swim with peers without disabilities, permission to wait for her bus in a more comfortable location than the shower room, and some input into her swimming routine. Mary's requests were well received, and the staff agreed to make some changes to accommodate her.

During an evaluation interview regarding *TAKE CHARGE,* her mother reported the following:

> As far as the project, I think it was really good because it...directed some of her energy into another way to look at things; instead of being so caught up on the negative, she had a lot of positive....she got to do a lot of things with the mentor and got to see another side to somebody else with a disability and how they dealt with things. It taught her a lot more....Like the school meeting. Taking charge of the talking, calling a meeting herself, you know setting the agenda, setting, you know, people there that she wanted, that were gonna participate with her....telling them her goals and following through with them.

Dave

Dave was a 19-year-old male with severe cerebral palsy. He was unable to speak and used a visual tracking communication board. Dave had virtually no use of his limbs: He used a power chair controlled by head movements and required complete assistance to meet all of his personal needs. Dave was also labeled with below-average cognitive abilities and received special educational services. Dave lived with his paternal grandparents in a modest home located in a rural area.

Dave met with his *TAKE CHARGE* facilitator on a weekly basis during the school year. He selected three major activity goals to pursue during the year. Dave's goals were to manage his daily helping routines, to learn about options for housing for people with disabilities, and to organize a team to support his goals.

Dave was introduced to his mentor, an adult with severe cerebral palsy who lived independently. Dave performed many activities with his mentor: improvisational dance lessons, riding in the sidecar of his mentor's bike, adaptive sailing, and spending the night at his mentor's home. Dave also attended monthly peer support workshops with six other youth participating in *TAKE CHARGE.* His grandparents were provided with the parent guide, monthly updates from his facilitator, and individualized support from a parent staff member of the local Direction Services program. Parent support focused on validating the many ways Dave's grandparents were supporting his independence, helping them to obtain respite funding, and supporting them as they attempted to respond to Dave's rapidly increasing demands for autonomy.

Dave problem-solved and prepared to convene monthly transition planning meetings attended by 12 representatives of agencies serving young adults with challenges, including the state Disabled Services agency, vocational rehabilitation, a supported employment program, the local Direction Service program, the independent living program, and the developmental disabilities program. Dave problem-solved strategies to communicate in the meetings, and he gradually assumed greater responsibility for setting and directing the agenda. Coaching focused on assisting Dave to clarify his long-term goals, to consider the outcomes of the preceding meeting, and to plan for the following meeting. By the end of the year, Dave was directing the focus of his meetings, asking members to complete specific activities on his behalf, and monitoring their follow-through. Several outcomes were achieved through the efforts of Dave and his team. Dave was able to hire a personal assistant to help him at home and in the community. Dave also established a plan for self-support that permitted him to save money to purchase a computer to create graphic images on a job the supported employment program was negotiating for him. Finally, Dave applied for both Section 8 housing and personal assistance services in preparation for independent living.

Dave devoted much of his time to learning and applying strategies for management of support. He identified the steps in his major helping routines and developed a support guide that he could show to helpers before they assisted him. Dave made plans to spend several overnight stays with an aide, during which he would practice directing his assistance. Dave agreed that his aide would do exactly what he communicated, no more and no less. Dave became increasingly proficient at directing his support, although on one occasion he became frustrated that his aide did not automatically bring some supplies when they went to the mall. After this incident, Dave indicated he wanted to discontinue his team meetings and was no longer interested in living on his own because it was "too much work." Dave's mentor and facilitator validated his frustration, while also reviewing the progress he had made and emphasizing the implications of disbanding his team. After some reflection, Dave decided that he wanted his team to continue assisting him and that he would continue to work on directing his personal assistance services.

At the conclusion of his participation in *TAKE CHARGE*, Dave decided to maintain his support team and requested that they assist him in making arrangements to spend one weekend per month away from home with a personal assistant. During this period, Dave also wanted to begin working part-time. Dave's team was able to assist him to achieve these goals, and currently he is employed and living in an apartment adjacent to his grandparents' home.

Dave's grandmother reported that *TAKE CHARGE* helped her to encourage Dave's decision making:

> He used to say, "Grandpa, you make something for me," and now he's trying to tell us, you know, that it should be done this way or that way. Well, he tells us that he doesn't want to do this or that…and I'll say, "Make up your mind," you tell me, and like the other day he wanted to get up and he laid there, and he said, "I don't know." I said, "Well, you got to make your mind up, I gotta know what." And so, we were talking and finally he said, "I want to take the manual chair." I said okay, that's all we wanted to know. Now he makes decisions.

IMPLICATIONS FOR PRACTICE

Results from qualitative and recently completed controlled, quantitative evaluation of *TAKE CHARGE* suggest that the model is effective in promoting the self-determination of youth (Powers, Turner, et al., 1995). *TAKE CHARGE* is configured as a highly flexible and collaborative approach that can be adapted to address the needs of diverse populations of youth. Although the integrated delivery of model components is likely to have the most dramatic effect on most youth, individual components can be successfully implemented to address specific youth needs or to accommodate to the resources available for implementation.

In addition to proposing specific intervention processes and options, *TAKE CHARGE* is configured to challenge thinking about effective approaches to promote the self-competence of youth. Approaches must respect youth as effective change agents in their lives, capable of exercising personal control and of decision making. Interventions designed to assist youth must provide for the primary implementation of strategies by youth, with other participants functioning as facilitators and support providers. To do so will require *major* revisions in existing practices and a shift in decision making responsibility at many levels. We must be willing to provide youth with access to information and experiences that will promote their decision making and convey confidence in their abilities to make effective judgments (Mitchell, 1988). Professionals must be provided with facilitative strategies to use for establishing collaborative relationships with youth and parents (Goetz, Anderson, & Laten, 1989; Slater, Martinez, & Habersang, 1989; Walker, 1989).

The collaborative implementation of *TAKE CHARGE* resulted in the development of a highly flexible approach in which model components could be delivered in various forms as a function of student needs and local conditions. Interagency collaboration also stimulated high-quality model development by promoting exchange of information and support among school and community programs. The reality is that the needs of youth and the organization of our society are far too complex to successfully compartmentalize programs in isolated settings. Many challenges facing youth cannot be successfully addressed within the confines of the school walls or by individual community agencies. Schools, agencies, and mutual support programs must work together to design integrated resource-efficient approaches to support adolescents and their families. The definition and scope of such collaboration is limited only by creativity and by willingness to think beyond our traditional notions about organizational roles and supports for youth.

There are many thousands of youth in America, with and without disabilities, who are struggling with underachievement, depression, dependence, and low self-confidence. Many of these youth have vague dreams for their futures but little awareness of the personal strengths or strategies they might use to move forward toward successful adult lives. Without intervention, they are likely to undergo a transition into marginal lives and to be overly reliant on societal support. These youth are capable of taking charge of their lives if provided with the opportunities, information, skills, and supports to do so. It is essential for us to join with them in this effort.

REFERENCES

Allsop, J. (1980). Mainstreaming physically handicapped students. *Journal of Research and Development in Education, 13*(4), 37–44.

Arborelius, E., & Bremberg, S. (1991). How do teenagers respond to a consistently student-centered program of health education at school? *International Journal of Adolescent Medicine and Health, 5*(2), 95–112.

Bandura, A. (1977). Self-efficacy: Toward a unifying theory of behavior change. *Psychological Review, 84*, 191–215.

Bandura, A. (1986). *Social foundation of thought and action: A social cognitive theory.* New York: Prentice Hall.

Bednar, R.L., Wells, M.G., & Peterson, S.R. (1989). *Self-esteem: Paradoxes and innovations in clinical theory and practice.* Washington, DC: American Psychological Association.

Bellamy, G.T., Horner, R.H., & Inman, D.P. (1979). *Vocational habilitation of severely retarded adults.* Baltimore: University Park Press.

Biran, M., & Wilson, G.T. (1981). Treatment of phobic disorders using cognitive and exposure methods: A self-efficacy analysis. *Journal of Consulting and Clinical Psychology, 49,* 886–899.

Bolles, R.N. (1995). *The 1995 what color is your parachute? A practical manual for job-hunters and career-changers.* Berkeley, CA: Ten Speed Press.

Boston, B.O. (1976). *The sorcerer's apprentice: A case study in the role of the mentor.* Reston, VA: Council for Exceptional Children.

Bricker, D.D. (1978). A rationale for the integration of handicapped preschool children. In M.J. Guralnick (Ed.), *Early intervention and the integrating of handicapped and nonhandicapped children* (pp. 3–26). Baltimore: University Park Press.

Brigham, T.A. (1989). *Self-management for adolescents: A skills training program.* New York: Guilford Press.

Brophy, J., & Good T. (1974). *Teacher-student relationships: Causes and consequences.* New York: Holt, Rinehart & Winston.

Brotherson, M.J., Backus, L.H., Summers, J.A., & Turnbull, A.P. (1986). Transition to adulthood. In J.A. Summers (Ed.), *The right to grow up: An introduction to adults with developmental disabilities* (pp. 17–44). Baltimore: Paul H. Brookes Publishing Co.

Brotherson, M.J., Houghton, J., Turnbull, A.P., Bronicki, G.J., Roeder-Gordon, C., Summers, J.A., & Turnbull, H.R. (1988, September). Transition into adulthood: Parental planning for sons and daughters with disabilities. *Education and Training in Mental Retardation, 23*(3), 165–174.

Brown, D.S. (1992, Fall). Empowerment through peer counseling. *OSERS: News in Print, 5*(2), 27–29.

Brown, L., Branston, M.B., Hamre-Nietupski, S., Pumpian, I., Certo, N., & Gruenwald, L. (1979). A strategy for developing chronological age appropriate and functional curricular content for severely handicapped adolescents and young adults. *Journal of Special Education, 13*(1), 81–90.

Clark, F.A., Mack, W., & Pennington, V. (1988). Transition needs assessment of severely disabled high school students and their parents and teachers. *Occupational Therapy Journal of Research, 8*(6), 323–344.

Clark, R.M. (1980). *Family life and school achievement: Why poor black children succeed or fail.* Chicago: University of Chicago Press.

Compas, B.E. (1987). Coping with stress during childhood and adolescence. *Psychological Bulletin, 101*(3), 393–403.

Conservation Company and Human Organization Science Institute. (1986). *Pennsylvania Evaluation Report.* Villanova, PA: Villanova University.

Cruikshank, W.M. (Ed.). (1976). *Cerebral palsy: A developmental disability.* Syracuse, NY: Syracuse University Press.

Crundall, I., & Foddy, M. (1981). Vicarious exposure to a task as a basis of evaluative competence. *Social Psychology Quarterly, 44,* 331–338.

Davis, S.E., Anderson, C., Linkowski, D.C., Berger, K., & Feinstein, C.F. (1985). Developmental tasks and transitions of adolescents with chronic illnesses and disabilities. *Rehabilitation Counseling Bulletin, 29*(2), 69–80.

DeJong, G. (1979). *The movement for independent living: Origins, ideology, and implications for disability research.* Ann Arbor, MI: University Centers for International Rehabilitation.

Des Jardins, C. (1986). Assertiveness is/is not. In F. Weiner (Ed.), *No apologies: A guide to living with a disability, written by the real authorities—people with disabilities, their families and friends* (pp. 122–123). New York: St. Martin's Press.

de Vries, H., Dijkstra, M., & Kuhlman, P. (1988). Self-efficacy: The third factor besides attitude and subjective norm as a predictor of behavioral intentions. *Health Education Research, 3*(3), 273–282.

Dolce, J.J. (1987). Self-efficacy and disability beliefs in behavioral treatment of pain. Special issue: Chronic pain. *Behavioral Research and Therapy, 25*(4), 289–299.

Dowrick, P.W. (1983). Self modeling. In P.W. Dowrick & S.J. Biggs (Eds.), *Using video: Psychological and social applications* (pp. 105–124). New York: John Wiley & Sons.

Dush, D.M., Hirt, M.L., & Schroeder, H.E. (1989). Self-statement modification in the treatment of child behavior disorders: A meta-analysis. *Psychological Bulletin, 106*(1), 97–106.

Edgerton, R.B. (1967). *The cloak of competence: Stigma in the lives of the mentally retarded.* Berkeley: University of California Press.

Ehrenberg, M.F., Cox, D.N., & Koopman, R.F. (1991). The relationship between self-efficacy and depression in adolescents. *Adolescence, 26*(102), 361–374.

Espinosa, L., & Shearer, M. (1986). Family support in public school programs. In R.R. Fewell & P.F. Vadasy (Eds.), *Families of handicapped children: Needs and supports across the life span* (pp. 253–277). Austin, TX: PRO-ED.

Fewell, R.R., & Vadasy, P.F. (Eds.). (1986). *Families of handicapped children: Needs and support across the life span.* Austin, TX: PRO-ED.

Fichten, C.S. (1988). Students with physical disabilities in higher education: Attitudes and beliefs that affect integration. In H.E. Yuker (Ed.), *Attitudes towards persons with disabilities* (pp. 171–186). New York: Springer-Verlag.

Fielder, C.M. (1988). Perceived psychosocial barriers related to physical disability: An investigation of alienation, internal processes and the application of practical skills. *Dissertation Abstracts International, 49*(6), 21–23.

Fisher, R., & Ury, W. (1981). *Getting to yes: Negotiation agreement without giving in.* New York: Penguin Books.

Folkman, S., & Lazarus, R.S. (1980). An analysis of coping in a middle-aged community sample. *Journal of Health and Social Behavior, 21*, 219–239.

Fredericks, B. (1988). Tim becomes an Eagle Scout. *NICHY Transition Monitor, 5*(4).

Gardner, N.S. (1986). Sexuality. In J.A. Summers (Ed.), *The right to grow up: An introduction to adults with developmental disabilities* (pp. 45–66). Baltimore: Paul H. Brookes Publishing Co.

Gaylord-Ross, R.J., Haring, T.G., Breen, C., & Pitts-Conway, V. (1984). The training and generalization of social interaction skills with autistic youth. *Journal of Applied Behavior Analysis, 17*(2), 229–247.

Goetz, L., Anderson, J., & Laten, S. (1989). Facilitation of family support through public school programs. In G.H.S. Singer & L.K. Irvin (Eds.), *Support for caregiving families: Enabling positive adaptation to disability* (pp. 239–251). Baltimore: Paul H. Brookes Publishing Co.

Goffman, I. (1973). *The presentation of self in everyday life.* New York: Overlook Press.

Goldenson, R.M., Dunham, J.R., & Dunham, C.S. (Eds.). (1978). *Disability and rehabilitation handbook.* New York: McGraw-Hill.

Gonzales, F.P., & Dowrick, P.W. (1983, October). *Effects of video self-modeling in "feedforward" training hand/eye coordination.* Unpublished manuscript, University of Alaska, Anchorage.

Graham, S., & Harris, K.R. (1989). Components analysis of cognitive strategy instruction: Effects on learning disabled students compositions and self-efficacy. *Journal of Educational Psychology, 81*(3), 353–361.

Granat, J.P. (1978). Assertiveness training and the mentally retarded. *Rehabilitation Counseling Bulletin, 22*, 100–107.

Haensly, P.A., & Parsons, J.L. (1993, December). Creative, intellectual, and psychosocial development through mentorship: Relationships and stages. *Youth and Society, 25*(2), 202–221.

Harter, S. (1981). *Minnesota symposium on child psychology: Vol. 4. A model of mastery motivation in children: Individual differences and developmental change.* Hillsdale, NJ: Lawrence Erlbaum Associates.

Heimberg, R.C., Montgomery, D., Madsen, C.H., & Heimberg, J.S. (1977). Assertion training: A review of the literature. *Behavior Therapy, 8*, 953–971.

Houghton, J., Bronicki, G.J., & Guess, D. (1987). Opportunities to express preferences and make choices among students with severe disabilities in classroom settings. *Journal of The Association for Persons with Severe Handicaps, 12*(1), 18–27.

Hoy, C. (1986). Preventing learned helplessness. *Academic Therapy, 22*(1), 11–18.

Hughes, C.A., Korinek, L., & Gorman, J. (1991). Self-management for students with mental retardation in public school settings: A research review. *Education and Training in Mental Retardation, 26*, 271–291.

Jakubowski, P., & Lange, A.J. (1978). *The assertive option: Your rights & responsibilities.* Champaign, IL: Research Press.

Jones, M.L., & Ulicny, G.R. (1986). The independent living perspective: Applications to services for adults with developmental disabilities. In J.A. Summers (Ed.), *The right to grow up: An introduction to adults with developmental disabilities* (pp. 227–244). Baltimore: Paul H. Brookes Publishing Co.

Kessler, J.W. (1977). Parenting the handicapped child. *Pediatric Annals, 6,* 654–661.

Kleinhammer-Tramill, P.J., Tramill, J.L., Schrepel, S.N., & Davis, S.F. (1983). Learned helplessness in learning disabled adolescents as a function of noncontingent rewards. *Learning Disability Quarterly, 6,* 61–66.

Larson, R., & Kleiber, D. (1993). Daily experiences of adolescents. In P.H. Tolan & B.J. Cohler (Eds.), *Handbook of clinical research and practice with adolescents* (pp. 124–126). New York: John Wiley & Sons.

Lewis, C.C., Pantell, R.H., & Sharp, L. (1991). Increasing patient knowledge, satisfaction, and involvement: Randomized trial of a communication intervention. *Pediatrics, 88*(2), 351–353.

Lindemann, J.E. (1981). Cerebral palsy. In J.E. Lindemann (Ed.), *Psychological and behavioral aspects of physical disability* (pp. 117–145). New York: Plenum.

Luchow, J.P., Crowl, T.K., & Kahn, J.P. (1985). Learned helplessness: Perceived effect of ability and effort on academic performance among EH and LD/EH children. *Journal of Learning Disabilities, 18*(8), 470–474.

Margalit, M., & Shulman, S. (1986). Autonomy perceptions and anxiety expressions of learning disabled adolescents. *Journal of Learning Disabilities, 19*(5), 291–293.

McCarthy, H. (1986). Making it in able-bodied America: Career development in young adults with physical disabilities. *Journal of Applied Rehabilitation Counseling, 17*(4), 30–38.

Mitchell, B. (1988). Who chooses? *NICHCY Transition, 5*(4).

Neistadt, M.E. (1986). Occupational therapy treatment goals for adults with developmental disabilities. *The American Journal of Occupational Therapy, 40*(10), 672–678.

Pearpoint, J., O'Brien, J., & Forest, M. (1992). *Path: A workbook for planning better futures* (version 1.1). Toronto: Inclusion Press.

Peterson, C., & Stunkard, A.J. (1989). Personal control and health promotion. *Social Science Medicine, 28*(8), 819–828.

Powers, L.E. (1993). Promoting adolescent independence and self-determination. *Family-Centered Care Network. Association for the Care of Children's Health, 10*(4).

Powers, L.E., & Ellison, R. (1995). *TAKE CHARGE: Student guide.* Lebanon, NH: Dartmouth Medical School.

Powers, L.E., & Matuszewski, J. (1995). *TAKE CHARGE: Parent guide.* Lebanon, NH: Dartmouth Medical School.

Powers, L.E., Singer, G., & Sowers, J. (1992). *A student-directed model for the promotion of self-determination.* (CFDA Grant No. 84.158K: Model demonstration projects to identify and teach skills necessary for self-determination.) Lebanon, NH: Dartmouth Medical School, Department of Education, Office of Special Education and Rehabilitative Services.

Powers, L.E., & Sowers, J. (1994). Evolving perspectives on transition: Promoting self-determination and natural supports. In S.N. Calculator & C.M. Jorgenson (Eds.), *Communication supports in regular classrooms for students with severe disabilities.* San Diego: Singular Press.

Powers, L.E., Sowers, J., & Stevens, T. (1995). An exploratory, randomized study of the impact of mentoring on the self-efficacy of adolescents with physical health challenges. *Journal of Rehabilitation, 61*(1), 33–41.

Powers, L.E., Turner, A., Wilson, R., Matuskewski, J., Ellison, R., & Rein, C. (1995). *A controlled field-test of the efficacy of a multi-component model for promoting adolescent self-determination.* Lebanon, NH: Dartmouth Medical School.

Powers, L.E., Wilson, R., Turner, A., & Rein, C. (1995). *TAKE CHARGE: Facilitators guide.* Lebanon, NH: Dartmouth Medical School.

Rhodes, J.E. (1994, Spring). Older and wiser: Mentoring relationships in childhood and adolescence. *Journal of Primary Prevention, 14*(3), 187–196.

Robinson, N.M., & Robinson, H.B. (1976). *The mentally retarded child* (2nd ed.). New York: McGraw-Hill.

Rousso, H. (1988). *Mentoring empowers! How to start a networking project for disabled women and girls in your community.* New York: YWCA.

Sailor, W., Gee, K., Goetz, L., & Graham, N. (1988). Progress in educating students with the most severe disabilities: Is there any? *Journal of The Association for Persons with Severe Handicaps, 13*(2), 87–99.

Santelli, B. Turnbull, A.P., Lerner, E., & Marquis, J. (1993). Parent to parent programs: A unique form of mutual support for families of persons with disabilities. In G.H.S. Singer & L.E. Powers (Eds.), *Families, disability, and empowerment: Active coping skills and strategies for family interventions* (pp. 27–57). Baltimore: Paul H. Brookes Publishing Co.

Saxton, M. (1983). Peer counseling. In N.M. Crewe & K.Z. Irving (Eds.), *Independent living for physically disabled people* (pp. 171–186). San Francisco: Jossey-Bass.

Scherer, M.J. (1988). Assistive device utilization and quality-of-life in adults with spinal cord injuries or cerebral palsy. *Journal of Applied Rehabilitation Counseling, 19*(2), 21–30.

Schunk, D.H. (1982). Effects of effort attributional feedback on children's perceived self-efficacy and achievement. *Journal of Educational Psychology, 74*, 548–556.

Schunk, D.H. (1989a). Self efficacy and cognitive achievement: Implications for students with learning problems. *Journal of Learning Disabilities, 22*(1), 14–22.

Schunk, D.H. (1989b). Social cognitive theory and self-regulated learning. In B.J. Zimmerman & D.H. Schunk (Eds.), *Self-regulated learning and academic achievement: Theory, research and practice* (pp. 75–99). New York: Springer-Verlag.

Seligman, M.E.P. (1975). *Helplessness: On depression, development, and death.* San Francisco: Freeman.

Seligman, M.E.P. (1990). *Learned optimism.* New York: Pocket Books.

Singer, G.H.S., & Irvin, L.K. (1989). Family caregiving, stress, and support. In G.H.S. Singer & L.K. Irvin (Eds.), *Support for caregiving families: Enabling positive adaptation to disability* (pp. 3–25). Baltimore: Paul H. Brookes Publishing Co.

Singer, G.H.S., & Powers, L.E. (1993). Contributing to resilience in families: An overview. In G.H.S. Singer & L.E. Powers, (Eds.), *Families, disability, and empowerment: Active coping skills and strategies for family interventions* (pp. 1–26). Baltimore: Paul H. Brookes Publishing Co.

Slater, M.A., Martinez, M., & Habersang, R. (1989). Normalized family resources: A model for professionals serving families with a chronically ill or handicapped child. In G.H.S. Singer & L.K. Irvin (Eds.), *Support for caregiving families: Enabling positive adaptation to disability* (pp. 161–173). Baltimore: Paul H. Brookes Publishing Co.

Sowers, J. (1989). Critical parent roles in supported employment. In G.H.S. Singer & L.K. Irvin (Eds.), *Support for caregiving families: Enabling positive adaptation to disability* (pp. 269–282). Baltimore: Paul H. Brookes Publishing Co.

Sowers, J., & Powers, L.E. (1989). Preparing students with cerebral palsy and mental retardation for the transition from school to community-based employment. *Career Development for Exceptional Individuals, 12*(1), 25–35.

Sowers, J., & Powers, L.E. (1991). *Vocational preparation and employment of students with physical and multiple disabilities.* Baltimore: Paul H. Brookes Publishing Co.

Sowers, J., Rusch, F.R., Connis, R.T., & Cummings, L.E. (1980). Teaching mentally retarded adults to time-manage in a vocational setting. *Journal of Applied Behavior Analysis, 13*(1), 119–128.

Starke, M.C. (1987). Enhancing social skills and self-perceptions of physically disabled young adults. *Behavior Modification, 11*(1), 3–16.

Steinhausen, H., Schindler, H., & Stephan, H. (1983). Correlates of psychopathology in sick children: An empirical model. *Journal of the American Academy of Child Psychiatry, 22*, 559–564.

Stopford, V. (1987). *Understanding disability: Causes, characteristics, and coping.* London: Edward Arnold.

Summers, J.A. (Ed.). (1986). *The right to grow up: An introduction to adults with developmental disabilities.* Baltimore: Paul H. Brookes Publishing Co.

Summers, J.A., Behr, S.K., & Turnbull, A.P. (1989). Positive adaptation and coping strengths of families who have children with disabilities. In G.H.S. Singer & L.K. Irvin (Eds.), *Support for caregiving families: Enabling positive adaptation to disability* (pp. 27–40). Baltimore: Paul H. Brookes Publishing Co.

Thomas, A., Bax, M., Coombes, K., Goldson, E., Smyth, D., & Whitmore, K. (1985). The health and social needs of physically handicapped young adults: Are they being met by the statutory services? *Developmental Medicine & Child Neurology, 27*(4)(Suppl. 50), 1–20.

Turnbull, A.P., & Turnbull, H.R. (1986). *Families, professionals and exceptionality: A special partnership*. Columbus, OH: Merrill.

Ulicny, G.R., Adler, A.B., & Jones, M.L. (1988, July–September). Consumer-directed attendance management. *American Rehabilitation*, 22–31.

Ulicny, G.R., & Jones, M.L. (1987). Consumer management of attendant services. In *Rehabilitation Research Review*. Lawrence: University of Kansas, Research and Training Center on Independent Living.

U.S. Department of Health and Human Services, Public Health Service, Health Resources and Services Administration, Maternal and Child Health Bureau. (1992, Summer). *Moving on: Transition from child-centered to adult health care for youth with disabilities*. Washington, DC: Author.

Varela, R.A. (1986). Risks, rules, and resources: Self-advocacy and the parameters of decision making. In J.A. Summers (Ed.), *The right to grow up: An introduction to adults with developmental disabilities* (pp. 245–254). Baltimore: Paul H. Brookes Publishing Co.

Vash, C.L. (1981). *The psychology of disability*. New York: Springer-Verlag.

Walker, B. (1989). Strategies for parent-teacher cooperation. In G.H.S. Singer & L.K. Irvin (Eds.), *Support for caregiving families: Enabling positive adaptation to disability* (pp. 103–119). Baltimore: Paul H. Brookes Publishing Co.

Wehman, P. (1981). *Competitive employment: New horizons for severely disabled persons*. Baltimore: Paul H. Brookes Publishing Co.

Wehmeyer, M.J. (1993). Perceptual and psychological factors in career decision-making of adolescents with and without cognitive disabilities. *Career Development for Exceptional Individuals, 16*(2), 135–146.

Werner, E.E., & Smith, R.S. (1992). *Overcoming the odds: High risk children from birth to adulthood*. Ithaca, NY: Cornell University.

Wilcox, B., & Bellamy, G.T. (1987). *A comprehensive guide to the activities catalog: An alternative curriculum for youth and adults with severe disabilities*. Baltimore: Paul H. Brookes Publishing Co.

Williams, R., & Long, J. (1979). *Toward a self-managed life style*. New York: Houghton Mifflin.

Williams, P., & Shoultz, B. (1984). *We can speak for ourselves*. Bloomington: Indiana University Press.

Zeaman, D., & House, B.J. (1960). Approach and avoidance in the discrimination learning of retardates. In D. Zeaman & B.J. House (Eds.), *Learning and transfer in mental defectives progress report No. 2*. NIMH, USPHS, Research Grant M-1099. City: University of Connecticut.

Go for the Career You Want

Tiffany Goupil

My name is Tiffany Goupil. I am 20 years old. This is my last year in high school. I was in a car accident when I was young and had a head injury. I have trouble remembering things. A lot of people have treated me like I couldn't learn things. A lot of teachers, even special education teachers, don't know how to teach people with brain injuries. I can learn just about anything if you take the time to teach me—it just takes me longer to learn things.

I love animals. I have a cat. I always wanted to work with animals. People thought I could only do cleaning. They got me a couple of cleaning jobs, but I got fired because I didn't like doing them.

I now am taking classes in how to work with animals. We have learned how to handle cats and dogs. I also helped deliver a calf. I have also been working at and getting trained at Silver Clippers Dog Grooming. Elaine, the owner, has taught me how to wash and brush dogs. I am going to New Jersey next month with Elaine to take my Grooming Assistant test—I'm nervous, but I know I will pass it. After I graduate and get my certificate I will keep working for Elaine, but I am also applying to other grooming shops in town, so that I can work full time. I feel really proud that I showed everyone that I could do it.

Here is some advice I have for other people who have a disability:

1. If you have a strong interest in doing a job you should go for it. If other people don't think you can do it, keep telling them that you really want to try. Write it down on a piece of paper and give it to them.

2. It is important to get real work experience—school is not enough. I have learned so much from Elaine.

3. You learn more from a job than just how to do a job. I learned that even when I was tired or in a bad mood, I needed to go to work and do a good job.

4. Working is sometimes really hard. After I started at Elaine's I wasn't sure I could do it. But I hung in there. My advice when things get hard is to just keep going at it and put your mind to it and it won't be so hard.

5. It really helps if your family believes in you. My mom kept telling my teachers that I could do more than clean things. She helped me believe in myself.

6. Working helps you pay for things yourself. I used my money to buy clothes. I am saving some of my money. I am proud that I have my own money and can help pay for things I want.

16

Strategies to Enhance Control of the Employment Process by Individuals with Severe Disabilities

Jo-Ann Sowers,
Rick McAllister, and Patty Cotton

Since the mid-1980s, the supported employment movement has begun to dramatically expand the work opportunities of individuals with significant disabilities (West, Revell, & Wehman, 1992,). Prior to supported employment, sheltered programs were the only work option available for most individuals with severe disabilities. It is estimated that well over 200,000 people have gained employment in regular work settings (West et al., 1992).

The existing supported employment model comprises the following components (Mank, Rhodes, & Bellamy, 1986; Mcloughlin, Garner, & Callahan, 1987). 1) A supported employment program obtains information about the individual, focusing on his or her current skills and abilities. 2) The program takes responsibility for seeking job openings in the community that best match the skills and abilities of the individual. 3) A job coach from the program takes responsibility for training the individual to perform the job. 4) The job coach returns to the job site to solve any job performance or work-related problems that may arise.

This model of supported employment has dramatically expanded the employment options and quality of work life of many individuals with severe disabilities (Chadsey-

Rusch, Gonzalez, Tines, & Johnson, 1989; Sowers & Powers, 1991; West & Parent, 1993; Williams, 1991). However, the model is primarily controlled by agencies. In the 1990s, there has been an interest in encouraging supported employment staff to shift from taking control of the process of employment to facilitating "natural" agents to play a greater role. Particular focus has been placed on having agency staff shift from directly training supported employees to perform their jobs to consulting with the employees' supervisors and co-workers about how to train and support them (Callahan, 1992; Fabian & Leucking, 1991; Hagner & Dileo, 1993; Nisbet & Hagner, 1988; Nisbet & Sowers, 1995). Some attention has also begun to be given to the use of planning and job development processes that include the individual and his or her family and friends to a greater extent (Sowers, Cotton, & Malloy, 1994).

Despite the beginning movements away from agency-controlled employment services, there remains much need for identifying and implementing strategies aimed at optimizing, to the fullest extent possible, the direction and control of the process by consumers (individuals who experience a disability) (Williams, 1991). West and Parent (1993) suggested a number of critical points in the employment process over which consumers should have the opportunity to have greater control, including choice of the type of occupation to pursue, choice of the agency and training staff who will assist them, choice of training methods, and choice of keeping or resigning from a job. Providing individuals with the opportunity to make choices is an important component of enhancing their control. However, providing the opportunity to make choices frequently is not sufficient, especially when providing relatively complex choices to individuals who have little prior experience in making decisions and whose disability may make decision making a challenge. A new and important role of employment consultants is to assist individuals in understanding the options they have and to support them in weighing the pros and cons of each in order to make the most fully informed decision possible.

Control of one's work life involves more than making choices; it also involves participating in and performing the actual activities that the employment process comprises. Research illustrates that the level of participation in a process results in a higher level of commitment to the outcome and to individuals' self-esteem and self-determination (Powers & Sowers, 1994; Sowers & Powers, 1995). Most employment specialists have experienced frustration when a person for whom they have worked hard to find a job quits after a few days or weeks. Because consumers usually put little or no effort into the process of locating the job, the level of their motivation to keep the job may actually be lower than that of the staff member. Dependence of supported employees on employment specialists often results in difficulties in performance maintenance when the staff member gradually attempts to spend less time at the job site. Most job coaches can even attest that some supported employees seem to develop problems in order to get the employment specialist back to the site.

This chapter focuses on four major areas related to enhancing the extent to which individuals with disabilities have control over the process of deciding what type of career to pursue, locating their job, and learning and keeping their job. We describe specific strategies that employment consultants can utilize to facilitate the choices and involvement of consumers in employment.

CAREER DEVELOPMENT AND PLANNING PROCESS

The common approach used in supported employment is to identify the type of job that will be sought for an individual with a severe disability based on assessment of the person's current skills and abilities. A typical assessment uses a checklist of functional skills and work-related behaviors as well as a description of work experience and training history. This information is collected primarily through record review and through meetings with professionals involved with the individual. Attempts are usually made to find out the extent to which the person liked those jobs he or she has previously performed and to determine his or her preferences related to such aspects as work schedule and location (e.g., close to home, on the bus schedule).

This focus on current skills and abilities and the limited time given by supported employment programs to career assessment is a direct reaction to more traditional employment paradigms applied to individuals with severe disabilities. In the past there was the belief that individuals could only work in community businesses if they had learned a long list of skill competencies needed for employment success. This was the basis upon which these individuals were kept in prevocational programs and in sheltered workshops where they were trained and assessed on these "work readiness" skills (Bellamy, Rhodes, Bourbeau, & Mank, 1986).

The supported employment approach was based on the belief that there are many jobs that individuals can learn to do, given their current skills, and that any training that they need can be more effectively provided within the context of the job situation in which they are employed (Bellamy, Rhodes, Mank, & Albin, 1988; Rusch, 1990). With this approach, a large number of people with disabilities have left segregated work programs, and many have not had to experience these programs. In contrast, the result of matching current skills to available jobs for the vast majority of individuals served through supported employment programs has been placement in cleaning-related occupations such as dishwashing and table bussing in restaurants and housekeeping in hotels and other businesses (O'Brien, 1990; Sowers, Cotton, & Malloy, 1994; West et al., 1992). These are the jobs with the lowest skill requirements and the highest rate of turnover, two factors that have made these jobs the focus of placement efforts of supported employment programs. Unfortunately, the high rate of turnover in these occupations can be attributed to a number of negative job characteristics, including low wages, high physical demands, low level of challenge and creativity, low status, and few opportunities for advancement. Not surprisingly, these are the same characteristics that have been found to contribute to job dissatisfaction for workers without disabilities (Friedman, 1964; Halle, 1984; Locke, 1983). Supported employment has taken few, if any, of these factors (e.g., status, advancement opportunities) into account in determining an appropriate job match or in assisting individuals to identify and pursue careers (Hagner & Dileo, 1993; Mank, 1994; Moseley, 1988; Sowers, Cotton, & Malloy, 1994; West & Parent, 1992).

It is critical that supported employment begin to move toward an expanded vision of the types of jobs and career options that individuals with severe disabilities are given the opportunity to pursue. This is important not only because it is the "right thing to do," but because it has a direct impact on the job satisfaction of supported employees and thus on job success. As suggested earlier, the rate of job retention among supported employment participants has been modest. Job loss estimates in supported employment range from 44% to 70% (Nisbet & Hagner, 1988). Supported employment professionals' response to these outcomes has focused on improved job coaching and follow-along strategies. Interestingly, it is widely acknowledged that few job losses can be attributed to employees' inability to perform the tasks, but rather to what is frequently called work-related issues (Greenspan & Shoultz, 1981; Hanley-Maxwell, Rusch, Chadsey-Rusch, & Renzaglia, 1986). These issues include poor maintenance of work quality and production when not directly supervised, as well as behaviors such as poor attendance and failure to follow a supervisor's instructions. All of these issues can be placed in the general category of poor work ethic when the argument is being made to blame the job loss on the individual or need for a return to "get ready" programs. However, it must be recognized that these issues are all behavioral indices of boredom and job dissatisfaction that are typical of employees without disabilities (Moseley, 1988).

The Rehabilitation Act Amendments of 1992 (PL 102-569) states that individuals should have access to "meaningful careers" based on "informed choice." A supported employment agency may ask an individual, "What kind of job do you think you would like to have?" Many individuals have very limited employment and life experiences. Many also have limited ability to fully comprehend this type of question or to respond to it. Families who help represent the person may have a limited vision of their family member's employment potential. Consequently, a common response to this question is to say "I don't know" or to identify those work tasks the person has been given the chance to perform previously, which are typically cleaning or rote assembly tasks.

The general career counseling field, which focuses on individuals who do not experience disabilities, recognizes that career interests often can best be realized by assisting individuals to identify their general likes and dislikes (Anthony, 1991; Bolles, 1994; Sher, 1979; Sinetar, 1978). For example, a strong affinity for being outdoors (e.g., the person chooses to spend time outside, likes to camp, hike, bird watch) may suggest looking into a career as a forest ranger. In addition, career counselors recognize the importance of general personality tendencies in helping people think about the jobs they may like to pursue. Examples of these traits are being organized, being extroverted, and being good at making people feel comfortable. A number of standardized tests have been used by professional evaluators for many years to assist individuals without disabilities and those with less significant disabilities in career planning. Examples of these tools include the Strong Interest Inventory (Levin, 1991) and the Myers-Briggs Type Indicator (Myers & McCaulley, 1985). Unfortunately, because of the nature of the questions contained in these instruments, they have little validity and utility for individuals with significant cognitive disabilities.

Since the late 1980s, assessment and planning processes have aimed at facilitating the efforts of family and friends of individuals with severe disabilities to reflect on and communicate the gifts, talents, and interests that are unique to the person and that may provide better insight into the activity goals (including career goals) the person should pursue. These processes have been called personal futures planning, circle of support, and MAPs (Making Action Plans) (Mount & Zwernik, 1988; Vandercook, York, & Forest, 1989). To date, the focus of these processes has been on gaining the input and support of family and friends in the development and attainment of goals. Clearly, personal support is extremely important. However, the role of the career planner, the individual with the disability, in these processes has been one of a recipient of the planning, with little attempt being made to facilitate his or her participation to the greatest extent possible. In the remainder of this section, a process is described that attempts to facilitate the career planner's involvement in and control of the career planning process.

"Planning My Career" Profile and Planning Process

The "Planning My Career" Profile and Planning process (Sowers, Goodall, Cotton, & McAllister, 1995) has three goals: 1) enhancing the extent to which individuals with severe disabilities have the opportunity to consider and pursue the full range of career options available to all individuals, 2) facilitating the extent to which the career planner takes the lead in the process, and 3) enhancing the extent to which the career planner has the information needed to make a fully informed choice about his or her career.

The career profile contains 15 topic maps through which a career planner can reflect on and summarize information about himself or herself that may be relevant to identifying a career path. The career profile is also meant to be a means for career planners (and adults) to maintain a journal or record of career-related experiences, including vocational education classes, work and internship experiences, and career exploration opportunities. As an individual gains additional experiences through his or her high school years and post–high school years, he or she can describe the activities and reflect on aspects about them that she or he liked and disliked. The 15 topic headings are the following:

- My likes and interests
- Things I don't like
- Things I am good at
- People I know who can help me figure out my career
- Internships and apprenticeships
- Paid jobs
- Volunteer work
- Home chores
- Vocational education classes
- Academic classes
- Businesses I have visited to explore
- Things I have read about jobs
- Vocational tests and assessments I have taken
- Help I will need at work
- Things I would like to be part of my job

Figure 1 shows the cover page and two of the Profile topic pages completed for a young man with a severe disability. The following summarizes the basic steps in facilitating an individual's participation in the career planning process.

Step 1: The career planner and family are oriented to the career planning process. The career planner and his or her family are provided with a written and verbal description of the steps in the process. It is emphasized that the employment consultant will meet with the career planner over a period of several weeks, during which time the career planner will be assisted to take the lead in going through the profile, identifying a career goal, and developing a plan to achieve this goal. This meeting is an important first step in communicating to both the career planner and his or her family that the career planner will lead this process and in showing the reasons why this is important. In particular, many parents of individuals with severe disabilities need to be encouraged to support and encourage the career planner to take charge, because they may not perceive the individual as being capable of doing so. The family needs to be reassured that the individual will be supported and assisted in the process and that the family will still play an important role.

Step 2: Meetings are held between the employment consultant and the career planner over a period of several weeks to go over and complete the profile topic pages and to identify possible careers and jobs to explore. During this period, the career planner may choose to get the input of other individuals who know him or her well. For individuals who are very limited in their ability to communicate information about them-

MY LIKES AND INTERESTS

Sometimes things you do for fun are things you can do for work. For example, if you like to draw you might want to be an artist. If you like to play basketball, you may not be able to be a professional player, but maybe you could be a sports reporter. Thinking about your interests can also give you hints about jobs that may not be directly related to one of your interests. If you like to play a lot of sports this might tell you that you would rather do a job that is active. So, even though you like sports, you might be happier loading trucks than selling sporting goods in a department store (because the loading job would be more active).

I LIKE TO DO
THESE THINGS FOR FUN

Sleeping late
Listening to music—all kinds
People who joke around
Ride my bike
Walk in the woods
Ride in cars
Going places

Going out to eat
Watching people
Hanging out
Watching cartoons on T.V.
Making pictures with colored pens
Pictures—photographs of family/friends

THINGS THAT I DON'T LIKE

Everyone has things that they like a lot, things they don't like a lot, but are just OK. Then there are things that you really don't like at all. These may be things like washing the dishes, having to get up early in the morning, math class, when your brother gets into your stuff. Things you don't like might also be things like when people treat you like a kid, when you are made to go fast, or a room that is cold.

List below things that you really, really don't like:

Getting up early
Pressure—being asked to do too many things at once. Trying to learn too many things.
Doing repetitive things
People who are uptight around me
People who are serious all the time
Doing things all by myself
Lifting heavy things

Figure 1.   "Planning my career": cover page and profile topic pages for youth with a disability.

selves, it is necessary to include others in the process from the beginning. The career planner and facilitator meet individually with family, friends, and professionals who may have information and ideas to share that will help in the process.

Step 3: The career planner summarizes the information from the topic pages on the career profile summary page. Figure 2 shows the career planning summary for Mike. This information reflects the elements that Mike thinks are the most important to keep in mind in considering the type of career he will choose and the type of job and workplace he will seek.

Step 4: The career planner develops a career goal and plan. A goal may be a very specific career that a person know she or he wants ("I want to be a car mechanic"). A career planner may be interested in a particular career area but may want to get more information before "going for it." For example, the goal may be "I want to find out more about being a car mechanic, so I can decide if I want to be one." Some people may want to find out about more than one career. Other people may have little or no idea about what their interests are after going through the profile. A goal for this person might be "I want to spend time thinking more about my general interests and talents and getting information about a lot of different areas."

Step 5: The career planner shares his or her plan and gets input from family, friends, and professionals who can assist him or her to carry out the plan and to reach the goal. For most individuals, this sharing and planning is done as a group meeting. It is critical that the career planner invites the people she or he wants. It is also important that the career planner be encouraged to have as many family and friends at the meeting as possible because these people likely know the person the best. The career planner may also choose to invite professionals such as the vocational rehabilitation counselor, case manager, and transition coordinator (if she or he is in school). The

---

CAREER PLANNING SUMMARY

Mike Grant

LIKES/DISLIKES

* *Being outdoors*
* *Going places*
* *Moving around*
* *Watching people*
* *Being around people*

JOB/TASK EXPERIENCE-
LIKED/DISLIKED

* *Liked: Supply delivery*
* *Didn't like: Shelving, packaging*

THINGS WANTED ON JOB

1.) *No dangerous machines*
2.) *Friendly co-workers*
3.) *Close to home*
4.) *To move around a lot*
5.) *Not a lot of heavy lifting*
6.) *At least 4 hours a day*
7.) *Not too early*
8.) *2 or 3 different jobs*

HELP NEEDED

1.) *Ride to/from work*
2.) *To help coworkers get to know me*
3.) *Low-key coworker to train me*
4.) *To learn one task at a time*
5.) *To learn one way to do something*
6.) *Tell co-workers how to not stress me out and what to do if I do start acting nervous*

Figure 2.   Career profile summary for Mike.

career planner is assisted to take as great a lead as possible in conducting the meeting, including the presentation of his or her profile summary, career goal, and plan.

Again, the aims of the process and the role of the employment consultant are to encourage the career planner to reflect on and identify things about himself or herself that may be important in selecting a career and to enhance the extent to which the career planner takes charge of the planning activities. The following facilitation strategies can help improve chances for success.

Do not try to complete the profile in a specified period of time or number of meetings. There is not a specific or magical number of hours or meetings. However, it is likely that it will take at least four or five sessions to really begin to develop a relationship with a career planner and for him or her to begin to think about and explore who he or she is and to consider what this might mean in terms of a career. Few individuals with significant disabilities have had the experience of really being asked to think about themselves, to describe their preferences, and to develop a course of action for themselves. Because it is a novel experience, many individuals may find it difficult and even uncomfortable at first.

Meetings should be kept conversational and casual. Encourage the person to expand on answers, to tell stories, and to get sidetracked into other areas and topics. For example, when Steve and his employment consultant got together, this conversation took place:

> [Consultant: How was your weekend?]
> "Great."
> [How come?]
> "Went to Uncle John's."
> [What did you do there?]
> "Saw his truck. He has big truck."
> [What kind of truck does he have?]
> "Big, silver truck. He let me sit in it. And I pushed the horn."
> [Did you go for a ride?]
> "No, but I sat in it—you have to climb up."

The employment consultant could have simply gone on to other things after Steve said he had a great weekend. By continuing to probe, he found out that Steve likes Uncle John and trucks a lot. These details add to the picture of who Steve is. If the employment consultant had simply turned to the profile page titled "Your Interests" and said to Steve, "Tell me things you are interested in." Steve might not have remembered or thought of the fact that he liked trucks.

The consultant should always ask leading questions to gain more information. Sheila was asked, "Did you like your work experience cleaning the cafeteria?" She responded, "Yes, I liked that job a whole lot." One conclusion might be that she liked working in cafeterias and doing cleaning work. However, questions such as "What did you like about it?" or "Did you like washing the tables?" might reveal that what she really liked about the job was that Lucille the cafeteria helper was really nice to her and gave her a cookie and soda each day after she finished her job.

The profile should be given to the career planner. This is a simple but important strategy in helping career planners understand that this is their process and that they can and should take charge of it. The profile should be provided in a folder or binder of some kind. The individual can then write his or her name on the front. When the career planner and employment consultant meet, the profile should be opened in front of the career planner, not the employment consultant. If the career planner is able to read, he or she should read the topic descriptions (with as much support as needed to read and understand them). The career planner should also be assisted and supported to "write" as much of the information on his or her Profile as possible. For some individuals, this may require help with spelling words they want to write. For other people, the employment consultant may do the actual writing, but use the career planner's words. If the profile is created on a computer, career planners can type in information on their profile.

The career planner should be asked to select when and where to meet. A professional's office is the locale in which a career planner may be least likely to reflect and share information. The employment consultant should let the career planner know that meeting in other places is an option and that he or she can choose where to meet. Other places include the school library or cafeteria, outside on the grass, at home, at a local restaurant over a soda, or a bench at the mall. In fact, employment consultants should encourage career planners to meet in a variety of different places. Individuals act differently and reveal different things about themselves in various settings. For example, Debbie and her employment consultant sat at a table in a mall drinking sodas and talking about her interests. Her employment consultant noticed how distracted Debbie got whenever a baby went by—she would stare and smile. Debbie never mentioned anything about babies as an interest until her employment consultant said, "Debbie, you were looking at all the babies go by. Do you like babies?" Debbie broke into a big smile and nodded yes.

The career planner should be assisted in creating a To Do task list after each meeting and in assigning tasks to himself or herself and to the employment consultant. This is one powerful way to enhance the extent to which career planners understand that career planning takes time and effort and that they can and should take the lead in it. An example of a To Do list is shown in Figure 3. Here is an example of how the employment consultant assisted Chris to generate his To Do list:

**CAREER PLANNING
TO DO LIST**

Chris

TASK	WHO	WHEN	DONE
1. Ask things I'm good at: Mom	Chris	Tonight	
2. Grandma	Chris	Saturday	
3. Mrs. Seymore	Jane	Friday	
4.			
5.			
6.			
7.			
8.			
9.			
10.			

Figure 3.   Completed sample To Do list.

[Today you thought of some things that you like to do. In working with other people I have found that their family and friends can sometimes help them think of things they are good at. Would you like to ask some of your family and friends about things you are good at?]
"Yeh."
[Which people do you want to ask?]
"My mom."
[Anyone else?]
"My Grandma."
[Is there anyone from school who knows a lot about things you are good at?]
"Mrs. Seymore."
[OK, what do you want me to write on your To Do list for you?]
"Their names."
[OK, and what are you going to ask these people?]
"Things I am good at."
[OK, I wrote "Ask Things I'm Good At" and "Mom, Grandma, and Mrs. Seymore." OK, do you want to talk to everyone on the list, or do you want me to talk to one of them?]
"You talk to Mrs. Seymore."
[OK, I will talk to her on Friday. When are you going to ask your Mom about things you are good at?]
"Tonight."
[Great—I'll write tonight.]
[When can you talk to your Grandma?]
"I'm going to her house on Saturday."
[I'll write Saturday. Now let's talk about what you are going to ask these people. Do you have an idea about what to say?]
"No."
[What are you and I doing together?]
"Working on jobs."
[Right, so how about saying something like "I am trying to figure out the kind of job I want to do."]
"OK."
[What do you want to ask these people?]
"Things I am good at."
[Right. How would you ask your Mom?]
"Tell me things I am good at."
[Good. OK, would you want them to write down what they think of on your sheet or on another piece of paper?]
"On another piece of paper."
[OK, I'll write here, "Tell me and write down things I am good at."

The New Hampshire Natural Supports Project has provided technical assistance to a number of school programs and adult services agencies related to the employment of individuals who experience severe disabilities. Data were collected on the extent to which the schools and adult services agencies place the individuals in jobs that were directly related to interests identified during the career planning process. Information was formally collected on 23 individuals, 8 of whom were placed in jobs directly related to interests identified during the career planning process. Only one (13%) of these individuals was fired due to poor performance. One person lost her job because the business was doing poorly and needed to lay off employees to reduce costs. Of the 15 placements made into jobs that did not directly relate to the person's interests, 7 (46%) were fired.

Many supported employment professionals argue that the person's co-workers are more important than the specific type of work he or she does in determining the job satisfaction of most supported employees. Connections with co-workers are highly important to all employees. However, few of us would want to have to choose—work with co-workers we like or do the type of work that is interesting. Most us feel that we should be able to strive to have both interest and connection with others in our employment situations, and individuals with disabilities should also be able to strive for both.

JOB SEARCH

Supported employment agencies have traditionally taken all the responsibility for contacting employers. Typically, most of these contacts are initiated by want ads and by calling or visiting businesses on a random basis and asking if any job openings are available. This approach is contrasted with the fact that research and experience has shown that the most effective approach to obtaining employment, for individuals with and without disabilities, is through personal contacts and networking (Bissonnette, 1994; Hagner & Dileo, 1993; Jackson, 1991; Kregel, Wehman, Seyfarth, & Marshall, 1986; Zadny & James, 1979). In other words, it is not necessarily what you know, but who you know that is crucial in obtaining a job.

Through the career planning profile, the individual identifies those personal connections who may be able to help in locating a job. Personal connections include family; friends and acquaintances, including neighbors, business connections from current and prior jobs, and personal business connections (e.g., doctor, dry cleaner, grocery manager); and connections through organizations (e.g., church, social club, health club, interest group). It is important for individuals to learn to use their personal connections and to learn how to expand these connections as career planning and job search strategies. For example, Sarah thinks that she might be interested in a career related to fashion (she loves to shop for clothes and to keep up with the latest fashion trends). Sarah understood that it probably would not be a good idea for her to work at the same small store as her sister. However, her sister did agree to introduce Sarah to her boss, who provided Sarah with input about different types of jobs in the fashion industry. She also provided Sarah with the names of people she knew in town who might give her additional information and might even have a job opportunity for her.

The job seeker should also be facilitated to have the greatest degree of involvement in the actual job-seeking activities as possible. As with the career planning process, active coaching and support will need to be provided to job seekers with severe disabilities in order for them to participate in the process and to learn to take charge of it. Here is an example of how Sarah was facilitated, coached, and supported in her job-seeking process:

> [Sarah, last week you got the names from your sister's boss of several clothing businesses. What do you think you should do next?]
> "Talk to them."
> [That makes sense. Let's see, you got five names. How many do you think you and I can contact by next week?]
> "I don't know."
> [Well, all five is probably too many to do in one week. How about two or three?]
> "Three."
> [OK, I'll read through the list and then you check off which ones you will contact. (She reads through list). Which three do you want us to contact this week?]
> "Fashion Beetle, Fashion Galore, and Denise's."
> [Great. There are a couple of different ways to contact businesses. One way is that you can go to the business and introduce yourself. A second way is that you can call up on the phone and ask for an appointment. Another way is to write a letter to the company. How would you like to try the three different ways with these three places?]
> "Sure."
> [Great. Let's start by writing a letter to one place. It's best to write a letter to places that you don't know very much about. Which of these three do you not know very much about?]

"The Fashion Beetle."
[That's a good choice. You have never been there and your sister's boss wasn't able to give you much information about it. Here is a letter that a lot of people use as an example in writing their letters to businesses. Let me read it to you…OK, Let's go down to the computer room so that you can change the letter to fit you. First, you need to address it to the Fashion Beetle and to the name of the manager. Next, you need to put in your interest in fashion and retail here. (The employment consultant had the sample letter already typed on the computer. The job seeker then had to type only the new information with the assistance of the employment consultant.) OK, your letter looks great. Here is a To Do List. What else needs to happen in contacting the Fashion Beetle?]
"Mail the letter."
[Yeah, I'll write that down here. What do you need to do to get it mailed?]
"Put it in the mailbox."
[That's one thing, but you need to put it in an envelope first, and what do you need on the envelope?]
"A stamp."
[Right, and you need to put the address on the front too. I'll write these two things down. Here is an envelope. Let me show you how to fold the letter with this piece of paper. Now you can fold your letter and put it in the envelope. Great, looks good. OK, you can check off that that task was done. Here is a stamp; go ahead and put it on (points to place on letter it goes). Great, can you check off another task on your list? Right, go ahead. OK, will you take the letter home today and put it in the mail?]
"Sure."
[Great, where can you put the letter to keep it clean and so you will remember to mail it?]
"In my notebook."
[All right.]

The employment consultant called Sarah's mother to tell her that Sarah had the letter and was supposed to mail it. The employment consultant asked her mother to ask Sarah what she had done that day during her career meeting as a way to help Sarah remember that she was to mail the letter. If this general question did not help her to remember, the employment consultant suggested that her mother ask her if she had any To Do tasks she had agreed to complete.

Whenever possible, the job seeker should accompany the employment consultant to talk with prospective employers. This may be an uncomfortable situation at a business with which the employment consultant has no prior experience or relationship. The business representative may not know what to say or how to act toward the individual with the disability, which may result in an unpleasant experience for both the job seeker and the business representative and may eliminate any possibility of the job seeker's obtaining employment at the company. Employment consultants should attempt to approach and meet representatives of businesses in their communities to establish a relationship with them to provide an understanding of supported employment and the capacity of individuals with disabilities to work and to gain knowledge of the business. This approach is done without any request for a job. We have found that when approached in this way, businesses are open to spending time talking about their workplace and gaining knowledge related to individuals with disabilities and their capabilities. When a job seeker then wishes to talk with the business about a job, the business representative has the knowledge base to feel comfortable doing so. The employment consultant has information about the representative and the business that will help the job seeker approach the company for a position. The employment consultant should help the job seeker rehearse an interview, including greeting the employer, answering frequently asked questions, and asking questions she or he wishes to ask the employer.

JOB TRAINING

Using a traditional supported employment approach, when a company agrees to hire an individual with a disability, an existing employee trains an agency job coach in how to perform the job; and this coach then takes all the responsibility for training the employee until he or she learns to perform the job duties independently. This responsibility includes identifying the adaptive and training strategies that will be used. If the supported employee experiences any significant performance or work-related difficulties, the company contacts the job coach, who returns to the site to provide additional training and to implement strategies to alleviate the difficulties.

However, it has begun to be recognized that this approach to training may have a number of shortcomings. First, it may result in the supported employee's viewing the job coach as the individual for and with whom he or she works, rather than with his or her "real" supervisor and "real" co-workers. This dependency is evident when a supported employee's performance does not "maintain" after the job coach leaves the business. An ongoing cycle of performance difficulties followed by job coach intervention, performance improvement, job coach fading, and repeated performance difficulties is not uncommon.

A number of authors have suggested that performance difficulties of supported employees may also result from the stigma they experience when being trained by a human services person. Most individuals who do not experience disabilities would be embarrassed if a "special" person came with them to their new job to teach them how to perform their work. Not only may the presence of a job coach have an impact on the employee's own expectations of success, but it may also affect the expectations of his or her co-workers for the employee's success, which in turn will be communicated to the employee. The following provides an example of a young man who was trained by one of his co-workers.

Dave was a high school career planner who was in the process of figuring out the type of career he desired to pursue. In the meantime he expressed a desire to work after school at a fast-food restaurant as his brother had done. Dave has autism and moderate mental retardation. He had participated in a work experience program through which he had been trained on a number of cleaning jobs by a job coach. His job coaches reported that Dave required intensive training to learn tasks and in fact had never made significant progress toward independence.

A local fast-food restaurant manager agreed to hire Dave as a front room table busser and cleaning person. The manager indicated that a co-worker is assigned to all new employees for the first few days to provide training, and he agreed that this would also be done for Dave. The staff person from the school indicated that she would provide input and consultation to the co-worker related to how to train Dave. The co-worker, John, who was selected by the manager to train Dave, was 21 years old and had no prior experience working with or training individuals with disabilities. The employment consultant (the school staff person) introduced and met with Dave and John.

(continued)

Case study *(continued)*

During the meeting, the employment consultant and Dave discussed with John a few things that he could do to help Dave learn his job (e.g., tell Dave what to do and show him at the same time, have Dave show John that he knows how to do the tasks before John leaves, keep checking back with Dave to make sure he is continuing to perform the task correctly and when he is tell him so). After only a few days of training, John and the manager said that Dave had learned to perform the job as well as any other new employee. Over the year that Dave worked at the restaurant, he experienced no significant performance or work-related difficulties. At the end of the year, Dave resigned to move on to another job more in line with his long-term career aspirations.

No one who knew Dave would have predicted that he would be able to learn his job in a few days with a professional job coach, much less a co-worker with no training experience. Anyone who observed Dave his first few days on the job and saw the manner in which he interacted with John would have little doubt of the positive impact of being trained by a co-worker had on his self-esteem and self-perceptions. The employment consultant spent several hours the first 2 days sitting in the restaurant in case John had any questions or concerns about training Dave. On the second day, Dave approached the employment consultant and suggested that she leave. The employment consultant asked John if it would be all right with him if she left. He said that Dave was doing extremely well and there was no reason for her to stay.

It is clear that Dave took great pride in being trained by a "real" co-worker rather than a "special" job coach, and he showed that he had skills and abilities that he had never before revealed. In addition, he made it clear to the outside staff person that he wanted to be left alone and that he was able to do the job without her assistance. The following suggestions can help involve the employee in the training and support given by a co-worker at a job site.

Assist the employee to participate in identifying and giving suggestions related to training and adaptation strategies. When a co-worker takes the lead in training an employee with a disability, it is important that the co-worker be provided with input about approaches and methods of training that may help the individual to learn and perform his or her job. To the greatest extent possible, the employee should be involved in and assisted by the employment consultant to participate in and to take as great a lead as possible in this process.

Chris was hired to work in an office performing clerical tasks (basic data entry, photocopying, and mailing), and the company agreed that a co-worker would train him. The employment consultant set up a half-hour meeting for Chris and the co-worker to become acquainted and for Chris and the consultant to share with the co-worker some methods that help Chris learn new

(continued)

Case study *(continued)*

tasks. The employment consultant first met with Chris and explained to him
that his co-worker (Sue) would be training him on his new job and that they
would be meeting with Sue to give her some ideas about helping him learn
new tasks. The employment consultant reviewed with Chris the points he
and others indicated during the career planning process helped him learn
and helped him to do a good job. The employment consultant described
each point and asked Chris if he agreed with it and would want to tell Sue
about it. She and Chris then worked together to type a Things That Help Me
Learn and Do a Good Job sheet for Sue (see Figure 4). As they talked about
each suggestion, the employment consultant typed on a computer how it
might be written and read it for Chris:

> [Chris, one thing that you agreed helped you learn something new was for the
> person teaching you to show you how to do it, not just to tell you what to do.
> How would you like to tell Sue this?]
> "Oh, I don't know."
> [How about show me how to do things—don't just tell me."
> "OK."
> [The next thing that you and everyone agreed was important was that the per-
> son teaching you should watch (the employment consultant emphasized this
> word by raising her voice and changing her tone) you while you try to do a
> new job a few times to make sure you understand what to do. How would
> you like to tell Sue this?]
> "Watch me."
> [Sounds good. How about if I type "watch me while I try to do a job"? I will
> give her an example of this."]

This process continued until there was a list of training strategies for
Sue to use. After they were finished, they went back over the list, and Chris
practiced what he was going to say to Sue. Chris was not able to read, and he
would not be able to remember all of the things on the list. The employment
consultant suggested to Chris that he give the list to Sue and say, "These are
things that will help you teach me my new job." She also suggested that he
say the first strategy on the list—"show me what to do." Chris practiced saying this to the employment consultant. When they met with Sue, Chris initiated the meeting by giving her a copy of his list and saying the things he had
practiced. The employment consultant then facilitated the remainder of the
meeting, going through the strategies on the list and encouraging both Chris
and Sue to discuss each of the suggestions.

*Assist the supported employee to participate in solving problems on an ongoing
basis.* When difficulties arise related to the performance of a supported employee on
the job, job coaches have traditionally taken the lead in identifying the strategies that
should be utilized to solve them (and, in most cases, taking responsibility for implementing them). The new natural supported employment approach focuses on the
employment consultant's encouraging and consulting with the employee's supervisor and co-workers to identify and implement these strategies. Once again, the supported employee should be included and supported to play a key role in this important
activity.

THINGS THAT HELP ME LEARN AND DO A GOOD JOB

Sue

1. SHOW ME HOW TO DO THINGS–Don't just tell me how to do them.
    For example, when you are teaching me how to photocopy, show me each of the steps,
    one at a time–The first thing you do is put the papers to be copied in here (put the
    papers in the feeder slot), next push the number on here of the number of copies you
    want (I want 1 copy, so I will push the 1–push the 1), the next thing you do is to
    push this green button (push it), so on....

2.

3.

4.

5.

Figure 4.   Completed sample form showing ways to enhance learning and performance.

Cindy was hired to work at a small company that manufactured electronics. She performed a number of subassembly tasks. Cindy was trained by the floor supervisor. On a weekly basis the supervisor, Cindy, and the employment consultant met for about 20 minutes to review how things were going—both the supervisor and Cindy would talk about how each thought things were going and discuss ways to resolve any concerns. At around the fifth week, the supervisor indicated she was concerned that Cindy's production was not improving enough and said she thought the major reason for the lack of improvement was that Cindy became distracted watching other things going on on the floor. Cindy agreed that it was hard keeping her concentration with all the other activity going on. The two then brainstormed different ideas about ways that might help her keep her concentration. The employment consultant asked Cindy if she had noticed what some of the other employees wore while they worked, and she said, "Walkmans." The supervisor explained that some people found listening to music helped them concentrate and that it blocked out other noises. Cindy said she would like to give a Walkman a try. The supervisor suggested that she thought Cindy was curious about the other things going on (the machinery being used), and if she took some time to show and explain to Cindy exactly what the machine did and what the people were doing with the machines, that it might help. Cindy liked that idea. The employment consultant suggested

(continued)

Case study *(continued)*

that it might help if Cindy had a way to keep count of how many circuit boards she had completed and how many she had left to do. The supervisor indicated that she could set up the specific number of circuit boards that Cindy should complete by break or lunch and then she would know how she was progressing. Cindy also thought that this would help.

SERVICE BROKERAGE: GIVING THE REAL POWER TO THE EMPLOYEE

Real control comes when individuals have the opportunity to choose among the array of services available (e.g., medical, plumbers, grocery stores) where they will do business and spend their money. In making these choices, people evaluate the quality and cost of the services available to determine which will give the most for the least amount of money. If we do business with a company and are not satisfied, we take our business elsewhere. There is growing recognition that real empowerment by individuals with disabilities will come only when they have the same relationship to the services provided to them as does any other citizen in choosing and using services in a free market society. Canada has taken the lead in attempting to put into practice approaches that will optimize the actual control of services and the money spent on services by consumers via a concept known as service brokerage (Bach, 1991; McClughan & Salter, 1988). This service brokerage approach is currently being replicated on a small demonstration scale in Concord, New Hampshire (Cotton & Sowers, 1995). In the brokering service, a consumer receives assistance through a personal agent. The personal agent is not employed by and thus not beholden to any funding, regulatory, or service provision agency, but rather only to the individual he or she represents. This relationship avoids the conflict of interest inherent in current developmental disability case management and vocational rehabilitation counselor arrangements.

Consumers receive three types of assistance from their personal agent. First, consumers receive life planing assistance, in which the personal agent works intensively to help the individual identify the type of career he or she wishes to pursue and to define other lifestyle goals. Individuals are encouraged to focus on their personal interests and unique talents as the most important factor in considering the type of career to which they would be best suited and in which they would be most motivated to succeed. Information and input is gained by the individual from his or her personal network; however, individuals are encouraged and supported to take as great a lead as possible. The agent also explains the different types of services and supports available. For example, the agent helps individuals understand the difference between receiving training from a job coach and receiving training from a supervisor or co-worker. The individual is then assisted to identify the most important characteristics of the employment services and supports they wish to obtain.

The person's agent then provides assistance to select the services and supports she or he wishes to receive. The agent identifies each agency and individual who may be able to offer services and supports desired by the person. This will usually include supported employment agencies in the local area. In addition, it may also include nonspecialized employment agencies, friends, or family. The agent assists the individual to develop a list of questions that she or he can use to interview each prospective agency and support person. These questions include the type of services the agency or person offers, whether the person or agency could offer the type specifically wanted by the individual, past outcomes in providing services to individuals (e.g., number of people placed into jobs, time that people have waited for a job, type of jobs, consumer satisfaction), and cost of services the individual desires. These interviews are audiotaped, and the agent and individual summarize and review the information obtained. The agent then assists the individual to identify the agencies or people he or she wishes to utilize.

Through the third phase of the process, the agent provides the individual with assistance to contract for services and to manage the contract. The agent helps the individual to develop a specific service contract that includes a detailed description of the services the agency or person will provide to the individual and the cost of these services. The contract stipulates that a monthly written report, invoice, and planned activities for the next month will be sent to the individual. The agent goes over the report and invoice with the individual. The individual may make additions to the report and will describe the extent to which he or she is satisfied with what has occurred during the month. After signing the report and invoice, the individual forwards it to the funding agency (e.g., Vocational Rehabilitation, Division of Developmental Disabilities). The individual may cancel the contract (with 2 weeks' notice) at any time. The agent assists the individual to discuss with the agency or person any concerns and possible remedies to these concerns.

Brokerage services have begun with five individuals through this demonstration project. It is too soon to assess the outcomes of the project. However, we hope and believe that the approach will result in better (and potentially less expensive) services for the individuals in the project. We also hope that this approach will over time encourage employment programs to understand that they should perceive themselves as directly accountable to the individuals from whom they make a living (i.e., the individuals with disabilities in their programs) and that they must work to satisfy their customers rather than the funding and regulatory agencies. Most of the supported employment agencies who have been interviewed and done business with individuals in the brokerage have welcomed this opportunity, indicating that it has encouraged them to think differently in how they plan and deliver services. The individuals who participated report that they feel for the first time as if they are being listened to seriously and that they are in control.

CONCLUSION

Great strides have been made in opening up employment opportunities for individuals with disabilities during the 1980s. Formerly, people with disabilities often expressed how empowering and confidence-building it was to get a "real" job, regardless of what kind of job it was and regardless of how much they were directly involved in the process. Groups of individuals in this society who have been depressed and discriminated against are usually willing to settle for a short while for opportunities that are little better than what they had before. However, in time these groups begin to demand better—to have the same opportunities as the rest of us. People with disabilities and their advocates are at this point reassessing work (as well as all areas of their lives). They no longer want those with disabilities to be relegated to the lowest-paid and lowest-status jobs, they no longer are willing to be trained by special staff from out-side their workplace, and they no longer are willing to turn over the decision-making power and control to employment agencies. Professionals have the obligation not only to respond positively to those individuals who express this desire for change, but to encourage change even for those individuals whom the system has made dependent.

These times also reflect the ongoing evolution of the field of rehabilitation for individuals with disabilities, particularly for individuals with developmental disabilities. Today the field continues to operate from a belief that professionals know best—that we have specialized expertise that enables us to make the best decisions for individuals with severe disabilities regarding the type of work they should perform and to have prime responsibility for determining the type of training and support they need, as well as the delivery of this training and support. However, we are slowly beginning to understand that a more appropriate role is one very close to that a rehabilitation counselor may play with a person with less significant disabilities. The rehabilitation counselor facilitates the person to understand the various options, to weigh these options, and to undertake the necessary activities to move toward his or her self-selected goal. Staff working with individuals with significant cognitive disabilities typically need to be more proactive and structured in their facilitation and counseling efforts than do traditional rehabilitation counselors. One might even say that employment consultants provide coaching! However, this coaching is focused not on specific work tasks, but on how to take the steps in the process of career planning, job seeking, and working with co-workers to resolve learning and performance issues.

Butch was 20 years old when he began participating in the New Hampshire Natural Supports Project. His school records revealed that he had had a number of serious emotional and psychiatric diagnoses and labels. Prior to project participation, he primarily attended resource room classes and participated in a special education unpaid work experience program. Through this program he had cleaned rooms at a nursing home and cleaned yards as part of a work crew. He also had a work experience stapling papers and stuffing envelopes in an office.

Via the career planning process, Butch indicated that he had a strong interest in drawing, in particular in cartoons and caricatures. The employment consultant also observed when meeting with Butch that he would often pull out a piece of paper and draw while he was talking. Often Butch would draw while he tried to explain his ideas. When going to pick him up for a meeting, the employment consultant would often find that he had been put into a room by himself because he had become agitated in class. He always spent this "cool down" time drawing. Butch indicated that drawing helped him to relax. Butch said, and it was confirmed by staff, that he had taken no art classes during his high school career. Butch also indicated, and the staff agreed, that he had been told by them that art was just something he could do for fun, and he had never considered it as something he might be able to do for a career. The employment consultant encouraged Butch to at least explore the possibility of an art-related occupation as a career. Because of his "reputation" in school, the art teachers were not particularly open to working with Butch.

(continued)

Case study *(continued)*

> With the help of the employment consultant, he met with a private art teacher, Eileen. She said that Butch indeed had a great deal of raw talent. She began meeting with him once a week to provide him with art instruction and to explore with him the type of career he might be best suited to pursuing. At first she encouraged him to learn line drawing, which might enable him to pursue a fine arts career. However, it became clear to Butch and to Eileen that his real talent and interest was in cartooning and caricatures. Through Elaine's personal connections, she has begun to assist him to build a business of performing caricatures and cartoons at art festivals, children's birthdays, and video stores (drawing caricatures of movie stars). Eileen serves as his manager, obtaining business opportunities including negotiating the payment. She also helps prepare Butch for the event and stays with him during the event if needed. The Division of Vocational Rehabilitation pays Eileen on an hourly basis for the assistance that she provides to Butch.
>
> Eileen suggested that he gain experience using computer programs that are used by artists. His employment consultant found a T-shirt design business that used such a program that indicated a willingness to train him on it and to perform other tasks related to the business. An apprenticeship was set up by the Job Training Council, through which the employer is reimbursed for training expenses.
>
> The following are some excerpts from a newspaper article (Milbouer, 1994) written about Butch and his experiences in pursuing a career:
>
> > "When I was in school, I worked in so many group homes, learning to do cleaning and serve meals to the elderly,"...In his heart, he said, he knew he didn't want a career doing janitorial work. However, he didn't know anything else was even available to him...."Now, I know I want to be an artist. . . . Now, I know I am an artist. Before, I felt like a prisoner. Now I feel like I am out of that prison." . . . I'm just a beginner. I know that. But I have so much talent and I can do anything I want to do," he said, without the slightest bit of self-consciousness. "He's right," his teacher [Eileen] said proudly.

REFERENCES

Anthony, R. (1991). *Doing what you love, loving what you do.* New York: Berkeley Books.

Bach, M. (1991). Giving choices to people with mental disabilities. *Perception, 15,* 33–36.

Bellamy, G.T., Rhodes, L.E., Bourbeau, P.E., & Mank, D.M. (1986). Mental retardation services in sheltered workshops and day activity programs: Consumer benefits and policy alternative. In F.R. Rusch (Ed.), *Competitive employment issues and strategies* (pp. 257–271). Baltimore: Paul H. Brookes Publishing Co.

Bellamy, G.T., Rhodes, L., Mank, D., & Albin, J. (1988). *Supported employment: A community implementation guide.* Baltimore: Paul H. Brookes Publishing Co.

Bissonnette, D. (1994). *Beyond traditional job development: The art of creating opportunity.* Chatsworth, CA: Milt Wright & Associates.

Bolles, R. (1994). *A practical manual for job-hunters and career changers: The 1994 what color is your parachute?* Berkeley, CA: Ten Speed Press.

Callahan, M. (1992). Job site training and natural supports. In J. Nisbet (Ed.), *Natural supports in school, at work, and in the community for people with severe disabilities* (pp. 257–276). Baltimore: Paul H. Brookes Publishing Co.

Chadsey-Rusch, J., Gonzalez, P., Tines, J., & Johnson, J. (1989). Social ecology of the workplace: Contextual variables affecting social interactions of employees with and without mental retardation. *American Journal on Mental Retardation, 94*, 141–151.

Cotton, P., & Sowers, J. (1995). *Empowering consumers through service brokerage: Demonstrations.* Project Product #5, Natural Supports Project, Institute on Disability, University of New Hampshire, Concord Center, Concord, NH.

Fabian, E., & Leucking, R. (1991). Doing it the company way: Using internal company supports in the workplace. *Journal of Applied Rehabilitation Counseling, 22*(2), 32–35.

Friedman, G. (1964). *The anatomy of work: Labor, leisure and the implications of automation.* New York: Free Press of Glencoe.

Greenspan, S., & Shoultz, B. (1981). Why mentally retarded adults lose their jobs: Social competence as a factor in work adjustment. *Applied Research in Mental Retardation, 2*, 23–38.

Hagner, D., & Dileo, D. (1993). *Workplace culture, supported employment and people with disabilities.* Cambridge, MA: Brookline.

Halle, D. (1984). *America's working man: Work, home and politics among blue collar property owners.* Chicago: University of Chicago Press.

Hanley-Maxwell, C., Rusch, F., Chadsey-Rusch, J., & Renzaglia, A. (1986). Reported factors contributing to job terminations of individuals with severe disabilities. *Journal of The Association for Persons with Severe Handicaps, 11*(1), 45–62.

Jackson, T. (1991). *Guerrilla tactics in the new job market.* New York: Bantam Books.

Kregel, J., Wehman, P., Seyfarth, J., & Marshall, K. (1986). Community integration of young adults with mental retardation: Transition from school to adulthood. *Employment and Training in Mental Retardation, 21*, 35–42.

Levin, A. (1991). *Introduction to the Strong for career counselors.* Palo Alto, CA: Consulting Psychologists Press.

Locke, E. (1983). The nature and causes of job satisfaction. In M. Dunnette (Ed.), *Handbook of industrial and organizational psychology* (pp. 1297–1349). Chicago: Rand-McNally.

Mank, D. (1994). The underachievement of supported employment: A call for reinvestment. *Journal of Disability Policy Studies*, 5(2), 1–24.

Mank, D., Rhodes, L., & Bellamy, G. (1986). Four supported employment alternatives. In W. Kiernan & J. Stark (Eds.), *Pathways to employment for adults with developmental disabilities* (pp. 139–162). Baltimore: Paul H. Brookes Publishing Co.

McClughan, G., & Salter, L. (1988). There when you need them. *Entourage, 3*, 26–32.

Mcloughlin, C., Garner, J., & Callahan, M. (1987). *Getting employed, staying employed: Job development and training for persons with severe handicaps.* Baltimore: Paul H. Brookes Publishing Co.

Milbouer, S. (1994, September 11). Art opens up his world: Program helps Butch Soto defeat disabilities. *The Sunday Telegraph*, p. A-10.

Moseley, C.R. (1988). Job satisfaction research: Implications for supported employment. *Journal of The Association for Persons with Severe Handicaps, 13*, 211–219.

Mount, B., & Zwernik, K. (1988). *It's never too early, it's never too late. A booklet about personal futures planning.* Minneapolis: Metropolitan Council.

Myers, I., & McCaulley, M. (1985). *Manual: A guide to the development and use of the Myers-Briggs Type Indicator.* Palo Alto, CA: Consulting Psychologists Press.

Nisbet, J., & Hagner, D. (1988). Natural supports in the workplace: A reexamination of supported employment. *Journal of The Association for Persons with Severe Handicaps, 13*(4), 260–267.

Nisbet, J., & Sowers, J. (1995). People with disabilities: Emerging members of the workforce. In R. Ritvo, A. Litwin, & L. Butler (Eds.), *Managing in the age of change: Essential skills to manage today's diverse workforce* (pp. 275–285). New York: Irwin Professional Publishing.

O'Brien, J. (1990, October). *Working on.... A survey of emerging issues in supported employment for people with severe disabilities.* Lithonia, GA: Responsive System Associates.

Powers, L., Sowers, J., & Stevens, S.T. (1995). An exploratory study of the impact of mentoring on the self-confidence and community-based knowledge of adolescents with severe physical challenges. *Journal of Rehabilitation, 61*(1), 33–41.

Powers, L., & Sowers, J. (1994). Evolving perspectives on transitions to adult living: Promoting self-determination and natural supports. In S. Calculator & C. Jorgenson (Eds.), *Including students with severe disabilities in schools: Fostering communication, interaction, and participation* (pp. 215–248). San Diego: Singular Press.

Rehabilitation Act Amendments of 1992, PL 102-569. (October 29, 1992). Title 29, U.S.C. 701 et seq: *U.S. Statutes at Large, 100,* 4344–4488.

Rusch, F. (1990). *Supported employment: Models, methods, & issues.* Sycamore, IL: Sycamore Publishing Co.

Scholtes, P. (1988). *The team handbook: How to use teams to improve quality.* Madison, WI: Joiner Associates.

Sher, B. (1979). *Wishcraft.* New York: Ballantine Books.

Sinetar, M. (1978). *Do what you love, the money will follow.* New York: Dell Publishing.

Sowers, J., Cotton, P., & Malloy, J. (1994). Expanding the job and career options for people with significant disabilities. *Developmental Disabilities Bulletin, 22*(2), 53–62.

Sowers, J., Goodall, S., Cotton, P., & McAllister, R. (1994). *The "planning my career" profile and planning process.* New Hampshire Naturally Supported Employment Projects, Institute on Disability, University of New Hampshire, Concord, NH.

Sowers, J., Malloy, J., & Cotton, P. (1994). *The New Hampshire natural supports project: Interim report of outcomes.* New Hampshire Naturally Supported Employment Projects, Institute on Disability, University of New Hampshire, Concord, NH.

Sowers, J., & Powers, L. (1991). *Vocational preparation and employment of students with physical and multiple disabilities.* Baltimore: Paul H. Brookes Publishing Co.

Sowers, J., & Powers, L. (1995). Enhancing the participation and independence of students with severe physical and multiple disabilities in performing community activities. *Mental Retardation, 33*(4), 209–220.

Vandercook, T., York, J., & Forest, M. (1989). The McGill Action Planning System (MAPS): A strategy for building a vision. *Journal of The Association for Persons with Severe Handicaps, 14*(3), 205–215.

West, M., & Parent, W. (1993). Consumer choice and empowerment in supported employment services: Issues and strategies. *Journal of The Association for Persons with Severe Handicaps, 17*(1), 47–52.

West, M., Revell, W., & Wehman, P. (1992). Achievements and challenges. I: A five-year report on consumer and system outcomes from the supported employment initiative. *Journal of The Association for Persons with Severe Handicaps, 17*(4), 227–235.

Williams, R. (1991). Choices, communication, and control: A call for expanding them in the lives of people with severe disabilities. In L.H. Meyer, C.A. Peck, & L. Brown (Eds.), *Critical issues in the lives of people with severe disabilities* (pp. 543–544). Baltimore: Paul H. Brookes Publishing Co.

Zadny, J., & James, L. (1979). Job placement in state vocational rehabilitation agencies: A survey of technique. *Rehabilitation Counseling Bulletin, 22,* 361–378.

17

Enhancing Friendships and Leisure Involvement of Students with Traumatic Brain Injuries and Other Disabilities

Jo-Ann Sowers, Ann E. Glang, Judith Voss, and Elizabeth Cooley

Since the 1980s, we have witnessed a growing belief that individuals with disabilities, including those with severe disabilities, should be fully included in school, work, and their communities (Nisbet, 1992; Taylor, Biklen, & Knoll, 1987). This belief has been accompanied by ongoing shifts in best practices and models. In areas of schooling, recommended practices have evolved from segregated schools, to self-contained classrooms in general schools, to inclusion in general classrooms (Jorgensen, 1992; Villa, Thousand, Stainback, & Stainback, 1992). In 1985, the only employment opportunities for most individuals with severe disabilities were in sheltered programs. The supported employment and job coach models have demonstrated that these individuals can work in typical businesses (Wehman & Moon, 1988; West, Revell, & Wehman, 1992). Through the job coach approach, supported employment staff have taken the primary

The preparation of this chapter was supported, in part, by Grant Nos. 90DN0014 from the Department of Health and Human Services, H158Q40054 from the U.S. Department of Education, and H128A40102 from Rehabilitation Services Administration. No official endorsement should be implied, nor does this chapter necessarily reflect the opinions or policies of any of these grant agencies.

responsibility for training new employees with disabilities. It has begun to appear that many businesses and co-workers are willing and able to provide much of the initial training when provided with proactive consultation from supported employment staff and that this approach may enhance both the long-term job retention and social integration of supported employees (Hagner & Dileo, 1993; Nisbet & Hagner, 1988; Sowers, 1995). Recent years have seen the widespread understanding that large institutions are not acceptable (although some continue to exist). Recommended practices for individuals with disabilities have moved from large group homes to smaller group living arrangements to the opportunity to rent and own homes (Klein, 1992).

Inclusion in typical leisure and social activities, including the development of acquaintances and friendships with individuals without disabilities, has been another important arena for evolving beliefs and practices since the 1980s. Earlier, "special" recreation activities were the widely accepted best practice approach to fulfilling the social and recreational needs of individuals with disabilities. It was assumed that these individuals' social and friendship network should and would primarily comprise other individuals with disabilities. Beliefs have begun to shift to an understanding that these individuals should have the opportunity to participate in regular and typical social and leisure activities and to develop acquaintances and friendships with individuals who do not experience disabilities (Grenot-Scheyer, 1994; O'Brien & O'Brien, 1993; Schleien, Meyer, Heyne, & Brandt, 1995; Staub, Schwartz, Gallucci, & Peck, 1994; Voeltz, Wuerch, & Wilcox, 1982).

In this chapter we provide an overview of the literature related to the implications of friendship and leisure participation on the self-determination of children and youth. We also provide a brief review of the major approaches that have attempted to enhance the friendships and leisure participation of individuals who experience disabilities. Two projects conducted by the authors are described in detail. The first is a comprehensive approach to enhancing friendships and leisure participation conducted with students who have experienced traumatic brain injuries. The second is a community bridge-building project aimed at students with severe disabilities transitioning from school.

FRIENDSHIP AND LEISURE: IMPLICATIONS FOR SELF-DETERMINATION

There is substantial evidence of the impact and importance of social relationships and leisure participation on the self-determination and self-esteem of children and youth without disabilities. Children and youth who perceive that they have supportive friends have higher self-esteem than those individuals who do not perceive the presence of supportive friendship networks in their lives (Mannarino, 1976; McGuire & Weisz, 1982; Townsend, McCracken, & Wilton, 1988). There is also the understanding of the impact that peer interactions and culture have on the development of autonomy and self-determination. For example, it has been found that once children enter child care and educational settings they very quickly develop a strong identity with their peers and engage with these peers in challenging teachers and adult caregivers (Davies, 1982; Rubin, 1980). It has also been shown that children attempt to gain control over fears, confusion, and curiosity evoked by the adult world through their participation in numerous play routines, rituals, and games (Garvey, 1984; Goodwin, 1985). The literature on typical adolescent development supports the important role that peers play for youth in the development of self-determination. As children reach adolescence, they report an increasing reliance on peers and friends for advice, understanding, and acceptance and as the means through which they can reflect and define themselves, their values, and their goals (Corsaro & Eder, 1990; Griffin, 1985; Wulff, 1988; Youniss & Smoller, 1985).

The critical role that participation in leisure activities has in the development of self-determination has been widely discussed in the child and adolescent development literature. For example, many have argued that individuals learn to direct their lives through setting goals, attempting to achieve them, and evaluating their progress toward reaching them (Lerner & Busch-Rossnagel, 1981; Sibereisen, Eyferth, & Rudinger, 1986). Oerther (1986) suggests that school and work settings provide relatively limited opportunities for these experiences because of the structure and control imposed by others on the activities engaged in by students and employees. In contrast, Oerther believes, free-time activities give individuals the best opportunity for self-determination experimentation. Dattilo (1994, 1995) has also suggested that leisure participation provides an excellent context in which to teach choice. He had developed and tested a systematic instruction approach for teaching leisure making choices.

A number of studies have looked at the extent to which adolescents choose to spend their free time in different types of activities. The most frequent free-time activity of high school students was socializing with friends (Csikszentmihalyi & Larson, 1984). Research suggests that membership in an organization is also common for many teenagers. The positive impact of formal organizational activities on participants' self-determination, both short-term and into adulthood, has been validated by a number of research studies (Hanks & Eckland, 1978; Hedin & Conrad, 1981; Spady, 1970).

REVIEW OF RELATED RESEARCH

Since the mid-1970s, a wide variety of approaches have evolved to enhance the friendship and leisure participation of individuals with disabilities. In this section, we review the major types of approaches that have been made and summarize the outcomes that have been achieved.

Pairing Individuals with and without Disabilities

Voeltz and her colleagues conducted one of the first organized and widely disseminated efforts to facilitate and enhance social interactions and friendship between elementary-age peers with and without disabilities (Voeltz, 1980, 1982; Voeltz, Kishi, Brown, & Kube, 1980). The "Special Friends" program recruited and matched peers without disabilities to play with students with severe disabilities during recess, lunch, and activity times. School personnel encouraged and facilitated social interactions and play between the peers and were specifically instructed not to allow instruction or helping behaviors by the peer without disabilities. Positive attitudes toward students with disabilities and peer relationships among the students were found to increase as a result of participation in the project.

Peer Tutoring

The second major line of social integration and interaction efforts has focused on peer tutoring (Haring, 1991; Odom & Strain, 1986). The results of research on peer tutoring have shown an increase in positive social and academic skills by the students with disabilities and an increase in positive attitudes of the peer tutors toward individuals with disabilities (Gartner & Lipsky, 1990; Haring, 1991). No research has illustrated an actual impact of peer tutoring on friendship or social activity involvement among peers with and without disabilities. The potential deleterious effect on the formation of reciprocal and equal social relationships of placing students without disabilities in a teaching and oversight role has been voiced in the literature (Kishi & Meyer, 1994).

Peer Involvement in Planning

A third social integration enhancement model identified by Kishi and Meyer (1994) is the involvement of peers in the educational planning of students with disabilities. Examples of these approaches are the circle of friends (Forest & Lusthaus, 1989), the McGill Action Planning System (MAPS) (Vandercook, York, & Forest, 1989), and the collaborative problem-solving approach (Salisbury & Palombaro, 1992).

Community Bridge-Building

Another important approach has been the facilitation of involvement of individuals with disabilities in regular community recreational activities. This approach has frequently been termed community bridge-building (Arsensault, 1990; Mount, Beeman, & Ducharme, 1988; O'Connell, 1988). Community bridge-building involves identifying formal and informal organizations and activities that offer opportunities for individuals to get to know each other and to develop relationships and friendships. It also facilitates the inclusion of individuals with disabilities into these groups and offers activities and connection with the other participants. A number of case studies have been reported of individuals (from young children to older adults) who were included in community groups and who made friendships with group members without disabilities (Arsensault, 1990; Perske, 1988; Strully & Strully, 1989).

Inclusion in General Classrooms

One of the primary rationales for inclusion of students with disabilities into general classrooms is the opportunity for these students to interact socially with their peers without disabilities in and outside of class (Stainback & Stainback, 1990). In general, research suggests that positive social relationships did occur between students with and without disabilities (Hall, 1994; Staub et al., 1994). However, there were substantial differences in both the amount and the nature of these interactions experienced by students who had disabilities. The amount and particularly the forms of the interactions and relationships for many students with disabilities with their peers is different from what is typical among students who do not experience disabilities, and it remains unclear which criteria and measures should be used to judge progress toward social inclusion of students with disabilities (Hall, 1994). One conclusion that perhaps can be drawn is that inclusion is sufficient for some students with disabilities to develop typical levels and forms of interactions with their peers, whereas for many students inclusion in typical classrooms is not sufficient, and other strategies must be utilized to facilitate social interactions and relationships. Strategies such as the active promotion by teachers of a relationship between a student with disabilities and a peer or peers is one strategy that appears to have some impact (Cole, 1986; Meyer et al., 1987; Voeltz & Brennan, 1984). The argument has been made for the utilization of strategies that promote positive interactions and relationships for all students, rather than using different approaches for students with disabilities (Uditsky, 1993). Cooperative learning strategies have been identified as holding promise for promoting relationships among all students (Gartner & Lipsky, 1990; Stainback & Stainback, 1990). Using a cooperative learning approach, teachers facilitate all students to teach and support each other and typically focus on participatory learning activities to encourage the active involvement of students in projects.

Entering the Work World

As with school inclusion, one of the primary reasons for moving individuals from sheltered to regular businesses was the increased social interaction opportunities with co-workers without disabilities that are available in the latter. There is no question that individuals who work in regular businesses have higher levels of social interactions with co-workers without disabilities during their workday than do individuals who work in sheltered workshops. Evidence also shows that co-workers are less involved with employees with disabilities who work in a group than with an employee who is individually placed (Rusch, Johnson, & Hughes, 1990). However, research has revealed that the amount and nature of the interactions among co-workers with and without disabilities were less than among co-workers without disabilities (Chadsey-Rusch, 1986; Lignugaris/Kraft, Salzberg, Rule, & Stowitschek, 1988; Storey & Knutson, 1989). In addition, it was also found that employees with disabilities were less likely to be involved in joking and teasing, social interactions that were found to occur at a high level among co-workers without disabilities (Lignugaris/Kraft et al., 1988).

The role of the job coach has been identified as one factor that impedes the development of social connections between co-workers with and without disabilities (Nisbet & Hagner, 1988). The groundwork for connections among co-workers typically occurs during the first few weeks and months on the job, when a new employee is trained and is helped to understand the workplace culture (i.e., the unwritten rules of fitting in) by other employees. When an agency staff person takes most or all of the responsibility for training an employee with a disability, these initial opportunities are lost. In addition, the presence of a job coach may serve to stigmatize, accentuate the employee's differences, and indicate to co-workers that only individuals with specialized training know how to interact with their new co-worker. There is a growing trend to encourage employees with disabilities to be trained by co-workers and for supported employment program staff to provide input to co-workers when necessary about approaches that may be unique to the learning needs and style of a particular employee (Rogan, Hagner, & Murphy, 1993; Sowers, 1995). Research on interventions has focused almost exclusively on teaching employees with disabilities social skills to use at worksites (Chadsey-Rusch, Karlan, Riva, & Rusch, 1984; Shafer, Brookes, & Wehman, 1985). For example, Breen, Haring, Pitts-Conway, and Gaylord-Ross (1985) taught students with a disability at a work experience a break-time conversation script that they could use with their co-workers.

As stated, the current hope is that the amount and type of social interactions between co-workers with and without disabilities will be enhanced if the new workers are initially trained by co-workers rather than by a job coach. No research has yet been conducted to determine if co-worker training approaches do result in this outcome. It has also been suggested that supported employment staff must focus much more of their time and effort on facilitating social connections among supported employees and co-workers, rather than just on addressing task performance issues. Again, no research is available illustrating the impact of proactive co-worker interaction facilitation.

Teaching Leisure Skills

A body of literature illustrates the effectiveness of systematic instruction and adaptation strategies in teaching a wide variety of leisure skills (Baumgart et al., 1982; Schleien et al., 1995; Wehman, 1977).

THE BUILDING FRIENDSHIPS PROJECT

Each year, approximately 165,000 children and youth survive traumatic brain injuries (TBI) sustained in motor vehicle accidents, falls, sports accidents, and physical abuse (Bush, 1986). Of these children, 20,000 annually are left with long-lasting alterations in social, behavioral, physical, and cognitive functioning (Kalsbeek, McLaurin, & Harris, 1980; Rosen & Gerring, 1986).

The loss of friends, decrease in social activities, and absence of social support that usually accompany TBI can be the most difficult effects for children and adolescents to manage (Singer & Nixon, 1995; Wagner, Williams, & Long, 1990; Willer, Allen, Durnan, & Ferry, 1990). After a brain injury, a student often loses the ability to function effectively in social situations; he or she may behave in ways deemed socially inappropriate (e.g., showing disinhibition, poor social judgment, insensitivity to others, or impulsiveness). Friends may be confused by the student's behavior and may gradually drift away. This problem is only exacerbated when the student has had to miss up to an entire year of school while undergoing rehabilitation. Same-age peers have moved on to a new grade level and established new friends and interests, and the student with TBI may feel left behind.

Just as a child never fully recovers from TBI, the child's friendships may never return to the way they were before the injury. Many survivors of brain injury report that problems with social isolation persist over many years (Thomsen, 1984) and that new problems in the area of social support often develop in the years following injury (Brown, Chadwick, Shaffer, Rutter, & Traub, 1981).

The Building Friendships project focuses on alleviating the social isolation experienced by students with TBI by developing and enhancing school-based social networks. The project uses an adapted version of MAPS for this purpose (Vandercook et al., 1989). The overarching goal of the Building Friendships project is to increase the quality of the student's social life through an ongoing, informal team process designed to bring together and mobilize key people in a student's life. The student, family, peers, and professionals participate in a four-phase process. These phases consist of gathering information, recruiting, conducting an initial team meeting, and holding regular follow-up meetings. Each is described as follows.

1. *Gathering information through interviews with student, parents, school staff, and peers.* Project facilitators conduct interviews to identify opportunities within school and community settings to create new friendships, to enhance current friendships, and to develop increased social opportunities. This information is used as a basis for the initial team meeting (see next step).

2. *Recruiting family members, school staff, and peers for involvement as team members.* Based on information gathered in interviews, key individuals are identified and invited to the initial meeting. The student and family members play the primary role in determining whom to recruit. Facilitators are responsible for making contact with potential team members, who must include peers, extended family, and school staff. In some cases, whole classes are giv-

en information about the purpose for developing the team; and interested peers are asked to participate.

3. *Conducting an initial team meeting to share information and to create visions for the future.* The team identifies individualized social goals and specific strategies to meet these goals.

4. *Holding regular review meetings.* Every 2–3 weeks, team members meet to review progress, revise plans and strategies, and reevaluate team membership and responsibilities.

Like other person-centered planning strategies, the Building Friendships process strives to create an environment that encourages the student and family to direct all aspects of the planning process. The process combines many of the features of the MAPs (Vandercook et al., 1989) and the circle of friends (Perske, 1988; Snow, 1989) strategies. Several adaptations in these strategies were made in order to accommodate busy schedules of team members and to emphasize social issues and follow-up activities. Following is a description of the adapted process.

Intent and Structure

The Building Friendships process, like MAPs, represents a dynamic and fluid person-centered planning strategy designed to increase the ability of students and families to guide their own solutions to problems of social isolation. The process emphasizes the importance of including peers as team members as early in the process as possible; hence, potential peers are identified by the student with TBI, family members, and teachers during the second phase.

The original MAPs process consists of seven key questions to help guide efforts of team members in increasing the successful inclusion of students with disabilities (Vandercook et al., 1989):

1. What is the individual's history?
2. What is your dream for the individual?
3. What is your nightmare?
4. Who is the individual?
5. What are the individual's strengths, gifts, and abilities?
6. What are the individual's needs?
7. What would the individual's ideal school day look like?

Whereas MAPs addresses a full range of student-centered issues, the Building Friendships process focuses solely on social issues and is thus of shorter duration. The steps involved in the initial team meeting are described as follows.

1. Who Is [the Student]?   Participants are encouraged to offer as many words and phrases as they can think of to describe the positive qualities and attributes of the student. These are shared out loud and recorded by the facilitator in colorful markers on a large sheet of paper. This first question sets the tone for the rest of the initial meeting in its upbeat focus on the student's strengths. Importantly, this step can also be emotionally charged for students and families unaccustomed to such an outpouring of positive feedback.

2. Hopes and Dreams   This question prompts team members to state their hopes and dreams for the student within the social domain. The student is given the opportunity to state his or her own hopes and dreams first. The facilitator checks with the student frequently to make sure that hopes and dreams offered by other team members are acceptable. The student is the only one who holds veto power for any hope or dream. As long as the student accepts the hopes and dreams offered by others, every response is recorded and nothing is censored. This serves to model a mindset that both empowers the student and expands the team's notion of what is possible. Important goals for the student often emerge from dreams which, initially, might seem unrealistic to achieve.

3. Circle of Friends   With the information previously gathered, a pre-prepared visual diagram is presented to the group to represent the key people currently in the student's life. This diagram consists of four concentric circles, with the student's name placed inside the innermost circle. Those closest to the student, trusted friends, acquaintances, and paid professionals are all listed on successive circles extending outward from the student. The intent of this activity is to graphically demonstrate the nature of the student's social network. In most cases, students with TBI have only a few close and trusted friends and an abundance of acquaintances and paid professionals in their circle. The goal of the Building Friendships process is to create positive social changes to allow expansion of the student's inner circle of trusted friends.

4. Goals   The next phase of the first meeting involves identifying several goals toward which the team can begin working. Often these goals are derived from the hopes and dreams created earlier by the team. As in the earlier steps of the process, the student decides whether chosen goals are acceptable. Goals are fluid and can be changed as needed, and it is important to remind the group that more goals can be added in future meetings.

5. Obstacles   Next the team identifies obstacles to achieving the identified goals. Team members are asked to think of all the reasons why the identified goals are not currently being addressed.

6. Strategies   The team then brainstorms specific strategies for overcoming the obstacles. Pushing the limits of commonly accepted practices is encouraged to facilitate the emergence of creative, untried approaches and solutions. Strategies might take concerted effort to implement or might be as simple as a schedule change to permit greater inclusion and opportunities with peers—the point is that at this stage, anything goes. To help initiate the brainstorming of ideas, certain strategies were described to team members as examples that have been found useful with other individuals. The following description shows how each of these strategies were used by one or more of the participants in the Building Friendships Project.

Schedule changes: modifying a student's schedule to increase social opportunities in inclusive settings. Rather than spend all day in the special education classroom, Janet's team changed her schedule so that she went to recess at the same time as other first graders and went to the first-grade classroom at the beginning of each day for several hours.

Peer education about TBI: presenting information about TBI to peers, with specific information about their peer's experiences. In his middle school homeroom class, Richard and his mother presented a slide show about his rehabilitation from a severe brain injury several years earlier. The presentation included slides of Richard prior to his accident, during coma, and in various rehabilitation activities at the hospital. Richard's mother discussed the effects of the brain injury on Richard and their family. Richard and his mother then answered students' questions.

Organized recreational activities: linking a student with recreational activities in the community (e.g., through parks and recreation departments and the local YMCA). As a result of his team's brainstorming and exploring of community-based social and recreational opportunities for focus students, Ted got involved in a church youth group. Joan joined a Camp Fire club, Bob began going to the YMCA with two friends several times a week after school to hang out and shoot baskets, and Ralph and another young man started working out in a gym three times a week.

Friendship clubs: shifting focus from one individual to a larger group while facilitating and maintaining a general group awareness of and sensitivity to pertinent social issues of group members. One special education teacher began the Building Friendships process specifically for her student Billy. But as peer interest developed and grew, the focus gradually shifted away from an exclusive focus on Billy. Soon Billy and his peers were meeting once a week to discuss concerns about friendships and were planning dances and other activities to be involved in together.

Buddy system for getting to and from class and at lunch and recess: asking peer volunteers to assist students who need help getting around the school campus and to spend time with students at lunch and recess. The facilitator for Helen's team was able to coordinate with other teachers whose students were interested in eating lunch with Helen and playing with her at recess. These artificial situations were helpful in allowing the children to get acquainted with one another and to establish a routine. After several months the peer team members decided that having a schedule was causing problems and was unnatural. The formal buddy systems were dropped, but the interactions with Helen and her peers continued.

Cooperative learning activities: structuring classroom activities so that groups of students work together toward a common goal. This strategy was not selected by a student and his or her team. An example of how this might have been used is classroom teaching implementing a process whereby small groups of students would work collaboratively to complete math problems or a science project.

Social events outside of school: planning a group activity in the community. Randy's team planned an after-school pizza and bowling party that was very well attended by the peers in the group. This experience served to strengthen group rapport, and it gave everyone an opportunity to get to know one another in a different way outside the academic setting. Randy's joking, usually viewed as inappropriate during class time, was well received and reciprocated in this recreational context.

Organizational systems: creating compensatory systems for keeping track of important information. Sally's team helped her create a book with pictures of her friends. Below each picture was the friend's telephone number. Each of the friends also had their own photo telephone books so that they could call one another. Ted's team suggested that he carry around a tape recorder at school. This enabled him to record information such as students' telephone numbers, and was a fun way for him to interact with other students as they taped messages for him.

Informal weekly get-togethers: lunch at school. Sam and the peers involved in his team decided they would all eat lunch together once a week. A classroom and the gym were reserved for them, and often they took turns bringing special treats. Sam and his peers looked forward to this special time to play group games and have organized discussions about topics of interest ranging from current events to quality of cafeteria food.

Classwide activities: disability awareness/community building. As part of their involvement in the Building Friendships project, the facilitator for Billy's team coordinated a Disability Awareness Week that was set up in the school gym. Each class spent their gym time rotating through various simulation exercises which were designed to provide students with the experience of having a number of different disabilities. The facilitator for Mark's team came to his block class several times and guided the student group as a whole through some of the steps in MAPS. This was a unifying experience for the students, and some of the pressure of being the focus of attention was taken off of Mark. Both Helen and Billy's special education teachers had an open door policy in their classroom, which made it very comfortable for students from different classes to come in and spend time with Helen and Billy and the other students.

Events outside the classroom: attending extracurricular school functions. Through the work and encouragement of team efforts, Ralph obtained a student body card and attended several school dances with his brother and a few friends. Ed became very involved working on the school newspaper and began to feel more comfortable participating in class field trips, and Randy earned extra money as a track helper.

7. Action Plan   Finally, the team prioritizes goals and strategies and develops a specific plan that details how team members will achieve their goals. The action plan itself consists of three columns: *What, By Whom,* and *When.* The action plan keeps team members clear on tasks and accountable for following through with agreed-upon commitments.

Because each student's situation is unique, the activities and strategies decided upon by the team vary considerably. The following presents a menu of sample strategies that might be included on a student's action plan.

Implementation of the Building Friendships Process

Students   The Building Friendships process was implemented with 10 students who had survived severe brain injury. School-based facilitators worked intensively with each student throughout the school year. Of the 10 students, there were 7 boys and 3 girls, ranging in age from 7 to 17 (mean age = 11.7). Prior to their injury, 6 of the 10 students were average to above-average students who attended their home schools, performed at grade level, and were not described as displaying behavior problems. The remaining four students were under age 5 and not yet enrolled in school when they were injured. According to parent reports, none of these students showed signs of physical, behavioral, or cognitive deficits prior to their injury.

When they became involved with the Building Friendships project, the students averaged 4.7 years postinjury (range = 2.4–9 years), well past the most rapid period of "spontaneous recovery." As a result of their injuries, they experienced significant deficits in physical, cognitive, and behavioral functioning. They received special education services in resource or self-contained settings. All of the students had experienced a significant decline in their social network. They described themselves as having few, if any, friends.

Facilitators   For six of the students, project staff facilitated team and peer group development; for the remaining four students, school-based educators were trained to facilitate the process in their schools. The trained facilitators included two special education teachers, a special education consultant, and an educational assistant.

Prior to getting started with their students, facilitators participated in a day-long training session. The training was designed to familiarize facilitators with the general goals, value system, and approach of the Building Friendships process. The steps in the MAPS were detailed as a foundation to the Building Friendships process, and case study information was provided about social issues specific to students with TBI and their families. The training served as an opportunity for facilitators to understand their role in enhancing social experiences for students with TBI and to discuss potential challenges to implementing the Building Friendships process with their particular students.

Measures To evaluate the effectiveness of the Building Friendships process, project staff interviewed students, parents, and teachers prior to and following their involvement in the project. In addition to gathering demographic information about participants, interviewers asked participants to complete several written measures.

Teachers and parents completed the School and Community Activity and Integration Assessment (SCAIA) (Sowers & Powers, 1991). This instrument assesses a student's level of social integration in school and community settings. The measure is administered to a parent for home and community activities and to a teacher for school activities. The measure asks the parent to indicate the number of times, in what context (e.g., telephone call, home visit, neighborhood play, club), and with whom the student has recently socialized. Parents also report how often the student has participated in the activity during the prior month, 3 months, and 6 months. The teacher scale includes analogous questions for school-related activities.

Parents, students, and teachers also completed social validation measures designed to assess their satisfaction with the students' social networks before and after their involvement in the project (5 = highly satisfied). Participants were asked to rate how satisfied they were with the quantity and quality of the students' interactions with peers.

Finally, at the completion of the project, participants were asked to provide their perceptions of the process as a whole. Participants were asked open-ended questions about their satisfaction with the process and its effects on the student.

Results

Table 1 depicts parents', teachers', and students' mean responses on pre- and postproject measurements for the 10 students involved in the Building Friendships project. As indicated in Table 1, the average number of friends reported by the students, their parents, and their teachers increased from pre- to postassessment. In the majority of cases, students named more friends than did their parents or teacher at both pre- and postassessments. At postassessment, parents reported that their child spent less time in the prior month with peers with disabilities than they had in the month prior to preassessment. Parents reported a substantial increase, however, in the number of activities their child did with a friend without disabilities. On the satisfaction measure (i.e.,

Table 1. Results of Building Friendships

Measure	Students		Parents		Teachers	
	Pre	Post	Pre	Post	Pre	Post
Number of friends	5	7	2	4	3	4
Involvement-peers with disabilities			.8	.67		
Involvement-peer without disabilities			4.6	10.0		
Satisfaction	3.2	3.0	2.3	2.8	2.5	2.9

Note: Pre (prior to Building Friendships participation) and Post (after such participation) refer to mean responses by students, parents, and teachers about the number of friends of students, the number of activities students participated in, with peers with and without disabilities, and the level of satisfaction with the students' social network.

satisfaction with the quantity and quality of the student's social network), the mean responses by parents and teachers increased from pre- to postassessment, whereas the students' average responses decreased slightly. Only one of the students' ratings on this measure actually decreased at postassessment; however, because of the small number of students in the sample, this student's scores decreased the group mean.

In postassessment interviews, students, parents, and teachers reported feeling very satisfied with the effects of the process on the students' social networks. Students were seen as having more opportunities to interact with peers and were spending more time with peers in home and school settings. Participants commented that the problem-solving process used in the meetings allowed the group to work collaboratively.

Parents and teachers also felt that the process helped their students feel more positive and confident at school. In many cases, they attributed the changes to the involvement of peers in regular meetings:

> Kim just made a complete turn-around. She knows how to communicate now...the meetings were extremely important. I was amazed at how much input we got from the kids. They were saying things that I was thinking but really couldn't say.

One teacher who worked with a student who had a history of aggressive behavior felt that as a result of being involved in the project, her student had learned more positive ways of interacting with peers:

> After we started this process David became a new kid...he doesn't have any behaviors that are really violent...kids come up and they want to play with David....He didn't have any friends before, everyone was afraid of him.

Discussion

Because of the lack of control group data and the variability in responses, the results presented here can be interpreted only as preliminary in nature. However, the results do suggest that after their involvement in the project, students, parents, and teachers reported increases in the number of activities the students did with peers without disabilities and in the number of friends the students had. Parents and teachers also reported increases in their satisfaction with the student's social life.

Results from the Building Friendships project have been encouraging. With minimal training designed to introduce an informal, creative approach for enhancing social participation of students with TBI, facilitators were able to promote positive changes in a limited period of time. The Building Friendships process requires ongoing effort to further increase and maintain its effects. While the facilitator role may decrease in intensity over time, it is likely that some form of continued guidance and monitoring of the team process will be needed. This section highlights additional factors that have been instrumental in the implementation of the Building Friendships process. Issues to be aware of that are specific to working with students who have TBI and their families are outlined, as are other insights gained along the way.

1. At least one adult member of the Building Friendships team needs to have a strong commitment to enhancing the student's friendships. This is absolutely essential to the success of the process. One person's ongoing commitment will help to ensure that necessary follow-through will occur.
2. The building administrator needs to be supportive of the project if team efforts are to succeed. The Building Friendships process introduces new approaches to facilitating social opportunities within school settings. With support of the

process from principals, team members often experience a greater sense of freedom to engage in creative problem solving and activities.

3. Ideally the friendship facilitator is a school staff member, or, at minimum, has close associations within the school. Because each school has its own culture, it can be difficult to implement the process as an outsider. Insider status can be helpful in recruiting team members, organizing activities and events, and maintaining adequate communication.

4. The facilitator needs to keep in contact with team members between meetings to maintain group cohesion and to determine whether any situations have arisen that will prevent team members from following through on specified commitments. Providing such "glue" is a key to success of the process. Linking team members in ongoing communication between meetings serves to deepen feelings of membership, and helps to establish and maintain the group's momentum.

5. Every child is different, so the process must be tailored to meet each student's unique needs. What works for one student may be inappropriate for another. Keeping the process creative, dynamic, and open to variation will further enhance its effectiveness. This flexibility is the essence of the Building Friendships process and helps keep teams from getting stuck in ruts.

6. To the extent possible, Building Friendships should be a student-driven and peer-driven process. Allowing students to direct their own process as much as possible is an empowering experience that is new for many people. Trusting in this approach can serve to strengthen student commitment to the process which, in turn, will result in greater ownership of outcomes on the part of the students.

7. Emphasis should be placed on reciprocity between the student and other peers. Horizontal, not vertical, relationships are the goal. The Building Friendships process aims to facilitate and support interactions among peers that are based on equality of status and are not hierarchical in nature.

Lessons Learned

Other issues and dynamics that became apparent during the course of the Building Friendships project are important to consider before attempting to increase social relationships for students with TBI. Weiss (1973) makes an important distinction between social isolation characterized by the absence of a peer network and emotional isolation that stems from a lack of deep, meaningful friendships. Early in the process of implementing the Building Friendships project, it became apparent that the friendship-enhancing strategies we were using were designed to address issues of social rather than emotional isolation. In providing a structure for increasing social opportunities with peers, the hope is always that over the long term, friendships will take root and develop.

Awareness of and sensitivity to the issues faced by family members is a critical aspect of the Building Friendships project. For some families, their child's loss of friends is a very difficult and sensitive issue. One parent told us, for example, that becoming involved in the process was frightening at first. For the first time since her son was injured, she was asked to confront the deep sadness she felt about her son's loneliness and to trust that this group of well-meaning professionals and peers might help him reestablish important social connections.

In some cases, we found that parents were pleased to attend meetings and support school efforts, but were unable to promote interaction in home and community settings. The reasons for their reluctance varied. Some parents were less concerned about their child's social network than they were about academic goals and devoted their necessarily limited energy to helping their child with schoolwork. For others, the day-to-day stresses they faced outweighed their desire to help their child develop friendships. Many of the families we worked with faced enormous financial and emotional drains on family resources. It is critical that schools begin to view their roles to include active, out-of-school supports. This new view may include the allocation of staff who are able to spend time away from the school building, during after-school hours (including evenings and weekends), to provide direct support and assistance to students related to leisure and social activities (see the next section, which describes the Community Bridge-Builder Project). Schools may also include providing financial resources directly to students and families that will assist in the cost of out-of-school community activity participation, including the cost of transportation and leisure activities.

CONNECTING TRANSITION-AGE STUDENTS TO YOUNG ADULT LEISURE ORGANIZATIONS AND ACTIVITIES

With the assistance of the New Hampshire Natural Supports Project (Sowers, 1994), Nashua High School in Nashua, New Hampshire, conducted a survey of students with significant developmental disabilities who had departed from school services between 1989 and 1991. Interviews with the school leavers and their families revealed that their greatest current concern was the lack of social and leisure activities in which the young adults engaged and their lack of friends and social acquaintances. With the exception of the Special Olympics, leisure activities for most of the students were limited to those done with their family.

In response to this survey and with a desire to enhance the postschool social lives of current students, Nashua High School hired a community bridge builder to assist students with significant developmental disabilities who were 18–20 years of age to participate in community leisure and social activities. The community bridge builder was hired through a small grant received from the New Hampshire Department of Education. The goal of this person was to facilitate each student to participate in at least one typical community organization or activity that provided the opportunity for the student to develop relationships with the other members of the organization or activity. The role of the community bridge builder was not to do activities with the students, but to facilitate and assist each student to become connected to and supported by the members of a typical leisure organization.

To fill the community bridge-builder position, the school district specifically looked for a person who met the following criteria. 1) The person had to be very familiar with and well-connected to the local community. A person who has lived for many years in a community and who is active there is able to quickly identify the organizations where the greatest opportunities for social connections exist. Such a person will also frequently know one or more individuals who participate in an organization there, thus making the approach to these individuals about including the students and young adults much easier and more natural. 2) The person had to be outgoing and able to easily communicate with and relate to a wide variety of individuals. Again, the role of the bridge builder is not to do activities with students, but to serve as a bridge between the students and individuals who belong to organizations and participate in activities. The activities to which students are connected are driven by their individual interests and thus include a wide array of groups and types of people who participate. A shy person or one who feels comfortable interacting with only certain types of individuals will have a difficult time successfully taking on this role. 3) The person had to be able to work afternoons, evenings, and weekends. Most young adult and adult social activities do not occur during the typical school day. Rather, these activities occur when young adults are not going to school or working. The bridge builder must be willing and able to work a schedule different from other school personnel. This schedule flexibility, of course, must also be accommodated by the school district. The funding provided to Nashua High School from the New Hampshire Department of Education permitted the hiring of an individual into the community bridge-builder position at the wage paid to a special education aide. The individual hired into the position was a young woman who had worked as an aide at the high school for a year, who knew the students and their families, and who was a native of Nashua and well connected there.

The Nashua community bridge-builder project was conducted for 1 year. In addition, other school and respite care organizations in New Hampshire are implementing similar projects. The following provides a description of strategies and recommendations that derived from what was learned through the Nashua High School and other subsequent community bridge-builder projects.

1. Investigate and develop a written document describing local community social and leisure organizations and activities. Every possible typical organization and group should be included, not only the most well-known or formal organizations. Include special interest groups (e.g., model train organization, book discussion groups, poetry groups, hang glider associations). In other words, don't focus on groups or activities based on a preconceived notion of what individuals with disabilities can do or would want to do. Also, bridge builders do not have to wait to begin connecting individuals to activities until every single group has been identified and surveyed–get the list going and let the individual's interest drive your further investigation. Community bridge builders should be faithful readers of the social and community news sections of their newspapers and bulletin boards posted at community organizations and businesses.

Again, developing a list and description of local community activities will be easier for bridge builders who are already very familiar with a community and well connected there. In investigating and compiling information for the Community Activity Guide (a name some of the bridge builders have used), bridge builders should attempt to actually meet with someone from the organization and attend an activity. Doing this will permit the bridge builder to begin to develop a connection with the organization and to gain the kind of information needed to determine if it is a place that will be supportive of a student and will provide opportunities for connections and to plan for facilitating these supports and connections. During initial contacts with an organization, a bridge builder should not emphasize his or her role as working for and with students with disabilities. In fact, we have found that a better title for a bridge builder is community liaison, a more common and generic term. The bridge builder from Nashua High School typically described her role as representing the school district's goal to develop and expand their connection with community businesses and organizations and to involve students in a variety of ways in community activities, including assisting students to become active members of positive and adult social and community organizations. The written document should have a brief description of each organization/activity, including the specific types of activities that occur there, the type of members that belong and attend events (e.g., age, gender, how supportive they seem to be), cost, schedule of activities, and accessibility.

2. Gain initial support of family. Most of the families were excited by the prospect that the school was going to provide resources to assist their sons and daughters to become involved in leisure and social activities. However, most of the families also assumed that this meant a school staff person would accompany their children to these activities on an ongoing basis. The families had a certain degree of fear about the prospect of having their children belong to and participate in typical social activities "on their own." Parental concerns included fears that the children's physical safety was threatened, that the young adult would be ridiculed or shunned, and that the young adult could not perform or participate in a meaningful fashion without outside support. The bridge builder found it important not to insist that the families make a full commitment to the idea that their son or daughter would eventually be supported naturally in order to proceed. The bridge builder assured the families that she would never place the student in a situation that was deemed unsafe or unsupportive and that she would provide as much support as needed to ensure that the student was safe, both physically and emotionally. The bridge builder discovered that when she was able to describe for the parent a specific organization, the individuals who participated there, their commitment to their son or daughter, and a plan for ensuring his or her safe and active participation, all of the families were willing to support the plan.

3. Identify the types of activities the individual enjoys. Some students have a very clear idea about what they want to do as a community leisure activity. One student was clear that she wanted to take horseback riding lessons. For students with clear leisure goals, the bridge builder can begin to immediately plan with him or her how to achieve this goal. However, many students do not have such a clear idea. For these students, bridge builders need to help them identify their leisure interests by asking such questions as these: What do you like to do for fun? What do you do for fun when you get home from school in the afternoons? What did you do yesterday afternoon, and/or what are you going to do today when you get home? What do you like to do on weekends? What did you do last weekend, and/or what are you going to do this weekend? Do you have any hobbies? Are there any classes at school you have really liked? With the assistance of the bridge builder the student should write these things on a sheet of paper with the title "Things I Like and Things I Like To Do For Fun." If a student is not able to understand these types of questions or to readily communicate more than basic needs, then it will be necessary to ask these questions of the family.

After the student has identified his or her interests, the bridge builder can then go through the Community Activity Guide with him or her, describing those organizations and activities that reflect his or her interests, and the student can choose a few that she or he wishes to investigate in order to decide which one to pursue. Students may also wish to spend time going through other sections of the guide and hearing about organizations and activities that may not have anything to do with his or her current interests. This effort may spark a new interest.

4. Identify what the student will need to attend and participate in an activity. The bridge builder should assist the student to think about the things he or she will need. We have found it helpful to begin with the following list: money, transportation, clothes, equipment, learning how to do the activity, Meeting and Getting to Know Other People. The student, with the assistance of the bridge builder, lists the things that are needed and then brainstorms possible ways these needs can be met. Money is typically a major issue. If the student works, he or she should be encouraged to contribute as much as possible to the cost involved in joining and attending. Social Security income should be another resource that is considered. Of course, using these resources often is not simply up to the student, but must be negotiated with the family.

This is a good time for the student and the bridge builder to meet with the student's family. The student should lead the discussion to the greatest extent possible. The student should give his or her parents the list of interests and the specific organizations and activities he or she wishes to explore. The student should also give his or her parents the list of needs and supports that was developed. The bridge builder should then facilitate a discussion with the family about the assistance that the family can and will be able to provide. Again, money is often a major issue. The bridge builder needs to encourage a family to permit the young adult to use his or her own resources for these purposes if he or she so chooses, while at the same time not making this a requirement for participation or a point of contention. Other resources should be offered if the family is unable or unwilling for the student's or their own resources to be used to pay for any or all of the costs. Other resources that have been tapped include The Developmental Disabilities Agency in New Hampshire, which provides a small amount of Family Support funds and respite care dollars to families. Families are permitted to use these dollars in any way they wish, including paying for memberships and other expenses involved in leisure activities for their sons and daughters. A few districts have been willing to pay for some of these costs, especially if the student happens to attend the activity during regular school hours or if the student attends school fewer hours because of his or her involvement in the activity during the evening or weekend that is paid for by the school. Finally, a number of health clubs provide a certain number of students (these arrangements were established not as "special" programs for students with disabilities, but for all students) with the opportunity to exchange a small number of hours of work weekly for a membership.

Transportation is also another major logistical issue faced by students wishing to participate in regular and typical community activities. Of course, whenever possible the student should use a public bus. However, the availability of public transport in most communities is extremely limited, especially during the hours when many social activities take place. Many families are not able (because of schedule restrictions) or wish not to provide transportation. This is especially true for parents of older individuals—they do not have the energy to leave the house after dinner to drive across town and then to return several hours later to pick up their son or daughter. Again, bridge builders should try to walk a line between looking for other options and encouraging families to provide some transportation because of the importance of the activity in their son's or daughter's life. We have found it useful for bridge builders to provide transportation for several weeks. This provides the bridge builder the opportunity to talk with and reassure the student before going into the activity and, at the end of the activity, to check in on how things are going. The bridge builder may be able to identify a person in the organization who can give the student a ride to and/or from the activity. This may be a person the student meets and gets to know. The student (with help from the bridge builder) could ask about getting a ride. A group leader may also be approached about identifying individuals who live in the same vicinity as the student and might be asked about a ride, or a ride request notice might be put up on a bulletin board. The student should offer the individual payment for providing transportation. Again, families may be leery about allowing their son or daughter to obtain a ride with someone they do not know. Most families seem to feel most comfortable with a female and with someone whom the student and bridge builder have gotten to know over several weeks or months. The issue of car insurance and liability are often raised when attempts are made to recruit someone to help provide transportation. However, it is important that these arrangements be viewed not as a program activity, but simply in the same way as a similar arrangement made by any person getting a ride from a friend or acquaintance (e.g., when typical students get rides with each other to school or to an after-school event, the issue of insurance is rarely raised).

The student, with support from the bridge builder, should have the opportunity to visit and observe several of the possible organizations or activities in which she or he might be interested. The manner in which this is arranged depends on each organization. For example, health clubs routinely give tours to interested individuals, and the student should go on a tour like any one else. A young adult interested in an aerobics class may choose to observe it for short period of time, to talk with the instructor, or to go one time and try it out. Once the young adult has observed each of the possible groups, he or she will choose which one to attend.

5. *Facilitate the young adults' participation and connection.* Once again, the role of the bridge builder is not to do activities with young adults, but to actively facilitate their connection to typical members of groups and to gain support from these members. This does not mean simply getting young adults into an organization and activity and hoping that all goes well. Rather it means proactively identifying individuals with whom the person might connect and receive support and providing the assistance for the support and connection to successfully occur. There is no formula for active facilitation—each young adult and each organization and activity dictates the kind and amount of facilitation needed. The following two case descriptions show very different kinds and amounts of facilitation given to two young adults by a bridge builder.

David had a chance to tour a small weightlifting club that was owned and run by two brothers, one of whom was Greg. Greg was not told by the bridge builder that David experiences a significant cognitive disability before meeting him. The bridge builder did tell Greg that David loved weightlifting (he lifted at home) and wanted to see if he would be interested in joining a club. Greg and David seemed to really connect at their first meeting, and David said he very much wanted to join the club. The bridge builder met with Greg and explained how enthusiastic David was and that he was going to join the club. She explained that he probably would need someone with him for several weeks to show him how to use the club and equipment and that the best possible person would be someone who knew the club well, and she asked if he knew of a member who might be able and willing to work with David once or twice a week. Greg said that he would like to be the person and he volunteered (without the bridge builder's asking) to spend 2 hours a week, twice a week with David after his shift at the club usually ended—this would allow him the time free from his other duties. This arrangement continued for several months. Transportation was paid for by the school program. At the end of the school year, David was able to use the club fairly independently and he was well connected to both owners and other club members and received any help he needed from them. He was so clear with his family of his desire to continue to attend the club that they readily agreed to transport him.

Sheila had never done aerobics before, but wanted to give it a try (she had seen people doing it and she knew it was a "cool" thing to do). The bridge builder had chatted with the aerobics teacher several times and thought she would be a supportive person. She also thought that the people in the class (it was one that had been ongoing for a long time, with a core group of regulars) would be supportive. The group did low-impact aerobics and emphasized the chance to move around a little. The bridge builder decided to sign up for the class herself, along with Sheila. They both went together for several weeks, the bridge builder helping Sheila to understand the basics of where to stand (and to stay in roughly the same place) and other social etiquette of aerobics. She practiced with Sheila outside of class to show her how to do some of the basic moves and how to watch the instructor and copy her. The bridge builder introduced herself and Sheila to other members of the group when the opportunity presented itself and was natural (e.g., standing next to the soda machine after class).

After several weeks Sheila felt comfortable in the class, and the instructor and many of the class members knew her and were comfortable with her. The bridge builder kept Sheila's mother informed about how things were going and took time after bringing Sheila home to share stories about what had happened that night and about the people in the class. Sheila's mother saw her enthusiasm and felt that she knew the class and that it was a safe and supportive place for her. The bridge builder then asked Sheila's mother's permission to begin to gradually spend less time with Sheila—her mother agreed. The bridge builder told the instructor that because of schedule constraints, she was not going to be able to attend the class regularly any more, but that Sheila wanted to keep attending. The bridge builder told the instructor that she would continue to drop off Sheila and pick her up and would chat with the instructor about how things were going. The instructor said that Sheila sometimes would wander into other people's areas and that they moved for her. The bridge builder suggested that others should simply remind Sheila when she began to stray to move back to her own area (and to point to where it was).

The bridge builder stayed to see how this process went—when Sheila started to wander, the instructor looked at the bridge builder, who nodded to encourage her to say something to Sheila. Sheila moved back to her area and all went well from then on. For several weeks, the bridge builder walked in with Sheila, stayed until the class was under way, and checked in several times during the evening. She then began to spend less and less time there until she was finally only dropping Sheila off and picking her up without going into the building.

Table 2 lists the activities in which students participated before receiving assistance from the community bridge builder. Two students participated in no organized leisure activities with or without their families. One student participated only in church-related activities, but she was always in the presence of her family. Another student only attended a special summer camp. Two students were active Special Olympics participants, and one these students also attended Sunday church services

Table 2. Activities of students before and after community bridge-builder project

Student	Preproject activities	Identified interests	Postproject activities
1	Church activities with family	Animals—horses in particular	Volunteered at horsebacking farm and took lessons—not "therapeutic" or "special" program
2	None	Books, history	Volunteered at Nashua Historical Society helping to set-up pictures and slides for displays
3	Special summer camp	Dance, music, theater	Took performance dance class
4	Special Olympics	Sports, weightlifting	Joined and went to weightlifting club several times weekly
5	Special Olympics, church with family	Sports	Joined and went to health club several times weekly
6	None	Socializing, hanging out	Joined and attended weekly low-impact aerobics group

with his family. In addition, none of the students and their families indicated that the student did any activity with a person without a disability considered a "friend" over the prior year. Only one of the students and his parent reported that he had done a social activity (other than Special Olympics) during the prior 6 months. Table 2 also provides a brief description of the primary area of interest identified by each of the students and the activity in which the community bridge builder assisted them to become connected.

CONCLUSIONS

Those individuals involved in attempting to assist people with disabilities to develop real social connections and friendships understand this is probably the most difficult challenge we face. At the same time, this goal is truly the most important and is at the heart of all other initiatives, including school inclusion, employment, and living in typical neighborhoods—we can achieve all of these objectives, but if people still don't make friends with their school peers, co-workers, and neighbors, what have we really achieved? In fact, the actual achievements in the area of friendships have been modest. We should not be surprised, given the relatively small amount of attention that has been and continues to be focused on friendships and leisure participation as compared with academics, functional skills, employment, and independent living.

The high school in which the community bridge-builder project was conducted had a sincere desire to assist their students in enhancing their participation in typical community activities and in connecting socially with young adults who did not experience disabilities. The district planned to continue the position of bridge builder with their own funding after the grant was completed. There were budget reductions, however, and the district had to weigh where their resources would be allocated. The decision was made that the priority was for aides to devote their time to other activities (academics, functional skills, employment) and that the aide who was the bridge builder would not be able to continue these activities to any substantial degree. This is not an indictment of this particular district, but rather of society's perspectives regarding the value of these activities and regarding what is needed and should be done to help young people with and without disabilities to achieve full and satisfying lives in terms of their friends and social activities.

There has been decreasing importance placed on the value of friends and connections. This has been a natural accompaniment in a mobile society in which the idea of putting down roots is almost a thing of the past. Careers and obtaining financial security (which seem to have a much higher standard than in times past) now seem to be the primary driving force. In this context, it should not be surprising that special education does not invest much time and resources on social and friendship issues. It should also not be surprising that it is hard to connect people with or without disabilities in this social context. There is the beginning of understanding that focusing on school inclusion may not be the most fruitful approach for achieving meaningful education inclusion for students with disabilities. Rather, the focus must be on school reforms that are aimed at making education more successful for all students—that returns schools to caring and supportive places for all students, including those with disabilities. We are beginning to understand that it may not be the best strategy to encourage businesses to support individuals with disabilities when they are not particularly supportive of any employee. Instead we need to focus greater amounts of our expertise and energy in helping businesses value diversity of all kinds and supportive workplaces for all employees. We need to begin to apply this approach to the area of friendship and social connections—to focus more of our energies on the bigger issue of how to facilitate and reinforce in our families, schools, neighborhoods, and communities the value of connection, support, and friendship.

The call for special education and rehabilitation personnel to begin to view their role as larger change agents does not obviate the need to continue facilitating social connections and friendships for the individuals with disabilities whom we know and to whom we provide "services." In fact, we must increase our efforts in this regard. Schools and adult resources are limited and are becoming more limited, and there will need to be prioritization of what areas are most important. Schools and adult programs should not view leisure participation and connections as extra—not a goal for when other individualized education program goals permit, but as a priority. Again, this focus should not be only for students with disabilities, but for all students. This suggestion is not given lightly. To make this commitment requires a significant change in how the American educational system views its role. Again, there is a growing consensus for the need for widespread and basic school reform, within which schools are examining their missions and practices.

The general lag in progress in the area of building connections between people with and without disabilities may in part also be attributable to the generally held belief that connections and friendships should happen "naturally." We understand and feel comfortable with the notion that individuals (both those with and without disabilities) need lots of assistance and support to learn academics and functional skills and to pursue careers. However, we feel uncomfortable actively facilitating social connections and friendships. When attempts have been made to proactively intervene to develop friendships between individuals, we are often frustrated that our typical ways of controlling and programming often are not "successful." Uditzky (1993) made a compelling argument that friendships cannot be engineered. In fact, we need to actively facilitate increasing the opportunities to bring people together. This includes ensuring that individuals participate in typical organizations and activities. We also need to help actively bridge relationships between individuals with and without disabilities—helping each to communicate mutual interests, helping individuals with disabilities to understand social mores and ways of interacting, and helping individuals without disabilities to understand how to relate to and communicate with the individual with disabilities.

At the same time, we should not expect quick successes from these efforts. Friendships take time (not just weeks and often not just months) to develop, and we should not expect that friendships will always or will even usually take hold—they do not always succeed for any of us. Given active facilitation, two individuals can decide if they wish to be friends, and we cannot and should not try to engineer that part of the friendship process. If two people decide not to be friends, we should not perceive of our work as a failure—we have helped them participate in the typical friendship development process. We must stop viewing the assistance we give as programs and interventions with 1-month, 1-year, or 3-year evaluation deadlines after which we decide, based on counts and numbers, if we were successful and if we should continue with the program.

REFERENCES

Arsensault, C. (1990). *Let's get together: A handbook in support of building relationships between individuals with developmental disabilities and their community.* Boulder, CO: Developmental Disabilities Center.

Baumgart, D., Brown, L., Pumpian, I., Nisbet, J., Ford, A., Sweet, M., Messina, R., & Schroeder, J. (1982). Principle of partial participation and individualized adaptations in educational programs for severely handicapped students. *Journal of The Association for Persons with Severe Handicaps, 7*(2), 17–27.

Brown, G., Chadwick, O., Shaffer, D., Rutter, M., & Traub, M. (1981). A prospective study of children with head injuries. III. Psychiatric sequelae. *Psychological Medicine, 11*, 63–78.

Breen, C., Haring, T., Pitts-Conway, V., & Gaylord-Ross, R. (1985). The training and generalization of social interaction during breaktime at two job sites in the natural environment. *Journal of The Association for Persons with Severe Handicaps, 10*, 41–50.

Bush, G.W. (1986). *Coma to community.* Paper presented at the Santa Clara Conference on Traumatic Head Injury, Santa Clara, CA.

Chadsey-Rusch, J. (1986). Identifying and teaching valued social behaviors in competitive employment settings. In F.R. Rusch (Ed.), *Competitive employment: Issues and strategies* (pp. 273–287). Baltimore: Paul H. Brookes Publishing Co.

Chadsey-Rusch, J., Karlan, G., Riva, M., & Rusch, F. (1984). Competitive employment: Teaching conversation skills to adults who are mentally retarded. *Mental Retardation, 22*, 218–225.

Cole, D. (1986). Facilitating play in children's peer relationships: Are we having fun yet? *American Educational Research Journal, 23*, 201–215.

Corsaro, A., & Eder, D. (1990). Children's peer cultures. *Annual Review of Sociology, 16*, 197–220.

Csikszentmihalyi, M., & Larson, R. (1984). Intrinsic rewards in school crime. *Crime and Delinquency, 24*, 322–335.

Dattilo, J. (1994). *Inclusive leisure services: Responding to the rights of people with disabilities.* State College, PA: Venture.

Dattilo, J. (1995). Instruction for preference and generalization. In J.S. Schleien, L.H. Meyer, L.A. Heyne, & B.B. Brandt, *Lifelong leisure skills and lifestyles for persons with developmental disabilities* (pp. 133–145). Baltimore: Paul H. Brookes Publishing Co.

Davies, B. (1982). *Life in the classroom and playground: The accounts of primary school children.* London: Routledge.

Forest, M., & Lusthaus, E. (1989). Promoting educational equality for all students: Circles and maps. In S. Stainback, W. Stainback, & M. Forest (Eds.), *Educating all students in the mainstream of regular education* (pp. 43–58). Baltimore: Paul H. Brookes Publishing Co.

Gartner, J., & Lipsky, D. (1990). Students as instructional agents. In W. Stainback & S. Stainback (Eds.), *Support networks for inclusive schooling: Interdependent integrated education* (pp. 81–93). Baltimore: Paul H. Brookes Publishing Co.

Garvey, C. (1984). *Children's talk.* Cambridge, MA: Harvard University Press.

Goodwin, M.H. (1985). The serious side of jump rope: Conversational practices and social organization in the frame of play. *Journal of American Folklore, 98*, 315–330.

Grenot-Scheyer, M. (1994). The nature of interactions between students with severe disabilities and their friends and acquaintances without disabilities. *Journal of The Association for Persons with Severe Handicaps, 19*, 253–263.

Griffin, C. (1985). *Typical girls?: Young women from school to the job market.* London: Routledge.

Hagner, D., & Dileo, D. (1993). *Working together: Workplace culture, supported employment and persons with disabilities.* Boston: Brookline Books.

Hall, L. (1994). A descriptive assessment of social relationships in integrated classrooms. *Journal of The Association for Persons with Severe Handicaps, 19*(4), 277–289.

Hanks, M., & Eckland, B. (1978). Adult voluntary associations and adolsecent. *The Socological Quarterly, 19*, 481–490.

Haring, T. (1991). Social relationships. In L.H. Meyer, C.A. Peck, & L. Brown (Eds.), *Critical issues in the lives of people with severe disabilities* (pp. 195–217). Baltimore: Paul H. Brookes Publishing Co.

Hedin, D., & Conrad, D. (1981, Fall). National assessment of experiential education: Summary and implications. *Journal of Experiential Education*, pp. 6–20.

Jorgensen, C. (1992). Natural supports in inclusive school: Curricular and teaching strategies. In J. Nisbet (Ed.), *Natural supports in school, at work, and in the community for people with severe disabilities* (pp. 165–178). Baltimore: Paul H. Brookes Publishing Co.

Kalsbeek, W., McLaurin, R., & Harris, B. (1980). The national head and spinal cord injury survey: Major findings. *Journal of Neurosurgery, 53*, 19–31.

Kishi, G., & Meyer, L. (1994). What children report and remember: A six-year follow-up of the effects of social contact between peers with and without severe disabilities. *Journal of The Association for Persons with Severe Handicaps, 19*(4), 277–289.

Klein, J. (1992). Get me the hell out of here: Supporting people with disabilities to live in their homes. In J. Nisbet (Ed.), *Natural supports in school, at work, and in the community for people with severe disabilities* (pp. 277–340). Baltimore: Paul H. Brookes Publishing Co.

Lerner, R., & Busch-Rossnagel, N. (Eds.). (1981). *Individuals as producers of their development.* New York: Academic Press.

Lignugaris/Kraft, B., Salzberg, C., Rule, S., & Stowitschek, J. (1988). Social-vocational skills of workers with and without mental retardation in two community employment sites. *Mental Retardation, 26*, 297–305.

Mannarino, A. (1976). Friendship patterns and altruistic behavior in preadolescent males. *Developmental Psychology, 12*, 555–556.

McGuire, K., & Weisz, J. (1982). Social cognition and behavior correlates of preadolescent chumships. *Child Development, 53*, 1,478–1,484.

Meyer, L., Fox, A., Schermer, A., Ketelson, D., Monton, N., Maley, K., & Cole, D. (1987). The effects of teacher intrusion on social play interactions between children with autism and their nonhandicapped peers. *Journal of Autism and Developmental Disorders, 17*, 315–332.

Mount, B., Beeman, P., & Ducharme, G. (1988). *What are we building? About bridge-building: A summary of a dialogue between people seeking to build community for people with disabilities.* Manchester, CT: Communitas, Inc.

Nisbet, J. (Ed.). (1992). *Natural supports in school, at work, and in the community for people with severe disabilities.* Baltimore: Paul H. Brookes Publishing Co.

Nisbet, J., & Hagner, D. (1988). Natural suports in the workplace: A reexamination of supported employment. *Journal of The Association for Persons with Severe Handicaps, 13*, 260–267.

O'Brien, J., & O'Brien, C. (1993). Unlikely alliances: Friendships and people with developmental disabilities. In A.N. Amado (Ed.), *Friendship and community connections between people with and without developmental disabilities* (pp. 9–40). Baltimore: Paul H. Brookes Publishing Co.

O'Connell, M. (1988). *Getting connected: How to find out about groups and organizations in your neighborhood.* Springfield, IL: Department of Rehabilitation Services.

Odom, S.L., & Strain, P.S. (1986). A comparison of peers: Initiation and teacher antecedent interventions for promoting reciprocal social interaction of autistic preschoolers. *Journal of Applied Behavior Analysis, 19*, 59–72.

Oerther, R. (1986). Developmental tasks through the lifespan: A new approach to an old concept. In P. Baltes, L. Featherman, & R. Lerner (Eds.), *Lifespan development and behavior* (Vol. 7, pp. 233–269). Hillsdale, NJ: Lawrence Erlbaum Associates.

Perske, R. (1988). *Circle of friends: People with disabilities and their friends enrich the lives of one another.* Nashville, TN: Abingdon Press.

Rogan, P., Hagner, D., & Murphy, S. (1993). Natural supports: Reconceptualizing job coach roles. *Journal of The Association of Persons with Severe Handicaps, 18*(4), 275–282.

Rosen, C., & Gerring, J. (1986). *Head trauma: Educational reintegration.* Boston: College Hill Press.

Rubin, Z. (1980). *Children's friendships.* Cambridge, MA: University Press.

Rusch, F., Johnson, J., & Hughes, C. (1990). Analysis of co-workers involvement in relation to level of disability versus placement approach among supported employees. *Journal of The Association for Persons with Severe Handicaps, 15,* 32–39.

Salisbury, C.L., & Palombaro, M.M.. (1992). *Collaborative problem solving: Peers and adults as advocates for inclusion.* Paper presented at the International Division for Early Childhood Conference on Children with Special Needs, Washington, DC.

Schleien, S.J., Meyer, L.H., Heyne, L.A., & Brandt, B.B. (1995). *Lifelong leisure skills and lifestyles for persons with developmental disabilities.* Baltimore: Paul H. Brookes Publishing Co.

Shafer, M., Brookes, V., & Wehman, P. (1985). Developing appropriate social-interpersonal skills in a mentally retarded worker. In P. Wehman & J. Hill (Eds.), *Competitive employment for persons with mental retardation: From research to practice* (Vol. 1, pp. 358–375). Richmond: Virginia Commonwealth University, Rehabilitation Research and Training Center.

Sibereisen, R.K., Eyferth, K., & Rudinger, G. (Eds.). (1986). *Development as action in context.* New York: Springer-Verlag.

Singer, G.H., & Nixon, C. (1996). A report on the concerns of parents of children with ABI. In G. Singer, A. Glang, & J. Williams (Eds.), *Families and children with acquired brain injury: Challenge and adaptation* (pp. 23–52). Baltimore: Paul H. Brookes Publishing Co.

Snow, J.A. (1989). Systems of support: A new vision. In S. Stainback, W. Stainback, & M. Forest (Eds.), *Educating all students in the mainstream of regular education* (pp. 221–231). Baltimore: Paul H. Brookes Publishing Co.

Sowers, J. (1994). *The New Hampshire Natural Supports Project—Project Report.* Concord: Institute on Disability, University of New Hampshire.

Sowers, J. (1995). Adaptive environments in the workplace. In K.F. Flippo, K.J. Inge, & J.M. Barcus (Eds.), *Assistive technology: A resource for school, work, and community* (pp.167–185). Baltimore: Paul H. Brookes Publishing Co.

Sowers, J., & Powers, L. (1991). *School and community activity and integration assessment (SCALIA).* Eugene: Oregon Research Institute.

Spady, W. (1970). Lament for the letterman: Effect of peer status and extracurricular activities on goal and achievement. *American Journal of Sociology, 75,* 680–702.

Stainback, W., & Stainback, S. (Eds.). (1990). *Support networks for inclusive schooling: Interdependent integrated education.* Baltimore: Paul H. Brookes Publishing Co.

Staub, D., Schwartz, I., Gallucci, C., & Peck, C. (1994). Children's perceptions of fairness in classroom and interpersonal situations involving peers with severe disabilities. *Journal of The Association for Persons with Severe Handicaps, 19,* 326–332.

Storey, K., & Knutson, N. (1989). A comparative analysis of social interactions of workers with and without disabilities in integrated work sites: A pilot study. *Education and Training of the Mentally Retarded, 24,* 265–273.

Strully, J., & Strully, C. (1989). Friendships as an educational goal. In S. Stainback, W. Stainback, & M. Forest (Eds.), *Educating all students in the mainstream of regular education* (pp. 59–68). Baltimore: Paul H. Brookes Publishing Co.

Taylor, S., Biklen, D., & Knoll, J. (1987). *Community integration for people with severe disabilities.* New York: Teachers College Press.

Thomsen, I.V. (1984). Late outcome of very severe blunt head trauma: A 10-15 year second follow-up. *Journal of Neurology, Neurosurgery, and Psychiatry, 47,* 260–268.

Townsend, M., McCracken, H., & Wilton, K. (1988). Popularity and intimacy as determinants of psychological well-being in adolescent friendships. *Journal of Early Adolescence, 8,* 421–436.

Uditsky, B. (1993). Natural pathways to friendships. In A.N. Amado (Ed.), *Friendships and community connections between people with and without developmental disabilities* (pp. 85–96). Baltimore: Paul H. Brookes Publishing Co.

Vandercook, T., York, J., & Forest, M. (1989). The McGill action planning system (MAPS): A strategy for building the vision. *Journal of The Association for The Severely Handicapped, 14*(3), 205–215.

Villa, R.A., Thousand, J.S., Stainback, W., & Stainback, S. (Eds.). (1992). *Restructuring for caring and effective education: An administrative guide to creating heterogeneous schools.* Baltimore: Paul H. Brookes Publishing Co.

Voeltz, L.M. (1980). Children's attitudes toward handicapped peers. *American Journal of Mental Deficiency, 84,* 455–464.

Voeltz, L.M. (1982). Effects of structured interaction with severe handicapped peers on children's attitudes. *American Journal of Mental Deficiency, 86,* 380–390.

Voeltz, L., & Brennan, J. (1984). Analysis of interactions between nonhandicapped and severely handicapped peers using multiple measures. In J.M. Berg (Ed.), *Perspectives and progress in mental retardation: Vol I. Social, psychological, and educational aspects* (pp. 61–72). Baltimore: University Park Press.

Voeltz, L., Kishi, G., Brown, S., & Kube, C. (1980). *The special friends program: A trainer's manual for integrated school settings.* Honolulu: University of Hawaii, Department of Special Education.

Wagner, M., Williams, J., & Long, C. (1990. The role of social networks in recovery from head trauma. *International Journal of Clinical Neuropsychology, 12*(3-4), 131–137.

Wehman, P. (1977). *Helping the mentally retarded acquire play skills: A behavioral approach.* Springfield, IL: Charles C Thomas.

Wehman, P., & Moon, M.S. (Eds.). (1988). *Vocational rehabilitation and supported employment.* Baltimore: Paul H. Brookes Publishing Co.

Weiss, R. (1973). *Loneliness: The experience of emotional and social isolation.* Cambridge, MA: MIT Press.

West, M., Revell, W., & Wehman, P. (1992). Achievements and challenges. I: A five-year report on consumer and system outcomes from the supported employment initiative. *Journal of The Association for Persons with Severe Handicaps, 17*(4), 227–235.

Willer, B., Allen, K., Durnan, M.C., & Ferry, A. (1990). Problems and coping strategies of mothers, siblings, and young adult males with traumatic brain injury. *Canadian Journal of Rehabilitation, 2*(3), 167–173.

Wulff, H. (1988). Twenty girls: Growing-up. Ethnicity and excitement in a south London micro-culture stockholm stud. *Social Anthropology,* No. 21.

Youniss. J., & Smoller, J. (1985). *Adolescent relations: Mothers, fathers and friends.* Chicago: University of Chicago Press.

18

First Steps
Toward Competence

Promoting Self-Esteem and Confidence
in Young Children with Disabilities

Carol Andrew and Nancee Tracy

Competence is a concept commonly applied to adults in relation to their ability to do a job or handle their affairs. How do we know when a young child is competent, and how can we promote the elements of competence for a young child, particularly a child coping with a disability? Identifying a child who is "handling his own affairs" may help to clarify the concept of competence in early childhood.

Michael, at age 3, came to the developmental clinic for a follow-up appointment and immediately walked to the playroom using his walker. His mother followed slowly behind, chatting amiably with the physician. As Michael entered the playroom he readily approached the examiner. Using gestures and words that were not clearly articulated, Michael indicated which toys he wanted to use and asked for help when he needed it. Throughout the evaluation, he was able to persist at tasks that were challenging for him because of the degree of his motor disability. He was ultimately successful at age-appropriate tasks, including independent free-play activities. When asked, his mother indicated that she just "followed his lead" and "helped him when he needed it."

Michael is obviously a competent and self-assured little boy. Despite being in an unfamiliar environment and being required to interact with a new person, he was comfortable and confident. He could request assistance when needed but was able to enjoy playing independently. He had remarkable persistence in attempting challenging tasks and did not seem to be upset by failures. He sought assistance, and he could also communicate when he did not need help and wanted to be independent and "try it myself."

Michael's mother was articulate about the experiences surrounding Michael's birth. Despite the difficulty of his first year as a result of the complications of a premature birth, his mother managed to maintain a philosophy of wanting to "help him to be the best he could be." She was able to see her son's strengths and referred to him as "feisty" and "a survivor." She was able to work collaboratively with the various therapists, physicians, and developmental specialists available to her; and she helped them to think beyond the standard therapeutic and educational approaches. She was able to ask many questions about how to encourage the next steps for her son. She was also able to maintain a balance between being nurturant when needed and promoting independence as much as possible. She was able to accept Michael's disability and move on emotionally, always finding ways to make things better.

Clearly Michael's mother had her own resources and had developed a support network as well. Families may need some help in finding the emotional, physical, and/or financial resources to achieve the level of competence that Michael's mother displayed. Professionals are most helpful when they can 1) increase family awareness about options and approaches for young children with disabilities, 2) assist families to develop a positive philosophy and approach to coping, and 3) assist in helping families to problem-solve and find necessary resources. It is essential that professionals work in a culturally competent, asset-oriented manner, collaborating actively with families and children as equal partners.

What are the antecedents of self-competence in infancy and early childhood? How do adults recognize the emerging indicators of competency in an infant or young child? How can families help their children to develop coping skills and self-determination? How can professionals enhance the capacity of families to raise children who have healthy self-esteem and resilience? What kinds of medical and early care and education practices can promote positive self-regard and future self-determination for young children with disabilities? This chapter addresses these questions and presents strategies within a developmental perspective that will promote self-confidence and resiliency in children from infancy through the preschool years.

WHAT DO COMPETENT, RESILIENT CHILDREN LOOK LIKE?

Resilient children have the capacity to withstand stressors; overcome adversity; and, in the process, achieve higher levels of self-mastery, self-esteem, and internal harmony (Poulsen, 1993). They are able to develop the ability to self-regulate as they respond to and recover from environmental challenges. They acquire a repertoire of responses to assist them in problem solving and in their adjustment to new situations. They have the flexibility to respond in a manner that matches the situation in terms of context and intensity. They are able to accomplish transitions smoothly and easily.

Infants are born with variable temperaments and varying abilities to self-soothe and self-regulate as newborns. Their innate capabilities can be promoted through interactions with their caregivers and their environment. Adults who can identify when infants are successfully trying to calm themselves and need little assistance are already promoting self-regulatory behaviors, which are antecedents for the development of a self-competent and resilient toddler.

Strong attachment also appears to provide "a secure base for the development of the advanced self-help skills and autonomy noted among children in their second year of life" (Werner & Smith, 1992). When parents promote the drive for independence of toddlers while at the same time providing consistent limits on behavior, they encourage the development of self-competence in their child. The toddler begins to develop self-esteem as a result of increasing competence and positive parental direction. Preschool children become capable of relating to others in positive, prosocial ways when they have had the opportunity to become resilient and caring and self-confident themselves and when adults allow them to negotiate the inevitable conflicts with supervision but little interference.

WHY DO WE PROMOTE SELF-ESTEEM AND RESILIENCE?

Children who are resilient and have high self-esteem are more able to acquire what they need from their environment for optimal learning and growth. Feelings of self-worth determine the use the child makes of his aptitudes and abilities (Briggs, 1975). Resilient children are happier and more flexible in the face of difficulties or challenges, which are inevitable in anyone's life. They are more open to relationships with others and can readily engage in helping behaviors, which in turn further promote their own feelings of success and competence. They may learn to tolerate making mistakes because of what they can learn from them, as opposed to becoming anxious about their errors and refusing to attempt further challenges. Self-confident children may be more challenging to the adults around them but will ultimately be more self-directed in their learning and relationships.

Because children with disabilities may have more need for direct assistance from the adults around them, they often experience challenges in developing their independence and self-competence. Adults need increased creativity and sensitivity as they try to help children with disabilities to develop the self-regulation, independence, and resilience that all children need to feel self-confident and prepared to face the daily challenges of relationships and learning. If children can develop resilience and self-competence during their infant and toddler years, they will have an advantage as they enter the world of school and friendships.

STRATEGIES FOR FAMILIES
AND EARLY CARE AND EDUCATION PROFESSIONALS

Newborns

Parents approach the birth of a child with various personal philosophies and experiences. Religious beliefs, education, parenting styles with which the parents themselves were reared, and previous experiences with young children all have an impact on the ways individuals perceive their parenting roles. Most families, however, do not anticipate the birth of a child with a disability; and shock and grief are consistently reported by families when the unexpected occurs (Affleck & Tennen, 1993; Murphy, 1982; Trout, 1983). The birth of a premature infant or the development of special health care needs in a young child are also situations that can stimulate a highly emotional response in families (Cameron, Snowdon, & Orr, 1992; Gould & Moses, 1985). Parental self-esteem and feelings of competence in the face of major life challenges significantly influence a family's ability to cope positively with the birth of a child with a disability.

Professionals can respond to the birth of a child with disability or ongoing illness in various ways. Denial of long-term problems (e.g., "Don't worry, he'll outgrow this") may have the effect of not validating parents' legitimate concerns regarding care and future progress of their newborn. Overidentification of all the potential problems that might exist (e.g., "There is a strong likelihood that your child will have severe cerebral palsy and probably mental retardation; it is unlikely that he will ever walk or talk") may eliminate hope and the valuable opportunity to experience the unconditional loving of new parenthood. Falling back on "medical-ese" in describing the problems of the infant (e.g., "In an infant with such severe intraventricular hemorrhage and bronchopulmonary dysplasia, chronic hypoxia is likely to produce further neuromotor deficits") effectively distances the professional from the personal meaning and emotion of the diagnostic process.

Parents often have strong feelings about the way in which they are informed of their child's disability or risk for disability. The manner in which they receive information regarding their child's diagnosis has a long-lasting impact and sets the stage for how they begin to cope with the news. Bernheimer, Young, and Winton (1983) report the following:

> The way in which professionals shared the diagnosis with the parents was a source of stress, regardless of the nature of the child's handicapping condition. Some parents related that the diagnosis was not shared with compassion or sensitivity. Others felt that professionals lacked respect for the child as well as the parents....Professionals were frequently viewed as unresponsive to the parent's need to talk, to ask numerous questions and to be told the answers over and over again. (p. 178)

Alternatively, family-centered, family-friendly information may be provided regarding the child's specific disability. Information is most effective when it includes attempts to impart a philosophy of acceptance of the infant and of helping the infant to be the best he or she can be. For example, a professional might say this: "You know that the tests have shown there is an area in your child's brain that has been injured. We know that sometimes this kind of injury can cause a child to have some difficulties in movement as she gets older. It will be important for us to work together to watch your child's development carefully. As she grows, we will help you to think of ways to encourage her mobility as well as other areas of her development." Other supportive strategies include 1) encouraging the family to know that they will ultimately be the expert on their infant, even if they do not feel like one at the time of the infant's birth; 2) providing assistance in helping the family to find resources in the community for support when they want it; and 3) providing opportunities for parents to meet and discuss their feelings with other parents who have experienced a similar situation (McGrath & Meyer, 1992).

Most important is the professionals' respect for the family's need to determine their own path. For some parents, seeking the support of their own family and friends is the only strategy they need to help them cope (Werner, 1989). Some families have a strong desire to be at home with their newborn without the aid of early intervention providers and community support workers. Implying an urgency for gaining access to community supports can disempower a family and decrease feelings of confidence and competence in parenting at a time when attachment to the infant is of primary importance. Families must be informed of all the options available and then supported in their decisions. They should have the opportunity to negotiate their own supports rather than be forced into a "one size fits all" system of services.

Young Infants

Ashley was an infant with an unknown and probably progressive brain disorder who was sent home to die. Her family did not wish to have referral to early intervention services because "there was no point." She was seen in the follow-up clinic, and a plan for development of oral feeding was instituted when it was discovered that her sucking could be facilitated. Her mother made several telephone contacts with the clinic therapist, and the plan was altered based on her description of Ashley's responses. Within 2 months, her parents had helped Ashley to take all of her feedings by mouth. When they returned to the clinic, the family had contacted a community early intervention program. They indicated that they still saw no need for direct services. Ashley's father said, "We know that we will need some help for her sometime. But right now, we know what to do and how to do it. She'll only be this little for a short time, and we want to just enjoy having our baby."

Attachment is identified as one of the earliest precursors to self-esteem and positive self-regard (Briggs, 1975; Poulsen, 1993). Attachment is thought to develop through prolonged, satisfying interactions between parent and infant (Coopersmith, 1967). When a parent is able to respond positively to comfort the infant and to provide what an infant needs in a prompt manner, the infant is able to reinforce the parent by calming and relaxing (Goldberg, 1972; McLean, 1989). The infant learns to trust his or her environment and to trust that there will be a satisfying response to the infant's communications. When the parent is unable to respond or responds in an inconsistent or incomplete manner, the infant is unable to calm and relax; and the interaction is unsatisfying for both parties (Prizant & Wetherby, 1990). The infant may learn to doubt the reliability of his or her environment and may become anxious or avoidant in interactions with others (Greenspan, 1992):

> During the first year of life a child usually learns to enjoy being with her mother and to trust that she will hold or feed her when she approaches. She also begins to feel some sense of accomplishment if she learns she can trust her body to do what she wants—to grasp a toy, reach something by crawling, or move something to her mouth. With proper care, even children with limited mobility can develop this basic trust in other people, the environment and themselves. (Cowan, 1991, p. 155)

The self-esteem of parents is a powerful predictor of how well they may support the process of attachment. Tronick, Ricks, and Cohn (1982) indicate that

> those mothers who feel positively about themselves and their early relationships have infants who feel secure in their primary relationship and, inferentially, in their own capabilities. (p. 87)

If a parent is depressed as a result of her own life circumstances or in response to the prospect of parenting a child with a disability, she may be less available emotionally to the infant. This decreased positive emotional responsiveness will likely affect the infant's feelings of self-worth (Murphy, 1982). Parents' coping skills not only allow them to be emotionally available for their children's needs, but also to serve as models of coping (Poulsen, 1993).

When an infant has a disability, the infant's ability to respond in ways expected by the family may be altered. Early behaviors frequently seen in infants with disabilities may include irritability, feeding difficulties, and erratic sleep/wake schedules (Brooks-Gunn & Lewis, 1982). In addition, prolonged hospitalization around the time of birth may limit contact between the parents and the infant. All of these components of the early parenting experience may contribute to feelings of inadequacy for parents and infants alike (Mintzer, Als, Tronick, & Brazelton, 1985).

Family-centered approaches to promote the involvement of parents during hospitalization can facilitate the attachment process by supporting parental coping (Cameron et al., 1992). Regardless of whether or not the child is hospitalized, the parents are the primary caregivers and need to be acknowledged as such. They should have an integral role as a member of the medical team. The parents should be invited to work in partnership with the hospital staff to provide both emotional support and medical care for their child. They are the "only constant in the life of their child," and therefore care practices need to revolve around the family (Turnbull & Summers, 1985).

Families should be encouraged to be present for their infant as consistently as possible to allow for optimal attachment to evolve over time. Hospital staff have a responsibility to include the family in decision making and to communicate clearly with the family. In addition, families need to be oriented to the hospital environment and need to feel comfortable within it. In order to be available to their baby, families may also need assistance from the community supports (e.g., to provide care for other children or to find transportation). Hospital and community personnel must communicate with each other, as well as with the family, to ensure that collaboration best serves the family's needs. Families must not be caught in the middle between hospital and community systems. An example of positive collaboration might be when the staff of the intensive care nursery invites the home nurse and early intervention provider to a meeting with the parents prior to discharge to share strategies and methods of promoting positive health and developmental progress.

Hospital staff should encourage dependable but flexible schedules for sleeping and feeding, based on family preferences and lifestyles. It is also essential that pediatric staff, in collaboration with parents, learn how to read infant cues and behaviors. Finding ways to help infants to remain calm and relaxed and promoting quiet, alert states allow babies to be as available as possible for social interaction. Saving some typical family chores such as feeding and bathing for times when a parent will definitely be present allows for maximum involvement of the family in the daily care.

Parents may experience conflicts between their duties at home and their desires to be with their infants. Professionals must be active listeners who can support parents' statements and assist them to problem-solve solutions that meet their various needs. Circumstances differ for each family, and staff should respect the needs of families and provide support when appropriate.

Even when an infant is not hospitalized, guidance is often needed to promote optimal feeding and sleeping routines. Beyond standard pediatric anticipatory guidance, infants with potentially disabling conditions may pose challenges in their daily care as well as in their developmental needs. For example, children with disabilities may need special nipples for bottle feeding, extra support to promote breast feeding, or adaptive equipment to assist with feeding positions. In these circumstances, parents may find support from early intervention professionals or developmental specialists who are able to spend longer periods observing the baby's care and discussing options for solving problems that might arise.

Professionals need to promote parental competence and self-esteem in all of their meetings with families. This is done by conveying trust and respect for the parents.

When parents are in frustrating or stressful situations, a professional who actively listens to their concerns and provides caring, thoughtful strategies strongly promotes parental competence and self-esteem. By demonstrating trust in the parents' abilities and respect for the parents' approaches, the professional models a style that parents may be able to apply in their interactions with their children. Teaching specific strategies that might help parents be successful in a particular situation allows families to take charge and feel independent and competent. Modeling of these strategies by professionals can be effective methods to help parents feel more competent and in charge, thereby enabling them to promote competence and self-determination in their child as he or she grows.

Older Infants and Toddlers

Jose, a handsome little boy of 12 months, came to the clinic with his parents. They were very concerned about the fact that he was unable to sit, but even more upset that he had periods of inconsolable crying that were solved only by holding him. Because he could not yet speak, they were at a loss to help him. He was able to roll from his stomach to his back, but not in the other direction. He was able to lift his head and push up on his forearms; but when he was placed in a typical sitting position, the tense muscle tone in his legs and lower back caused him to fall over backwards. For the purposes of testing, he was helped to sit in a booster chair with a small table; and he proceeded to demonstrate age-appropriate skills. He was able to select one of two toys offered to him. His ability to make that kind of choice was used as an example to demonstrate to his parents his capacity for nonverbal communication. Much to the surprise of his parents, he also did not cry during the evaluation at all, except when he was returned to lying on the floor.

The biggest developmental tasks of the period from approximately 9 to 18 months relate to the child's development of independence in motor skills and control of his or her environment by means of movement and communication. For children with disabilities, it is often the case that neither of these tasks is readily achievable. Alternative methods for developing competency must be developed in order for the child to continue to build feelings of self-efficacy and positive self-regard. Since "infant competence is generated and maintained by the quality of the infant's interactions with the environment" (Tronick et al., 1982, p. 89), the environment needs to be flexible, responsive, and attuned to the individualized needs of the child.

The relationship with the caregiver continues to be a primary determinant in how confident a child appears and in how willing he or she is to seek control of his or her own environment. Tronick et al. (1982) identify three types of parent elicitation of behavior: overcontrolling, undercontrolling, and elaboration. Independence and infant effectiveness are best promoted by elaborative techniques, such as standing back to allow the child time to experiment in productive ways; by facilitating activities to ensure that the child is helped enough to avoid frustration; by following the child's interests; and by timing activities to optimally utilize the child's attention for learning. These goals can be achieved by promoting and responding to nonverbal as well as verbal communication, by offering choices of activities, and by setting appropriate limits on negative behaviors.

If the parent or caregiver is overcontrolling and prevents the child from experiencing failure, artificial barriers to self-acceptance are set up. Even a very young child may interpret overprotection and overcontrol to mean that the caregiver thinks the child is a failure and cannot do anything for himself or herself. An undercontrolling parent may also have a serious impact on the young child's feelings of competency. A child who cannot control his or her environment through sensorimotor capabilities depends upon the parent to find alternative methods for learning. An undercontrolling parent who is reluctant to organize the infant's behavior or the environment for learning and play may experience significant frustration with the developmental progress of the child who cannot "just develop automatically" but depends upon others to promote learning opportunities.

Professionals can help most with the care of a toddler with disabilities by identifying the strengths of the child and by framing the difficulties faced by the child in positive terms. Validation of parental concerns is an essential component of this process. Families need to feel that they are being heard by the professional and that the professional is giving full attention to the parents' stated concern. Pointing out strategies for promotion of independence and communication help families to feel they are taking positive, proactive steps on behalf of their child. It is important for professionals to work in partnership with the parents, actively problem-solving and adjusting approaches to meet the changing needs of the child and family. Recommendations without follow-through may be unsuccessful, and families are likely to become frustrated if professionals cannot be flexible and creative in strategizing.

If a child feels that his or her urge for independence is being fulfilled through strategies that promote movement and communication, he or she is more likely to be emotionally positive, and negative behaviors are more likely to dissipate. Helping the child to "see himself as a problem-solver" (Gerber, 1987, p. 47) by talking the child through the solution to a dilemma rather than "fixing it" for him or her will promote self-determination and self-esteem for any young child.

Professionals and caregivers can support the development of competence and, ultimately, self-esteem through their approach to the daily activities of the child. They can encourage the child to be in control of play, feeding, and other activities as much as is possible and reasonable. For example, offering a choice between two objects can allow a nonverbal child to communicate his or her wishes by looking at the one object that is preferred. When a child has the ability to initiate an activity, following the lead of the child promotes engagement in a learning opportunity. When a child needs help in engaging in an activity, active participation by the child allows him or her to remain attentive to the process and promotes incidental learning as well as boosting self-esteem.

Helping the child initiate actions and then allowing him or her the satisfaction of completing a task is another way to ensure success and perseverance. However, knowing how to fade assistance is also an important component of this approach. As children grow and mature, they need to take more of the responsibility for trying a particular task. Self-esteem will falter if a caregiver is unable to allow the child to try over and over again, making some mistakes along the way. The key is to intervene only enough to avoid overfrustration, not to alleviate all frustration from the life of the child (Williamson, Zeitlin, & Szczepanski, 1989). "Children need the opportunity to test reality and experience limitations" (Cowan, 1991, p. 155).

All of these strategies require substantial time and patience. Time is necessary for nurturance. Children need help more at some times than at other times, and they need encouragement rather than demands. A relaxed approach, wherein the adult is able to accept approximations of responses as steps on the way to learning, is important. The adult needs the capacity to remain focused on longer-term goals. The child will be motivated by prompt and reasonable praise; helping words or phrases; and patient, positive approval.

Toddlers normally need consistent expectations and clearly communicated limits as they try out various behaviors to determine what is appropriate and what is not allowable (Greenberg, 1991). Toddlers with disabilities are no different. However, when the ability to move around independently is limited by disability or illness, testing behaviors may present in different ways than one might expect, such as vomiting, setting off monitor alarms by breathholding, and other maladaptive strategies. Toddlers with disabilities still need to have some limits placed upon them for appropriate behavior. For example, if they throw food they can be included in the process of cleaning up as a logical consequence of their behavior. Another example might include polite social acknowledgments such as "please" and "thank you," through gestures or symbolic communication systems:

> Adaptive coping generates a sense of mastery that is usually reflected in subsequent coping efforts. Maladaptive coping interferes with productive interaction with the environment and therefore hinders learning. Over time maladaptive coping leads to a sense of incompetence and expectations of failure. (Williamson et al., 1989, p. 5)

The social give and take of communication is also important to the positive self-regard of a young child. Part of the child's developing sense of independence comes from feeling that he or she can contribute to the activities of the family and is not just a "passive recipient" of whatever the environment has to offer (Beckwith, 1976). Harter (1990) states that "self-judgments depend heavily on social comparison, normative standards, social similarities and behaviors that enhance interpersonal interactions and social appeal" (p. 356). Thus, even during the toddler years, parents may provide opportunities for positive social comparisons and interactions with others by setting expectations for helping behaviors that contribute to the family's well-being. Using eye gaze or pointing to choose what shirt to wear or which food to be fed can facilitate the active involvement of a child in his or her own daily care. Simple strategies such as positioning children so that they can drop a cup into the water to be washed or hold onto several pieces of silverware as the table is set allows toddlers to feel like a valued member of the household or classroom as they help with daily activities to the best of their abilities. Praise for true accomplishments of that nature certainly promotes positive self-regard.

Providing adaptive equipment to allow for independent mobility or independence in self-care is another strategy that is important during the late toddler years. Use of walkers and electric wheelchairs or go-carts can further promote the independence craved by toddlers. For those who cannot yet speak, the ability to move away from something they do not want is essential to the development of autonomy. This allows the child to clearly communicate by physical approach or distancing from the object. Negative behaviors sometimes exhibited by toddlers with developmental challenges may be avoided. Augmentative communication strategies, such as the use of picture boards or computer-generated speech, are likewise essential to the child's ability to utilize adaptive, proactive strategies for achieving autonomy.

Preschool Children

Kevin was a blond, blue-eyed little 4½-year-old boy with severe developmental delay. He had sensory and motor impairments that created further challenges. He was placed in a child care setting 4 mornings per week. He was the only child with a disability in the classroom and had the opportunity to interact with children between 3 and 6 years of age. Although he had a personal aide, the program staff did not seem to have any strategies to include Kevin fully in the daily routines of the program. As a result, he seemed passive and apart, having little or no interaction with his peers. Personal care activities were "done to him" with little opportunity allowed for him to participate. For example, he was able to lift his arms to indicate that he wanted to be picked up but was seldom given the opportunity to do so (as when being taken for a diaper change). Classroom activities were seldom adapted appropriately to meet Kevin's needs as an integral member of the class. Although the classroom materials might have been adapted to allow for Kevin's decreased visual acuity and motor impairment by making the materials larger, brighter, and easier to handle than those used by the other children, this was not done.

The most important developmental "task" of the preschool years is promoting the child's ability to interact socially with adults and other children. Preschoolers need to learn to channel their energies into constructive opportunities for learning, a process that usually extends into the elementary school years. Caregiving adults set the tone for all children in the development of sharing, respect, kindness, politeness, and soothing behaviors. Play can be facilitated by adults, and conflict resolution can be modeled by adults to allow for positive learning opportunities. In Kevin's situation, an adult could have encouraged the other children to help Kevin participate in some of the classroom activities. A computer had been purchased for Kevin's use and other children were drawn to his computer activities. They could have been encouraged to ask Kevin for a turn or to negotiate whose turn would be next, thus including Kevin more fully in typical classroom interactions. Cooperative play experiences might have included Kevin in the kitchen area, dress-up corner, or block area, where he might receive assistance from his classmates with support from the classroom aide. As much as possible, adults should be able to eventually fade their assistance so that each child can find his or her own way in the social world. Children with disabilities learn a great deal from these types of opportunities for interaction and generally require progressively less intervention from adults.

The preschool child often has the desire to begin to move away from the safety of home and family to the more expansive world of peers. Individual children vary in their drive to enter the social world, with some children being hesitant and others almost demanding opportunities to interact with children of their same age. The preschool child with disabilities is no different in his or her need to expand horizons.

In providing services for a preschooler with disabilities, it is essential to carefully evaluate the desires of the family as well as the behaviors of the child. For example, some parents do not believe in preschool for any child until age 5; yet they may be receptive to related services such as speech therapy or occupational therapy to meet their child's needs. Still other parents may wish to teach their child with a disability through home schooling as they have done with the other children in their family. Preschool professionals should provide a flexible approach to the child's education to ensure that, for example, the option exists for children to receive services in their homes rather than being required to enroll in a preschool program.

When home services are the preferred approach, specific therapies and educational strategies must take into account the schedule of the child and family, avoiding nap times and dinner times, for example. The current health status of the child certainly influences the ability to attend to stories or specific tasks. Frequently, the most engaging tasks are those that are typical within the home environment of the child. For example, finding ways for the child to participate in cooking, doing laundry, setting the table, or washing dishes will often provide motivation as well as facilitate learning of such concepts as temperature, measuring, color matching and naming, and counting. As always, promoting the child's drive for independence and contribution to the family can be the best motivation for learning for a young preschool child.

When it is deemed time for the child to move into an out-of-home program such as a nursery school, Montessori school, or preschool program, therapies and educational strategies still must focus on helping the child to benefit from the activities being presented to all of the children in the classroom. Rather than pulling the child out of an opportunity such as circle time to do a specific therapy or to receive specific tutoring, therapy and learning goals can be woven throughout the natural classroom activities. Aides can be used to best advantage by including them in program planning in advance so that they can promote the involvement of the child in the activities of the entire class. They might be trained by the therapist to position the child to best advantage or by the speech pathologist to facilitate the use of a picture board so that the child can fully participate in circle time activities. Aides might also prepare adaptive materials ahead of time that will motivate the child and encourage learning opportunities similar to those of the other children in the classroom.

For some children with disabilities, tools for augmentative communication and adaptive equipment can be essential for success in the preschool environment. Play opportunities expand when a child is at eye level with his or her peers, whether the child is in a walker or in a wheelchair. Use of computers and voice synthesizers draw other children to the child with disabilities and allow for communication options not available otherwise. To be most effective, adaptive equipment must be available to the child as early as possible prior to preschool. This allows the child with disabilities to become familiar with the equipment and to be able to use it effectively by the time the preschool experience begins.

Another important component of the preschool experience for children with disabilities is providing them with opportunities to get to know children with whom they will go to elementary school. Providing a preschool program with multiple therapies but limited chances to meet and play with other children who will be classmates in elementary school is a waste of an important opportunity. Preschool children are typically far less judgmental and are more willing to accept differences than are elementary-age children (Sparks, 1989). Allowing a child to develop friendships in the preschool years offers that child the opportunity to maintain those friendships for several years to come, as is shown in the case of Amy.

Amy was a bright-eyed and enthusiastic little girl with Down syndrome who had the opportunity to participate in a typical preschool program at the town nursery school. She was completely accepted by most of the young children in that preschool and made friendships that brought invitations to parties and play times. Although she sometimes had some challenging behaviors, her behaviors were no more challenging than were those of the other preschool children around her. She constantly watched and participated, as did the other children. She also learned self-help skills and independence in dressing, toileting, and snack activities. Specific therapies were offered outside of preschool hours to allow her optimal continuity of activities in the classroom.

Now, at the age of 11, Amy has maintained her friendships with many of the children who went to preschool with her. She is active in Girl Scouts and on the swim team, and she is frequently invited to birthday parties and other outings. She is an active member of a regular fourth grade class and receives assistance as needed on school assignments from other children as well as from the aide assigned to her classroom. She is a happy, confident, and secure little girl who is well known and well liked by many other children.

STRATEGIES TO PROMOTE SELF-COMPETENCE IN TODDLERS AND PRESCHOOLERS IN MEDICAL SETTINGS

Toddlers and preschoolers with disabilities may have frequent interactions with medical care providers. Multiple evaluations, medical procedures, and hospitalizations can have a marked effect on the young child's feeling of control over the environment. Young children at this age are coming to terms with themselves as separate individuals who need opportunities for mastery and independence. For this reason, the health care professionals need to gear their caregiving to be more child-oriented. It is possible to engage the child in a partnership with the professional rather than place the child in a passive or oppositional relationship with the professionals. Several simple strategies can be implemented in routine medical care practices with toddlers and preschoolers, whether in a hospital, office, or home-care setting.

Environment

The environment must be "child-friendly" and must include furniture that is child-sized, decor that is child-oriented (e.g., pictures at child's eye level, toys that draw attention and alleviate boredom). The less stark and clinical the room is, the better. It should be warm and welcoming. Professionals must look at the environment from a child's height. For example, intimidating pieces of equipment may be stored at children's eye level but be unnoticed by adults. Children should have access to toys with which they can occupy themselves. Toys need to be physically accessible to all children. There should also be adaptive toys that are readily available for play.

Practitioners should realize that children may associate people in white coats with pain or discomfort because of past traumatic experiences. They should therefore dress in white only when painful procedures might be required. Likewise, bed spaces need to be "safe havens" as much as possible, with painful procedures being done in treatment rooms or outside of the child's own space.

Communication

All practitioners who associate with young children need to first greet the child and acknowledge his or her presence. They must understand the necessity of clear communication directly with the children as well as with the parents.

Children should be informed about the activities that will occur, regardless of their age and presumed ability to understand. This will allow them to anticipate and prepare themselves for what will happen next. It is important to give the child a chance to respond before beginning the action (Gerber, 1987). For example, it is preferable to say, "I am going to pick you up and put you on the exam table now," rather than to place the child on the table without warning. Directions should state only what needs to be done, leaving no room for choice unless choices are appropriate. For example, it is preferable to say, "It's time to look in your ears," rather than to say, "Will you let me look in your ears now?" or to just insert the otoscope without telling the child first. When appropriate, choices should be offered, such as "Which do you want to do first, look in your ears or look in your eyes?" Even a child without verbal skills may be able to point or otherwise indicate which would be preferred.

In order to build a trusting relationship with the child, it is important to continually engage in an interactive dialogue, regardless of the child's verbal ability. Children should be viewed as active partners in health care practices and not as passive recipients. Engaging children in this way will decrease the likelihood of uncooperative behavior on the part of the child. It gives the child a sense of control and independence in a setting in which these two attributes are not often promoted.

Young children are concrete thinkers and therefore most often take what adults say literally. For example, "stool" may mean a piece of furniture and "shot" may mean wounded with a gun. Asking the parents what the child's familiarity is with particular terms or asking parents to help to interpret and reassure when appropriate is certainly an important aspect of health care. At the same time, honesty is required when potentially painful procedures will occur. It is not appropriate to tell a child that drawing blood is not going to hurt. It would be better to say, "You will feel a prick and then need to hold still until the tube is full, then you get a bandaid" (Stanford, 1991, p. 261).

All children, including those with disabilities, can understand more than they can express. Care should be taken to include a child in the conversation. However, if there is information that must be conveyed to the parents or practitioners in private, care must be taken not to talk in front of the child, assuming that he or she will not understand. For example, when giving a diagnosis of a chronic illness or developmental disability, allowing the child to play with supervision in a separate room will allow the parents the freedom to ask many questions or to cry without needing to worry about the immediate impact on the child. In this way, they can determine the best way to inform the child as they see fit. In addition, parents will be more able to focus on the information without the distraction of having to watch their child while listening and trying to formulate questions to clarify the information they are receiving.

Scheduling

Health care providers tend to work on a schedule based on efficiency and adult needs; young children's routine schedules often do not coincide. Scheduling appointments during a child's typically free times rather than during naps or mealtimes is one option that is especially important for children who spend a great deal of time in medical care situations. Inpatient laboratory tests should not take precedence over a child's sleep patterns. Likewise, too many different procedures scheduled in one short period of time can overstress a child and cause a loss of feelings of competency and control. The result may be an increase in negative coping behaviors (e.g., sleep disorders, tantrums, decreased appetite) for a prolonged period after the stressful event. Providers should be aware of not keeping a child waiting for more than a maximum of 10–15 minutes. This requires that appointments be scheduled to allow adequate time for each patient, as opposed to double-booking appointments for the sake of office efficiency.

CONCLUSION

Many factors influence the development of coping, self-esteem, and competence in children. For young children with disabilities, the ability of the family to cope in positive ways is one key factor in instilling a "can-do" attitude in the child. Providing menus of services to allow families to determine what best suits their lifestyles and the needs of their child can also facilitate family empowerment. Families who are empowered and confident, are, in turn, more free to positively promote the care, learning, and development of their children. They are also more able to advocate for their children in the early years. They are more able to allow their children the freedom to experience frustration, to cope with failures, and to come through adversity stronger and more able to direct their own lives. In the long run, children who have families who cope positively with difficult times are more likely to cope positively as they mature into adolescence and adulthood (Werner & Smith, 1992).

Medical and child care providers can help or hinder the process of family and child coping by the way they interact with the family. Respect and empathy, an understanding of the developmental issues of all children, and an understanding of the issues of disability in the very early years of life are all prerequisites for professionals who wish to positively influence the development of independence and mastery in young children:

> The ultimate goal is to instill in parents a sense of competence while assisting them to see their child, regardless of handicap or medical condition, as a competent developing individual. (Hedlund, 1989, p. 8)

REFERENCES

Affleck, G., & Tennen, H. (1993). Cognitive adaptation to adversity: Insights from parents of medically fragile infants. In A.P. Turnbull, J.M. Patterson, S.K. Behr, D.L. Murphy, J.G. Marquis, & M.J. Blue-Banning (Eds.), *Cognitive coping, families, and disability* (pp. 135–150). Baltimore: Paul H. Brookes Publishing Co.,

Beckwith, L. (1976). Caregiver–infant interaction and the development of the high risk infant. In T.D. Tjossen (Ed.), *Intervention strategies for high risk infants and young children* (pp. 119–140). Baltimore: University Park Press.

Bernheimer, L., Young, M., & Winton, P. (1983). Stress over time: Parents with young handicapped children. *Developmental and Behavioral Pediatrics, 4*(3), 177–181.

Briggs, D.C. (1975). *Your child's self-esteem.* Garden City, NY: Dolphin Books.

Brooks-Gunn, J., & Lewis, M. (1982). Affective exchanges between normal and handicapped infants and their mothers. In T. Field & A. Fogel (Eds.), *Emotion and early interaction.* (pp. 161–188). Hillsdale, NJ: Lawrence Erlbaum Associates.

Cameron, S., Snowdon, A., & Orr, R. (1992). Emotions experienced by mothers of children with developmental disabilities. *Children's Health Care, 21*(2), 96–101.

Cooley, W.C., & Moeschler, J.B. (1993). Counseling in the health care relationship in families. In G.H.S. Singer & L.E. Powers (Eds.), *Families, disability, and empowerment: Active coping skills and strategies for family interventions* (pp. 155–174). Baltimore: Paul H. Brookes Publishing Co.

Coopersmith, S. (1967). *The antecedents of self-esteem.* San Francisco: W.H. Freeman.

Cowan, N.S. (1991). Family life and self-esteem. In E. Geralis (Ed.), *Children with cerebral palsy: A parent's guide* (pp. 131–174). Reisterstown, MD: Woodbine House.

Gerber, M. (1987). *A manual for parents and professionals.* Los Angeles: Resources for Infant Educarers.

Goldberg, S. (1972). Social competence in infancy: A model of parent-infant interaction. *Merrill-Palmer Quarterly, 15,* 323–340.

Gould, P., & Moses, L. (1985). Mild developmental delays from a parent's perspective. In *Equals in this partnership* (pp. 14–17). Washington, DC: National Center for Clinical Infant Programs.

Greenberg, P. (1991). *Character development: Encouraging self-esteem and self-discipline in infants, toddlers, & two-year-olds.* Washington, DC: National Association for the Education of Young Children.

Greenspan, S. (1992). *Infancy and early childhood: The practice of clinical assessment and intervention with emotional and developmental challenges.* Madison, CT: International Universities Press.

Harter, S. (1990). Self and identity development. In S. Feldman & G. Elliott (Eds.), *At the threshold: The developing adolescent* (pp. 352–387). Cambridge, MA: Harvard University Press.

Hedlund, R. (1989, December). *Fostering positive social interactions between parents and their severely handicapped/medically fragile infant.* Paper presented at the Sixth Biennial National Training Institute of the National Center for Clinical Infant Programs, Washington, DC.

McGrath, M., & Meyer, E. (1992). Maternal self-esteem: From theory to clinical practice in a special care nursery. *Children's Health Care, 21*(4), 199–204.

McLean, L. (1989, December). *Communication intervention with infants and toddlers: A transactional approach.* Paper presented at the Sixth Biennial National Training Institute of the National Center for Clinical Infant Programs, Washington, DC.

Mintzer, D., Als, H., Tronick, E., & Brazelton, T. (1985). Parenting an infant with a birth defect: The regulation of self-esteem. *Zero to Three, 5*(5).

Murphy, M. (1982). The family with a handicapped child: A review of the literature. *Developmental and Behavioral Pediatrics, 3*(2), 73–81.

Poulsen, M. (1993). Strategies for building resilience in infants and young children at risk. *Infants & Young Children, 6*(2).

Prizant, B., & Wetherby, A. (1990). Assessing the communication of infants and toddlers: Integrating a socioemotional perspective. *Zero to Three, 11*(1), 1–12.

Sparks, L. (1989). *Anti-bias curriculum: Tools for empowering young children.* Washington, DC: National Association for the Education of Young Children.

Stanford, G. (1991). Beyond honesty: Choosing language for talking to children about pain and procedures. *Children's Health Care, 20*(4), 261–262.

Tronick, E.Z., Ricks, M., & Cohn, J.F. (1982). Maternal and infant affective exchange: Patterns of adaptation. In T. Field & A. Fogel (Eds.), *Emotion and early interaction* (pp. 83–100). Hillsdale, NJ: Lawrence Erlbaum Associates.

Trout, M. (1983), Birth of a sick or handicapped infant: Impact on the family. *Child Welfare, 62*(4), 337–347.

Turnbull, A.P., & Summers, J.A. (1985, April). *From parent involvement to family support: Evaluation to revolution.* Paper presented at the Down Syndrome State-of-the-Art Conferences. Boston, MA.

Werner, E., & Smith, R. (1992). *Overcoming the odds: High risk children from birth to adulthood.* Ithaca, NY: Cornell University Press.

Williamson, G., Zeitlin, S., & Szczepanski, M. (1989). Coping behavior: Implications for disabled infants and toddlers. *Infant Mental Health Journal, 10*(1), 3–13.

19

Helping Young Children with Behavior Problems Develop Self-Determination Through Behavioral Skill Building

Joanne Singer and George H.S. Singer

With increases in poverty, crime, and divorce in our society has come an increase in the prevalence of serious behavioral and emotional disorders in young children. Childhood behavioral problems fall into two major categories: externalizing and internalizing disorders. Children who exhibit externalizing, disruptive behavior in school pose the greatest challenge to successful inclusion efforts in schools today. An extensive research program has begun to produce evidence of developmental pathways for major behavioral problems. There is an increasing body of evidence that 3- and 4-year-old children who exhibit aggressive and noncompliant behavior are likely to continue to have serious difficulties with their behavior in their schools and communities as they mature. Internalizing behavior disorders, such as depression and anxiety, often go undetected and untreated, although they commonly manifest themselves early. Children with internalizing disorders are frequently quiet, well behaved, and compliant in school settings. In increasingly large classrooms that are short of staff and resources, these children often go unnoticed and suffer in silence.

A common developmental pathway for both major internalizing and major externalizing disorders is disrupted parent–child relationships. We argue that building self-competence in children is better supported through the appreciation that behavioral challenges, by their very nature, threaten the typical development of a strong, positive relationship between parents and children. Interventionists have concentrated so narrowly on child interventions and parent training aimed solely on compliance that they have often missed understanding that parents and children most frequently attempt to relate to each other in the best way they currently know. Whether the behavioral challenge is caused by the child's language delay, attention problems, a developmental delay, parental stressors, or other environmental factors, the result is that the daily patterns of building relationship have been, in part, derailed. We argue that, rather than perceiving of these disrupted, or derailed, relationships as pathological, attention needs to be provided to strategies that promote self-esteem and self-competence in parents and their children, building on the existing strengths in the relationship. After reviewing current evidence for the prevalence and developmental causes of problem behaviors, we present a set of cognitive behavioral interventions aimed at restoring disrupted relationships.

PREVALENCE AND CHARACTERISTICS OF CHILDHOOD PSYCHOPATHOLOGY

Prevalence estimates of childhood psychopathology range from 14% to 22% (Brandenburg, Friedman, & Silver, 1990; Costello, 1989). Children who exhibit externalizing behaviors are the most noticed, and the consequences of their behavior are one of the most important concerns in the United States today (Gabel & Shindledecker, 1991). There are major disruptive behavioral disorders listed by the *Diagnostic and Statistical Manual of Mental Disorders,* 4th ed. (DSM-IV) (American Psychiatric Association, 1994): attention-deficit/hyperactivity disorder (ADHD), conduct disorder, and oppositional defiant disorder. Comorbidity combined with the severity, frequency, and complexity of externalizing behavior disorders create impressive challenges for parents and interventionists hoping to raise and educate children in a manner that prevents the development of these disorders.

Among researchers and mental health professionals, agreement on definitions of internalizing disorders has proved difficult to attain. Generally, internalizing disorders are characterized by the turning inward of emotions associated with problems such as loneliness and social withdrawal and by psychiatric disorders of depression and anxiety (Bucy, 1994). Internalizing disorders have serious, long-term complications. Alarmingly high percentages of children who experience internalizing disorders ultimately drop out of school, attempt suicide, or require psychiatric hospitalization.

In addition to those who have major psychological disorders, many children in our society struggle to develop into self-reliant and self-competent young adults. While they may not experience symptoms severe enough to warrant a psychiatric label, many children fail to live up to their potential as a result of nonclinical behavioral problems.

Although many risk factors exist that increase the likelihood of threat to children's mental health, distinct, single causal links among particular risk factors and later mental health problems have not been unequivocally established for any childhood behavioral disorder. Certain risk factors, such as having a mother who is seriously depressed, having divorced parents, being the victim of abuse or trauma, and living in extreme poverty, predict an increased likelihood for mental health problems for the child. A multitude of other factors also buffer against damage or amplify risk factors. For example, the risk factors for a child being raised by a divorced mother who is financially secure and has a strong support network might be less than those for a child raised by a socially isolated mother on welfare. Behavioral problems appear to arise as a result of complex interactions between characteristics of the child, characteristics of the parents, environmental buffers, and environmental stressors. In most cases, the developmental pathway to childhood disorder is marked by disrupted parent–child relationships.

RISK FACTORS

Prevention and intervention for children at risk for developing serious emotional and behavioral disorders would be greatly simplified if there were a direct, causal link between parent, child, and environmental variables. The difficulty in trying to pinpoint causal links for child behavioral disorders is complicated by an enormous number of potential variables and causality relationships that are often bidirectional. To further add to the complexity, it is likely that many key variables do not behave in a linear fashion. Some factors may cause risk, while others may play a protective role for the child. An important child risk factor is temperament, particularly a difficult temperament, including noncompliant behavior, irritability, and aggression or a tendency to respond to environmental challenge with anxiety and withdrawal. Language delays clearly increase the risk for emotional, behavioral, and academic problems (Jenkins, Bax, & Hart, 1980). Beitchman, Inglis, and Schachter (1992) found that 48% of 5-year-old children with psychiatric disturbance had language delays. Middle ear disease, which is common in young children, can lead to language delays and ultimately to attentional problems in elementary school. Cognitive delays, attentional difficulties, and ongoing special health care needs can also affect the mental health of children.

Children, however, do not come in neat packages with neat labels. A child may have a difficult temperament much of the time, but also be extremely articulate and have an engaging sense of humor that softens the reactions of parents and other adults to the child's inappropriate behaviors. A child may arrive at preschool with a strong tendency to withdraw from peers and adults. However, adults and children may regularly initiate positive interactions with the child as a result of the child's physical attractiveness.

Many parent variables may present risk or causal factors for the emotional and behavioral development of children. A parent with mental health problems, such as depression or anxiety or drug and alcohol abuse, represents a potential risk for children; but parent variables also do not fit into neat categories. For example, a parent with limited cognitive abilities may have many friends or relatives who provide compensatory support. Numerous environmental variables may also increase child risk, including divorce, low socioeconomic status, sibling conflict, stressful life events, being subjected to or witnessing coercive interactions, and antisocial peers. The complexity of interactions among the child, parent, and environment are evident, and ascribing direct causal links for the development of behavior disorders is clearly problematic.

Some researchers have tried to establish these causal pathways. Rubin and Mills (1991) described a causal pathway to internalizing disorders, which included a child's temperament problems interacting with a primary caregiver with negative attitudes and a stressful environment to produce a child who is likely to be insecure, socially withdrawn, and incompetent. Thomas, Chess, and Birch (1968) describe infants and toddlers with "difficult temperament" as having 1) irregularity of biological functions, 2) withdrawal from novel stimuli, 3) slowness to adapt, 4) intense responses, and

5) predominantly negative mood. McDevitt and Carey (1978) found 19% of 350 preschool children had difficult temperaments. A theory of "goodness to fit" between difficult-temperament infants and their mothers was discussed by Campbell (1990). A difficult-temperament infant born to a highly stressed, nonresponsive mother is at much higher risk than one born to a calm, responsive mother. Tynan and Nearing (1994) reported that 50% of the children identified as impulsive with difficult temperaments as toddlers did not fit the criteria for ADHD at later ages. Mothers having negative perceptions of their child's behavior were the most likely to have a child who was later diagnosed with ADHD. The interaction of difficult temperament with a particular parenting style created a developmental pathway to a psychiatric disorder. In this case, the interaction of parent and child characteristics gives rise to serious behavioral and emotional problems. The disrupted parent–child relationship appears to shape preexisting tendencies in the child into long-term problems.

Similarly, Biederman, Rosenbaum, Chaloff, and Kagan (1995) have documented the development of anxiety and avoidant disorders in young children. They identified a group of 50 infants who at birth had temperaments that predisposed them to withdraw from environmental stress. Compared with their peers, these infants were more distressed and had higher levels of physiological arousal, such as elevated heart rates, when stressed. Kagan et al. followed these children for a 5-year period and found that children whose parents were overprotective and overanxious with their infants were more likely to become anxious preschoolers. In particular, they identified the parents' behavior in setting limits as decisive. Parents who responded to potentially dangerous behavior from their toddlers (e.g., playing in the garbage) by setting limits and giving explanations, had preschoolers who were less anxious and withdrawn than did parents who did not set limits or provide explanations and who responded to unsafe behavior by anxiously removing the child from the situation without a statement of limits or explanation. Again, an interactional pattern between a child with a particular predisposition appears to give rise to a long-term behavioral or emotional problem.

Patterson (1982) developed a model for explaining the development of externalizing disorders in children. He describes a scenario in which parents and children develop two-way coercive interactions. These interactions have an escalating quality. Parents and child each try to control the other's behavior, and their interactions increase in negativity and intensity. The child learns from the parent that the way to get what you want is through coercion. The child also is able to obtain increased adult attention (even though it appears quite negative) via escalating inappropriate behavior, especially around compliance issues. Patterson indicates that sibling fighting commonly occurs in families where there are coercive interactions between parents and children. The child learns how to get rid of peers that she perceives as negative and to obtain increased adult attention by fighting. By the time a child from a family with coercive interactions is 6 years old and entering school, he or she is likely to generalize home behavior to school and be noncompliant with teacher requests and aggressive with peers. Noncompliance, in turn, is associated with academic failure. Aggression with siblings tends to generalize to aggression with school peers and eventual association with an antisocial peer group.

The models of Patterson (1982) and Rubin and Mills (1991) are very compelling and worthwhile attempts to clarify risk factors for the purposes of prevention and intervention. However, these and other models are new, need to be validated, and do not explain the variety of outcomes that do not fit the models. Years of research may be needed to discover reliable causal pathways, and it is likely that a large degree of uncertainty will always prevail in attempts to explain the development of behavioral disorders. The causes for negative outcomes in human behavior, with all of its complexity, are not analogous to discovering the biological causes of disease. The equivalent of breaking the genetic code for cystic fibrosis is not likely in the study of the causes for emotional and behavioral disorders in children. One alternative to identifying highly specific causal pathways is to call upon a different level of analysis that focuses on broader sets of variables. For example, Bednar, Wells, and Peterson (1989) have marshaled evidence that a condition common to most emotional disorders is low self-esteem. Similarly, it is highly likely that the majority of parent–child relationships in young children who develop behavioral or emotional disorders in early childhood fall outside culturally established norms for interactional patterns.

DISRUPTED RELATIONSHIPS AS
A COMMON PATHWAY TO CHILDHOOD BEHAVIORAL DISORDERS

In the following discussion, we examine the impact of disrupted parent–child relationships for children 3–6 years old. Considerable work has been published in recent years concerning relationships between mothers and infants. This body of work has centered on the concept of mother–infant attachment and the impact of poor attachment on later behavior (Ainsworth, 1993). Here we are concerned about parent–child relationships in preschool and early elementary school–age children. We assume that many of the children who are identified as having internalizing or externalizing problems in school settings have had early problems in their development of secure attachments. However, because the links between infant–parent relationships and later behavioral and emotional problems in the early school years have not been thoroughly studied, we emphasize a set of later developmental skills and their parenting corollaries that are important for young children to adapt to school environments. We begin with the non-controversial assumption that most children who are identified as troubled in early childhood experience disruptions in their relationships with parents.

Given the great diversity in developmental pathways to child behavioral and emotional disorders, is there a construct that is sufficiently broad that it can apply to a majority of types of behavior problems but yet is not so nebulous as to have no practical implications? We believe that the concept of a *disrupted relationship* provides a unit of analysis that fits. Disrupted relationships consist of behavioral, cognitive, and emotional interactions that are primarily negative in affective tone, frequently set the stage for inappropriate child behavior or the extreme absence of appropriate child behavior, and establish powerful contingencies that maintain problem behaviors. The use of the term *disrupted* is normative, assuming that there are culturally normative interactional patterns that are desirable and are not taking place in a disrupted relationship. The focus on *relationship* implies a transactional emphasis that assumes parents influence children and vice versa. The assumption is that a disruption in the normative interactional patterns between parent and child can occur from a wide variety of causes, including child developmental or language delays, parental stresses, or environmental stresses on either the child or the parent. Our intention is to assist in a clear analysis of what is occurring between parents and children when a disruption in their interactional patterns has occurred rather than to place blame or judgment on either children or their parents. The target of intervention is, therefore, the parent–child dyad or triad. The locus of the problem is assumed to reside in the system created by parents and children, rather than solely within the parent or the child.

In order to be useful, the idea of disrupted relationship should contain some common relationship characteristics that are likely to exist regardless of the particular child problem behavior. In keeping with the structure of the theory, these common character-istics should have cognitive, behavioral, and affective elements. At the affective level, disrupted relationships are characterized by abnormal levels of negative affect includ-ing anger, sorrow, disgust, or shame. Behaviorally, these affects are characterized either by abnormal levels of externalizing behavior or by abnormal levels of internalizing behavior. Cognitively, they are characterized by idiosyncratic patterns of appraisal and labeling that represent distortions and biases when compared with the cognition of parents and children whose relationships fall within a culturally normative range. For children over the age of 8, one cognitive–emotional characteristic that is common to most childhood behavioral disorders is low self-esteem. Parents are also likely to suffer from a sense of low self-esteem in regard to their parenting. Psychological problems involve a mismatch between the individual and his or her social environment and usu-ally involve negative feedback from significant others in the social environment. Par-ents and children are likely to feel bad about themselves when their relationships are highly disrupted.

CYCLE OF NEGATIVE INTERACTIONS

One way to focus on practical approaches to the development of emotional and behav-ioral challenges in young children is to look at what happens to the interactions between a parent and child when the relationship has been disrupted and damaged, regardless of the cause. As discussed above, there are many complex pathways to the development of emotional and behavioral disorders through the interactions of parent, child, and environmental variables. What is proposed here is a conceptual framework for a general understanding of what happens to the parent and child when their rela-tionship is damaged, how the negative influences in the relationship tend to perpetuate themselves, and how early child behavioral difficulties become more serious, stable conditions. We assume that for many children who develop problematic behavior in early childhood, there have already likely been some significant disruptions of normal attachment and of normal parenting. The child is very likely by early childhood to already be exhibiting behaviors that are aversive to the parent. At some point, parents reach a threshold, and they begin to develop negative attributions about their child. Parents enter the cycle of negative interactions with their child once they are so con-vinced of the correctness of their negative views that they begin to interact with the child predominantly based on those negative beliefs. The following scenario describes one of many patterns that we believe occur once a parent has developed a negative cog-nitive bias about the child. There are, of course, many variants on how a disturbed rela-tionship can unfold.

A parent who is about to cross the threshold into a cycle of negative interactions with a child is characterized as someone who is increasingly making negative attribu-tions toward the child. This parent is typically often angry and irritable with the child and begins to believe that the child is either intentionally behaving inappropriately or that deficits in child behavior are the fault of the child. When the child's behavior is ambiguous, the parent is quick to assume the child's behavior has negative connota-tions, rather than positive or neutral ones. Resentment of parenting responsibilities grows. The threshold is crossed when the parent begins interacting with the child based on negative attributions.

Once a parent is frequently making negative attributions toward a child, the nega-tive cycle begins as the parent decreases the amount of positive attention he or she provides and generally withdraws from the child. The decrease in positive attention and withdrawal from the child is sometimes sufficient for the parent to not recognize and acknowledge when the child is acting appropriately. Ill intent on the part of the parent is usually not the reason parents begin to focus on difficulties with the child. For instance, a child with a sleep disorder may be extremely irritable upon rising in the morning or may regularly disrupt the parents' sleep. The scenario of parent and child, deprived of sufficient sleep, having to accomplish all the morning routines before the parent leaves for work is fraught with the possibility of promoting negative and mutually aversive interactions. Due to lack of sleep, the parent is having to deal on an ongoing basis with a child who is unlikely to be cooperative at the same time the parent has the least amount of patience. The parent's intention may be very positive, but the situation does not promote starting the day feeling positive about the child.

A parent, acting from predominantly negative beliefs about the child, is likely to decrease the amount of positive interactions with the child, to withdraw from the child, and to increase negative interactions with the child. With reduced access to parental attention and with the tendency of the parent to not recognize positive behavior, the child learns to elicit increased parental attention for inappropriate behavior. Two common pathways for receiving this kind of parental attention are via noncompliance with adult requests and via sibling fighting. However, a selectively noninteractive child might find that *not* interacting or responding verbally to a parent might require the parent to spend more time with the child, playing charades and guessing what the child might want. The parent may be irritated while spending this time, but, the child regularly gains undivided adult attention through not speaking. Both parties are attempting to control the other through their behavior, but they are both successful only in exacerbating the situation. Parental withdrawal and reduced parental attention for positive behaviors leads the child to increase the use of negative and deficit behaviors to at least obtain negative parental attention. The problematic behavior from the child serves to reinforce and solidify the parent's negative attributions about the child, leading to more negative reactions to the child's behavior and more parental withdrawal from positive interactions. In addition, the cycle frequently expands to include sibling fighting and marital disputes over child-rearing practices, leading to disrupted and negative sibling and marital relationships.

This negative cycle of interactions, left untreated, has severe consequences for the child. The predominantly negative interactions the child is having with the parent solidify over time, become internalized by the child, and lead the child to reenact the negative cycle at school and in the community. When the most important adults in a child's life are continually making negative attributions about him or her, it is difficult for the child to develop self-esteem. The child has no reason to assume that new adults in his or her life will be positive and approaches new adults in a confrontative or avoidant manner. Children who grow up in families where there are negative cycles of interactions are unlikely to easily bond with future adults in their lives. The child has no practice in positive social interactions at home and is at a loss and socially incompetent when old enough to begin interacting with peers and other adults at school and in the community. Whether the causal pathway leading to the child's disrupted development leads to externalizing or internalizing problems, it is likely that the child will repeat the interaction patterns of home with his or her first teachers and peers.

Adults at school and in the community react to the child's negative behavior patterns as if these patterns were proof that the child had identifiable, unchangeable traits. With increasing frequency, children are being labeled as ADHD, socially withdrawn, incorrigible, shy, a "loner," aggressive, or depressed, to name a few, when they are only 3 years old. Once the child has been informally labeled with negative traits and is allowed to continue the negative cycle of interactions with teachers, there is a great likelihood that this continued cycle will disrupt learning and academic achievement. An insecure, withdrawn child is less likely to raise his or her hand to be called on by the teacher, and the same child is easy for the teacher to ignore because he or she is not demanding attention. The externalizing child who is noncompliant with adult requests, irritable, and aggressive frequently finds him- or herself excluded from instruction through time-out procedures or teacher avoidance. Teachers may view periods of compliant behavior by externalizing children as times to withdraw from contact with the child (i.e., "let sleeping dogs lie"), and they may reduce contact and positive interactions in the same way that these children's parents interact with them.

Behavioral parenting interventions have been widely studied and disseminated since the 1970s. These treatment methods usually focus on specific techniques for changing children's problematic behavior by teaching parents new interactional skills. While these methods have been successful in remediating a wide range of problem behaviors across the life span, they are not usually discussed as ways of improving parent–child relationships or of improving children's self-esteem. Such discussions have usually been considered the province of psychodynamic or object-oriented therapists. However, in our experience, well-designed and well-implemented behavioral treatments can be effective in healing the disruptive, negative feedback loop that characterizes disrupted parent–child relationships in early childhood. In the following discussion, we explain some of the key procedures that can lead to improved parent–child relationships.

BEHAVIORAL TREATMENT PROCEDURES FOR DISRUPTED RELATIONSHIPS: LEARNING NEW APPRAISAL AND LABELING BEHAVIORS

Two keystones of disrupted parent–child relationships are negative appraisal and labeling of the child's intentions and behavior. Negative appraisal and labeling develops from a social context in which inappropriate behavior in children is viewed as willful; parents' natural frustration at being unsuccessful in getting their child to cooperate with requests; and a lack of understanding that appropriate behavior involves extremely complex and difficult learning, especially for a child with weaknesses in language development or a child with a difficult temperament. Unfortunately, difficulties arising from negative appraisal and labeling are too frequently exacerbated by educational and mental health professionals when they become involved belatedly with the child and family.

A trip to any supermarket in our country will give an observer the opportunity to see the typical reaction of onlookers when a young child is misbehaving in public. Onlookers typically stare, whisper to the people they are with about the behavior, exhibit facial expressions that indicate criticism of the parent and the child, and sometimes voice their negative opinions about the child's behavior to the parents (e.g., "I find you need to set limits with children when you go to the store" or "Is something wrong with your child?"). Parents with children who do not easily cooperate often find themselves being subjected to critical looks, uninvited advice and criticism, or obvious avoidance. Parents of young children with behavior disorders report that relatives and friends are frequently critical of their parenting abilities and exclude their children from family and social functions (Singer, 1993). Parents are left feeling stigmatized by their child's behavior and frequently feeling badly about themselves as parents when they are in public or with friends and relatives.

The combination of social pressure to have a child behave appropriately, strongly paired with the negative interactions suffered from others when the child's behavior is inappropriate, contributes to parent frustration at being unsuccessful in getting the child to cooperate and comply with simple directions and routines in daily life. Parents feel the "double whammy" of having to contend with aggravation from ongoing resistance by the child and frequently hearing negative messages from their social environment and community about parents who cannot "control" their children. In our experience, by the time parents seek help for their child's problem behaviors, they are usually engaged in negative appraisal and labeling toward their child. As we have learned from the description of the development of a negative interactional cycle between parent and child, this negative appraisal and labeling often accelerates the cycle of escalating negativity between parent and child.

Negative attributions about the child often involve characterological blame. Instead of saying that the child has troublesome behaviors, the child comes to be viewed as troublesome. Parental attributions emphasize the generality and stability of the problem behavior, even though it may be situational to an outside observer. For example, one parent referred to her 4-year-old as "my little cross to bear" and described him as a "bad kid." The parent can arrive at the viewpoint that the locus of the problem is in the child rather than in the transactions between the child and the environment. Furthermore, parents in disrupted relationships are likely to view the child's troublesome behavior as deliberate and willful and aimed in a very personal way at causing pain to the parent. When combined, these attributions can establish a negative bias in which the parent perceives and interprets the child's behavior negatively.

In the midst of all of this negativity, the goal of raising a child who will have confidence in his or her abilities, be able to face challenges directly and responsibly, and make independent, productive choices can be lost. The issue with parents, and later with teachers, can deteriorate into one of control instead of nurturing toward independence. We believe that the first step to repairing the disrupted parent–child relationship is for parents to learn to make positive appraisals and engage in positive labeling of their child's appropriate behavior. Unless parents can understand for themselves the nature and function of the negative interactions they currently have with their child, convincing them to change their behavior is extremely difficult. If the parent believes that the child is intentionally misbehaving, starting to be more positive with appraisal and interactions with the child may not make sense to the harried parent. One of the goals of intervention for the parent–child dyad is to gradually provide the parent with a different model of problem behavior, one that alters attributions in three ways: 1) away from believing that the problem behavior is permanent and general to recognizing that it is situational and only a part of the child's total repertoire, 2) away from attributing the locus of the problem entirely in the child to understanding there is an interaction between the child and the environment, and 3) away from viewing the behavior as willful and deliberate and instead seeing it more as a result of factors that are less under the child's control, such as delays in language development.

In our experience, these changes in parental attributions are often slow in developing and require an ongoing effort by the interventionist. We were involved in training a mother who had a child with extreme noncompliant and self-abusive behavior to provide the child with reinforcing planned activity times and to allow him to partially participate in helping her with the laundry and making dinner. The mother and child were both successful in changing their behaviors, with the mother providing structure and praise for appropriate behavior and the child playing and participating without engaging in noncompliant or self-abusive behavior. However, the mother continued to make negative appraisals about the child. As interventionists, we needed to shadow the mother while she was interacting with her son and point out to her whenever the child was cooperating, hugging, smiling, and laughing in response to his mother's efforts. This mother did not intend to view her son negatively. The drain of years of being unsuccessful in getting him to cooperate and being treated judgmentally by teachers and relatives had made it difficult to let go of the old patterns of viewing her son. Often parents have to experience a significant improvement in the child's behavior before they are open to new ways of thinking about their relationship.

We recommend that the interventionist actively work to educate parents about causes of problem behaviors in ways that lessen the onus placed on the child while also not inducing parental guilt. One useful view of behavior problems centers on the idea that the problem is a matter of disrupted learning rather than willful intent. The interventionist works to remove blame from both the parent and the child by emphasizing what both parties need to learn to be more effective in their relationship. Initially, the interventionist can focus the parent on some of the child's positive qualities and positive behavior by asking about times when the child is more enjoyable to the parent. An early homework assignment for the parent can be to keep data on times when the child behaves well. The interventionist can communicate to the parent the positive qualities she sees in both the parent and the child and can encourage the parent for using more positive attributions about the child.

Parents need to understand that behavior involves complex learning, similar to academic skills such as reading, spelling, and math. When a child has difficulty with a spelling word or math computation or a motor task such as tying shoelaces, parents and teachers typically assume the child needs more instruction and more practice to master the new task or skill. In contrast, many parents and professionals believe that children somehow automatically learn how to behave appropriately, almost by a process of osmosis. Any number of factors can disrupt the natural process of learning social behavior, such as a language delay (even a slight delay can have significant impact on learning appropriate social behavior), developmental delays, medical challenges, a parent who is depressed, a chaotic home life, or high stress.

We are coming to understand that the challenging behavior of most children has communicative intent. Carr and Durand (1985), working with children who experience severe disabilities, found that even the most extreme forms of inappropriate behavior often have communicative functions, usually expressing a desire for more attention or assistance or the desire to avoid requests or tasks. For example, anyone who has spent time with young children is likely to be familiar with the overtired baby or toddler who cries at length, refusing to be fed or distracted, until he or she eventually falls asleep. Overtired toddlers frequently go through a period of time of seeming hyperactive and highly noncompliant before being willing to lie down and sleep. Most of us realize that this behavior is a function of exhaustion and being too tired to control difficult emotions that arise. That cluster of overtired behaviors (before bedtime or when a nap is missed) are so common that most people do not assume negative intent on the part of the child. The behaviors likely function in bringing additional attention and assistance from parents and in further exhausting the child so it is easier to "give in" to the exhaustion and sleep. Later, through a long process of training, some children learn to recognize that they are tired and can verbally complain about it, thereby setting the stage for the parent to let them rest.

However, from a combination of mistaken assumptions about negative intent, young children's limited ability to communicate their feelings and intentions, and parents' lack of skill in seeing and appreciating the communicative function of their child's behavior, there are many occasions for misunderstandings about the child's intent. For example, here is a vignette from a home observation:

> A 4-year-old is watching his mother as she changes the diaper of his baby sister. The mother is tickling, cooing, and smiling at the baby. Afterwards, she hands her 4-year-old son his clothes and says, "Go get dressed for preschool." He replies, "No, I can't!" The mother says, "You know how to dress yourself, go do it. I'm going to be late for work." The 4- year-old throws down the clothes and runs into another part of the house.

At this point, it is not unusual for a mother to think that her son is purposely trying to aggravate her and to make her late, both negative assumptions. In her frustration, she might use these phrases with her child.

As part of an intervention in this situation, an interventionist would try to provide an understanding that, although the son does not have the proper words yet to let his mother know that he is feeling jealous of the attention his baby sister is receiving, his behavior is communicating it in the best way that he can. From the child's perspective, apparently, if you are helpless and do *not* know how to dress yourself, then you get Mom's undivided, positive attention. In addition, although his mother's attention was not positive when he refused to dress and ran away, he subsequently received attention from her that was not divided with his little sister. If his mother had been able to see and appreciate what the child was feeling while she was dressing the baby, she might have started the interaction with her son in a different way. The mother might have provided some positive attention that was age-appropriate, but similar in quality, to what the baby was receiving, such as, "I'm so proud that you know how to dress all by yourself! I'm going to give you a hug and a tickle as soon as you are dressed!" The interaction would likely have had a more positive outcome.

One of the most common misunderstandings of parents and teachers arises when they see a child exhibit an appropriate behavior in one setting, but not another. We do not commonly appreciate that social behavior involves a vast array of learned skills. For many children, social behavior, just like academic learning, requires effective teaching, modeling, and practicing in easy and more difficult settings. The understanding that there is a difference between "unfirm" and "firm" skills in the realm of social behavior is an unfamiliar idea to most parents. Learning the multiplication tables for the first time when home alone studying does not ensure success on the first timed test in class. A child who can play a piano piece flawlessly at home or with her teacher might still become frightened and forget how to proceed when in front of an audience for the first time. Change in setting and contexts make newly learned skills more difficult to perform.

When a skill is new and can be reliably performed only in "easy" contexts, then we refer to it as "unfirm." When the skill can be performed successfully, regardless of the context or setting, then we refer to it as a "firm" skill. The same holds true for social behavior. Learning to respond quickly when your entire preschool class is lining up to go in for snack may be a much easier context than when your mother arrives to take you home and some of your friends are able to stay and play until their parents arrive later. Getting dressed independently for school may be easier than getting dressed for bed when older siblings get to stay up and watch TV. For many children, parents and teachers need to explain ahead of time what the expectations for behavior are in a new context, provide time to practice before the behavior is required in the difficult or new context, and provide practice after errors occur. For example, a preschool child may have difficulty leaving a fun activity to go home with his mother. In many other situations, the child may willingly comply with the mother's directive, "Come with me now." However, simply because the child can follow this direction in some situations does not mean that the behavior has been mastered in other more difficult settings.

Children need to learn social behavior through a variety of examples with practice opportunities, useful (not punitive) adult corrections for errors, and positive feedback for correct attempts. For the child who does not want to go to the car when his mother arrives at preschool, he might be helped by practicing at the beginning of recess what he will do when he sees his mother. The teacher could give him a 2-minute warning about needing to leave when he sees the mother's car arrive. As the mother approaches, the teacher might say, "It's time to leave. Would you like to go by yourself or hold my hand?" She would praise compliance and walk him by the hand, if he resisted, without talking. The mother might bring a small, favored toy for the child to have in the car on the days when he goes along right away. Appreciating that a skill may be new and unfirm in a young child and that some contexts are more difficult than others can assist in preventing negative appraisals and labeling and can encourage parents and teachers to do more "teaching" of behavioral expectations.

IMPROVING DIRECTION GIVING AND DIRECTION FOLLOWING

A common focus of troubled interactions between parents and young children is compliance with parental requests. The issue of compliance can be complicated when the goal is to foster self-reliance, self-determination, and self-esteem in a young child. Young children need the chance to express their positive and negative feelings and to make independent choices when possible, but adults should not lose sight of the fact that basic cooperation and compliance are necessary for all learning. Adults can err on two fronts, by assuming that noncompliance is an expression of negative intent and by believing that the child's displeasure should always be respected and that no effort should be made to require compliance. A belief in negative intent on the part of the child leads to negative appraisals and labeling and coercive attempts to force compliance. Yet a refusal to follow through with requests when the child shows any resistance can lead to disruption of one of the basic modes of regulating the behavior of children, asking them to do something. Fortunately, there are positive and practical procedures and strategies for breaking the cycle of negative interactions surrounding issues of compliance with directions in young children (Forehand & McMahon, 1981).

Adults who are parenting or teaching highly noncompliant children tend to make frequent demands of them. Perhaps uncertainty or anxiety about the child's willingness to cooperate invites adults to give repeated directions to these children, but the effort is doomed to failure. Noncompliant children respond to repeated demands by ignoring them or becoming quickly resistant in their behavior. Repeated requests frequently occasion an escalating negative cycle of interactions (Patterson, 1982). The first practical strategy adults can use is to not make unnecessary requests, and to only make requests for which they intend to follow through. Offering choices in a positive manner is another practical strategy that allows the child to feel more in control and fosters self-determination. We recommend providing the child with frequent opportunities to choose activities such as what to wear, what to eat, and which book to be read when those choices are not problematic for parents or teachers. Frequently, requests requiring compliance can also be expressed in a way that allows some degree of choice: "It's almost time for dinner. Would you like to bring the plates to the table or to set each place with silverware?" or "Before we go to the park you need to brush your teeth and put away your toys. What would you like to do first?" These questions are usually easier for a child than comments such as these: "It's time for dinner; take the plates to the table," or "You can't go to the park until you brush your teeth and put away your toys." In addition, parents and teachers willing to take time to play with young children where they follow the lead and interests of the child, instead of insisting on being in control, foster good will from children who do not have many opportunities to be "in charge."

Parents and teachers sometimes make the error of thinking that because choice making promotes self-determination and cooperation, they offer choices with *every* request. This teaches a misrule, since people do not go through life always getting to make choices when expected to do something. If we want to be paid for our work, we do not get to wake up each morning and decide whether we want to go to work or to the beach. Children should not have the option to go to school or stay home and watch videos, and they will not have the option, once they are at school, to go to math or stay longer at recess. In order to learn complex skills such as reading and math, children need to persist in following the teaching protocol presented to them. Children can benefit from having regular opportunities to make independent choices, but they need to have a firm foundation in cooperation and compliance with most adult requests in order to learn and adapt to the school environment.

When delivering requests, parents and teachers should use a bright, clear, positive tone of voice, assuming success. A shrill, harsh, whining, or hesitant voice can be sufficient to make a highly noncompliant child resistant. Giving only necessary directions and avoiding repeated requests is important. Forehand and McMahon (1981) suggest only giving one direction at a time, using simple language and only a few words. Give directions as a positive statement, such as "Put your toys in the clean-up bucket," and avoid indirect statements such as "Don't you want to clean up your toys now?" Physical proximity is important. Be close and within the child's view when asking him or her to do something. If the adult is not present to follow through with requests and to positively encourage with feedback, the chances of a child being compliant are greatly reduced. In preschools where teachers roam the room making direct requests with children and following through before moving on, there is much greater compliance than when teachers stay in one place, expecting that all the children hear and understand what is expected of them.

Giving up a reinforcing activity to follow an adult request is frequently difficult for young children. This difficulty can be eased by giving the child a few minutes of advance notice or warning that a transition is coming soon. With a particularly noncompliant child, in addition to advance notice, engaging the child in a few positive interactions before making the request can be helpful. Table 1 summarizes a recommended procedure for teaching children to follow directions.

This procedure appears deceptively easy. Parents and teachers who have a disrupted relationship with a child may need some coaching on how to use this type of direction-following procedure without engaging in negative talk if the child is resistive or argumentative and on how to eliminate angry-appearing body language that can escalate negative interactions. When used correctly, the procedure provides a great deal of instruction for the child. First, the child learns, over time, that he or she always

Table 1.   Following direction procedure

1.	Give direction in a bright, positive voice (wait 4–5 seconds for compliance).
2.	If the child is compliant, deliver enthusiastic praise.
3.	If the child is not compliant, repeat direction in a flat tone of voice (wait 4–5 seconds for compliance). Avoid sounding angry, sharp, or frustrated.
4.	If the child is compliant, praise with minor enthusiasm.
5.	If the child is not compliant, physically prompt correct response using minimal assistance. Minimal assistance means that only the amount of assistance is used to ensure compliance. If the child resists, this may require physical prompting; but at any time that the child begins to cooperate, the physical assistance is faded. Do *not* make eye contact, talk, or prompt with an angry manner or excessive force. The purpose of the prompting is to teach the correct response, remove attention for noncompliance, and to ensure that noncompliance does not result in avoidance of the request or an escalation in negative interactions.
6.	When the task or request is completed with minimal assistance, tell the child, "That's how to _____," or "That's what I wanted you to do."

gets the most positive attention when he or she complies after the first request. If the child heeds the second request, the experience is still positive, even though the attention is diminished. Resistance and noncompliance *always* result in the least amount of positive adult attention; escaping compliance is not possible, and a small amount of practice in doing the task correctly is always provided. We have found that the elimination of verbal arguing between the adult and the child as a way for the child to obtain attention and the easy access to positive, enthusiastic praise for compliance has dramatic effects on the compliance of young children. Once again, using this procedure only for necessary requests and ensuring that the child has many other opportunities for choice making and independent play is essential.

TEACHING CHILDREN TO PLAY INDEPENDENTLY

One of the chief characteristics of home life for young parents is that they are faced with multiple competing demands during much of the time that they are home. Women in families with traditional role structures are expected to prepare food, clean house, watch children, pay attention to other family members, and get everyone ready for school and work. Periods of undivided attention from young parents is rare. Having young children who are able to play appropriately with minimal adult supervision is of great help to parents and an important developmental milestone for children.

Researchers have studied ways that parents can teach their young children as well as children with disabilities how to play independently. Sanders and Dadds (1993) developed a procedure called planned activity training (PAT) that they demonstrated to be effective in reducing child problem behavior. Powers et al. (1992) used PAT with parents of children with severe disabilities and demonstrated that it was an effective technique in home and community settings including shopping malls, grocery stores, and church. Because PAT has been described in previous publications we describe the procedure only briefly. PAT includes the following steps: 1) to get ready for PAT, the parent and child identify play activities that the child prefers (e.g., puzzles, coloring, playing with toy cars, electronic games); 2) the parent offers the child a choice of activities; 3) the parent helps the child get started with the activity; 4) the parent praises the child for playing and explains what he or she will be doing (e.g., "I'll be in the kitchen cooking. I'll come back and see you play in a few minutes."); 5) the parent intermittently walks back to the child and praises him or her for playing; and 6) if the child stops playing, the parent redirects him or her to the activity or offers a choice of other new activities. In the event that the child begins to engage in a problem behavior, the parent redirects the child back to the play activity. If the child still persists in the problem behavior, the parent briefly removes the child from the play setting, waits until the child has calmed down, and then begins the PAT procedure again.

PAT assumes that the child already knows how to play with some toys or objects. For children with developmental delays, teaching play skills prior to implementing PAT may be necessary; PAT is more of a proactive behavior management method than a procedure for teaching new play skills. We recommend enlisting the help of the child's school teachers to give instruction in new play skills.

INCREASING COMMUNICATIVE ALTERNATIVES TO PROBLEM BEHAVIOR

If we accept that problem behavior has communicative intent, then it is essential to teach children alternatives that are equally effective and to respect what they are trying to communicate. Children need positive replacement behaviors. Attempts to just eliminate inappropriate behavior, when there is an underlying need or desire that is being ignored, are ultimately unsuccessful. A child who is disruptive at home or in school when given a task that he believes is too difficult needs to be assured that it takes time and practice to learn new skills and taught how to ask for help. The child needs to learn a range of ways to ask for help that will work in different settings. It is fine to call out for help at home while working on a difficult puzzle, but raising your hand and asking for help when you are called on by the teacher might work better at school. When a child is learning a new and more appropriate way to communicate, the new behavior needs to be effective and efficient. If the child asks for assistance, parents need to provide it immediately or let the child know when they can provide it. If the child has learned to avoid difficult tasks and get negative adult attention when tasks seem too difficult, parents and teachers need to be quickly responsive to the child's new efforts to ask for assistance. If they cannot provide immediate help, they can let the child know they appreciate the request for help and let the child know how soon they will be available to provide it.

Children can be taught positive ways to ask for attention from adults: "Can you spend some time with me now? I want to show you what I am doing." Some families schedule short private time with each child, during which the child can have the parent's undivided attention without having to share the parent with siblings. Besides positively responding to children's efforts to ask for attention in a positive manner, teachers can be very effective in positively pointing out appropriate efforts to obtain teacher attention.

Anger can spark aggressive behavior in young children. Too often attempts to teach anger management with communicative alternatives are done only in settings where anger does not arise. Initial training may be fine in an easy, neutral context, but training in the problem setting is important to ensure that the child can learn a new way of responding while feeling difficult emotions. As we mentioned earlier, adults sometimes assume that children already know how to behave and are just choosing to behave otherwise in this instance. Adults frequently respond to young children who are physically fighting by saying things like, "Use your words." This response assumes that expressing anger verbally is already a firm skill, when the child is clearly showing by his or her behavior that it is not. Children need direct assistance on what to say when they are angry, not general platitudes. A child also needs to know that it is fine to express the feeling with words. For example, a young child may need the adult to say, "No pushing!" or "You need to tell Sammy, 'Don't grab that truck from me!'" Older children may need to learn more sophisticated ways to express their feelings and to problem-solve. However, adults sometimes err on the side of dismissing the young child's feelings and expressing their own anger at the child's aggression or by involving young children in too lengthy and complicated discussions about emotions that just functionally gives the child a great deal of attention for inappropriate behavior. Communicative alternatives for problem behavior need to match the child's level of understanding and communication, and they need to be at least as effective and efficient as the inappropriate behavior.

SETTING CLEAR AUTHORITATIVE LIMITS

Children need limits so that they have a clear picture of the boundaries for appropriate and inappropriate behavior. There are two common patterns of problematic parenting in regard to limit setting: being authoritarian or being too permissive. Living under authoritarian rules is no different for children than it is for adults. The tendency is either to have one's spirit broken or to be rebellious whenever possible. Harsh, unreasonable, or too frequent commands without explanations can create troubled relationships with young children. Possibly out of fear of being too authoritarian, parents and teachers are sometimes afraid to set limits; and the child is left without any clear picture of what is safe and dangerous or what is acceptable and unacceptable behavior. We are all familiar with the child who spends his day continually "testing" what the limits might be.

What is most effective for children is for adults to set clear and reasonable limits in a matter-of-fact, but nonpunitive manner while providing the child with an explanation of why there is a limit (e.g., "You need to play ball in the fenced backyard, because I'm afraid you might accidentally chase a ball into the road if you play in the front yard," or "You need to go to bed at 8:30 so that you will get enough rest for school tomorrow."). The limits or "fence" needs to be modified and moved as the child grows and develops, but the child needs to know there are clear boundaries in his family and community. For an older child it might be, "You need to drive for 6 months after getting your license without any tickets or accidents before you can drive your friends to the mountains to hike," or "If you are going to be home later than 11:00 P.M., I need you to call me so I won't worry about you." Children may seem disgruntled at having adult limits in their lives, but in addition to giving them parameters in which to govern their own behavior, it lets them know that their parents are watching after them and care. As a child becomes more competent, it is possible to negotiate about some limits so that he or she can acquire some experience at self-management.

TEACHING PERSISTENCE

Studies of children with behavior disorders suggest that they frequently suffer from extremely low self-esteem (Simeonsson, 1994). Contemporary theory about self-esteem points to the importance of learning to deal with difficulty and failure experience as a key to developing a healthy self-concept (Bednar et al., 1989). Central to promoting of self-determination in children is the teaching of persistence in the face of difficulty. Some ways that parents and teachers can promote persistence include recognizing small attempts to behave appropriately, encouraging attempts to use communicative alternatives to problem behavior, supporting efforts to accept limits in their lives, and encouraging children to try again after making errors. Adults should openly show appreciation of these efforts. Parents and teachers who recognize and praise effort in children teach them the value of persisting through difficulties and promote healthy development. Coping involves the willingness to face difficulties directly and responsibly; it does not require that a person is always successful with every attempt.

An important element of teaching children to persist is to link their efforts with their accomplishments. For example, a parent might say, "Look what you did, you practiced your spelling words last night and today you got a good grade on your quiz. See what you can do when you work hard!" The same approach can be taken toward self-management of problem behavior: "Your brother was making you angry and you tried to tell him instead of hitting him. I really appreciate it when you try hard like that." Interventionists need to encourage parents to persist in their attempts to improve their child's behavior and the quality of their relationship with their child. Interventionists need to show appreciation and respect for the efforts of parents as well as children.

CONCLUSION

When the primary relationship between a parent and child becomes problematic, children are at risk of developing behavioral disorders that interfere with long-term adjustment. Disrupted relationships are characterized by parental negative cognitive bias and negative emotion, resulting in a suspected negative impact on the child's developing sense of competence and self-worth. It is difficult for parents to promote the self-determination and self-esteem of young children whose behavior is often aversive. Cognitive behavioral methods can be useful for improving parent–child interactions and for interrupting an escalating cycle of negativity in which both parents and children can progressively become locked into rigid behavioral habits that are mutually aversive and damaging to healthy development.

We have presented descriptions of key behavioral treatment techniques that can be helpful in improving parent–child relationships, and we have suggested ways of using these techniques to enhance children's self-determination. These methods include giving clear directions and teaching children to follow them, providing children with appropriate and ample opportunities for choice making, using authoritative discipline practices by setting clear limits and rewarding good behavior, teaching children communicative alternatives to problem behavior, teaching children to play independently and engage in planned activities, and teaching children persistence in the face of difficult tasks.

REFERENCES

Ainsworth, M.S. (1993). Attachment as related to mother infant interaction. *Advances in Infancy Research, 8,* 1–50.

American Psychiatric Association. (1994). *Diagnostic and statistical manual of mental disorders* (4th ed.). Washington, DC: Author.

Bednar, R.L., Wells, M.G., & Peterson, S.R. (1989). *Self-esteem: Paradoxes and innovations in clinical theory and practice.* Washington, DC: American Psychological Association.

Beitchman, J.H., Inglis, A., & Schachter, D. (1992). Child psychiatry and early intervention: I. The aggregate burden of suffering. *Canadian Journal of Psychiatry, 37,* 230–233.

Biederman, J., Rosenbaum, J.F., Chaloff, J., & Kagan, J. (1995). Bahavioral inhibition as a risk factor for anxiety disorders. In J.S. March (Ed.), *Anxiety disorders in children and adolescents* (pp. 61–81). New York: Guilford Press.

Brandenburg, N.A., Friedman, R.M., & Silver, S.E. (1990). The epidemiology of childhood psychiatric disorders: Prevalence findings from recent studies. *Journal of the American Academy of Child and Adolescent Psychiatry, 29*(1), 76-83.

Bucy, J.E. (1994). Internalizing affective disorders. In R.J. Simeonsson (Ed.), *Risk, resilience, and prevention: Promoting the well-being of all children* (pp. 219–238). Baltimore: Paul H. Brookes Publishing Co.

Campbell, S.B. (1990). *Behavior problems in preschool children.* New York: Guilford Press.

Carr, E.G., & Durand, V.M. (1985). The social-communicative basis of severe behavior problems in children. In S. Reiss & R. Bootzin (Eds.), *Theoretical issues in behavior therapy* (pp. 219–254). New York: Academic Press.

Costello, E.J. (1989). Developments in child psychiatric epidemiology. *Journal of the American Academy of Child and Adolescent Psychiatry, 28*(4), 836–841.

Davies, P. (Ed.). (1976). *American heritage dictionary.* Boston: Houghton Mifflin.

Forehand, R.L., & McMahon, R.J. (1981). *Helping the noncompliant child: A clinician's guide to parent training.* New York: Guilford Press.

Gabel, S., & Shindledecker, R. (1991). Aggressive behavior in youth: Characteristics, outcome, and psychiatric diagnoses. *Journal of Clinical Child Psychology, 20*(6), 982–988.

Garrison, C.Z., Addy, C.L., Jackson, K.L., McKeown, R.E., & Waller, J.L. (1992). Major depressive disorder and dysthymia in young adolescents. *American Journal of Epidemiology, 135*(7), 792–802.

Jenkins, S., Bax, M., & Hart, H. (1980). Behavior problems in preschool children. *Journal of Child Psychology and Psychiatry, 21,* 5–18.

McDevitt, S.C., & Carey, W.B. (1978). The measurement of temperament in 3–7 year old children. *Journal of Child Psychology and Psychiatry, 19,* 245–253.

Parker, J.G., & Asher, S.R. (1987). Peer acceptance and later personal adjustment: Are low-accepted children "at risk"? *Psychological Bulletin, 102*(3), 357–389.

Patterson, G.R. (1982). *Coersive family process.* Eugene, OR: Castalia Publishing.

Powers, L.E., Singer, G.H.S., Stevens, T., & Sowers, J. (1992). Behavioral parent training in home and community generalization settings. *Education and Training in Mental Retardation, 27*(1), 13–28.

Rubin, K.H., & Mills, R.S.L. (1991). Conceptualizing developmental pathways to internalizing disorders in childhood. *Canadian Journal of Behavioral Science, 23*(3), 300–317.

Sanders, M.R., & Dadds, M. (1993). *Behavioral family intervention.* Boston: Allyn & Bacon.

Simeonsson, R.J. (Ed.). (1994). *Risk, resilience, and prevention: Promoting the well being of all children.* Baltimore: Paul H. Brookes Publishing Co.

Singer, J. (1993). *A qualitative study of the coping strategies and social support in the lives of parents having a child with a serious emotional or behavioral disorders.* Unpublished manuscript. University of Oregon, Eugene.

Thomas, A., Chess, S., & Birch, H.B. (1968). *Temperament and behavior disorders in children.* New York: New York University Press.

Tynan, W.D., & Nearing, J. (1994). The diagnosis of attention deficit hyperactivity disorder in young children. *Infants and Young Children, 6*(4), 13–20.

Index

Page numbers followed by "f" or "t" indicate figures or tables, respectively.

On the Road to Autonomy